Family Desk Reference
to Psychology

Chuck T. Falcon, Counseling Psychologist

Sensible Psychology
Lafayette, Louis

D1445444

The author and the publisher hold no responsibility for the personal problems of any reader. This book is not meant as a substitute for counseling when personal problems may have unfortunate or dangerous consequences.

Cover Design by Beth Glass and Chuck Falcon

Publisher's Cataloging in Publication

Falcon, Chuck T.
 Family desk reference to psychology / Chuck Tilton Falcon.
 p. cm.
 Includes bibliographical references and index.
 LCCN: 2001090305.
 ISBN 0-9628254-2-5

 1. Problem Solving. 2. Change (Psychology) 3. Behavior modification. 4. Adjustment (Psychology) I. Title.

BF449.F35 2002   158

Printed in the United States of America
First edition printed: 2001

Table of Contents

Table of Contents

Table of Contents

Introduction

You have the power to control your own destiny.

Knowledge is power. The more you know,
the closer you are to self-control.

This is the first psychology self-help book to cover all the most common personal problems and describe how to solve them in very simple, practical terms. It brings you psychology's most up-to-date, useful advice and describes things in easy language so anyone can use it as a handbook and benefit. Besides the standard counseling information taught in schools for psychologists, the author gathered the best guidance from new scholarly books for psychologists on each area of human life problems, recent research studies reported in technical journals and periodicals, and hundreds of new counseling manuals, self-help books, and psychology textbooks.

Unlike most self-help psychology books, this book covers the whole range of personal problems, which are often interrelated. Deceptively short chapters on each personal problem in Part 2 refer to many other related chapters, adding up to comprehensive instructions for each issue. Each chapter with further resources for people who want in-depth discussions of that particular personal problem, including the best new books on the topic (research books appear in the select bibliography), national support groups (both phone numbers and Internet addresses), and hotline numbers.

To a great degree, we determine our own fates by our thoughts, feelings, decisions, and actions. Learn the characteristics of happy people, exactly what love is, and how to think, feel, and act to your best advantage. By teaching life skills, this book gives you the tools for personal growth. Although clarifying examples do appear, we waste no time discussing the personal histories of therapy clients, their actions or feelings, or details of therapy sessions.

Understanding basic facts can do much to help avoid painful mistakes. Knowing how to judge love and recognize the signs of trouble in relationships helps you choose a mate wisely. Gain insight on how to keep the fire of marital love burning brightly forever. Discover what you can do to conquer each negative emotion, make friends, find a job, ease the transition of divorce, overcome addictions, gambling, nervous habits, insomnia, or sex problems, lose weight, avoid rape, prevent anyone abusing your child, and avoid expensive, attractive nursing homes that neglect or abuse the elderly. Learning about common patterns can provide much reassurance when you face troubling emotions or experiences like anger toward the deceased in grief or hallucinations in grief. A comprehensive chapter on raising children teaches how to develop a close, warm, loving relationship with them, how to avoid major problems, how to help them do well in school, how to best discipline them, and how to deal with various child stages and troublesome behaviors.

Find out how to avoid incompetent psychologists and psychiatrists, those who have training in ineffective types of psychotherapy, and those who don't keep up with the field, perhaps using hypnosis, guided suggestion, or other techniques improperly and harming their clients. Avoid the scams of subliminal audiotapes and recovered memory therapy. Recovered memory therapy often creates false memories and destroys peace among family members; it has broken up thousands of families and led to hundreds of lawsuits. Understand the very real possibility of counseling ruining lives by causing multiple personality and how this might happen. See how many psychologists exaggerate the importance of childhood experiences and blame people's parents for their problems. We also discuss the controversy over electroshock therapy.

Chapter 11 teaches you how to succeed in making great changes by working on a few simple things at a time. People who attempt to change too much at one time or to make great, dramatic changes all at once often overwhelm themselves and give up. Chapter 11 also teaches you how to fight denial, keep motivated, and combat the natural tendency to backslide in personal problems, including the importance of beginning efforts again immediately after any slip or setback and how to avoid later problems after succeeding in changing.

Most people have a good intuitive understanding of mental health and function well, but we all have negative emotions and personal issues that could use work. Fortunately, by following the advice in this book, most people, even those with serious problems, can change and improve themselves without counseling. Telephone surveys show recovery from alcoholism most often occurs outside hospitals, psychotherapists' offices, or self-help groups. Preliminary research suggests reading a therapy book on how to change works as well as group or individual therapy for depression or alcoholism. Recent studies have found phobic people with great fears can improve as much following the procedures described in manuals like this on their own as they can doing them with a therapist. New research shows self-help groups often help people improve as much as counseling from psychologists and psychiatrists with 30 or 40 years of experience.

Never lose hope and give up, even if a psychiatrist or psychologist says you have a mental disorder—you may not need counseling and you may have great potential. People diagnosed mentally ill often function satisfactorily, having only temporary setbacks due to stressful events in their lives. As we shall see in chapter 41, diagnoses don't really mean much and may just be insulting nonsense that foolishly labels you and makes you feel unable to change. Even famous, very productive people have diagnosable disorders. Abraham Lincoln, Winston Churchill, and Isaac Newton were deeply depressed much of their lives. Albert Einstein had a nervous breakdown at age 16 and his teachers considered him mentally slow, unsociable, and lost in fantasies. Charles Darwin was a recluse, a hypochondriac, and probably agoraphobic. Florence Nightingale suffered from extreme anxiety and was bedridden much of her life. Many great writers and artists were alcoholics or mentally disturbed. Beethoven, Leo Tolstoy, Michaelangelo, Charles Dickens, Mark Twain, Ernest Hemingway, Tennessee Williams, Eugene O'Neill, John Keats, Walt Whitman, Cole Porter, and Georgia O'Keefe suffered from either manic depression or major depression. Problems and crises are opportunities to learn, change, and grow; this book will show you how.

Two problems are particularly important and should be your first priority in changing: addiction and a bad temper (regular outbursts of yelling). We don't normally think of a bad temper as especially significant and devastating, but the way you deal with your own anger is very important to the quality of your relationships, problem solving, self-esteem, and the levels of stress and happiness in your life. Poorly controlled anger destroys warmth, closeness, and trust in relationships. If you have ever been violent, be sure to work on controlling anger first, perhaps along with addiction.

Learn how to safely leave an abusive relationship and how to assert yourself and use the legal system effectively despite the unhelpful attitudes of many prosecutors and judges. The latest research emphasizes the importance of leaving any abusive relationship. Batterers' counseling programs often don't help at all and may actually increase your risk by leading to a false sense of security. Arresting your abuser may or may not help, depending on the type of man. Couple's therapy without a clear focus on a partner's violence is dangerous because discussing difficult and emotional issues can easily lead to violence.

For those who don't know what problems they have or who simply want to understand themselves better, chapters 39, Understanding Yourself, and 40, Dreams, describe how to explore personal issues. If you need to get over the past, chapter 38 teaches how to contact and express avoided emotions and work with and finish the past, so you can let it go forever. Chapter 13, Help from Other People, tells you how support groups work, how to find or organize local branches, and points out that small membership groups may communicate with fellow members by mail.

By using the suggestions in this handbook, you can change yourself and conquer your personal problems if you put forth enough effort. Overcoming one personal problem may take days, months, or even years. Most will take from several months to several years to conquer, depending on how much effort you put into it, how constantly you stay aware of the problem and work on it, and how many thought, feeling, or behavior changes in the problem area you need. Research suggests a major lifestyle change such as overcoming alcoholism or drug addiction requires three to five years to become stable. Any dramatic change in your habits generally requires practice, practice, and more practice, but you will find everything you need to know in this book.

Part 1:

General Information and Advice

May you always live with love and in truth,
speak with warmth and understanding,
and live life fully in all its panoramic glory.

Part 1 describes important areas of human life everyone should understand in order to work on personal problems or toward happiness. Part 1 also describes general approaches and techniques useful in working with many kinds of problems. Later chapters of this book will often refer to points made and described in detail in Part 1.

1. Happiness

*Honest, hard working, kind, generous people
are seldom emotionally disturbed.*

Grief and joy are a revolving wheel.
(Tamil proverb from India)

It is never too late to turn around and choose a better path.

Happiness is enjoying and appreciating life and feeling good about yourself. Happy people do not feel joyous constantly. Everyone has peak joy experiences and great sorrows.   Life inevitably brings with it failure, disappointment, rejection, negative emotions, pain, and sorrows, but happy people gracefully accept these trials as an integral part of life, while doing what they can about their problems. Happiness is a courageous choice in the face of life's suffering, a stance. It involves loving life, with all its pleasures and suffering, and loving the world, with all its good and evil. True happiness comes from love—love of nature, other people, ideas, activities, things, and yourself. Happiness—this love of life, the world, and oneself—relates to certain kinds of thoughts, feelings, and actions.

First, happy people, as the great psychologists Abraham Maslow and Viktor Frankl realized, find meaning in life by doing good works and striving for ideals and righteousness.   In this way, they are morally pure, always fighting the evil within. (Since ancient times, people have described the human tendency for evil by saying there is a wild beast, dark side, or devil in all of us.) Happy people have personal commitments to the virtues: kindness, helpfulness, generosity, sensitivity to others, loyalty, patience, reliability, responsibility, honesty, work, persistence, self-control, self-reliance, achievement, humility, justice, the courage to do what is right, good judgment that considers future consequences of actions, tolerance, etc. These ethical, loving behaviors are so important that all the major religions point the same way with a central teaching, the Golden Rule: "Do for others what you want them to do for you." You can find it in the Christian Bible (Matthew 7:12), the Jewish Talmud (Shabbat 31a), Islam (Forth Hadith of an-Nawawi 13), Buddhism (Udana-Varga 5:18, also Samyutta Nlkaya v. 353), and Hinduism (Mahabharata 5:1517, also Mencius Vii.A.4).   It also appears in Confucianism (Analects 15:23, also Doctrine of the Mean 13.3), Taoism (Tai

Shang Kan Ying P'ien), Jainism (Lord Mahavira, 24th Tirthankara) and Zoroastrianism (Dadisten-i-dinik 94:5).

In many ways, our thoughts, goals, and ideals determine what kind of people we are. We can lower ourselves with evil thoughts and selfishness or we can lift ourselves by striving for our ideals. Performing good acts and putting the virtues into practice in our lives lead to good self-esteem, peace of mind, and harmonious relationships with other people. Virtually any positive act (friendliness, sharing an interest with someone, performing your job well, etc.), no matter how large or how small, feels righteous and adds self-satisfaction to your life. Moreover, accomplishing things, improving ourselves, or helping people also benefits our social lives. A good reputation can help dramatically in making friends.

Happy people also take an enthusiastic interest in a well-rounded variety of interests and activities, which keep the mind off negative thoughts and emotions and give satisfaction, pleasure, and relaxation. Many interests and activities provide feelings of accomplishment and a sense of adding to this world, and many add to social skills by providing the basis for sharing and interesting conversation. In all of these ways, interests and activities increase happiness and self-esteem.

Another important characteristic of happy people is their ability to give themselves, to love, and to have deep relationships. Relationships involve warmth, closeness, companionship, trust, and sharing interests, activities, ideas, and values. In relationships, we receive acceptance, respect, and love. Friends may also provide reassurance, emotional support, helpful ideas, or material resources such as transportation, shelter, babysitting, money, etc. Love enriches our lives in many ways. In intimate relationships, we can confide our joys, fears, hopes and sorrows. We feel needed and useful when we help or give to friends and loved ones. Emotional bonds with other people add to self-esteem and give a sense of belonging to the world.

Love is so important to happiness that much of this book involves simply treating others in loving, respectful ways. A great deal of evidence suggests the importance of love in our lives. Until the 1920s, nearly all infants in orphanages died simply because people didn't realize that to survive, babies need someone to pick them up, hold them, carry them around, and play with them several times a day. Married people describe themselves as very happy much more often than do never married people or those who have divorced. Married people have lower rates of alcoholism, mental illness, suicide, illness, hospitalization, and death than do single, widowed, divorced, or separated people of the same sexes and ages. A variety of research studies even suggest close, trusting relationships with others may help prevent illness, speed recovery, and promote longevity. An analysis of 42 studies involving 125,826 people shows religious people definitely live longer than others, probably because of taking better care of their health and because of social support and friendships at religious services.

Satisfying friendships and close relationships are important in happiness. The ability to make and keep friends improves the prognosis when psychological problems occur. Emotional support from others reduces the likelihood of depression and improves adjustment to stresses such as grief, job loss, severe illness or injury, natural disaster, retirement, and aging. Neurotic and psychotic people have fewer friends and less satisfying relationships with friends than other people do. Psychologists believe it is best to have a number of relationships, ranging from very close to less intimate friendships. Yet many people are happy with just one good friend. Even people whose closest friends have moved away or died are often happy if they keep their focus on good things, such as interests and activities, good works, appreciating the simple things in life (sunshine, nature, food, etc.), and ideals such as virtues or religious beliefs.

Finally, happiness involves attitudes of acceptance, optimism, hope, and other positive thinking habits. Because science has eliminated many painful diseases, made our lives more comfortable than ever before, and provided medicines for every minor ache and pain and even for emotional problems such as depression and anxiety, people now tend to feel suffering is intolerable.   But life inevitably brings with it pain and a variety of disappointments and sorrows. Happy people keep a positive attitude by accepting sadness and suffering as normal parts of life, while doing what they can about their problems. A graceful or cheerful acceptance of life's trials makes us more pleasant company and promotes mental health and happiness. Happy people focus their minds on good works and good things. In chapter 5, we shall see the importance of optimism and positive thinking in almost every area of our lives and will learn how to change the negative thinking habits contributing to depression and almost every life problem.

Fortunately, we can control our thoughts and feelings much more than most people realize. With enough work and effort, you can change habitual thoughts and feelings. Don't worry about whether you are happy. Develop interests, activities, and friendships, be kind, help other people, strive to be virtuous, accept emotional pain, work on conquering your personal problems, and improve your thinking habits. These things will lead to happiness.

2. Love

Love by Truth and Deed. (Bible, John 3:18)

The best way to find love is to give love.

Loving other people and giving of yourself is a very important part of mental health, loving yourself, happiness, and self-esteem. Love is so central to mental health that many sections of this book teach how to act more loving. Let's define exactly what love is.

Love is caring about the well-being, happiness, and growth of people you love. Love is not just a feeling; true love shows itself in actions. Love is protecting your loved ones from emotional or physical pain, helping and strengthening them, and improving their lives, without asking to be repaid. Love is considerate, kind, patient, gentle, tender, respectful, and loyal. Love is sensitive to the feelings and needs of other people. Love accepts imperfection in others. Love is never rude, selfish, irritable, nor prone to anger. Love is not happy with evil but delights in the truth. Love does not envy other people, nor hold grudges.

People who love take interest in the activities, feelings, and ideas of those they love. They accept other people as they are, believe in them, express affection, and give approval, praise, comfort, encouragement, and moral support. They perform acts of kindness, helpfulness, and service, even when they must sacrifice to do so. Forgiveness shows love, too. Forgiving someone showers the other person with caring and respect, reduces tensions, and makes it easier for the other person to grow. Forgiveness also frees you from your resentment, anger, or pain because you have chosen to let go of these negative emotions.

Finally, love finds the strength to continue loving, supporting, believing in, and helping loved ones even when it becomes difficult. There is no limit to its faith, hope, and patience. True love proves itself in times of trouble, when difficulties and hostilities mount. It is easy to act in loving ways when no problems exist and your relationships with loved ones are harmonious. But when love shines brightly with the kinds of feelings and behaviors described above through hard times and despite bad feelings with loved ones, you can be sure true love exists. People need love the most when problems weigh heavily upon them and they are at their worst, not when they are happy and their worlds seem bright and beautiful.

3. Humor

Create fun in your life, relieve frustrations,
and bring peace to conflicts with humor.

Gods and goddesses of laughter and mischief, fools, clowns, court jesters, and comedians are all expressions of the important aspect of humor in human culture. Such humorous and fun-loving characters occur in many cultures and date back far into history. Many of these characters commanded great respect as awesome spiritual beings. Even rats laugh but they laugh in high pitches we can't hear.

In medieval days, doctors prescribed court jesters to aid in healing. Even today, many people believe humor promotes healing. Some people claim using humor helped them conquer terminal illnesses, and a few doctors argue for the physical benefits of laughter, but very little scientific work exists in this area. Nevertheless, some hospitals across the United States set aside rooms for humor and laughter and stock them with classic comedy in movies, television shows, and audiotapes. These hospitals send patients who seem to be giving up hope to the laughter room for a few hours, which sometimes results in a renewed interest in life. Many people note humor and laughter can take their minds off physical or emotional pain for a while. (This is also true of interesting activities such as stimulating conversation.)

Most people recognize the psychological benefits of humor and laughter. Humor is joyous and takes our minds off our troubles. Seeing the humor in our circumstances relieves frustration, tension, and stress. Laughter physically relaxes the muscles and brings a more relaxed posture. Research suggests laughter can trigger the brain to release endorphins, hormones that create a natural high or euphoria that can be more effective than a tranquilizer in reducing muscular tension and anxiety. One study suggests laughter can reduce the level of stress hormones in the body.

Laughing at ourselves or our troubles gives us a better perspective on the all-too-human messes we get ourselves into and our difficulties and sorrows. Seeing the humor in our problems involves a wise acceptance of the human condition, with its mistakes, weaknesses, conflicts, and misfortunes. Humor lightens the heaviness of frustration, anger, conflict, grief, and suffering. Viktor Frankl, who survived the prison camps of Nazi Germany, reported humor, more than anything, helped the prisoners to gain some distance and rise above their desperate plights, even if for only a few seconds.

Humor can also express negative feelings in positive, friendly ways. Cultures all over the world use humor as a safety valve for expressing aggressive and sexual feelings in acceptable ways.

A good sense of humor is an asset in our relationships, creating fun and excitement and bringing us closer to others. It helps us bear our burdens without being unpleasant to other people and can comfort others. A good sense of humor is a part of good mental health. It seems to relate to joy, hope, love, and the will to live. One need not laugh heartily to reap the benefits; just seeing the humor in things will help. Good humor is always friendly, pleasant, and relaxing, not callous, insensitive, or offending, not a weapon for retaliation. Use humor carefully so you don't make other people uncomfortable. Sometimes, despite the best intentions, a joke will irritate or offend someone. If this happens, apologize and clear up any misunderstanding.

Develop and improve your sense of humor. Spend some time every evening thinking over the events of the day and finding humorous ways of looking at things. Think of funny things you could have said. Poke fun at yourself, other people, and the situations you find yourself in. Your own flaws, mistakes, and conflicts with other people make very good material. Look for the absurdities in life, the labor in vain, and the times of much ado about nothing. Experiment with using either gross exaggeration or great understatement to find the humor in a situation. Exaggerate or understate facts, feelings, situations, action, number, size, or comparison. Use the element of surprise. Develop unique associations connecting mismatched feelings, facts, situations, or objects. Experiment with plays on words such as puns and double meanings. Memorize jokes, funny lines, and amusing stories you hear and practice telling them. Sources of humor include your own experiences, friends, humorous books, television, comedians, bumper stickers, T-shirts, and buttons.

If you have children, use your sense of humor to brighten the time you spend with them. Children love silliness and humor. Set aside time with them each day to practice seeing the humor in the day's events using the above techniques. This is a fun activity that helps your children take their frustrations less seriously.

4. Thinking

*Optimism improves your social life
and motivates you to never give up,
which turns failures and setbacks
into comebacks and successes.*

Your thinking habits can make your life a heaven or hell.

Thinking, emotions, and behaviors intertwine very closely and each can change the others. In this chapter, we focus on the importance of our thoughts, how they help or trouble us, and what to do about our counterproductive thought habits. Much of the discussion in this chapter derives from the pioneering work of the great psychologists Aaron T. Beck and Albert Ellis.

Voodoo deaths, faith cures, the placebo effect, and hypnosis all provide dramatic evidence for the power of thinking. Voodoo deaths seem to come from the great anxiety and loss of hope in the cursed person caused by one overwhelming thought, the belief that death inevitably awaits. Faith cures at religious sites or by charismatic healers may come from a newly acquired serenity, acceptance, confidence, and vigor due to belief in the cure that reduces helplessness and allows one to notice small improvements and pay less attention to symptoms or problems. Faith in the cure may help some people to stop gaining sympathy and attention for the sick role. Perhaps believing in the cure reduces anxiety and the experience of pain. Such changes may alleviate an emotional problem or overcome a physical one. Perhaps these improved feelings and behaviors produce beneficial effects on the disease processes themselves.

In the placebo effect, believing someone gave you an effective cure can sometimes improve emotional or physical problems, especially pain. Researchers mislead patients by treating them with *placebos*, inactive imitations of medicines such as sugar pills or injections of saltwater. New research combining 114 studies of placebo shows that placebos don't help nearly as many people as believed in the past. Many studies found no placebo effect at all. However, the new research shows patients in pain studies given placebos report an average of a 15% reduction in pain and shows a smaller placebo effect in other studies with subjective measures such as ratings of how much symptoms bother the patient.

Placebos occasionally cause unpleasant side effects: heart palpitations, insomnia, weakness, nervousness, drowsiness, dizziness, dry mouth, headache, nausea, vomiting, rashes, hives, swelling of the lips, constipation, diarrhea, etc. When the patients stop taking the placebo, the side effects disappear. The simple belief that one took a potent drug causes these reactions. Researchers don't understand the placebo effect, but all the possible explanations for faith cures noted above may also apply here. Psychologists often take advantage of the placebo effect by giving glowing testimonials about the effectiveness of their techniques, because they know making believers of their clients will result in more cures. Hypnosis, treating people with the power of suggestion, also highlights the power of thinking.

Our thoughts are important to us in many ways. We emphasized certain patterns of thinking in our previous discussions of happiness: acceptance, a focus on good works and virtues, and humor. Our negative and positive thoughts can also cause our expectations to come true, a self-fulfilling prophecy, by affecting how we see things and act. If you attempt a task thinking, "I know I'll mess it up. I can't do anything right," you probably won't feel like trying very hard and you may interpret your progress as unimpressive. This pessimism may lead you to give up, perhaps blaming the poor outcome on your lack of ability or other circumstances. In contrast, if you have hope and optimistically think your efforts will make a difference, you will keep trying for much longer. Positive thoughts such as, "Maybe this will work," motivate you to spend more time thinking and trying various things. These behaviors increase your chances of success.

In many situations, success comes from repeatedly trying and from refusing to give up because of failure. Optimistic people tend to keep working and thinking success will eventually come, but pessimistic people often give up and make their poor expectations come true. One researcher studied 500 incoming freshmen at a university and found a test of optimism predicted their grades the first year better than did either their SAT scores or high-school grades. Perhaps this was because optimistic people tend to stay motivated despite frustrations and failures.

The self-fulfilling prophecy can also operate in your social life. Suppose you go to a social event thinking to yourself things like: "I'm such a bore," "Nobody will like me," "I never make a good impression," and "I'll never make any friends." Thinking pessimistically, feeling inadequate, and fearing inevitable rejection, you will probably talk and mingle very little and never offer invitations. You might even see events in a distorted manner, assuming people hadn't come over to talk to you or they eventually walked away because they didn't like you, or you might assume the man looking at you must think you are weird. Although withdrawn behavior rarely leads to friendships, you may decide making no friends there gives further proof of your dullness. Alternatively, suppose you go to a social event feeling just as awkward, but telling yourself things like: "Lots of people are nervous at first. Concentrate on being friendly," "Everyone has to get used to rejection," "I don't need to be perfect. Quit worrying and go," and "The more I do it, the smoother I'll be." These thoughts help you mingle and practice your conversation skills. You may not make a friend there, but your thoughts and actions are more likely to lead to a friendship sometime, somewhere.

Our thoughts greatly influence our emotions and personal problems. Negative thoughts are common in bad moods and depression, and positive thoughts go with feeling good and happy. Experiments show spending time thinking about happy, sad, or angry situations often causes these feelings to arise. Consider how bad you would feel if you spent twenty minutes thinking about the worst things people ever said or did to you, the worst times of your life, and all your faults and mistakes. Habitually thinking about negative things tends to drag you down into depression. Angry thoughts make it more difficult to calm down, to see the other person's point of view, and to act in respectful ways. If no negotiation or solution occurs, angry thoughts simply keep us tense, our feelings inflamed, and our mood disturbed. Similarly, upsetting thoughts help cause anxiety, thoughts of needing addictive substances help cause addiction, dwelling on loss helps cause grief, etc.

Changing habits of negative thinking helps a great deal in changing emotions and improving personal problems. Negative thinking is counterproductive, self-defeating thinking that makes you feel worse, see things in a worse light, and act in ways that often interfere with goals. The more you think negatively, the worse you feel. Positive thoughts help you feel better, see things in a better light, and act more sensibly and effectively. Optimistic, hopeful thoughts improve your chances of success in work and social life. Much research suggests optimism in facing losses and failures promotes mental health, whereas pessimism does the opposite. Let's look at some categories of negative thinking and some positive thought alternatives for each, on the following pages.

These examples make it clear how our thoughts can influence our feelings and problem behaviors. When a problem frustrates us, we should either do something constructive about it or learn to accept it. Negative thinking resigns you to problem emotions and keeps you from feeling calm

Negative Thoughts	Helpful Alternatives

Inferiority

Other people seem so much more confident (or successful, popular, etc.) than me.	In all areas of life, you can always find people who are better or luckier than you and people who are worse or
I don't have any talent.	less fortunate than you.
I have no discipline, no will power.	I'll try to do the best I can.
I'm a complete failure.	I'm not going to give up!
I'm worthless, no good.	Making mistakes is only human.
I have no patience whatsoever.	My qualities include ... (make a list)
I'll never be able to ...	I can do anything if I put enough time
I don't have any brains.	and effort into it.
I'm a born loser.	I have a good family life. That's all
I'm so weird.	that matters.
Dwelling on concerns about status.	Many things are more important than
Dwelling on unattractiveness.	looks.

Lack of Charm

Who would want to date me?	The more I do this, the smoother I'll
I have no sense of humor.	be.
I'm such a bore.	People are often nervous at first. Just
I'm so dull.	concentrate on being friendly.
I make a lousy impression on other people.	Well, it was easier than last time.
I'm a wallflower and I always will be.	I was nervous, but people usually don't notice. I'll improve.
I don't know how to flirt and I never will.	You don't need to be funny all the time.
I'm the worst conversationalist in the world.	Even popular people sit in a corner sometimes. You have to share the
I always say the wrong thing.	limelight.

Lack of Ability, Mistakes, Failure

I can't do it. It'll be awful.	I'll try to do the best I can.
I'm too nervous. It'll never come off right.	If at first you don't succeed, try, try again. If I give up, I'll fail.
See! I'll never be any good at this.	Practice makes perfect.
I know I'll mess it up.	I don't need to be perfect. I'll learn.
I just know I'll make a fool of myself.	Maybe this will work.
I don't want to try. I could never do it.	Mistakes are the stepping stones of
I'm not smart enough. I might as well not try.	learning. I'm going to hold my head up high.
That proves I'm a total jerk.	Well, I know that doesn't work. What else can I try?

Negative Thoughts	Helpful Alternatives
What's the use? I give up. I can't do anything right.	If I work hard and refuse to give up, I'll get it.

Pessimism about Life or the World

The world is going downhill. Things
    just get worse and worse.
Life is futile and meaningless.
Life is just one problem after another.
    It never ends.
Life is misery and then you die.
Life is unfair.
People don't care anymore. They're
    out for whatever they can get.
I have nothing to look forward to.
Nothing ever works out for me.
I'll never have what I want.
	Problems have been around since time
	    began, but so have cleverness and
	    courage.
	We have spices, fruits, and material
	    comforts that Medieval kings would
	    have envied.
	Most people are pretty good.
	Life is what you make of it.
	A winner gets ahead by working for his
	    goals.
	I'm willing to do what it takes to get
	    the things I want.

Lack of Love, Rejection in Romance

Nobody understands me.
I just don't belong.
I'm so all alone.
I know he won't find me interesting.
I knew she'd reject me. I'm so boring.
I can't live without her.
I'll never get over him.
I'm going to be an old maid (or lonely
    bachelor) all my life.
Nobody cares about me and nobody
    ever will.
What's the use? I'll never find love.
Without a lover, life is endless
    depression.
How could anyone ever love me?
She's the only one I could ever care
    for.
	Nobody likes rejection, but I'll get
	    over it.
	I'll pick the places I'd like to go to
	    meet people.
	Moaning for a lover will turn people
	    off. What interests and activities can
	    I develop?
	I wish she hadn't left me, but it'll be
	    fun to start dating again.
	Rejection is a normal part of life.
	I'll find someone I get along with
	    better someday.
	It's not the end of the world. Being
	    cheerful will help me find someone
	    new.
	Maybe she's too busy or deeply
	    involved. I'll ask someone else.

Social Hostility or Rejection

They really think I'm no good! There
    must be something wrong with me.
I made such a fool of myself. I can't
    ever go back there.
	I know I'm living a good life. That's
	    all that matters.
	People respect a guy who can hold his
	    head up after a mistake.

Negative Thoughts	Helpful Alternatives
It's not fair they're against me. I can't stand it!	It's not worth getting upset about. Plenty of people like me as I am.
This is just awful. They hate me.	You can't please everyone, no matter how hard you try.
It's my fault she doesn't like me anymore.	I wonder why he's so moody.
He seems angry. I must have done something wrong.	Maybe he's having some kind of personal problem or maybe he's just
The way he acts just tears me apart.	having a bad day. I guess I shouldn't
I just know he doesn't like me.	take it personally.

Chained to the Past

I'm this way because my parents ...	I'll keep trying until I can ...
I'm this way because when I was growing up ...	It'll take time and effort, but I'll see it through.
My folks never taught me to control my bad habit of ...	I'll get over it.
I've never been the kind of person who could ...	Today is a new day. From here on in, I'm going to ...
I just don't have the will power to change.	I'll take one day at time.
My dad had a very bad temper. That's why I ...	It's hard to change, but this time I won't give up.
People will never change their opinion of me.	It's never too late to change. If I stick with it for long enough, people will see I've changed.
I've been this way for so long. It's too late to change now.	While I look for new friends who won't lead me to my old ways, I
I'll never change. I might as well not even try.	need to keep busy and do things I enjoy.

Depression, Excessive Grief

Thoughts from any of the previous sections: Inferiority, Lack of Charm, Lack of Ability, Mistakes, Failure, Pessimism about Life or the World, Lack of Love, Rejection in Romance, Social Hostility or Rejection, Chained to the Past.	Time heals all things. Maybe if I start reading some books, going to clubs, and learning to cook, I'll feel better. Thank goodness for my friends.
Dwelling on sorrows or problems.	Once I get started, I won't feel so tired.
I can't shake how I feel.	Let's not drown in my own tears.
Why did it have to happen?	What interests would I like now?
I'll never get over this.	This isn't the first time I've been down and out! I'll get over it.
I just don't feel up to it.	It's hard to lose someone you love, but I can accept my pain.

Negative Thoughts	Helpful Alternatives

I can't help how I feel.
I don't have any energy.
Nothing interests me anymore.
I feel so exhausted. I wish I could stay in bed all day.

Enough of this self pity!
I've been dwelling on this long enough. It's time to get back in the swing of things.

Anger

I'll always have a bad temper.
I can't control my anger. I just blow up.
When I get angry, there's no stopping me.
I don't have any patience. I never did.
Dwelling on a quarrel.
Dwelling on a humiliating episode or an insult.
That rotten creep. I can't stand her!
Thoughts about cursing and insulting the target of your anger.
That burns me up! I think he does this just to make me angry.
I can't get over it! The nerve! Who does she think she is!

A bad temper is just a habit. I can change it if I keep working on it.
From now on, whenever I'm angry, I'll wait until I calm down before I try to settle anything.
I don't like it, but I'll get over it.
No use getting upset over it. What's done is done. I can't change it.
No use dwelling on it. I guess I'll call someone and go to a movie.
Well, at least now I know not to trust him so much.
I guess I'll call a friend and get it off my chest.
Later when I'm calm, I'll decide what to say to her.

Anxiety, Worry, Fear, Phobia

Worrying about possible problems and real problems.
Other people seem so much more relaxed than me.
I'm so nervous. It'll be horrible.
I'm better off not going. I'll be so nervous, I'll look like a fool.
I can't help it. It just comes over me.
I've tried, but I just can't shake it.
I'm too nervous. I can't do it.
I can't stand it. I tremble, my stomach gets queasy, and I have to turn back.
No! I couldn't stand it!

That's not very likely.
Never sweat the little stuff.
Everybody gets the jitters. People usually don't notice.
Just concentrate on being friendly. It'll be fine.
Being anxious won't hurt anything.
It won't be so bad. I'll feel great when it's over and done with.
It'll get easier with practice.
My fear will come and go. It's OK.
It will be over in no time.
I'll try my best. I'll just have to fake it until I make it!

Negative Thoughts	Helpful Alternatives

Insomnia

I wish I could just get some sleep.	It's so nice to thoroughly relax and let
Oh no! It's already 2 A.M. Darn it!	my mind wander where it will.
I never get enough sleep. Oh, I hate	My body will get the rest it needs.
insomnia!	If I don't sleep much tonight, I'll make
When will I ever get to sleep!	up for it tomorrow night.
It's been one hour already. I just know	Just relax and get some good rest. No
this is going to be a bad night.	use worrying about it.
If I don't sleep soon, tomorrow will be	I guess I'll read a book until I get tired.
awful.	It's so cozy to just lie here and rest.
It always takes me forever to fall asleep.	This is really pleasant.

Addiction

Dwelling on desires, cravings.	I need new activities to keep my mind
I'll never be able to quit for very long.	off my addiction. I'll do gardening,
I've been an addict for too long. I	jogging, and artwork.
wouldn't know what to do without it.	If I can flirt drinking, I can learn to do
Life would be boring without my	it without drinking.
highs.	It's going to be tough, but I'm
I hate doing chores without getting	determined to succeed.
high!	I'll get used to partying and doing my
I can't flirt without drinking.	chores without getting high.
Withdrawal would be horrible. I can't	Maybe I won't have any withdrawal
go through it.	symptoms.
Withdrawal is too hard. I give up.	Once this withdrawal ends, I'll be free.

Marital Problems

I can't stand it when she does that!	No use letting it upset me. We've
Why did I ever marry her!	talked about this before. Just forget
I'm going to get a divorce. Then he'll	it.
be sorry!	I'll have to bring this up tonight when
He's a rotten husband!	I've calmed down.
I feel so bored in this marriage. I have	We used to have fun. We should start
to get out.	going dancing and camping again.
There's no love or romance left in our	All marriages have problems.
marriage anymore.	You can save any marriage if you
We don't even like each other	really want to. First I'll work on
anymore.	showing more interest and warmth
We're just too different to ever make	toward her.
this marriage work.	Let's set aside some times for problem
If only I had married ... instead of her.	solving.

and content and confronting problems in constructive ways. Instead of seeing problems as normal, tolerable, manageable, or challenges to overcome, people with habits of negative thinking often overreact and blow things out of proportion. Negative thoughts continually create bad feelings and cause misery or upset over life circumstances.

Sometimes firmly fixed negative beliefs color our worlds without our realizing it. We may never consciously think the negative thoughts. Rather, our feelings indicate we hold the negative beliefs or assumptions. For example: When you feel inadequate, some of the negative thoughts listed above concerning inferiority, lack of charm, or lack of ability may feel true to you, whether or not you ever actually think them. When you feel overwhelmed, some of the negative thoughts concerning pessimism or depression may describe your feelings well. If perceiving dislike, hostility, or rejection devastates you, you probably feel like endorsing some of the negative thoughts concerning social hostility or rejection. If you have a bad temper, you can probably easily relate to the angry thoughts listed above, whether or not you ever actually think them.

When grouped together in a list, negative thoughts are obviously negative. Detecting your own negative thoughts is much more difficult, but you can recognize many negative thoughts by their extreme nature. The following thoughts all paint things in extreme terms: "I am the worst conversationalist in the world," "I always mess things up," "I have no sense of humor," "Anything I try turns out terrible," "Nobody understands me," "I'll never be able to dance," and "I can't stand it!" Notice in these examples and in the above lists that many of the negative thoughts are overgeneralizations using the words *always, no, anything, nobody, everyone, never,* and *can't.*

Some negative thoughts involve the use of negative labels, such as complete failure, bore, born loser, rotten creep, lousy mother, etc. When you apply a negative label to another person in anger, you keep yourself angry or upset. When you habitually think of yourself in terms of a negative label, you define yourself in a way that reduces your hope for change. People who do this often resign themselves to the social role it implies. Children whose parents constantly scold and insult them often come to believe their parents' descriptions of them are true. With low self-esteem, these children have little hope of changing and put little effort into improving. This is another kind of self-fulfilling prophecy. Similarly, when adults come to think of themselves as boring, bad tempered, alcoholic, addicted, sluttish, homosexual, neurotic, mentally ill, or criminal, they often resign themselves to the social roles these labels imply.

The best way to find your negative thought habits is to write down negative thoughts. Some people prefer to tape record them. Write down your thoughts anytime you notice one that might be negative or seems to contribute to your feeling bad. Then spend a minute or two every hour or so reviewing the time interval for possible negative thoughts to jot down. At the very least, review your thoughts four times a day. If you review them only once or twice a day, you will forget many because negative thoughts tend to be habitual and automatic. Pay particular attention to your thoughts when your mood changes for the worse. Your thoughts at these times are the most likely to be counterproductive. Write these thoughts down even if you don't think they contribute to the negative emotion. Never evaluate these thoughts when your mood changes for the worse; always evaluate them later, in a calm, content mood. Negative thoughts will be more obvious when you don't feel angry, depressed, or emotional. The following questions help in judging whether the thoughts you collected are negative. These questions also help you look at problem situations in more constructive ways.

Questions for Evaluating and Fighting Negative Thoughts

How does this thought make me feel? Does it help keep me depressed or angry? Nervous, anxious, or fearful? Frustrated or upset? Grieving? Guilty?

Am I being negative?

Am I dwelling on something negative? A flaw? A mistake? Something I want but don't have?

Am I minimizing qualities in myself?

Am I overlooking good in other people or the situation?

Am I frustrating myself by wishing something I can't change wasn't true or by feeling something I can't change shouldn't be?

Am I overreacting or blowing things out of proportion?

Am I blowing one detail out of proportion?

Am I overgeneralizing by using words like *always, no, anything, nobody, everyone, never,* and *can't?*

Is it really true? Why? How do I know? What is the proof?

Have I asked what they really said or thought or did?

Could this situation have had nothing to do with me?

Can I look at this another way? How else could I interpret it? And how else?

What would I think if I felt better or wasn't so worried?

What would I say to a friend in this situation if I was trying to help?

What would a counselor, minister, or wise person trying to help say?

How likely is my fear?

Am I focusing on facts that are not relevant to this immediate situation?

Is the event really less important than I first thought?

Did a similar situation ever work out satisfactorily, better than I now feel this situation will?

Haven't I experienced something similar before, survived, and gotten over it?

Am I underestimating my ability to cope, to deal with it?

Haven't I felt this way before? What did I do then? What could I do better now?

Can I do something about this?

Do I need to learn to accept this?

Changing your thinking habits can make many things less disagreeable. If you don't like your job, for example, you may habitually think about what a chore it is, how much you hate it, and how much you'd rather do something else for a living. You may think negative thoughts about your job from the time you get up to go to work until you get home, and this may keep you miserable all day long. You will feel better about working at a job you dislike if you practice positive thoughts such as: "At least it pays the rent," "I sure do like my paycheck," and "I'm going to do the best I can."

After identifying your negative thoughts, write several positive statements for each negative one. Most of the questions in the above list aid in generating ideas for more helpful thought alternatives. First, focus on what you can do about the problem. Replace unfulfilled longing with realistic goals or plans for change. When you can't do anything to change a problem situation, work toward acceptance. Use thoughts like, "I don't really need it." You may need to change your priorities to fit the reality of the situation. Write optimistic, rather than pessimistic, views of it. Instead of dwelling on sorrows, practice thankfulness for your friends, pleasures, strengths, and other blessings. When you compare yourself to other people negatively, emphasize that no matter what trait you consider, you can always find people who are either more fortunate or less fortunate than you. Find the good part of your failures, problems, actions, experiences, or situations. You can find good in almost anything. View failure as a learning experience teaching you what doesn't work, so you can succeed in later attempts. If you have trouble with your child, take pride in setting limits to teach your child, in supporting, and in forgiving your child. Relabel crying, vulnerability, or anxious, upset feelings as sensitivity.

Don't use overly simplistic, general thought alternatives such as: "It's not so bad," "That's not true," or "Look at the bright side." Statements like these become trite when you use them in a variety of situations. An effective alternative focuses on helpful aspects or views of the particular situation. A positive thought alternative should also sound convincing and help you feel the way you want to feel, act in your own best interest, and avoid further problems.

Whenever you find yourself thinking one of your habitual negative thoughts, think "STOP!" This makes you more aware of negative thoughts and helps you reject them. Then practice substituting more helpful thought alternatives every time. Keep a list of your most common negative thought habits and positive alternatives for each. Refer to this list whenever negative thoughts arise, until you can substitute helpful alternatives from memory or immediately make up new thought alternatives to counter the negative thoughts. When a negative thought arises and circumstances make it impossible to read your list, read it at the next convenient moment.

In addition, read all of your positive thought alternatives several times each day. This helps you build new positive thinking habits. It also helps make up for the times negative thoughts arise and you forget to read your list or you can't stop and read it. Because of similarities between many habitual negative thoughts, you can often counter new negative thoughts with some of your planned alternatives. If none of your alternatives seem appropriate, write down the new negative thought and create some positive alternatives for it later.

Like other bad habits, negative thinking can be very difficult to change. You can only change it by practice, practice, and more practice. The more you flood your mind with positive thought alternatives by reading and practicing them, the more your thoughts and feelings will change for the better. Many people witness the power of positive thinking when they practice and repeat affirmations for spiritual growth such as, "I will face each new day with peace and love in my heart." It may take months of daily effort changing your habits of negative thinking before you notice much change in your feelings, however.

Recommended Additional Readings and Support Groups:

Please refer to the end of the next chapter, Emotions, for helpful readings and
  support groups for negative thought habits.

5. Emotions

Act the way you want to feel and the feelings will come.

If you don't control your emotions, they will control you.

Some emotions are so basic and primeval many animals exhibit them: interest, affection, fear, being startled, and emotions about sexuality and aggression, including those associated with winning and losing in aggressive encounters. But people all over the world do not share the same emotions. The most obvious example is trance states of possession by spirits, gods, demons, or ancestors. These emotional states are very unfamiliar in Western cultures, but occur today in places such as Latin America, Africa, Turkey, Israel, India, Cambodia, and Bali. To some degree, we learn and develop our emotions. Each culture has its own standards of socially acceptable behavior for when and how to show emotions. Children learn these ways early in life. Cultures may differ greatly in their emphases on particular emotions and in how to view emotions. For example, Western cultures greatly emphasize romantic love, but many other cultures put little emphasis on it. In Tahiti, people consider disliking a particular food a fear. People in French-speaking West Africa may experience acute anxiety as an attack on the body by witches, with a threat of immediate death.

The Semai Senoi of West Malaysia are a very peaceful people who share many of their possessions. Authorities received no reports of assault during a 15-year period in their homeland. These people lack strong, hostile anger and view violence as puzzling and very peculiar, but they constantly fear storms, strangers, supernatural beings, and animals. All of them report fears and view fear as normal and socially acceptable. Many other cultures around the world are very peaceful. The Utku Eskimos of the Hudson Bay rarely feel anger, perhaps because they emphasize an acceptance of life's problems and desires to help and protect others. Some Eskimo tribes have no word for anger; the closest word equivalent means childish.

In contrast, other cultures used to be full of suspicion, anger, treachery, and hatred. The Mundugumor of New Guinea, former headhunters and cannibals, were one such quarrelsome culture. The Mundugumor called their leaders "really bad men." The leaders were the most aggressive, fearless men who bought or stole the most wives, quickly saw insult and took revenge, and betrayed others with impunity. The society mourned these men at death more than others. Often brothers fought each other with weapons, husbands abused wives for becoming pregnant, and babies died of neglect. Other especially quarrelsome cultures included the Dobu of Melanesia, the Chukchi of Siberia, and the Yanomamo of the Amazon jungle. The Yanomamo men often raided other villages for women. If a Yanomamo group tired of constant warfare and moved to a new garden site, the new neighbors might have invited them to a feast and killed all the men to take the women. Yanomamo men frequently punished disobedient women, sometimes brutally with weapons.

Cultures view sadness and sorrow in very different ways, too. Western cultures avoid sadness and classify deep depression as a mental illness. In Chinese, Tahitian, Inuit Eskimo, and the African language of Yoruba, it is difficult to translate the words *sadness* or *depression.* In Chinese tradition, negative or disturbed feelings indicate mental illness, shame the self and the family, can lead to physical illness, and now indicate unhelpful, antisocial political thinking. Among Yoruban Nigerians, guilt is rare but depression may produce burning sensations, crawling sensations of maggots in the body, or claims of being a witch. Some African languages use a single word for depression and anger, and some American Indian and Malaysian cultures had no words for depression.

Buddhists, however, find important meaning in sorrow, believing life is suffering and attachment to worldly pleasures and desires causes suffering. Buddhists strive to detach themselves from desires, usually through meditation, to reach enlightenment. For Buddhists, hopelessness and a loss of a sense of pleasure are important first steps toward enlightenment, rather than symptoms of depression. Many Asian cultures, then, greatly value sadness as a wise step toward salvation. The Shiite Muslims of Iran find important religious meaning in sorrow, too, viewing life as tragic because just people face an unjust world. In this context, deep sorrow is the mark of a wise man. Similarly, diaries of England and America from the 1600s show people were proud of responding to interpersonal problems with sadness, and they associated sadness with patience, wisdom, humility, and religious strength.

Cultures also differ in how much they express emotions. The Chewong of Malaysia have only eight words for emotions and show little emotion in their faces or in gestures, but they seem to emphasize fear and shyness. The Balinese of Indonesia and the Thai-Lao of northeast Thailand believe in restricting emotional extremes for a calm inner state. In contrast, the Kaluli of Papua New Guinea express many emotions openly and very dramatically.

The Kaluli often express anger in a frightening rage, express grief in sobbing speech and loud wails, and express embarrassment, fear, compassion, and other emotions in dramatic ways. The Kaluli even use traces of musical notes from tropical bird songs in their intonation to express different feelings. The Ilongot of the Philippines also tend to express passionate feelings openly.

Emotional problems, too, vary greatly through history and among cultures. During the Middle Ages in Europe, _dancing mania,_ a mass hysteria, erupted in city after city; when afflicted, people jumped, screamed, foamed at the mouth, and danced wildly and convulsively. When Freud studied patients in Vienna, hysterical paralysis, blindness, and numbness were much more common than they are today. In this century, rates of severe schizophrenia, particularly the catatonic type with its bizarre postures, repetitive movements, immobility, or muteness, are decreasing, while rates of paranoid schizophrenia and depression are increasing.

The eating disorder anorexia is far more prevalent in Western, industrialized cultures than in less developed countries. Some researchers argue the following problems are also specific to Western culture: premenstrual syndrome, overdose, shoplifting, Type A personalities (impatient, aggressive, workaholics), agoraphobia in women, exhibitionism in men, and child abductions by fathers from divorced women with custody. In Nigeria, men (and in rare cases, women) may report missing sex organs after exchanging greetings with a stranger, feeling the stranger used witchcraft to steal the organs. Examining the organs usually doesn't convince these people; they often respond that the body part has changed since the greeting. In Senegal, hysterical mobs killed eight people in one week, convinced foreign sorcerers shriveled sex organs with a handshake.

All of these interesting examples of varying emotions among different cultures emphasize the social role aspects of our emotions and emotional problems. We grow up with certain cultural expectations about what people normally feel and how to express emotions and we learn to think and feel accordingly.   For example, in our society, women generally report experiencing both positive and negative emotions more intensely than do men. If we learn from our society to emphasize certain emotions and limit others, we can certainly learn to change our emotional behaviors, with enough work and practice.

In fact, learning to control our emotions is very important. We must learn to restrain impulsive desires to live harmoniously with others and to work toward goals.   We must learn to deal with negative emotions constructively to be happy and resolve conflicts. Emotional self-control is the basis for good character, maturity, satisfying relationships, self-esteem, happiness, and accomplishment. The following research highlights the importance of this skill. The study used a marshmallow test to measure impulsiveness in four-year-olds at a daycare center and then followed these children until the end of high school. In the marshmallow test, somebody puts one marshmallow in front of a child in a room and leaves the room to run an errand, giving the following instructions: You can eat the marshmallow at any time, but if you wait for me to return, you can have two marshmallows. About one-third of the children grabbed the marshmallow, usually within seconds of the experimenter leaving the room. Those who waited the 15 or 20 minutes to earn the larger reward, however, tended to grow up to be more mature, confident, trustworthy, dependable, assertive, achieving adolescents. On the average, these teenagers had dramatically higher SAT scores and were less likely to become angry, upset, immobilized, or disorganized by stress or frustrations. The children who grabbed the marshmallow were more likely, as adolescents, to have low self-esteem, shy away from social contacts, be stubborn or indecisive, and provoke arguments and fights with their bad temper.

Fortunately, we have more power to change our emotions than people generally assume. Our thoughts, emotions, and behaviors are very much interrelated, and each of these can change the others. People tend to believe events *make* them feel happy, sad, depressed, angry, upset, etc. Events help cause our emotions, but we are free to respond to any event in many different ways. We can respond to problems with great anger, mild frustration, calm problem solving, depression, humor concerning life's trials, etc. When we believe circumstances *made* us feel a particular way, however, we feel stuck with an emotion that seems inevitable given the life circumstances. When you blame circumstances or other people for your emotions, learn to take responsibility for your emotions by thinking or saying, "I made myself feel ... when that happened. I didn't have to feel that way." Thinking of your emotions in these ways helps you gain control of them.

Often the fastest way to change emotions is to change behavior. Lonely, depressed people who begin to attend various club meetings feel much better after finding a social club they enjoy. Very timid people who find other people taking advantage of them may gain much self-esteem and confidence after once confronting another person. Acting the way you want to feel, frequently helps you change your feelings. Depressed people who act cheerfully for a few weeks often begin to feel more cheerful, particularly when other people respond favorably. Shy people who perform very outgoing acts gain practice and self-confidence that help them become more extroverted. People with great fears who force themselves to remain in fearful situations find the fear lessens. This book describes the most effective things you can do to change problem emotions.

Another way to change emotions seems paradoxical but can work. At times going deeper into a problem emotion can help you overcome it. Crying is an excellent way to release and finish emotional pain. Allowing yourself to sink deeply into a problem feeling may bring on or remind you of images, thoughts, ideas, urges, expectations, ambivalent feelings, and fantasies that relate to it. This can teach you plenty about the sources of those problem feelings and possible solutions.

Deeply experiencing a problem emotion and accepting it as a normal part of life can help resolve the emotion in a way that was impossible when you tried to avoid it. Sometimes it seems the more you try not to feel a negative emotion, the more it plagues you. Perhaps we become obsessed with the problem emotion because we constantly worry about avoiding it. Perhaps the acceptance involved in deliberately and fully experiencing the emotion makes it less important and less troublesome when it does occur. In any case, by reaching, experiencing, and accepting our deepest depression, we often become more able to feel joy. Every time we face our worst fears and fully experience and accept them, we reduce their hold on us. By experiencing our anger and expressing it appropriately, we can often leave our resentments behind and feel love again.

Repression is either the deliberate avoidance of upsetting memories or emotions until you completely forget them or the unplanned, automatic rejection of them from the conscious mind. When a person is no longer aware of repressed memories and emotions, psychologists say they are in the person's _unconscious mind_. Sigmund Freud believed repressing upsetting emotions uses up mental energy and interferes with happiness and productivity. People who explore important avoided or forgotten traumas, reexperience the upsetting emotions, and work through these emotions, often find this finishing process leads to increased happiness and productivity. It seems unrecognized emotions have great power over us and often lead us to repeat negative patterns. Recognizing and talking about strong feelings helps to organize the experiences, work through them, and loosen their hold on you.

Channeling your painful emotions into creative mediums such as art, poetry, short stories, music, or interpretive dance helps in resolving them. A dismal drawing or painting from depressive imagery can help finish depression. By producing works of art or creative writing, we rise above and beyond the negative emotions. Even the darkest despair sometimes results in great works of art. Of course, it helps to express your negative emotions in creative mediums even if the results are of poor quality. Please refer to the lists of music and art activities in chapter 8 for ideas.

Many people believe feelings are irrational and interfere with good decision making. Strong emotions can certainly lead to unwise decisions, but in general, feelings help you make personal decisions you will be happy with. Emotions are vital to our personal relationships. Sharing feelings heightens intimacy, deepens understanding, and aids problem solving. Expressing irritations as they arise and finding solutions to these problems helps us avoid our resentments mounting into rage. Recognizing and expressing emotions is essential in communicating, asserting yourself, controlling your anger, maintaining friendships, marriage, and raising children.

Many people are in poor touch with their own feelings. We suppress our feelings early in life because of stereotyped notions that feelings are unimportant, irrational, or a sign of weakness and that boys and adults shouldn't cry. You may claim you don't feel anything in a particular situation, while other people sense you really do have feelings but you are unaware of them. If you don't recognize and express your feelings very often, other people can easily misinterpret them, and close friends may become frustrated by your lack of emotions.

Improve your relationships by practicing communicating your feelings more often. It may seem awkward and difficult at first, but it will become easier with practice. Become more aware of your own feelings by asking for feedback. Ask other people what they thought you were feeling and how you came across. Ask them why they thought so. Ask your friends to pay attention and point out any feelings they notice or think they perceive in you. Keep an open mind to the answers you receive. Your friends will be right about your emotions more often than you initially think they are. Become more aware of your facial expressions and your nonverbal communication.

Physical symptoms can make excellent clues to buried emotions. A list of physical symptoms that may result from burying an emotion such as anger, anxiety, or depression follows on the next page. Symptoms such as these may sometimes be your only clue to a buried emotion. A buried or avoided emotion may result in a physical symptom even when you feel and express other emotions.

List of Physical Symptoms Perhaps Caused by Buried Emotions

clammy hands	louder voice
constipation	lump in the throat
diarrhea	psychosomatic outbreaks
facial tension	(ulcer, asthma, eczema, etc.)
faster breathing	restlessness, faster movements
faster heartbeat	shortness of breath
fidgeting	sweating
gritting teeth	tight abdomen
headache	tight chest
heart palpitations	tight muscles
hunger attacks	tired all the time, fatigued
loss of appetite	twitching muscles
loss of energy, slowed down	upset stomach

Exaggerate the tiny feelings you notice to practice feeling and expressing them. Bring forth the hidden intensity by magnifying faint flickers of emotion. Do this for practice in recognizing feelings and for preparing to express the emotion effectively in real life. If you notice slight frustration or irritation, for example, you can turn it into anger, either at home by yourself or with a trusted friend. Complain loudly and angrily. Once you contact your anger, practice using this anger effectively in a convincing, appropriate complaint.

Finally, use the following list of feelings to practice expressing your emotions. Many people need to practice recognizing and expressing their emotions to improve their relationships: unemotional or unassertive people, people with anger control problems, and those who want to learn to share their feelings without antagonizing other people. The list helps you understand more clearly what you feel and helps you express your feelings to others more precisely. Practice by using "I feel ..." statements at least twice a day. Be very careful with your "I feel ..." statements, however—use the advice in the section on Criticism and Conflicts in chapter 6 to avoid communicating blame. Certain words in this list describe perceptions relating to feeling states: cheated, ignored, ridiculed, insulted, imposed upon, wronged, degraded, abused, persecuted, tormented, etc. When using these words, emphasize you are describing your feelings and perceptions, not necessarily deliberate acts or the truth.

List of Feelings

abandoned	bitter	cruel	elated
abused	blamed	crushed	embarrassed
accepted	bold	curious	encouraged
accepting	bored	cynical	energetic
accused	bothered	daring	enjoyment
adamant	brave	defeated	enterprising
adequate	broken-hearted	defensive	enthusiastic
adore	brutalized	defiant	envy
admiration	bullied	degraded	evil
adventurous	burdened	delighted	exasperated
affection	calm	demanding	excited
afraid	capable	demoralized	fair
agreeable	care	dependent	fascinated
aggressive	cautious	depressed	fear
agitated	challenged	desire	fellowship
agony	charitable	desirable	feminine
alarmed	cheated	despair	firm
alone	cheered up	desperate	flirtatious
altruistic	cheerful	determined	foolish
amazed	childlike	devilish	forgiven
ambitious	clever	devoted	forgiving
ambivalent	close	dignity	frantic
amused	cold	disappointed	free
angry	comfortable	disapproval	friendly
annoyed	comforted	discouraged	frightened
anxiety	compassion	disgraced	frustrated
apologetic	competitive	disgust	furious
appreciated	compliant	disillusioned	gay
appreciate	concerned	dislike	generous
apprehensive	confident	disoriented	glad
approval	confused	dissatisfied	gloomy
arrogant	conspicuous	distant	good
ashamed	contempt	distress	grateful
assertive	content	distrust	grave
astonished	controlled	disturbed	greedy
attracted	cooperative	dominated	grief
awe	cowardly	dominant	grouchy
awful	craving	doubt	guilt
awkward	crazy	driven	happy
bad	creative	duty-bound	harassed
baited	critical	eager	hard-hearted
betrayed	criticized	ecstatic	hate

hated	irritated	passionate	rude
helpful	jealous	passive	ruthless
helpless	jovial	patient	sacrificing
homesick	joy	peaceful	sad
honored	judgmental	persecuted	satisfied
hopeful	justified	pessimistic	screwed up
hopeless	kindness	petrified	secure
horrible	lazy	pity	self-conscious
horrified	left out	playful	self-pitying
hostile	lenient	pleasant	self-respect
humble	lethargic	pleased	selfish
humiliated	like	pleasure	sensitive
hurt	lively	powerful	sentimental
hypocritical	lonely	powerless	serious
hysterical	longing	prejudiced	shaky
idealistic	lost	pressured	shocked
ignored	love, in love	privileged	shy
immature	loved	proud	silly
impatient	lucky	prudish	sincere
important	lust	pure	skeptical
imposed upon	manipulated	puzzled	sociable
impressed	masculine	quarrelsome	soft-hearted
impulsive	mean	quiet	sorrow
inadequate	mischievous	rage	sorry
incapable	miserable	rebellious	special
incompetent	moody	regret	spiteful
indecisive	mouthy	rejected	spontaneous
independent	moved	relaxed	stable
indifferent	naughty	relieved	startled
industrious	needed	reluctant	stingy
infatuated	need	remorse	strict
inferior	nervous	repulsed	strong
inhibited	neutral	resentment	stubborn
insecure	noble	reserved	stupid
inspired	obsessed	resigned	submissive
insulted	OK, okay	respect	suffering
intelligent	opposed	respected	sullen
interested	optimistic	responsible	superior
intimidated	outraged	restless	supported
intrigued	overjoyed	revengeful	sure
irresponsible	overwhelmed	ridiculed	surprised
irreverent	panicky	righteous	suspicious
irritable	partial to	romantic	sympathy

tactful	touched	uninterested	vulnerable
tactless	trapped	unloved	wanted
talkative	treasure	unlucky	warm
tempted	triumphant	unprepared	wary
tender	troubled	unsatisfied	weak
tense	trust	unselfish	wicked
terrible	unadventurous	unsociable	wild
terrific	uncomfortable	unstable	willing
terrified	understanding	unsure	wise
thankful	undesirable	unsympathetic	wish
thoughtful	uneasy	unwelcome	wonderful
thrilled	unhappy	unworthy	worried
timid	unimportant	upset	worthless
tolerant	uninhibited	used	wronged
tormented	uninspired	virtuous	

Recommended Additional Readings:

The Feeling Good Handbook. by David D. Burns. NY: Penguin Books, 1989. for
feelings, thinking habits, communication skills, anxiety, fear, phobia.

Feeling Good: The New Mood Therapy. by David D. Burns. NY: Avon Books,
1980. for feelings, thinking habits, anger, guilt, depression, love addiction.

Emotional Intelligence. by Daniel Goleman. New York: Bantam Books, 1995. for
the importance of controlling emotions, but not thinking habits.

Handbook of Culture and Mental Illness: An International Perspective. by Ihsan Al-
lssa, ed. Madison, CT: International Universities Press, 1995.

Support Groups and Hotlines:

Emotions Anonymous 651 647 9712 support groups for any personal problem, pen
pals. on-line: www.emotionsanonymous.org

Recovery Inc. 312 337 5661 support groups for any personal problem, on-line:
www.recovery-inc.com

National Mental Health Association 800 969 6642 referrals for treatment, brochures
on depression, grief, warning signs of mental illness, and other mental health
topics. on-line: www.nmha.org

Co-Dependents Anonymous 602 277 7991 support groups for love or sex addictions
or dealing with a loved one's problems. on-line: www.codependents.org

Overcomers Outreach 800 310 3001 Christ-centered support groups for any
personal problem. on-line: www.overcomersoutreach.org

6. Communication Skills

Once you say something selfish, hurtful, or foolish,
you can't block the impression you gave, nor its effects.

Be quick to hear, slow to speak and anger. (James 1:19)

Good communication is a very important social skill that can deepen understanding, aid problem solving, and reduce tensions. Communication is vital to any relationship. How wonderful it feels when we talk out our feelings, impressions, misunderstandings, and conflicts and each person truly understands the other person's point of view. Teaching communication skills often improves troubled marriages. Any friendship or relationship will benefit from the practice of good communication skills. Let's look at a list of common problems in communication.

Communication Problems

Threats and Intimidation can destroy good relations and open, honest communication faster than anything else.

Yelling in Anger escalates frustrations into a battle of wills in which nobody looks for solutions and nobody will compromise. Chronic anger and yelling undermine warmth and closeness. If you tend to yell in anger, please refer to chapter 28.

Avoiding Issues by Refusing to Discuss Them, Walking Out, Ignoring, Withdrawing, Distracting, or Giving the Silent Treatment leaves problems unresolved. When you use these tactics regularly, intimacy is shallow and needs go unmet. Without communication and problem solving, relationships become dead, empty shells.

Manipulative Communication to Get What You Want (Deceiving, Crying, Pouting, Sulking, or Lying) harms relationships. You build trust with honesty, not feigned emotions. Manipulative behaviors cause resentment, damage trust, and reduce closeness.

Using Personal Knowledge of Sensitive Issues to Hurt Someone is a vicious act that increases hostility.

Bringing Up Old Resentments or the Past is counterproductive unless it has direct relevance to the present problem, because it antagonizes the other person. Instead, focus on issues in the present.

Nagging causes resentment and rebellion. Cooperation is more likely if you problem solve, make polite requests, praise or reward desired behaviors, make contracts, or set reasonable consequences.

Negative Labels (Inconsiderate, Mean, Lazy, etc.) and Insults cause anger, judge a person as flawed in character, and show a lack of faith in the person's ability to change. The use of negative labels can also lead to more of the behavior suggested by the label, particularly in children. This occurs because of anger or low self-esteem and becoming resigned to the negative social role.

Blaming and Attempts to Induce Guilt cause resentment. Avoid telling other people what they *should* do, feel, or want. When attempts to understand the development of a problem deteriorate into battles in which each person tries to blame the other, focus on problem solving. Remember that nobody *makes* you feel hurt, angry, or upset. You are responsible for your own feelings.

The Attitude "I'm Right and You're Wrong" prevents problem solving by interfering with your willingness to compromise. Always keep an open mind during conflicts, and remember your view is not the only way to look at the situation.

Assuming You Know What People Think or Feel and Telling Them, Interpreting Their "True" Wishes or Motivations, or Psychologically Analyzing Them often causes anger, whether you are right or wrong. Examples include: "You're jealous because ...," "You think I can't wait to ...," and "I think it goes back to your relationship with ..." When you are wrong, you unjustly accuse the other person. When you are right, the other person may become angry because they can't face or the truth or don't want to admit it. Instead of stating your views as facts, ask people what they think or feel. If you need to bring up your impressions, clearly describe them as a guess and ask for feedback. For example: "Is it possible you ...?" or "When ... happens, I get the impression ... What are you thinking and feeling when you do that?"

Demands and Ultimatums often result in anger or rebellion. Don't angrily scream a command, and never threaten or hint at extreme, dire actions in an attempt to force cooperation. More effective alternatives include polite requests, problem solving, praising or rewarding desired behaviors, making contracts, or setting reasonable consequences.

Overgeneralizations using such words as *always, never, all, anything, ever, forever,* and *every time* exaggerate things and condemn the other person.

For example: "All you ever think about is ...," "You are forever ...," "You always act like ...," and "You never do anything around here!"

Getting Off the Subject interferes with problem solving. Focus on one specific issue at a time until you find a solution. Don't ramble on to other related issues or similar problems until you resolve the first problem.

<u>Cross-Complaining</u> is a version of getting off the subject in which two people respond to each other's complaints with their own complaints about the other person. Instead of retaliating in this way, focus on problems one at a time until you find solutions to each.

Too Many Interruptions can annoy people, especially when a speaker tries to present details of feelings and perspectives on a problem. Interruptions show you are not listening carefully.

Mixed Messages give contradictory impressions at the same time. For example, one becomes confused when someone says, "That's nice," in a hesitant manner with a worried facial expression. Similarly, a loud voice often contradicts words insisting on the absence of anger. If you feel confused because a tone of voice or facial expression conflicts with the spoken message, point out the reasons for your confusion and ask what the speaker really feels.

Dominating a Conversation by speaking too much is self-centered. Take an interest in other people's activities, feelings, and ideas by listening and asking questions. Chapter 15, Social Life, discusses conversation skills in detail.

Too Many Questions can sometimes annoy other people. Even in the closest relationships, people sometimes need privacy. At other times, too many questions may indicate a lack of trust.

Positive Communication

First and foremost, good communication is predominantly positive. Strive to normally use positive statements many times more often than negative statements, complaints, and criticisms. Focusing yourself on the good in life contributes to happiness and mental health and helps develop the social skill of positive communication. Of course, we occasionally need to discuss negative things to solve problems or share our emotional burdens and receive comfort from other people. In general, however, relationships deteriorate and happiness sours when negativity prevails. A good conversationalist generally avoids burdening other people with personal troubles and complaints.

You can communicate in a variety of positive ways. Share details of your recent experiences and activities, interesting or useful information, ideas, and stories. Show an interest in the ideas, interests, activities, and feelings of the other person. Spice your conversation with wit and humor. Give other people thanks, compliments, praise, approval, encouragement, and emotional support. Practice pointing out things they have done well, things you like about them, and personal qualities or admirable feelings. Be sure to express warmth, affection, and loving concern in your friendships and close relationships.

Unfortunately, it is too easy to take other people for granted and to give little positive feedback to our close friends and family. Great rewards come from practicing positive communication in our close relationships. Psychologists often improve troubled marriages by simply prescribing the daily practice of compliments and affectionate behavior. At first this may seem forced, artificial, or manipulative, but people soon enjoy the new behaviors and learn to communicate comfortably in positive ways. Remember, you can often change your emotions the fastest by changing your behaviors.

Helpful Listening Skills

When you listen in passive silence, the speaker may think you are not paying much attention. By doing a few simple things, you can show you are listening carefully and understand the speaker's point of view. Maintaining regular eye contact, rather than looking around much of the time, indicates interest and attention. Occasional nodding and words or sounds that acknowledge the speaker's message ("yes," "yeah," "uh-huh," "Oh," "hmm," etc.) clearly indicate your attention. Asking questions and clarifying points not only shows undivided attention, but also helps make sure you understand the speaker's message. Your facial expressions and tone of voice may show anything from interest, attention, enthusiasm, warmth, or concern to disinterest, boredom, impatience, coldness, dislike, or disgust.

Good listening skills include acting friendly and respectful toward other people, even when you disagree with them. People deserve respect even if their attitudes, ideas, and feelings are very different from yours. You can act friendly and respectful despite viewing a message as repulsive or immoral. Cultivate an attitude of accepting other people. A good listener will temporarily put aside personal reactions and try to understand the speaker's point of view. This involves trying to put yourself in the person's place and share the speaker's world, feelings, and thoughts. Doing this allows the speaker to become more comfortable, trusting, and honest and to open up more (especially valuable in conflicts between parents and children).

Psychologists use good listening skills to help people look at their feelings and organize their thoughts better. When you ask questions about other people's intentions, views, thoughts, or feelings, you clarify the information for yourself and often help them sort through and define exactly what they think and want. Questions asking for yes or no answers can help, but questions that elicit more information often help even more. Ask questions beginning with who, what, where, when, which, or how.

Another useful listening technique is to occasionally paraphrase the essence of what the person is saying. Don't repeat the person's exact words and don't add your own interpretation of the other person's thoughts or feelings. Just use the given information and reword it. Watch for the speaker's positive and negative feelings and point them out as you paraphrase. People often don't recognize their emotions and often deal with them poorly. By pointing out emotions, you help them feel understood and look at this important part of the situation. Try to pick the right words to match the intensity of the speaker's emotions. Paraphrasing the important points of a rambling explanation helps the other person stay on the subject, review and sort out thoughts and feelings, and pinpoint and clarify things. After a long discussion, summarizing the most important points, ideas, feelings, and decisions helps in getting a good perspective of the whole situation. Psychologists often summarize at the end of a therapy session for this reason.

Even when people feel upset about problems, they often ignore or resent advice they receive. Instead of giving advice right away, try gently leading people to make their own decisions by asking questions, clarifying points, occasionally paraphrasing the essence of what they say and feel, and asking them what they think they should do. Decisions they make while you help them sort their feelings and thoughts will usually please them much more than decisions you suggest. Save your advice until you thoroughly understand the person's situation, viewpoints, and feelings. Suggestions made in the light of such understanding have the greatest chance of being helpful.

Criticism and Conflicts

Criticism can provide valuable feedback and give you the opportunity to learn and grow. People respect those who are mature enough to take criticism well and learn from it. Pay particular attention to any feedback you receive more than once, especially when the same criticism comes from different people. Make sure you fully understand any criticism you receive, by listening carefully and asking questions to clarify the feedback. Ask for specific examples about concrete behaviors. Don't settle for vague complaints. Find out exactly what you did that led to the complaint. If you did something wrong, acted selfishly, accidentally hurt the person's feelings, or did something that caused an inconvenience, apologize and take steps to correct your behavior. Try to make up for what you have done in some way, perhaps by performing kind acts to make the person feel better.

Of course, not all criticism is useful. Consider the other person's motive for criticizing you. Is the person criticizing you in jealousy, revenge, or anger? Did the person have a hard or bad day? Is the person oversensitive or biased? Even if criticism is unfair or exaggerated, there may be a kernel of truth in it. What can you learn from this feedback? If you find some truth in the criticism, say so and apologize. For example, "Well, I'm sure I can sound cold and indifferent at times. I'm sorry I hurt your feelings."

The ability to apologize is an important communication skill. Everyone occasionally makes mistakes and hurts other people's feelings. If you have done something wrong or been negligent, an apology shows a righteous acceptance of responsibility for your mistake, but whether or not you are at fault, an apology is a kind attempt to soothe the person's feelings. The ability to apologize shows wisdom and strength, not weakness. If you find it difficult to apologize, practice by starting with minor, unthreatening issues. For example, "I'm sorry I forgot to take out the garbage. I'll do it now."

Trying to win an argument generally leads to escalated hostilities. Instead, focus on understanding each other, negotiation, and compromise. The ideal compromise, completely satisfying both parties to a conflict, is only occasionally possible. Compromise often means neither party likes the solution very much or both parties dislike the solution, but they can tolerate it and agree upon it.

First, of course, you must alert the other person to the conflict, so problem solving can occur. Always strive to do this in tactful, polite ways to increase the chance of cooperation. Begin with a polite request. If it doesn't result in cooperation, you must express your negative feelings to show the problem needs solving. Deal with minor, but troubling, problems in constructive ways before you become very frustrated or angry. Letting things go may result in mounting tensions and explosive anger. If you become too angry to express your feelings tactfully, wait until you calm down. If you find it uncomfortable or difficult to express negative emotions or if you rarely recognize your feelings until you explode in anger, practice "I feel ..." statements at least twice a day using the list of feelings at the end of chapter 5. Start practicing by sharing unthreatening feelings such as, "I feel a little edgy. Would you please quiet it down a little?" Then gradually work up to more difficult confrontations.

The best way to avoid blaming and hostility when you need to voice frustrations is to use the formula: "When ... happens, I feel ..." Describe what frustrates you in very specific, concrete terms about actual events or behaviors (actions, words, tone of voice, and facial expression). For example, "When you act immature, I feel ..." is not specific. Saying "Whenever you come home in a bad mood and get angry with me, I feel ..." is not specific enough, but saying "Yesterday, when you yelled at me about coming in late, I felt ..." is very specific. Speaking very specifically about the precise event that bothered you avoids exaggeration and overgeneralization. Describing what you feel starting with the word "I" helps avoid negative labels and blaming the other person for your feelings. For example, saying "I feel angry" is much less accusing and hostile than saying "You made me angry."

In using this formula, make sure you always put an emotion after saying "I feel" or "I felt." Otherwise, your statement may come across as hostile or accusing. For example, "When you ..., I felt you didn't care about me," comes across almost as negative and accusing as, "You don't care about me." Never follow "I feel" or "l felt" with a negative statement about the other person. Don't describe the other person's attitudes, character, or intentions. Just describe exactly what happened in observable events and then describe your feelings. You may want to refer to the list of feelings at the end of chapter 5 for help in choosing a precise emotion. Using the formula "When ... happens, I feel ..." to share frustrations in a friendly tone of voice makes it much more likely the other person will consider your feelings and cooperate with you.

In relationships, sharing vulnerable feelings of hurt, fear, disappointment, doubts, uncertainty, and insecurity tend to trigger empathy and promote closeness more often than do stronger feelings like anger, resentment, and thoughts having to do with assertion, power, and control. Very often, the vulnerable feelings are associated with the angrier feelings, and choosing to express the vulnerable ones produces better results. Thus, if you feel like showing anger, try to find the pain, disappointment, or fear underneath and to express, perhaps, your hurt and doubt about the person's love or caring, or fears about the loss of the relationship or whether compromise is coming.

If sharing feelings doesn't result in the problem solving you need, suggest what specific behaviors would satisfy you. State what you want, not what you don't want. If the other person refuses your suggestions, use stronger, more insistent "I" messages such as, "This really bothers me. I must have a solution to this problem!" If this doesn't help, you can offer a reward for cooperation: "If you did ..., I'd be willing to ..." If the other person is not in a good mood, schedule another time to discuss the issue and problem solve.

Make your complaint less negative by adding a positive statement to it. Examine yourself for any positive feelings that can reduce your hostility and put the complaint into better perspective. For example: "I love keeping a nice house for you, but when you bring muddy shoes into it, I really get upset." Or you might say "I really appreciate all your work around here, but I get irritated when you ..." When scolding your child, you might say "I love you and want you to be happy more than anything, so I can't let you "

Recognizing the other person's point of view helps make the person feel understood. Examples include: "I know you're tired, but ...," "You must be pretty upset by now!" and "I'll bet that made for a rough day!" Agreeing with parts of the other person's argument that make sense to you also promotes good will. Admitting that your actions, or perhaps lack of them, contributed to the development of a problem reduces hostility and helps make the other person more willing to accept some responsibility. It can help to point out that each person's perceptions and judgments are subjective and both parties must therefore negotiate and compromise. Sometimes people view the same event in very different ways because of what each noticed, expected, and their respective locations, desires, and needs.

When other people communicate in negative ways such as regularly interrupting, using negative labels, ignoring, nagging, or yelling, point out the problem, discuss how it makes you feel and affects your relationship, and negotiate for change. If strong emotions such as embarrassment or hurt feelings interfere with your ability to discuss a problem with someone, write a letter. Letters have several advantages over face-to-face confrontations. You can reword a letter to make sure you convey precisely the right information, feelings, and impressions. You can present your feelings and thoughts in their entirety without interruption. And the other person has plenty of time to think over what you have written before responding and can reread the letter while considering the issues.

7. Nonverbal Communication

Let your love shine.

Learn about others by looking carefully.

The great majority of our impressions about other people come from nonverbal cues such as facial expressions and body language. Our ability to read these clues to other people's feelings and motives is an important social skill that helps us deal with them more effectively. Preliminary research with thousands of people in many countries suggests people who are more sensitive at reading feelings from nonverbal cues may tend to be better adjusted emotionally, more popular, and more outgoing than less nonverbally sensitive people.

Some **facial expressions** are universal. People all over the world, even in isolated, primitive tribes, recognize the same facial expressions for the following emotions: happiness or pleasure, surprise or amazement, fear, sadness or grief, anger or rage, interest or attentiveness, and disgust or contempt. Some researchers believe the facial expressions for skepticism or distrust, anxiety, pity, pride, or bitterness are also universal. Facial expressions can also blend emotions in very complicated, shifting mixtures, and people often assume facial expressions for social reasons. For example, people often hide boredom and act interested, or hide negative feelings by smiling and acting cheerful. Cultures differ in this, however. Anglo-Saxons are more likely than Latinos to control facial expressions consciously, and Asians tend to avoid expressing many emotions in public.

Vocal qualities, too, convey a great deal of information. Voice can play an important role in showing the following emotional qualities:

accusing	confidence	firm	sad
anger	confusion	happy	sarcasm
alarm	defiance	hurt	surprise
amusement	demanding	irritation	tender
anxiety	dislike	joy	timid
boredom	disgust	mockery	unsure
caring	disinterest	nervous	upset
cheerful	enthusiasm	relaxation	warmth
coldness	excitement	relief	weak
concern	fear	resigned	whining

The speed and volume of speech often help convey emotions. Fast speech may indicate anger, anxiety, fear, or joy. Slow speech may indicate sadness or boredom. Louder voices contribute to impressions of anger, dominance, confidence, assertiveness, or extroversion, and quieter voices contribute to impressions of boredom, sadness, submission, timidity, or warmth and affection. Pitch variation helps make a voice sound happy, pleasant, dynamic, animated, and extroverted, but a voice with monotonous pitch often sounds depressed, uninterested, uninteresting, submissive, bored, or lacking in confidence. A nasal voice also gives a negative impression. Speaking relatively fast, using strong volume, answering questions without long pauses, and pausing before important points help give impressions of competence. Dominant people will interrupt someone speaking more often than do other people.

Cultures assign specific meanings to many **gestures**. In greeting, we often smile, nod our heads, raise our eyebrows, or shake hands. We shake our heads to indicate no, and we wave hello or goodbye. We clench our fists in anger, and we shrug our shoulders to express indifference or giving up. Cultures often differ in the meanings assigned to gestures. Raised eyebrows signify yes in Samoa but no in Greece. We think of hissing after a performance as a rejection of the performance, but the Basuto of South Africa applaud by hissing. Many cultures consider spitting a sign of disrespect and contempt, but the Masai of Africa consider spitting a sign of affection and blessing.

Some widespread gestures are natural. People all over the world kiss to express affection, especially toward little children, although some cultures avoid kissing among adults in public. People of many cultures use a smile and a momentary raising of the eyebrows for greeting and for flirting, probably because these gestures closely resemble the facial expression of friendly surprise. The common gesture of shaking the head to indicate no may relate to the similar motions of shaking off an unwanted touch or object (other mammals and birds do this) or of a satisfied baby rejecting the breast by turning its head away. A few cultures use other natural ways to say no: jerking the head back and closing the eyes (a reaction of repulsion), pushing the lips out to pout, and wrinkling the nose and closing the eyes (a reaction to horrible smells).

In conversations, we show emphasis and suggest taking turns with gestures and with **looking behavior**. In our culture, speakers generally look away from their listeners when they begin to talk and look at their listeners during grammatical breaks in their speech, at points of emphasis, and at the end when it is the other person's turn to talk. When people want to start speaking, they usually move their head slightly toward the other person's face and may begin hand gestures. If a listener signals a desire to start talking and the speaker wants to continue, the speaker will shorten pauses, maintain or increase loudness, glance away as if to overlook the other person's hints, and perhaps continue gesturing. When people of different status interact (doctor and staff, director and employees, etc.), the person of higher status tends to talk more, speak louder, and interrupt more than do people of lower status.

Eye contact and looking behavior communicate many things. We look more at other people we like or find interesting or attractive. Thus, you can often gauge curiosity, interest, attraction, and the willingness to communicate by looking behavior and regular eye contact. The pupils of the eyes enlarge as interest increases or with a pleasant focus of attention and narrow when interest reduces or with an unpleasant scene or subject. This includes sexual arousal or positive or negative responses to another person's personality, attitudes, or values. Pupils enlarge with happiness and joy and narrow with sadness or sorrow. The amount of enlargement or narrowing shows the intensity of the emotion. Some psychologists pay attention to pupil changes to understand people better. The avoidance of eye contact generally signals a lack of interest in communicating. For example, a waiter or waitress who is too busy will avoid eye contact with you, and children in school who don't know the answer to a question and don't want the teacher to call upon them avoid eye contact with the teacher. The amount of eye contact between a couple provides a clue to the level of intimacy and satisfaction in the relationship. (Other clues include physical distance and touching behavior.)

With strangers, eye contact for much over one or two seconds often feels impolite and uncomfortable, at least at fairly close distances. Longer gazes invade one's privacy and may appear hostile, threatening, or lewd. Looking away after one or two seconds of eye contact with a stranger shows consideration and respect for privacy. People often use slightly longer eye contact (two or three seconds) or more regular eye contact, perhaps with a smile, to signal an interest in communicating or to flirt. Prolonged eye contact with facial tension looks threatening and hostile.

During conversations, people generally look at each other's faces half the time, using many repeated glances of a few seconds to five or seven seconds apiece. We normally look at the listener about 40% of the time we speak and the speaker 60% of the time we listen. Dominant people, experts, and powerful people look more at their listeners while speaking and look less at the speaker while listening, while lower status, more submissive people do the opposite. Weak or submissive people frequently look away when you look at them. Depending on the situation and on other clues, looking at your conversation partner for much less than 50% of the time may give a variety of negative impressions: coldness, indifference, anxiety, shame, embarrassment, unassertiveness, introversion, insecurity, incompetence, evasiveness, or dishonesty. A high, but normal, amount of looking during conversations, between 60 and 70% of the time, often gives impressions of friendliness, sincerity, honesty, competence, persuasiveness, self-confidence, assertiveness, and extroversion. One study suggests poor eye contact may reduce your chance of being hired in a job interview. Practice more eye contact if you use low rates of it during conversations.

Posture also conveys much information. Relaxed, erect, good posture (such as standing straight and tall with both feet planted firmly on the ground) gives an impression of confidence and assertiveness. When seated, positions with open, sprawled (not symmetrical) arms and legs, relaxed hands, and a sideways or backwards lean come across as relaxed and friendly. Tense or stiff symmetrical positions suggest anxiety and perhaps unassertiveness. In formal situations, people generally use better posture and less relaxed sprawling. When people of differing status (boss and employee, teacher and student, etc.) interact, the person of higher status is more likely to assume a more relaxed posture than the person of lower status.

Leaning slightly toward someone or turning the head or body a little toward the person indicates some willingness to communicate. When talking, slightly turning or leaning toward the person shows some warmth, liking, or interest. Open arms, open legs, and arms positioned toward other people also show warmth. Closed positions, such as crossed arms and legs or keeping the arms and legs near the body, suggest timidity or unassertiveness, especially when bodily tension accompanies them. When flirting, men and women use typically masculine and feminine stances. Men assume better postures, square their shoulders, and pull their stomachs in. Women often put their chests out or cross and uncross their legs. Sometimes a very relaxed position in a chair, lying way back or sideways, is flirtatious and almost sexual. Women who find a man uninteresting may use prim and proper gestures or folded arms, along with an unwillingness to orient their body toward the unlucky suitor.

Touch varies by sex, race, age, status, and culture. In our society, women touch other women much more than do any other combination of sexes. Touch between people of opposite sexes is more frequent than touch between members of the same sex, with men touching women more often than women touch men. The sex differences in touching in short-lived relationships may not hold true in longer, established relationships, however. Rates of touching are high for little children, then decrease until high school, with women touching children more than men do. Adult touching apparently remains stable until retirement age, when it increases quite a bit. Preliminary research suggests touching is as much as three times more frequent among blacks than among whites. It seems that black males touch each other the most, black females touch each other almost twice as often as white females do, and white males touch each other the least. Both blacks and whites touch their own race more often than they do the other race. People of high status touch low status people much more frequently than vice-versa. Touching is much more frequent in Arabs, Latin Americans, and southern Europeans than it is in northern Europeans and Americans.

Touch can communicate support, reassurance, appreciation, warmth, affection, sexual attraction, or playful aggression. It can help make someone feel included, get attention, enforce obedience, or signal meeting or leaving. Touch is one of the most effective ways to comfort and reassure someone who needs emotional support. Studies repeatedly show that touching someone helps persuade the person. For example, touching someone increases the likelihood of shoppers signing a petition or completing a short rating scale.

Social rules exist for how close by we should approach other people, and we seldom violate these rules, except in crowded situations. Edward Hall first described these standard **social distances**. In general, only loved ones come closer than 1 1/2 feet from us. While talking to most people, including good friends, we generally keep a distance of between 1 1/2 feet and 4 feet. In job interviews and other formal situations, we often stay farther away. If someone moves too close, we often move farther or lean away. We normally accept closer distances between females than between males. We accept closer distances, too, as we get to know people, if we like them, or if we feel attracted to them. Distances become greater in anxious or angry situations. Increasing distance during an interaction may give a negative impression and destroy trust. There are cultural differences in these rules that can result in discomfort during cross-cultural social interactions. Germans prefer more social distance than we do. Latin American, French, Arab, and Mediterranean people normally use closer distances than we do.

Our **physical appearance** tells other people a great deal about ourselves. Our clothes, hair, jewelry, neatness, and cleanliness give clues to our social class, wealth, job, credibility, group membership, likability, conformity and rebellion, and sexual availability. Neatness, cleanliness, and either normal or conservative clothing give impressions of responsibility and conventional morals. Uniforms communicate power or powerlessness and generally make the person seem more competent and likable. Dark, conservative suits and normal hair length help give professional men credibility. Physical appearance plays a great role in forming first impressions of other people.

Physical **attractiveness** greatly influences the way we see and treat each other. It is unfair, but people consistently view attractive individuals in a better light and treat them better in almost every setting studied. Parents and teachers seem to expect attractive children to do better academically and socially. Parents tend to expect misbehaving attractive children to improve. In dating, attractive people have more opportunities and end up spending more time talking to people of the opposite sex. They go to more parties and report more satisfaction with their long-term relationships with the opposite sex than do less attractive folks. We see attractive people as more likely to be sensitive, strong, sociable, sexually warm and responsive, credible, and persuasive. We often judge their work to be of better quality than that of less attractive people. Attractive counselors get judged more competent, intelligent, trustworthy, and likable than less attractive counselors. We are more willing to help attractive people, and we tend to disclose more about ourselves to them. In mental health evaluations, attractive people are less likely to get referred to psychiatrists or to become diagnosed extremely maladjusted. Courts less often convict attractive people, especially women, of crimes. Finally, the more attractive we are, the more positive our self-esteem is likely to be. This is especially true during adolescence.

Many of the things we have talked about influence **likability**. We like people better if they dress to meet the expectations of the people with whom they interact. We also like those who signal interest, attention, and warmth with voice, eye contact, direct body and head orientations, head nodding, open body positions, close interaction distances, forward leans, socially appropriate touching, and smiles in context. Out of context or excessive smiling makes a person seem untrustworthy, less credible, or unassertive. People who use appropriate volume in their voices and who vary pitch and volume to express emotions and warmth are more interesting and liked than people who use a narrow range of pitch and loudness. Animated facial expressions and gestures also help, unless they are excessive.

We may recognize **anxiety** in a variety of ways: tense muscles, rigid posture, twitches, jerky movements, shakiness, tugging at clothing, wringing the hands, fiddling with objects, restless movements, excessive scratching, nervous habits, or many shifts in posture. Fast speech can indicate anxiety. Hesitant speech, repetitions, mistakes and corrections, stuttering, or many useless noises ("er," "uhm," "ah," etc.) indicate anxiety or low self-esteem and suggest incompetence. Anxiety may result in short eye contact or shifting, darting eyes. The pupils of the eyes enlarge with fear. Hesitancy when approaching or speaking to other people, poor eye contact, downcast head or eyes, drooping, hunching forward, poor posture, or any of the signs of anxiety noted above may signal low self-esteem, timidity, or unassertiveness. The same is true of a voice that is weak, quiet, monotonous in pitch, whining, pleading, hesitant, or apologetic.

Clues to **anger** and aggressiveness include facial tension, tight lips, stiff posture, and narrowed or glaring eyes. Hostile gestures include clenched fists, fist pounding, and sharp finger pointing. An angry voice often sounds fast, loud, tense, or demanding. A confronting, erect stance directly in front of someone may indicate hostility, especially with hands on hips, tense muscles, or other signs of anger. Sadness, **depression**, or **grief** may result in drooping, hunching forward, poor posture, a head angled downward, frowning, eyes looking down and away, poor eye contact, sluggish actions and movements, and slow or quiet speech, especially with little pitch variation.

Many nonverbal characteristics occur more frequently during **lying** but may also appear in people telling the truth. In detecting lies, no one clue is enough and the discomfort suggested by many body movements, facial expressions, or vocal changes may come from something else besides attempts to deceive. Of course, the more nonverbal behavior differs from what is being said, the more likely the person is lying. Despite stereotypes, people telling lies do not avoid eye contact, smile, or make awkward posture shifts any more than do people telling the truth. Perhaps liars suppress these responses to avoid detection.

Compared to people who are telling the truth, liars tend to use more negative statements, irrelevant information, overgeneralized statements, and fewer words in response to questions. They tend to have more speech hesitations and changes in pitch and make more mistakes—repeating words, stuttering, grammatical errors, useless noises to fill pauses ("uh," "er"), slips of the tongue, etc. They are more likely to speak slowly and take a longer time to answer questions, perhaps because they must plan their answers rather than answer spontaneously. They tend to move their heads less, blink their eyes more, and engage more often in nervous habits such as scratching, touching the face or body, or playing with their hair.

Pupil dilation from anxiety is more common during lying, with the pupils enlarging at the moment of deception, more so if you feel worried about being caught. Other signs of anxiety include blushing, blanching (whitening) of the skin, sweating, and changes in breathing patterns. Facial expressions are not very helpful in catching lies, but liars tend to fake smiles more and have less genuine, happy smiles. People tend to move their hands less to illustrate their speech when they are lying, because they are less spontaneous and more focused on what they are saying.

Women smile and laugh almost twice as much as men do during conversations, except in childhood, when studies find no differences. Women cry more often than men do. Friendships between women tend to involve more intimacy in self-disclosure, expression of feelings, and affectionate physical contact than do friendships between men. Women are also generally better than men at verbally and facially expressing emotions and at recognizing nonverbal communication, except when it comes to anger. Recent evidence suggests women are worse than men at expressing and recognizing anger, especially at recognizing anger in men.

If you want to recognize nonverbal communication more often, practice watching for facial expressions, vocal characteristics, and body language. Be careful in dealing with people from other cultures, however. Their meanings for gestures and their standards for things like volume of speech, eye contact, touching, and personal space may differ from yours.

8. Interests and Activities

*Enthusiasm for interests and activities
makes you a fun person to know.*

A healthy mind is an active mind.

*The simplest way to beat depression, anxiety, or an addiction
is developing interests and activities.*

Interests and activities are very important in mental health. They give satisfaction, help make you feel good about yourself, and keep your mind off problems and negative thoughts and emotions. Simply cultivating them can sometimes cure depression, grief, addiction, explosive anger, anxiety, excessive worrying, or guilt, especially if you do the activities whenever you feel the negative emotion. Interests and activities are important social skills. Sharing them with other people builds a satisfying social, marital, and family life. They give you pleasant and interesting things to talk about, improving your conversation skills. Developing them contributes to self-esteem and happiness, thus making you a more pleasant friend, marital partner, and parent. Understanding the importance of interests and activities, Freud made sublimation his only positive or mature defense mechanism. *Sublimation* is the expression of energy in productive or creative activities.

Having only a few interests and activities doesn't help very much in fighting depression or other problems. A small number of interests and activities (10 for example, not including listening to various kinds of music and the simple interests in the list below) tends to become routine and boring at times. You can best improve mental health by developing many and practicing many of them until you do them well. Truly happy and productive people love life and often enjoy 50 to 100 of them, besides listening to music and the simple ones. Strive toward the ideal of the *Renaissance man*—a well-rounded person with broad social, cultural, and intellectual interests and skills.

There are three main kinds of helpful interests and activities: pleasurable, constructive, and altruistic. Of course, pleasurable activities give us enjoyment. We may do them just for fun or relaxation. Constructive activities produce or accomplish something and give a sense of pride. Examples include getting things done around the house, working on a project, practicing a skill, or studying a subject that interests you. Altruistic activities help other people. Examples include teaching a neighbor child a craft, taking an elderly person shopping, or volunteer work. Altruistic activities make you feel useful, effective, and generous and give you companionship, gratitude, and a sense of pride. Helping others is one of the best ways to lift yourself spiritually. Helping less fortunate people can also give a healthy sense of perspective. For example, your personal problems may appear trivial after a day volunteering with mental patients or dying cancer patients.

Interests need cultivation. People often don't enjoy a new activity right away. It may take time to become accustomed to it and for interest and pleasure to grow. You may need to learn to relax in the new situation or to develop some expertise or skill before you can learn to enjoy it. Don't reject new activities before giving them a chance. Try any new activity at least several times, with an open mind. Bored or depressed people often reject new interests and activities without trying them or after one attempt. Their negative thoughts about many activities interfere with their happiness. Anyone who wants or needs to develop new ones should counter negative thoughts with positive alternatives each time they occur. Examples include: "I'll give it a try. Who knows, maybe I'll really like it," "Hey, that wasn't bad. I enjoyed it some. Maybe if I try it a few more times, I'll really like it," "Why sit here and feel bored? I'll try ...," and "Not bad on my first try, but I'll get better with practice. That was kind of fun."

You may find it difficult to think and come up with new interests and activities. We often forget many we once enjoyed or we were once curious about. Depressed or bored people are especially likely to have forgotten previous interests and activities. The following list helps a great deal in finding new ones.

List of Interests and Activities

Simple Interests
arranging flowers, dry grasses
barbecues
bicycling
braiding hair
building or watching a fire
camping
card games (blackjack, rummy, bridge, etc.)
crossword puzzles

cutting or chopping wood
decorating your home
drying or pressing flowers
exercise, jogging
family reunions
field trips, parks, nature walks
fishing
flirting
flowers (appreciation, smell, identification)

flower gardens
flower garlands, leaf laurels
friends (visiting, inviting)
garage sales, auctions
giving a party
going to museums
going to restaurants
going to the beach, skipping stones
going to the mountains
going to the zoo
helping people
home movies
housework
jokes (telling, hearing)
looking at architecture, buildings,
   cathedrals
making new friends
movies
outdoor work
owning a pet (dog, cat, bird, etc.),
   training them
peace and quiet
people watching
picnics
plants, terrariums
playing with babies or children
radio
rearranging furniture
religious worship, praying
reminiscing, talking about old times
riding in the country (bike or auto)
shopping or browsing in stores
sounds of nature
sunbathing
travel
TV
visiting elderly folks
watching clouds, storms, sunsets
watching planes at the airport
walking
walking barefoot
whistling, humming
writing a diary
writing letters or cards to friends

Food (Preparation, Growing)
appetizers
barbecuing
beverages, mixing
breads
cake decorating
canning food
casseroles
cheese dips, other dips
cocktails
cookies, candy
crock pot cooking
ethnic cuisine (French, Chinese, etc.)
jellies & preserves
microwave cooking
pies, pastries
soups, salads
vegetable, herb gardens
vegetarian cooking
wok cooking

Music
a cappella
barbershop quartet
Black soul music
classical music, opera
country & western
drums
early instruments
easy listening, show tunes
ethnic music (reggae, etc.)
folk music, ballads
gospel music
jazz, ragtime, blues
big bands
rock & roll, hip hop
string instruments: guitar, violin, etc.
synthesizer
tribal percussion
wind instruments: flute, clarinet, horns,
   saxophone, harmonica, etc.
piano, organ

Dance
ballet

ballroom
belly dance
clogging
dance clubs
discotheque
folk, polka, etc.
interpretive
limbo
square dancing
tap dance

Reading
adventure
animals, pets
astrology, occult
biography
comic books
cook books
drama
family & child care
fiction
gardening
health & fitness
history
humor
literature
magazines, newspapers
mystery
poetry
politics
psychology
religion
romance
science
science fiction
sports
travel
westerns

Other Common Interests
African cultures, crafts
American Indian cultures, crafts
antique shops
archaeology
art history

astronomy
auto identification
bee keeping
bird watching, identification, bird song
Blacks in history
bonsai tree growing
boomerang throwing
budgeting
butterfly appreciation, identification
cars, ships, trains, planes
cave exploration
Christmas caroling
church activities
circus, circus trivia
Civil War facts
clearing land
computers
country fairs
country stores
covered bridges
dinosaurs, other extinct animals
Eskimo cultures, crafts
explorer facts
farm work
first aid, lifesaving
family history, genealogy
flags
fortune telling (Tarot, I Ching, etc.)
fossils
fraternities & sororities
going to a health club
greenhouses
Halloween costumes
ham radio
handwriting analysis
historical tours, factory tours
horseback riding
impersonations
knights and chivalry, coats of arms,
    royalty, castles
knots (kinds of, tying them)
landscaping your yard
leaf, tree identification
learning about wild animals

local history
marine animals
massage (body, face, feet, shoulders)
meditating
meteor watching, stars
Morse code
observing animals in the wild
pet shows
photography (architecture, nature,
  people, wildlife, etc.)
prehistoric human life
presidents
primitive cultures
puppet theater
real estate
riding a motorcycle
river touring
rocks and minerals
rock gardens
rodeos
school meetings
school reunions
seashells
self-defense
shorthand
sign language of the deaf
social problems
song writing
speed reading
states and state capitals
tracks of animals
trail blazing
typing
ventriloquism
vocabulary building
writing poetry
weather study
women in history
yoga

For Kids of All Ages
alphabet hunt (in a vehicle)
animal, plant, place, or object (20 yes
  & no questions)

arm wrestling
assembling toys (Lincoln Logs, etc.)
back bends, flips
baton twirling, cheer leading
bean bag games
bingo
blind man's bluff
board games (checkers, Monopoly,
  Scrabble, etc.)
buildings of stacked cards
card, match, or coin tricks
charades
clay designs and figures
climbing trees
coin or button toss games (into cups or
  on targets)
computer games
croquet, darts, horseshoes
dice games
dominoes (playing, toppling rows)
finger painting
jacks, marbles, yo-yo
jigsaw puzzles
juggling
jumbled words
keeping balloons afloat
kites, Frisbee
magic tricks, magic shows
monkey in the middle
obstacle course with blindfolds
password (other words as clues to a
  hidden word)
pinball
races: piggy-back, sack, one-legged,
  three-legged, wheel-barrow, relay
scavenger hunt
skipping, hopscotch
somersaults
swinging, seesaws
tag, hide-and-seek
tug of war
walking on your hands
water balloon fights
Who am I? (20 yes & no questions)

Collecting
Americana
angels
animal figurines or artwork (owls,
    rabbits, cats, etc.)
antiques (furniture, books, etc.)
art (see category of Artwork)
autographs
beads
bells
books
bonsai trees
bottles
boxes
buttons
candles
coins
crystal
dolls, doll houses
dragons
driftwood
eggs, painted
fine art fabrics
fossils
gems
hats
Indian artifacts, arrowheads
jewelry, imitation jewelry
lace
maps
match books
miniatures
Native American artwork
old photographs
Oriental rugs
plates, dishes, etc.
post cards
pottery
rocks & minerals
stained glass
stamps
tapestries

Sports
acrobatics

aerobics
archery
auto racing (circuit, rally)
ballooning
baseball
basketball
bicycling, bicycle racing
boating (sailing, rowing, motorboat),
    racing
bowling
boxing
canoeing
fencing
football
golf
gymnastics
handball
hang gliding
high jumps, hurdles
hiking
hockey
horse, dog racing
hunting
ice-skating, figure skating
jogging
judo, karate, self-defense
jump rope
marksmanship
motorcycle racing (circuit, motocross)
mountain climbing
Olympic games
pole vaulting
polo
pool (pocket billiards)
racquetball, squash
rafting
rock climbing
roller-skating, roller-blading
scuba diving
sledding, tobogganing
skate-boarding
skiing (water, snow, cross country)
sky diving
snow boarding

soccer
swimming, diving, surfing, races
table tennis
tennis
track
trampoline
volleyball
water polo
weight lifting
wind surfing
wrestling

Crafts (Making, Collecting)
aerial photography using kites
arranging flowers, dried grasses
basket making (reeds, stick, fabric)
batik (clothing, wall hangings)
bead craft
Bible crafts
bird feeders, bird houses
blown glass
bookbinding
bread dough craft
cabinet making
calligraphy
cameos
candle making
ceramics, pottery
ceramics for jewelry
clock repairing
collage
decoupage
doll making (foam rubber, stuffed
    fabric, papier-mâché, etc.)
doll house making & furniture
eggshell craft
fabrics, dying, hand painting
fashion design
furniture refinishing
garden sculpture
gem cutting, grinding, polishing
gourd carving & painting
gourd rattles
hand weaving (reeds, fibers, sticks)

hooking rugs
ice or snow sculpture
interior decorating
jewelry making (gold, silver, etc.)
lamp making & lamp shades
leather craft
kite making
macaroni craft
macramé
map making
mask making
metal craft (etching, engraving,
    sculpture)
miniature craft
mobiles, hanging
model ships, cars, trains, etc.
mosaics
musical instruments (wood flutes,
    dulcimers, violins, etc.)
nail craft
necklace stringing (soaked cloves,
    soaked Indian corn, etc.)
origami (Japanese paper folding)
papier-mâché
pincushions
puppet & marionette making (cloth,
    stuffed cloth, carved wood, papier-
    mâché, etc.)
reed or wicker craft
restoring antiques
rubbings (gravestones, leaves, manhole
    covers, etc.)
sand paintings (under glass, in jars or
    vases)
scissored paper designs, repeating
scrimshaw
seashell craft
seed craft
sewing (crewel, crocheting, knitting,
    cross-stitch, embroidery, needlepoint,
    quilting, tatting, clothes, appliqué or
    stuffed fabric scene wall hangings,
    stuffed fabric animals, embroidery
    wall scenes, small wall quilts, etc.)

sign painting
silvering plants, leaves, weeds, shells
stained glass
taxidermy
tie-dye (clothing, wall hangings)
tile craft
toy making
upholstery
wine making
wire craft
wizard, witch, or shaman dolls
wood carving (whistles, animals, etc.)
   wood inlays
wood staining, finishing
wrought iron

Artwork

art of various civilizations (Greece,
   Egypt, Africa, China, Inca, etc.)
block printing (wood, linoleum, etc.)
cartoon drawing
chalk, crayon, felt markers
charcoal, oil pastels
enameling, cloisonné
engraving, etching
film making
historical, bird, or marine
movements in art (Impressionist,
   Pointillism, Cubist, Surrealism, etc.)
painting (oil, acrylic, watercolor)
   graphic arts, airbrush
pencil, pen & ink
portraiture, caricatures
screen printing, silk-screen
sculpture (soap, wood, stone, relief)
still life, landscapes

Performing Arts

announcing
broadcast news
choreography
comedy, impersonations
costume design
directing
production

radio, TV, movies
set design
stage lighting
stage make-up
theater, acting
ushering
writing

Fixing Things

appliance repair
auto body refinishing
auto maintenance, repair
carpentry
electrical wiring
heating and cooling systems
home improvements
plumbing
radio, TV repair
sewing repairs

Subjects (Interests, School, Career)

accounting, finance
advertising, marketing
agriculture, animal husbandry
anthropology, archaeology
architecture
astronomy
biology
business
chemistry
city planning
computer science
criminal justice
draftsmanship
economics
elementary education
engineering
English grammar
geography
geology
health
history
home economics
journalism
languages (French, Spanish, etc.)

literature (American, World, Spanish American, Black, etc.)
mass communications
mathematics
medicine
nursing
oceanography
philosophy
physics
political science
psychology
public relations
sociology
special education
speech pathology
statistics
surveying
writing (poetry, short stories, etc.)
world religion

Helping, Volunteering, Organizing
alcoholic, drug treatment centers
animal shelters
battered women shelters
Big Brothers, Big Sisters
crisis centers
daycare centers
disaster victims, refugees
ecology groups
free babysitting for working parents

give clothing or food
Girl Scouts, Boy Scouts
Goodwill, Salvation Army
group homes or halfway houses
help find a job
homes for the disabled
hospitals, nursing homes
invite to a meal or family outing
lonely, elderly, sick, disabled, poor, or grieving people
Meals on Wheels
orphanages
political action groups
prisons
psychiatric wards or hospitals
rape victim centers
Red Cross
relieve caretakers of the chronically ill
schools, tutor children
send a needy child to camp
senior citizens' centers
share interests
suicide prevention centers
supervise playground
take on errands, shopping, appointments
teach crafts
tutor foreigners in English
visit regularly, telephone, write
YWCA, YMCA

Sharing new interests and activities with friends often makes them more fun and sustains interest. For example, exercising with a friend makes it easier to stay motivated. You can also join or establish a social club based on the interest or activity. Be sure not to reject any of the listed interests as unworthy of serious pursuit! You might feel that only children would enjoy bread dough craft, for example, but Central American peoples traditionally make hard bread dough figures with lavish ethnic costumes and ornaments in brilliant colors, and museums display these elaborate figures.

Resource:

Volunteer Match 415 241 6872 information, referrals to 10,000 groups nationwide that need volunteers. on-line: www.volunteermatch.org

9. Problem Solving

Settling one problem prevents many others.

Who begins too much accomplishes little. (German proverb)

Solve problems in a calm and relaxed manner, choosing a time when neither party to the conflict feels angry or upset. Work on just one problem at a time, staying focused on it until you find a solution. Use polite requests, good listening skills, the formula: "When ... happens, I feel ...," negotiation, and compromise. Carefully avoid communication problems (nagging, negative labels, etc.) using the advice in chapter 6; they often block problem solving. Remember compromises completely satisfying both parties to a conflict are only occasionally possible, and both parties may need to tolerate unpleasant terms to find a solution both can agree on.

Begin practicing problem-solving skills on easy, unthreatening problems. After each problem-solving session, discuss the helpful behaviors that occurred, the negative ones interfering with progress, and what others would have helped. Use this chapter and chapter 6, Communication Skills, as guides for your analysis. In teaching children problem-solving, start with simple problems about which nobody feels upset or angry.

Vague problems are difficult to solve because vague problems such as *a bad attitude, not getting along very well anymore, a lousy mother,* or *a lousy husband* may mean very different things to each person involved. What can you do about vague problems? Define them more precisely by thinking of examples. Think of specific times and places in which the problem bothered you. Exactly what happened? Define the specific problem behaviors with observable actions, words, tone of voice, or facial expression. Perhaps something you wanted or expected to happen did not? In this way, you might define more precisely the vague problem of *not treating me right* as chronic yelling, ignoring, and lateness. A vague problem of *getting on my nerves* may refer to constant criticism of your housework, cooking, and physical appearance. *Growing apart* may mean a lack of shared activities and affectionate behaviors. Once you define your interpersonal problems in specific, observable terms, both parties can negotiate for changes, find solutions, and easily determine whether progress occurs.

Vague solutions, too, don't help very much. Solutions should always tell you exactly what to do in specific, observable behaviors. Planning to be nicer to your wife, for example, is too vague. Instead, you might plan to compliment your wife several times a day, to ask about her day every day, and to hug her, hold her, or kiss her at least once a day. A plan to socialize more often is not nearly as helpful as a plan to go to a community activity where you can meet new people (clubs, volunteer work, nature walks, museums, etc.) at least once a week and to start a few conversations each time you go.

Make vague personal problems such as _unassertiveness_ or _a bad temper_ more workable by defining them in observable behaviors from specific episodes, too. One man may find his unassertiveness mostly involves failures in complaining to strangers and coworkers. His unassertive responses may include a weak, barely audible voice, poor eye contact, and tension in the body. These observations suggest he should practice complaining to strangers and coworkers with a louder voice, better eye contact, and relaxed muscles. A bad temper usually means yelling in response to certain kinds of frustrations. Similarly, the vague problem of depression becomes much more workable when you observe specifics such as negative thinking, a lack of varied interests and activities, personal problems, chronic complaining, drooping posture, poor eye contact, and monotonous tone of voice.

Solutions involving plans to avoid problem behaviors are too vague. It is much easier to follow a plan of action than to try not to do something. For example, don't just plan to stop arguing. Instead, plan to take turns listening to each other's feelings and perspectives, compromise, and take a break from the negotiations whenever your voice gets louder. Similarly, don't just plan to quit drinking alcohol. Instead, plan to distract yourself from desires for alcohol with new interests and activities, attend Alcoholics Anonymous meetings, and read a list of your reasons for quitting every time you feel the urge to drink. Plans to do specific acts are much more clear and workable than plans to avoid certain behaviors.

The first step in problem solving is to study the problem. With simpler problems, a short analysis of who, what, where, when, how, and why may define the problem in specific, observable terms and provide enough information about it to solve it successfully. If the problem involves two or more people, share your feelings and views about it. Thoroughly understanding a problem often yields clues that help in finding a good solution. The best way to study it is to observe problem episodes carefully over time. Three weeks of observation and record keeping is generally enough for problems occurring nearly every day, but one week may suffice if the problem occurs several times a day.   If the problem only occurs occasionally, you may need to observe and study it for months to understand the variety of situations involved.   Sometimes simply counting the episodes of a fairly automatic, habitual problem behavior (such as nagging or smoking cigarettes) actually results in an improvement because paying extra attention to each episode gives you many opportunities to decide against the behavior.

Shortly after each problem occurs, if possible, write down the details of the situation using the following questions as a guide.   Who is present when the problem occurs?   Who does it affect?   Where did it occur?   When?   How long did it last?   In what situation or circumstances?   Why?   What was happening when the problem occurred?   What were your thoughts and expectations?   What feelings, perhaps conflicting or ambivalent, did you experience?   What are the other people involved likely to think, expect, and feel?   If possible, ask them.   What did you and other people do?   What happened next?

To study a problem emotion such as depression, anxiety, or anger, measure the intensity of the emotion each time it occurs in the following manner.   Rate the emotion on a scale from 0 to 100, with 0 representing *did not feel the emotion at all* and with 100 representing *extreme emotion, the strongest I have ever felt it.*   Each person will rate emotions differently, but the important thing is developing some consistency in your own rating system.   After using your scale for a while, you should have a good idea what kind of emotion will rate 10, 30, 50, 75, 90, 98, etc.   This helps you compare your emotions in different situations, so you can better find patterns relating to the problem emotion.

After gathering information for long enough to see many episodes of the problem, ask yourself the following questions.   How often does it occur?   Is the problem more likely to occur with certain people than others?   Is it more likely to occur with certain categories of people, such as authority figures, coworkers, strangers, acquaintances, the opposite sex, or the same sex?   What other patterns exist?   What do you do or don't you do that allows or invites the problem to occur?   Does the situation or the feelings you experience during the problem remind you of anything from your past?   Could powerful emotions from your past color your view of present events?

Surprising relationships may become apparent.   Events occurring either before or after the problem might seem unrelated, yet be important.   An argument between the parents or boredom in children often leads to children's behavior problems.   People on diets often notice that frustrations such as boredom or criticism lead to eating sprees. Events after problem behaviors often serve as rewards for the negative behaviors. When tantrums succeed in getting children what they want, the tantrums often become more frequent. In relationships with poor communication and problem solving skills, crying, screaming, manipulating, or threatening may prevail as the surest methods of getting results. The warmth, sympathy, and attention shown to depressed or grieving people often reward chronic complaints and negative thinking. Whenever studying a problem, always consider events both before and after the problem for their possible importance.

After studying the problem situation, brainstorm possible solutions. Be creative and think of many possible solutions. Try to see the problem in new ways. Consider unusual, wild ideas—don't be critical of wild thoughts at this stage. Your best ideas may come from changing, combining, or improving other ideas. Consider previous attempts to solve the problem and how you could improve on them. Ask yourself repeatedly what else you could do. Imagine how a counselor, minister, or wise person might deal with the problem. Ask other people how they would go about solving it. If possible, make a list of alternative solutions with clear plans for action, before evaluating them. This helps avoid the tendency to choose the first workable solution when brainstorming may lead to more effective alternatives.

When negotiations between two or more people seem unproductive, a break often helps. Be sure to take a break if any party to the conflict is becoming tired or irritable. During the break, get advice from other people. When no compromise seems possible, you may simply agree to live with your differences. Another possibility is to find a _mediator_, an impartial outside party who helps the conflicting parties negotiate and compromise.

When you evaluate alternative solutions, consider what difficulties might arise and the probable effectiveness of each. How much trouble is each solution? How do you feel about each? Are there certain circumstances in which a particular solution wouldn't help? If so, how can you best deal with these exceptions? Using these criteria, choose the best solution. Make sure the solution specifies clear behaviors. What actions will occur? Who will perform them? When? Where? How? If any solution fails to help or becomes unacceptable for some other reason, start problem solving again. Frequency observations taken while studying the problem situation become very useful when you want to measure progress to see if your solution is helping.   Without these measurements, you may not notice small improvements in the frequency of problems such as nagging, fights, depressive thoughts, children's hitting behavior, etc.

Another problem-solving strategy helps in making difficult decisions between two alternatives.   Ben Franklin first proposed this method of decision making and he used it himself on many occasions.   First, make comprehensive lists of the advantages and disadvantages of each alternative course of action, four lists in all.   Then look over your two lists of advantages and find positive items on each side that, in your judgment, weigh about equally.   Cross out these items of equal importance.   Next, consider your two lists of disadvantages and cross out negative items on each side that weigh about equally in your feelings.   Sometimes two or three items on one side may weigh equally with one item on the other side and you can cross out all of them.   When you finish, you will have a short surplus list of advantages and disadvantages of both alternatives that you can weigh in importance fairly easily.   Compare the surplus advantages and disadvantages to make your decision.

There is a simple way to do your own therapy session about a troubling issue in your life.   Begin by writing down every thought or feeling you have about the person or situation in your life, without hiding anything.   Write down anything that comes to mind about the issue in a spontaneous way, whether sensible or silly.   When you exhaust your whole range of thoughts and feelings on the issue, sort them all out.   Which ones do you want to emphasize?   Which ones are good or wise goals or feelings?   Which ones should you eliminate because they are selfish or unwise?   Decide how to work toward your goals, and brainstorm to solve any remaining problems.

Time Management

Time management deals with using your time effectively.   Organizing your time better can increase your productivity, while giving you more free time.   Most people can save quite a bit of time by planning meals, shopping, and errands in advance to organize these trips more effectively.   Combine several errands into one trip, avoid driving during rush hours, and do your banking, shopping, and other errands when the lines are short.   Some people enjoy working early or late to get things done without interruptions and avoid traffic jams.   Save time by taking more control of your visitors, interruptions, phone calls, free time, and children's behaviors.   Working or studying in the library helps avoid many of these interruptions.   In an office or at home, taking the telephone off the hook or using an answering machine can help.

With an answering machine, secretary, switchboard operator, or voice mail, you can screen calls or ignore the phone and then prioritize and return them when you are ready.

Organizing all your tasks and goals increases your efficiency. Good planning can avoid the wasted time in haphazard approaches. First make a thorough list of them, then set your priorities. Which are the most important? Which can wait until you finish more important tasks? Long-term goals require continuing effort over a long time. Which simple tasks can you finish now to provide feelings of accomplishment while you continue to work on long-term tasks? To make difficult, complicated, or huge tasks much more manageable, break them into many small, simple steps, so each part is easy to accomplish. If spring cleaning seems overwhelming to a mother with young children, she can clean one room at a time for one hour each day. Reward yourself occasionally for finishing a few steps of your plan, perhaps with a movie or special dessert.

If you feel overwhelmed by your tasks and responsibilities, consider the following questions. First, are you trying to do too much? Perhaps you need to eliminate one or more responsibilities, so you have a little more time to relax and enjoy yourself. Do you find it difficult to refuse requests? If so, please refer to the chapter 16, Assertiveness. Can you delegate some of your responsibilities and tasks to coworkers, subordinates, or family? Do you procrastinate too much and then become overwhelmed when you must finish many tasks at once? Avoid this problem by starting tasks right away and setting early deadlines. Are you a perfectionist? You may attempt too much, trying to be the perfect parent, spouse, employee, or citizen, or you may become inefficient by spending too much time perfecting every task, when a more reasonable amount of time would still result in a job well done. If you are a perfectionist, learn to reduce your demands on yourself or to spend less time overdoing each task.

Highly active and accomplishing people often organize their time very precisely with a schedule for the whole week. Organize your activities for increased productivity by making a weekly chart of your planned activities for each half hour of the day. Be sure to include some time each day or at least several blocks of time each week for relaxation and recreation. Such time is not wasted. Everyone needs some time to relax and enjoy themselves. By updating your activity chart with any changes in schedule or problems that occur, you can review a typical week to find out how you normally waste time. Then you can find ways to avoid wasting it in the future.

10. Stress

*In silence is peace and joy.
Once you find it, use it as an anchor in the rough seas of life.*

*Fight stress and refresh your spirits with simple stretches,
fun and silliness, plenty of time with loved ones,
plenty of sleep, optimism, good nutrition, and exercise.*

We all know that the death of loved ones, losses to fire or theft, time in jail, military combat, illness or injury, marital or family problems, divorce or separation, losing a job, financial problems, legal problems, and arguments are stressful. Most people understand major disagreements, problems with a boss or teacher, important examinations, deadlines, traffic jams, failure, and small nuisances such as a busy signal on the telephone are stressful, too. But people often don't realize many pleasant things can add stress, such as marriage, a pregnancy, starting a new job, or adding a child or an elderly person to the family. Even starting or finishing college, getting a promotion, retirement from work, vacations, the Christmas season, large financial gains, and outstanding achievements can be stressful.

Any major change in your life can be stressful. Changes in living arrangements such as moving, getting a new roommate, or a family member going away to college or getting married can increase stress, as can a change in work hours, conditions, responsibilities, career plans, or schools. Even going on a diet or changing the amount of time you spend relaxing, socializing, or having fun can be stressful.

Why are changes often stressful? First, changes often disrupt familiar and comfortable routines and present new and unknown situations. Changes may place new demands and responsibilities on you. They may disrupt your existing relationships, ending them or drastically reducing the amount of time you can spend with loved ones. Changes may also require you to develop new work or social relationships, require new activities, or alter the amount of time you can devote to relaxation or recreation.

Environmental factors such as high temperatures, noise, and crowding increase stress. Hot weather sometimes seems linked to increased reports of violence. People who work in noisy factories or live near airports often report more tension than people who work or live in quieter surroundings. Rats living in crowded research conditions show withdrawn and aggressive behaviors more often than do rats living in less crowded areas. People living in cities generally report more tension than those in country areas. Poor, crowded inner city neighborhoods generally have higher murder rates than do country or more affluent, less crowded areas.

Stress plays an important role in many psychological problems, such as anxiety, depression, insomnia, fatigue, and suicide. People vary greatly in their tolerance for different forms of stress, such as noise, temperature variations, travel, changes in sleeping habits, arguments, etc. What one person finds stressful, another person may not. Some people are extremely afraid of heights, closed spaces, dogs, bridges, snakes, or open spaces. Certainly most people don't find these things stressful enough to lead to states of panic.

Our bodies respond to severe stress in ways that prepare us to fight or run, for reasons dating back to prehistoric days when people lived in caves. When early humans felt challenged or threatened by a dangerous situation, they needed to fight or run quickly, so our bodies release the hormone adrenaline when we sense danger. Adrenaline prepares us for crises by causing the heartbeat to race and our breathing to speed up, so more oxygen is available in our blood, bringing increased alertness in the brain and preparing the muscles for action. It also causes many muscles to tense in readiness and the stomach to stop digesting food, so we don't waste energy on digestion. You have probably noticed some of these physical changes when you suddenly felt alarmed, such as when narrowly avoiding a dangerous accident. Many minor frustrations may also cause similar, but smaller changes in the body.

Stress is a factor in many illnesses, such as tension headaches, migraine headaches, chronic back pains, allergies, ulcers, asthma, colitis, high blood pressure, eczema, psoriasis, hives, herpes, arthritis, diabetes, lung ailments, accidental injuries, sexual problems, and even cirrhosis of the liver, cancer, and heart disease. Researchers believe Type A personalities are more prone to high blood pressure and heart disease because of their hostility and stressful lifestyles. *Type A personalities* are very competitive, perfectionist, impatient, hostile, and aggressive workaholics who hurry a lot and spend little time relaxing. Studies suggest highly hostile people tend to engage in excessive eating, smoking, drinking, and substance abuse, so the increased cardiac problems of Type A personalities may come from obesity or these other behaviors. The American Academy of Family Physicians states that two-thirds of all visits to doctors are stress related.

How does stress relate to physical problems? Chronic neck muscle tension plays a great role in tension headache, and chronic back muscle tension plays a great role in many backaches. Tense muscles can also lead to cramps. Stress is clearly associated with increased susceptibility to infectious diseases and reduced immune responses. One study found separated or divorced men had significantly more recent illness than did married men. Two epidemiological studies found family conflict and disorder predicted later infectious illnesses. When researchers put cold viruses in people's noses, stress showed a linear relationship to both the rates of infection and full-blown colds. Researchers have noted decreased immune system measures associated with marital hostility, divorce, marital separation, the loss of a spouse, taking care of a spouse with Alzheimer's Disease, and medical school examinations.

Such studies lead researchers to suspect the hormonal response to danger and frustration may account for many of the illnesses associated with stress. The adrenal glands produce adrenaline and other hormones through complicated chemical relationships with the pituitary gland and the brain. Excessive, prolonged, or chronic arousal of this endocrine system may lead to disease. The cells of the immune system have receptors for many hormones and brain chemicals and are exposed to them in the blood and lymph nodes. Recent studies suggest the immune system receives signals from the endocrine and central nervous systems and sends signals to both. Thus, stress may reduce the ability of the immune system to fight disease.

There are several problems with these studies, however. First, a statistically significant finding of a reduced level of an immune system component may have little biological importance. In addition, stress often influences many behaviors that can affect health. Excessive eating or the chronic use of drugs such as cigarettes and alcohol as coping mechanisms can certainly lead to many diseases. Stress often influences the quality of our sleep and behaviors such as exercise and diet. Perhaps these things cause many of the observed changes in immunity and susceptibility to infection. There has not been enough attention to these factors in the research to date. Finally, most studies of the relationship between stress and infectious disease do not meet contemporary scientific criteria in measurements and control groups.

Coping with Stress

Because problems are stressful and happiness and good mental health help in coping with stress, all the skills described in this book for constructively dealing with personal problems and negative emotions help in coping with stress.   Clearly, dwelling on negative thoughts and feelings increases the stress in our lives, but attitudes of acceptance, positive thinking, humor, and good problem solving reduce stress in our lives.   Much research suggests optimism in facing losses and failures promotes mental health and perhaps even physical health, whereas pessimism does the opposite.   Interests and activities help in reducing stress by providing feelings of pleasure and accomplishment and by distracting us from our problems and negative feelings.   Everyone should balance their work time and life stresses with enough relaxation, fun, and time for rewarding interests and activities to make each week enjoyable.

Be sure to spend plenty of time with loved ones.   Close, trusting relationships add joy and provide emotional support and helpful ideas and resources in times of stress.   Simply sharing your problems with an understanding and sympathetic friend is often a great relief. Developing love and virtues within ourselves, good communication skills, and the abilities to compromise and apologize all help reduce stress in our relationships.   Many studies suggest emotional support from others may protect the immune system from the effects of stress and that a lack of social support may worsen the effects of stress on the immune system.   Large, well-controlled epidemiological studies suggest social isolation is a major risk factor for death, with effects as strong as those noted for health risks like smoking, obesity, and low physical activity.   One study found emotional support altered brain chemicals in a way believed to lower blood pressure and relax the heart. Owning a pet helps by providing an important loving bond.   One study found people's blood pressure was lower in stressful situations if a pet was present.

Keeping our bodies healthy promotes mental health and increases our ability to cope with stress.   Good nutrition, getting enough sleep and exercise, and avoiding drugs such as alcohol and cigarettes help us cope better with stress.   Even a simple stretch of a muscle group (neck, shoulders, legs, etc.) or a short time spent deep breathing or visualizing a pleasant scene can release tension and provide a short mental vacation.   When your stress level is high, pamper yourself with hot soaks in the tub, massages, music, good food, etc. If your life has been chaotic recently, it may help to establish more regular routines and avoid making any unnecessary major changes in your life. If you have too much to do, eliminate some activities and spend more time relaxing and in leisure activities. You may need to delegate tasks or hire a babysitter. If someone you can't change contributes a great deal of stress in your life, you may need to end or drastically limit your relationship with that person.

Exercise

If you don't exercise, by the time you are middle-aged you will lose muscle mass, strength, and energy. Exercise can restore strength, energy, and vitality to your life. Regular exercise can also reduce stress, make you feel better about yourself, and lift your spirits. Research shows walking and other forms of exercise trigger the brain to release endorphins, hormones with effects similar to those of Valium and morphine. This natural high or euphoria from exercising can be more effective than a tranquilizer in reducing muscular tension and anxiety. Exercise can also increase certain measures of immune functioning.

Researchers at Purdue University studied people who didn't exercise and people who used walking as a major part of their fitness program. The researchers found exercise not only fought anxiety and depression, but also increased motivation and improved self-esteem, manual dexterity, and decision-making. Regular exercise reduces your chances of heart, lung, and circulatory diseases. A huge study of women found walking briskly 3 hours a week reduced the risk of heart attacks and strokes by 40%; you can do this by walking less than half an hour a day. Walking this often can relieve the pain of osteoarthritis in the knees, the stiffness and pain usually caused by normal wear and tear on the joint. Exercise of either the stomach or back muscles can reduce back pains. Exercise plays an important role in avoiding obesity, which increases your risk for arthritis, diabetes, gout, strokes, many cancers, and other problems (see chapter 35). The Centers for Disease Control and Prevention recommends adults get half an hour of moderate exercise every day.

Dr. Hans Selye, one of the world's leading authorities on stress, conducted an experiment that dramatically shows the power of exercise in reducing stress. He regularly stressed ten inactive rats with blinding lights, deafening noises, and electric shocks. All ten rats died within one month. He exercised another ten rats on a treadmill until they were in excellent physical condition and subjected them to the same stressful lights, noises, and shocks, and they were doing fine one month later.

Increasing your level of daily activities is a simple way to get more exercise. Walking fast is a cheap, easy, very safe, and popular form of exercise. Substitute walking for short trips in the car. Walking is a nice way to see neighboring areas of town or view scenic areas such as parks, the countryside, historic districts, etc. Start with short walks of five or ten minutes and work up to longer, faster walks. Dancing and participating in sports are fun ways to burn many calories, or put on a symphony and work up a sweat conducting the orchestra. Many new interests and activities add exercise; develop these for fun and physical fitness.

Increase your level of exercise slowly or gradually. This often avoids your dreading exercise and quitting the regime. Wait until you become accustomed to each small increase in exercise levels and desire more exercise before increasing the amount again. If you don't push yourself too hard, you can find an exhilarating and satisfying amount of exercise that eventually leads you to want more.

Although today's health clubs have weight equipment that is easier to use and more safe than those of ten years ago, you should ask the staff to teach you how to use the equipment. In this way, even old folks and couch potatoes can safely work out in spas. Of course, exercising at home with calisthenics, which works with your own body weight, is the cheapest and safest form of exercise for beginners. Some excellent exercises for cardiovascular fitness include vigorous dancing, jumping jacks, jump rope, and jogging. For muscular strength, try push-ups, partial sit-ups (bend your knees and don't anchor your feet), deep knee bends, and back extensions (lying down on your stomach and raising your head and chest off the floor).

No matter how physically fit, anyone who experiences any of the following symptoms while exercising or immediately after, should stop and see a doctor before exercising again: pain anywhere in the body, weakness, dizziness, faintness, confusion, or pain or pressure in the chest, arms, or throat. People over 40 years old, more than 15 pounds overweight, smokers, those who regularly drink moderately heavy amounts of alcohol, or whose hearts beat more than 80 times a minute at rest should check with their doctors before starting any reasonably vigorous exercise program. You should also get a checkup from your doctor before exercising if you have chest pains, dizzy spells, irregular heartbeats, high blood pressure, diabetes, kidney disease, liver problems, or bone or joint diseases or deformities. People with a family history of high blood pressure or heart disease should also see a doctor first. Ideally, this checkup should include a physical examination, blood and urine tests for cholesterol and diseases, and both resting and exercising measures of heart functioning. Electrocardiograms (measures of the heart's electrical activity) and blood pressure measurements taken both while resting and exercising on a treadmill or exercise bicycle can detect signs of heart trouble that won't show up on these measures taken only while sitting or lying down.

To keep your heart healthy and lower your chances of getting heart, lung, and circulatory diseases, you must exercise in a reasonably vigorous way three times a week for at least twenty minutes each time. Use some mild warm-up exercises and stretches both before and after any exercise period to reduce your chance of injury. Although reasonably vigorous exercise will noticeably speed up your breathing and heartbeat, don't exercise so hard that you are out of breath and you can't comfortably carry on a conversation—this deprives the working muscles of needed oxygen and forces the body to burn protein and muscle instead of fat.

Using the following formula, you can determine how hard you should exercise. First, after a period of relative physical inactivity and after lying and relaxing for a few minutes, count your pulse at your carotid artery. You can easily feel your pulse at this artery about 1 inch on either side of your Adam's apple and slightly up. The number of heartbeats during one minute is your resting heart rate. Next, find the number we will call a by subtracting your age from 220. Now find b by subtracting your resting heart rate from a. You will use the number b twice: once to figure your ideal minimum exercising heart rate and once to figure your ideal maximum exercising heart rate. To get your ideal minimum exercising heart rate, multiply b by 3/5 and then add your resting heart rate. To get your ideal maximum exercising heart rate, multiply b by 4/5 and then add your resting heart rate.

This formula gives you the ideal range in heart rate (heartbeats per minute) you should reach when you exercise. While you exercise, check to see if you are within the proper range by stopping and counting your pulse for 15 seconds and by multiplying the number of heartbeats you get by 4. This procedure avoids counting for a minute while the heart slows down. If your exercising heart rate is under your ideal minimum heart rate, you are not exercising hard enough to significantly help your heart or improve your physical fitness. If your exercising heart rate is above your ideal maximum rate, your overly strenuous exercise works much of your body without giving it the amount of oxygen it needs. As you become more physically fit, your resting heart rate and exercising heart rate will gradually lower because the heart becomes more efficient.

Many people enjoy going for walks, jogging, and other exercises more when they share the activity with friends. Exercising in groups helps keep you motivated. When two people agree to jog together every morning at dawn, they generally try to be punctual and regular because they know each relies on the other for companionship and motivation. Friends may encourage or coax you when your motivation lags. Consider group activities such as family outings, participating in sports such as neighborhood volleyball games, exercise classes, classes to learn sports or improve sport skills, going to a health spa, etc.

Relaxation Skills

Relaxation physically combats stress by reducing tension and physical arousal throughout the body, slowing the same bodily systems adrenaline speeds up. Relaxation changes the action of many hormones in the body. The regular practice of deep muscle relaxation (described below) often improves anxiety, depression, addiction, insomnia, irrational fears, muscle spasms, headaches, backaches, neck pains, high blood pressure, and chronic pain in a variety of medical conditions. Don't expect serious pain to lessen before you practice for a month or two, however. Studies suggest deep muscle relaxation may possibly slow the progress of heart disease, reduce the chance of heart attacks, help control glucose and insulin levels in diabetes, cure some cases of infertility, and help improve prognoses in cancer. One study found practicing relaxation exercises increased measures of immune system functioning.

Ancient traditions in cultures all over the world emphasize the importance of regularly practicing silence, meditation, and relaxation to reach states of profound calmness and serenity. The Eastern philosophies Hinduism, Buddhism, Taoism, and Zen emphasize the practice of stillness. Some Islamic sects practice silence for similar purposes, and quiet times of solitude are important in Judaism and Christianity. Spiritual leaders such as Abraham and Jesus often went into the desert or mountains to pray alone. People of religious orders and monastic traditions all over the world have long recognized the importance of times of silent meditation.

Psychologists believe deep relaxation, whether achieved by meditation or relaxation therapy, leads to both physical and psychological benefits.

Research shows deep muscle relaxation is better than meditation for moderate or severe anxiety, however. You can develop the skill of deep relaxation only by practice. Most people must practice the following relaxation techniques for thirty minutes each day for a month or two to reach deep states of relaxation. Both psychologists and people from various cultures all over the world emphasize the *daily* practice of relaxation and meditation for maximum psychological or spiritual benefits.

To practice meditation or relaxation, make yourself comfortable and your surroundings quiet and free of distractions. Remove eyeglasses or contact lenses and shoes and wear loosely fitting, comfortable clothing. Turn off the television and radio and take the telephone off the hook or turn the ringer off and use an answering machine in another room. Ask other people to keep quiet and avoid interrupting you. Shut the door to the room to increase privacy and reduce noise. Use dim lighting in the room, if possible. It often helps to close your eyes. Although many people benefit from practicing meditation or relaxation while sitting comfortably, psychologists recommend lying down to deepen the relaxation. If your position becomes uncomfortable, move in a relaxed way to become comfortable again. Most itches soon disappear, but if an itch persists and distracts you, feel free to scratch it.

When practicing meditation or relaxation, you may sometimes feel normal tingling or floating sensations. They will go away. Also, certain muscles may twitch or jerk; this, too, is normal. You have probably experienced sensations such as these when you were becoming very relaxed and falling asleep. Just ignore them. Inevitably, during meditation or relaxation, noises, thoughts, worries, or daydreams will distract you. With practice, however, you will learn to gently put these irritations aside, merely noticing and dismissing them without paying much attention to them, and you will experience moments of inner peace. These feelings of serenity will deepen and become more frequent as you continue practicing meditation or relaxation. At times, these feelings may approach peaceful bliss.

There are three main kinds of meditation. One focuses on meaningful words, often in a rhythmical or repetitive way, to achieve moments of inner peace. Christians use prayers such as the Lord's Prayer. *Mantras* are words of spiritual significance people repeat slowly, again and again, in meditation. "Om," signifying the ultimate oneness of the universe, is the most famous mantra. The use of mantras has spread from Eastern civilizations to the Western world, but Christians had a similar practice for centuries—they often said the name "Jesus" repeatedly as a prayer or meditation. You can make up your own mantras. Some people meditate by slowly repeating "Peace" or "Love" as mantras, or you may repeat "be calm," "just relax," "calm down," "peaceful relaxation," or "serene calm" to clear your mind and relax.

Chanting, another form of meditation with words, is used by people of various religious sects and others. Nowadays, many people enjoy using music for relaxation. Researchers note New Age music, environmental sounds, and classical music without crescendos and climaxes do reduce physical and emotional arousal, but other types of music do not. (People who fear lightning may not be able to relax to rain and thunder, and people who can't swim may not be able to relax to ocean sounds.) These kinds of music are especially effective when combined with the breathing or relaxation techniques described below.

The second major kind of meditation focuses on clearing the mind by letting thoughts, worries, and daydreams simply arise and fade away without dwelling on them. The goal is to attain the pure experience of being, without the desires and ideas of the thinking mind. As one learns to still the mind more often and for longer periods, feelings of serenity develop. People of Eastern civilizations traditionally believe that long practice of this kind of meditation brings one closer to supreme harmony and enlightenment, a merging with the divine principle of the universe.

The third type of meditation focuses on relaxed, rhythmical breathing to still the mind of its thoughts and worries. Breathing meditation has long been important in many Eastern civilizations. Christians too, historically used breathing with prayers such as the repetition of the name of Jesus and the Lord's Prayer. Slowing and deepening the breath act physically to promote relaxation. Begin making your breathing relaxed and rhythmical by taking several very deep breaths, taking in as much air as possible, so your body has plenty of oxygen and can begin to slow down its breathing. Then let your stomach rise each time you inhale and sink each time you exhale, so your lower lungs seem to do most of the breathing. This breathing from the abdomen rather than the chest is more relaxing. We naturally breathe this way in our sleep. Deep breathing in this way for just thirty seconds will start to calm you. While breathing this way, focus your mind on the sensations of the air flowing into and out of your body. Some people count "one, two, one, two, ..." or say "in, out, in, out, ..." with each inhalation and exhalation, or you might say "peaceful, calm, peaceful, calm, ..." or "quiet, joy, quiet, joy, ..." You can also use prayers or mantras with the breathing practices.

Psychologists have developed three kinds of relaxation therapy: the tension-relaxation sequence, deep muscle relaxation, and visualization. The tension-relaxation sequence is the best way to learn to become aware of tension in the muscles and learn to relieve it. Use the tension-relaxation sequence for the first two weeks of daily practice of relaxation therapy. If you don't practice every day, use it for 14 sessions. Then switch to deep muscle relaxation, which skips the tension exercises and focuses only on relaxing more deeply. Anytime you feel very tense or very anxious and you find it difficult to relax, however, use the tension-relaxation sequence to find and relieve tension in each muscle group.

When you practice the tension-relaxation sequence, squeeze each muscle group tightly during the tension phase. Always release the tension very gradually, paying attention to the difference between almost completely relaxed and completely relaxed. Use the whole five-second period for gradually releasing the tension in your body part. Next, spend some more time further eliminating any remaining tension and feeling the relaxed state of the muscle group. This procedure is important in learning to notice and eliminate small amounts of muscular tension. If a muscle cramps, you have probably squeezed it too tightly.

Instructions for the tension-relaxation sequence follow. You can arrange for a friend to read the instructions to you each time you practice it, or read the instructions into a tape recorder for playback. Read the instructions using a slow, calm, rhythmic voice and a watch or clock to time the pauses in parentheses. Just before you practice this procedure, minimize your distractions in the ways described previously and make yourself comfortable.

Instructions for the Tension-Relaxation Sequence

Lie down with your arms at your sides and make yourself as comfortable as you can. Close your eyes and take several very deep breaths to start the relaxation process. (Pause for 20 seconds.) Let your breathing assume a natural, relaxed rhythm by letting your stomach rise as you inhale and fall as you exhale, so you seem to breathe mostly from the lower lungs instead of the chest. This is the most relaxed way you can breathe. We breathe this way when we sleep. (Pause for 15 seconds.) Wait for your breathing to become slow and regular. (Pause for 30 seconds.)

Now let's focus on the muscle groups of the body. First, wrinkle the forehead by raising the eyebrows. (Pause for 5 seconds.) Now slowly relax the forehead. (Pause for 5 seconds.) Feel the relaxed forehead and let any tension dissolve away.

(Pause for 10 seconds.) Squeeze the eyes tightly closed. (Pause for 5 seconds.) Slowly relax the muscles around the eyes. (Pause for 5 seconds.) Let these muscles thoroughly relax. (Pause for 10 seconds.) Now smile as widely as you possibly can to feel the cheek muscles tensed. (Pause for 5 seconds.) Slowly let your smile go away, feeling the tension in your cheeks disappear. (Pause for 5 seconds.) Enjoy the relaxed feeling of your cheek muscles and let any remaining tension melt away. (Pause for 15 seconds.) Squeeze your lips tightly together. (Pause for 5 seconds.) Now slowly relax your tongue and lips. (Pause for 5 seconds.) Be aware of the feel of your tongue and lips as you relax them completely. (Pause for 10 seconds.) Grit your teeth together tightly. (Pause for 5 seconds.) Gradually let your jaws loosen and relax, noticing the tension fade away. (Pause for 5 seconds.) Now feel your whole face at rest. Totally relax your forehead, face, and mouth. (Pause for 5 seconds.) Feel no muscle stirring in the face at all. The face is completely limp. (Pause for 10 seconds.)

Next, let's feel the tension in your neck. Push your head forward and reach for your chest with your chin. (Pause for 5 seconds.) Slowly lay your head back down and relax the neck. (Pause for 5 seconds.) Now push your head backward against the surface you are lying on. (Pause for 5 seconds.) Gradually release all tension in your neck. (Pause for 5 seconds.) Now let your neck have no muscle activity and your head lie softly back on the surface with no effort. Let go of any tension left in the head and neck. (Pause for 15 seconds.)

Now raise your shoulders as high as you can toward the top of your head. (Pause for 5 seconds.) Slowly let your shoulders drop. (Pause for 5 seconds.) Feel your shoulders calm and limp. (Pause for 15 seconds.) Tighten your upper arms, flexing the biceps so these muscles bulge. (Pause for 5 seconds.) Slowly release the tightness in your upper arms. (Pause for 5 seconds.) Make fists and tighten the muscles of your forearms and wrists. (Pause for 5 seconds.) Release slowly and gradually. (Pause for 5 seconds.) Now thoroughly relax your head, neck, shoulders, and arms, so they are still, comfortable, and relaxed. (Pause for 15 seconds.) OK, let's tighten the muscles of the chest and stomach. (Pause for 5 seconds.) Gradually relax them. (Pause for 5 seconds.) Arch your back to feel the tension there. (Pause for 5 seconds.) Slowly release. (Pause for 5 seconds.) Now feel your head, neck, upper torso, and arms perfectly at rest. Let them fall completely limp. Imagine they feel heavy and you cannot move them. (Pause for 25 seconds.) Good.

Now let's work on the lower body. First, tighten your buttock muscles. (Pause for 5 seconds.) And let them gradually relax. (Pause for 5 seconds.) Release any remaining tension and feel your buttocks sink comfortably down with gravity. (Pause for 15 seconds.) Squeeze the muscles of your thighs and knees. (Pause for 5 seconds.) Let the tension in your thighs and knees slowly disappear. (Pause for 5 seconds.) Feel your thighs and knees lose all remaining tension and come to rest. (Pause for 15 seconds.) Tighten your calves, your lower legs. (Pause for 5 seconds.) Now slowly release. (Pause for 5 seconds.) Feel your legs completely still and relaxed. (Pause for 15 seconds.) Curl your toes upward toward your face. (Pause for 5 seconds.) Slowly relax the toes. (Pause for 5 seconds.) Curl the toes downward, away from the legs. (Pause for 5 seconds.) Let the toes and feet gradually come to rest. (Pause for 5 seconds.) Now feel your feet totally at rest. (Pause for 10 seconds.)

Now feel the pull of gravity on your calm, still body and give way to the deepening relaxation. (Pause for 25 seconds.) You are relaxed from the top of your head to the tip of your toes. Each time you practice this, you achieve a level of relaxation that can help calm you in daily life. Note the comfortable, peaceful feeling of this kind of relaxation. (Pause for 15 seconds.) Observe your breathing now, the endless cycle of bringing life and vitality into the body and breathing out wastes. You will become even more relaxed as you do nothing but observe the sensations of the air coming into and leaving your body. (Pause for 1 minute.) Good. Now imagine your limp body feels heavy, as if there were small lead weights all over gently pulling you down. (Pause for 20 seconds.) You may stay in this relaxed state for as long as you like: one more minute, 5 minutes, or 20 minutes longer. When you finally get up, do so leisurely and avoid any abrupt movements. (Silence.)

After 2 weeks or 14 sessions of practicing the tension-relaxation sequence, switch to deep muscle relaxation, so you can achieve deeper states of relaxation. You won't need a friend or an audiotape for this, and you won't squeeze or tense any of your muscles. Focus on body parts from head to toe, one at a time, spending about twenty seconds or more noticing and releasing tension in each body part, making it go completely limp. Keep repeating the whole sequence of relaxing all of your body parts; do this at least three times. Each time you come back to a body part and concentrate on releasing tension there again, you become more thoroughly relaxed. Taping this procedure is not a good idea. Research shows taped relaxation training is not helpful in learning to use the skill of relaxation in different situations. It is best to learn to relax deeply on your own, without a tape.

Imagery can help you relax more deeply while you practice deep muscle relaxation. Occasionally imagine warmth or relaxation flowing and spreading into other body parts. Occasionally imagine gravity or small lead weights gently pulling you down, making you so heavy you can't move. Some people enjoy imagining lying on a warm heating pad, soaking in warm bath water, or lying in the sun. Make a note about these helpful images and read it as a reminder before each relaxation session. No matter how expert you become at relaxing your whole body, always focus on each body part, one at a time, during deep muscle relaxation. This procedure helps you notice small amounts of muscle tension you would otherwise easily miss.

Unfortunately, nearly everyone carries unnecessary tension in their bodies much of the time, every day. In subtle ways, we often stand, walk, sit, or work with great amounts of muscle tension. The neck, shoulders, face, jaws, stomach, and back are very common places to hold excess tension. People often have tense neck and shoulder muscles while they sit and lean forward to eat, work, study, drive, etc. Some people tend to tighten their lips, tongue, and jaw while writing or concentrating. Others tend to squint a little while reading.

Practice noticing subtle tension by making yourself go limp, but still erect, many times each day while sitting, standing, walking, talking, driving a car, resting, etc. Spend a few seconds doing this every hour. You will find a surprising amount of unnecessary tension in your body while you watch television, eat lunch, work, etc. Learn where you hold your tension and relieve it many times each day. Gentle stretches can help. This will add calmness and reduce stress in your life.

Poor posture plays a great role in excessive amounts of tension in the body. Straighten your back and consciously relax to eliminate much of this tension. When you stand or walk, perfect posture means tucking in your buttocks a little by pushing your groin area slightly forward and up. Learn this movement of tucking in your buttocks by standing with your feet and back flat against a wall and moving to eliminate or greatly reduce the gap between the small of your back and the wall. Forget the military style of pulled back shoulders; that is tight, not relaxed. Allow your shoulders to go limp.

Breathing deeply, stretching, improving your posture, or releasing muscle tension can help whenever you feel stressed and before and during tense, anxious, or upsetting situations (such as confrontations, public performances, etc.). Experiment with different types of relaxation and meditation and switch from one to another any time you please. You may start with ten minutes of deep muscle relaxation, then decide to focus on rhythmic breathing for the next ten minutes, or you might start with the meditation of clearing the mind, then switch to prayer or a mantra.

You can also use visualization with other relaxation techniques. Visualization is creating a scene in your imagination. Use pleasant scenes like a favorite vacation spot, a hike in wooded mountains, a cabin with a spectacular view and a warm fire, a favorite memory, a beautiful fantasy, etc. Prepare for any visualization by first spending a minute or two in rhythmic breathing or deep muscle relaxation. Visualization works best when you create the scene in detail. If possible, include how you feel and what you see, hear, smell, sense by touch, and perhaps taste. Don't picture your own body in the scene; picture the scene as you would see it if you were actually there. Use slow movement during much of the visualization. Scenes without movement don't promote relaxation for very long, and fast movement doesn't lead to clear visualization.

You can create your own imaginary scene each time you visualize, or you can write out a scene and read it into a tape recorder with pauses for visualizing. Writing and tape recording is a good way to begin practicing because it allows you to prepare scenes carefully, so they change regularly and slowly and you include feelings, sights, sounds, etc. Once you learn to visualize, try to do it without the tape, so you can use this skill more effectively in other situations. Many people enjoy visualizing the following beach fantasy. Ask a friend to read it to you while you visualize, or read it yourself into a tape recorder. Again, read the instructions using a slow, calm, rhythmic voice and a watch or clock to time the pauses. When you visualize, remember to minimize your distractions and make yourself comfortable in the ways noted previously.

Instructions for a Visualization

Lie down with your arms at your sides and make yourself as comfortable as you can. Close your eyes and take several very deep breaths to start the relaxation process. (Pause for 20 seconds.) Let your stomach rise as you inhale and fall as you exhale, so you seem to breathe mostly from the lower lungs instead of the chest. (Pause for 15 seconds.) Wait for your breathing to become slow and regular. (Pause for 30 seconds.) Now focus on each part of the body as I mention it and release any tension you feel there. First the head, face, and neck. (Pause for 20 seconds.) Relax the shoulders and arms. (Pause for 20 seconds.) Torso. (Pause for 15 seconds.) Upper legs. (Pause for 15 seconds.) Lower legs and feet. (Pause for 15 seconds.) Now your whole body should feel very comfortable and still. (Pause for 15 seconds.)

Now imagine you and a few good friends are standing at the start of a trail to the ocean, looking at the scenery ahead with anticipation. The trail winds up and down a number of sand dunes, spotted with grasses, flowers, bushes, and stunted trees. (Pause for 20 seconds.) Your group begins walking uphill, carrying beach towels and a cooler full of food. With each step you take, warm sand spills over and around your feet, creating patterns up and down the hill. (Pause for 15 seconds.) Going over a few small ridges, you admire the grasses, wildflowers, and bushes around you and occasionally smell the fragrance of wildflowers. (Pause for 20 seconds.) The trail now passes through lush bushes to approach the top of a ridge with bent, stunted pine trees. (Pause for 15 seconds.) As you reach the top of the ridge between two twisted pine trees, you stop to appreciate the view: one more sand dune, spotted with yellow and green vegetation, and the turquoise ocean beyond. (Pause for 20 seconds.) You walk slowly downward, sinking with each step in the sand, as the view of the ocean disappears behind the sand dune. (Pause for 10 seconds.) As you walk up the last dune between yellow and green expanses, you notice the sound of the surf crashing on the shore. (Pause for 15 seconds.)

Arriving near the ocean, you put your things down. The shallows have a sandy bottom and the ocean beyond is deep blue-green. The scent of salt is in the air. (Pause for 20 seconds.) You happily watch seagulls floating in the sky and listen to their noisy chirping. (Pause for 15 seconds.) You sit down, close your eyes, and enjoy the sun's intense warmth combined with a nice breeze. (Pause for 10 seconds.) After baking in the sun for a while, you decide to go for a swim. As you get up and walk slowly to the water, you watch the waves crashing into white foam and washing up the beach and back again. (Pause for 20 seconds.) You walk into the refreshing, cool water and each wave pushes higher on your legs. (Pause for 20 seconds.) As the water reaches your hips, you deliberately fall into the water and let each wave push you back and forth. (Pause for 20 seconds.) You begin to play with the surf foam, first allowing it to crash on your back a few times. (Pause for 20 seconds.) Next, you fall down with the crashing surf a few times amidst all the bubbles. (Pause for 20 seconds.) Now you gleefully dive over the surf and get pushed a few feet along with it. (Pause for 20 seconds.)

You leave the ocean and go back to your friends to sit, talk, and enjoy the view. (Pause for 20 seconds.) Someone suggests eating and you open the cooler to pass out food and drinks. (Pause for 15 seconds.) Now imagine the sight and taste of your favorite picnic food as you savor eating it with your friends. (Pause for 15 seconds.) Before long, the sun begins to set. People talk quietly and others simply watch as the fireball creeps toward the horizon. (Pause for 5 seconds.) You feel peaceful as you watch the colors of the sunset: lemon yellow, a flaming orange sun, pink, lavender, and robin's egg blue above. The dunes behind are pearly white. (Pause for 15 seconds.) The colors deepen, pink becoming maroon, yellow becoming deep amber, and purple becoming navy blue. (Pause for 15 seconds.)

Now you and your friends build a bonfire. (Pause for 20 seconds.) You sit cozily and gaze at the dancing fire, occasionally talking with your special friends. (Pause for 20 seconds.) Now you walk up the beach away from the campfire. (Pause for 5 seconds.) Frothy suds flow up on the beach, sparkling with tiny seashells that catch the moonlight. Streaks of rippled moonlight stretch into the ocean. (Pause for 20 seconds.) Listening to the eternal sound of the ocean, you wander in and out of the edge of the water. With the shifting wind, you occasionally smell the aroma of a patch of greenery nearby. (Pause for 15 seconds.) You approach a large sand castle. (Pause for 5 seconds.) Water washes up near the sand castle and falls back, again and again. (Pause for 10 seconds.) You turn around and head back toward your friends by the distant campfire, feeling the cool, wet sand on your feet. Above you, millions of stars shine deep in the distance. (Pause for 15 seconds.) As you walk in the sand along the water's edge, you occasionally smell foliage or burning logs from the campfire. (Pause for 15 seconds.) Finally, you join your friends again at the campfire and feel a quiet contentment as you watch the flames dance, watch the occasional spark, and hear the logs crack. (Pause for 25 seconds.) Now rest as long as you please, perhaps focusing on your breathing, deep muscle relaxation, or just enjoying this peaceful state of relaxation. When you get up, do so leisurely and avoid any abrupt movements. (Silence.)

Recommended Additional Readings:

Stress Management: A Comprehensive Guide to Wellness. by Edward A. Charlesworth and Ronald G. Nathan. NY: Ballantine Books, 1984.

11. Easy, Small, Successful Changes

Take one small step and one day at a time.

The first step in solving any problem is to admit you have it and to take responsibility for it, rather than make excuses or blame other people or circumstances. We often refuse to admit, even to ourselves, that we have a problem until it causes trouble time and again. People sometimes remain oblivious to their own problems long after their friends and family members have noticed them. Addicted people are notorious for denying their problems, even while their careers and personal lives go to ruin. No matter what other people do or what circumstances befall us, we are free to respond with helpful or destructive emotions and behaviors. We, more than anyone or anything else, are responsible for our own personal problems. If you tend to deny a problem or blame other people or circumstances for your emotions, practice statements like: "I have a problem with ...," "I am responsible for ...," "I *chose* to feel ....," or "I *made* myself feel ... when that happened. I didn't have to feel that way." Write down such sentences fitting your particular problems and read them every day or several times a day to fight these bad habits.

Psychologists always recommend working on just one or two simple changes at a time to avoid becoming overwhelmed and giving up. Each step toward your goal should be easy enough to provide success more often than not. Never go on to a new step until practice has perfected the last step, making it easy and comfortable. Trying to make too many changes at once or a great, difficult change in one huge effort often leads to failure and discouragement.

Break down large, complex, or difficult problems into simpler steps and work on these steps one or two at a time. For example, a troubled marriage usually involves poor problem-solving skills, a variety of communication problems, poor control of anger, and a lack of affectionate behaviors. Work on the troubled marriage might begin with each spouse agreeing to improve one chronic communication problem, such as nagging or yelling. After several weeks of success in this area, the couple might establish weekly problem-solving sessions and agree to increase affectionate behaviors every day. Thus, the overwhelming marital problems become more manageable. Similarly, depression may involve negative thinking, personal conflicts, social isolation, chronic complaints, and a lack of variety in one's interests and activities. Here, too, start by working on each of the parts of the problem, one at a time.

When you can't break a difficult problem down into smaller problem areas, find easier situations in which to practice dealing with it. If you fear heights, climb a fire observation tower only as far as you feel comfortable going and then just a little bit farther. If you fear large dogs, observe a large dog from a long distance every day. If you fear bridges, begin with small bridges over creeks and gradually work up to larger ones. Gradually increase your skills as you become comfortable with previous steps.

If you feel shy with strangers and particularly awkward with attractive strangers of the opposite sex, practice your conversation skills whenever possible in elevators, on bus rides, etc. When you feel very comfortable with this, begin practicing talking and flirting in small group settings. Next, practice talking and flirting at parties, perhaps going to parties with a friend for a short while and then to other planned activities. You can also practice talking and flirting with less attractive members of the opposite sex (without leading them on, of course). The easiest way to begin practicing many skills is by acting out the situation, either by yourself or with a trusted friend for feedback and coaching. Chapter 14 contains a full discussion of this technique, called the behavioral roleplay.

Certain kinds of lists help you keep motivated and fight denial. Make a list of negative things about your problem behavior, including its resulting burdens, consequences, possible future consequences, and the ways in which it has hurt, disappointed, or inconvenienced other people. Be graphic about the worst possible outcomes. If you want to quit smoking cigarettes, include on your list endlessly coughing and fighting to breathe in the hospital with emphysema. If you go on a diet, include on your list obesity and repeated, painful rejections in romance. Ask your friends to think of ways in which your problem has hurt or burdened them, and add these to your list. Make another list of the benefits of change and improvement. Read both these lists every day to keep motivated.

After carefully studying the problem situation as described in chapter 9, make a list of the situations in which the problem is most likely to occur. Label these your high-risk situations. Next, use the suggestions in this book to make a list of coping plans or rules to follow in high-risk situations and whenever the problem occurs. Reading these lists every day keeps you aware of possible problems and helps you deal with them more effectively. Always keep your coping plans with you, so you can refer to them whenever necessary. Your coping plans are your most important list.

Put these lists in strategic spots, so you can't miss them: on your desk, on the bedroom or bathroom mirror, etc. Keep a copy in your purse or wallet. Don't defeat your purpose by ignoring a list or note every time you see it. Read all your lists at least once a day, perhaps every morning at breakfast. You might read your coping plans again when you come home from work. Or you could read a list every time you perform a frequent activity, such as brushing your teeth, talking on the telephone, drinking a cup of coffee, or smoking a cigarette, keeping your lists in the location of the activity. Other chapters can also help. Replace the negative thinking about problems that reduces motivation with more helpful alternatives every day, as described in chapter 4. The suggestions in the two following chapters, 12 and 13, also help a great deal in motivation.

Never lose hope and give up because of making a mistake or having a setback; this only guarantees failure. Losing hope and giving up involves self-defeating, negative thinking about your lack of will power, ability to change, or ability to overcome the problem. It is very important to remain motivated. Don't let a mistake or setback lead to giving up and backsliding farther, even for just a few days. The sooner you go back to work on your problem, the better. Instead of giving up, worrying about the mistake, or feeling guilty about the problem episode, learn from it. What kind of situation was it? How could you have responded better? Study the problem situation and plan strategies that will help you deal with similar situations more successfully in the future. If you can practice the ideal responses in behavioral roleplays (chapter 14), do so.

Once you succeed in changing or overcoming a problem, it is still very important to occasionally check on your continued progress. It is amazing how easily old habits tend to creep back on us. As noted previously, a major lifestyle change requires three to five years to become stable. Review your life every two months during the first year and every 4 months thereafter for any further instances of the problem. Write a note to remind yourself to review your continued progress and place it where you will occasionally see it. If you have made a number of behavioral changes in one problem area, keep a list of these changes for future reviews. Also keep your lists of reasons for changing, high-risk situations, and coping plans. If your old problem reappears, renew your efforts at self-improvement. After you feel sure you have overcome the problem again, begin the process of periodic reviews again. This approach makes you aware of backsliding when it occurs and helps ensure long-term success.

12. Help from Other People

Don't be afraid or too proud to ask for help;
it can make the difference between succeeding and failing.

To overcome personal problems, involve as many family members and friends as possible—this greatly increases your chances of success. Ask them for help and encouragement.   The more people monitoring your progress, giving you suggestions, reminding and encouraging you, the better. Ideally, they should learn as much as possible about the problem and about approaches for solving it.   One excellent way to do this is to read the relevant parts of this book.

When you ask people for help, use clear, specific terms to tell them exactly what you would like them to do. Asking for emotional support is too vague. Instead, ask them to check on your progress at least twice a week in detailed conversations.   Ask each person to explore your feelings, the difficulties you face in trying to change, and how you could have coped with the problems more successfully and to give you advice whenever possible. Ask them to give you encouragement, sympathy, and praise for your efforts. If you ask only a few friends or relatives for help, ask each of them to talk with you about your progress every day.

Many friends and family will agree to receive telephone calls or visits from you in times of trouble, day or night.   In this way, they can provide sympathy, encouragement, and advice whenever your problem is particularly upsetting or overwhelming.   For example, addicted people should ask their friends and relatives for emotional support and for reminders of their reasons for abstinence on an emergency basis when they feel unable to fight cravings or temptations alone.   Similarly, people with explosive anger or strong suicidal feelings should call friends or relatives (or a crisis line) for help in calming down, etc.

Ask friends and relatives to remind you about your plans and reasons for change whenever you act in ways that show you are not thinking about your need for self-improvement. Equip them with a thorough list of your reasons for wanting to change. They can use this information to argue with you when your motivation lags. Helpers can also monitor your continued effort and progress directly. For example, a wife can help a dieting husband count calories. Relatives should always make sure psychiatric patients are taking their medicines. Stopping medication prematurely is the most frequent cause of relapse. Often patients improve and decide they don't need their medicines when, in fact, the medicine is the only reason they feel better.

Helpers may participate in behavioral roleplays (chapter 14), so you can practice new behaviors or improved responses to troubling situations. People can also help motivate you by providing rewards or penalties. A husband could buy his obese wife a new dress each time she loses an additional ten pounds. An alcoholic and his steady girlfriend might agree they will go out only if he abstains from alcohol during the previous week and that she is free to date other men during weeks in which he drinks.

Instead of criticizing or nagging the person with the problem, make every effort to notice and praise any positive efforts and constructive behaviors. We tend to notice only what bothers us, and we often fail to appreciate any good or improvement that occurs. Even when someone requests your help, criticism or nagging may result in resentment and rebellion. For example, alcoholics often view nagging as a justification for drinking alcohol. Helping friends and relatives, then, should always emphasize the positive, accept mistakes, recognize effort and improvement, practice good communication skills, and use humor in a friendly way.

People often view unrequested encouragement, advice, and reminders as meddling and nagging, rather than kind helpfulness. This may provoke resentment and lead to additional problems. If you want to help people with their problems, try to use great tact and sensitivity to their feelings to avoid making them resentful of your interference. Gently get permission before using pleasant reminders, so they don't feel nagged.

If certain people act in ways interfering with your progress, explain this and ask for the changes you need. Addicted people should ask all their friends not to offer addictive substances, and people on diets should ask all their friends not to offer sweets and desserts. If you don't receive cooperation, you may need to see less of certain friends or even eliminate those friends in favor of more helpful ones.

Sometimes the loving acts of loyal friends and relatives innocently contribute to our problems. Efforts to cheer up a depressed person with sympathy, affection, or help with chores can contribute to depression by rewarding complaints and inactivity. The friends and relatives of addicted or violent people often make it easier for the problem to continue by tolerating it, hiding the problem from friends and employers, and helping with social, financial, or legal problems. Returning defective merchandise and confronting other people for a timid person may enable that person to avoid learning assertiveness skills. Running errands for a person who greatly fears driving a car may enable the person to avoid learning to drive.

Always consider how you might contribute to the person's problems. What do you do that allows the problem to continue, and what else could you do to help end the problem? One possibility is a loving group confrontation. If you believe someone needs to make drastic changes but the person disagrees or refuses, gather all the friends and family you can find who agree with you. Perhaps some concerned neighbors or coworkers see the problems and would be willing to participate. Ask all these people to come together at one time to discuss the issue with the person. In this group confrontation, participants should talk about their concerns for the person, one after another. Anyone who has ever been hurt, disappointed, inconvenienced, or affected by the person's problem behavior should explain how. Ask all the participants to prepare beforehand by thinking over the past, making a list of problems they remember, and another list of ways the problem has hurt or burdened them. Make the confrontation tough, yet loving. Start by emphasizing that everyone present loves the person and has come to help because of that love. Make sure each participant shows some warmth to the person. End your confrontation with everyone urging the person to get professional help. (Please read chapters 40 and 41 for important advice on getting counseling.)

Such group confrontations often persuade people to go to counseling. If the person insists on making changes without professional help, use this book as a resource and insist that if improvement does not occur in a reasonable amount of time, the person must go to counseling. All the people in the confrontation should offer their help, monitor the progress in the ways described in this chapter, and insist on counseling when they agree improvement has not occurred in a reasonable amount of time.

Support groups can help in many of the same ways as friends and relatives. *Support groups* are self-help groups in which people meet to share their feelings and experiences and help each other with a common problem. People with problems often feel terribly alone and find great relief in support groups in which others share many of the same concerns, disappointments, thoughts, feelings, and actions. Support groups provide an atmosphere of sharing and acceptance, but nobody has to disclose private information if they don't feel like it. The members maintain confidentiality about whatever any member decides to share. Members share ideas and practical help for their common problem. Some support groups use a buddy system in which members pair up to provide emotional support and help in times of difficulty between scheduled meetings. Support groups may meet in church halls, public buildings, or members' homes. Some have guest speakers, newsletters, or telephone hotlines. There are now over 1,000 self-help groups available on the Internet. Small membership groups may communicate with fellow members by mail, and some groups do political lobbying for their common concerns.

Alcoholics Anonymous is the most famous support group, with the largest membership and most local chapters. There are national support groups for almost every imaginable problem. Groups exist for narcotics addicts, the families of alcoholics, neurotics, people with emotional problems, former mental patients, the families and friends of the mentally ill, gamblers, and the overweight. Other groups help parents who have lost children to death, the families and friends of young people with behavior problems, single parents, widows and widowers, homosexuals, the families and friends of homosexuals, and people with anorexia or bulimia. Many support groups are for dealing with physical problems: people with heart diseases, blind people and their families, parents of children with cancer, people with muscular dystrophy and their families, women who have had mastectomies, etc.

Find out about support groups in your community by calling the local information and referral center, crisis hotline, social service agencies, or mental health centers. Public libraries usually have books listing self-help organizations and their national headquarters. If a support group interests you and there is no chapter in your area, the central office can give you information that helps in organizing a local group. You can often find members by putting notices in local churches and newspapers.

Recommended Additional Readings:

When Someone You Love Has a Mental Illness: A Handbook for Family, Friends, and Caregivers. by Rebecca Woolis. Los Angeles: Jeremy Tarcher; New York: Perigee Books, 1992. Friends and relatives of the mentally ill will find this book very helpful in getting along with the person, in encouraging taking medicines, and with practical matters such as housing, jobs, and stigma. It also gives useful advice for dealing with anger, delusions, hallucinations, and confusion.

13. Rewards, Penalties, and Contracts

Gifts strengthen affection and love.

Exchanging gifts of improved behaviors can turn bitter hostility to harmony.

Rewards for success and penalties for failure can motivate you to achieve your goals. In countless research studies with both animals and humans, rewards for behaviors often increase those behaviors. Reward yourself with anything you want or enjoy doing. The reward may be a common pleasure or a special treat. A teenager who enjoys throwing parties may decide to motivate herself in school by reserving this privilege until she has achieved all A's and B's on her tests for a full month. An unassertive man may motivate himself by treating himself to a meal in his favorite restaurant after any week in which he refused to accommodate all annoying requests. A cigarette smoker may shave the mustache he loves dearly and plan to reward himself with growing the mustache back if he abstains for two months. A woman who feels ashamed of her sloppy apartment may motivate herself by quitting going on dates until she cleans and scrubs it.

Your penalty for failure may simply be the loss of your reward or it may be an additional penalty, to add more motivation. For example, a depressed man who wants to buy a television may use it to motivate himself to develop more interests and activities. Every week in which he increases the amount of time he spends on interests and activities beyond his normal level, he will put $15 aside for the TV. In addition, for further motivation, any week in which he fails to increase his time spent on interests and activities, he will take $10 away from the amount saved for the TV.

Never reward yourself before achieving your goal. People who do this often lose motivation and fail to follow their plans. If you go on a diet, for example, never reward yourself today and promise you will eat only fruit and salad all next week. Reward yourself only after having eaten nothing but fruit and salad for a week. Use small rewards for easier goals and save your larger rewards for more difficult ones. Some penalties benefit you or others. A teenager might decide every time she yells at her sister, she will study mathematics, her worst subject, for two hours on each of the next three days. A woman may specify that every time she fails to follow her plan, she will give $25 to charity, clean out the garage, or pick up litter in the neighborhood.

Fit your rewards and penalties to your goals in a reasonable manner. Make sure if you really try, you can achieve the reward more often than not. If your goal is too difficult, you will only frustrate, not motivate yourself. To help avoid unreasonable goals, consider the frequency of your problem when you choose your goals and rewards. Consider the above example of the teenager who plans to study mathematics each time she yells at her sister. If she normally only yells at her sister about once a week, a penalty of two hours study for three days each time she yells may fit her well and help. But if she normally yells at her sister frequently, often several times each day, this penalty is excessive; she would probably earn endless penalties and give up hope. Expect some improvement of yourself, but don't push so hard for your rewards or to avoid your penalties that progress is difficult to maintain.

Rewards work best for those who dislike or don't care about their work. Research suggests rewards decrease creativity, reducing the risk taking of exploring new possibilities. Working for rewards, we tend to do only what it takes to earn the reward and no more, not striving for excellence. Rewards may also reduce our interest in the task. If you are a parent, offer rewards to your children occasionally, not every time you see the desired behaviors. Surprise your children with rewards, so they are not motivated only by rewards. Use plenty of praise and instill pride for improved behaviors, effort, work, and achievement. When you do reward, point out specifically what worthy behaviors earned the reward.

Contracts involve agreements between two parties, such as husband and wife, parent and child, etc. Contracts may deal with increasing positive behaviors or decreasing negative ones. The simplest form of contract exchanges behaviors desired by the other party. These agreements take the form: "I will do ..., if you do ..." For example, a husband may promise to discuss his day and to ask about his wife's day at supper daily in return for his wife's promise to stop complaining about his weekly poker game. A wife may agree to cook her husband's favorite desserts once a week if her husband will do the laundry on weekends. The parents of a teenager may allow their son to stay out later on weekends if he gets his homework done and if he treats them with respect, defined as politeness and no cursing or yelling.

These simple, informal agreements are the most pleasant, friendly kind of contract, but they can backfire if the spirit of cooperation is not strong enough. In cooperative relationships, one party may forgive the other for failing to perform the promised behaviors, and both parties may renew their efforts to honor the agreement. But when one person fails to perform the promised behaviors, the other person often retaliates and soon nobody tries to follow the contract. Thus, people at odds with one another may require a more complicated kind of contract.

For such people, the ideal contract uses separate rewards or penalties for each person that have nothing to do with the other person's side of the agreement. If the reward or penalty affects the other person at all, it should not be a chore or burden for that person. Let's use the previous example of a husband's discussing daily events at supper in return for his wife's elimination of complaints about his weekly poker game. If either person fails to perform the promised behaviors and cooperation deteriorates, they might revise the contract as follows. Only if the husband discusses the day's events with his wife each day at supper, he can play his weekly game of golf; otherwise he must cancel it. Only if the wife never complains about his poker game all week, she can hire a babysitter for one free afternoon for herself during the next week. In this kind of contract, anyone who fails to perform the promised behaviors loses the reward without interfering with the other half of the contract, the terms of the abiding partner. The parties in this arrangement are less prone to anger, because each person can earn the reward even when the other party fails to do so. As long as the terms of the agreement seem fair and workable to both parties, this kind of contract can survive repeated failure by either party.

The problems and goals in reward and penalty plans or contracts must always focus on specific, observable behaviors, rather than on vague behaviors. That is why a previous example defined the vague notion of treating the parents with respect in a more clear and helpful way as politeness, no cursing, and no yelling. Please refer to chapter 9, Problem Solving, for a full discussion of this important point. You can write and sign your reward and penalty plans for yourself or your contracts with others to make them more official. People who need the complex kind of contract using separate rewards and punishments for each party should certainly write down and sign the agreement.

Rewards, penalties, and contracts help in motivating people but when circumstances change, you may need to alter them. If complaints about a contract arise, you may need to revise it by renegotiating to fit the changing needs of each person. When you succeed and reach your goals and you always earn your reward, you may decide to end your plan or perhaps to set a higher standard of performance to improve yourself further.

14. Roleplay

We are all actors on the stage of life.

You never really know or understand other people
until you have walked in their shoes.

Roleplay involves using your imagination to act out roles for a variety of possible reasons. Despite the acting, roleplay is not as artificial as it first appears. We are all actors playing many different social roles in various situations. We act the roles of friend, student, worker, husband, wife, father, mother, boss, customer, etc. There are four kinds of roleplay: behavioral roleplay, teaching roleplay, interpersonal roleplay, and dialoguing.

Behavioral roleplay uses acting to rehearse new or desired behaviors or prepare behavior for a future situation that concerns you. Imagining you face the problem situation and acting out the planned behavior is a safe, easy way to become comfortable with the situation and to learn what to expect of yourself and other people. Try to find a trusted friend who will act the part of the other person in the conflict. The more lifelike the situation and the acting, the better. Ask your friend for suggestions and feedback on the skills you need to practice. If you do the behavioral roleplay by yourself, rehearse in front of a mirror and, if possible, tape record your roleplays, so you can watch, listen, and study your own efforts. In a variety of roleplays, experiment with different situations, your own responses, possible reactions from the other person, and positive and negative outcomes. Work on using your facial expressions, gestures, voice, and posture to communicate emotions and impressions you want to convey. What could have been better in your performance? Keep experimenting until you feel you have found the best responses for each possible situation. Keep practicing your responses until you feel confident about dealing with each possibility. In this way, you will feel prepared for whatever might happen.

Although acting out the scenes in behavioral roleplays is the best way to rehearse, you can also spend time imagining the situations and your responses. This is an excellent way to get extra practice when you can't act out the scenes, on the subway, at lunch, etc. You can use behavioral roleplay and rehearsal in the imagination in many kinds of situations. Alcoholics should rehearse dealing with peer pressure to drink, until they develop a variety of effective, comfortable responses. People who find it difficult to express their emotions can practice in roleplays with trusted friends or loved ones. If you have a bad temper, you should roleplay typical situations provoking your anger, so you can practice assertive, yet calm and respectful responses. Assertiveness groups run by psychologists use many behavioral roleplays, so the participants can practice expressing warmth, making requests or demands, refusing requests, complaining, confronting, and dealing with anger and pestering.

Teaching roleplays use reversed roles to help young children learn to take a more adult perspective. In *reversed roles*, two people change places and roleplay each other in a reenactment of a situation. This technique clearly shows each person the perspective of the other. Teaching roleplays in which the parents play the misbehaving children and the children play the parents help show little children why their misbehavior must change. You can easily distract little children from their misbehavior with this technique (when you don't use it too often) because they love playacting the adults trying to correct and scold their children. During the roleplay, help your children formulate and take adult perspectives by pouting or mimicking reluctance and asking why. This pushes your children to think and give reasons why the behavior is wrong. Always follow teaching roleplays with plenty of praise for the adult perspectives verbalized by the child. After the roleplay in a quick, friendly discussion, you can also add other reasons for improved behaviors.

Teaching roleplays with reversed roles can also help little children with fears. The fun of helping mom or dad calm down and confront the fear helps children deal with the fear better. If you succeed in playacting in the presence of the actual feared situation, perhaps from a distance at first, the roleplay may lead to quick improvement in the child.

The next two types of roleplay, interpersonal roleplay and dialoguing, explore personal issues and are very effective at contacting emotions. In rare cases, however, these two techniques can be dangerous. Both can sometimes uncover sensitive issues and stir up stronger emotions than the person can handle alone. People with severe problems, overwhelming problems, or many chronic problems, in particular, should not use either of these techniques without the guidance of a psychologist. *Anyone* considering the use of either interpersonal roleplay or dialoguing should read the first paragraph in chapter 41 on Counseling. If you have any of the problems listed there, don't use interpersonal roleplay or dialoguing without professional guidance. Even happy people may experience strong and troubling emotions when exploring personal issues with these two techniques.

Interpersonal roleplays reenact a conflict between people to deepen understanding of the problem situation.   Never use interpersonal roleplay during a hostile conflict; use it later when everyone is calm.   Start with a simple reenactment of each significant event in the conflict, one after another. Then repeat the dramatization with reversed roles, so each party roleplays one another and experiences the other point of view.   Such roleplays often relieve tension as the participants feel silly and laugh.   Children often enjoy exploring family conflict in roleplays because acting is a fun way for them to express their feelings and perceptions.   Subtle differences between the simple reenactment and the dramatization with reversed roles often appear.   A mother may appear more nagging and insensitive when portrayed by her daughter, and the daughter may appear more cross and disrespectful when portrayed by the mother.   By seeing each interpretation graphically portrayed, regardless of which portrayal is actually more correct, all the participants learn about the feelings and impressions involved.

An interpersonal roleplay may also include an *aside,* another technique helping illuminate different perspectives among the participants.   An aside is very much like an actor's soliloquy, when the actor turns aside and reveals to the audience what the character in the drama really thinks or feels.   Any participant can stop the action to inform the others of personal thoughts, feelings, wishes, or motivations—even confusion or ambivalence.   You might stop a roleplay to say, "Aaaugh!! He's always telling me what to do and how to do it.   I'm so sick of that!"   Asides allow you to be more honest than you could be in the real situation.

Finally, all the participants talk over what they experienced in the roleplay.   Discuss the events that led to the problem, the perspectives and feelings of each participant, how it felt to reverse roles, and how to deal with similar situations in the future.   Interpersonal roleplays also help in resolving feelings about the past.   Psychologists conducting group therapy may coordinate this kind of roleplay to help a client uncover and express buried emotions, deal with them, and recover from the past.   For more information on this, please refer to chapter 37, Getting over the Past.

Dialoguing is a type of roleplay in which people use fanciful conversations to explore their own issues, conflicts, roles, thoughts, and feelings.   In dialoguing, you speak aloud both sides of an imaginary conversation by yourself.   The spontaneity of these imaginary dialogues is an important element that allows feelings and parts of yourself to emerge, so never think beforehand about what you will say.   Improvise and talk rather impulsively. Free yourself of restraints and inhibitions. Be silly, playful, and dramatic. A playful dialogue might help you understand more about yourself than you could by thinking about the problem in an intellectual way. Don't hide anything. Always dialogue with important issues, conflicts, situations, feelings, or people in your life; otherwise your dialogues will be trite and artificial. Even when working with important issues in your life, you will probably feel, at first, that your dialogue sounds contrived or artificial. You may feel somewhat ridiculous. Don't let these feelings bother you. Keep talking and experimenting despite them. Eventually, if you are working with important issues in your life, you can access buried emotions, learn about parts of yourself, and resolve issues.

You can dialogue alone for privacy and totally uninhibited self-expression or in the presence of other people such as trusted friends, a psychologist, or therapy group members. Tape record your dialogue, so you can listen to it and study the feelings, thoughts, issues, conflicts, and parts of yourself you expressed. When dialoguing with other people present, you carry on both parts of the imaginary conversation yourself, although the other people may help by suggesting things for you to try. For example, a psychologist may coach you to develop an emotion, believing your portrayal has not truly reached your buried emotion. The psychologist may ask you to try a particular phrase, keep repeating it with more emotion each time, or keep repeating an angry phrase louder and louder. Other people can also help by offering feedback after the dialogue. They may point out feelings, issues, or conflicts they noticed or may label a part of your personality you expressed. Whenever someone else gives suggestions, you remain the final judge of whether or not the dialogue or interpretation rings true or holds meaning for you.

Begin your dialogue by speaking with a clue to your conflicts you would most like to investigate. You may begin with a problem person in your life, conflicting parts of yourself, a physical symptom that might come from buried emotions, or a strong, negative, or troublesome feeling in your life. No matter what you start with, the dialogue may lead you to other people, parts of yourself, or feelings. Feel free to switch to a new dialogue whenever a new feeling arises, when your dialogue reminds you of another person or emotion in your life, or when it seems to express one personal characteristic or side of you and neglect your opposite side. Let your dialogue wander with whatever intuitively seems most important. Always refer to both speakers with "I," the first person singular. Always express thoughts and feelings in the present tense, even if your dialogue concerns a long-past event. Use "I am angry," not "I was angry;" "I think ...," not "I thought ...;" "I wish ...," not "I wished ...;" etc. Doing this helps you express your inner feelings and thoughts.

Dialogue about a person only when you have intense, conflicting, or troublesome feelings about the person. Otherwise, the work tends to be unproductive and meaningless. To dialogue about a person, create an imaginary confrontation and speak both parts aloud yourself. You may change position, voice, and/or facial expression when you switch from one person to the other. Be more honest and blunt than you can be in real life. Don't censor or hide anything and don't try to be logical. Exaggerate each person's feelings and point of view. The purpose is to explore your issues and inner feelings, so express even your irrational or troublesome thoughts. Let each person argue back and forth, explaining feelings, views, and reactions to the last detail. Then examine the dialogue and consider how to deal with the feelings, thoughts, and issues that emerged. This can increase your understanding and help you deal with the problem person more effectively in real life.

When you dialogue with a feeling or physical symptom that might come from buried emotions, you pretend the feeling or symptom can speak like a person. Carry on a whimsical conversation, perhaps finding out what your depression or tight neck would say if it could talk. You may speak to your loneliness, fear, anger, boredom, tears, upset stomach, headache, lump in the throat, trembling hand, twitching muscle, fidgeting, etc. Any problem emotion or any physical symptom listed in chapter 5 as perhaps from buried emotions is a good candidate for this kind of dialogue. You might ask it a question such as: "Why are you bothering me?" or "What do you want from me?" Be silly and experiment. Let go. If you work with an important feeling or symptom, you may find the words ring surprisingly true.

Dialoguing with parts of the self helps in exploring and resolving ambivalent feelings or conflicts in yourself. Whenever you are torn between two ways of feeling or behaving, dialoguing with the parts may help. You can dialogue with any feeling or characteristic and its opposite, as long as you have some trouble with the opposing tendencies, some conflict. Conflicts you might want to explore follow.

Possible Conflicts to Explore with Dialoguing

careful me / fun-loving me
angry me / forgiving me
angry me / loving me

angry me / sensible me
invulnerable me / hurt me
invulnerable me / devastated me
affectionate me / distant me
assertive me / helpful me
proud me / embarrassed me
good parent / pleasure-seeker
good parent / friend and equal to my child
cheerful me / open and honest me
optimistic me / realistic me
responsible me / rebellious me
strong me / the part of me needing help
strong me / kind me
strong me / the part of me in touch with my emotions
independent person / loving mate
concerned, worried me / wild me
the part of me that is hurt and wants distance / lonely me
kind me / harsh me
kind me / manipulative me
good me / bad me
extreme perfectionist / realist
inadequate failure / determined me
dependent me / independent me
real self / ideal self

Note that certain characteristics appear on this list more than once, with different opposites each time. Depending on the situations and feelings, different people may choose various opposites to the same characteristic.

Create an imaginary discussion or argument between the opposite sides in your personality. Start by making one part explain how and why you feel or act that characteristic way. Next, argue from the opposite part of yourself, explaining the merits of its position and criticizing the statements of the first side. Go back and forth, bringing up new points and trying to destroy the arguments of the other side. Improvise playfully. Feel free to be emotional or illogical. Exaggerate each position. Both sides will have good points and bad points. After expressing the feelings, views, and counterarguments of each side to the last detail, review the dialogue and consider what solutions you can find. You may decide to accept more fully the two conflicting emotions or sides of yourself and find a more comfortable balance between them, either a midpoint between the extremes or a versatile ability to emphasize one or the other in appropriate circumstances. Or you may decide one side is unproductive or troublesome and the opposite side of yourself needs more emphasis and development. Use what you have learned to make changes in your life.

Let's consider some examples illustrating the different kinds of dialogues and how and why one might go from one type to another. The first example concerns a frustrated man who holds an imaginary confrontation with his girlfriend.

Man: You make me sick! You never want to see me unless you happen to be in the mood. Anytime you have someone else to go out with, you act as if I don't exist. You don't really love me!

Man roleplaying girlfriend: You're right, I don't really love you, but we have a nice thing. I like you and know I can always come back to you.

Man: When you feel bored or lonesome.

Man roleplaying girlfriend: Right.

Man: What about me? What can I do when you've got someone else? I really get hurt. I feel neglected, lonesome, and used.

Man roleplaying girlfriend: I don't really care how you feel, when you come right down to it. You're convenient. I can leave you whenever I please and I know you'll be willing whenever I want to see you again.

In this dialogue, the man speaks the thoughts of both parties according to his deepest feelings. In real life, neither he nor his girlfriend would ever admit to such feelings. By dialoguing with brutal honesty, he faces feelings and impressions he normally avoids. The painfully honest dialogue leads to feelings of depression, a chronic problem, so he decides to dialogue with his depression.

Man: What would you tell me, depression, if you could talk?

Depression: It's no surprise I'm always around. I'm always bothering you because you have real problems and keep avoiding them. You tolerate a girlfriend who doesn't care about you, you act as if you could never find another girlfriend, you sit around all day and drink beer, and you never do anything but work, watch TV, and worry about that so-called girlfriend of yours. You only go with her because it's easier than making yourself the type of man a woman would want. Why don't you do something for yourself! Just cutting down on the booze would make you feel better. You always wanted to learn to cook and to play the flute. If you don't make some changes, I'm going to plague you all your life!

Of course, most dialogues won't be so productive right away. It may take a half or full hour of experimenting to produce the main ideas summarized above. If you work with issues that really bother you, you will eventually produce meaningful dialogue that may give you insight. An honest, intellectual study of your own feelings, thoughts, and issues will often produce the same results, but sometimes the spontaneous, uninhibited approach of dialoguing with emotional issues reveals much about yourself quickly. The next example involves a woman with chronic headaches. She starts by dialoguing with the headache.

Woman: Why do you keep bothering me, headache?

Headache: I keep bothering you because you cram so much into me. A head is only so big and you cram all your work into me. First, it's your career. I have to take that. Then you cram all your community activities into me. I have to take that. You cram all of your social activities into me. I have to take that. Then you add all these things you need to remember to do, must try to do well, need to do to please yourself, and must do well to please the people you're doing it for. I have to take that. I feel like I'm a small shoe with a big foot in it, as if there's no room for anything else. So I hurt you. Notice I don't hurt you if you stop, sit down or lay down, and rest for long enough. If you would just quit trying to do so much, I wouldn't push against the sides of your head and hurt you.

Now the woman realizes she has some very ambivalent feelings, a great conflict between desires for more relaxation and desires to be an outstanding and perfect community member, so she holds a dialogue between these sides of herself.

Part craving relaxation: You're never going to get rid of those headaches if you don't learn to take it easy occasionally.

Outstanding community member: What do you want me to do? You want me to turn into a lazy, average person! I like being known as the best employee on the job. I help a lot of people in my community activities. What's wrong with being great instead of average?

Part craving relaxation: You can be great, but at what cost? Do you want to have headaches almost every day of your life? You can't just do everything well. No, you have to overdo it. You have to be great! If you keep this up, someday you're going to die of a stroke or heart attack. That's what happens to workaholics who can't slow down. Then you won't be any good to anybody.

Outstanding community member: I don't care. At least I'll go out accomplishing things and helping people instead of sitting on my rump in boredom. You're just a lazy, good-for-nothing bum. Is that what you want people to call me?

Part craving relaxation: That's your other problem. You think nobody will like you for what you are. You think you have to please everyone, to do everything for everybody. People will still respect you and love you if you slow down a little. You don't need to quit everything. I know you enjoy your work and your accomplishments, but you aren't superhuman. Drop a few things and take more time to enjoy yourself and your friends.

Outstanding, perfect community member: That's not such a bad idea, I guess.

In this dialogue, the resolution occurred during the roleplay itself as the two sides managed to find a compromise. When this happens, the solution to your problem appears in the dialogue itself. Otherwise, you must consider the issues presented in the dialogue and decide how to begin working on the problem.

The above examples should clarify what a dialogue is, how to do it, and how it can help explore personal issues. Chapters 37, 38, and 39 in this book discuss more uses for dialoguing. If you want a deeper understanding of this technique, please refer to the recommended book below.

Recommended Additional Readings:

Gestalt Therapy Verbatim. by Frederick S. Perls, compiled and edited by John O. Stevens. Moab, Utah: Real People Press, 1959. Fritz Perls, the inventor and undisputed master of dialoguing, leads people in exploring their personal conflicts with dialogues. The book contains many examples of dialogues using imaginary people, feelings, physical symptoms, body parts, and dreams.

Part 2:
How to Solve Personal Problems

*Problems, crises, and failures
are all crossroads on our paths.
Choose to learn from them
and you blossom in wisdom.*

Change yourself and your luck will change.

Part 2 describes how to solve a variety of common personal problems. Although Part 2 often refers to especially relevant information in the general chapters of Part 1, referring to those earlier chapters whenever possible would have resulted in endless repetition. Therefore, use the information in Part 1 whenever it is relevant, whether or not the book specifically advises you to do so for any particular personal problem. For example, chapters 11, Easy, Small, Successful Changes, 12, Help from Other People, and 13, Rewards, Penalties, and Contracts, help increase your chances of success in conquering any personal problem.

15. Social Life

Reaching out is the first step toward lasting friendship.

In friendship and dating, a good reputation has great value.

$\mathbf{A}$ good social life is important in happiness and mental health. Psychologists often teach the social skills of conversation skills, good communication skills, anger management, appropriate eye contact, other nonverbal communication skills, and friendship formation to reduce the chance emotional problems will develop and to improve the ability to cope when emotional problems do occur. Having friends helps make life satisfying and rich. Close relationships provide warmth, companionship, acceptance, respect, love, understanding, reassurance, emotional support, help, and sometimes useful ideas or material resources. Even an ideal marriage partner cannot meet all your emotional needs, however. Unfortunately, many isolated people don't realize this until they lose their spouse and find themselves unable to cope.   Psychologists believe it is best to have a variety of relationships, from very close to less intimate friendships. Well-rounded, happy people have several very close friends and a number of other friends, some closer than others, with whom they can share different activities and parts of themselves.

Loneliness and Shyness

Everyone experiences times of loneliness and sometimes we must learn to accept such feelings. Indeed, each person is ultimately alone and separate from fellow human beings in an utterly final sense. Each person has private thoughts and feelings, suffers pain alone, and is destined to lose loved ones and to make the journey of death alone. Our ability to love other people enables us to bridge this gap and become close to others. More important than having a romantic, intimate love for one other person is the love of humanity and the ability to care and give to other people that brings us closer to others.

Loneliness often comes from lack of a well-rounded variety of interests and activities and simply developing more of them may end the loneliness. Loneliness also often indicates a need to reach out to other people and develop friendships. Use the skills in this chapter to develop new habits of speaking to, helping, and getting to know other people. If you don't enjoy being alone, you need to develop more interests and activities you can enjoy alone, work on changing habits of negative thinking, and perhaps work on relaxation skills, anxiety, depression, or other problem emotions. Never attempt to pull sympathy or attention from friends with your loneliness, or attempt to make your friends feel guilty for not spending time with you. Doing these things emphasize your loneliness, manipulates other people, and alienates them. Using casual sex, food, or addictive substances as outlets for your loneliness is even more destructive. Volunteer work is especially useful to lonely people, providing companionship, feelings of usefulness and being needed, and many opportunities to make new friends. Owning a pet may help. Pets such as dogs and cats provide a constant source of comforting companionship and uncritical affection.

Anxiety is very common when you are in unfamiliar situations, with unfamiliar people, with authority figures, with people of high status, performing a new role, or being evaluated. It is also very common in large crowds or parties, when trying to make a friend, when dating, in dealing with rejection, or in sexual intimacy. In one study, 48% of American adults reported shyness. Cultures differ in this, however. For example, in Israel only 30% of college students report being shy, but in Japan and in Taiwan, 60% do. Social anxiety may seem painfully obvious to the anxious person while other people see little or no indication of anxiety. People at parties often feel they are the only anxious person there, when most of the people at the party actually feel some degree of social anxiety. A certain amount of social anxiety, then, is quite normal.

Shyness or social anxiety involves negative thinking that keeps you anxious. People who feel very anxious in social situations often expect to feel nervous, make mistakes, and be rejected. Please refer to the discussion of negative thinking in chapter 4 and use its advice to write positive thought alternatives and practice them daily. Many socially anxious people need to work on their poor self-esteem, and many of them need to improve their nonverbal communication skills. Low rates of eye contact, looking down toward the floor too much, a lack of warm facial expressions, or the use of certain postures may betray anxiety or poor self-esteem or create a false impression of lack of interest in communicating.

Use the skills in this chapter to talk more to other people. Begin with those with whom you feel more comfortable, such as children, old people, or other shy people, and then learn to talk to people you meet anywhere. Practicing these skills to be friendlier to everyone will help you a great deal when you want to reach out to someone in particular. If a particular social situation makes you very anxious, prepare yourself for it, perhaps using behavioral roleplays. It may help to practice meditation or deep relaxation beforehand. Be sure to breathe deeply and to relax muscle tension or stretch just before and during the situation. Distract yourself from your anxiety by finding out as much as you can about other people or focusing your mind on colors, textures, and patterns you see. Chapters 11, 12, 13, and 29 also help with problems of shyness or social anxiety.

Conversation Skills

You can start a conversation in countless ways, limited only by your imagination. Sometimes the situation will determine the way to begin. You may simply greet the other person, introduce yourself, and ask the person's name. You may ask other people's permission to join them, or invite someone to join you or your group. You might offer to share a snack, information, help, or something else. Perhaps you need information, advice, or some kind of help. Begin some conversations with a comment or question about the other person's activities or something you both have in common, such as children, school, work, waiting in line, the place you are both in, etc. People often comment or ask opinions about the weather, news, sports events, entertainment, or politics. A compliment is a very nice way to begin a conversation. The compliment may deal with the person's clothing, hair, jewelry, personal qualities, smile, laugh, skills, etc. Try asking questions about the other person or sharing information about yourself. Topics include such things as how the day went, places of origin, work, family, interests, hobbies, activities, experiences, feelings, areas of expertise, or accomplishments. When you talk to someone you don't know very well, you should probably avoid very personal information such as finances, sex, and perhaps age.

In initiating a conversation with someone new, be brief. Test the other person's interest in talking by using simple statements or questions before giving a very detailed explanation or telling a long story. See if the other person responds very briefly, with several details, with friendliness, or with polite boredom. If the other person shows some interest, you can talk for longer periods. People often ramble from one topic to another during conversations, with questions, answers, and topics triggering others. Developing a wide variety of interests and activities gives you more to talk about and improves your conversation skills. Keeping informed about current events and other subjects by reading newspapers and magazines helps. Entertainment such as movies, plays, music, sports, and television make good topics. Jokes and interesting or funny things that have happened are also good topics.

The art of conversation involves a nice balance between talking and listening. Don't dominate a conversation by talking too much; this may bore other people or appear self-centered. On the other hand, talking too little may give the impression you are uninterested, bored, or cold. Good conversation involves a give and take of information. When someone asks you a question, feel free to give more information than is necessary, more than just yes or no. This shows your interest in talking and gives the other person more topics for conversation. If the other person seems bored with a subject that interests you, change topics or ask the other person questions.

Take a genuine interest in other people and learn to bring out their feelings, ideas, and interests. Encourage them to speak by asking questions that call for more than just yes or no answers. Questions beginning with what, why, or how tend to require longer answers. Cultivate acceptance for other people and toleration for different points of view. Show your interest and attention both verbally and nonverbally. Verbal ways of showing interest include both comments and noises: "That's interesting," "Yeah," "Hmm," "Uh-huh," etc. Nonverbal ways of showing interest include turning toward the person, nodding your head occasionally, maintaining regular eye contact, and friendly, interested facial expressions and tone of voice. Of course, when a person shares problems or upsetting events with you, you should respond with a concerned, perhaps softer tone of voice, a sadder face, and emotional support.

Good conversation is predominantly positive. Strive to normally use positive statements many times more often than negative statements, complaints, and criticisms. It is unpleasant to be around a person who often complains or finds fault with other people. Break habits of complaining or discussing health problems. Don't speak poorly of other people if you can help it; doing so reflects poorly on your character. Please refer to the section on Positive Communication in chapter 6 for more details on this issue and for specific ways to practice positive communication.

People who feel awkward talking to strangers need to practice their conversation skills. The following list is a useful reminder of ways to begin conversations and things to talk about. Copy it and carry it with you in a pocket, wallet, or purse, so you can refer to it whenever necessary.

Ways to Begin Conversations and Things to Talk About

ask a question about the other
person
ask for help, advice, information
comment on activity
compliment
funny or interesting personal
experiences
interests, hobbies, activities
introduction and request for name
jokes
movies, sports, music, television
news, current events, politics

offer invitation to join
offer help or information
opinions, feelings, experiences
question about activity
request permission to join
share information about yourself
situation you are both in
something you both have in
common
weather
work, family, origin

Develop a repertoire of funny or interesting personal experiences and jokes. Write down particularly good stories and jokes you hear from other people and read them occasionally to refresh your memory. Practice telling these stories with your friends or alone with a tape recorder or looking in the mirror. Don't memorize and recite them word for word. Just practice them until you can tell them in a relaxed, natural way during a conversation.

Any conversation will include occasional breaks or short silences. If you feel anxious during lulls in the conversation, practice accepting them comfortably. You may use these periods of silence to think of new questions or topics of conversation or to enjoy your surroundings, watching people, scenery, architecture, etc. If you tend to talk anxiously just to fill the void, count slowly to five or ten before talking to become accustomed to silences.

Nonverbal communication often plays a role in ending conversations. Positions that begin to move away from the other person (such as increasing distance slightly, turning the body away a bit, and perhaps moving a leg toward your direction of exit) suggest your intention of leaving. People also signal their intention to leave by using less eye contact. At a party you might look around at other people before wandering away from someone. There are many ways to end a conversation. You may explain what you need or want to go and do, or you may announce your decision to leave in a friendly way without explaining any details. You may stand to leave or perhaps shake hands good-bye. In any case, end your conversations on a friendly note. Say something positive like: "I really enjoyed talking to you. Bye now," "Thank you for the dessert. I enjoyed the visit," or "Nice to see you again." A hug good-bye is very nice for close friends or friends you don't see regularly.

Meeting People and Making Friends

If you want to make friends, develop the attitude that anyone you meet is a potential friend. Say hello or strike up a conversation with the people you meet anywhere, especially when you see the same faces regularly in your neighborhood, at the store, in your church, etc. Whenever you speak to or want to speak to someone, pay attention to nonverbal clues of friendliness and interest such as regular eye contact and a friendly facial expression. Brief answers to questions followed by looking away from you indicate a lack of interest in you. Turning slightly toward you or turning body parts such as an arm or leg toward you suggests interest or openness.

Whenever you approach an informal group of people, see if some of them turn slightly toward you, use friendly facial expressions, ignore you, or turn away from you. People who are willing to let you join them often shift positions, so you have room to move in closer. At a party all you need to do to join a group is position yourself with it. You can then listen to the conversation and contribute to it when you have something to say. If you find it difficult to gain the attention of other people in a group, moving closer, using hand gestures, or tapping someone lightly on the arm or shoulder may help. When conversation is moving fast, you may need to speak loudly and squeeze in your comments during very brief pauses.

Bars and some restaurants are well suited to meeting people, but busy restaurants and formal supper places are not. You need inexpensive places where you enjoy occasionally spending some time and chatting with other people. Less hectic restaurants, coffeehouses, diners, delicatessens, bakeries with some tables and chairs, health food restaurants, department store restaurants, or drugstore restaurants are good. Linger over your coffee or drink, sipping occasionally and talking to other people. Stop in such places regularly, perhaps eating a leisurely meal such as a Saturday brunch. Relax and read a newspaper, your favorite magazine, or a few pages of a book while you are there. Sitting at a counter, rather than at a table, makes it more likely you will meet people. Even sitting at a table, you can invite someone to join you or you can get up and join someone else. If someone seems friendly, you might ask "Do you feel like having company this morning?" By starting a conversation with someone nearby, you can ask to join the person if you get a friendly response.

You can meet people in many other places, too. Nature walks, parks, bird watching trips, beaches, lakes, pools, and camping and hiking trips all offer the opportunity of meeting other nature lovers. The Sierra Club is a national organization whose members enjoy group outings in the wild. People with cultural interests go to libraries, museums, historical walks or tours, art films, foreign films, lectures at universities, concerts, theater, ballet, opera, and other cultural events. Singing in a choir, playing a musical instrument in a group, taking dance lessons, or joining a dancing social group also help in meeting people. Clubs help people of common interests to meet: photography clubs, game clubs (bridge, chess), gardening clubs, sewing clubs, etc.

You can also meet people at sporting events such as football, basketball, or baseball games, gymnastics or swimming meets, etc. Try taking lessons or joining clubs for particular sports like skiing, horseback riding, bowling, etc. Adult evening classes make nice places to meet people. They offer many choices, including cooking, art, foreign language, dance, personal improvement, craft, hobby, home maintenance skills, and technical skills. Another way to meet people is to spend time at community recreation centers or city parks. Many communities have recreation and social centers specifically for senior citizens. Volunteer work is an excellent way to meet people. Many people find paid work for extra cash, for something to do, and to meet new people.

Find out about the events and activities in your area. Local newspapers often list events, activities, and club meetings. Get on the mailing list of organizations that interest you. Clubs often have newsletters and art galleries often mail notices of scheduled events to people who express interest. Colleges and universities usually have several sources of information for campus events open to the public. College music departments often hold free concerts and recitals. Most universities show movies on campus and sponsor lectures open to the public. Check the campus newspaper for this information.

When finding ways to meet new people, choose only places you enjoy and activities that interest you. Otherwise, you may defeat your purpose by appearing bored, lonely, unhappy, or needy. Of course, when you go places to meet people and make friends, you must make regular attempts to start conversations. If you feel uncomfortable going places alone to meet people, bring a friend with you the first few times. But learn to enjoy going alone. Always needing a friend with you greatly limits your socializing.

If you want to meet people at a scheduled event such as a movie, class, or nature walk, go early so you can look for someone alone that seems interesting, friendly, and approachable. Talk to other people during scheduled breaks in classes or meetings. Many clubs, meetings, and community events include a period of socializing after finishing business. With a little assertiveness, you can meet other people, even when everyone rushes out of an activity to go home. After a movie, concert, or class, you might introduce yourself and start a conversation with someone getting ready to leave, walking alone, or going your way.

Friends and acquaintances are a great resource for making new friends. Many people exchange occasional cordial words with their neighbors but don't really know them. Why not invite a friendly neighbor over for dessert? Are there casual acquaintances at work or school with whom you have been friendly? Why not have lunch with some of them or invite them to share one of your activities? If you see a familiar face from your past, introduce yourself, explain how you met, and ask the other person's name. Invite an acquaintance with whom you've never socialized to go to your favorite restaurant. We often lose contact with old friends. Try looking up an old friend and rekindling the friendship. Go with your friends to cultural events, sports events, clubs, parties, or other activities and meet their friends. When you go to parties or other events, mingle with the crowd. Don't just stay with your friend. Another good way to meet people is to have a party or small gathering of friends and ask each person you invite to bring someone else.

Don't be too picky about finding someone who suits you perfectly. Sometimes special bonds can form between very different people, and someone with whom you wouldn't want to spend all day might make a great partner for tennis, bowling, movies, or some other activity. People who don't seem to be your type can also introduce you to new interests and activities you enjoy. With time, you may learn to appreciate someone who didn't seem to suit you at first, and that person may become one of your best friends.

Trying to make new friends inevitably means facing the possibility of rejection. Everyone must learn to deal with rejection; it is a normal part of life. Rejection may be a painful blow to the ego but with practice, you can handle it gracefully and accept it comfortably. Don't waste your time dwelling on a rejection; this only keeps you depressed. Remember that the rejection may have nothing to do with you. The person may have been in a bad mood, may be dealing with important personal problems, may be too busy at present, may prefer spending free moments in a new romance, or may already lead a satisfying, busy social life. Cultivate the attitude that each rejection is an opportunity to practice comfortably accepting rejection and a step along the path to finding new friends. Each time someone rejects you, be proud you mustered the courage to ask.

You can often avoid outright rejection by using vague invitations and seeing how much interest the other person shows. Examples include: "We should get together sometime," "You'll have to come over sometime," "Are you interested in art movies?" and "Do you enjoy going to parks?" If the other person responds enthusiastically, continue with a firm offer about a specific time or activity. If the person shows little interest in the activities you mention or half-heartedly or politely agrees you should meet again and leaves, the lack of enthusiasm implies a lack of interest. Watch for eye contact, posture, facial expression, and other nonverbal clues of interest.

People often use compliments or expressions of warmth before direct invitations. For example: "I've really enjoyed talking to you. Would you like to meet me for lunch sometime?" or "You're so interesting! Would you like to come to dinner Friday?" A person who claims to be busy for many invitations and who doesn't suggest alternative times is probably uninterested. You could compliment someone or express some warmth and request the person's phone number. Some people are very careful about giving out their phone number but may accept yours. If someone requests your phone number, feel free to deny this request politely. You might say "I don't like to give out my phone number but thanks for asking." When first calling someone on the phone, briefly describe who you are and where you met to help the person remember you.

New options for making friends include the Internet and personal ads in newspapers. If you try one of these, however, be careful and protect your safety. Some people use these approaches to find victims to rape, rob, or attack. Before meeting anyone through the Internet or personal ads, verify information. Ask the person for both home and work phone numbers. Check home phone listings. Call to verify the person does work at the named business. Never arrange a first meeting in either of your homes. Meet in a busy public place. Women should wait several dates and make sure they feel very comfortable about the man before inviting him to their home or going to his home. Women should avoid any man who uses even subtle sexual language (looking for a sensual woman, etc.) on the Internet or in a personal ad. This is a clue he mostly desires sex and not a real, caring relationship.

Friendship takes time to grow, with much sharing. Developing a wide variety of interests, activities, and skills gives you more to share with others and helps in making and keeping friends. As people get to know each other, they share deeper and more important feelings in a mutual, reciprocal way. Some people find it difficult to make friends because they present themselves in a bad light, saying many negative things about themselves or emphasizing their weaknesses, rather than strengths. Besides time spent together, shared interests, and mutual self-disclosure, true friendship requires the development of trust.

Keeping Friends and Relationships

Keeping social relationships and living in harmony with other people involves unselfishness, practicing certain kinds of behaviors, and developing personal qualities. Nobody's perfect, but sincere efforts to behave in the ways described here will help you get along better with other people and will establish a good reputation that can help dramatically in making friends. First and foremost, getting along with other people involves caring about them. This includes taking an interest in others, helpfulness, kindness, generosity, sensitivity toward their feelings and needs, and providing emotional support. Please refer to the description of love in chapter 2.

Good communication skills, both verbal and nonverbal, and the ability to deal constructively with negative emotions (anger, depression, etc.) are important in getting along with other people. We have already noted the importance of a wide variety of interests and activities in conversation skills, friendship formation, and keeping friends. A positive outlook makes you more pleasant to be around. Thus contentment, acceptance of life's sorrows, cheerfulness, and optimism are important social qualities. Humor, playfulness, and enthusiasm for interests and activities make you a fun person to know. Appreciation for simple pleasures (such as sunshine, scenery, the company of friends, bird song, and the sound of rain) also helps. Appreciation for other people's qualities and the routine things they do for you also helps make you pleasant.

Developing your virtues increases respect from other people, making you more valuable to them and improving your social standing. Besides loving helpfulness, kindness, generosity, and sensitivity to feelings and needs, other important virtues include loyalty, patience, reliability, responsibility, honesty, work, persistence, self-control, self-reliance, achievement, humility, justice, the courage to do what is right, and good judgment that considers future consequences. Work and perseverance command respect, as do the resulting accomplishments or productivity. Keeping your body, clothes, and home clean and odorless shows pride in yourself and good judgment, reducing the chance of disease. Taking precautions to avoid spreading disease by covering coughs and sneezes and by responsible intimate behavior is an important social duty.

Kindness includes treating children and old, sick, disabled, unfortunate, unhappy, and unpopular people with respect and consideration. Those people who get along the best with others make a habit of performing small acts of kindness such as holding doors open for others, visiting the lonely or sick (perhaps with food), showing generosity to unfortunates, and giving emotional support to unhappy or unpopular people. Never make fun of people for their looks, disabilities, weight extremes, shyness, weirdness, nervousness, or awkwardness. Even silent ridicule by facial expressions between friends may be noticed and is unkind. Such acts show you to be callous and cruel.

Kindness also dictates that you handle changing relationships honestly, yet tactfully. If you want to spend less time with a friend who calls with an invitation, describe your plans honestly. If you prefer to finish some chores or visit someone else, gently say so. Your friend needs honest information to deal with the situation constructively. After you reject a number of invitations, most people will take the hint and call less often. If a friend continues to call frequently and you regularly disappoint the person, you should kindly, but firmly, describe your new interests. For example, "I feel awful saying this and I still cherish our friendship, but I'm really enjoying spending a lot of time with Lee lately, so I'll be seeing you less often. I'd rather explain how I feel than keep disappointing you."

If someone seems less interested in seeing you, describe your perceptions and ask how the circumstances have changed. If your impression is wrong, your friend will tell you so. If your friend admits to new interests, friends, or priorities, however, you must accommodate yourself to your friend's feelings, painful though that may be. Offer to call less often. A mature person realizes people are free, friendships change, people sometimes grow apart, and even the best relationships sometimes need distance. This kind, understanding approach makes the change in the relationship less painful for both of you, and your unselfishness may even prolong the friendship or deepen it later.

Flirting and Dating

Although most single people dream of falling in love, a preoccupation with finding romance is generally frustrating and disappointing. Yearning for a romance to make you happy is looking in the wrong place for happiness. Although finding a mate can help make you happy, your best chance of finding a mate depends on developing a different set of priorities. Looking for a romance to save you from your loneliness and unhappiness is a rather desperate, needy search that alienates other people. Your personality cannot sparkle with this kind of focus in your life. Instead, focus on enjoying the single life, meeting people, and making friends. Accept you may be single for a long time and get on with your life. You need a wide variety of interests and activities, and you need to enjoy and value your friendships. Having these priorities will make you more pleasant, give you practice in socializing, and increase your chances of finding romance. With interests and activities and a good network of friends and acquaintances, your painful longing will cease.

It is wise to date a good variety of people before settling down. This makes you a better judge of character and human nature and less likely to settle for an unfulfilling, explosive, or abusive relationship. People make better marital choices and are more happy with their mates if they date widely before settling down. In making friends, in flirting, and in dating, try not to be overly picky about looks or other personal characteristics that are less important than good character. With time, we often learn to value the personal qualities of people who initially didn't seem suited to us.

If you feel uncomfortable with flirting and dating just for the fun of it, you will probably find yourself awkward and anxious when you try to flirt with or date someone who seems ideal for you. You can practice dating skills by asking out friends and acquaintances, starting with those who are most likely to accept. Never lead anyone on by feigning romantic attraction. Describe the scope of your relationships honestly. You might explain "Don't misunderstand me. I'm not feeling romantic. I just like you and thought we could have fun going out together." Some psychologists offer practice dating services in which shy people can meet and practice asking each other out, conversation skills, and flirting. Most participants report becoming more comfortable with dating.

A common, very painful mistake in dating is to become completely engrossed in a person who shows little true concern for your needs and feelings. Perhaps your partner only wants to see you occasionally or when other relationships end. Perhaps your partner is selfish and repeatedly inconsiderate of your feelings or needs. Staying in any unfulfilling relationship ties up much of your time and deepest emotions. The danger in staying in an unfulfilling relationship is you become accustomed to unhappy situations, making you an easy target for people who will use you. Unfortunately, plenty of people will use you if you let them. Your time and emotional energy are better spent developing interests, activities, ways of meeting people, and a more suitable love relationship. Never settle for less in a relationship—hold out for what you really want.

If, despite an unfulfilling relationship, you sometimes resort to sexual activity with a person to relieve negative emotions such as loneliness, boredom, depression, or anxiety, plan more constructive ways of dealing with these emotions. Keep busy, avoid the problem person, find better ways to have fun and to relax, and practice rejecting the person's advances in behavioral roleplays. If you find it very difficult to stop having sex with a problem person or to stop engaging in unfulfilling or dangerous casual sex, the support groups and resources at the end of the chapter can help. If lowered inhibitions due to drinking alcohol or using other drugs play a role in your continuing an unfulfilling relationship, plan ways to avoid this problem. Chapter 33 describes how to conquer addictions.

In the previous sections of this chapter, we noted many ways to meet people and described the importance of eye contact, facial expression, posture, and vocal characteristics in expressing interest and the willingness to communicate. When you go someplace with a friend and want to meet other people, stand or sit with your body turned partly away from your friend and signal your interest in meeting people by looking around at others, rather than looking mostly at your friend. This makes other people feel more welcome to join you. Better yet, leave your friend so you can stand or sit somewhere by yourself where there is plenty of room for other people to join you. If you sit huddled with your friends, other people will think you are busy and don't want to meet anyone.

Common ways to flirt include raising the eyebrows, winking, asking someone to dance, moving in closer than 1 1/2 feet away, whispering in the ear, and a quick touch or brushing of the knee, hand, arm, or shoulder when laughing or emphasizing a point. A woman should feel free to flirt, approach a man, or ask a man out. Women today need not feel confined to a passive role; things have changed. If a person persists in making advances toward you despite your showing very little interest, you can change positions and speak to someone else or politely end the conversation and walk away. If someone asks you out or asks for your phone number and you don't know how you feel yet, admit you don't know and ask to talk for a while longer. Instead of giving your phone number, you can always take a phone number.

Most people prefer to talk, flirt, and establish some rapport before asking someone out. This allows both parties to gather some first impressions and allows you to gauge whether the other person seems interested before you risk rejection by asking. Watch for eye contact, warm or bored facial expressions and voice, and warm or distant posture. Does the other person take an interest in you and ask questions, or politely respond to questions with short answers? Talk with you while looking around for other people of interest? How does the person respond when you move closer, whisper in the ear, or touch briefly and flirtatiously? With cheerfulness? Increased warmth and intimacy? Facial tension? Increased distance? A date's responses to such warm gestures may give clues to the person's willingness to kiss or embrace you.

Computer dating services match members. After paying a fee, you fill out questionnaires about your personal characteristics, interests, and requirements. The computer uses the data to make the matches. Some dating services include party facilities where members can meet each other. Computer dating services are especially useful for people who don't frequent bars and for older folks who may have lost a spouse and often find it difficult to meet people their own age. Beware, however. Many dating services disappear or fail to fulfill their promises. Dating services that have been in operation for years are safer than new companies. Investigate any dating service before joining by checking with the Better Business Bureau and the Consumer Affairs Department for complaints. If the company owns facilities, visit them before you join. Get any promises made to you (such as a promise half their customers are your age) in writing and signed or initialed by the salesperson.

Is This Relationship Good for Me?

People often continue friendships or love relationships that are unsatisfying, troublesome, emotionally abusive, or even violent. Unhappy people and people with an unhappy childhood are particularly likely to mistake an unsatisfying relationship or an unrequited love for true love. In the previous section, we noted the dangers of staying in an unfulfilling relationship and that our time and emotional energy are better spent developing interests, activities, ways of meeting people, and a more suitable love relationship. How do you decide when a friendship or romantic relationship is not good for you?

First, consider the description of love in chapter 2. Nobody can act in perfectly loving ways all the time, but any good, satisfying close relationship includes the kinds of consideration, caring, and emotional support described in chapter 2 most of the time, every day of the week. Study the behaviors in the relationship. Do you often notice indifference to your activities, interests, ideas, feelings, or problems? Does the person often compromise in little things, such as where to go or what to do? Admit making mistakes and apologize? Forgive you? Show patience in anger? Is the person selfish? Have you often felt very disappointed, hurt, or upset in this relationship? Do you often feel manipulated? How does the person treat you when feeling angry? When things go wrong? When you have many problems? When you feel upset or depressed? Does the person ever hit walls, throw or break objects, or hurt animals in anger? Is the anger frequent, unnecessary, or sometimes very intense? How does the person treat other people in anger? Has the person ever threatened or intimidated you or anyone else? Ever hit you or anyone else?

Communication is an important part of any relationship. Can you spontaneously say what you feel, or do certain topics result in bad feelings or trouble? Is the person open to your expressing your needs in the relationship or occasionally unwilling to listen and discuss things? Can you discuss and resolve problems and sensitive issues? Do you both compromise on problem issues, or does one person always dominate and the other give in? Is the person honest, dependable, and trustworthy? Have there been many lies or deceptions by not telling the whole truth?

Do you feel comfortable and relaxed together? Can you enjoy yourself and have fun? Do you respect each other's values and goals? Does the person show good judgment that considers the future consequences of any actions on both of you? Do you notice an alcohol or drug problem? Does the relationship bring out the best in you or bring out negative things? Does it contribute to your problems, such as depression or alcoholism? Are you both proud to be seen together? In a dating relationship, never meeting the person's friends and family suggests the person feels ashamed of you or doesn't want you to know much about parts of the past or present. A date who doesn't see you on a steady basis or who has been absent without explanation several times may be lying to you and using you only when no other relationship is satisfying.

These questions concern very important dimensions of any close friendship or romantic relationship. Answering more than a few of these questions negatively indicates important flaws in the relationship. Any close relationship that doesn't live up to the kinds of consideration, caring, and emotional support described in chapter 2, Love, most of the time, every day of the week, needs serious work that results in improvement over time, needs less closeness and time spent together, or needs eliminated. In considering a romantic relationship, if you answered more than a few of these questions negatively, you should probably end the relationship and look for a new romantic partner. You should also end it and find a new romance if you don't feel you receive the kinds of consideration, caring, and emotional support described in chapter 2 most of the time, every day of the week. How your partner behaves in conflicts with other people reveals more about how that person will treat you in the distant future than does how the partner behaves in conflicts with you during the romantic days of courtship. How people feel about their family members, especially those of your sex, and their previous romances are also very important indicators of things to come.

The questions about hitting walls, throwing or breaking objects, hurting animals, frequent or unnecessary anger, very intense anger, threats or intimidation, and hitting concern danger signals that the person may eventually become violent towards you. Wise people end relationships at the first violent or intimidating episode or threat and end relationships with regular yelling or insults. If the person regularly criticizes or insults you or has ever threatened, hit, or physically hurt you, please refer to chapter 36, Abuse.

Recommended Additional Readings:

Beyond Shyness: How to Conquer Social Anxieties. by Jonathan Berent and Any Lemley. NY: Simon & Schuster, 1993. for shyness, social anxiety, social phobia.

The Complete Idiot's Guide to a Healthy Relationship. by Judy Kuriansky. New York: Alpha Books, 1998. teaches judging love, compatibility, and commitment, marital skills, affairs, parent interference, sex, when to get help for a sex problem.

Obsessive Love. by Susan Forward and Craig Buck. NY: Bantam Books, 1991.

How to Survive the Loss of a Love. by Melba Colgrove, Harold H. Bloomfield, and Peter McWilliams. Los Angeles: Prelude Press, 1991. for the end of a relationship, whether by breaking up, divorce, separation, or death.

Support Groups:

For support groups for sexual or love addictions, please refer to the end of chapter 18, Sex.

16. Assertiveness

*Be polite but never let anyone
ignore your needs or take advantage of you.*

Assertive behaviors insist that your needs are as important as other people's needs. It includes honest and direct expressions of your feelings, opinions, and preferences and maintaining or defending your rights. People often don't realize their behaviors irritate you until you tell them so. Assertive people vent their frustrations constructively, instead of burying them until they explode in anger. They set limits to their duties and responsibilities whenever necessary to stop other people from overburdening them. You may need to be bold to assert yourself, but assertive behavior is not hostile. Assertiveness improves communication and helps in resolving conflicts with other people.

All the following questions deal with the skills of assertiveness. Can you comfortably express warmth, liking, or love toward other people whenever you want to? Is it sometimes difficult for you to make requests? Can you comfortably make demands or tell people what you expect from them? Put forth your opinion and make sure other people consider it? Is it sometimes difficult for you to disagree with others? Can you comfortably and firmly refuse or say no whenever you want to? Can you complain or confront someone without undue anxiety? Express your anger constructively? Deal with another person's anger fairly comfortably? Deal effectively with unkind, overly critical, or vicious comments from others? Can you put a stop to pestering from others? Stop unwelcome coercion or forwardness by politely ending the conversation or walking away? When you feel bored, can you politely end the conversation? Can you politely end a conversation with a chronic complainer? With a drunk? A braggart? Can you do all the above things even if the other person tries to avoid what you have to say? Even if you are dealing with an authority figure? Even if it will bother, irritate, hurt, or upset the other person? Even if the other person will view your actions as unreasonable or ridiculous?

Unassertive behavior, in contrast, is behavior that allows other people to take advantage of you, whether deliberately or inadvertently. Unassertive behavior allows other people to ignore your feelings, refuse to accommodate you, push or coerce you against your will, rudely interfere, control you, or violate your rights. It includes hiding your anger, giving up and submitting to others, sacrificing your rights, and failing to clearly state your feelings, opinions, and preferences. Unassertive people often try so hard to avoid conflict, avoid ever hurting anyone, or please other people that they sacrifice their own needs, desires, and feelings. A lack of assertiveness interferes with happiness and self-esteem.

Certain common beliefs and negative thoughts may interfere with your willingness to assert yourself. Consider the following list of thoughts. Whether or not you ever actually think sentences like these, these underlying beliefs may interfere with your willingness to assert yourself.

Thoughts That Interfere with Assertiveness

Saying no to a request is selfish.

Always be helpful and think of other people first.

Never impose upon other people.

Always be cheerful and never complain.

A good friend will understand your needs and desires without your having to explain them.

It is best to simply agree with authority figures.

I should never say or do anything that would disturb or hurt anyone.

I don't want to be too aggressive.

I don't want to be too unfeminine.

A complaining wife will drive her husband away.

I try to be the perfect father, mother, employee, etc.

I'm just too shy to return this to the store and complain.

I just can't do it. I can't tell her how I feel.

If any of these sentences describe your feelings well and seem to interfere with your willingness to assert yourself, use chapter 4, Thinking, to write more helpful thought alternatives and practice them every day. Follow the advice in chapter 4, too, if you feel negative about your ability to assert yourself. Some possible helpful alternatives follow.

Helpful Thought Alternatives for Assertiveness

From now on, I'm going to stand up for my rights.

With practice, I'll become more comfortable with asserting myself.

It is foolish to consider the needs and feelings of other people but not my own.

If I learn to say no, I won't feel used so often.

I deserve to have my needs and feelings considered by other people.

To resolve problems, I must make my feelings known.

Sometimes you must complain to get your needs met.

Standing up for my rights doesn't make me any less feminine.

Politely and persistently insisting on my rights is not aggressive.

How can you confront someone or stand up for your rights without hostility or verbal attacks? The section on Criticism and Conflicts in chapter 6, Communication Skills, describes a number of ways, including polite requests, polite discussions of the problem using tact, the "When ... happens, I feel ..." approach, and persistent repetition of your needs and requests. Please refer to chapter 6 for a thorough discussion of these and other techniques. Be very careful to use "When ... happens, I feel ..." in exactly the way described there; improper use renders the approach worthless. If you seldom express your positive or negative feelings, practice "I feel ..." statements at least twice a day, perhaps using the list of emotions in chapter 5 as a guide. You can find tips on dealing with another person's anger in chapter 28.

Certain types of language give impressions of timidity and clue other people that they can refuse your wishes or ignore your feelings. Regularly using the sounds "uh," "er," or "um" or regularly hesitating during conversation makes you sound less sure of yourself and less assertive. Apologizing before a request or confrontation also makes you sound less firm. Examples include: "I'm sorry to say this, but ...," "I hate to ask, but ...," "I hope you don't mind, but ...," and "I hope it's not too much trouble to ..." Sometimes people discredit their own feelings or arguments by saying things like: "Maybe this sounds silly, but ...," "It seemed like ...," "Maybe there are reasons I don't know about, but ...," or "Maybe I'm wrong, but ..." Another mistake is describing your complaint or feelings with the qualifiers "kind of," "sort of," or "pretty much," as in statements like: "I kind of felt ...," "I sort of would like it if ...," or "I pretty much thought ..." Stop making these mistakes.

Nonverbal communication also influences impressions of assertiveness or timidity. Avoid laughing or inappropriate smiling when you need to defend your rights. Act serious. A strong, clear, firm voice sounds very different from a weak, soft, pleading, or monotonous voice. Good rates of eye contact are more assertive than looking away or looking down too much. Facing the other person with good, but not rigid, posture is also assertive. Please refer to chapter 7, Nonverbal Communication, for more details on anxious or timid presentations.

We all occasionally need to refuse requests for money, time, permission, help, a date, etc. Generally, you should refuse requests in very direct, simple ways by starting your answer with the word "no" and keeping your answer short. Be sure to sound firm and sure of yourself. Otherwise, people may feel they can persuade you by arguing. Use only good reasons for your answer. If you use poor reasons or excuses, people may argue the merits of your decision. A long explanation for saying no gives many points for possible discussion and argument. Feel free to give no reason whatsoever. You can say no simply because that is what you want to do. Even when other people ask you repeatedly or why not, you don't need to give any reasons and you don't need to argue with them. You can simply say "I'm sorry but that's just how I feel," or "I said no and I don't want to argue about it." You may need to say no repeatedly, to ignore someone who continues to pester you, or to leave the situation.

Some unassertive people habitually agree to requests and don't realize when they want to say no. These people should pay attention for other feelings as clues they want to say no. Obvious signs include feelings of resentfulness or of being manipulated, taken advantage of, or burdened. Hesitancy in agreeing is a less obvious clue that you really want to say no. Sometimes your only clue that you really want to say no is facial tension, tightness in the mouth, muscle tension in the body, or the onset of a nervous habit.

Whenever you have mixed feelings about granting a request, feel free to ask questions or postpone making your decision. Don't allow other people to pressure you. Ask for information to help you decide or ask why the person chose to ask you. You might say you would like to think it over and will contact the person when you decide. Perhaps you could suggest an alternative to the request, another activity you would prefer or another way to solve the problem.

Persistent repetition helps in asserting yourself. Always repeat in a calm, but firm way. Besides repeating no, you can also repeat requests, opinions, demands, or complaints until you receive satisfaction. Repeating won't always work, but people often don't get what they want simply because they give up too easily. Persistence proves how determined you are. Repeat again and again until the other person agrees or compromises with you. Focus on the issue important to you. Don't let the person change the conversation and argue related issues. You have no obligation to argue other issues. Occasionally, you may need to repeat yourself more loudly, firmly, insistently, or even angrily to get what you want. Perhaps you can go to a person's superiors to get your demands met. You can talk to a child's parents, a store clerk's manager, governmental regulating agencies, a professor's dean, etc. If you want help with a complaint against a business or an institution, call your local information and referral agency or public library for ideas.

Begin working on assertiveness by studying the problem situation, using the list of questions at the beginning of this chapter to identify your problem areas. Next, determine the situations in which each problem area is most, less, and least difficult. With authority figures? With strangers such as salespeople or waiters and waitresses? With acquaintances? With coworkers? With the opposite sex? The same sex? In crowded situations? Practice the assertive behaviors first in easier situations and later in more difficult ones, gradually working up to the most difficult situations as you become more comfortable.

Don't just wait for opportunities to assert yourself. Find ways to practice this behavior. For example, you could practice speaking loudly in public and acting boldly despite public attention in the following manner. Ask a friend to help by going ahead of you into a public place such as a shopping mall and walking slowly. When you enter and see your friend ahead, yell the person's name so that many faces turn toward you. Ask your friend not to notice you if you don't yell loudly enough. Use plenty of behavioral roleplays to practice assertiveness skills you need to develop, such as refusing, complaining, expressing warmth, making demands, etc. Practice the nonverbal aspects of assertiveness, too. Psychologists always use behavioral roleplays in assertiveness groups.

Enlist your friends to help you work on assertiveness in behavioral roleplays and in the ways described in chapter 12. If certain friends or family members perform acts of assertiveness for you (returning merchandise, intervening in your conflicts, etc.), ask them to refuse to do these things, so you must stand up for your own rights. Use rewards and penalties to motivate yourself to work on assertiveness. Using meditation or deep relaxation skills before asserting yourself may help, and be sure to breathe deeply and stretch or relax any muscle tension in your body before asserting yourself and during the encounter. If great anxiety interferes with your ability to assert yourself, please refer to chapter 29.

Recommended Additional Readings:

The Complete Idiot's Guide to Assertiveness. by Jeff Davidson. NY: Alpha Books, 1997.

17. Job Hunting

Spend as much time job hunting as if it were a full time job.

Many people look for jobs in newspapers, but newspapers don't list nine out of ten job openings. It is much more effective to look up every company in the yellow pages that might have the kind of job you want and to contact them, finding out if they have an opening and who does the hiring, then going to talk to that person. If a company seems ideal but they have no openings, fill out an application and ask if you can check with them again in a month or so. Show your enthusiasm and sell yourself. You should also ask everyone you know, even acquaintances, if they know of any job openings in your area. Commercial, government, or college employment services can help. Professionals may find jobs through executive search firms or in magazines or journals in their field.

Many employers for skilled and unskilled jobs use fairly brief, uncomplicated interviews to look for eager, friendly, responsible workers. Some employers for skilled jobs will train new employees, but others require that you demonstrate your skills on the first day of work. Professionals face more complicated job interviews requiring careful preparation and a resume.

The first step is often to fill out a job application. When you go to do this, bring a pen and dress nicely, but conservatively. Remember that your appearance gives them their first impression of you, and the person taking the application may screen applicants for the interviewer. Find out what people normally wear on the job and dress a little more formally than the job requires. Don't wear sandals, flip-flops, shorts, tank tops, hats, or nose rings. Make sure your hair, teeth, and fingernails are clean. Fill out the application completely and accurately, with complete sentences. This makes a better impression than answering with short phrases. Grammar, spelling, and neatness in writing count. Be prepared with your social security number and with school, employer, and supervisor names, addresses, and phone numbers.

If you become very anxious in job interviews, practice them in behavioral roleplays. The friend acting the part of the interviewer should ask all the standard job interview questions listed in this chapter and any more questions that come to mind. Encourage your friend to make the interview rather difficult by asking tough questions and trying to find fault with you. After roleplaying many interviews, practice your skills in real ones, starting with those for your least favorite jobs. These interviews will give you realistic practice, yet provoke less anxiety than interviews for more desirable jobs. If a less desirable employer offers you a job, you can ask for time to hear the results from other interviews.

Begin preparing by writing out your answers to all the standard interview questions in this chapter. Improve them until you make the best answers you can, then memorize them. Reciting the answers into a tape recorder allows you to perfect your presentation.

Try to avoid showing anxiety in job interviews. Work to avoid nonverbal signs of anxiety such as rigid posture, tense muscles, trembling, fidgeting, many shifts in posture, poor rates of eye contact, fast, hesitant, or repetitious speech, or many useless noises such as "er," "uhm," "ah," etc. Meditating or relaxing deeply before you go may help. While waiting for your interview, breathe deeply and release any tension you find in your body. You can also carefully release bodily tension during the interview in a way the interviewer won't notice. Never drink alcohol to relax for an interview. Any smell of alcohol on your breath or slurring of words would ruin your chances of getting the job. If you find your hand trembling slightly or find yourself showing anxiety in some other way, accept it and do the best you can. The interviewer will only assume this job is very important to you.

Make sure you arrive at the job interview on time. Leave plenty of extra time for bad weather or traffic jams. Arriving even a few minutes late creates a very poor impression, making the employer think you don't really care about the job or you will often arrive late to work. If you have never been to the location, go there on a day before the interview, so you won't get lost. Time the trip, so you will know exactly how long it takes to get there under normal traffic conditions. You may chew gum or use a breath mint on the way, but never enter the job interview with anything in your mouth.

Get plenty of sleep the night before your interview, so you can make the best impression possible. Dress nicely, but conservatively and a little more formally than the job requires. Professional men should wear a suit or sport coat and a tie, depending on how formal the dress required on the job. Groom yourself well, with clean, combed hair, brushed teeth, and clean fingernails. Professionals need conventional hair styles. If you use any perfume or cologne, make it quite weak. Women who use make-up or jewelry should use them sparingly. Men should not wear jewelry in job interviews, except perhaps a nice watch.

Your task during the interview is to sell yourself to the employer. Don't bring up any of your weaknesses or faults, unless the interviewer specifically asks you to. Don't smoke during the interview. Use good, but not rigid, posture. Use your best language; don't use slang. Never show any irritation, annoyance, or anger.   No matter what your opinions, never contradict the interviewer. Besides work skills, an interviewer looks for your ability to communicate well, get along with others, friendliness, cheerfulness, intelligence, neatness, tact, responsibility, and confidence. Be friendly and positive. Don't complain. Be confident, but don't brag or be arrogant. Act determined to learn, improve yourself, and help the company, but not determined to move on and leave the company.

Interviewers always ask about your qualifications for the job. Prepare a discussion of the relevant duties and responsibilities in your previous jobs and relevant training, education, skills, volunteer experiences, or accomplishments. If you have a college degree or if your education relates to your job, prepare answers to questions about your studies in school, your grades, how you financed your education, and your extracurricular activities during school. Professionals should prepare a resume of previous jobs, educational qualifications and honors, and relevant skills or experiences. Public libraries have books describing resume style. Your resume is your first introduction to possible employers, so type it on good quality paper, with no typographical errors. Letters of recommendation from previous employers or professors also help in winning professional jobs. Even if you have sent a resume or letters of recommendation, bring several extra copies to the job interview and proof of your relevant accomplishments, such as a college transcript, special awards, and perhaps examples of your work, such as published papers or a newsletter you created.

Professionals should always find out minimum requirements for the job and desirable additional qualifications. Although the interviewer will familiarize you with the job and the company, researching the company in depth before going shows serious interest and may help you win the job, especially in highly professional job interviews. You can investigate the establishment of the company, major changes in its history, operations, and products, or the variety of jobs available. You may gather information from the company's library, brochures, or annual report, company or employee newsletters or papers, or certain reference books or trade magazines in a public library (ask a librarian for help). Talking to employees at the company may help answer your questions about working conditions.

In any job interview or resume, describe your previous jobs carefully. Try not to mention or list too many jobs you held for less than six months.

Doing so creates the impression of an unreliable employee who constantly jumps from one job to another. Feel free to mention any job that you left soon to take a new job with more responsibility and a higher salary, however. Try not to leave out a job that adds skills relevant to the job you want, particularly when none of your other jobs or experiences includes those skills.

The interviewer will probably ask questions about time between jobs, reasons for leaving previous jobs, or frequent job changes. Prepare answers that do not give the impression you are lazy, unreliable, immature, or troublesome. Acceptable explanations for gaps between jobs include vacations, traveling, spending time with your family, or working on a long project, such as helping someone build a house. If you have numerous gaps between jobs, try to emphasize your accomplishments during these periods to avoid giving the impression of laziness. Good explanations for changing jobs include gaining new work experiences, finding a better job, getting more acceptable working hours, or wanting to live elsewhere. If you left a job because of problems or complaints, plan your explanation carefully. Try to avoid criticizing or speaking poorly of your previous employers; doing so will reflect poorly on you. If you must describe a conflict with a previous employer, do so logically, unemotionally, and briefly. A lengthy description of a conflict in which you try to justify yourself or explain personality clashes generally raises more questions than it settles.

Some interviewers hunt for problems with more direct questions, asking about your frustrations in previous jobs, feelings about your bosses, good and bad points about previous jobs or employers, or previous disagreements with employers. Keep the above advice in mind when answering such questions. They may ask you for permission to contact previous employers as references. If they do call a previous employer or anyone else you gave as a reference, they will probably ask questions concerning your work performance, character, ability to get along with other people, and perhaps reason for leaving a previous job.

If an employer fired you in recent years, you should probably eliminate the job from your resume and not mention it during your interviews. One reason is your answer to the common question about why you left each of your recent jobs would probably ruin your chances of being hired. Also, the interviewer may ask you for permission to contact your recent employers as references.

Prepare an answer for the question "Why do you want to work for us rather than for some other company?" Another common interview question is "What do you want from your job or employers?" Answer with skills, experience, or other benefits you will get as an employee. Find out the typical salary in your field before going to your interviews because an employer may ask you what kind of salary you want. If you don't know, you can always say "A competitive offer."

Interviewers often ask you to describe your personal strengths and weaknesses or what you did well and poorly in your previous jobs. Describe such strengths as job skills, interest and enthusiasm for the field, motivation, or personal qualities such as honesty, industriousness, reliability, etc. Answer questions about your weaknesses carefully. Try to find minor faults that won't affect your job performance or that you can easily correct, such as lack of certain job skills due to lack of experience. Find something, though. Don't deny you have any personal weaknesses and don't insist you can't think of any. The interviewer prefers to see a healthy self-awareness, rather than an ignorance of your weak points.

They may ask why you are the best person for the job or why they should choose you out of all the applicants. Answer by speaking not only about your qualifications, but also about your interest, determination to do well, honesty, reliability, or other personal qualities useful to the company. If they ask about your career goals for the next few years or five years, answer in a way that gives the impression this particular company fulfills your needs perfectly for at least the next several years. You might describe a desire to excel and plans to move up in the field. Make the interviewer feel this particular job is your ideal job now or one of your best job possibilities.

Plan how to respond if asked to describe yourself or how you use your free time. Most interviewers also give the applicant a chance to ask questions. Show your interest by asking for details about job responsibilities, possibilities of promotion with a job well done, salary and other benefits, and perhaps qualifications they prefer. If you have researched the company, you can demonstrate your knowledge at this point with intelligent questions. Certain job interviews may include a test of typing skills or professional knowledge.

The interviewer may ask you questions about plans to have children, sexual preferences, prior mental health treatment, or previous trouble with the law. Realize that your answers to such questions may affect their decision about hiring you and plan accordingly. If you believe you have been denied a job because of race, religion, gender, or disability, including mental health problems, the Equal Employment Opportunity Commission (see next page) may be able to help you. In many states and cities, job interview questions about sexual preference are illegal.

Recommended additional readings:

What Color is Your Parachute? A Practical Manual for Job-Hunters & Career-Changers. by Richard Nelson Bolles. Berkeley, CA: Ten Speed Press, 1998. comprehensive book covering how to decide what kind of job you want, how to research companies, job hunting on the Internet, deciding if you need a career counselor, how to choose a good career counselor, tips for special populations such as high school students, college students, women, etc.

Trashproof Resumes: Your Guide to Cracking the Job Market. by Timothy D. Haft. New York, NY: Villard Books, 1995.

Hotline:

Equal Employment Opportunity Commission (EEOC) 800 669 4000 a federal agency that investigates cases of job discrimination due to race, religion, gender, or disability, including mental health patients. Qualified women who believe an employer denied them work because of plans to have children can take their cases to this agency, too. on-line: www.eeoc.gov

18. Sex

Sex is only part of love, one physical
expression, a drop in the ocean of love.

Sex reaches its highest glory, most ecstatic joyfulness, and greatest fulfillment in the context of a deeply loving and respectful relationship. The most comprehensive and scientific sex survey ever done, *Sex in America: A Definitive Survey* (Michael et al., 1994), shows married couples and couples living together have the most satisfying sex lives, both physically and emotionally. It found single people dating and having sex with one partner come a close second in sexual satisfaction, and married people with an outside affair are less happy with their sex lives. The lowest rates of satisfaction are among unmarried men and women, those not living with a partner, and those with two or more sex partners.

Americans are very monogamous, with 83% reporting one or zero sex partners a year. Nearly 75% of married men and 85% of married women say they have always been sexually faithful. About 1/3 of Americans have sex two or more times a week, about 1/3 have sex a few times a month, and about 1/3 have sex a few times a year or not at all. Married couples and unmarried couples living together are twice as likely as single people not living with a partner to report having sex two or more times a week. About 95% of men report always or usually reaching orgasm during sex, but only 75% of married women and 62% of never-married women not living with a partner report this level of response. Statistically, every American is likely to confront a sexual problem (if you include lack of desire), with 43% of women and 31% of men reporting one at any given time. Men have more sex problems as they grow older, but women report more when they are young, especially if they are single. Only 1 in 10 men and 1 in 5 women seek help, however.

Chapter 2, Love, describes the kinds of caring, closeness, tenderness, trust, loyalty, and sharing that predominate in deeply loving relationships. Sex demands great responsibility because it stirs up deep feelings within people, because people are vulnerable when they become sexually involved, and because of the possibilities of pregnancy and sexual diseases. You must take precautions to avoid hurting other people, unwanted pregnancies, and sexual diseases. As detailed in chapter 19, Pregnancy, parents of unplanned or unwanted children face great financial and emotional burdens that may lead to lifelong poverty, abuse, juvenile delinquency, or children's social or psychological problems. If you suspect you may have a sexual disease, having sex without warning your partner is immoral. It is also immoral to lie, deceive, or feign affection to have sex with someone. Forced sex is both immoral and a crime. In fact, a man can be guilty of rape by pressuring a woman for sex when she says no or feels unsure about what she wants, because women often feel intimidated by the size or physical presence of men.

Several studies show rates of sexually transmitted diseases (STDs) in the United States are 50 to 100 times higher than in other developed nations. For example, 150 out of every 100,000 people in the U.S. have gonorrhea, compared to 3 per 100,000 in Sweden and 18.6 per 100,000 in Canada. Thousands of people die annually because of complications from STDs, and many STDs show no symptoms until it is too late. Learn how to recognize and protect yourself from STDs with brochures from your public health clinic. For a more detailed discussion of this problem and reasons for it, refer to the section on Discussing Sex with Your Children in chapter 22.

Sexual Communication

People often want different degrees of affectionate or intimate behaviors, both in dating and marriage. Never assume you know what the other person wants. Rape may occur when a woman says no, but the man thinks she means yes or wants him to persuade her. Be sensitive to the other person's feelings and pay attention to all verbal and nonverbal responses. If you have any doubts about what your partner wants, stop and talk about it.

Most people in our culture grow up with great inhibitions about openly discussing sex. These inhibitions influence us even when we get married and need to discuss feelings about sex with our spouses. Couples may also avoid communicating about sex because of the fear of hurting each other's feelings by complaining. Telling your spouse a particular type of stimulation doesn't feel good may result in feelings of rejection or inadequacy as a lover. Men, in particular, may take offense because of feeling they should know how to please women. Feedback during sex invariably improves your sex life because no one can feel the inner sensations of another person.

Sexual communication also improves our sex lives because our sexual responsiveness to various kinds of stimulation changes over time. The same physical act may greatly excite you on one occasion and give much less pleasure on another. Over time, you may become bored with certain kinds of stimulation and find another kind more pleasurable. Your sexual life will be more satisfying if you can discuss sexual acts and say things like: "Slow down ... ooh, that's better," "Mmm, would you do that a little faster?" or "Would you rub over here a little?" Give feedback by talking or using sounds of pleasure, touch, or other signals. You might move your partner's hand to help direct the stimulation you desire.

Although many people feel awkward talking during sex, with enough practice, anyone can become comfortable doing so. The best way to overcome discomfort is to practice sexual communication throughout your love-making, by taking turns providing a nearly constant commentary on what feels good, better, etc. Some very common problems often receive attention when people begin to talk about sex. Women often feel men are too aggressive and prefer a more considerate, slower sexual approach. Women often need prolonged stimulation before coitus. Otherwise, they are often still in the early phases of sexual excitement when their men reach orgasm. Men often desire a more active sexual partner and greatly appreciate women touching and stimulating them. Most couples report they would prefer both partners to initiate sex equally but they also report that the man usually initiates it.

Discuss how you communicate interest in, initiate, and reject sex. Nonverbal communication often plays a role. Responding to caresses with vocal sounds of pleasure ("Mmmmm") or reciprocal touching shows interest in sex. A complete lack of responsiveness or turning away from caresses indicates lack of interest. Couples often reject sex in ways giving mistaken impressions of anger or lack of love or attraction. Develop warm ways of rejecting sex that don't hurt your partner's feelings. You might say: "I love you darling but I'm too tired. I would really enjoy just curling up with you and going to sleep," or "I'm really not in the mood right now, sweetheart. Could we make some time Friday to relax and have a romantic evening?"

Men and women experience periods of low sexual drive in which they prefer not to have sex. Show understanding and patience—this demonstrates your love and sensitivity to their needs. Your lover trusting you and feeling safe is much more important than whether you have sex today, tomorrow, or next week. The dangerous notion that it is a wife's duty to provide sex whenever her husband wants it, often leads to marital dissatisfaction and may even lead to a woman's inability to reach orgasm. Both partners in any relationship should always feel free to reject sexual advances from the other partner.

Sexual Myths

One common sexual myth is that men and women cannot have multiple orgasms, two or more orgasms in a short time. Either sex may reach multiple orgasms with continued stimulation after the first orgasm. Multiple orgasms are possible for women of any age, but not for most men approaching old age. Men usually lose their erections after reaching orgasm and need at least a short time before they can regain them; the time needed increases with age. With very exciting sexual stimulation, however, young men can sometimes maintain an erection after an orgasm and continue sex until they reach another orgasm or two.

Another common myth is that oral sex is wicked, perverted, or unsanitary. Although some people enjoy oral sex and others don't, the genitals are just as clean as any other part of the body, with normal habits of cleanliness. A clean vagina has fewer germs than the mouth. People have engaged in oral sex since the days of ancient civilizations. Archaeologists have found erotic art including oral sex dating back to prehistoric times in many parts of the world.

Many people fear having sex during the woman's menstrual flow, which is the safest time of the woman's cycle if you wish to avoid pregnancy. The flow of blood generally stops during coitus, but a dark towel placed under the woman will absorb any blood flow. Some women will notice more blood flow for a short time after sex, but this temporary increase poses no problem—don't worry about it. Some women enjoy sex more during their menstrual periods and others enjoy it less. Many people don't realize that sex during a blood flow may cause pregnancy if the woman menstruates and ovulates irregularly or if the bleeding does not come from true menstruation.

Another myth is that people who don't reach orgasm from coitus alone have sexual problems. Many men and women enjoy coitus but don't reach orgasm from coitus alone. Instead, they generally reach orgasm by adding masturbation (manual self-stimulation) or manual or oral stimulation from their partner before, during, or after coitus. These are very common patterns sex therapists consider normal and treat with reassurance that there is no need for sex therapy. Some people believe lovers should always try to reach orgasm at the same time. Although reaching climax simultaneously is nice, always striving to coordinate your orgasms will often frustrate you.

Many people mistakenly believe masturbation is wicked or dangerous or leads to acne or even insanity, but masturbation has a number of uses and benefits. The survey *Sex in America* found 63% of men and 42% of women masturbated in the previous year. Masturbation is a good alternative when your partner doesn't want sex, making it easier for you to accept this decision in a loving way. Regular masturbation (or regular sex) often reduces the severity of menstrual cramps in women, because these cramps involve poor blood flow in the genitals and sexual excitement concentrates blood there and then suddenly disperses it, leading to better blood flow. We shall soon see masturbation helps in curing many sexual problems and that regular masturbation (or regular sex) has beneficial effects in old age.

Aphrodisiacs are also myths. Many people believe alcohol or certain other drugs, such as marijuana or cocaine, increase sexual desire. Any increase in sexuality associated with these drugs is due to the person's expectations. When researchers mislead people about whether or not they are drinking alcohol, sexual arousal increases with their belief they are drinking, not with the actual intake of alcohol. Finally, the myth that sex will weaken athletes is false.

Homosexuality

Many people mistakenly believe homosexuality is wicked, perverted, or sick or indicates mental illness. The American Psychological Association reviewed the research and publicly stated in 1973 that being homosexual does not imply any impairment in social skills, work skills, judgment, stability, or reliability, establishing that homosexuality is not an illness, emotional disorder, nor psychological disturbance. Psychotherapy with homosexuals now often focuses on first relationship, relationship, and self-esteem issues. Other issues include substance abuse, sharing sexual orientation with other people (coming out), and assertiveness in facing negative attitudes, taunts, and discrimination. Research suggests homosexuals have a higher rate of alcoholism and drug abuse than heterosexuals.

Another myth is that homosexuals are often child molesters. Research studies of sex offenders in prison and of early sex experiences recalled by people in the general population show homosexuals are no more likely to molest children than are heterosexuals. The belief that people are always either completely homosexual or heterosexual is another common misconception. Many people with one preference have experimented with the opposite behaviors. Indeed, many homosexuals are parents. Bisexuals enjoy both heterosexual and homosexual behaviors, often without their heterosexual partners knowing it. The comprehensive, scientific survey *Sex in America* shows 9% of men and just over 4% of women have had homosexual sex at some time since puberty, but that only 2.8% of men and 1.4% of women consider themselves homosexual or bisexual. Sometimes a person's sexual preference changes.   Experimenting with homosexual behavior is not unusual and does not mean the person is or will become homosexual, but repeated homosexual experimentation may lead to a homosexual lifestyle, especially if you begin to think of yourself as a homosexual or if other people do and reject you in heterosexual romance.

Unfortunately, only 10 states have laws protecting homosexuals from job discrimination.   In all the other states, an employer can fire someone simply because of sexual orientation.   Courts often forbid child custody or visitation rights to homosexual parents, even after they have raised the child from birth.   Families, even those long-estranged from the homosexual, may refuse to allow visits by long-term, live-in lovers at sickbeds, hospitals, and funerals, perhaps even taking the shared home, property, or money of the partner after death.   In 159 cities and counties in the U.S., homosexuals have some civil rights protection, and courts in large cities tend to honor the implied rights of homosexual partner, but homosexual couples should consult a lawyer knowledgeable about homosexual relationships to safeguard their rights.   You can set up agreements about living together that specify the division of property in case of separation or death, custody and visitation of children, wills, and mutual durable springing powers of attorney for the right to act as next of kin in medical emergencies.

If you want to stop homosexual behavior, you can work on this as you would work on any other addiction. Make heterosexual friends and practice flirting with and dating members of the opposite sex. Replace thoughts that you can't change or can't live without sex with more helpful, hopeful thoughts. Realize people in other cultures often went from homosexual to heterosexual as a normal part of growing up and that sexual abstinence can help you by increasing desire.   Replace homosexual fantasies during masturbation with heterosexual fantasies earlier and earlier, farther from orgasm. The support groups for sexual or love addictions at the end of the chapter can help a great deal.   Males with sexual performance concerns should read the section in this chapter on erection problems.

Sex in Old Age

Although many people lose interest in sex as they approach old age, many other men and women report active sex lives well into the latter years.

Several studies have found increased sexual frequency and satisfaction among married couples when their children grow up and leave home, probably because they have more time for each other. Sexual relationships in widowed or divorced older folks can help prevent depression, counteract stress, encourage weight control, and increase self-esteem.

Certain physical changes from aging affect sexual functioning. As men approach old age, they often become erect more slowly and need more stimulation to become erect than they did in the past. In orgasm, men nearing 50 and older often produce less ejaculate and a less forceful ejaculation than younger men. When fully erect, older men may be less firm than they were in the past. They may find they don't reach orgasm every time they have sex or they only occasionally reach orgasm during sex. Even so, less than 25% of men over 60 can't have any intercourse because of erection problems. Regular sex or masturbation helps maintain sexual functioning and reduces the chance of prostate problems in older men. Many women appreciate the extra time a man takes to become erect because prolonged foreplay often helps women reach orgasm. Sex without orgasm in the man can also give the woman more time to reach orgasm.

Women produce reduced levels of sex hormones after menopause, which causes the vaginal walls to become thinner and reduces the amount of vaginal lubrication. These changes may make sex less comfortable for older women than it was when they were younger. A lubricant helps make sex more comfortable. Use a water-soluble lubricant (available in drugstores) because lubricants that are not water-soluble make vaginal infections more likely. If a lubricant doesn't make sex more comfortable, a gynecologist can prescribe sex hormones that may help. Regular sex helps maintain women's sexual functioning, too.

Men Who Reach Orgasm Too Quickly

Some men become so excited in lovemaking, they reach orgasm within the first minute or two of coitus, a short time that often fails to satisfy their mates. Other men climax even before penetrating the vagina. Fortunately, a number of effective solutions exist. Men can often solve this problem by simply continuing the sexual stimulation until coitus can resume, perhaps to a second orgasm. It will take longer to reach the second orgasm, and the extra time spent in coitus should satisfy the woman. After the first orgasm, most men need anywhere from a few minutes to half an hour or more to regain their erections. If sexual stimulation doesn't result in a new erection, the couple may fondle each other, kiss, cuddle, talk, or sexually stimulate the woman for a while before trying again.

Another effective solution for men reaching orgasm too quickly is to pause occasionally during lovemaking, stopping the sexual stimulation to reduce the level of excitement. Pause until your erection becomes a little less firm and then continue. During coitus, the pause procedure is to stop all movement until the male's erection weakens noticeably. It takes some practice to master the pause technique. Many men pause too late and accidentally ejaculate. Men who reach orgasm before penetrating the vagina and men who pause but who reach orgasm too quickly anyway should add another step to the pause technique: squeezing the head or glans of the penis quite hard with a couple of fingers for a few seconds. During coitus, the man must withdraw from the vagina to squeeze the head of his penis. Never squeeze the penis while having orgasm, however, as this would forcibly prevent the ejaculation.

Men can gain experience in controlling their level of sexual excitement by practicing these pause techniques during masturbation. Pause when you near the feelings of climax, so you learn to gauge how early you must interrupt your stimulation to successfully avoid orgasm. Prolonging masturbation in this way for an extra ten or twenty minutes prepares you to use these pause techniques during lovemaking. Practicing these pause techniques during manual stimulation by the female before trying to do them during coitus also helps. Finally, you may find wearing a condom during sex reduces your excitement and helps prolong intercourse. If wearing one condom doesn't help, two or more condoms may.

Problems with Female Orgasm or Male Erection

Because women with concerns about reaching orgasm and men with concerns about becoming or staying erect often share the same problems and attitudes and require the same solutions, we shall discuss them together. The real root of many women's problems with orgasm and many men's problems with erection is the marital relationship. Most people realize great anger often eliminates the desire for sex, but many people don't realize chronic anger or subtle, underlying hostility or unhappiness in a relationship can reduce enjoyment of sex. In contrast, a warm, loving, affectionate relationship promotes a satisfying sex life. If you think a poor-quality relationship may contribute to a sexual problem in your marriage, please refer to chapter 21.

Negative feelings about sex are another common reason for problems with orgasm or erection. Guilt or shame about sex or feeling it is dirty or bad can interfere with sexual pleasure and performance. Work on changing these feelings by replacing your negative thought habits with more positive alternatives every day, as described in chapter 4. Use the facts in this chapter to write statements that help you feel the way you want to feel. Religious people will find the paperback book *The Act of Marriage* (LaHaye & LaHaye, 1978) very useful in placing sex in a positive, Christian perspective and relieving guilt, shame, or anxiety about sex. If past experiences contribute to your negative feelings about sex, you may need to resolve and finish your feelings about the past (chapter 37), so your feelings about sex can change. People with strong negative feelings about sex may need to use the techniques in chapter 29 to combat their anxieties or fears.

Worry, anxiety, and fears about whether or not you will reach orgasm, become erect, or stay erect can interfere with your sexual pleasure and cause these problems. Many factors can temporarily interfere with sexual pleasure or performance: illness, back problems, painful genital infections, fatigue, anger, stress, depression, using too much alcohol or drugs, or trying to have sex when you really aren't in the mood. Fatigue, anger, or stress can also reduce interest in sex. Depression is a major cause of low sex drive for both males and females. The physical changes of middle or old age may occasionally interfere with orgasm or erection. Simply misunderstanding a normal, temporary problem and becoming anxious about sexual performance can cause chronic problems, but understanding the reason for it helps avoid chronic sexual problems.

Lovers have a profound impact on the sexuality of their partners. A lover who demands sex or nags or complains about it may actually cause a sexual problem in the mate. In contrast, an affectionate lover who is patient and encouraging about a sexual problem helps to overcome it. Never scream about your sexual frustrations to your mate, and never use labels of frigidity or impotence as insults. This just adds to your mate's sexual performance concerns and makes the situation worse. Carefully avoid any angry, bitter, or rejecting comments about your lover's sexual functioning.

The solutions for problems with orgasm or erection often attempt to eliminate the pressure and anxiety to perform sexually. Develop the helpful attitude that sex can be satisfying without reaching orgasm or becoming and staying erect. Many people view the intimacy, affection, and giving in sex as the most important aspects of it. Unfortunately, people with orgasm or erection problems generally find it very difficult to find satisfaction in these aspects of sex. Your desperate preoccupation with achieving orgasm or erection causes the problem. You must give up trying so hard to reach orgasm or to become or stay erect, in order for these things to happen.

Replace worries or negative thoughts about reaching orgasm or erection with more helpful thought alternatives every day, as described in chapter 4. Use the information in this chapter to write statements that help you feel the way you want to feel, such as: "Quit worrying! I'm just going to enjoy the closeness and giving we share," or "Our love is the only important thing." Read these thought alternatives several times every day and each time the negative thoughts occur.

Sexual fantasies can distract you from worries about performance. Try fantasizing during sex about exciting sexual episodes, past sex experiences, or sex with different partners. Most couples find fantasizing can heighten pleasure. Sometimes simply experimenting with fantasies can result in orgasm or erection.

Sex therapists strongly recommend developing other ways to reach sexual satisfaction besides coitus, such as manual stimulation to orgasm, oral sex, and mutual masturbation. This helps solve problems with erection or orgasm in two ways. First, when the couple regularly satisfies each other in these alternate ways, the achievement of erection or of orgasm during coitus becomes less important and provokes less anxiety in the partner with the problem. Second, these alternate practices allow the partner with the problem to sexually satisfy the other partner each time they have sex. Sex therapists tell their clients to always satisfy the other partner, not only because this benefits the marital relationship, but also because a sexually satisfied partner will be more patient and understanding and will spend more time trying to satisfy the partner with the problem.

People with sexual problems often have negative attitudes about masturbation and oral sex. They often feel surprised to learn that many couples with no sexual problems have experimented with masturbating together as a variation on the sex act. If you have negative feelings about masturbation or oral sex, follow the previous advice on changing negative attitudes. If you feel inhibited, anxious, or repulsed when you first try oral sex or mutual masturbation, develop these behaviors gradually. Start by just looking at each other's sex organs and identifying the parts with the help of an anatomical drawing. When this becomes comfortable, try licking nearby or masturbating in the dark for a few seconds. Slowly and comfortably, you can develop the new behaviors in stages and for longer times.

Exercising a certain muscle every day can help men and women improve their sexual functioning. Sex therapists often recommend that people with orgasm or erection problems practice Kegel exercises, named after the man who first discovered the importance of exercising this muscle. You use the muscle whenever you stop your flow of urine. Do this once, so you know how to exercise the muscle. You can exercise it any time, perhaps while driving to work or sitting and watching television. Repeatedly contract the muscle, as if you were often stopping a flow of urine, until the muscle tires and you cannot easily contract it. Many sexually active people can easily contract it eighty or more times without stopping to rest, but people with sexual problems may find it difficult to repeat the contractions even ten or twenty times. Exercise this muscle several times a day until you can contract it at least fifty times without stopping to rest.

The treatment programs described here for problems with orgasm or erection, like all sex therapy programs today, incorporate many of the techniques and much of the logic of William H. Masters and Virginia E. Johnson's landmark contributions to sex therapy. Begin working on your problem by abstaining from sex for two weeks. In this first phase of the treatment program for couples, enjoy the sensuality of your bodies together without direct sexual stimulation. As often as you please, you may hold each other, kiss, affectionately touch and stroke each other, take showers together, and cuddle up together, all without sex occurring. In addition, at least three times a week, you must take a shower (preferably together) and then take turns stimulating and massaging each other for twenty or thirty minutes each, all over the body except for the sex organs. Experiment with different kinds of strokes using fingertips, palms of hands, whole hands, fast strokes, slow strokes, delicate pressures, and moderate pressures. Try kissing, licking, or blowing air on the different parts of the body. Feel free to play with various parts of the body. The toes, fingers, armpits, back, neck, stomach, buttocks, legs, and back of the knees can all be surprisingly sensual and exciting.

Some couples schedule the stimulation and massage sessions on the same nights, one after the other, and other couples prefer to schedule them on separate nights, so no partner must get up and give a massage after having received the relaxing stimulation. Either arrangement works fine, as long as each partner gives twenty or thirty minutes of stimulation to the other partner at least three times a week. During these first two weeks of sensual activities, you should also begin practicing sexual communication. While receiving the massage, each should talk about what feels good, what feels better, etc. Each person will probably prefer different kinds of stimulation.

The first two weeks of sexual abstinence and sensual pleasure are very important in treating problems with female orgasm or male erection. Refraining from sex increases the desire for sex and the likelihood of successful sex later. The instructions help the couple relax and learn to enjoy their bodies again, without worrying about orgasm or erection. With sex forbidden, they can become more aware of their bodies and the different kinds of stimulation they enjoy. The sensual activities also help restore romance and affectionate sharing to relationships that have fallen into a routine of sex without much play.

Now let's focus on advice specific to women with problems in reaching orgasm. Until recently, many people believed women shouldn't enjoy sex or that sexual women were bad women. If you suspect attitudes such as these, ingrained early in your life, may contribute to your problem, use the previous advice for replacing negative beliefs or attitudes with more helpful thoughts or facts. Another common reason for women's difficulties with orgasm is ignorance about parts of the vagina. Because many people rarely discuss sex openly, some couples simply don't know the location of the clitoris or that stimulating it produces the most intense sexual feelings of the vaginal parts. These couples often find identifying the clitoris with an anatomical diagram and stimulating it leads to orgasm.

Perhaps the most common reason for women's difficulties with orgasm is lack of foreplay before coitus. As mentioned previously, women often need prolonged stimulation before coitus. Otherwise, they are often still in the early phases of sexual excitement when their men reach orgasm. Research shows two-thirds of all women do not reach orgasm through coitus alone; they also need manual stimulation to reach orgasm. Sex therapists simply encourage these couples to indulge in plenty of foreplay, and perhaps also to use manual stimulation, either by the man or by the woman herself, during coitus.

Women who normally lie still during sex, often find actively thrusting enhances their pleasure and makes orgasm easier to reach. Any woman with a problem with orgasm should realize that the average woman with no sexual problem doesn't reach orgasm every time she has intercourse. The scientific survey *Sex in America* found only 29% of women said they always had orgasms during sex, but about 40% reported being extremely pleased physically and emotionally with their sex lives. Women often feel satisfied with the intimacy, affection, cuddling, feelings of being desired, and the other aspects of the sexual experience.

Women with problems in reaching orgasm despite a happy marital relationship, good attitudes toward sex, and following the previous advice, should begin the following sexual treatment program. First, however, consult a gynecologist to see if a physical problem might play a role. Estrogen, testosterone, or Eros (a clitoral suction device that increases blood flow) can help. Painful coitus indicates a physical problem, except as follows. Virgins often find coitus painful at first and often need gentle, considerate lovers and much foreplay to learn the pleasures of lovemaking.

This treatment program is very successful in teaching women to reach orgasm during coitus. It begins with the important two weeks of sexual abstinence, sensual body activities, and communication about sensual preferences described previously. Next, the woman uses masturbation to learn what kinds of stimulation feel best to her. Masturbation is the fastest and easiest way for a woman to learn to reach orgasm. Finally, the woman gradually shifts the orgasmic response to coitus.

The masturbation phase of the treatment begins with the woman locating and identifying the parts of her vagina with the help of a mirror and an anatomical drawing. Find a medical book with drawings of sexual anatomy at a public or university library. When the woman feels very comfortable with looking at herself and has identified all the parts of the vagina, she can begin touching and rubbing the various parts of her genitals to compare sensitive areas and to pleasure herself for short periods. If this rubbing or self-stimulation causes discomfort, a lubricant will help. Use a water-soluble lubricant (available in drugstores) because lubricants that are not water-soluble make vaginal infections more likely. As she becomes comfortable with this, the woman should stimulate herself for longer periods of time and experiment with different strokes, speeds, and pressures. Women who have never had an orgasm generally reach orgasm within a month with this kind of experimentation and practice for thirty minutes or more, at least three times a week.

The next phase of the treatment, shifting the orgasm to coitus, begins with the woman learning to masturbate comfortably in front of her mate, so she can teach him the kinds of stimulation that best arouse her. After he watches her masturbate a few times, she guides him in stimulating her with his hands, so he learns to bring her to orgasm manually. If the couple feels very uncomfortable about this, they should begin by allowing the man to identify the parts of the vagina and look at these parts with the woman. Then the woman can play with herself for short periods of time while the man kisses, licks, holds, or strokes her body. When they feel comfortable with this, she can play with herself more and more in front of him, until she can masturbate in front of him. Finally, she can teach him to perform the kinds of manual strokes that bring her to orgasm. This sequence of becoming comfortable with sharing masturbation and teaching the man to bring her to orgasm may take a month or more. The woman should bring the man to orgasm in some way each time they have sex.

The last step in shifting the orgasm to coitus is giving the woman more control over coital movements and using manual stimulation during coitus, so she can reach orgasm. Coital positions with the woman on top make it easier for her to gain control over the movements and learn to enhance her own pleasure. Either the woman or the man can manually stimulate her clitoris during coitus. Once the woman regularly achieves orgasm during coitus (which may take months), the couple may prefer to stop the clitoral stimulation just before orgasm, so the thrusting movements result in the orgasm. Gradually, they can stop clitoral stimulation longer and longer before her orgasm, so her orgasm becomes more and more a result of coitus. Most women, however, will always prefer plenty of foreplay and perhaps some manual stimulation during coitus.

Now let's consider advice specific to men with problems in becoming erect or staying erect. Common lore holds that men always want sex and are always ready for it, but as we have seen, men sometimes fail to perform sexually for a variety of reasons, including simply not being in the mood. Concerns about sexual performance can be particularly troublesome for men because they need an erection to engage in coitus. In contrast, women may engage in coitus and satisfy their mates without much sexual excitement.

Physical problems affect men's erections much more often than they affect the female sexual response. Illnesses such as heart, liver, or circulation problems, diabetes, and some neurological diseases can cause erection problems, as can high blood pressure medications and some sedatives, ulcer medicines, and over-the-counter drugs. Alcoholism can cause erection problems, but problems due to short-term alcoholism generally clear up after a few months of sobriety. Alcoholism continuing for ten years or more may result in permanent erection problems or may contribute to problems with erection much later in life. Alcoholism is the most common reason for impotence after previous sexual functioning in men between forty and sixty.

However, many erection problems come from psychological causes such as marital problems or anxieties about sexual performance. Several clues can help you determine whether physical or psychological factors cause the problems. First, men normally wake up occasionally with a morning erection, although most men have poor memory of them. Second, men normally have a few nighttime erections during sleep. Your mate can observe you all night long for nighttime erections. Absent or weaker than normal morning or nighttime erections indicate a physical problem. Third, weaker than normal erections during masturbation indicate a physical problem. If any of these clues are present, consult an urologist for medical advice. New medicines such as Viagra and surgical interventions can help. Even when irreversible physical disorders cause erection problems, anxieties about sexual performance often complicate the situation, and the following treatment program can help maximize sexual functioning.

Begin with the important two weeks of sexual abstinence, sensual body activities, and communication about sensual preferences described previously. Next, you need at least two weeks of sensual body activities, three times a week, with the following instructions. The play should now include manual or oral stimulation of the sex organs, but coitus is still forbidden. The woman should manually or orally stimulate the man's penis for twenty or thirty minutes each time they have sex, but the man should not try to become erect. Stimulation may continue on a partially erect penis, but if a firm erection occurs, the woman should stop until the erection becomes soft. The man should bring the woman to orgasm each time they have sex, either manually or orally.

These instructions help make erections more likely by providing sexual stimulation while eliminating the need for erection. Only when the man quits trying to become erect, will erections naturally occur. The man must learn to enjoy the sensations of sex with a soft or partially erect penis, without worrying or becoming upset. Letting all the firm erections go soft helps in becoming comfortable with losing an erection, because the man soon learns another erection will arise if he just doesn't worry about it. Letting the erections go soft also eliminates the common tendency to immediately and anxiously try to use any erection in coitus, hoping the erection will last long enough to complete the sex act. These desperate attempts to use any erection for coitus often cause the sex problem. The sex without male orgasm builds up sexual desire and helps make coitus successful later.

Any man who becomes disturbed by losing an erection, even men with no sexual problems, can benefit from letting an erection go soft and then getting a new one. Practicing this many times makes the loss of an erection less threatening. Single men can gain some practice during masturbation in becoming comfortable with sexual performance concerns by occasionally including fantasies in which they either can't get an erection or lose the erection, but in which they later become erect and perform satisfactorily.

Continue the second phase of the program, the sensual body activities with manual and oral sex but no coitus, until the man regularly gets firm erections the couple allows to go soft. This often occurs in two weeks, but may take months if the man cannot give up trying to become erect. Next, the treatment program introduces coital activities in a way that avoids performance anxieties. Again, the man should bring the woman to orgasm each time, but now the sex play should include the man's rubbing his soft penis on the vagina and occasionally pushing it into the vaginal opening. This sex play may continue with a partially erect penis, but if a firm erection occurs, the man should stop and let the penis go soft. Having a soft penis during coital play generally upsets men with erection problems. These instructions eliminate the performance demands and help these men become comfortable with sex with a soft or partially erect penis.

Continue this until the man has many, many firm erections, which the couple allows to go soft. Next, besides rubbing the penis on the vagina and insertion, the man can use the resulting firm erections for short times of coital thrusting, beginning with just a few seconds. After a few seconds of penetration with a firm erection, the man should withdraw and let the erection go soft. After feeling confident from having done this many times, he may extend the coitus to five or six seconds with a firm penis before withdrawing and letting the erection go soft. Later, with much more practice and confidence, he can thrust within the vagina for ten seconds. Gradually increase the length of coitus as experience with the previous times builds sexual confidence. Withdrawing and letting the penis go soft at the end of the time period eliminates the performance demands, while gradually building up confidence. Sexual desire increases with the lack of orgasm. Trying to rush the process with prolonged coitus too soon may result in performance anxiety and failure.

It may take many months for a man to achieve prolonged erections and eliminate anxiety about losing erections, particularly if the sexual problem has been long standing. Men working on this problem should realize all men sometimes become less firmly erect during coitus; this is perfectly normal. If you don't worry about it, coitus can go on and sexual excitement can build up again. Middle-aged men should realize the aging process may reduce the firmness of their erections. When a man achieves prolonged coitus, he should still occasionally stop thrusting, let his erection go soft, then regain it, in order to remain comfortable with losing an erection. Also, he may want to switch to manual or oral sex at times during coitus to enhance his sexual excitement.

Recommended additional readings:

The Act of Marriage: The Beauty of Marital Love. by Tim LaHaye and Beverly LaHaye. Grand Rapids, MI: Zondervan, 1978. Religious people will find this paperback book very useful in relieving guilt, shame, or anxiety about sex. It discusses sex in a positive way, placing it in a Christian perspective.

Sex in America: A Definitive Survey. by Robert T. Michael, John H. Gagnon, Edward O. Laumann, and Gina Kolata. New York: Little, Brown, & Co., 1994.

Sex for Dummies. by Ruth K. Westheimer. Foster City, CA: IDG Books Worldwide, 1995. sexual relationships, sexual problems.

The New Male Sexuality. Bernie Zilbergeld. NY: Bantam Books, 1992. sex, sexual problems.

The Complete Idiot's Guide to a Healthy Relationship. by Judy Kuriansky. New York: Alpha Books, 1998. teaches judging love, compatibility, and commitment, marital skills, affairs, parent interference, sex, when to get help for a sex problem.

Support Groups and Hotlines:

National Council of Sex Addiction and Compulsivity 770 541 9912 information, referrals, support groups. on-line: www.ncsac.org

National Sexually Transmitted Diseases Hotline 800 227 8922 education, referrals, free pamphlets, research, public policy. on-line: .www.ashastd.org

Sex Addicts Anonymous 713 869 4902 support groups, information, newsletter. on-line: www.saa-recovery.org

Sexaholics Anonymous 615 331 6230 support groups, information, newsletter. on-line: www.sa.org

Sexual Compulsives Anonymous 800 977 4325 support groups, information, referrals, newsletter. on-line: www.sca-recovery.org

Co-Dependents Anonymous 602 277 7991 support groups for love or sex addictions or dealing with a loved one's problems. on-line: www.codependents.org

Parents, Friends, and Families of Lesbians and Gays 202 638 4200 support groups. on-line: www.pflag.org

19. Pregnancy: Facts and Decisions

Pregnancy is the joy of creating
a new wonderful life full of potential.

Pregnancy is a blessing for happily married couples who want children, especially when they have the financial resources to raise a family, but anyone who becomes pregnant or decides to raise a child needs to understand the enormous psychological and behavioral consequences of having one. The constant, never-ending chores of feeding, playing with, bathing, and dressing a baby are stressful for all parents, no matter how happy they feel about having the child and no matter how ready they feel to take on these responsibilities. For many months, the parents often cannot even get eight hours of sleep without interruption.

Even the happiest parents may experience conflicting feelings at first. A new father often finds taking care of the infant makes the young mother too busy and tired to pay as much attention to him as before. Both parents find they have much more work to do, less time to spend with friends, and more stress in their lives. Noise and confusion increase. New parents lose the freedom to do almost anything they want whenever they want to. New mothers often feel very lonely, especially if they are single, they have moved far from home, or their friends are busy dating, going to school, etc. The financial burdens of raising a child often make simple pleasures, such as going out to dinner or the movies, a rare treat. For all these reasons, many people become depressed after having a child. Hormonal changes in the mother also probably make depression more likely after childbirth.

You should consider the long-term consequences of having a child. Children require 18 years of continuous work, love, and attention, including feeding, playing, dressing, cleaning, teaching, scolding, and discipline. Clothes, food, and dentist and doctor bills cost plenty of money. How will these things affect what you want? Will they interrupt your educational or career plans? Can you work hard enough to both raise a child and work or go to school?   Could you handle a difficult, retarded, handicapped, or emotionally disturbed child? Raising children has its joyful moments, but nobody can deny raising children is a great deal of work. Women who have babies to save their marriages or keep a boyfriend at home make a serious mistake; having a baby increases stress. Women who have babies to fill a void in their lives, feel needed, or end their boredom or depression also make a serious mistake; having a baby generally only compounds their problems.

Pregnant women and breast-feeding mothers should consult a doctor before using any drug. Even common, seemingly harmless over-the-counter medicines can cause drastic problems during pregnancy. For example, the overuse of aspirin during the latter part of the pregnancy can cause severe bleeding in mother or baby at childbirth. Never take leftover prescription medicines from before your pregnancy or medicines a doctor prescribed to someone else. Prescription drugs that are safe for someone who is not pregnant may be very dangerous to a developing fetus. Pregnant women must get good nutrition from well-balanced meals to have healthy babies. Doctors recommend taking one ordinary multivitamin each day, but no more than one. Taking too much of certain vitamins can cause serious problems.   For example, one study suggests taking 15,000 units of vitamin A each day early in pregnancy can cause facial deformities or serious heart or nervous system defects in a baby.

Caffeine, cigarettes, alcohol, marijuana, and other drugs are dangerous during pregnancy. Researchers have correlated high caffeine intake with miscarriage, stillbirth, Sudden Infant Death Syndrome (SIDS or crib death), and other problems in both people and animals. Studies suggest drinking more than 2 cups of coffee per day can prove harmful. Remember that tea, cola drinks, and chocolate all contain plenty of caffeine. Mothers who smoke cigarettes or use cocaine increase their risk of miscarriage. Maternal cigarette smoking also increases the risk of stillbirth, premature birth, low birth weight babies, cleft palate birth defect, and SIDS. Preliminary evidence suggests heavy use of marijuana may increase the risk of miscarriage, stillbirth, premature birth, low birth weight babies, and birth defects. Low birth weight alone increases the risk of vision, hearing, and speech problems, learning disabilities, Attention Deficit Disorder, mental retardation, and cerebral palsy. Parents who smoke cigarettes greatly increase their baby's risk of bronchitis, pneumonia, and SIDS during the first year of life.

Mothers who drink alcohol increase the risk of miscarriage, stillbirth, birth deformities, and mentally retarded babies. Consuming three alcoholic drinks per day during pregnancy may result in _Fetal Alcohol Syndrome (FAS)_, with mental retardation and deformities of the baby's head, face, and heart. One case report suggests just one night of heavy drinking resulted in FAS. About 10% of babies whose mothers drank one or two drinks per day have milder forms of FAS. Researchers find one or two drinks per day can lower your baby's intelligence and that just three or four drinks per week can result in harm. Alcohol-exposed children without the physical deformities may still suffer from attention problems, hyperactivity, aggression, and psychiatric illnesses. Doctors advise that pregnant women never drink alcohol. If you foolishly do so, drink only rarely and never more than one or two alcoholic drinks in any 24-hour period. One drink equals 8 ounces of beer, 4 ounces of wine, 2 ounces of sherry, or 1 ounce of hard liquor. Unfortunately, a mother may drink alcohol during the first few months of pregnancy before she knows she is pregnant and this often causes FAS.

All pregnant women, then, should use any medicine or drug with extreme caution. The risk of harm to the fetus from dangerous medicines or drugs greatly increases with chronic use or large amounts.

According to the Institute of Medicine, most pregnancies (57%) in the United States are unintended (either mistimed or unwanted) and about half of unintended pregnancies end in abortion. Research links unintended pregnancy (especially unwanted pregnancy) to higher rates of smoking cigarettes and drinking alcohol during pregnancy, low birth weight, infant mortality, and social problems such as poverty, subsequent divorce, child abuse, children's psychiatric problems, and juvenile delinquency. Several comprehensive government studies conclude that child abuse prevention should begin with pregnancy planning and affordable birth control services. Both psychologists and the U.S. government's Institute of Medicine believe the world would be a better place if every child was an intended child. This makes sex education, birth control, adoption, and abortion very important.

Unfortunately, studies document widespread misconceptions about sex in teenagers and major gaps in adults' and parents' knowledge about basic sexual information. Few women realize birth control is safer than childbearing, that they can obtain emergency birth control after sex or a broken condom, and that oral contraceptives have health benefits. Sexually active people need to know about the kinds of birth control, their success rates, and their proper use. Because of the complexities of using many forms of birth control, longer-acting hormonal implants and injections, IUDs, and reversible sterilization are becoming more popular. Sex education frequently persuades young people to delay starting sexual activity, use condoms, and have fewer sex partners. For a full discussion of all the points made in this paragraph, as well as a description of the most effective sex education programs and other policies that can reduce teenage pregnancies, please refer to chapter 42, Preventing Violence and Crime.

Social service agencies often arrange adoptions, but in many states, a clergyman, doctor, or lawyer can arrange an adoption that might include money for hospital, living, and legal expenses. Make sure the mother has the right, written into the contract, to change her mind and keep the baby, even after signing the papers. Half of all states require parental involvement when minors seek abortion, and 61% of minors who have abortions do so with at least one parent's knowledge. The great majority of parents support their daughter's decision to have an abortion. Most teenagers who choose adoption or abortion are from the middle or upper classes.

Pregnant Teenagers

In the United States, about 1/4 of women become pregnant before age 19. Because teenagers often underestimate the risk of pregnancy, almost 9 out of 10 pregnancies of unmarried teenagers and over 1/2 those of married teenagers are unwanted. Teenagers are at higher risk for pregnancy when their families live in poverty or their parents are divorced or have alcohol problems. In making pregnancy decisions, teenagers must face complicated emotions and difficult moral issues.

Unfortunately, teenagers often make these important decisions unwisely. Many decisions about pregnancies are based on desires to be grown up, on rebellion from parents, what their friends have done or said, the mistaken idea having a baby will improve their unhappiness or boredom, or the wish to keep a boyfriend at home. Others choose foolishly because of their desire to be needed or important, overly romantic notions about having fun taking care of her own adorable baby, or overly romantic assessments of their boyfriends' promises to be good fathers and good providers. Despite promises by boyfriends, more than half of teenage mothers are not even living with the child's father by the time the child reaches grade school, and only 20% of never-married mothers receive child support. In contrast, 4 out of 5 women who wait until age 24 to have a baby are still living with the child's father when the child reaches grade school, and 2 out of 3 of those children have never lived in poverty. In all social and economic groups, growing up without the father in the home doubles the risk of children having behavioral or emotional problems, dropping out of school, poor work histories, juvenile delinquency, becoming teen parents and unmarried parents, and divorcing.

Teenagers who think they want a child should keep a baby for a weekend, giving its parents a weekend off. After experiencing the joys and burdens of caring for an infant first hand, these teenagers should imagine what it would be like to care for a child for 18 years with no vacations. Another good learning experience is Baby Think It Over, an electronic doll that cries, requires attention from one teenager as regularly as a real baby, and records any neglect or abuse (see the company's number listed under hotlines at the end of this chapter).

These days, unmarried teenagers produce 4 out of 5 teenage pregnancies. About 75% of all teenage marriages end in divorce, but when pregnancy was the primary reason for marriage, almost 90% do. Although 7 in 10 teenage mothers complete high school, 9 out of 10 women who postpone childbirth finish high school. Many teen mothers drop out of school and never go back. Of all teen mothers, 1 out of 4 has a second child within two years of their first. The high divorce rate means most teen mothers end up raising their children alone, which makes it very difficult for them to go back to school or go to college and get jobs with high salaries. Thus, teenage pregnancy often leads to a lifetime of poverty. Research shows 55% of all teenagers who have children end up on welfare within one year and 77% within five years. Studies also indicate the children of teen mothers are more likely to have lower intelligence test scores, have poor school adjustment, repeat a grade in school, end up in prison, go unemployed as young adults, and have children before 18 years of age.

About one-third of pregnant teens receive inadequate prenatal care. Poor medical care and poor diet contribute to many problems in pregnancy. Teenage mothers are at higher risk of dying while delivering the child, miscarriage, birth complications, and having premature and low birth weight babies than are other mothers. (We noted above the increased risk of serious mental and physical problems in low birth weight babies.) Twice as many babies of teenage mothers die during their first year of life, compared to babies of older mothers. Good medical care during pregnancy can prevent most of these physical problems, but other factors often cause additional problems later in these children's lives. Children born to unmarried parents, a category that includes most children of teenage mothers, are more than twice as likely to experience physically abuse as are children born to married parents. The fact that most children born to teenagers are unwanted also adds to the risk of problems, as described previously.

Sexually active teenagers, then, need to understand the facts presented in this chapter and to practice effective methods of birth control. Unfortunately, a government survey in 1999 found 42% of the sexually active students in high school don't use condoms. Many of those who do use contraceptives don't understand the proper ways to use them or use them inconsistently. Half of all premarital pregnancies occur within the first six months of sexual activity. If pregnancy should occur, the facts presented in this chapter can help teenagers make better decisions in these important matters, which will undoubtedly affect them for their entire lives.

Recommended Additional Readings:

The Best Intentions: Unintended Pregnancy and the Well-Being of Children and Families. by Sarah S. Brown and Leon Eisenberg, eds. Washington D.C.: National Academy Press, 1995.

The Complete Adoption Book. by Laura Beauvais-Godwin and Raymond Godwin. Holbrook, MA: Adams Media Corp., 1997.

Support Groups, Hotlines, and Resources:

Planned Parenthood 800 829 7732 information, support, referrals for contraception, emergency contraception, abortion, adoption. on-line: www.plannedparenthood.org/main.htm

Pregnancy Hotline 800 848 5683 referrals for information, support, shelters, baby clothes, adoption. on-line: www.nationallifecenter.com

Pregnancy Hotline 800 238 4269 Christian information, support, referrals to free pregnancy testing, foster and adoption centers. on-line: www.bethany.org

Internet site for emergency contraception information: www.not-2-late.com or http://ec.princeton.edu

Internet resources for learning about adoption, including avoiding fraud: www.adoption.com, www.adoptioncenter.com

Baby Think It Over 800 830 1416 a 6.5-pound, electronic infant Baby used in classroom instruction, at-risk teenager programs, or group counseling. It has a crying cycle corresponding to the times when a real baby would want to eat, need a diaper, and otherwise require attention. The $250 model stops crying only when you insert a key in its back and hold it at a certain angle for up to 25 minutes at a time. This key attaches to the teenager's wrist on a tamper-proof, nontransferable hospital bracelet. Sensors detect and record if the parent figure ignores the doll's cries for over one minute or drops, hits, or violently shakes it. A computer readout reports such neglect or abuse on command. The more realistic $350 RealCare Baby model requires feeding with a bottle or breastfeeding device, changing diapers, holding while rocking and burping, and its head falls back when not supported. It cries, coos, burps, coughs, and makes breathing and feeding sounds recorded from real infants. Again, a tamper-proof wristband makes it impossible for someone else to take care of the baby. All models are available as a male or female, Caucasian, Afro-American, Hispanic, American Indian, Japanese, or Asian. Parents can ask schools to order it and begin programs, perhaps getting local organizations such as Kiwanis, Lions Club, or Knights of Columbus to pay for it. on-line: www.btio.com

20. Before Getting Married

Only by waiting is character known.
(Hausa proverb from Africa)

Judge people by their actions, not words.

Consider all the issues in this chapter to measure your compatibility with your partner, predict likely problem areas, and help avoid the mistakes in love and marriage that lead to divorce. First, many people confuse the intense feelings of sex with true love or believe great sex indicates true love. Good sex, however, simply involves certain kinds of physical stimulation, which people may perform with or without love, and great sex can exist in selfish or even in physically or emotionally abusive relationships. People who marry because of mistaking sex for love, often divorce when the glow of new romance fades and the spouse's selfishness becomes more clear. Many people mistakenly believe marriage will settle a person down because it establishes a warm home life that eliminates promiscuity and late night carousing. Many people do settle down when they get married, but you can't rely on marriage to settle someone down, because many people continue their wild or promiscuous ways after marrying. Many people wrongly believe marriage will make them happier than they've ever been before. Although getting married can add much joy and happiness to one's life, after the initial glow of romance fades, marriage involves plenty of work, sacrifice, and compromise.

The younger the couple at the time of marriage, the more likely is divorce. As noted previously, teenage marriages end in divorce about 75% of the time. Divorce rates also increase when a couple marries after having known each other for only a short time. It is unwise to marry someone without having known that person for at least one year. Without one year's acquaintance, you really don't have enough time to judge how the marriage might go after the initial glow of romance fades. You need to draw upon at least one year of shared experiences to judge compatibility and evaluate the important issues described in this chapter.

People often get married for the wrong reasons. Pregnancy is a poor reason. Divorce is very common when pregnancy was the major reason for marriage. Before marrying someone after a pregnancy, you should evaluate the relationship as described in this chapter and ask yourself the following question. If this pregnancy had never occurred, would this person still seem to be a good marital choice? Some people marry primarily because they already have children and they feel children need two parents; this, too, is unwise. The quality of your relationship with the person and the feelings you have for each other should be your primary considerations. Of course, the quality of the person's relationship with your child or children should also weigh heavily in your decision.

Other poor reasons include marrying to cure your loneliness or depression, overcome inferiority feelings, feel more wanted or attractive, find happiness, or escape from an unhappy home. Other mistakes include marrying because it is a grown up thing to do, because you don't know what else to do with your life, because everyone gets married, and so you won't end up a lonely old bachelor or maid. Sometimes people marry primarily for sex, because they had sex, or for money. A few people get married because they don't want to hurt the other person's feelings by turning down the offer of marriage. Some push their sweethearts into getting married by threatening to leave them if they don't marry them soon. All of these are poor reasons to get married and may lead to heartbreak and divorce.

If your romantic partner has ever hit or physically hurt you or threatened or intimidated you, get rid of the person. Unfortunately, anger and physical abuse generally become worse during marriage, increasing in frequency and severity after courtship is over and the initial glow of romance fades. If your partner has ever hit you, realize this may happen again and things may get much worse, no matter what the person says. In chapter 36, Abuse, we shall see that men who commit violence against women are unlikely to stop their violence, even with counseling.

Several clues help in evaluating a person's ability to love. One is whether your partner has close nonsexual friends of the opposite sex. Having these kinds of relationships is a good sign, whereas not having them suggests an inability to truly love. Another clue is how the person treats parents or family members. People who hate their own parents or family members, especially those of your sex, or who do not treat them with respect, warmth, kindness, and consideration are likely to make poor mates later on. You should also ask your partner's family, coworkers, friends, and neighbors about problems. Anyone who doesn't get along well with several of these other people may be the problem. If someone denies having any family, close friends, or coworkers, find out from the police department if the person has a criminal history or have a detective check the situation out more carefully.

If you are considering getting married, be sure to evaluate your relationship using the section Is This Relationship Good for Me? in chapter

15, Social Life. When considering spending the rest of your life with a person, alcoholism or drug abuse becomes particularly important. Pay careful attention to the questions in that section concerning danger signals of possible violence toward you. If you had to answer negatively more than a few of the questions in the section on evaluating relationships or if you see any of the danger signals described there, you should not marry this person and you should probably look for a new relationship. End the relationship, too, if your romantic partner abuses alcohol or drugs. If your relationship meets any of these criteria but you want to continue it, insist on waiting not only for the needed improvements, but for at least another year, preferably two years, to see that the improvements last, before marrying the person. Improvements persisting for one or two years are more likely to continue after the marriage than those that have lasted a test of only six months.

Another sign of trouble in romantic relationships is breaking off the relationship one or more times during dating or either person's seriously considering breaking up. Research shows couples who have broken up or had doubts about the wisdom of getting married divorce more often than do couples who never broke up, nor had any serious doubts about the relationship.

Even in the happiest relationships, people must occasionally express anger to bring forth issues and resolve conflicts. In this way, marriage is difficult work. Be sure to carefully discuss your communication and problem-solving patterns with your prospective spouse. Read chapter 6 together, point out any communication problems and skills you notice in your relationship, and work on improving them. Do you have different ways of expressing or of not expressing emotions? Different communication styles? Read chapter 9 together and consider how you can improve your normal styles of problem solving. Beware if you cannot discuss certain issues without anger or upset feelings—this suggests you will never resolve the conflict. Wise people understand that a person who regularly avoids issues makes a poor mate and look elsewhere for someone truly willing to work to improve interpersonal relationships.

Yelling in anger, avoiding issues, negative labels or insults (inconsiderate, mean, lazy, etc.), and regular criticism are important issues in any relationship. Avoiding issues may involve refusing to discuss them, walking out, ignoring, withdrawing, distancing, or giving the silent treatment. Walking out is only helpful when it avoids yelling. You should get rid of any romantic partner who ever does any of the above things and won't work on it enough to show continuous improvement over time.

There are many other areas couples need to discuss honestly and openly. Discuss intimacy. Which partner has more need for intimacy? Can both express intimacy equally comfortably? How do you express affection, appreciation, and commitment? Which affectionate behaviors would you like more often? What does each expect for sexual practices during the marriage? What about the frequency of sex? Ways to indicate desire for sex? Are you both comfortable with these sexual expectations? Do both agree to be sexually faithful? Have there been outside sexual affairs since the engagement to marry? This may indicate things to come! Discuss birth control until you are ready to raise children, whether you want children, how many you want, how close together you want to space them, how much time each of you will spend with them, and how you will discipline them.

Discuss power and decision making, too. How will you make decisions? Will each of you control certain areas, such as paying the bills and raising children, or will both share in most decisions? Does one person insist on having control and the other usually give in? Which of you is more assertive? Do you plan things together? Do both have input into major decisions? Are these aspects of power and decision making comfortable for both? Who is more dependent? Who has lower self-esteem? More anxiety? More depression? Anger? Fears? Worry? Guilt? Do these characteristics bother the other partner? How do you deal with this? Do the actions of the other make the problem worse or help improve it? Could any of these problems burden the other partner in the future? What kind of loyalty is likely if an emotional problem or obesity should develop in one of you? What are your biggest worries about marriage with the other person? What do you expect from a spouse? How much time do you expect sharing thoughts and feelings?

Who will hold a job and for how long? What kind? If the wife works and you plan to have children, will she go back to work after childbearing? How soon? Will both partners control the money? Who will write the checks? How do you feel about credit cards and loans? Is one of you so impulsive with money that keeping up with the bills becomes troublesome? This, too, may indicate things to come! What kind of priorities (automobile, education, apartment or home, interests and hobbies, clothes, etc.) will determine your habits in spending and saving money? How important is education to each of you? Where will you live? In what kind of apartment or home? Will you have pets? What will you do for vacations? How and where will you spend Christmas and other holidays? How will you divide or share household chores (cooking, cleaning, washing dishes, shopping, repairing things, etc.)? How will you spend leisure or recreation time, both together and separately? How much time would each person like with friends, away from the other partner? Is one partner so jealous it will be hard to maintain outside friendships with other men and women?

Discuss your feelings about each other's friends. Can you accept your partner's friends even if some of them aren't people you would want to spend much time with? How open will your home be to other people? Discuss your feelings about the family of each partner. How much time will you spend with each other's families? How important are religion and morals in each of your lives? Do you agree on whether to attend church? If both plan to go, do you agree on what church to attend and how often? Do both partners hold the same standards of appropriate behavior? Are your life goals and priorities similar or very different? What kinds of personal information would each partner prefer kept private?

By considering all the above issues, you will have a much better idea of how compatible the two of you are and likely problem areas. Ask yourself if you can live with your differences and the negative characteristics you see in your partner. Never marry someone with hopes of changing the person after marriage. Although some people do change and grow after marriage, other people become worse after the initial glow of romance fades. If you don't want to tolerate the problems you see in the relationship for a lifetime, either wait for lasting changes before getting married or look for another mate. With major problems, as noted previously, you should wait not only for the needed improvements, but also to see if the improvements last for another year or two before marrying. If you don't want to tolerate a less serious problem, you can wait for improvement and another six months to one year of lasting change before getting married.

Recommended Additional Readings:

The Complete Idiot's Guide to a Healthy Relationship. by Judy Kuriansky. New York: Alpha Books, 1998. teaches judging love, compatibility, and commitment, marital skills, affairs, parent interference, sex, when to get help for a sex problem.

Obsessive Love. by Susan Forward and Craig Buck. NY: Bantam Books, 1991.

How to Survive the Loss of a Love. by Melba Colgrove, Harold H. Bloomfield, and Peter McWilliams. Los Angeles: Prelude Press, 1991. for the end of a relationship, whether by breaking up, divorce, separation, or death.

Support Groups:

For support groups for sexual or love addictions, please refer to the end of chapter 18, Sex.

21. Marriage and Couple's Problems

Never let a day pass without
a compliment, a hug, and saying I love you.

Encourage another day by day. (Hebrews 3:13)

Never go to bed angry.

Some animals, such as coyotes, jackals, geese, swans, and certain species of monkeys, small tree apes, mice, ducks, cockatoos, ravens, and other birds form life-long, devoted, sexually faithful pairs. Coyote pairs almost seem to show romantic love, hunting together, greeting each other with elaborate displays of wagging tails and licking, howling together, and curling up together to sleep.

Please refer to chapter 2 for a description of the true love that characterizes happy relationships. Of course, no one can act in these ways all the time, but striving to feel and act in the ways described will enhance any marriage. Happy couples show sensitivity to each other's feelings and needs. They act in kind, helpful, respectful, tender, patient, forgiving, and loyal ways. Happy couples help each other with chores such as cooking, washing dishes, child care, shopping, work from the job, etc. They also act in considerate ways like calling to let each other know when they will be late coming home or leaving notes describing their whereabouts and the time they are due home. These many little warm acts add up to a pleasant relationship and keep the marriage strong.

At first the joys of romance and marriage make life seem almost perfect. People with personal problems often feel unusually happy during courtship and for a time after getting married, because the deeply satisfying romance temporarily overrides their problems. Eventually, the initial glow of romance fades as the spouses begin to see each other more realistically, the stresses of daily life become more obvious, the pleasures of sex become more routine, and the appetite for sex decreases. Married or committed people tend to gradually take each other for granted. Affectionate behavior, compliments, and statements of appreciation tend to decrease, and criticism tends to increase. The partners often become less considerate and perhaps more selfish than they were during courtship. If you don't constantly cultivate love in a relationship, love will weaken and the relationship may deteriorate.

Make a point of regularly showing your appreciation for routine things your spouse does for you every day and for anything else your spouse does that you like. Watch for personal qualities you can compliment. These things help you stay aware of the positive aspects of your relationship. Giving thanks and compliments tell what you appreciate and make it more likely your partner will continue to do these things. Happy couples also show interest in each other's daily lives and share interests and activities. Make some time every day to find out how your partner's day went and what your partner is feeling or thinking. Share interests and activities such as walks, nature parks, barbecues, games, swimming, watching sports, etc. Teaching your mate a skill you possess (cooking, taking care of the car, etc.) gives the relationship flexibility in accomplishing chores and gives the mate more independence and self-esteem. Plan fun things to do together, both now and in the future. Occasionally do fun things on the spur of the moment. Reminisce together about past good times once in a while, too.

Keep your relationship alive by keeping the romance in it as the years pass. After being together for a while, many couples feel no need to express affection to their partners, assuming they well know the strength of their love. It seems that men may value sexual intimacy more than verbal intimacy, whereas women value verbal intimacy more, but everyone enjoys expressions of affection. Make a habit of kissing and hugging when you greet each other, when you part, before going to bed, and for no particular reason. Hold hands while watching television, going for a walk, etc. Use pet names such as sweetheart or darling. Express your love regularly. If you find it difficult to say, "I love you," just practice every day. With regular practice, you will become more comfortable.

Call each other sometimes just to say hello. Surprise each other occasionally with something pleasant such as cards, cheap presents, a rose, breakfast in bed, a favorite meal, a special snack, an evening out, etc. Occasionally dress and groom yourselves extra nicely just for each other. Have a candlelight dinner together once in a while. Try some body massage, too, or perhaps just a neck rub when your partner seems grumpy or tired. Many couples enjoy going to bed at the same time and sharing a private conversation together. Showering together or having sex by candlelight is very romantic. Some couples go out on dates together just as they did before they got married, hiring a babysitter if necessary. On these dates they dress to please and take a special interest in each other's thoughts, feelings, and recent activities. Don't forget to show your affection by remembering holidays, birthdays, and anniversaries.

Sharing feelings, rather than facts, seems strongly related to marital satisfaction, probably because of the loving responses of understanding and acceptance. Share your feelings so you can receive emotional support and your partner can respond appropriately to you, instead of trying to respond based on guesses and intuition. Some research suggests unhappy couples may misunderstand each other more often than happy ones. If you find it difficult to express your feelings, practice at least twice a day.

Happy marriages use honest, open communication about conflicts as the basis for negotiation, compromise, and problem solving. Such communication helps uncover areas needing work to make the relationship stronger and deeper. Of course, constantly living with someone inevitably leads to irritations, disagreements, and conflicts. Some people try to cope by ignoring the problems and forgetting their bad feelings. This unwise strategy solves nothing and may allow irritations to build into explosive anger.

Bring up your negative feelings and problem issues tactfully, in ways that are not hostile or blaming, to avoid hurt feelings, arguments, and marital dissatisfaction. Use chapter 6 to carefully evaluate and improve the communication problems in your relationship. Couples need good problem-solving skills focusing on choosing very specific behavioral goals for change. Read chapter 9 and consider how you can improve your own normal styles of problem solving. Pay particular attention to problems that recur.

In many relationships, outbursts of anger, yelling, and verbal abuse occasionally occur. Such fighting releases tension and brings forth each person's perspective on important issues the couple needs to discuss. This can feel good and may sometimes even solve problems, but is an inefficient and often destructive method of communicating and problem solving.

If you begin to practice good communication and problem-solving skills, you will quickly see these skills are much more productive and much less troublesome than simply arguing when your problems become intolerable. If outbursts of anger or yelling occasionally occur in your relationship, set aside time each week for problem-solving sessions devoted to exploring feelings, problems, patterns of behavior that seem negative, and recent improvements. Please refer to chapter 28 for important advice on controlling anger, techniques that help turn arguments into problem solving, and advice on dealing with an angry person.

Every marriage needs a certain amount of humor and acceptance. Don't lose your perspective on the overall relationship because of a few frustrating problems. Happily married couples often have recurring, long-lasting frustrating issues, but they can back off and de-escalate the conflict using humor, gentle teasing, appreciation, and affection to give support and break up the tension caused by the problem. Notice and appreciate the strengths of the relationship. Avoid the common tendency to view your mate's bothersome behaviors as horrible or intolerable rather than simply frustrating. Agree to disagree on certain things and learn to live with your differences.

Often a couple's frustrating differences actually create a needed balance for the relationship as a whole. For example, men's tendencies toward strong independence often balance women's tendencies toward strong intimacy and allow the relationship to have a healthy balance of each. When one spouse is much more critical than the other, the critical spouse may contribute very careful observation and judgment, while the noncritical spouse contributes acceptance of others. Whenever differences frustrate you, consider if the traits might be useful in certain situations and try to learn from the other spouse's trait.

Forgiveness is particularly important in a marriage, reducing tensions, pain, and resentment. Try not to hold grudges about past events that hurt you. Don't bring up the past when you discuss problems with your mate. A person who regularly brings up the painful past has not been able to forgive and strains the relationship.

In the happiest marriages, the partners treat each other as equals. Each spouse will consult the other on any important decision affecting both, and both partners feel they have some power in the relationship and over areas of their lives. Many couples feel comfortable with the traditional sex role in which the man dominates and the woman submits to his ultimate authority. This often interferes with the compromise and negotiation needed for problem solving. It may work well when a kind man always considers the feelings and input of his spouse, but whenever one person's decisions or feelings generally dominate over the other's, the potential exists for the marriage to suffer when the needs of the submissive partner receive insufficient attention. One study suggests couples with dominant husbands have more conflict about family responsibilities than other couples do.

Traditional sex roles of male authority, working male and female housewife, and sex-typed interests tend to make changes less likely. Another study suggests men whose wives work outside the home help much more in child care but only slightly more in housework, compared to men with housewives. A long-term study suggests men who do housework are physically healthier, less likely to avoid marital conflict, and less overwhelmed by their wives' emotions than men who don't do housework. A submissive partner who wants to become more assertive should refer to chapter 16 for advice. Money is a common source of marital conflict, so try to work together on the monthly budget and long-term financial planning.

Both partners need interests, activities, and friends of their own, as well as time spent enjoyably together as a couple, away from their children. Married people with intimate outside friendships seem to have more satisfying marriages. Separate interests and activities give independence and things to share with the other partner. Separate friendships allow partners to receive emotional support and to express different facets of their personalities with various people. Warmly accept your spouse's friends. To reject one of them is to reject an important part of your spouse's life. A lonely marital partner may simply need more interests, activities, or outside friendships, but loneliness may also mean the marriage lacks enough communication, affectionate behavior, acts of kindness, or shared interests and activities. Work on these problems using the appropriate chapters of this book.

Excessive jealousy that interferes with your partner's outside activities or friendships involves negative thinking, and perhaps low self-esteem. Replace thoughts dwelling on jealousy, fears of losing the mate, and angry or anxious thoughts with more positive thought alternatives every day in the ways described in chapter 4. For example, "Quit worrying! She's always been faithful to me. I don't want to take away all her freedom. She needs time for herself. It will make our marriage stronger." When your spouse is busy with outside activities or friendships, cultivate your own interests and activities and renew old friendships or develop new ones, so you won't dwell on jealousy, anger, anxiety, or fears of losing your spouse. If great anxiety interferes with your ability to give your spouse freedom, use chapter 29 to work on it.

For a happy relationship, be honest, reliable, and responsible. Try to show good judgment and consider the present and future consequences of your actions. Don't abuse alcohol or any other drugs. Live within your finances and budget. Stay healthy and fit. Don't criticize your mate in public or make any negative comparisons to a previous spouse, sweetheart, or date. Show pride in your partner and try to say only good things about the partner or your relationship in public. Most couples can enhance their sex lives by improving their sexual communication in the ways described in chapter 18, Sex. Chapter 18 also includes useful information for couples about sexual myths, sex in old age, and treatment for sexual problems.

The following exercises help couples explore and improve their marital relationships. Start with just the first exercise, spending a few days writing down your answers and adding to your list whenever you think of another answer. Then share your answers with your spouse and discuss any feelings that arise. Move to the next exercise and repeat the procedure, spending a few days compiling your answers, and then sharing and discussing them. Do this for each of the six exercises.

Exercises for Exploring and Improving Your Marriage

1. Make a list of all the things you like about your partner and your marriage, including personal qualities, things your mate does that you appreciate or enjoy, and things you would like to thank the person for.
2. Make a list of things you regret in your relationship and things you would like to apologize to your partner for.
3. Make a list of your happiest times in the marriage, the most fun times, the most special and touching moments, and the times when you felt the closest to your partner.
4. Describe what you hope your marriage will be like someday.
5. Make a list of specific behaviors you can do to improve your marriage. Try to think of behaviors that would help make the other spouse feel more loved, more appreciated, or happier. Consider decreasing or eliminating negative behaviors, too.
6. Make a list of specific behaviors you think your spouse can do to improve your marriage or make you feel more loved, more appreciated, or happier. Again, consider decreasing or eliminating negative behaviors.

Use your answers to exercises 5 and 6 as menus for choosing pleasing and loving activities and as the basis for problem solving or creating contracts that exchange desired behaviors of fairly equal difficulty (I will do ..., if you do...). Agree to make changes whether or not the other partner keeps the agreement and without any other rewards or punishments. In marriage, both people need to choose to work to improve the relationship. If simple contracts don't result in cooperation and improved behaviors, use the more complicated form of contract with separate rewards and penalties for each party, described in chapter 13.

Personal problems can weaken or damage a marriage. For example, a spouse with a bad temper can destroy marital harmony, and a depressed spouse can make the marriage dull and lifeless. A depressed person may notice and recall mostly a partner's negative behaviors or may angrily overreact to conflicts, perceiving criticism or a lack of emotional support. Working on personal problems often improves the relationship. Sometimes people repeat feelings, actions, or patterns of interaction from the past in their marital life because they haven't completely resolved past conflicts. If upsetting experiences from your past or problems from your family of origin seem to affect the quality of your marital life now, please refer to chapter 37 for advice on how to explore, work with, and finish the past, so you can leave it behind.

Other marital problems involve conflicting habits from the spouses' two families of origin. The families may have different religions, views of career roles, ways of expressing or not expressing emotions, or ways of showing affection, appreciation, or commitment. They may vary in communication styles, decision-making methods, balances of power and control between husband and wife, degrees of independence and dependence, or degrees of assertiveness and passivity. Other problems may come from different standards for sharing friends, sharing finances, time with in-laws, balances of outside interests versus family togetherness, or time spent sharing thoughts and feelings. Some of these underlying assumptions and standards may be automatic and not particularly conscious. Look for common themes or feelings in various upsetting situations. You might ask "What is upsetting about this?" Just understanding how your different families affect your relationship makes each spouse less self-righteous in these conflicts and more sympathetic to the other point of view. Of course, the couple must resolve such conflicts using good communication and problem-solving skills.

Both partners jointly cause and maintain most marital problems, so both will have to change to improve the marriage. Often both blame each other in conflicts, feeling the actions of the other spouse cause their own negative behaviors and feeling helpless to change the other spouse's negative behaviors. Learn to recognize your typical circular patterns of interactions. For example, when child care and housework are issues, wives may become overwhelmed and angrily demand help with a number of chores, triggering avoidance in their husbands. Humorously describing this as "The Screaming Army General Wife and Deserter Husband Syndrome" can help a couple get a better perspective on the pattern, and each can work to improve their roles in it. Once you see how the pattern normally progresses, you can change your own behaviors to interrupt the cycle. Look for each partner's actions that helped escalate the conflict.

When discussing upsetting conflicts or arguments, try to focus on the early stages of the problem, even what was going on before the problem began.   Couples can easily place blame and become frustrated again in discussing the escalating argument, when both probably acted in negative ways.   The conditions before the argument and the early stages are generally more understandable and acceptable and may suggest triggers and early actions or decisions that led to later escalation.   You will know you are making progress when you can discuss problems and negative patterns you share in a descriptive, detached way, rather than fighting about them and trying to place blame.

A number of studies show husbands and wives have very different perceptions of their interactions, even during brief time periods such as 24 hours, with unhappy couples agreeing less often than happier couples.   We all notice different details of interactions and interpret them in various ways, based on our feelings, beliefs, what we expect, etc.   Unhappy couples seem to underestimate the number of pleasant events that occur between them by 50%, according to the observations of trained raters in the home.   Couples may have very different memories of their relationship history, with many upsetting, negative events remembered by one but not by the other.

Our goal, then, should be to find out what happened as best we can and to learn factors that influenced problems and good times to occur.   Carefully study the problem situations as described in chapter 9.   When problems occur, replace negative thoughts about how terrible or intolerable it is or hating your marriage or partner with more helpful thoughts every day in the ways described in chapter 4.   That chapter also includes examples of negative thoughts about marriage and positive alternatives for them.   Consider what both partners did differently when things were better, perhaps the last time you got along better.   How did you make that happen?

In relationships, our moods often depend on the conclusions we make about the reasons for or causes of our spouse's behaviors and on our predictions of what will happen in the future.   These conclusions and predictions can be automatic, not particularly conscious, and wrong. Carefully record the detailed wording of your thoughts when your emotions and behaviors change for the better or worse in the relationship.   It may take consistent monitoring and study to find your conclusions and predictions. Consider what it meant to you when your partner said or did something that you didn't like.

Most marriages go through periods in which the partners feel unhappy with each other and the marriage.   These discouraging times are normal. Don't worry about feeling you are no longer in love with your mate.   Most people equate being in love with the intense feelings of an idealized new romance. Of course, these feelings fade in time because of the inevitable conflicts of marital life, especially if the couple fails to work at keeping romance in the relationship. Some couples may feel they no longer love each other or they hate each other, but people use the word *love* in a confusing variety of ways, with varying amounts of romance, affection, closeness, jealousy, etc., and hate is often simply love in anger.

Any couple can save their troubled relationship if they put enough effort into making the necessary changes. Marriages that successfully overcome troubled periods grow deeper and stronger with the knowledge the couple can overcome crises and their love has endured. These spouses also acquire a deeper acceptance and more realistic love of each other as fallible human beings. Never have a child in an attempt to improve or save a troubled relationship. If you think about doing so, please read chapter 19, Pregnancy. Adding a baby to a troubled marriage generally compounds the problems in it.

Psychologists often succeed in improving troubled marriages by simply ordering an increase in positive interactions. Work on increasing the kinds of loving behaviors described earlier in this chapter: acts of helpfulness, giving thanks, compliments, questions that show interest in your spouse's daily life, affectionate behavior, etc. Fortunately, kindness and positive interactions generally lead to more of the same. Your actions toward your partner help determine the kind of treatment you receive in return. Start by practicing two of these loving behaviors every day, and then gradually add more of them. At first practicing these loving behaviors may seem forced, artificial, or manipulative, but as noted in chapter 5, Emotions, changing your behavior is often the fastest and easiest way to change your emotions. If you practice loving behaviors as an experiment for several weeks, you will find they quickly become natural and comfortable and your marriage improves. Sometimes this can bypass marital problems.

Develop good communication and problem-solving skills, effective control of anger, and positive thought habits about your partner and marriage, as suggested previously. The five exercises for exploring and improving marital relations help in reviewing the strengths of the marriage, apologizing for mistakes, and finding behaviors useful for problem solving and helpful contracts. Make sure each partner has a well-rounded variety of interests and activities and that the spouses have both separate and shared interests and activities. Any time your mate performs behaviors or makes changes you appreciate, reward your mate with attention, compliments, thanks, and affection. This helps increase the behaviors.

Even when only one partner actively works on improving the relationship, that person can make much progress by initiating more pleasant interactions and improving negative patterns of anger, communication, and problem-solving.   You may need to use the advice in chapter 16, Assertiveness, to insist, without hostility, on problem solving or behavioral changes. Remember, polite requests and assertiveness work much better than anger.   Your anger can lead to a vicious cycle of arguments, anger, and retaliation that contributes to the problem behaviors of your spouse.

Setting firm negative consequences for your partner's chronic problem behaviors may help. For example, each time your mate insults you in public or comes home very drunk, you might immediately leave and spend the next day with a friend or family member away from home. In general, however, more positive approaches such as increasing positive interactions, making contracts, and rewarding behaviors you like, are best.   Use negative consequences only as a last resort and only along with more positive approaches that will strengthen the marriage.   If your spouse has been sexually unfaithful, realize that punishing your spouse by refusing sex for too long might promote the extramarital affair.

Certain problems may prove so resistant to change that unless you get a divorce, you must simply learn to be happy despite the problem. Spouses of alcoholics may find themselves in this position. (Chapter 33 describes how to best deal with an addicted person.) If you are considering getting a divorce, please refer to chapter 23 for advice on how to best make this important decision and go on with the divorce. Nobody should tolerate emotional or physical abuse. If your partner has ever emotionally brutalized you with chronic insults or criticism, threats, temper tantrums, or sexual exploitation, or if your partner has ever physically hurt you by hitting you, pushing you, kicking you, or throwing an object at you, please refer to chapter 36, Abuse.

If you have concerns about how well you will handle a particular situation with your mate, prepare for it with behavioral roleplays, so you can deal with it effectively. Meditating or relaxing deeply before the encounter may help. Breathe deeply and stretch or relax muscle tension in your body just before and during the situation. Sometimes you can use an interpersonal roleplay to explore a conflict in the relationship and help each partner more fully understand the other person's perspective. Work on only one or a few simple behavioral changes at a time, and use the advice in chapters 11, 12, and 13 to keep motivated and help ensure success in working on your relationship problems.

Recommended Additional Readings:

Couple Skills: Making Your Relationship Work. by Matthew McKay, Patrick
   Fanning, and Kim Paleg. Oakland, CA: New Harbinger Publications, 1994.
   marital communication skills, finding and fighting automatic thoughts about your
   mate, coping with anger, separating your partner from your childhood parent
   issues.

The Complete Idiot's Guide to a Healthy Relationship. by Judy Kuriansky. New
   York: Alpha Books, 1998. teaches judging love, compatibility, and commitment,
   marital skills, affairs, parent interference, sex, when to get help for a sex problem.

Resources:

For readings or hotlines on sex, please refer to the end of chapter 18.

22. Raising Children

Brighten your children's lives with silliness and fun.

*Children need many times more hugs, smiles,
and praise than lectures and discipline.*

Nothing can compare to the joys of raising children and seeing them grow into responsible adults, yet raising children is also a great deal of work. Using the advice in this chapter makes the task of raising children much easier and increases your chances of raising good, happy children. Don't overwhelm yourself with all the advice in this chapter. Work on just one or two changes at a time and occasionally reread the appropriate sections to maintain your progress and choose new improvements to make.

Members of the healthiest families have a variety of friends outside the immediate family and plenty of interests and activities they enjoy. These friends, interests, and activities make excellent resources when family problems occur. The parents can share their feelings with friends or with other parents who have experienced similar problems. The children also have friends outside the immediate family with whom they can share their feelings. In these healthy families, the children grow up learning to enjoy many interests and activities, which provide not only constructive ways to use time, but also much self-esteem. The parents have satisfying lives and don't live through their children, and the children don't feel burdened by emotionally needy parents.

All too often, families with problems don't have these times off for relaxation, outside friends, and interests and activities. All parents need some time off from the demands of raising children, both individually and as a couple. Psychologists understand the great importance of relaxation away from the children and prescribe such free time for overwhelmed parents. At the very least, try to have a few hours of free time away from the children for each parent at least once a week and a few hours of free time away from the children for both parents together at least once a week. Occasionally take over the child care duties for your spouse, hire a babysitter, take advantage of daycare facilities, or take turns with other families providing group outings or group play at home. Do these things, too, when you want to devote special time to just one child.

Babies

Despite being fed, bathed, and changed regularly, most babies in orphanages and institutions in the early 1900s lost interest in life, became withdrawn, lost weight, and eventually died. In some institutions, every infant under two years old died. In the 1920s, people finally discovered they could prevent these deaths by simply giving each baby regular human interaction. Babies need someone to pick up, hold, carry around, and play with them several times a day to survive. This shows how important human contact and interaction are for babies.

Breast-feeding provides many important advantages over using a bottle and helps satisfy the baby's needs for intimacy, touch, interaction, and affection. Mother's milk is the perfect food for an infant. It includes antibodies, white blood cells, and certain useful bacteria that all help the baby fight infections and diseases. Because of this, breast-fed babies get fewer infections and fewer viral and bacterial diseases than do bottle-fed babies. Breast-fed babies get less constipation, less diarrhea, spit up food less often, have less smelly stools, and fewer allergies than do bottle-fed babies. New research suggests breast-feeding (and mothers not smoking after delivery) reduces the chance of unexplained deaths of healthy babies under one year old, called Sudden Infant Death Syndrome (SIDS or crib death). Breast-feeding, even for just a few months, increases your baby's intelligence and reduces the chance of your child starting school overweight or obese, with the most benefits coming from exclusive breast-feeding to six months old and continued breast-feeding past the child's first birthday. Breast-feeding is much cheaper and easier than buying formula and cleaning and sterilizing bottles. Breast-feeding helps mothers regain their figures, because the hormones involved help the uterus return to its normal size and because of the calories used up by it.

If you bottle feed your baby, hold it while feeding, to help satisfy your baby's great needs for human contact and interaction. Use only water in a bottle when you put a baby down to sleep or rest, because a bottle with milk, formula, or fruit juice keeps sweet fluids in the mouth for a long time and promotes tooth decay. A pacifier also works well in this situation.

At first you must feed your baby anywhere from 6 to 12 times a day, with each feeding lasting from 5 or 10 minutes up to 30 or 40 minutes. The baby will wake you up at night for some of these feedings for the first three or four months. Some babies sleep often and don't eat much for the first few days of life, especially those born to mothers under sedation. After the first week of life, most babies need to feed only about six or seven times a day. Babies swallow air while feeding, so you must burp your baby once or twice during the feeding and again after the feeding to avoid gas pains. The best way to burp your baby is to put it over your shoulder and lightly pat it on the back. Whenever you lay your baby down after a feeding, place the baby on its side for a while to avoid choking if the baby spits up any food.

People of Western civilizations hold their babies less than do the people of many other cultures. Many Eskimo and African tribal mothers carry their babies on their backs in a wrapped cloth pouch throughout much of the day. One study showed African women videotapes of American mothers with their children and found the African women puzzled or horrified at our lack of mother-child physical contact, asking questions like, "Why do they hate their children?" Many people note babies held more in these cultures cry and fuss less than do babies in Western civilizations. One study found carrying babies only two more hours each day reduced crying and fussing by 43%. Buy an infant pouch with straps for carrying your baby on your back or chest and wear it whenever possible, perhaps while you do household chores, run errands, or visit friends. This better satisfies your baby's needs for human contact and interaction, and you can hear or smell if the baby wets or soils its diaper and immediately clean up. This can reduce diaper rash and gives the baby the security of having its needs quickly met. Many parents enjoy sleeping with their baby or lying down with it until it goes to sleep. Both of these intimate activities are wonderful, even if you only occasionally do them.

Newborn babies sleep an average of 17 hours a day, but may only sleep for one or two hours at a time. Always place your baby on its back to sleep and never on top of soft, fluffy bedding such as comforters and pillows. Research shows these two precautions help avoid Sudden Infant Death Syndrome (crib death). It seems likely that sleeping on the stomach or on soft materials covers the baby's mouth and nose, and it dies of carbon monoxide poisoning because of breathing the trapped air it has exhaled. Using a sleeper for warmth instead of blankets is safer, but if you use a blanket, use a thin one and tuck it around the mattress so it reaches only as far as the baby's chest. Infants placed on their sides can easily roll over and sleep on their stomach, so if you put your baby down on its side after feeding to prevent choking on vomit, check on it regularly and move it onto its back to sleep later on.

Little children often feel somewhat neglected or left out when a baby arrives in the family, because parents and friends pay so much attention to the new baby. Help your other little children adjust by making sure they still get special attention from you. Make an effort to regularly play with them and compliment their behaviors. Occasionally asking them to help you with the baby also improves adjustment, even if this only means holding the baby for a minute, bringing you something you need for it, or watching so the baby doesn't get into trouble or make a mess while you do something. Make the other children feel important for helping. Tell visiting friends and family to spend a little time with the other children and not just with the baby. Many little children misbehave more after a baby's birth. This is one way they try to get more attention. Realize this is a normal reaction to losing plenty of time and attention to the newborn, but use consistent and firm discipline.

Babies cry when they are hungry, thirsty, wet, soiled, tired, bored, or uncomfortable for any reason. When you have met all your baby's needs, you can often calm it by rocking, stroking, holding, carrying, walking in a rhythmic manner, giving a pacifier, or playing with it. Play with your baby by touching or gently jiggling various parts of the baby, bouncing it on your knees, talking, singing, or dancing with it. Swaddling the baby snugly in a blanket may help, and sometimes soft music will calm a baby. Toys may also entertain your baby. Some devices made for infants and toddlers can entertain with movement: many baby swings operate for a time after you turn a crank, and some bouncing seats attach to a doorway and allow the baby to bounce around a little. If a baby swing allows your baby to lie down, you can use it before the baby can hold its own head upright. Don't use any device requiring a seated position until the baby has good neck muscle control and can easily hold its own head upright, generally at around three months.

Unfortunately, babies also cry for no reason at all. Although this can happen at any time, many parents note unsatisfiable crying often occurs during the first three months of life. Experts don't understand such crying very well, but it seems to peak at six weeks of age. Perhaps indigestion from an immature digestive system or irritability from an immature and hypersensitive nervous system causes it. Fatigue can also cause unsatisfiable crying, especially when it occurs mostly at certain parts of the day, such as late afternoon or evening. Don't become upset or overreact to this common stage or to the normal fussiness of a tired baby. Anxious parents who fuss too much over an unsatisfiable baby can further upset it.

You can often differentiate between normal crying and crying because of a serious physical problem, such as an ear infection. Crying that occurs during certain times of day and not at others is probably normal crying. Crying that begins with irritable whimpering and only gradually builds up to intense crying is also probably normal. If you can temporarily calm your baby by holding or playing with it, the problem is probably not serious. In these cases, you can either try some of the methods above or let the baby cry itself to sleep. But if your baby has a weak, whiny cry or cries without tears, consult a doctor. Other signs of illness in an infant include great irritability, poor sucking, sunken eyes, pale or grayish skin that is cool and clammy, no urination for 6 hours, acting as though moving hurts, or a fever of over 100.4 degrees in a baby under 2 months old.

Never shake an infant in anger because of its crying. You can accidentally kill a baby, put it in a coma, break its neck, rupture blood vessels, or cause learning disabilities by shaking it (Shaken Baby Syndrome), because babies under six months old have heavy heads and weak neck muscles. Although uncontrollable crying is frustrating, don't let this make you feel angry, upset, inadequate as a parent, or depressed. For a deeper understanding of the stresses of caring for a baby that can help you cope, please refer to the first two paragraphs of chapter 19, Pregnancy. These paragraphs also describe why many parents of infants become depressed.

Beginning at about three months old, start teaching your baby to cry less. When it starts to play a little after waking, instead of crying immediately, make an effort to go to the baby while it is quiet and change or feed it, if necessary, or just play with it. Make sure you often notice the quiet baby and give it attention for being quiet. Gradually, the baby will learn it doesn't need to cry to get its needs met or to get someone to pay attention to it. Similarly, when the baby plays quietly during the day, check on it regularly, even if all you have time to do is touch it, say a few words, and perhaps rearrange a toy in the crib. This reduces the baby's boredom and helps it feel you are always around, so it doesn't feel neglected. When enough time has gone by for hunger or soiling to possibly have occurred, meeting these needs without your baby needing to cry helps.

Ignoring your baby's crying in certain situations can also help teach it not to cry so much. When your baby cries, of course, check to see if it needs feeding, cleaning, etc. If you have met all the baby's needs, you may or may not have much time to comfort or play with it. If you don't, a pacifier may quiet the baby. Often, simply moving it into the room where you are busy helps because it then receives comfort from seeing you. If you have met all its physical needs and it continues to cry, you can safely ignore the crying, as long as you play with your baby many, many times a day, so you don't neglect its social needs. Sometimes a baby will eventually give up crying after you turn on loud music or television or a vacuum cleaner. Even if it continues to cry, loud noises can help you ignore the crying. Again, make sure you spend a little time paying attention to the baby when it does quiet down.

Babies often cry when you bathe, diaper, or put them to bed. Don't let your baby control you by fussing at these times. If you calmly continue these activities while ignoring the crying, your baby will eventually cry less during these routines. If you interrupt these activities to comfort the baby when you know you have met its physical needs, you only prolong these ordeals and teach the baby to repeatedly manipulate you by crying. Parents can gradually eliminate bedtime comforting, for example, going from rocking and singing to rocking, then just patting, then sitting nearby and responding to crying less, etc.

At around the age of three or four months, start trying to get your baby to sleep through a night. Feed the baby more than normal just before you go to bed. Let your baby sleep during the day, but pay attention to how long it normally sleeps and start waking it after shorter times. When your baby wakes up and cries at night, try to keep it calm and quiet during feeding or diaper changes, so it can go back to sleep. Avoid bright lights, using minimal lighting when necessary for diaper changes. When the baby is five months old, you can wait before responding to crying at night and it will probably go back to sleep in a few minutes. As the baby grows older, it will need less sleep. By one year old, babies sleep an average of 13 hours a day; by two years old, 11 hours.

By the third month of life, a baby may only feed four or five times a day. Begin feeding your baby solid foods between four and six months of age. Don't start it on solids any earlier than this. Doing so increases the chances your child will develop allergies or obesity. Start your baby with only one solid meal a day and with commercially prepared baby foods or soft cereals such as cream of wheat for the first few weeks. You can identify allergic reactions if you introduce new foods and wait four or five days before starting another new food. Begin vegetable purees before the sweeter fruit ones, so your baby won't reject vegetables. In the following weeks, gradually use solid foods at more meals and begin using bits of vegetables and fruits. Start meats later. If anyone in the family has a food allergy, consult a doctor about starting your baby on solid foods.

Babies naturally play with their food when you feed them. This is one of the ways in which they try to explore the world. Don't yell or become angry when your baby plays with its food. You don't even need to clean up immediately. By staying calm and cleaning up occasionally, you avoid making this a battle of wills. Start teaching your baby about mealtime behavior by responding playfully to messes with something like, "No, yeccht. Well, now we need to clean up!" Give very small portions of food and teach an older child to say, "more please." Make mealtime as pleasant as possible to avoid trouble, using plenty of smiling, talking, and playing to make it fun. When your baby gets older, you can get it to pay more attention to eating by letting it help you hold the cup or spoon. Babies are often reluctant to try new foods. Offer them in between other foods, again and again. Try to be patient and cheerful even when your baby repeatedly spits out new food. If you keep offering the new food, your baby will eventually eat it. It may help to alternate between a favorite food and the new food or to mix small amounts of the new food with a favorite food, later increasing the proportion of the new food in the mixture.

You can speed up your baby's learning in many ways. In the first three months of life, babies learn to focus their eyes on objects and then learn to visually track objects, follow moving objects with their eyes. Hang mobiles made of soft objects over the crib to encourage your baby to learn to follow the objects with its eyes. Mobiles with great dark and light contrast best attract a baby's attention. Bold black and white patterns are ideal. Place the mobile between 12 and 18 inches away from the baby because it can focus its eyes only on close objects at first. Play games that develop visual tracking by moving yourself or an object within your baby's field of vision and waiting for the baby's eyes to follow.

The more stimulation your baby receives, the more it will learn. Encourage exploring objects by giving your baby a variety of safe objects to see and touch. The best toys for the first six months of life fit into two categories. One is any safe object small enough that the baby can pick it up and move it from one hand to the other, yet big enough that the baby can't swallow it. Another category is anything that clearly responds to a baby's action, so the baby begins to learn cause and effect relationships. This includes rattles, toys that make a noise when the baby squeezes them, mobiles that move when touched or when the crib shakes, etc. Frequently changing toys also stimulates the baby and helps avoid boredom.

Environmental stimulation promotes learning, too. Prop your baby upright whenever possible, so it can look around. Carrying your baby in a pouch or using seated swing or bouncing devices help by providing a constantly changing environment. Don't leave your baby in a boring crib or playpen for too long. Move your baby in the room, from room to room, and outside to give it a variety of things to see. If you use a playpen, move it and change the toys in it often. Whenever possible, move your baby so it can see you work in the house. Babies enjoy being able to see or hear you nearby.

Between the ages of three and six months, babies learn to reach for, grasp, and hold objects. Help your baby develop its grip by putting something in its hands and then playfully tugging on it or shaking it. At this age, babies can also begin learning object permanence, that objects still exist whether the baby sees them or not. The game peekaboo helps teach this: hide your face behind your hands or something else and then suddenly uncover it while enthusiastically saying, "Peekaboo!" Teach object permanence, too, by hiding one of your baby's favorite toys behind your hands or something else and playfully asking, "Where did it go?" Then surprise your baby by taking it out and saying, "Here it is!"

A baby's interactions with its parents play an extremely important role in the development of its intelligence. By frequently talking and playing with your baby, you can speed up its progress in talking and learning things. Whenever you try to teach it something, remember babies have very short attention spans, so they get distracted easily and lose interest in things after a short time. Keep your teaching playful and fun, and stop whenever your baby begins to lose interest.

When you talk to your baby, make sure it can see your face. Your baby learns to talk by watching you talk and by babbling back to you. Encourage babbling by keeping your house quiet. Help your baby pay attention to its own noises and babbling by imitating the sounds. At six or seven months old, make this game a little more sophisticated by occasionally making variations on the noises your baby makes when you imitate them. Try prolonging the sound, speeding it up, adding a sound to it, shortening it, or changing the pitch. At the same age, give your baby a pacifier less often, perhaps using the pacifier mainly for naps, crying, and thumb sucking. Using a pacifier too much can reduce your baby's babbling and delay the development of talking.

At some point, make sure your baby can hear you. Surprise it by quietly approaching from behind and making a loud clap. This should startle your baby. Some other time, quietly approach your baby from behind and softly say something to it. See if your baby tries to look your way. If your baby never responds to this, consult a doctor about your baby's hearing.

Babies will repeatedly drop things and want you to pick them up. Don't let this upset you. They simply find pleasure in their newfound talent of holding things and dropping them at will, and your picking them up so they can do it again is a new social game they have invented. Don't turn this into a battle of wills by angrily scolding the child. Play the game whenever you please, but quit whenever you get bored with it. The baby will soon learn you don't want to do this forever.

Many books say babies learn to roll over between three and six months old and learn to crawl between six and nine months old, but new research suggests putting babies on their backs to sleep to prevent Sudden Infant Death Syndrome (SIDS or crib death) has changed this. Babies lying on their stomachs roll over to see more and learn to crawl when squirming moves them, but babies who sleep on their backs roll over and crawl later, with one-third of these babies never crawling before they walk. Even so, babies of both sleeping positions start walking at around one year old, on average.

You can encourage rolling over by playfully moving so your baby must try to roll over to see you. When your baby can roll over, don't leave it alone on a bed or changing table, even for a short time, because falls are common baby injuries. Encourage crawling by putting your baby on its stomach during the day, reaching under its stomach, lifting it a little, and helping it move and by putting things just beyond its reach. Whenever possible, give your baby room to crawl around and explore. An adjustable expanding gate that fits any doorway can create a space for this. Any time you leave your baby alone, you must childproof its environment. Keep all sharp objects, small objects it could swallow, breakable objects, pet water dishes it might drown in, toxic houseplants such as philodendron it might taste, and chemicals far out of your baby's reach. Never store chemicals such as cleansers, medicines, spray cans, and alcoholic drinks in low storage areas. Put caps on all the electrical outlets because a baby's face can become terribly disfigured by sucking on an electrical cord juncture or by biting into an electrical wire. Remove lamps or tables the baby could pull over.

You can encourage standing up and walking by holding your baby upright by its hands. Gradually let your baby do some of the work when you pull it upright. Help your baby learn to pull itself up by grabbing onto furniture, and help it learn to stand or to walk a little while holding onto furniture. Research shows using a baby walker actually slows learning to sit up, crawl, and walk. Baby walkers are associated with more injuries (including skull fractures, concussions, and many deaths) than any other baby product, and most of these accidents happen right in front of adults. If you insist on using one, buy only safety certified walkers, which are either stationary, too wide for standard doorways, or have a mechanism to stop it if one wheel goes over a step. If you use any other walker or have a wider than average stairway, be sure to fix a gate on any stairway the baby might fall down. Babies generally learn to walk short distances around ten months to one year old. When your baby can walk, childproofing involves making sure it can't reach the stove, pull over hot foods, burn itself with a scalding hot water faucet, nor reach the toilet where it might drown. Set the water heater at a lower temperature to prevent scalding.

Between the ages of six months and one year, babies learn a great deal about language. By the age of one, many can say a few words and understand and follow simple instructions. Of course, your baby will learn these things only if you frequently talk and play with and teach it. For example, you can teach your baby to come to you by repeatedly saying, "Come here," while physically getting your baby yourself. Teach the names for many things by pointing to them and naming them, again and again. Point out and name body parts on yourself, on your baby, on dolls, or in pictures. Make a game of finding objects. Playfully ask where the dog is and then take your baby's hand and point it at the dog while you enthusiastically say, "There's the dog!" Make a game of passing an object back and forth, petting a cat or dog, rolling a ball, hiding an object, smelling a flower, etc. All the while, describe the action to your baby while you play. For example: "Here comes the ball. It's rolling right up to you!" or "Is the doll behind the chair? No. Is the doll on the desk? Yes! Here it is!" Introduce your baby to books and magazines and name the objects pictured in them as one of you points to them.

When your baby makes a noise that sounds like a word, make a big fuss over it. Give enthusiastic praise. Show excitement whenever it even tries to say a word. The first attempts won't be very clear. Gradually teach your baby to be more precise in saying words. In teaching your child, describe not only objects, events, feelings, and actions, but also some very simple reasons, explanations, and causes. It doesn't matter whether your baby is old enough to understand you. The more you talk and explain things, the more it will learn. The baby will absorb much of what you say and this process helps it develop language and learn about the world.

Toddlers

At around 1 1/2 years old, most toddlers can walk upstairs by themselves using the wall for support. By 2 years old, most start putting together two words at a time, such as, "Go bye-bye?" Around the age of 3, most toddlers start putting together very simple sentences such as, "I wanna go!" The brilliant scientist Albert Einstein didn't talk until he was 4 years old, however. Most parents become concerned if their child doesn't talk by 2 or 3. If your child doesn't talk at the age of 2, you have probably eliminated the need for talking by getting things when your child points and makes gestures. Insist that your child make attempts at speaking to get breakfast, be picked up and carried, etc., but don't make it too difficult or frustrating. Begin by enthusiastically rewarding attempts at talking. Gradually teach and demand more precision in speaking. Eventually, teach your child the use of sentences.

Toddlers can really worry and upset their parents with stubborn misbehavior. They often delight in breaking rules and in yelling, "No!" Parents often fear their children will turn out to be horrible little monsters, but the terrible toddler stage is a normal part of growing up. Toddlers must learn rules for behavior in every area of life, from toilet training to getting along with others, so they naturally want to assert their independence. Misbehaving is the mark of the child's budding individuality and independence and is great fun because it results in plenty of parental attention. Despite this phase, the vast majority of children turn out all right.

Have faith in your child. Don't use negative labels by constantly saying things like, "You're so bad!" As we shall soon see, constantly scolding and insulting your child may cause low self-esteem and further misbehavior, in a self-fulfilling prophecy. Instead, parents need to catch their children being good as often as possible and to reward good behavior with attention and appreciation. Toddlers also need a great deal of training to play nicely with other children, share toys, take turns, show kindness, help around the house, etc. Use the techniques in this chapter to avoid problems and develop good behaviors. The fun activities in the section on Making Learning Fun in this chapter also help keep a toddler busy and out of trouble.

Hide toys your toddler has tired of and use them again weeks later. Try to get to know your neighbors, so they can become part of your child's social life. Children eight years old or older can make great babysitters if you stay around. They can match the toddler's energy level and add common sense to activities. Responsible adolescents can generally care for toddlers alone. Because toddlers are so much work, you might relax your standards a little for meals and household duties. Perhaps popcorn and a peanut butter and jelly sandwich will do for supper one day.

Try to use the same caretakers for your toddler regularly; constantly changing them is very stressful. Close friends or family members are ideal. If possible, arrange to visit with a new babysitter or daycare several times before leaving your child there. Begin with brief separations, perhaps leaving several of your child's favorite toys, and gradually work up to longer times. If you can, stay until your child settles in. Describe your child-rearing values, approach to discipline, and your toddler's likes, dislikes, strengths, vulnerabilities, worries, fears, and daily routine to the babysitter or staff. Describe special events at home (visiting grandparents, movies, etc.), so the caretaker can discuss them with your child. Concrete reminders of your love can help. You might leave a family photo album to show and discuss later, your picture, or an audiotape of you talking or singing to your child or telling a story. Try to visit at lunch or call on the phone.

Despite controversy over the effects of child care, researchers agree daycare has far less impact on children's mental and emotional development than does the family environment. The most important things are the attention, responsiveness, and intellectual stimulation from the parents and their emotional maturity. Good quality daycare can help improve intellectual abilities such as language, memory, knowledge, and vocabulary. But the best government study found an unexplained correlation between time spent by toddlers in any kind of child care, whether with nannies, relatives, or daycare centers, and aggressive, disobedient, and defiant behaviors later, between the ages of 4 and 1/2 and 6. In the study, 17% (a small minority) of children who spent over 30 hours a week in child care later showed the problems, but only 6% of those who spent less than 10 hours a week in child care did. It is unclear if child care causes this. Perhaps stressed families tend to use more child care, or perhaps parents who use more child care have wilder children in the first place. Perhaps the mediocre quality of most child care is to blame. We also don't know if the problems persist as the children grow up.

Choose the daycare with the best ratio of staff to children. The more staff members per child, the more individual attention each child receives, the more effective the supervision, and the more your child will learn, both intellectually and socially. The ideal ratio is three to five toddlers per adult, with each adult assigned to specific children for maximum familiarity and security. The presence of another adult gives emotional support, time for needed breaks, and reduces the likelihood of abuse. Large groups of children are noisy, create distractions, and are less easy to manage, even with enough adults present. A group size no larger than eight or ten children meets children's needs better and allows playfulness without the need for rigid group control.

A good daycare will have many opportunities for developing motor and visual skills through play and exploration. Look for such things as toys you build, puzzles, playground equipment, housekeeping utensils for imaginative play, dolls, action figures, play furniture, musical instruments, dress-up clothes, play dough, and painting equipment. Try to occasionally stop in unexpectedly at the daycare. This is the best way to make sure the supervision, safety, nutrition, and discipline are as they should be and that no abuse is occurring.

Toilet Training and Bedwetting

Don't attempt toilet training until your child is two years old, because children have a very hard time learning to control the urinary and anal sphincter muscles before this age. Some clues your toddler is ready for it include staying dry for longer periods and urinating a larger amount at one time instead of many smaller episodes. Choose a time free of stresses such as a death in the family or travel.

Always toilet train your toddler in a relaxed, pleasant, and unhurried manner. Rushing in the morning, pushing your child too hard for success, scolding, punishing, or becoming angry for a failure in control can start a battle of wills or make your child so concerned that anxiety may interfere with progress. Use a friendly, patient, understanding, approach. Remember toilet training takes time and all children have plenty of failures before they learn control. Even after a child gains good control, failures are normal for a time, especially during stressful times or when an interesting or fun activity preoccupies the child.

During toilet training, make sure your toddler always wears clothing that is easy to remove without your help. Buy either a small potty chair or a child's potty insert for the regular toilet. These devices make using the toilet much easier and much less scary because a toddler can fall halfway into the adult toilet and must learn to balance on it. A child's potty chair with a tray (see Kids Stuff catalog at the end of this chapter) makes it easy to give the toddler a book, toy, or snack while waiting.

The first step is to teach words for the bodily functions and what you want your child to do. Many parents use the words "pee" for urination and "poop" for defecation. When you clean diapers or soiled clothes, you can show where the feces go by putting them in the toilet and flushing it. Playing with dolls and pretending the doll needs to use the toilet can also help. Dolls that can take water in the mouth and release it as urine are particularly useful. Be sure to excitedly praise the doll for proper elimination. Act out successful elimination with dolls many times to teach your child what to do.

Ask your child to tell you whenever the urge to eliminate arises. This will take time. At first your child will probably come and tell you after wetting or soiling clothes. You can help by paying attention to natural patterns and behaviors that may indicate the need to eliminate. Begin by writing down the times of day when your child urinates and defecates for four or five days. Next, look at this list for any patterns. Many children tend to eliminate after certain meals or at certain times of day. The urge to urinate often makes a child grab the groin area or become animated, and some children strain or grunt at the urge to defecate. If any of these things happen, put your child on the potty. If nothing happens, bring a toy or book and keep the child there for a few minutes to relax and let it happen, but not more than five minutes—you don't want to make this a battle of wills. When your child does eliminate in the right place, use plenty of praise to instill pride. You can also reward success with a cookie or some other treat. Teach girls to wipe themselves from the front to the back, so feces from the anus don't get into the vagina and cause infection.

Another helpful technique is causing your child to need to urinate when you want to practice, by giving plenty of fluids to drink. Soon you can put your child on the potty and announce the success. If you do this a number of times and allow the child to tell you when the urge to urinate arises, the child can learn what sensations to look for at a time when you both know the sensations will arise. Occasionally using this method, along with the previous approaches, can speed up toilet training. Never force drinking excessively if the child doesn't want to, however; this would probably interfere with toilet training.

Children generally continue to wet the bed at night for a time after daytime failures in controlling elimination become rare. Within the next six months after successful toilet training, most children stop wetting the bed because of increased experience in daytime bladder control. Some children take much longer and have bedwetting problems until they are three or four years old. You may want to keep using diapers at night until the bedwetting stops. Don't scold, punish, or become angry about the wet bed. Remember that anxiety can interfere with your child's improvement. You should eliminate any drinking of fluids after supper, ask your child to use the bathroom before going to bed, wake your child up to use the bathroom when you go to bed, and praise your child on mornings when the bed is dry. If your child urinates frequently and is constantly thirsty, see a doctor about the possibility of diabetes.

A waterproof mattress cover helps in dealing with bedwetting at any age. You can make a very cheap waterproof mattress cover out of a thick plastic tarpaulin by cutting it big enough to tuck under the mattress. If bedwetting continues after the child's fifth birthday, continue the previous approaches and add the following. Train your child to change the bed, clean the mattress cover, and put clean sheets on the bed at night whenever the bedwetting occurs, putting the wet sheets into a plastic trash bag or some other convenient place. Once your child knows how to do this, let the bed stay wet if your child refuses to clean it. Calmly emphasize your child now holds this responsibility. Remember to use plenty of praise on mornings when the bed is dry. This often helps cure the bedwetting, probably because having to perform this chore in the middle of the night adds some extra motivation for solving the problem.

Certain urinary exercises can also help older children.   Teach bedwetting children who are at least five years old to practice holding their urine. This means becoming accustomed to a full bladder by drinking plenty of water or other fluids and then resisting the urge to urinate. Learning to resist the urge to urinate for a longer time, thereby holding more fluid in the bladder, helps in establishing nighttime bladder control. Kegel exercises, contracting the muscle that stops the flow of urine, also help. After learning to contract the muscle by stopping a urine flow, your child can practice contracting this muscle more easily and more often by doing it at other times, without the flow of urine.

The DRI Sleeper (see the listing in resources at end of the chapter) and the Wet Stop system (Sears catalog) are both electronic devices that help older children who wet their beds. Sensors detect wetness and immediately set off an alarm at the first sign of wetness, so the child can finish urinating in the bathroom. The first few nights, you may need to wake a child who sleeps deeply through the alarm.

When children over five years old wet their beds and especially when a child regresses to bedwetting after having had nighttime bladder control for a period, you should consult a urologist because the problem may involve urinary infections or certain other problems with the urinary system. Even without a physical problem, the doctor can prescribe the bedtime use of DDAVP, a new nasal spray containing a hormone that reduces urination. Very often, psychological pressures cause the late or regressive bedwetting. Consider what stresses or problems exist in the child's life or family. Parental conflict or even the birth of a new baby may cause the problem. Working to improve these problems or to reduce their impact may help cure the bedwetting.

Thumb Sucking, Nail Biting, and Stuttering

Thumb sucking, biting fingernails, and stuttering shouldn't particularly worry parents of preschool children. Thumb sucking is a natural behavior that occurs even in the womb, generally peaking around the baby's seventh month. Reduce this habit without decreasing feedings by waiting until your baby is three months old, then giving your baby a pacifier whenever it sucks its own thumb. Babies who use a pacifier want to quit as toddlers, but toddlers who suck their thumbs may continue the habit for much longer. Bored children suck their thumbs more, so playing and keeping your child busy will reduce the habit. Many children suck their thumbs more when they feel tired. If you notice this pattern, try putting your child to bed earlier.

Thumb sucking for hours every day can cause protruding teeth (buckteeth), but this can't happen before four years old or without a great deal of sucking. There is no need to say or do anything else unless your child still sucks the thumb for hours every day at four years old. Don't show anger, tease, nag, scold, or punish your child for this habit. These responses increase stress and make thumb sucking more likely. Putting substances that taste terrible on the thumb is also ineffective.

If your child still sucks the thumb for hours every day at four years old, explain that this bad habit can cause the teeth to grow outward as buckteeth. Tell your child not to worry because it takes a very long time and a great deal of sucking for this to happen. Then say you will help with this bad habit and describe the following procedures. First, you will give reminders to stop sucking whenever you notice it. (Always do this in a calm, pleasant tone of voice.) Whenever you notice thumb sucking while watching television, you will turn off the TV for 15 minutes. If your child is over six years old, make the consequence turning off the TV for half an hour. If other family members are watching the TV, however, you will simply send the child out of the room for the penalty period.

Make the stressful transition period easier by keeping your child busy to reduce thumb sucking and giving plenty of praise for taking the thumb out of the mouth. Rewards can also help, but don't be too strict and make your child feel like a failure. Count how often you notice thumb sucking each day, and reward small improvements with a later bedtime, desserts or extra snacks, by playing favorite games in the evening, etc. You can reward good weeks with picnics, special trips, movies, etc.

The habit of biting fingernails is harmless enough that parents can simply ignore it. If you notice this habit just developing, however, you can use gentle reminders and offer to trim your child's nails whenever you see the biting. You may motivate girls to quit with a promise to allow the use of nail polish after they quit nail biting. If you see no improvement in about a month, stop giving the reminders and ignore the nail biting. Never let this issue become a battle of wills. Parents who nag, scold, yell at, or punish their children for nail biting add unnecessary stress that can make the problem worse. If an older child expresses a desire to quit, teach the techniques in chapter 34, Nervous Habits.

Occasional speech disturbances are a normal part of learning to talk, but perhaps 1 in 30 preschool-age children stutter for several months. Without treatment, most eventually stop. Only about 1 in 100 school-age children continue, with boys outnumbering girls by 4 to 1. You can help your child end early symptoms of occasional stuttering with a few simple actions. Listen patiently and show you are paying attention by making eye contact or using sounds like "yeah," "uh-huh," "Oh," or "hmm" to acknowledge the message. Encourage your child to speak more slowly and to repeat unclear words. Role model by pausing before you reply, then answering slowly and calmly. Spend at least five minutes a day in relaxed conversation with your child. Encourage family conversation at meals, and read and tell stories frequently.

Don't correct, finish sentences, tell your child to relax or think before talking, make your child start over or perform speeches, encourage talking faster, nag, scold, rush, punish, nor become angry, upset, or very concerned. These responses add pressure and prolong the problem. If stuttering frustrates the child or continues for several months, consult a speech therapist. Speech therapy with preschool children may take only weeks. Rates of complete success from speech therapy are highest in preschool children, but older children can benefit. Older children will benefit from practicing reading aloud favorite stories or subjects.

Bedtime, Mornings, and Meals

Parents often think they need to nag their children constantly to get them to bed at night, ready for school on time in the mornings, to behave during meals, or to finish their meals in a reasonable amount of time. Unfortunately, nagging frustrates both parent and child and rewards the dawdling or misbehavior with attention.

Some fussing at bedtime is quite normal, but creating a bedtime routine reduces problems like complaining, begging, or finding excuses to get back up. Bedtime routines prepare children by giving plenty of advance warning, establishing some quiet time that helps them settle down, and using a pleasant, familiar routine that helps them learn and accept bedtime rules. First, choose a reasonable bedtime. Then about one hour before bedtime, tell your child it is time for calm, quiet activities because bedtime is near. Don't allow any wild behavior, loudness, or physical exertion during this last hour because an excited child probably won't want to go to bed. Next, point out when bedtime is about 10 or 15 minutes away and ask your child to get ready for bed.

Once you choose a bedtime routine, use it consistently, so your child becomes familiar with it. Many parents enjoy indulging in some wild play, perhaps with some tickling or tumbling, before the quiet period. The quiet period may include a long bath playing with toys or a snack just before brushing the teeth and going to bed. Young children love to end the day with bedtime stories. With older children, you might read sections of longer books each night or share interesting library books (on astronomy, American Indians, etc.) with plenty of pictures. Bedtime is a good time to discuss the day's events. Ask your children how the day went, what was fun or nice, what was worrisome or disappointing, what good or kind acts they performed, what they did well, and what they could have done better. Keep it pleasant, however. Don't lecture or scold. You can encourage reading by allowing a bedtime half an hour later if your child is quietly reading in bed. Any bedtime routine you create should end with a kiss or hug good night.

Make sure your bedtime routine shows your love for your child. Don't rush though it, even if you feel tired. If an uncooperative or misbehaving child fails to get ready for bed on time, a natural consequence is to eliminate the snack, long bath with the toys, or bedtime story, but try to remain calm and friendly. Don't threaten a punishment. Use a friendly reminder to hurry so your child won't miss the story or toys in the bath. Show your love by being a little flexible at times. If a child is unusually active, you might allow a later bedtime that night. You might occasionally allow a child to stay up late or sleep with you, as a special treat. But make sure most of the time and under most conditions, you enforce the fixed bedtime. This helps your child learn and accept the rules.

Never yell "Go to sleep!" Children can't just go to sleep at will. Instead, tell them to relax and enjoy resting and sleep will follow. Toys or books in bed or a night light or radio in the room can help. Encourage toddlers to soothe themselves when they go to bed or wake up at night. They can hug their pillow or a special stuffed animal or talk or sing softly to themselves. You might ask them to talk to themselves about the things they will do when it is time to get up. Many toddlers respond well to a musical mobile with a soothing lullaby.

Teaching a toddler to sleep alone for the first time can be troublesome. Temporarily allowing full light or sleeping in a sibling's room can help.

Another approach involves explaining you will ignore all talk or screaming and you will close the door until the child remains quiet, then you will open the door. If the child cries for twenty minutes, give a reminder that you're ready to open the door as soon as you hear silence. This works with most children. You must ignore any crying or questions and remain firm to teach your child to accept the new rule. Even occasionally giving in slows training by indicating a temper tantrum will sometimes work. If your child gets up and comes out of the room repeatedly, use a gate on the door. For taller children, you may need two gates, one above the other. Without gates, calmly explain your rule and put the child back to bed each time. Don't argue, talk about anything else, nor show affection. These things reward your child with attention for getting up. A plastic cup of water nearby may comfort, but the first few nights, it may result in an angry child throwing the water.

A toddler cannot calm anxieties about sleeping alone and stop fussing for some future reward, but rewards and penalties can help in establishing new bedtime rules for older children. You can reward going to bed on time without fussing with a privilege, such as quiet use of the radio in bed. Bedtime problems should result in the loss of the privilege. Don't waste your time nagging, nor provoke rebellion by yelling about bedtime behaviors. Simply state the rule and enforce the consequences. With school-aged children, you may want to build a reward system (see the section on Discipline in this chapter) that includes bedtime behavior.

Nightmares are quite common in preschool children and decrease in frequency as children grow older, although many adults report regular nightmares. After a nightmare, simply offer comfort and reassurance. Don't ask questions about the dream; this may only prolong the feelings or make it worse. Allow your child to talk, and then offer reassurance about safety, emphasizing that no harm will come. As your child calms down, you can change the topic of conversation to more pleasant things, and you might leave a light on for a while for extra comfort and security.

You can wake a child from a nightmare to end it. In contrast, it is very difficult to wake up a child from sleep terrors. Sleep terrors (or night terrors) usually begin with a panicky scream and last one to ten minutes. They are far less common than nightmares. The child appears intensely afraid and may yell, cry, talk incoherently, kick, thrash about, breathe heavily, sweat, or sleepwalk. When you try to give comfort, the child may push you away, hit you, try to get away, or stare at you without recognizing you. Although children often don't really wake up during these episodes, they usually appear to fall asleep immediately afterward and don't remember it.   If the child wakes up, no detailed dream is recalled.

Do not try to wake children from sleep terrors.   Remain calm and remember they will go back to sleep and won't remember it.   Gently restrain a child who tries to get out of bed.   Be sure to explain the problem to any babysitter.   Frequent or long sleep terrors are rare.   If they persist, let your child get plenty of sleep.   This will help by decreasing the deep delta sleep associated with sleep terrors.   Waking these children at the right time can help, however.   First, observe how long after the child goes to sleep, the sleep terrors normally occur.   Then wake your child each night 10 or 15 minutes before the normal time of the sleep terrors.   If these usually effective treatments don't help, ask a doctor for medicines that may help.

Sleepwalking may include walking up or down stairs, urinating in the wrong place, eating, talking, or even going outdoors.   A minor episode may just involve sitting up and perhaps talking.   Most episodes last from one to thirty minutes.   The child may wake up and be confused or may go back to sleep and never remember it.   Don't bother trying to wake up sleepwalking children; this is often difficult to do.   Just guide them back to bed.   Because sleepwalking children may injure themselves, lock all your windows and doors, clear the bedroom area of toys or furniture they might trip over, and put a gate across the top of stairs.

Many parents find it difficult to get their children dressed and ready for daycare or school on time.   First, of course, children must learn to dress themselves.   When buying clothes for toddlers, get mostly easy slip-on clothes rather than tiny buttons or bow ties.   Before teaching how to put clothes on, teach how to recognize the inside, outside, front, and back of clothes while you dress the child, making it a game and giving plenty of praise for correct answers.   At first praise any attempt to get dressed, even if your child puts clothes on wrong and you must do it over.   Make it easier by breaking down the tasks into small steps, with you helping less and less as time goes on.   Children can help pull up pant legs before they can get their feet through them.   It is much easier to sit down to put their feet through pant legs than trying to do it while standing.   Teach them to put on pullover shirts and sweaters over the head first, so they can see to get their arms in the right places.

Let your child choose between outfits to increase feelings of independence and reduce opposition.   Give praise for every little skill in getting dressed, no matter how much help you must provide.   Children naturally play and get distracted and dress slowly. Remain calm. Begging, nagging, or getting angry rewards them with attention for taking too long and makes things worse. Both you and your child should get up early enough so you can keep the chore pleasant. If your child has just learned to get dressed alone, check every few minutes and give plenty of praise for progress in dressing.

Several rules help in dealing with children on school mornings. Insist that they completely finish dressing before eating breakfast, that no child can watch television until all the children are dressed, and that taking too long to dress eliminates breakfast. If your children like to watch cartoons while having breakfast or before leaving for school, they will encourage each other to get dressed so they can watch. The rule about missing breakfast may seem harsh but is very effective; you won't need to enforce it very often. You can also use the rule about missing breakfast for preschool-aged children if they don't cooperate and slow you down too much while you try to dress them, but you should give them bread or crackers to eat on the way to where you are going. Don't nag or yell. Use a calm voice to occasionally remind your child not to miss breakfast by taking too long. If you don't want to use the rule about missing breakfast, use other privileges. If an uncooperative toddler slows you down in the morning, you might forbid watching TV that afternoon.

Mealtimes are excellent times for the whole family to come together and communicate. Consider waiting to serve a meal until all the family arrives. Include your children in the conversation by asking them questions and discussing topics that interest them. If you talk only to the adults at a meal for a time, boredom may lead children to misbehave. Don't make mealtimes unpleasant by heaping food on your children's plates and nagging them to eat it all. Avoid a battle of wills by serving them only as much food as they normally eat. You can always offer a second helping when a child finishes a plate. Encourage your children to eat a nutritious variety of foods with the following rule: people who don't finish their plates may not eat dessert or any snacks before the next meal. Often a child who doesn't eat well at meals simply isn't hungry because of snacking between meals. If your child repeatedly misses dessert and snacks because of one disliked food, put a very small amount of it on the child's plate the next time you serve it. This encourages the child to earn dessert and snacks by eating it. Then gradually increase the amount of disliked food as your child becomes accustomed to eating it.

Some parents allow their children to wander out of their seats and act silly at mealtimes, and then wonder why they can't control them when company comes for supper or when they go out to eat. Train your children to behave at meals every day. For good hygiene, insist that they wash their hands before any meal. Teach them never to spit out food, play with their food, nor leave their seats to play unless they have finished eating. Use time out to enforce these rules. If a child old enough to know the rules requires more than one time out during a meal, take that child's plate and refuse any dessert or snacks before the next meal; you won't need to enforce this effective rule very often.

If your children play and talk and take too long to eat, set a reasonable time limit for the meal, one that allows for pleasant conversation but not for excessive dawdling. Gently remind your children when they are not eating and when the time limit approaches. If they don't finish eating by the time limit, take their plates and refuse any snacks before the next meal. Again, you won't need to do this very often. Never give in to a hungry child who has lost the right to finish a meal or eat snacks, because this only teaches the child not to take you seriously.

Helpful Ways of Showing Your Love

Affectionate behavior helps avoid problems by keeping you close to your children. Many ways to show affection use the sense of touch. You can gently stroke your children, lovingly ruffle or play with their hair, hug or kiss them, massage them, or pat them on the arm, head, shoulder, back, hand, etc. You can also show affection by telling your children you love them, by saying what you enjoy or appreciate about them, smiling, using loving facial expressions, and with an occasional special treat or privilege. Do these things often, not just when they have done something good.

Show your love by spending plenty of time talking, playing, and doing things with your children. No matter how busy you are, make a special effort to devote a little time completely focused on each child every day. This helps make each feel loved. Spend some of this time listening to your child's ideas and feelings and asking about recent activities. Use the good listening skills described in chapter 6, Communication Skills, to invite your child to say more and deepen understanding. Explain you always want to listen but if you are too busy, you will make time to listen later. Spend time sharing interests and activities with your children, too. You might include family outings, games, singing, reading aloud to one another, or many of the interests and activities listed in chapter 8.

Spending plenty of time with them in the above ways helps avoid problems by keeping you close to your children and naturally allowing communication. Children whose parents often ignore them will misbehave a great deal to achieve the parental attention and involvement they desperately need. You can sometimes use activities or working together on a project to open up communication when you suspect a problem and your child might not be comfortable with the issue. The activity makes it less of a focus of the encounter and therefore less threatening and less likely to seem like prying. Sharing activities with your children also helps develop interests and activities, which are important in happiness and mental health. Children who feel close to their parents and develop a wide range of interests and activities have more self-esteem and less severe behavioral problems than others do.

Praise your child regularly. Few parents realize how effective and how important praise is. No matter how troublesome a child is, you can always catch the child in good behavior and praise or thank the child. Each time you do this, you encourage more good behavior and build up a self-image as a good person. This is much more effective than simply giving punishments for bad behaviors. A child's self-image comes mostly from the parents' evaluations, and a good self-image gives the child the confidence to improve. Focusing on the good increases closeness and cooperation by keeping your relationship warm and positive. You can also occasionally use rewards such as extra play time outdoors, a late bedtime, your own time and attention playing games, or a special treat for good behavior, but make your reason for rewarding the child clear.

To make praise effective, use it much more often than you scold or discipline your child. Very young children especially need regular praise for good behaviors. It repeatedly teaches them what behaviors you want and appreciate. Notice and praise good behavior in very young children many, many times a day, at least five or ten times as often as you scold them. This only takes a few seconds each time but it can do wonders. Praise or thank your child for the simplest things, such as playing quietly, kindness toward the cat, using a book carefully, waiting patiently while you talk on the phone, taking turns, or sharing. As children grow older and develop a positive self-image, they won't need praise so often, but you should never stop praising. Even teenagers need regular thanks and praise for their talents, virtues, routine chores, and helpful acts. Occasionally give praise in front of other people or to your spouse when the child can hear you.

Be careful to avoid praising your child for not doing something bad, however. For example, never say "Good! You're not being mean!" or "I'm so glad you're not bothering the cat! That's wonderful!" Thanking your child for not doing something bad ruins the positive emphasis of praise, implying that the child's normal behavior is much worse. By mentioning bad behavior, it can also suggest the idea of misbehaving. Instead, say "Good! You're being so friendly!" or "You're treating the cat so carefully and nicely! That's wonderful!" Always describe praiseworthy actions in a positive way by describing the good behavior, rather than the avoidance of bad behavior.

Unfortunately, it is all too easy to ignore good behavior and to notice mostly the bad things your child does. Some parents make the mistake of often calling their children negative things such as bad, brats, stupid, mean, shy, etc. Repeatedly using negative labels may cause a child to have low self-esteem, to believe the label fits, to feel unable to change, and to act accordingly. During childhood, despite an angry refusal to accept such labels, being bad (or stupid, mean, a brat, etc.) can seem like a fact of life the child cannot change without superhuman effort. In a self-fulfilling prophecy, these children may give up trying to improve themselves and may live up to the social role implied by the negative label.

Good communication skills help avoid the use of negative labels. Parents naturally have both good and bad feelings about their children, but you can express your anger over their behaviors in useful ways or in unkind or aggravating ways. Many of the communication problems described in chapter 6 tend to make your child more angry and less cooperative, but the communication skills in chapter 6 help keep your focus on problem behaviors (actions, words, tone of voice, and facial expression) and help avoid attacking your child's character.

Parents should also express love by encouraging children and showing faith in their abilities. Encourage and expect your child to develop talents, but avoid unrealistic demands. Demanding perfection frustrates your children and may even lead them to rebel or give up. Because parents' evaluations are so important to a child's self-image, showing confidence in your children helps them grow in confidence and self-esteem. Point out developing skills in your child. Learn to notice small improvements. Praise the progress, even if the child still needs to do much more. Praise work and effort, even after failure. Your child will occasionally need cheering up or reassurance. Always try to give hope, but emphasize that many things come only with long, persistent effort.

Certain research emphasizes the importance of adults' expectations in children's development, repeatedly showing teachers' expectations of young children may become self-fulfilling prophecies. When researchers mislead teachers about the intelligence and ability of their students, children who receive superior labels more often improve on later IQ tests than do those who receive average labels, although teachers never tell children about the labels. Several studies observed teachers to find out how their expectations affected children and noted differences in the way teachers behave toward supposedly superior, average, and poor students. When interacting with supposedly superior students, teachers tend to ask them more questions, lean forward more, use more eye contact, nod their heads more, smile more, and attempt to teach more information to them than supposedly slower students. With slower students, teachers tend to explain more and repeat themselves more often, which may slow the learning process. In these subtle ways, teachers made learning more fun and interesting for supposedly brighter students. Perhaps this led to the gains in test scores.

Parents' expectations are also important in their children's moral character. If your child has done wrong, express your disappointment and anger, set an appropriate punishment, forgive, and then show faith in the child's basic goodness and expect improvement. Even after a serious mistake or two, try to trust that your child will eventually mature and make wise decisions. If you lose faith in your child, you may communicate your negative expectations directly or inadvertently and this only compounds the child's problems, increases frustration, and damages the child's self-esteem. This may lead to a deteriorating relationship between the two of you and to further misdeeds in a self-fulfilling prophecy. Forgiveness bathes the child in love, and faith in your child's basic goodness encourages improvement.

Setting a Good Example

Actions speak louder than words.
(English proverb)

Children naturally observe and imitate what they see other people doing, especially their parents, and this helps them learn how to act. They learn by imitation the kinds of behaviors and feelings they see around them every day. To raise good children, then, parents must set a good example. As role models, parents must develop qualities and virtues if they want their children to show these qualities and virtues. Children will often do as you do, even if you insist they shouldn't do such things. You will make mistakes, of course, but you should strive to act virtuously and to practice what you preach.

When parents treat each other and their children with politeness, kindness, and helpfulness, the children generally learn to act similarly. By growing up with love, children learn how to love. If both parents give thanks and show appreciation for routine acts of helpfulness, their children usually learn to appreciate such things, too. If you listen carefully and help children when they have problems, you increase the likelihood they will listen to you and cooperate when you feel upset. If you show patience, express your anger in effective ways, and compromise to resolve personal conflicts, you give them the opportunity to learn these skills, too.

If you act rudely or yell and fight, your children will probably behave in similar ways. If you don't have much patience and you regularly shout at family members, instead of normally treating them with respect, your children will probably lack patience, shout frequently, and show disrespect, too. Studies suggest yelling excites youngsters, so they become more likely to misbehave. It's fine to raise your voice a little above your normal conversation level to give it the authoritative quality of a command. Parents do occasionally need to shout at their children to get their attention during a commotion. No parent is perfect, of course, but parents who yell every day or many times a week teach anger, rather than patience, by the example they set. Yelling also creates negative feelings that make your children less likely to cooperate. If you often shout at family members, work on this problem using chapters 28, Anger, and 6, Communication Skills.

Parents must also practice honesty and not just preach it. Parents who tell fibs to avoid trouble or make social situations go more smoothly generally find their children are not very honest with them. For example, asking your child to tell someone on the phone you are not home only teaches the child that lying is both useful and acceptable. Deal with money honestly, never take things home from work that don't belong to you, try to find the owner of any lost items, and play games honestly. Doing otherwise only teaches your child to cheat and steal. Make a point of living up to your word and promises. Forgetting to live up to your word teaches irresponsibility, if not dishonesty, by your example. Honesty also includes the noble action of admitting your mistakes. Apologize whenever you show excessive hostility, criticize your child too harshly, act in unfair ways, or hurt someone's feelings. This teaches your child the importance of taking responsibility for mistakes.

Act as a good role model in the area of addictive substances, too. Children often ignore their parents' pleading and punishments to follow their parents' example in using cigarettes, alcohol, and other addictive substances. Occasionally drinking too much alcohol and getting hangovers teaches by your example that the abuse of addictive substances is a legitimate form of entertainment. Moderation with alcohol reduces the likelihood your children will become addicted to alcohol or to other drugs. Parents who lecture their children about drinking and driving but who occasionally do so themselves make very poor role models.

Setting a good example makes it easier to train your children. Parents who neglect household chores or who complain or argue about chores find it more difficult to train their children to do chores than do parents who do their work in a calm, cheerful manner without fussing. Children learn habits of good hygiene more easily, too, if they see their parents consistently following them.

Teaching and Training Your Children

Children learn to take care of themselves, get along with other people, and become decent, contributing members of society only through regular and repetitious instruction and training. Start training your children in the ways described here very early in life. By learning these personal and social skills early, a child develops the ability to love and grows in happiness and self-esteem. These personal and social skills also help avoid problems and make family life more peaceful. Early training is much easier than trying to train after the child has developed a poor self-image and poor habits of self-discipline.

At first you must explain things in simple language so little children can understand. A child will often act appropriately if you explain what happened and what to do about it. Don't just lecture. Listen to the child's point of view and give feedback, describing reasons for appropriate behaviors. Clear commands or rules that explain exactly what you expect also help. For example, upon entering a grocery store with a toddler, calmly say "Stay with me. And remember, if you beg or touch anything without asking, you can't have it." Showing your appreciation for good behaviors and developing skills is also important. Give lavish praise or show your appreciation with thanks, smiles, loving strokes, hugs, etc.

Train your children to perform complex new tasks (such as chores or brushing teeth) by teaching the actions and by helping for months until they can do it well alone. At first give praise for doing a less-than-perfect job, only gradually increasing your expectations. Be patient. Scolding, yelling, and hostility only make the training unpleasant and may provoke rebellion. Once your child understands things better, learns the skills, or knows the rules, train with friendly reminders or gentle questions. This is much more effective than scolding. Ask questions that help your child evaluate the situation in more adult ways. When your child walks into the house with muddy shoes, you could say "What should you do with muddy shoes on this floor?" If you use a pleasant tone of voice, you will probably receive an answer and cooperation. In other situations, you could ask questions about how another person probably feels, the effects of a behavior you notice on friendships, or what would happen if everyone acted that way. Again, use praise and thanks for appropriate behaviors.

Firm and consistent discipline is important in training, too. For example, in training a toddler in how to treat objects such as crayons and books, the following rule helps: if your child misuses such an object, take it away for few days and then only allow the child to use it under adult supervision for another few days. Encourage older children to help you train your younger children, and praise them generously for such help. Finally, teaching roleplays are fun and can help you in training. Little children love to play this game in which they get to scold mom and dad and tell them how and why to behave.

Good Hygiene

Begin teaching your children good health habits at two or three years old. Instruct them to wash their hands before meals, cover their noses when they sneeze, cover their mouths when they cough, and always sneeze and cough in directions well away from people or food, either turning the body away or bending over to sneeze or cough downward. Explain that when they have colds, they must wash their hands more often, keep their fingers out of their eyes, and not share cups or eating utensils. Repeatedly explain the reasons for these rules, talking about how germs spread illnesses and infections. Children two and three years old can also start learning to brush their own teeth. First, of course, you must show them how to do it, many, many times. Once they begin to get the idea, let them have fun with the toothbrush and then quickly finish the job yourself. Eventually, when they can show you how to thoroughly clean all the surfaces of the teeth without your help, you can let them perform this task alone.

Kindness and Other Virtues

Toddlers need a great deal of training to play nicely with others, share toys, and take turns. Little children find it difficult to understand how other people feel, so you will often need to explain how to best get along with other people and how other people think and feel in particular situations. Use simple commands and point out how behavior such as hitting or taking a toy makes the other child feel. In reasoning with your child, you might ask "What if I had a new toy and never let you play with it?" Repeatedly explain that kindness and sharing leads to friendship and fun times, but that selfish or bad behavior makes people not like you, avoid you, or act unkindly in return. Toddlers playing together need plenty of adult supervision. If your toddler continues to misbehave despite your directions, you can punish with the same kind of behavior (hit, take a toy away, etc.) to show your child exactly how it feels.

Talk about love regularly. Point out and encourage love for family, friends, and pets. Explain love is wanting to make other people happy and doing so by performing little acts of kindness. Encourage and praise sharing with others, helping, complimenting, encouraging, and forgiving others. Treat conflicts as opportunities to teach manners and virtues. Teach your children that when other people do them wrong, they shouldn't do wrong in return. Instill a sense of honor and pride in doing what is right, even when provoked. Use plenty of praise and occasional rewards for honorable behavior when angry or in difficult circumstances.

Beginning at age two and three, teach your children good manners and never tolerate rudeness. Instruct them to give thanks, excuse themselves when they interrupt, and apologize when they have annoyed, inconvenienced, or hurt the feelings of other people. Calmly asking your child to rephrase rude language, start over, or warmly asking if the child really meant that can teach while saving face. Teach respectfulness and kindness toward old, disabled, unfortunate, unhappy, and unpopular people.

Train sensitivity by pointing out needs and insisting on cooperation. Explain you occasionally need time for yourself without interruptions, so you can talk on the phone, take a nap, write a letter, etc. If you don't want to hear the radio or television for too many hours, establish quiet times in the house. Teach them to recognize other people's feelings and act especially considerate when other people seem to feel low. For example, "He's quiet and doesn't seem relaxed, so he may not be in a very good mood. Why don't you surprise him by bringing him the newspaper? Then go and play outside, so he can have peace and quiet." Praise your child for showing sensitivity to other people's needs. Occasional rewards also help. For example, you could reward your children with ice cream for being quiet during your nap.

Teach the importance of honesty. Emphasize that friendships and all good relationships require honesty and that dishonesty in relationships destroys trust. Insist on honesty with money and in games, homework, admitting mistakes or wrongdoing, and trying to find the owner of a lost item. Point out that living up to one's word or promises is an important kind of honesty. Don't tolerate repeated excuses for not doing so.

Teach patience and encourage self-discipline. Don't tolerate obnoxious, repetitive begging. Establish the rule that if a child begs, you will refuse permission. Make sure your children learn the value of persistent effort, of trying repeatedly. Emphasize accomplishments generally come only after long effort. Encourage your child to keep working on problems and to finish projects. Explain that success may come even after many failures and that mistakes and failures are our friends because we can learn from them how to make a more successful plan. Develop a sense of pride for striving to do the best possible job. Encourage the attitude that any job worth doing is worth doing well. Promote self-discipline with money by establishing a savings account for your children. Don't force them to put money into the account, but teach them the value of saving money and encourage them to save for special purchases. Teach them to avoid impulse buying and to shop wisely by comparing prices.

Always striving to be respectful, kind, honest, reliable, patient, and hardworking leads to respect and admiration from other people. Teach the importance of having a good reputation. It can help dramatically in making friends, too. No matter what troubles you experience in your life and no matter what disasters or losses occur, a good reputation is always an asset nobody can take away, except you by your own wrongdoing.

Problem Solving

Whenever problems arise, teach the skills of problem solving. Encourage your children to think of possible reasons for the problem, to brainstorm a number of possible solutions, and to evaluate these solutions before choosing the best alternative. Always let them suggest causes and suggest and evaluate solutions before you do, so they will learn more. Encourage thinking carefully and looking for clues to help solve problems. If necessary, point out clues and ask them to tell you what the clues mean. Ask questions to help them produce and evaluate possible solutions. "What else could you do to solve the problem?" "What else might work?" "What would happen if you did that?" Then help them choose the best solution, making sure that it involves a plan for specific behaviors. If the solution doesn't work, start all over.

In conflicts, help your child consider the feelings and perspectives of other people. Describe the importance of compromise in finding an impartial, workable solution, even if the compromise doesn't particularly please any party. You can develop children's problem-solving skills even when it is too late to do anything about the problem. Help them analyze what went wrong, and ask what they could have done that would have been better.

Chores

Training children to do chores helps develop a sense of responsibility. When you begin to teach children to pick up toys, clean up their rooms, do dishes, or most other chores, you must do most of the work. At first the help of very young children may slow you down. Only gradually, over a period of weeks or months, will they learn to do the job alone. Don't demand perfection; just expect some real effort. Lavish praise and thanks on them for helping. After the child has learned how to do the chore, you can still occasionally help to show you care. Your help is especially useful when your child is not really in the mood or feels frustrated. Remember, your example of helpfulness and cheerfulness in doing chores has a great influence.

Perhaps the first chore to master is putting toys away. Make sure there is enough storage space for all the toys. Training to help you with dishes can begin by simply asking children to bring you the dinner plates. Next, teach them to rinse all the dishes after meals, so you can wash them easily. Other common childhood chores include making their beds, cleaning their rooms, taking out the garbage, feeding pets, and yard work such as mowing the lawn, raking leaves, or weeding a garden. Giving a choice between two chores often improves cooperation. As children reach adolescence, they should also learn how to do laundry, cook, sew buttons on, sew torn clothing, change tires, and car care (at least, to keep oil in the car). If you have an infant in the house, instruct your children how to take care of it. If you know how to fix things and a child shows interest, teach your skills. This helps prepare an adolescent for independence and adult life.

Fears

Childhood fears are quite common.   Don't make fun of fearful children, even if their fears seem ridiculous. Instead, give emotional support and encourage them to talk about their feelings. Provide realistic information to help reassure them, and tell them these fears are a normal, temporary phase that will pass.   Describe times when you were afraid.   If talking and reassurance don't help, try some of the following strategies. One fun way to work with a child's fear is the teaching roleplay described previously.

Little children often overcome fears by imitating other little children, so encourage another child to help. The ideal choice would be a child of the same age without the fear because your child will identify most easily with one the same age, but a slightly older sibling or friend nearly the same age can often help as well. Parents can also help their children overcome fears by rewarding small, gradual improvements. At first reward your child for approaching the feared object a long distance away and staying long enough to become comfortable.   After this accomplishment, give a reward for approaching a little closer and staying until comfortable. Tiny night lights that fit into wall sockets can help with fears of the dark.

Artwork also helps in working with children's fears. First, ask your child to draw things that other children fear, such as bugs, big dogs, large animals, heights, etc. This emphasizes various fearless areas and helps in realizing that many other children have fears. Next, encourage your child to draw the feared object or situation conquered or eliminated in some way. Those who fear monsters, for example, can draw themselves putting the monster in a cage or destroying it. Looking at these drawings can add humor and help calm children when they feel afraid.   Then ask for a drawing of themselves unafraid with the feared object or situation also in the picture. Reassure your child that this fearless drawing will come true in time. You can also use puppets, dolls, or action figures to help children express feelings and work on the fear: one action figure can help another overcome the fear or one puppet might conquer or eliminate the feared object.   If none of these approaches work, please refer to chapter 29, Anxiety, Worry, Fear, and Phobia.

Shyness

About half of extremely shy toddlers don't seem shy in later childhood. Occasionally using the services of a daycare not only gives you free time, but also helps a great deal by making your child learn how to play with many other children. You might volunteer at the daycare a few times to ease the transition. Don't describe your child as shy. Repeatedly using this label develops a shy self-image that interferes with progress. When other people call your child shy, explain that your child seems to be getting over the shyness and is really friendly.

Give your child plenty of opportunities to interact with other children, but don't pressure your child to be very social. Invite playmates over occasionally. At first your child may be more comfortable playing with slightly younger children. Make family trips to places children congregate, such as playgrounds, public swimming pools, roller-skating rinks, etc. Whenever you introduce new children or situations, don't send your child out alone. Begin by taking time together to simply observe what is going on. Make comments about what you see, especially anything familiar to your child. Then go along and help draw your child in. If you see another child who looks like a good match or companion for yours, you might start a conversation with that child and let things go on naturally. Stay near until your child seems to be consistently enjoying things, giving emotional support when necessary. After that, waving from a distance or occasionally moving close may be enough.

Add new activities gradually. Adjustment may be more difficult for this child than for others. Don't ask for permission or interest. A shy child will often refuse or say no. Instead, set up the activity and introduce it in a positive, assertive way. You might sign your child up for swimming lessons, then inform the child, saying, "I know you'll enjoy it!"

Teach using the phone and how to introduce themselves, start conversations, and initiate play. Point out when siblings and other children initiate interactions. Imitation will come naturally. Instruct how to maintain and end conversations, praise and give compliments, cooperate, express feelings, and make and refuse requests. Teach assertiveness when needed. Point out the nonverbal aspects of social interactions. When you initiate, does the other person respond with friendliness or short answers and boredom? Turn or lean toward you or turn away a little and look away much of the time as if the other person would rather do something else? Emphasize good eye contact to prevent appearing cold, sad, nervous, or unwilling to interact. In joining a group of children at play, a child is more likely to gain acceptance by first observing the action and understanding what kind of play is in flow before joining. Those who try to change the subject or action, disagree, or try to take the lead too soon are more likely to face rejection.

Teach these things using puppets, dolls, action figures, or behavioral roleplays. After developing some skills, help your children practice in real life. Ask them to practice one of these behaviors when they go to a public place, and discuss the results when they come home. Give praise for attempting to initiate interactions, even if the other child didn't respond well, and point out that everyone must risk rejection. When you go out in public with your child, encourage socializing and watch the results, perhaps giving tips on position, speaking loudly, eye contact, etc. If you notice problems and your child doesn't want to talk about it, you might use dolls, puppets, or action figures to set up a similar play scene and ask how the doll feels. At times, children can discuss things easier indirectly through toys. Explore feelings, reasons for them, and alternative solutions.

Ask siblings, playmates, and other children to help encourage your child, to initiate play with your child, to include your child in group play, and to give praise for interacting more. Occasionally reward your child for initiating interactions. Encourage after-school activities, because they help improve social skills and naturally lead to friendship networks. Sign your child up for clubs, such as the Boy Scouts or Girl Scouts. Emphasize everyone feels awkward in social situations at first but with more practice, confidence will increase.

Ask your child's teacher to work with shy children in school. Suggest assigning class work to pairs of students and changing partners every day to help shy children learn to interact with others and make friends. Teachers can focus on shy children's interests and abilities to promote sharing, ask them to hand out supplies or take charge of other routines, or give rewards to the class for completing a set number of interactions and play activities with them on the playground.

Impulsiveness and Attention Deficit Disorder

We discuss Attention Deficit Disorder (ADD) along with impulsiveness in this section because all the practical advice for impulsiveness helps in treating ADD. The symptoms of ADD involve inattention and impulsiveness, perhaps with hyperactivity. In tasks, schoolwork, and play, you may notice careless mistakes, failure to pay close attention to details, failure to follow through on instructions, difficulty sustaining attention, a tendency to easily become distracted by outside stimulation, difficulty getting organized, forgetfulness, loss of needed materials, and failure to complete activities. Such problems may lead to the child avoiding, disliking, or reluctantly participating in tasks that require sustained mental effort, such as schoolwork. Some of these children don't seem to be listening when you speak to them. You may notice difficulties in waiting their turn. Some will blurt out answers before hearing the whole question or often intrude or interrupt in conversations, games, etc. If hyperactivity is a part of the problem, they will fidget or squirm, talk far too much, or inappropriately leave their seat in class, in church, etc. They may move about excessively, perhaps running or climbing all over the place or finding it difficult to play quietly.

As children with ADD mature, symptoms usually become less obvious. By late childhood and early adolescence, fidgeting may remain, but excessive running and climbing and not remaining seated become less common. Adults with ADD may outgrow the hyperactivity and behavior problems but still have difficulties with concentration and restlessness that may lead to low frustration tolerance, problems in maintaining relationships and developing careers, and perhaps drug or alcohol problems. Many adults with ADD learn to function adequately, however, using coping skills such as time management and making lists to organize themselves.

Critics of the diagnosis note that the incidence of ADD is much lower in other Western cultures, that the U.S. uses drugs to treat ADD at a rate five times higher than in the rest of the world, and that most children diagnosed with ADD are white, middle-class boys. Some argue that ADD medicines are a quick fix for the increase in poor and single-parent families and the lack of control in today's classrooms, large class sizes, and lowered academic and behavioral standards.

Although the American Medical Association (AMA) says there is no evidence doctors are widely overdiagnosing or overprescribing medicine for ADD, some children are misdiagnosed. Many other disorders mimic its basic symptoms. Inattention, impulsiveness, disorganization, and distractibility may come from anxiety, depression, emotional problems, verbal or nonverbal learning disabilities, physical or sexual abuse, neglect, or psychiatric disorders. Certain medical problems such as traumatic brain injury, epilepsy, disorders of sleep or arousal, thyroid disorders, or lead poisoning can mimic ADD. Children from disorganized or chaotic homes with family problems may show very similar uncontrolled behaviors. Sometimes referrals to counseling or special education might be more appropriate.

Up to 90% of children with ADD improve with one of the stimulants used to treat it. This helps make learning and counseling more effective.

Improvements in overactivity, impulsiveness, and ability to pay attention help them obey, cooperate, increase their efforts, and decrease negative behaviors. Unfortunately, the most common, methylphenidate (Ritalin) and amphetamines such as Adderall or dextroamphetamine (Dexedrine), are very addictive and very often stolen, sold, or abused. Stimulants can also cause side effects such as insomnia, poor appetite, stomach pain, headaches, jitteriness, thinking problems, and, in rare cases, psychosis, but most side effects are mild, short lived, and responsive to dosing or timing adjustments. Most scientific studies conclude while Ritalin and other stimulants may improve classroom behavior, they do not have long-term positive effects on adjustment, learning, academic achievement, or adult outcome.

Be sure to get a thorough evaluation by a doctor or psychiatrist with plenty of experience in ADD before allowing your child to be labeled with ADD and medicated. Diagnosing ADD requires a careful history from parents, teacher's reports, and evaluation of the child, impossible in a typical 15-minute doctor's visit. Many children with ADD also have mood, conduct, or learning disorders, which may require counseling or other specialized treatment. Support groups specifically for parents of these children may help you cope. When stimulants don't work for ADD, tricyclic antidepressants or bupropion (Zyban or Wellbutrin) may help. Some people, however, promote unscientific remedies with no proven effectiveness, such as special diets, the elimination of food additives, identifying and avoiding allergens, megavitamin therapy, the regulation of blood sugar levels, anti-motion sickness medication, diets reducing candida, and biofeedback.

Both children with ADD and many other children need to learn to control impulsiveness. As detailed in chapter 5, Emotions, this basic skill underlies working toward goals, harmonious relationships, good character, maturity, self-esteem, happiness, and accomplishment. Much of the advice in this book becomes especially important with impulsive children. Parents need to set a good example and teach good communication skills, anger management, conversation skills, and problem solving. Impulsive children may need extra focus on listening skills and the conversation skills of staying on a topic and taking turns talking. Teach children who interrupt to recognize pauses in conversations and to wait for them. Teach them to give compliments, to cooperate, and the nonverbal skills involved in initiating social interactions and play, as described in the previous section on shy children.

Pay particular attention to the next sections in this chapter, on Discipline and on Reducing the Need for Discipline. Informal contracts exchanging improved behaviors for desired rewards or privileges, and the reward systems described in the section on Discipline are very helpful. Impulsive children need plenty of praise. Notice and praise good behavior many, many times a day, at least five or ten times as often as you scold them. You need to work on your own negative thinking habits if you tend to use negative labels and overgeneralize when your child does something wrong. Search for anything your child does well and nurture that hobby or activity. Developing a skill can do wonders by improving self-confidence and self-esteem. Children with ADD can be particularly frustrating, but don't yell, nag, or lecture—it doesn't work. Calmly focus on one behavior at a time, be consistent, and let the little things go.

Regular routines and clear rules help impulsive children a great deal at meals, bedtime, and play, with homework, and in the classroom. (Regular routines even help in training animals!) Keep regularly used objects in designated places, so your child can find them easily. Try to give your commands when there are no outside distractions. Use a friendly tone of voice and make direct eye contact with your child. Make your commands simple. Avoid complicated commands with multiple steps. Give one instruction at a time. Then ask your child to repeat the command back to you and clarify any misunderstandings. Repeat the command as often as necessary in a calm tone of voice. When you want some time for yourself to read, talk on the phone, take a nap, or visit with company, explain the situation beforehand and ask your child to help. Then make a plan together with some small reward for no interruptions, perhaps a game, visit to a neighbor, or dessert. When the time arrives, ask your child what you have planned.

When you go to places like stores, restaurants, movies, or church, anticipate the problems that normally arise. Before you arrive, talk about what you expect from your child. Some common rules are stay close to me, don't touch, and don't beg. Then explain what the reward will be for obeying and what the punishment will be for problems. Asking children for input on the rewards and punishments can help, but quick consequences are best. Delayed rewards and punishments are much less effective with impulsive children. Change your rewards regularly to avoid boredom, perhaps going back to a previous reward later. Immediately before entering the public place, ask your child to repeat the rules and consequences. Frequent feedback also helps. Use plenty of praise and reminders.

The following procedure helps in training impulsive children. You might use it to teach steps to use to complete homework assignments or to train careful thinking in the problem-solving skills discussed previously (looking for clues, brainstorming solutions, analyzing them, choosing the best). First, you role model the use of self-instructions by saying the steps to the procedure out loud while you do the task. Next, ask your child to perform the task while you speak the instructions. Then ask your child to perform it while speaking the self-instructions aloud at the same time. After this accomplishment becomes smooth and consistent, switch to doing the task while whispering the self-instructions. Finally, your child does it while thinking through the self-instructions privately.

Reward impulsive children for slowing down. Remind them always to stop, look, listen, and think. In problem solving, encourage them to spend more time thinking about the problem and evaluating alternatives before settling on a solution. Always praise them for paying attention, thinking carefully, taking their time, using the proper steps, and their efforts, whether they succeed or fail. Teach them to be proud of careful thinking and careful work, no matter what the outcome. Break down large tasks into small chunks, using lists to organize tasks if necessary. Eventually, as the impulsiveness improves, you can reduce and then eliminate the use of repeating back instructions.

If your child has ADD, make sure the teachers at scool use the strategies in this section. If possible, get your child into a school or class with fewer students or where students keep the same teachers for two or three years. These things help reduce discipline problems and make learning more effective. Avoid open classrooms; four walls and a door reduce distractions. Both counseling and tutoring in deficient subjects are also very important. Ask for your child's placement near the teacher and away from distractions such as high-traffic areas.

All impulsive children can benefit from colored folders for each subject and a notebook for keeping track of assignments and materials they need to bring home and to school. Ask the teacher to check your child's assignment book at the end of the day for completeness. Instruct your child to work on the easier parts of classroom assignments while waiting for the teacher's help. Encourage good organization, with class notes and graded work in chronological order. The section in this chapter on Helping Your Children Do Well in School is also very important. When you help your child learn rote facts such as multiplication tables, use short, spaced practice sessions instead of long, boring sessions and be sure to make visual aids like flashcards.

Teachers can also help students with ADD by shortening work periods, assigning fewer problems at a time, alternating more interesting tasks with less interesting ones, alternating tasks that involve standing or moving with tasks that require sitting, and occasionally allowing children to work with partners or in small groups. Break tasks down into smaller parts assigned at different times, so tasks change more often. Put less material on each work sheet and test. Using visual aids and game formats whenever possible will help by increasing interest and attention. Write short outlines or a summary of the directions on the board for easy reference. Use charts, pictures, and graphs to support verbal or written information. Use manipulable, hands-on materials and activities that require active participation whenever you can. Call children to work on the board, so they don't sit too long. Use calculators, computers, and tape recorders as learning tools. Use activities such as cleaning the board, running errands, or handing out papers as rewards; they help by reducing boredom and using up extra energy. Ask children to repeat new information aloud. In the classroom, reduce your emphasis on competition and on speed.

Reducing the Need for Discipline

We have already discussed many things that can reduce a parent's need for discipline. Setting a good example for your children, affectionate and trusting relationships with them, spending plenty of time talking and doing things with them, early teaching and training, frequently noticing and praising good behaviors, and developing a variety of interests and activities can all do much to prevent problems. Consistent household routines help a great deal. Children who know they must rinse their dishes after each meal or pick up after every activity cooperate more than those whose parents occasionally and irritably demand these chores. Another effective technique is scheduling unpleasant jobs before fun activities.

Rewards for good behavior also help. You can use popcorn, cookies, ice cream, other snacks or desserts, new games, comic books, crafts, toys, movies, picnics, or trips to museums, parks, or beaches. You don't need to spend money, however. One of the best rewards is simply extra time and attention from parents, perhaps spent playing games. The privileges of playing outdoors late, staying up late, visiting or spending the night with friends, going to a party, or throwing a party also make useful rewards. Surprise your children with material rewards only occasionally, so they are not motivated only by these rewards. Make sure your child knows the specific reason for the reward each time.   Use praise, thanks, and compliments liberally to instill pride.

Because boredom often leads to problems, keep your children busy with things to do and things to play with. Avoid problems at mealtimes by including them in the conversation, and avoid problems while traveling in the car by frequently chatting with them, singing, playing games finding numbers or letters, etc. In the grocery store, keep your child busy with frequent conversation or ask for help in finding, getting, and carrying things. Distract from a developing problem with a new activity. When a toddler tries to pull a toy away from another child, distract by offering something else to play with. When you notice mounting frustration, suggest a new activity or game or use a snack as a diversion.

Childproofing helps prevent problems. Using seat belts reduces wild behaviors in the car, and putting your child in a shopping cart increases control in the store. Keep matches, dangerous objects such as curling irons, and anything you don't want children to play with out of reach, and use locks on closets with dangerous chemicals inside. Childproofing also includes fencing your yard for better control of toddlers, using the back burners on the stove whenever possible, turning handles on saucepans backward, and using unbreakable plastic cups and plates at meals. Set aside an area for messy play, perhaps outside or on an old worktable.

You can also avoid problems with the well-timed use of affection, closeness, whispering, humor, or helpfulness. Calm a cranky or angry child with a hug, by playing with the child's hair, or with some other gesture of affection. Moving physically closer to a rebellious child increases your authority and may lead to cooperation. Whispering into an ear can make a command seem warm and playful. Whispering can also avoid public embarrassment that might provoke a power struggle. Friendly humor helps prevent problems by relieving tension. Helping a child who is starting to become frustrated can often prevent anger or other problems.

One of the most important ways to reduce the need for discipline is the use of firm, consistent, clear limits for behavior and enough parental vigilance to enforce these limits. Make it very clear you won't tolerate certain behaviors and that nothing will change that. Check on little children regularly to notice inappropriate behaviors. Always try to know the whereabouts, companions, and activities of your children, even in adolescence, so you can detect inappropriate behaviors. Make your rules firm because regularly changing your limits makes your rules seem arbitrary and unimportant. Don't argue with your spouse about a rule in front of the children. This makes the issue less clear and undermines your authority. Whenever possible, either follow the stand taken by the first parent or discuss your differences of opinion in private and present a united stance to the children. Enforce your rules consistently—children will break them often if they know they can occasionally get away with it.

Avoid unreasonably strict rules, which only cause unnecessary problems. For example, you can teach a child to use caution around mud and not get filthy, but remember that normal children often get a little dirty while playing outside. And although parents have the right to regulate moral behaviors and to forbid outlandish clothing or hair styles, don't try to force your opinions and personal tastes on your child. Doing so often provokes resentment and rebellion. Children need the freedom to choose their own opinions, interests, likes and dislikes, friends, and goals. After all, they must grow in independence and learn to lead their own lives.

Make your reminders, requests, and commands politely. You will receive more cooperation if you use the word *please* and a gentle, pleasant tone of voice than if you use an irritated or harsh tone of voice to scold or nag. State your reminders, requests, and commands positively rather than negatively. Talk about what you want, rather than what you don't like or won't tolerate. Use "Please pick up your clothes now, honey," rather than saying, "Stop leaving your clothes everywhere!" Instead of saying, "Quit fussing!" to your child, you could say "There's no reason to become upset. Do you remember what patience is?" A gentle question can often serve as a friendly reminder. You might ask "Where do your toys go after you finish playing with them?"

Avoid constantly using words like *no, don't, stop, quit,* and *can't.* Children who hear these words too much tend to ignore them. Using these negative words emphasizes that something is wrong and the child is at fault. You can often state a rule or even set consequences in a positive way. For example, instead of saying, "If you don't pick up all of your toys, you can't go to Billy's," you could say "If you pick up all of your toys, you can go over to Billy's for the rest of the afternoon."

Giving your child a choice when you issue a command or warning or when you make a rule also helps. For example, when you refuse a child's request for an activity, give some other fun alternatives, or if you want a chore done and your child wants to do something else, give choices about when to do it. Instead of issuing orders or imposing solutions, let your children help you find a good solution. This increases cooperation by giving them input, by treating them with respect, and by taking their feelings, views, and needs into account to create a better solution. A child can even help choose an appropriate punishment. You might ask what kind of penalty would help make sure the chores got done on time. Children often suggest an appropriate punishment when you ask. If a problem occurs more than once, make sure you both choose a very motivating penalty for further problems.

Family meetings that involve children in decision making also help. Wait until your children enter grade school and then begin with short meetings once a week, lasting perhaps 15 or 20 minutes. As they grow older and family problems become more complex, the meetings may last longer, but limit meetings to 45 minutes to an hour. If you can't resolve an important problem in this time, schedule an extra meeting the next day because long, unpleasant meetings may interfere with progress and the family probably needs a break to relax and mull over issues.

During each family meeting, allow each person to bring up a problem for discussion. The family can choose appropriate rewards for improvement and penalties for problem behavior. Family meetings help children learn how to solve problems and think beyond their own desires to the needs of the group. If a child refuses to participate, meet anyway and make decisions that concern the missing child. This will provide motivation for attending future meetings. During these meetings, if possible, try to focus on good things as much as bad, so they don't become negative and burdensome. Ask what went well during the last week. Ask your children to describe recent accomplishments or acts of kindness, helpfulness, or honesty. Express warmth and encouragement. Give each child a chance to participate in family decisions about recreation and trips. Ending each family meeting with a treat, such as popcorn or ice cream, can help.

Contracts can also prevent problems with your children. You and your child might agree to stop yelling at each other, or perhaps if your teenager stops yelling at you, you will allow attendance at rock concerts. Make reasonable, not harsh, contracts. Expect some improvement, but don't make success so difficult that your child often fails and then gives up hope. Contracts swapping desired behaviors or using privileges as rewards can reduce tensions and improve cooperation, even with juvenile delinquents.

Discipline

Contrary to popular opinion, physical punishment is a poor method of discipline and many parents raise fine children without ever spanking them.

Research shows that plenty of teaching and avoiding physical punishment results in better-behaved children. Studies show that parents who don't use physical discipline have the least violent children, and the more physical punishment used, the more violent the children, with abusive parents raising the most violent children. The use of physical punishment angers children and teaches them by example that violence is an acceptable response to frustration and anger. Five European countries (Denmark, Austria, Finland, Sweden, and Norway) have outlawed physical punishment of children, including spanking.

Avoiding physical discipline helps in teaching that violence is never acceptable. Never spank when you are very angry because this can lead to accidental child abuse. If you use physical punishment, reserve it for times when your child has done something dangerous, deliberately damaged something, or deliberately hurt someone. You might teach a toddler why hitting is wrong by showing how it feels. Try to hit the toddler with the same force that was used in striking the other person. Do this without anger. Just say something like, "See! That's how it felt when you hit him." Never spank a child under two years old—the danger of injury is too great. Don't spank or hit adolescents, it doesn't help and may make them worse. Never throw a child or hit with anything but an open hand on the rear end or extremities, as doing so can cause injuries. A slap that accidentally lands on the ear can create enough air pressure to break the eardrum.

Use a variety of punishments in disciplining your children. Save your harsh punishments for the most serious problems. Using harsh punishments for less serious problems may provoke anger and rebellion. In most situations, reasonably mild punishments are more effective than harsh punishments, but if a punishment fails to teach your child to behave more appropriately, set a stronger consequence.

Discipline alone is not very effective. It works best when you have a close relationship with your children, spend plenty of time training them, and reduce the need for discipline in the ways described previously. The purpose of discipline is to teach your child to be a better person. Make this purpose very clear whenever you enforce a consequence. Many, many times, explain that you must use a punishment because you love the child and you want to teach the child to be a happy, useful person. Always try to discipline in a firm, yet calm and tactful way, so it will be easy to believe that your discipline comes from loving concern. Never angrily ridicule or insult your child during discipline. If anger interferes with your ability to remain calm and tactful, try breathing deeply, relaxing muscle tension, imagining your parents and grandparents, boss, or a policeman watching, and counting for as long as necessary to calm down before responding.

Remember, regularly yelling at your children sets a bad example in patience and respectfulness and may provoke resentment and further problems. Another problem in discipline is that angry parents often take revenge upon their children and hurt them, rather than focusing discipline on teaching appropriate behavior. Remember, regularly insulting your child with negative labels may damage self-esteem and lead to further problem behaviors. During discipline, criticize only problem behaviors (actions, words, tone of voice, and facial expression), not your child's personality or character.

Make a point of enforcing the consequences whenever a child breaks your rules. Children will break your rules often if they know they can occasionally get away with it. Don't let your child get away with breaking a rule out of sympathy or because of arguing, complaining, begging, pouting, whining, crying, or temper tantrums. Never describe a consequence for further misbehavior that you wouldn't enforce. If you don't follow through on a specified punishment for further misbehavior, you teach your child not to take you seriously. If you feel that, in anger, you have threatened to impose an overly severe punishment, explain this and apologize for doing so, but try not to make this mistake too often. Only firm, consistently enforced rules help in guiding children.

Some parents fail to enforce their rules consistently or soon enough because they try too hard to be understanding, loving, and tolerant. Unfortunately, these parents often end up wondering why their children are so troublesome. Parents of unruly children should follow the advice in this chapter and never say they don't know what to do with them or have lost control of them. Remember, whenever possible, parents should present a united stance on discipline to the children.

Stop problem behaviors early, before they escalate and get out of control. Remind children to cooperate when a conflict grows louder. Stop and punish any angry yelling among children, so these arguments don't escalate into physical aggression. Although pleasant reminders can prevent a brewing problem, never use warnings for problem behaviors, such as angry yelling or insults. Immediately enforce your consequences for any problem behaviors. Giving even one warning weakens your authority by allowing children occasionally to get away with the misbehavior.

Don't give children too much attention for misbehaving.   Extra attention rewards misbehavior. Be short and to the point if you talk of your anger or disappointment, explain why the behavior is wrong, or describe punishment as a teaching tool. Don't reward your child by showing affection during discipline or immediately afterward. Children often become very angry when you punish them. They may even yell "I hate you!" Of course, discipline is no fun. Although they can have very strong feelings, their feelings often change quickly. Don't expect them to approve of the way you discipline them, and don't worry or feel guilty about punishment. Discipline with punishment is necessary and won't interfere with the love between the parent and the child. Children respect you for setting firm limits. When a child feels very upset but follows your demands, it is wise to ignore venting of anger.

Whenever you establish a new rule, you can expect more trouble than usual for a few days to several weeks. Children often rebel against new rules, perhaps to try to make their parents give up enforcing the rule or to see if they can escape the consequences. If you consistently enforce the rule, your children will gradually learn to accept it and abide by it.

Psychologists highly recommend *time out* as an excellent way to discipline toddlers and pre-teen children. Time out helps in dealing with most childhood problems, including tantrums, disobeying, yelling, fighting, etc. It is similar to making a child sit in a corner for misbehaving but has special rules that make it more effective. During time out, the child may either stand or sit, but must face a wall or a corner of a room. Make sure there is nothing to do in the spot you choose. Time out should be boring. Don't pick a place where the child can look out a window or watch people or television. Don't put children in their rooms for time out because they can play with toys, look out the window, listen to the radio, etc. Never use a scary place, such as a dark closet.

Any time you notice misbehavior, briefly point out the problem and then tell your child to go to time out. If possible, do this immediately. If your child doesn't cooperate, you must physically take the child to time out and perhaps hold the child there for a while. This mostly occurs while children are learning the procedure. In any case, enforce time out calmly. If you show anger or scold your child during time out, you may provoke a power struggle and further problems. Violence (hitting, throwing something at someone, etc.) or destructiveness should result in some other punishment as well, such as the loss of a privilege.

Time out should last for a minute for each year of the child's age. A 2-year-old gets 2 minutes, an 8-year-old gets 8 minutes, and a 12-year-old gets 12 minutes, etc., beginning when the child quietly remains in place. Any time your child leaves the location for time out, misbehaves, cries, talks, yells, or makes any other noise, the time out begins over. It ends only after the child remains completely quiet in the proper location for the required time. Ignore your children during time out, except perhaps to occasionally remind them that time out doesn't begin until you hear complete silence. If you ignore any screaming, cursing, or crying, the child will settle down faster. Don't worry if a child claims to enjoy time out. Many children pretend to enjoy time out when they feel angry. Make sure you don't forget your child in time out, perhaps by using a timer with an alarm.

When time out ends, ask your child why the behavior was wrong and what response would have been better in the problem situation. Don't scold or nag. Just hold a brief, logical discussion. You will end up repeatedly talking about the same things in response to similar kinds of misbehavior, but this is good. Each time you do this, you teach your child better ways to deal with problem situations.

If your children yell, refuse to talk, whine, still seem angry, or give answers that indicate they are not taking the situation seriously, time out starts over. End time out only after a very appropriate discussion of the issues. An angry child or one who won't discuss proper behavior with you will probably get into trouble again. Don't let your child manipulate you by acting silly or arguing and then quickly agreeing to cooperate when you have started the time over. If it was necessary to start it over, follow through and make the child prove being ready or willing to behave by waiting through more time.

Time out works by removing children from the problem situation, requiring that they calm down, punishing without the excessive harshness that can provoke anger and rebellion, giving very little attention for misbehaving, and teaching constructive ways of dealing with problem situations. As with any new rule, you can expect trouble at first. If your children complain when you first describe time out, ask them whether they would prefer that you spank them every time they do something wrong. Everyone who disciplines the child, including relatives and babysitters, should learn the procedure and use it. All the family should take care not to talk to anyone in time out. If any child teases or makes unkind remarks to someone in time out, put the offending child in time out at another location. Outdoors, you can choose a particular tree as the time out location. In a store, you can choose any convenient place. In a restaurant or car, you can tell your child to bend over toward the knees with folded arms and eyes closed.

Some of the best consequences teach responsibility by clearly relating to the misbehavior. When a little child makes a minor mess, calmly make the child clean it up. If children seem particularly irresponsible in making a mess, require cleaning up the mess and some extra house cleaning. For hurting someone, give a punishment and make your child apologize and do something helpful for the victim, perhaps lending the other child a toy or saving money and buying the other child a treat. For cheating in a game, penalize with much more than the child would have gained. For cheating in school, require extra hours of homework every night. When children break or damage other people's property (perhaps accidentally while misbehaving), make them pay for the damage or object in some way. Perhaps your child could make up for a damaged toy by giving up a toy to the other child. A child might pay for damaged property by losing allowance money for a time or working around the house for money. If your child damages an expensive object and can't pay for it, require the payment of at least part of its value. If a child loses objects too often, refuse to replace them or insist on payment for them.

Extra work is a useful punishment. If two children fight, you might make them clean up one room apiece. You could punish a child for lying to you by making that child wash the supper dishes for a week. Another useful punishment is the loss of a privilege. If your children have been arguing, feel free to send them to bed early or deny them the privilege of having friends visit. You might subtract a quarter from a child's allowance that week every time a particular problem behavior occurs. Other privileges you can deny for misbehavior include the right to play outside, go shopping or roller-skating (even when the child or someone else offers to pay), ride a bicycle, watch television, use the record player or radio, etc. You can cancel any special trip or activity (movies, beach, roller-skating, etc.) because of troublesome behavior, even during the outing itself. Grounding a child is denying the privilege of leaving the house for a time, except for going to school. If you ground a child but you work and can't directly supervise after school, occasionally call home to check on the child or ask neighbors to help enforce it. Another possibility is to ground the child only when you are home, such as evenings and weekends.

Whenever you punish children by taking away a privilege, start with a short time such as a day or two, unless the misbehavior involves a severe problem. No television in the evening is a reasonable punishment for physical fighting among children during the day, but don't forbid TV all week long. For lying to you, you might forbid TV for four days. For coming home much too late without calling you on the telephone, you might ground a child for two days. In this way, you teach lessons without being unreasonable and you can easily add more days of restriction for further misbehavior without overwhelming your children or provoking anger and rebellion. Don't let restrictions add up to more than a few weeks. If problems build up in this manner, try switching to more motivating penalties, contracts, or reward systems (described next).

A *reward system* is a complex form of contract that helps in disciplining children with behavior problems.   Psychologists have successfully used reward systems to train self-care, symptom improvement, social interaction, education, and job training in various patient populations, including psychiatric patients, mentally retarded people, juvenile delinquents, criminals, alcoholics, and drug addicts. People have successfully used reward systems in homes, daycare centers, schools, and institutions. Use reward systems to improve behaviors, and eliminate them when your children have developed better habits. It is much better to develop pride and self-esteem in doing things right than to constantly bribe your children with rewards.

Reward systems generally involve a chart with areas for the days of the week, the expected behaviors, the criteria determining the rewards and penalties, and marking whether the person performs each behavior. Emphasize the privileges the child can earn by putting them in the title. Make sure you reward and penalize your child consistently. Reward systems for children under seven years old should involve only one or two behaviors for change. Draw a smiling face or a star on the chart for successful times and use minus signs or zeros for failures. When young children are frequently troublesome, divide the day into morning, afternoon, and evening in order to count many successes. Using the chart in Table 1, for example, Suzy has a chance to earn $1.75 allowance with a perfect week.

Table 1   **Suzy: Earning Allowance Money**

	Sun	Mon	Tue	Wed	Thur	Fri	Sat
Morning							
12pm - 5pm							
Evening							

Notes: Suzy earns a star for each block of time free of angry yelling and receives a zero for times with angry yelling. For every 3 stars, she earns 25 cents for next week's allowance. For every 3 zeros, she loses 25 cents allowance.

You can tailor a reward system to fit any particular child and situation. Consider the example in Table 2. If Billy's parents felt that Billy also needed to work on aggression and destructiveness, they could easily add these categories to the bottom of the chart, along with *yelling at a parent*. The instructions could state that any of the behaviors in the lower part of the chart eliminates the right to play outside the next day. Ideally, they should define aggression as *aggressive gestures or trying to hit or physically hurt anyone* and destructiveness as *trying to damage or break anything*. These definitions wisely forbid even attempts at aggression or destructiveness and such things as threatening someone or karate kicks that come close to someone. If karate kicks are a regular problem, you should define a karate kick within three feet as an aggressive gesture. Billy's parents might also require an apology and helpful acts or payment to make up for acts of aggression or destruction.

Table 2   **Billy: Earning Privileges**

	Sun	Mon	Tue	Wed	Thur	Fri	Sat
Only one wake up call							
Make bed							
One hour studying							
Clean room							
Brush teeth each meal							
Bed on time, no fussing							
Yelling at a parent							

Notes: Billy may fail to perform two of the items in the upper list and still watch TV the next day, but if he fails to perform three of the upper items, he may not watch TV the next day. If Billy yells at a parent, Billy may not play outside the next day. If he never yells at either parent all day, he may play outside the next day.

There are many ways to structure reward systems. Some assign different privileges to each of their tasks (see Table 3) and others assign various points to specific behaviors and tally the points to determine the privileges (see Table 4). Study these examples to understand these two types. Using the reward system in table 4, it is theoretically possible for Mike to earn the bicycle in two months with perfect behavior.

Let's consider one more example. Karen, a teenager, received poor grades in school and often argues with her parents about what time she should come home in the evenings. Her parents created the reward system in Table 5. In it, Karen can earn the use of the car and 1 1/2 hours later curfew with perfect behavior. Her parents feel the extra studying warrants a later curfew. Because Karen only yells at her parents about once a week, the high penalty for yelling can motivate her to improve without overwhelming her with failure.

Table 3   **Tina: Earning Privileges**

Behavior (Reward)	Sun	Mon	Tue	Wed	Thur	Fri	Sat
Finished homework (watch TV)							
No angry yelling (have guests or visit with friends)							
Clean room (use radio)							
Bed on time, no fussing (late bedtime, 11pm)							
Trying to hit or physically hurt anyone (special activities)							

Notes: Performing the tasks in the upper list results in earning the privileges listed for the next day. If Tina avoids all attempts at aggression on the previous three days, she may attend special activities when the opportunity arises, depending on family circumstances. Examples include movies, parties, trips to the beach or parks, supper at a salad bar, spending the night with a friend, or having a friend spend the night.

Table 4   **Mike: Earning a Bicycle**

Behavior (Points)	Sun	Mon	Tue	Wed	Thur	Fri	Sat
Only one wake up call (1)							
Make bed (1)							
Rinse all supper dishes (1)							
Clean room (1)							
Brush teeth after meals (1)							
Bed on time, no fussing (1)							
Angry yelling (-3 each time)							
Trying to hit or physically hurt anyone (-10 each time)							
Daily Totals							

Notes: When Mike earns 336 points, he will receive a bicycle. Along with losing 3 points for angry yelling, Mike will receive a time out. For each attempt at aggression, besides losing 10 points, Mike will be grounded for one day and must apologize and do something nice for the wronged person.

Table 5   **Karen: Earning Car Privileges and Later Curfews**

Task (Points)	Sun	Mon	Tue	Wed	Thur	Fri	Sat
Only one wake up call (2)	*						*
Clean room (3)						*	*
2 hours homework and study (20)							
Angry yelling (-20 each time)							
Home over half an hour late (-10 per half hour)							
Daily Totals							

Notes: Karen must earn 100 points to use the car next week. After she earns the right to use the car, Karen may earn a later curfew for the next week with any remaining points. For each 10 points she has left, she can come home half an hour later.

          * On these days Karen need not perform the behavior and performing the behavior earns no points.

Reward systems work best when you carefully tailor them to fit the child and the circumstances. It is essential you make the reward system easy enough so your child can succeed more often than not. If you make it too difficult, the child may refuse to cooperate or give up. Require some effort and improvement but don't overdo it. You can always make the terms of the reward system more strict later when you see some improvement. The best way to tailor a reward system is to observe your child's behaviors carefully for a few weeks before making it. Without telling the child, count how often problem behaviors and desired behaviors occur. This helps you in planning realistic goals.

Tactfully introduce the reward system as a technique that will help your child become a better person. Children, of course, don't like having to earn routine privileges in a program of discipline or training. Emphasize that when your child does well with the reward system for a time, perhaps for several months, you will eliminate it as unnecessary. If you should ever decide to increase the expectations in a reward system to encourage further improvement, praise your child lavishly for the gains already made. When good behavior makes the reward system unnecessary, praise your child lavishly but make it clear repeated problems would make the system necessary again.

Keep the chart for the reward system in a prominent place to remind your child of its terms and remind yourself to keep track of it. Good places include doors, walls, the refrigerator, and bulletin boards. If possible, immediately record the expected behaviors and problem behaviors to help avoid forgetfulness and disputes over what happened. Always praise your child for meeting the terms of the reward system. Make your child proud of improvements, and use affection. Give hugs for good days.

If your child refuses to follow the reward system, withhold the rewards in it until you see cooperation. If your child has no interest in it, you may need to find more motivating rewards and privileges or to make success easier. Don't confuse normal testing and sabotaging of new disciplinary measures with failure of the reward system, however. If you think the rewards and privileges are good incentives for your child and you think the child can meet the expectations of the reward system with a little effort, continue to enforce its terms.

Children more readily accept reward systems with very attractive rewards, such as bicycles. A reward system with long-term goals should include some short-term consequences for important problem behaviors.

Long-term rewards can seem very far off to a child and are less motivating than short-term consequences, particularly when the child feels angry. You might increase acceptance of a reward system and make it more fair to the child by including a parental problem behavior. For example, each time a parent yells at a child, the child might get ten points to use toward rewards or privileges.

You can make any kind of discipline less upsetting and more agreeable in several ways. First, as noted previously, giving a child some choice of punishments can help. Discipline children in private whenever possible to reduce embarrassment, anger, and the likelihood the child will rebel to show off. Parents can allow their children to work off punishments they have already received. For example, if you have taken your teenage son's right to use the car for two weeks, you could allow him to shorten the loss of this privilege by one day every time he spends two extra hours studying his worst subject in school.

In discipline, you don't have to treat your children alike. You can give privileges to a well-behaved child that you deny to a troublesome one or to one who fails to perform chores. Use your sense of humor to help avoid feeling overwhelmed by problems with your children. When their actions really upset you, realize that disciplining patiently is all you can do. Try to have faith in your child's basic goodness, even when it is difficult to do so. Even if the two of you haven't been getting along for months and serious problems have begun to occur, develop the attitude your child will eventually improve and become more wise. Remember that losing faith in your child may lead to further problems in a self-fulfilling prophecy. If very serious problems such as chronic stealing or drug use occur, please refer to the section on Teenagers in this chapter.

Temper Tantrums

Temper tantrums are wild displays of angry screaming and crying, often accompanied by violent movements of the arms or body and sometimes accompanied by aggressive or destructive behavior. Children throw temper tantrums to force their parents to yield to their demands. Never give in to demands or promise a toy or treat because of a tantrum. This only rewards the tantrum, teaches the child that tantrums are effective, and makes further tantrums more likely. During a tantrum, it usually doesn't help much to yell at or to try to reason with the already upset or furious child.

Time out is the best way to deal with temper tantrums. Reduce the likelihood of tantrums in public places by running your errands early in the day, so your children won't feel tired and cranky. You can also punish tantrums with the loss of privileges or create a reward system to deal with them. Occasionally, children may try to hurt someone or break something during a tantrum. When this happens, you should physically hold them until they calm down. Punish them for any aggressive or destructive behavior, and insist that they do something nice for the other person or pay for the damaged object in some way. Remember the importance of noticing and praising your children's good behaviors. Give praise and attention for discussing upsetting problems or behaving well.

Sibling Rivalry

Children naturally argue and fight with their brothers and sisters. In doing so, they practice assertiveness, negotiation skills, and conflict resolution. Many of the previous sections of this chapter help prevent excessive angry yelling and fighting. Early teaching and training in kindness, love, sensitivity to the needs of other people, and problem solving helps, as does setting a good example of politeness, helpfulness, and patience. As noted previously, parents who yell every day or many times a week teach their children by their own example to lack patience, yell frequently, and show disrespect. Frequently noticing and praising good behaviors and keeping your children busy with varied interests and activities also help. Use polite reminders and commands, phrased in positive terms. For example, instead of angrily scolding ("Stop arguing!"), remain calm and politely ask your children to think of a fair way to solve the problem. Be sure to stop problems early, before they escalate and get out of control. Remind children to cooperate when a conflict grows louder, and stop and punish any angry yelling, insults, or name calling, so these arguments don't escalate into physical aggression.

Time out is the best way to deal with angry yelling or fights among children. In general, you should give time out to both the arguing children. In this way, neither wins the argument and you motivate both to prevent further problems. Sometimes a parent needs to intervene on behalf of one child, however. If one child always bullies another, punish only the bullying child. Use great care in this, because children often instigate problems and then make it look as if they were the victims. Punish both unless you see that one child is clearly at fault. When you discuss the problem situation with the child at the end of time out, emphasize appropriate responses to verbal teasing and insults, such as ignoring verbal attacks or leaving the room.

When children argue or fight over something, give them time out and take it away from them. If they argue over a game, give time out, end the game, and put it away for the day. If they argue over what channel to watch on TV, give time out and turn off the TV for half an hour. If one child hits another or even tries to, punish with time out, require an apology, and make the child do something nice for the other child. If the child really hurt the other, add the loss of a privilege, too. Feel free to deny children privileges anytime they misbehave, especially on particularly bad days. You can also use reward systems to deal with problems between siblings.

When two children regularly argue or fight, encourage them to make contracts that trade behavioral improvements (I will do ..., if you do ...). For older children who often quarrel, require each to make a list of ten things they like or admire about the other. Don't do this immediately after an argument, of course. Sharing these lists with each other can improve their relationship. Don't worry too much about children's fights. Despite bitter fighting, most siblings end up as good friends in adulthood.

Profanity and Lying

Setting a good example by avoiding profanity helps prevent this problem, but even if you never use profanity, your children will probably experiment with it at some time. When they do, try not to become upset or overreact. If your children discover that profanity can upset, anger, or shock you, they may enjoy this power over you and curse more often. The best way to deal with profanity is to calmly treat it like any other kind of insulting language by punishing the child with time out or loss of a privilege. During the problem-solving phase of time out, point out how profanity made the situation worse by offending you. Explain cursing is impolite, disrespectful, and hostile, without labeling your child as bad, immature, disgusting, etc. If your child curses excessively, you could make a contract or set up a reward system to deal with it. Remain calm and have faith your child will eventually improve, remembering that your opinion has a great influence on your child's self-esteem and ability to improve.

Toddlers and little children often interweave fact and fantasy. Don't overreact to a little child's normal tendency to exaggerate or tell stories. Storytelling is an important part of children's learning about the world and language and it helps prepare them for reading. You can often have fun by encouraging family members to tell stories. But toddlers do lie, especially when they want to avoid getting in trouble. Sometimes older children exaggerate excessively and insist their stories are completely true. In this case, gently confront the child by showing your skepticism in a friendly way.

Parents can in many ways unwittingly encourage their children to lie. Parents telling fibs set a bad example teaching that lying is sometimes useful and acceptable. Never lie to avoid trouble or for any other reason. For example, don't lie about your child's age to save money when going to the movies or buying a bus ticket. If you feel tempted to, consider whether you want your children to lie to you. One subtle way of provoking a lie is to ask whether your child did something wrong when you already know it is so. Asking angrily, in particular, adds pressure and so the natural response is to want to lie. If you know your child has done something wrong, use your knowledge in a direct confrontation and give a punishment. Trapping your child in a lie when you already know the truth unnecessarily helps build the self-image of a liar in the child.

Don't angrily interrogate your children about a possible misdeed and then harshly punish them after they admit the wrongdoing. When faced with this sequence repeatedly, people naturally want to lie to avoid the harsh punishment. Instead, make it clear you will punish misdeeds more severely if your children lie about them. Question calmly. You may be suspicious or skeptical and ask probing questions, but avoid extreme anger. If your child admits having done wrong, show appreciation for the child's honesty and courage in doing so. You may even show a little affection to a young child for telling the truth, but give a suitable punishment. If your child admits insulting someone, you might require an apology and another kind act for the person. If your child insulted someone and then lied to you about it, you could require the apology, the kind act, and impose the loss of a privilege. Lying about a misdeed should either double the punishment or result in two punishments, one for the misdeed and another for lying.

Teach that lying damages friendships and relationships and can result in losing friends and respect from other people, lowering one's self-esteem. Emphasize life is sad and bleak when people can't trust their loved ones, and once other people begin to think of you as a liar, it takes a long time to gain their respect and trust again. When your children first lie to you or if your children rarely lie to you, consider the lie a crisis in your relationship. Express your deep disappointment and explain that you don't want them to hurt themselves with this kind of behavior. After giving a punishment for this mistake, forgive the child and don't bring it up again.

If your child lies to you regularly, eliminate the common mistakes described above encouraging children to lie. Avoid anger, arguments, and threats because your battle of wills only contributes to the problem. If your disappointment over the lies hasn't helped, stop letting them ruin your mood. Your disappointment or anger may act as a reward for the child, a victory in hurting you. Never call your child a liar. You don't want this label to become a part of the child's self-image. Instead, teach the importance of trust in relationships and the damaging consequences of lies, but once you have made your position very clear, keep your statements short and to the point. Don't reward your children with too much attention for lies. Explain that you must punish each lie to help them learn from these mistakes. Show confidence that your children will eventually learn, because they need this support.

Increase your vigilance and occasionally check on the truth of statements. Children need to know you won't tolerate lies and you will try to find out whether they are lying to you. Explain you regret needing to do this and you look forward to the time when their continued honesty allows you to stop checking. Don't go to extremes and constantly check on your child or act like a detective, however. Continually raking up evidence for lies shows you don't trust the child to improve. Also, children, adolescents in particular, need some privacy. Parents can sometimes push their children to start lying by prying too much, so avoid severe interrogations about their private lives.

Pay attention to what your children lie about. This may give clues as to what might help. Those who lie to other people about money or possessions may need part-time jobs, so they can get some of the things they want. Some lies relate to overly strict rules. If your rules about where your children may play result in lies, for example, perhaps you should change these rules.

Stealing

Toddlers often take things that belong to other people because they don't understand property rights or find it difficult to consider the other person's perspective. Parents must train children to understand these things. One effective way to do this when your child takes something that belongs to another child is to take one of your child's favorite toys and give it to the other child for one day. When your child complains or becomes upset, say something like, "See! That's how he felt when you took his jacket." If your child takes something of yours, teach the same lesson by taking a favorite toy or possession and putting it away for a day.

When an older child steals something, treat it as a major crisis. Express your deep disappointment and anger, and describe stealing as violating other people's rights. If the stolen item came from a store, point out that this crime forces all innocent customers to pay higher prices. Make it clear stealing lowers self-esteem, results in loss of respect from other people, and may result in the loss of friends or even in jail. Insist that your child both return the stolen object and apologize. If it came from a store, make your child return the object, apologize, and pay the merchant its price without receiving it, to help make up for the merchant's other theft losses. If use of the stolen item makes returning it impossible, insist on an apology and on paying double for it. In addition, give away one of your child's favorite objects or clothes, to create the experience of a similar loss to a theft. Plus, set a harsh punishment. This is no time to be lenient. A young child might lose both allowance money and TV privileges for three weeks. An older child might lose use of the car for a month. Explain you must be harsh because theft can ruin a person's life.

Don't label your child a thief, no good, rotten, etc. These labels can help develop the self-image of a thief or evil person. Think of your child as good but having made a serious mistake. Your child needs your respect and faith that improvement will occur. Several other things can reduce the likelihood of further problems with stealing. Pay attention to the child's finances and purchases, so you will notice and can punish any further stealing. Perform this as a parental duty, but don't really expect further problems. Encourage your child to work part-time to keep busy, earn spending money, and build self-respect as a worker. If peer pressure helped encourage the theft, use behavioral roleplays to practice different ways of handling pressure and refusing to steal. Finally, if your child's stealing continues, please refer to the section in this chapter on Teenagers for ways to deal with severe behavior problems.

Making Learning Fun and Developing Skills

Children learn to think and communicate primarily by listening and talking. The more you explain about life and everyday things to your toddler, the more the toddler will learn. Frequently listening to your children is as important as frequently talking to them. Your child's ability to carry on a conversation and describe things is the basis for the ability to communicate well and write well in school. So chat with your children frequently while driving the car, having supper, etc. Give them plenty of opportunities to describe what they did or saw, and encourage them to go into more detail. Using good English at home also helps put your children ahead in school.

Inspire your children to observe the world with interest and pleasure by showing enthusiasm when you talk about things you see, because their interest will depend greatly on your liveliness and pleasure in observing things. Occasionally use expressions of wonder and excitement, such as, "Isn't that something!" Cultivate curiosity, exploration, thought, and questions in your child. You can do this during almost any activity. For example, children love playing in big cardboard boxes from furniture or large appliance stores. You might make a toddler think by asking, "Why is it dark in that box?" If your toddler says the sunlight is outside but not inside, point out that cardboard blocks sunlight and ask if sunlight will go through clothes, a roof, or a window. Give enthusiastic congratulations for correct answers and you have made a little game of it.

Nature is a wonderful thing to observe. Play outside with your child and look at birds, dogs, cats, butterflies, fireflies, ants, etc. Ask questions and use your knowledge to cultivate your child's curiosity. For example, explain birds like to eat seeds, insects, and worms and they spend much of their time looking for them. Or explain plants don't look like they're doing anything, but they really catch sunlight all the time and use it for energy, something our bodies can't do. Point out seasonal changes in weather and plant and animal life. Identify sounds such as cows mooing and the noises made by crickets rubbing their wings together.

Look at man-made objects in the environment, too. Toddlers enjoy going for walks in the neighborhood and looking at and talking about mobile homes, churches, schools, parking lots, satellite dishes, chimneys, telephone poles, cars, trucks, motorcycles, etc. Discuss the uses of these buildings and objects, perhaps finding opportunities to watch older children on a school playground, inspect a motorcycle up close, or let your child get up in a truck. Next, plan other trips farther from home. Take your child on a bus, meet the bus driver, and explain the use and purpose of bus fares and schedules. Browsing in stores is very entertaining and educational for little children. Spend time in many kinds of stores. Find elevators and escalators to use and talk about; children love them. If possible, go to visit a subway, a boat, a train, and an airport to look and talk about what goes on. Children can watch airplanes for hours.

Expose your children to a wide variety of experiences to stimulate their minds. Go to different playgrounds and parks. Teach about animals by going to the zoo, pet shops, and fish and aquarium stores. Go on nature walks, including those with exhibits or guided by rangers. Visit flower gardens. Go camping. Expose them to forms of nature they have never seen, such as lakes, the ocean, a cave, cliffs, mountains, snow, or a desert. Another excellent way children learn about the world is to see and talk about the different kinds of jobs people do. Explore a truck stop, fire station, police station, post office, construction site, shoe repair shop, and butcher shop. Children also enjoy visiting a farm, with its animals and tractor. Go to see artists such as potters, painters, glassblowers, or weavers. Many factories and public buildings allow tours.

Cultural experiences such as theater plays and musical performances also help. Go to churches to view stained glass windows. Go to the library and visit museums. Visit areas with historic interest, such as exhibits, homes, and tours. Some areas also have mills or river locks, either functioning or abandoned, you can visit. Perhaps you can find a planetarium near your town or an astronomical observatory associated with a university that you can visit for a better understanding of the universe.

Many fun activities that entertain children and keep them busy and out of trouble also develop manual dexterity (finger muscle coordination), which makes learning to write easier. Toddlers who play with blocks, hammer pegs into holes, and screw and unscrew nuts on bolts learn important basic skills for writing. Promote the use of pencils, pens, crayons, finger paints, and paintbrushes for drawing, coloring, and painting. Give your children activities that require cutting, folding, pasting, and gluing, such as making collages. Ask them to make masks out of paper bags, paper plates, construction paper, etc. that slip over the head or tie around the face with string. Children can make paper dolls by cutting out pictures in magazines and gluing them on cardboard cut to the same shape. They can make puppets out of socks, mittens, paper bags, or construction paper using felt, magic marker, glue, and other materials. Find more ideas in books from the public library about entertaining children.

Many other things that children love to do develop manual dexterity. Working with play dough or clay, lining up dominoes and toppling them, balancing and stacking playing cards to make buildings, and playing with jacks all help. Toys that children fit and assemble, such as Lincoln Logs, Tinkertoy, Erector, Lego, and Mega Bloks, also help, but when buying for toddlers, be sure to get the larger versions made for them to avoid choking. Encourage your children to string popcorn or beads, perhaps asking them to copy a design in beads you have made. Provide them with materials for crafts, such as gluing designs with dried beans, macaroni, stones, nails, seashells, seeds, string, or toothpicks. Popsicle stick craft, folding paper flowers, rock painting, and origami (Japanese paper folding to make birds, dragons, etc.) are also fun, as are jigsaw puzzles, string tricks, card tricks, making knots, drawing mazes, and making models (cars, ships, etc.).

Creative play develops children's minds. Encourage make-believe games of all kinds. Find props for make-believe games at toy stores, garage sales, and used clothing stores. Props include purses, wigs, hats of all kinds (women's hats, cowboy hats, helmets, Indian headdresses, etc.), swords, old jewelry, badges, cloaks, old eyeglasses or sunglasses (use a tiny screwdriver to remove any glass or plastic that corrects for vision), play stethoscopes, etc. You can even make some props, such as crowns, black eye covers, beards of felt, wedding veils, etc. Inspire older children to give dramatic performances, either on the spur of the moment or planned and rehearsed.

Other fun activities help develop thinking and children's enjoyment of language. Nursery rhymes such as "Pat-a-Cake," "Hickory Dickory Dock," and "Little Jack Horner" encourage children to memorize. Go to your public library for nursery rhyme books. Tongue twisters, sentences that are difficult to repeat quickly without making a mistake, also provide fun with language. "Peter Piper" is both a nursery rhyme and a tongue twister. Make up your own tongue twisters. Play with language and encourage memorizing by telling jokes and urging your children to do the same.

Songs, too, promote memorization. Teach children's songs such as "Twinkle, Twinkle Little Star" and "This Old Man." Children also enjoy folk songs, such as "Oh Suzanna," "Cumbaya," and "500 Miles." You can find these songs and many other perennial favorites in books at your public library. Sing as you clean house or cook. This not only lifts your spirits but sets a good example for your children. They will naturally want to learn some songs, sooner or later.

Telling stories is an excellent way to develop thinking and communication skills. Tell your children stories and encourage them to make up stories. Settings for your stories may include far-off places such as China, Africa, a desert island, a tropical paradise, jungle, or polar regions. You might pretend you are a king, queen, knight, superhuman hero, wizard, magician, scientist, millionaire, the President, or the strongest person on Earth. Science fiction stories may deal with traveling in space, being invisible, an alien visiting Earth, or living on the moon, other planets, or another galaxy.

You can often create an interesting story by simplifying movies you have seen or books you have read or by telling stories about your own life or what your grandparents were like. Stories about your life may deal with earliest memories, childhood events, things you used to do, favorite friends, how life was different when you were young, the best thing that ever happened to you, and times you felt very happy, kind, helpful, surprised, angry, afraid, or sad. You can also base stories on your wishes, things you would like to do, or daydreams, or perhaps describe a utopia, a perfect society or world.   Other stories may involve overcoming great obstacles and succeeding when failure seemed likely or detailing real events that seem impossible or believe-it-or-not fact and fiction.

Of course, many of the stories told at home will be short fantasies rather than long productions with plots. This is particularly true of children's first stories. Try to gradually increase the depth in stories your children tell. Encourage them to tell a whole story with a beginning, middle, and end. Another fun activity is starting a story yourself and letting your child finish it, or a group of children can put one story together, taking turns adding sections, perhaps with you starting it. Another twist is giving your child a phrase or sentence to work into the story. You might ask your child to create a story including the sentence "First she grew wild-eyed and then she panicked!" or "Then he fell a long, long, long, long way." Your family may enjoy repeatedly telling certain favorite stories. Other fun activities include drawing pictures of events from stories, drawing sequences of pictures that tell a story, or acting out stories, perhaps using homemade face masks or puppets.

Rhymes, comparisons, and riddles also bring fun with words and language. You might simply ask "What rhymes with cat?" Encourage brief stories in rhymes. For example:

> *The mouse said to his wife,*
> *"Would you pass the knife?"*
> *Then he said "Honey, please,*
> *won't you pass the cheese?"*

Teach children how to make comparisons by asking them to finish one. You might ask your child to finish the phrase "ran as fast as ..." or the sentence "The giant was as tall as ..." Play with riddles, too. Thinking of a tree, you might ask "What is bigger than our house but shakes with every breeze?" And make up riddles in which the answer rhymes with a previous word. For example:

First he hires them,
then he fires them.
He is so cross,
one day he screamed "I am the ...!"

Many games help teach language and promote thinking. While driving a car or riding a bus with a toddler, make a little game out of finding many things of one color (yellow, red, etc.). The game Simon Says helps teach children body parts, directions, counting, and memorization. The leader, called Simon, performs an action while describing it. Other players must copy the action, but only if the leader begins the description with the words "Simon says." Children will laugh when some accidentally copy actions and follow instructions that came without the words "Simon says." Instructions like, "Simon says pick up your right leg and grab the right toe with your right hand" help teach right from left. More complicated instructions teach counting and memory tasks. The leader might tap the table or stomp the feet eight times or instruct the children to repeat sequences of numbers or words.

The riddle game I Spy helps children to describe things, notice similarities, and think. Take turns choosing an object that everyone playing the game can see and giving clues by describing it until someone guesses it. You might choose a door and say, "I spy something big and heavy but very easy to move." If nobody can guess it, you might add "People grab only one small part of it to move it." Charades, Password, and Twenty Questions are good language and thinking games for children, but adults enjoy them, too. In Charades, people take turns choosing a word or phrase and then trying to convey it to the other players by acting it out in pantomime, either syllable by syllable or as a whole. Start by using your fingers to indicate the number of words, which word you will work on first, and perhaps how many component pantomimed words you will use to convey the word. Motion and shake your head yes and no to indicate when the other players come close to the word you want, wander farther away from it, or guess the word exactly. Indicate small words by holding your fingers close together. Indicate bigger and smaller words with hand movements. Pointing to your ear indicates the word you want sounds like another word you plan to pantomime or a player has guessed.

In the game Password, people take turns trying to convey a chosen word to the other players by describing it with other words. You may not use shorter or longer forms of the same word in your description, however. In the game Twenty Questions, people take turns choosing something and announcing its category: person, place, animal, plant, or object. Other players try to guess it by asking no more than twenty yes or no questions. The person who has chosen the object may answer only yes or no. Ask questions that help you narrow down the possibilities before you start guessing. When you do guess, save questions by asking whether any of several guesses is correct.

Social skills (such as sharing, interacting with others, and following directions) and helping your child enjoy learning during the preschool years are much more important than learning academic skills early. Although you can begin teaching preschool children counting, reading, or writing, never force or pressure them to learn when they want to do something else or when frustrated or uninterested. If they begin to complain, let them do something else. Pressuring a preschool child to learn may provoke resentment that results in disliking schoolwork. Pay attention to your own feelings while teaching. If you become frustrated, bored, or angry, stop for a while. Keep your teaching pleasant and fun, and stop whenever it isn't. Use enthusiastic praise when your child remembers a fact or solves a problem. Child development experts agree learning through warm interactions and playing with parents is much more beneficial than computerized learning games.

Help children understand numbers by asking them to count things. Count how many birds are in the backyard or people came to visit. Simple card games such as War and Go Fish encourage counting. When you drive the car or ride a bus, count how many buses, police cars, bridges, or barns you see. Teach the meaning of zero. Once your child learns to count, ask your child to compare numbers. "Are there more people or chairs in the room?" If there are more people, we should bring in extra chairs from the kitchen. This teaches your child the purpose of numbers. A fun way to teach comparing numbers is to adjust the number of objects when children close their eyes, and then ask them to look and tell you if there are more or fewer objects now.

Preschool children can gain some understanding of addition, subtraction, and fractions. Don't bore them with long sessions and memorizing; just occasionally expose them to the ideas in playful ways. "If I put these crayons with those crayons, how many crayons do I have altogether?" or "If I take four crayons, how many do I have now?" Memorizing that six minus four equals two is not nearly as helpful as learning what it means to take four from six and get two. Your child won't really understand this abstract mathematical concept until you show that the answer always remains the same, no matter what objects you use. If your child wants to learn to add or subtract, make flashcards to make memorizing fun.

Cut flashcards into the shapes of animals, cars, airplanes, boats, trains, motorcycles, bicycles, stars, fruits, vegetables, or geometric shapes. You might make them out of brightly colored construction paper. A simple way to make very realistic shapes is to find pictures of the right size, cut them out, and use them as patterns for the flashcards, perhaps simplifying the shapes. If you can't find the size you want, enlarge or shrink the closest size you find. Don't worry about making the shape perfect.

Playing with cup and teaspoon measures introduces children to fractions. Start by teaching them how to read the fractions on cup and teaspoon measures while you cook. Then occasionally allow your child to play by measuring water. Later, ask them to experiment and find out how many 1/4-cup measures it takes to fill a cup measure. Do the same with 1/3-cup and 1/2-cup measures. By writing down the results, you can point out the relationships between each of these and 1 cup, illustrating the reason for the names of each measure. Show enthusiasm, perhaps by saying, "Surprise!" You could tease your child by arguing that 1/4 is bigger than 1/2 because 4 is bigger than 2, and then proving yourself wrong. Ask your child to tear up a piece of paper into 16 pieces to prove that 1/16 is much smaller than 1/2.

Teach your children how to tell time in small, easy steps. Start by occasionally describing or drawing a picture of where the clock's hands will be when it is bedtime, time to leave for school or a movie, or time to take the brownies out of the oven. Then teach just hourly positions of the clock handles (12:00, 1:00, 2:00, etc.). After your child masters these, teach half-hour intervals, then later 15-minute intervals. To learn 5-minute intervals, your child must learn to count by 5s. Finally, teach 1-minute intervals on the clock.

Help children understand the calendar by asking them to put a big *X* through each day on the calendar as it goes by, perhaps as part of your bedtime routine. They can occasionally count the days to special events, such as holidays, birthdays, weekends, planned outings, or movies. When your children ask you how many days until something happens, look at the calendar together, instead of just telling them. If you grow plants indoors, mark the calendar each time you water the plants, and occasionally ask your child to count days since the last watering to decide if it is time to water yet or not. Eventually, your child may want to memorize days of the week and months of the year.

Another useful skill is learning to compare things and group or classify them. Children can sort objects for characteristics such as color, shape, size, texture, and use. They can categorize people by age, height, weight, or width. Place objects inside paper bags, tell children to put their hands in the bags without looking, and ask them to make comparisons such as weight, texture, height, width, or size. Another game that helps in learning to classify objects is presenting your child with four or five objects, one of which doesn't match, and asking which one doesn't fit in the group. Play this game verbally, too. For example, "I'm going to name some objects. You try to decide which object I name is different from the rest and doesn't match. Ready? Brick. Wood. Steel. Apple." A variation of this game is to list a group of objects and ask your child to name something else that fits in the same category.

Develop an appreciation of science, too. Children enjoy using rulers and yardsticks to measure size and distance between objects. Ask them to compare which object is farther or taller. They also enjoy weighing objects, including family pets. Little children often believe greater size indicates greater weight. You can prove otherwise to them by playing a little game. Present a variety of objects and ask them to guess which is heavier. Sometimes you can fool them with a small object that is heavier than a large one. End the demonstration with an obvious comparison like a balloon and a coffee mug. Little children often make mistakes in comparing volume, too. Teach your child not to mistake shape for amount. Do this by comparing the same amount of water poured back and forth between a tall, thin container and a short, fat container, perhaps using different vases.

While cooking, teach about solids, liquids, gases, evaporation, and dissolving. Explain that heat rises and let your child feel the hot air over your cooking pot. Show your child boiling water and explain that some of the water evaporates, changing from a liquid to a gas, and mixes into the air. Prove your point one day by boiling away all the water in a pan. Melting chocolate is an example of a solid becoming a liquid. Cooking scrambled eggs is an example of a liquid becoming a solid. Demonstrate sugar or salt dissolving in a hot liquid. When little droplets of water form on the outside of a container removed from the refrigerator, point this out. The water condenses out of the air because of the cold surface, the opposite of what happened when you boiled water.

There are picture books or coloring books of various animals, dinosaurs, planets, seashells, and forms of transportation, which help teach children about science. If you can't find some of these, field guide books with plenty of pictures also work well. Your children don't need to be able to read to enjoy the pictures. Many other activities also teach children about science. Plant seeds and start plants from cuttings, counting how many days it takes for a seed to sprout or for a cutting in water to start a root, and measuring the plant's growth in inches each month. Test what floats in water and what doesn't. Find out what conducts heat and what doesn't, by putting things partly into boiling water. A metal spoon will get hot, for example, but a wooden or plastic spoon won't.

Static electricity is fun to investigate. If you rub a balloon on your hair, it sticks to the wall because of static electricity. If you take your clothes out of a dryer at night with the lights out and separate clinging clothes, the static electricity flashes. Skip the fabric softener in the dryer for this experiment—it reduces static. In the dry air of winter, hair may float away while you comb it because of static electricity. If you notice hair doing this, comb it in a dark room at night, so your children can see the static electricity in it.

Play with magnets, magnifying glasses, and prisms, too. Iron and steel attract magnets, but let your child test various other substances, too. Then put a small nail on one end of a magnet and another on the bottom of the first. The second nail becomes temporarily magnetized and sticks to the first. (The tiny magnets holding knickknacks to a refrigerator may not have the strength to do this.) See how many nails you can put together. Now put paper or glass or wood between the magnet and the nail. It still works! Explain that mariners have measured the Earth's magnetism with the compass to tell directions and navigate overseas for many centuries. Use a magnifying glass to take a close look at skin and many other objects. Light a match by concentrating heat from sunlight onto the match head with a magnifying glass. Prisms or tiny faceted prism pendants show how many frequencies of light compose white light by separating them into the colors of the rainbow.

Another interesting activity is playing songs or making up tunes using the vibrations of glass drinking cups or rubber bands. To play tunes on glass cups, fill them with varying amounts of water, tap them with a spoon, and then arrange them in order from lowest pitch to highest pitch. If you use identical glass cups, the more water you put in, the lower the pitch because the weight of the water slows the vibration of the cup and because slower vibrations give lower pitches. To play tunes on rubber bands, stretch them between nails in a board. The pitch or speed of vibration will depend on the size of the rubber band and how tight you stretch it.

Nature is a wonderful source for science activities. Go on nature walks and take field guides with good illustrations of plant and animal life, bringing along a magnifying glass and binoculars. Open a flower and look at it closely, identifying the parts. Talk about how bees collect nectar and fertilize the flowers by bringing pollen from the stamen to the pistil. Open seeds or fruits that you find, too. Find stones that write or sparkle or contain bands indicating that different layers got shifted together. Point out sandstone formed of sand in shallow seas, granite cooled underground from molten rock, or limestone made of minerals from marine plants and animals. If you have a microscope, take samples to look at. Discuss how you can tell if something is alive or not. Talk about tadpoles becoming frogs, eggs becoming birds, and caterpillars becoming butterflies. Don't worry if your child asks a question you can't answer. Just make plans for a trip to the library.

Interest your child in astronomy. Find a well-illustrated astronomy book and talk of the moon, planets, celestial movements, eclipses of the sun and moon, comets, meteors, stars bigger and brighter than our sun, and star clusters. Discuss double stars that orbit each other, variable stars that regularly brighten and dim, galaxies, stars that explode and leave gas clouds, gas clouds that give birth to stars, and black holes that gobble up anything coming near. Drive away from the city on clear, moonless nights with your child and look for our spiral galaxy, the Milky Way. It appears as a hazy band of distant stars stretching most of the way across the sky. We can't even see the middle bulge of the Milky Way galaxy from our spot 2/3 of the way out a spiral arm because of distance and clouds of dust. Watch for meteors after midnight away from the city on clear, moonless nights. With these good conditions, you should see 5 or 10 meteors each hour by just lying down and watching the skies. The two best meteor showers peak on August 12 and December 13, but you can observe them on days just before and after the peak day. When these showers fall on moonless nights and you escape distant city lights, you may see as many as 50 meteors each hour. Describe the rare meteor storm in 1833 that lit up the sky with so many meteors, it seemed to snow meteors. In this storm, about 26,000 meteors fell each hour for 9 hours. Take your child to look in a telescope at astronomy club meetings, planetariums, or astronomical observatories.

Older children often become interested in identifying trees, rocks, flowers, wildflowers, birds, butterflies, etc. You can find field guides on all of these, as well as books on fishes, mammals, insects, reptiles, dinosaurs and other prehistoric animals, Indian cultures, astronomy, seashells, rocks and minerals, and fossils. Weather is another topic of scientific interest. Children can identify the billowy, white clouds of good weather and the darker clouds that threaten rain. They might enjoy identifying types of clouds with the help of a book. Perhaps tornadoes, hurricanes, or volcanoes interest them. Many children enjoy collecting and identifying leaves. Preserve leaves by pressing them between two pieces of wax paper with an iron, protecting the iron and the ironing board with several layers of newspaper.

Many parents enjoy teaching their children to read and write early. By reading regularly yourself, you encourage your children to want to read. Introduce a toddler to books by looking at pictures together and describing what you see. Don't bore your child; start with just one or two minutes of this activity. Toddlers can't pay attention very long, so quit whenever they seem to lose interest. At around age two, begin reading very simple stories to your child. Start with picture books that contain very little text. The fastest way to develop a child's interest in books is to set aside a few minutes for reading stories every day. Keep it fun; never force your child to do this. Offer to read a story every day, and stop reading when your child begins losing interest. At first a few minutes is long enough. Even four-year-olds often don't want to sit through a long story. Feel free to stop in the middle of a story, but if this happens regularly, even with new stories, you need shorter ones or books with short sections you can use one at a time. Go to the library to find new stories. Although children often enjoy repeatedly hearing the same stories, they do need variety to avoid boredom.

Your children will enjoy the stories more if you read with enthusiasm and use tone of voice to make the story more alive and understandable. Change your voice to portray different characters. Give bigger, stronger characters stronger voices and give tiny characters, such as mice, weak voices. When events in the story tend to provoke emotional responses or the words indicate emotion, try to create the appropriate feeling in your voice. With practice, you can read and use vocal qualities to indicate happiness, amazement, warmth, confidence, sadness, anger, fear, surprise, timidity, mockery, worry, etc. Look at your child regularly while reading; this helps in keeping attention.

Your child will learn more if you occasionally ask questions during the story or if you talk about it afterwards. Don't make this hard work; just ask a few questions for fun. Use questions like: "Why did she do that?" "What do you think he should do about his mistake?" "Who do you like so far?" "Why?" "How would you feel if that happened to you?" "How can she solve this problem?" "What do you think will happen?" "How was that story like real life?"

Praise children for looking at books, and make sure they treat books with respect. Explain that throwing a book or carelessly dropping a book can damage it. If a child throws a book, take it away for a few days, even if it belongs to the child. If your children damage a book, take all of their books for a few days, and then allow them to use the books only in your presence for a week. When you feel sure they understand the importance of taking care of books, you can return them.

Teaching your children to recognize letters, sound out words, and read can be fun. When looking at pictures in books together, start teaching them to recognize words. Point out the first letter in a word, read the whole word, and tell them what sound the letter contributes. Find this letter repeatedly, perhaps using large letters from colorful advertisements, until your child can find the letter without help. You can also make a pile of letter flashcards, with three or four of each letter in the alphabet. Then your child can pick out and match identical letters, while you identify each letter and the sound it makes. Later, show how to match capital (upper case) and small (lower case) versions of the same letter. For another flashcard game, make picture flashcards (draw them or cut them out of magazines), then ask your child to identify the pictured object and to guess what letter it starts with.

Small blackboards for use at home can make learning letters fun, too. Write letters on the blackboard for your child to copy. Some blackboards come with letters printed at the top, which help children learn the alphabet. You might buy letters from art stores or make your own letters out of construction paper. One fun game using a pile of letters or letter flashcards is to look in a magazine or picture book, ask your child to pick and identify any pictured object, and then you both spell the word together. As you call out the letters in order, your child hunts for the letters in the pile and arranges them to spell the word. Or try seeing how many words you can think of that start with the same letter. In the letter hunt game, played while riding in a car or bus, your child searches license plates, signs, and other objects for examples of a specific letter you choose.

The alphabet song, sung to the tune of "Twinkle, Twinkle Little Star," helps children learn the alphabet. Once your child knows the alphabet and sounds that go with each letter, play alphabet games. In the alphabet word game, each player takes turns thinking of words that start with each letter of the alphabet, one after the other. Help your child with difficult letters in this game, particularly *x,* or you can deal with the letter *x* by waiving the requirement that the word start with *x* and allowing the use of any word that contains *x*. The alphabet word game may continue through the alphabet several times, but you may not repeat any word. In the alphabet hunt game, people look for each consecutive letter of the alphabet while riding in a car or bus. Children and adults may compete, trying to find all the letters in proper order and trying to win by finding z first. On short trips just see who gets the farthest in the alphabet by the time you get to your destination. Of course, parents who play while driving must keep road safety their first concern.

Point out and read words around you every day, such as traffic signs, store names on buildings, and labels on boxes of cereal or candy. Occasionally write down what your children say and read it back to them. They enjoy this activity and will look over the words you wrote. Write down stories your child tells, or ask your child to draw a story or picture and make up a story about the picture. Either way, you write the story on the pictures. Label photographs you or your children take, perhaps with funny captions, or make up funny captions for drawings or pictures cut out of magazines and pasted on pages. Even if you don't try to teach your child to read, do some of these fun activities to develop a good attitude about reading.

Some picture books and coloring books label the names of depicted foods, animals, articles of clothing, and common household items. These books can help but they won't teach your child to read without your help. When you ask children what a word in the book says, they can often guess by looking at the picture. Instead, make a game of covering pictures, sounding out the words, and then uncovering the picture to see if the child read the word correctly. Your child might eventually enjoy playing this game alone. Make your own picture dictionary. Ask your child to cut out pictures of objects and paste them onto pages, and then you label them.

Start your child reading whole words with a flashcard game in which your child hunts for cards with the same short word (cat, dog, sit, sun, hot, box, etc.) written on them. Encourage your child to sound out the words. Later, make this game more complicated by varying the use of capitalization, sometimes using a capital letter only to start the word, sometimes using all capital letters, and sometimes using all small letters. Next, show flashcards with words for household objects and ask your child to sound out the word and then point to the real object in the home. Another game uses flashcards with pictures (children can make them) and flashcards with the words identifying the pictured objects; the child finds the matching flashcards. If you make flashcards of simple actions (wave hello, jump, clap your hands, touch your nose, spin around, kneel down, act like a dog, etc.), your child can sound out the words and do the action. If you make flashcards that sometimes correctly and sometimes incorrectly identify the color of the card or picture on the card, you can ask your child to identify the cards as correct or incorrect.

When playing these reading games, don't frustrate your children with failure. If they can't read a word within about five seconds, help them sound it out. Playing these games will help them learn to read simple children's books. Give praise for reading anything, even signs and cereal boxes. Lavish praise on them for reading stories or books. If your child can read simple sentences but points to the words while reading, discourage this bad habit, which interferes with reading speed and the mental grasp of the whole phrase that gives sentences the flow of spoken language. When your child reads a story to you and has difficulty with some of the harder words, don't spend too much time waiting for the sounding out of words, especially if many words give trouble. Instead, keep the story pleasant by quickly helping. You might say the first half of the word or sound out the word aloud.

Even when your children can read stories, keep reading to them. Read more difficult stories and books they can't read alone. Encourage them to read to you, too. Reading aloud helps children learn to read with the proper intonation to make sentences sound like speech. This skill increases understanding in reading, even when they read silently.

Give your children interesting things to read, including comic books. Find articles in magazines or newspapers on topics they enjoy. Take them to the library to find interesting books. Later, encourage them to read literary classics, such as *20,000 Leagues Under the Sea* by Jules Verne or *Moby Dick* by Herman Melville, but don't choose books that are beyond their ability. Reading for pleasure should be fun, not difficult. Try to reduce TV viewing and encourage more reading for pleasure. Allow your child to stay up half an hour later if reading in bed. Some parents and school systems pay children money for reading books. Reading is much better for them than constantly watching television.

Encourage your children to look up words they don't understand in the dictionary. There are simple dictionaries available for children. Set a good example by using the dictionary yourself when you see a word you don't know. Encourage your child to keep a list of troublesome words and occasionally practice them. Do this yourself, too, if you keep forgetting the meaning of certain words. Buying an encyclopedia also helps. Children can use it to do homework reports or look up interesting facts or topics occasionally.

Parents can teach their children to write early, too. Don't worry about whether your child is left-handed or right-handed. Forcing children to use a hand other than the hand they naturally prefer can make writing frustrating.

Prepare for writing by asking your children to copy straight lines (horizontal, vertical, and slanted) and wavy lines. When they can do this well, make circles, squares, and triangles in dotted lines for them to trace. After this skill develops, ask them to copy circles, squares, and triangles freehand, and then to trace dotted letters and words. Later, write letters and words and ask your children to copy them freehand. Just for fun, use crayons and magic markers as well as pencils and pens. The first thing many children want to write is their names. A fun activity is writing what your child says and letting the child copy it.

Don't be too critical of your child's early, poor attempts to write. Use praise to give encouragement. Instead of making too many corrections, just point out a few of the worst mistakes. Realize that some letters are much harder than others. Many children will reverse letters such as *b* and *d* and make mistakes with letters such as *g, p,* and *q* well into the early years of grade school. Later, when mistakes are less frequent, you can point out more of them without causing discouragement. Let your child make the corrections—children learn less if you make the corrections.

When your children can read and write, encourage them to write down telephone messages they might forget. Establish a policy that family members leave notes about where they have gone, when they left and will return, and perhaps how to reach them. Children enjoy writing letters to friends and relatives. Encourage writing letters and suggest keeping a journal or diary of daily events, thoughts, and feelings. Certain games help cultivate spelling and writing skills. Hold your own spelling bee, in which children compete to see who misses a word first. In spelling bees with children of different ages, try to tailor the words you ask to their levels of ability, perhaps by using previous spelling homework from school. Simple crossword puzzles also help cultivate spelling skills. Word jumbles are fun, too, made by picking a word and mixing up the order of its letters. The child tries to untangle the jumble, perhaps with a clue from you.

Helping Your Children Do Well in School

Many parents don't understand the great importance of success in school. School failure is a very important risk factor for alcohol and drug abuse, teen pregnancy, delinquency, violence, and crime. Problem behaviors such as drug use or violence often begin as ways for children who feel hopeless and powerless to gain acceptance from peers.

How can you help your children do well in school? First, put your child in daycare occasionally for experience in supervision by teachers and in how children interact in large groups. You might volunteer there a few times to ease the transition. When your children approach school age, take them to visit the school a few times to acquaint them with it. If possible, use the route your child will take to get there. Go when the school is empty and wander around the halls, looking in classrooms and pointing out things. Play on the playground. You might take a picture of your child at the school, draw a picture of it, or ask your child to draw the picture. Go back again when school is in session, so your child can also see this. Discuss the child's expectations and clear up any fears or misconceptions. Describe the importance of school and how people use what they learn there the rest of their lives. Explain school rules and the need for them. Suggest your child will like both school and learning. Be sure to feed your child breakfast before school; researchers believe this improves learning.

Children learn attitudes about school, learning, and work from their parents. If you want your children to do well in school, you must show, by example and interest in your child's work and progress, that education is very important to you. If only one parent does this or seems to feel education is very important, the child will have less motivation to do well. Rewards may actually interfere with a motivated child, but you can help an unmotivated child learn to take pride in achievement by rewarding time studying, effort, and handing in work on time. This is much better than using rewards for good grades on the report card. Show learning is important to you by reading books and using dictionaries and other books to look up answers to questions that arise. Parents also set an important example by working hard and doing the best they can in whatever they do. Parents who complain about their own work or do only what is necessary to get by will find it difficult to encourage their children to achieve. Allowing your child to miss school without a good reason shows that you don't place much importance on school. Don't try to sympathize by revealing you didn't like or did poorly in a subject. This encourages your child to lose interest and motivation in it.

Research shows when parents become actively involved with education and cooperate with teachers, improved student achievement, better school attendance, reduced dropout rates, and reduced juvenile delinquency results. Nagging about doing schoolwork and improving grades is not a good way to help, and paying attention to progress only when report cards come out isn't enough. First, set aside a block of time for homework each day. During this time, children must work quietly. Give them a quiet place to work with good lighting, turning off the television and radio. Find out what homework your children have each day and when tests are scheduled. After finishing all the day's homework, they may spend the rest of the time on long-term homework projects, extra studying, or pleasure reading. Setting aside time for homework and quiet, intellectual activities is much better than simply making the rule that children must complete their homework before watching television. It encourages your children to do more than necessary to finish their homework and watch television. If you can't be home during the study time, ask another responsible adult to supervise and assist, especially if your child is doing poorly in school.

The best way to show your interest in your child's homework is to always read it. In this way, you make sure your child has made a real effort. Pay attention to the grades earned on all homework assignments and tests, praising improvements, good grades, and extra effort. Occasionally reward these things, perhaps by making a special dessert, allowing a later bedtime one night, or renting a movie to watch. During early grade school, display your child's better schoolwork on your refrigerator or walls. Help children memorize facts. Make flashcards for addition, subtraction, multiplication, and division when your child studies them in school. Be sure to provide your help in good humor and encouragingly. Don't be critical; show patience. Remember, your attitudes are important in shaping your child's self-image. If you can't help without becoming frustrated or angry, the child may be better off without your help.

Talk to your children's teachers at least twice a year about their progress and behaviors. Are they consistently completing all the homework? If not, your child may be lying to you about homework, and you should ask the teacher to send signed homework slips every day. Ask if there are other problems. If bullying is a problem, meet with the school principal and encourage the school-wide changes discussed in chapter 28, Anger. If your child does poorly in school or the teachers complain of inattention, ask for a full learning disabilities evaluation. If this rules out learning disabilities, find out if the work is either too hard or too easy for your child. Frustration or boredom can cause inattention or underachievement. If your child has regular problems with staying in the seat, following teacher commands, finishing tasks, keeping hands away from other children, disruptive talking, provoking other children, aggression, or destruction, the following program can help. Ask the teacher to send a daily report card home on these issues, so you can impose or refuse rewards, such as desserts, TV time, movies, late bedtimes, etc. Moving the child's desk to the front of the classroom may also help.

Make sure your child can read by the third grade. If your child can't, either teach your child to read yourself or hire a tutor. If your child receives poor grades in any particular subject, spend time teaching and helping on that subject yourself or get tutoring for it. Older students often make good peer tutors. Avoid lecturing, nagging, scolding, or threatening children about school problems, as encouragement and a positive attitude will work better. For example, instead of scolding about not finishing the last questions, you might say "You did part of your homework very well, honey. Let's see if you can finish the last few questions."

If you find out your child cheated in school, give a punishment and make your child spend plenty of time on homework, perhaps two hours a day. Don't let the child stop after completing the day's homework. Enforce extra studying. You must teach the importance of learning and make it very clear you won't tolerate cheating to get by.

When the school assigns written papers or reports, encourage your child to make rough drafts of them to edit and improve. Inspire your child to think of more descriptive words and better vocabulary. *Roget's Thesaurus* of synonyms can help a great deal. Get extra reading material on subjects or topics that interest your child. Encourage striving high but don't demand perfection. Be realistic in what you expect. Support your child in failure, emphasizing that success often comes after learning from failure, continuing to work toward your goals, and refusing to give up.

For extra practice, you might have your children ask questions and give answers on a tape recorder, going back on the tape to self-correct and make improvements. Another good strategy is making and taking their own practice tests. During summer vacations, ask them to read books and perhaps write book reports.

When your children must learn numerous facts, teach them to take careful notes at school with as much detail as possible. Teach studying and test-taking skills. Teach them to memorize by using key words and first letters. By memorizing a few of the most important words, key words, it becomes much easier to memorize a definition or an important idea. To memorize a list, take all the first letters of the words and rearrange them to make a word or nonsense word you can easily memorize, then use this word or nonsense word to help you memorize and recall the whole list. Use the first letters of key words to help memorize definitions or explanations. Another useful trick is to make funny or striking associations between words to help you remember key words or nonsense words standing for first letters.

On tests, teach your children to answer all the easier questions first, coming back to the difficult items later, so they don't waste time.

Finally, don't let your child work at a part-time job any more than twenty hours a week during the school year. Working longer hours tends to interfere with the studying needed to do well in school, and many teenagers who work too much become overwhelmed and drop out of school for the financial independence of working full-time. A nationwide survey published by the Journal of the American Medical Association found junior high and high school students working twenty hours or more per week were more likely to use alcohol and marijuana and to start having sex earlier than other students.

What about Television?

Television is a wonderful invention that brings the pageant of life into our homes at the touch of a button. We can choose from an incredible variety of shows, including nature, historical documentaries, studies of other cultures in the world, science, health, musical performances, plays, comedies, adventure, etc. Shows like "Sesame Street," "Barney," and "Mr. Rogers' Neighborhood" on public television and "Blue's Clues" on Nickelodeon teach children about letters, numbers, books, problem solving, sharing, empathy, cooperation, disabled people, and different races, cultures, and religions. Children can learn a great deal from television.

Television captivates our attention with its fast pace and beautiful photography, but it also lures viewers with the excitement of violence, crime, danger, and sex. Certainly violence in art speaks to us of the human condition—think of Greek drama. But television seems preoccupied with violence, crime, and sexual attractiveness and innuendo. The obsession with violence and sex on TV is constantly escalating. The Parents Television Council reported that the incidence of prime-time sex, violence, and foul language tripled in the 1990s, with references to oral sex going from 0 in the first 4 weeks to 1989 to 20 in the first 4 weeks of 1999.

One study found 73% of violent acts on TV went unpunished, 47% of violent acts shown resulted in no observable harm or pain to victims, and only 16% of violent programs showed any resulting long-term problems—physical, emotional, or financial. Only 4% of violent shows had an anti-violence theme or showed any alternatives to violence. Another study reports 61% of all shows on TV contain violence and that 87% of shows on premium channels like HBO and ShowTime contain violence. Unfortunately, weekend daytime children's TV contains the most violence, is least likely to show bad effects of violence, and is most likely to make violence seem funny.

Many groups oppose excessive violence on television, most notably the American Medical Association and the National Parent-Teachers Association. The violent activity involves 2/3 of the leading characters. Violence is a common method of TV revenge. Most male TV roles are violent. Sadly, this often portrays violence as a powerful personal quality or skill that solves problems. Murder, assault, and armed robbery are the most common crimes on TV. A study by the American Psychological Association estimates the average child, watching 27 hours of TV a week, will see 8,000 murders and 100,000 acts of violence between ages 3 and 12.

About 3,000 research studies show TV has a variety of harmful effects on children and adults. First, watching violence on TV causes violent behavior in normal people of all ages, from preschoolers to adults, although TV violence is most likely to influence angry people, poor people, victims of child abuse, and those who grow up in urban areas witnessing violence. Many studies exposed children to violent movies or TV and noted an increase in aggressive and violent incidents afterward. For example, one study found that many children try to jump-kick their peers after watching the Saturday morning children's cartoon "Power Rangers." Aggression and violence do not increase after children watch nonviolent shows. Controlling for all other socioeconomic factors, children who watch more TV have less satisfying relationships, fewer interactions with others, and are more aggressive, violent, and destructive than those who watch less TV.

Violent acts portrayed in the media sometimes lead to crimes. After seeing a movie about gang warfare called *The Warriors,* 12 youths in New York terrorized and assaulted subway passengers until police subdued them. This movie was also linked to two fatal attacks in California. A movie about drug dealers called *New Jack City* led to violence, shootings, a rampaging crowd, and a murder at various theaters. Britain and Ireland banned the movie *Natural Born Killers* after copycat murders in Massachusetts, Louisiana, and France, and this movie later led a man in New York to kill a firefighter. One man burned his wife to death half an hour after watching Farrah Fawcett play a real battered wife who killed her husband that way in the movie *The Burning Bed.* Two armed men forced the owner of an audio store and customers to eat Drano and put duct tape over their mouths, imitating the movie *Magnum Force* the day after watching this movie three times. Some criminals report studying the imaginative scripts of crime dramas to learn how to escape detection for crimes. Media portrayals of suicide can also lead to deaths. After seeing the game Russian roulette in the movie *The Deerhunter,* over 20 people killed themselves this way.

Films have become increasingly violent since the early days of film making, to give greater thrills to the audience. Many people believe this makes violence seem more normal than it should and that seeing so much violence on TV and in movies makes people more willing to use violence in anger. Some research evidence suggests exposure to violent entertainment may make people more cold-hearted. Many studies found children were more tolerant of hostile and aggressive behaviors among their peers after a violent film than after seeing no film or after seeing a nonviolent film. Other studies found physical measures of arousal to violent scenes were weaker, a numbing of emotional responsiveness, in children with heavy TV viewing habits than in those who watched less TV. The concerned people of Canada, Germany, France, New Zealand, and other countries refuse to allow as much violent TV programming as Americans allow.

Television also promotes an unhealthy preoccupation with sex and attractiveness. Sexual innuendo and seductive acts and clothing dominate the advertisements and programming. More than 2/3 of all network prime-time shows contain sexual content, averaging more than five sex scenes per hour, a rate that would make porn stars jealous. The vast majority of sex on TV involves unmarried couples with little commitment to one another. Portrayals of premarital sex outnumber sex within marriage by eight to one. Sex on TV often involves violence, rape, or other sex crimes and seldom portrays sexual relationships as warm, loving, or stable. Television often depicts sex as exciting fun free of cares and risks, a competition, or a way to define masculinity. In a study of 1,351 randomly selected network and cable shows, not one scene with implied or actual sexual intercourse mentioned the dangers or potential consequences of sex, birth control, abortion, or sexually transmitted diseases. Television overemphasizes sexual attractiveness, with little or no focus on responsibility for people's feelings or looking for a partner with virtue and good character. Thin body types dominate on TV, and thinness is consistently associated with favorable personality traits. The American Psychological Association estimates TV exposes children to 14,000 sexual messages each year. One survey of 750 children ages 10 to 16 found that 62% believe TV encourages them to have sex too young.

Educators worry about the correlation between watching television and lowered reading skills, intelligence test (IQ) scores, and academic achievement. On the average, the more TV a child watches, the worse the reading skills, the lower the IQ, and the worse the school achievement.

Children with high IQs and children in high school tend to achieve less, especially in reading, if they watch even one or two hours of TV per day. Children with the lowest IQs and poorest school achievement are the ones most likely to watch more than four hours of TV per day.

Individual children may differ from these group patterns, but the more TV a child watches, the less time remains to devote to reading, writing, homework, and hobbies or interests that can result in learning. Most experts see television as an important factor interfering with reading skills and literacy in the world today. Research suggests a link between heavy TV viewing and less imagination and creativity in children. In one study of children in a Canadian town before and after the arrival of TV, creativity dropped and within two years of the introduction of TV, rates of hitting, shoving, and biting among 1st- and 2nd-graders increased by 160%. Adults also show a strong link between education and TV viewing habits. On the average, adults with fewer completed years of school watch more TV than do more educated adults.

Television also portrays drinking alcohol and using other drugs as common and harmless. In 1982, the National Institute of Mental Health noted that on TV, people drank alcohol 15 times as often as they drank water and 14 times as often as soft drinks, rarely with any negative consequences. Although this has improved with growing awareness of the problem, children often see old syndicated shows, and many new movies, comedy shows, and music videos on TV portray the use of alcohol, marijuana, and other drugs as harmless, exciting fun. A recent study found 81% of drug depictions in popular songs and 52% in movies give no sense of consequences, which promotes a false feeling of invulnerability in children. Sadly, another study found between 6 and 10% of the drug use in music videos involved what appeared to be children. Music videos often pair tobacco and drinking with at least mildly sexual behavior. MTV (Music Television) has the highest percentages of videos with tobacco and alcohol use.

Television also contributes to obesity in children, primarily because children watching TV are inactive and because of the foods being advertised. Children who watch TV heavily are more likely to be obese than are those who watch less TV. The more TV children watch, the less nutritional knowledge and the worse nutritional habits they tend to have. Quick snacks account for much of the eating on TV, and TV advertisements for food products generally promote high fat, high cholesterol, high sugar, and high salt foods. One study counted 223 food commercials during 4 hours of cartoons one Saturday morning. Of these, only nine commercials promoted foods with acceptable levels of fat and sugar. Children with heavy TV viewing habits request, buy, and eat more junk foods, such as candy, potato chips, soda pop, and hot dogs, than other children. Young children with heavy TV viewing habits more often believed candy is highly nutritious or that certain cereals could make them strong. Other countries use laws to help combat poor nutritional habits in children. For example, in Holland any advertisement for candy must include a toothbrush in the corner, and in Quebec, Canada, no advertiser may aim a commercial at children under 12 years old.

One excellent way to reduce the negative effects of TV and movies is to limit the kinds of shows your children may watch, perhaps using the V-chip, program ratings, and the guide to movies listed at the end of this chapter. You can forbid violent shows and shows that deal with crime or depict selfish attitudes toward sexuality. It also helps to avoid shows with selfish, greedy, or vengeful characters. Plenty of good shows remain to watch—educational, musical performances, plays, nature, science, children's stories, and shows about children and their families.

Keeping televisions and computers in the family room helps parents monitor viewing without the children feeling like you are prying. Use family-friendly Internet service providers or computer filtering software, too. Consider limiting the amount of TV your children may watch to one or two hours each day. One study reported limiting TV to one hour per day for one month reduced aggressiveness in one child, reduced shyness in another child, and increased grades in a third child. Be a little flexible, however. If your child's favorite TV shows fall on a particular evening, let your child skip TV another day to watch extra television on that day. Setting aside certain hours for homework, extra studying, and quiet reading, reduces the time spent watching TV in a subtle way. Considering the research, it is wise to limit any child receiving poor grades in school to one or two hours of TV per day.

Don't use television as a tranquilizer. Replace the family habit of watching TV with more worthwhile interests and activities, using the list in chapter 8 for suggestions. Reading good books aloud to one another is an excellent family activity. If you plan plenty of fun and interesting activities (singing, dancing, etc.), your children won't even miss TV. These shared activities increase family closeness and communication.

Reduce the negative impact of TV by talking to your children about it. Ask their thoughts and opinions on different shows and answer questions that arise. Explain the difference between TV shows about real life and make-believe TV shows for fun and excitement. Describe in simple terms how people make TV shows. Help your child learn to recognize what is real and what isn't real on TV. Explain that in real life, sarcasm and insults hurt people's feelings, break down closeness, and cause arguments. Point out that on TV, exciting, dangerous automobile stunts, complete with fires and explosions, never lead to injuries, yet you never see seat belts. Discuss the role stunt men perform for high salaries.

Teach your child at an early age why people make advertisements and that advertised products may not be as useful, fun, or healthy for you as the ad suggests. Make sure your child understands that although fighting and violence on TV can be fun to watch, real violence hurts people, has terrible consequences, and is a crime. Research suggests the more parents talk about such things on TV, the more the child's opinions tend to agree with the parent, and that making a negative comment about the violence on TV reduces children's tendencies to endorse violence or to copy it.

Watching an educational TV show with a child and interacting during the show increases the child's learning from it. Unfortunately, most of the time when parents watch TV with children, they watch what they want to watch, without trying to encourage learning from it, and the children often see programming intended for older viewers. Parents can use many TV shows for learning purposes. Help a young child understand the action, implications, feelings, and conflicts in TV shows. When your child gets a little older, discuss the sexual, age-related, and racial stereotypes on TV and discuss the difference between the apparent harmlessness of alcohol on TV and its serious consequences in real life. Point out the overemphasis on physical attractiveness, on violent sexuality, and on pleasure seeking through sex. At times, television can be very useful in opening communication on sensitive issues with older children. You can use shows that deal with teen pregnancy or premarital sex to begin a serious conversation with your older child in which you help them see the issue in a more mature way.

Discussing Sex with Your Children

Parents can reduce the chance of a variety of serious problems by discussing sex openly with their children. Establish open communication about sex very early by using good vocabulary for the parts of the body. Use the words *vagina, penis, breast,* and *anus.* Proper terms are less confusing than baby talk such as *weewee* or vague words like *bottom, bad parts,* and *down there.* Using the proper terms also promotes the healthy attitude that sex organs are ordinary parts of the body, rather than forbidden, bad, or secret parts. Children often develop a great interest in forbidden or mysterious things.

When toddlers absent-mindedly touch their genitals, either ignore it or distract them. Becoming upset, pulling the hands away, or punishing a child for touching genitals makes the forbidden behavior more interesting and may provoke a power struggle. Many parents become upset, shocked, or very angry when little children rub their genitals excessively in front of other people, expose themselves to others, or indulge in sex play or sexual exploration with other children (while playing doctor, for example). Sexual experimentation is common and normal in little children. Try not to overreact if you find your child doing any of these things. Little children often love to wield power over their parents by indulging in behaviors that shock or upset them. A calm response minimizes the chance of future problems.

The first time one of these things occurs, assume your child didn't know any better and gently explain the situation. Describe self-stimulation as normal behavior that should occur only in private because it offends other people, and describe self-exposure as offensive to others. Point out that self-exposure or public self-stimulation may result in social rejection or even in criminal charges or rape by other people. Then give your child time out for it. If further problems occur, give time out and impose loss of a privilege, perhaps not letting the child play outside for the rest of the day. Don't use severe punishments that exaggerate the importance of these common childhood problems. Remain calm and deal with the problem as if your child had broken any other rule.

Parents can also help a child who experiments sexually by satisfying the child's curiosity about sex differences. Explain that curiosity about sex differences is normal but you can provide the best information. Then describe the penis and the vagina by drawing diagrams or using illustrations from a medical book. Answer any questions that come up, keeping the subject in a healthy, natural perspective.

The best sex education is an informal, comfortable approach of answering any questions that arise. Start with simplified answers for little children and answer with more detail as they grow older. If a 5-year-old child asks where babies come from, you can probably satisfy the child's curiosity by answering something like, "Babies grow in the bellies of their mothers. Remember when Helen was pregnant and had that big belly?" An older child might think to ask for more details. Keep it simple but feel free to go into as much depth as necessary. If a child asks how a baby gets into the mother, explain it takes both a man and woman to make a baby and that women always have eggs for babies, but one of the eggs must become fertilized by the father's loving to make a baby. If an older child asks for more details, explain that a special fluid from the man fertilizes the egg in the woman during lovemaking, so a baby starts to grow. You might compare this process to pollen fertilizing a plant, so its seeds can grow into baby plants.

Making sure your child can comfortably discuss sex with you helps in preventing childhood sexual abuse. Research indicates 1 out of 4 or 5 girls is a victim of sexual abuse before the age of 18 and that approximately 1 out of 7 girls and 1 out of 15 boys has a sexual experience with an adult before puberty. Around 1/4 of all child sexual abuse occurs to children under seven years old. Family members, relatives, neighbors, or trusted friends most often sexually abuse children, although unrelated people, strangers, and acquaintances sexually abuse boys much more often than girls. Child molesters exist in cities, suburbs, and rural areas. Even highly respected members of the community may molest children.

Protect young children from sexual abuse early, preferably before starting school, in the following way. Make sure your children know which parts of the body are private and should remain hidden and untouched by other people. If you feel very uncomfortable with using the proper terms for body parts, use the words *private parts* and explain this means the parts of the body that underwear hide. Explain that some adults with personal problems bother children by hugging them, kissing them, or showing or touching genitals. Tell your children if any adult or family member ever suggests or tries anything like this, they should immediately leave, screaming and running if necessary. Explain the person will want to keep it a secret and may even threaten them, but they should tell you about it anyway, no matter who the person is. Several times, emphasize the importance of telling. Using roleplays with feedback improves understanding and helps your children practice assertive responses.

Make this just one normal part of training your child about safety rules. For example, you should also teach your preschool children their full names and addresses and how to dial the operator or emergency phone number 911. Teach them to go to policemen, store personnel, or females if they get lost (women are much less likely to sexually abuse children than men are). Teach your children not to accept invitations, candy, money, gifts, or rides from people they don't know well. Teach them not to get near a stranger's car, help a stranger look for a lost child or animal, nor give information on the phone to strangers. If afraid for any reason, they should scream and run toward other people and not into empty places. If a car follows them, they should turn around and run in the opposite direction. If someone tries to take them away against their will, they should scream "Help, I'm being kidnapped!"

Police recommend using the safety game to teach child safety. Play by asking your child for the best behavior in response to problem situations or by asking about the possible consequences of certain actions. For example, "What could happen if you put your homework paper on the stove?" Teach children what the smoke detector alarm sounds like, to roll on the ground if their clothes catch on fire, to crawl low under smoke, and never to go back into a burning building. Police also encourage the use of secret code words to identify friends who may legitimately transport your child. If the code word is *keyhole,* for example, the child should never go with anyone who claims to be sent by the parents unless the person tells the child the code word *keyhole.* Teaching early grade school children about the dangers of drugs in the ways described in the section on Teenagers in this chapter is another important part of child safety training.

Unfortunately, many parents never discuss sexual intercourse, contraception, masturbation, and other important sexual facts with their children. Most older Americans grew up with the notion people don't talk about sex. Many parents would like to inform their children about sex but don't know how to bring it up, and many children would like to talk to their parents about sex but never ask because they don't know if their parents would feel comfortable. Many natural opportunities to discuss it occur in every home, however. You can initiate a discussion of human sexuality when a friend of the family becomes pregnant, after the children see a pregnant woman in public, when a family pet has babies, or when neighborhood dogs or cats go to heat or mate. Or you can begin discussing it after TV shows or movies depicting sexual situations or consequences of sexual intimacy. For example, after viewing an aggressive sexual sequence with your child, you can ask questions and discuss real affection and love versus selfishness in sexual relationships.

If you have never discussed sex with your child, don't try to cover everything in one or two sittings. Make sure your children know you are willing to talk about sexual matters whenever they have a question. Don't worry if you don't know the answer to a question. Find a book or call Planned Parenthood or a health clinic for the information and share what you learn with your child. If you have given an answer that, upon your thinking it over, could have been better, tell your child so and give your new thoughts on the matter.

Adolescents need to be well informed about sex. As detailed in chapter 42, Preventing Violence and Crime, rampant misconceptions and lack of knowledge about sexuality and birth control lead to much higher rates of teenage pregnancy in the United States than in other developed nations. The lack of knowledge also leads to more sexually transmitted diseases (STDs). Several studies show rates of STD infection in the United States are 50 to 100 times higher than in other developed nations. Of the estimated 12 million new STD infections in the U.S. each year, 8 million occur in people under 25 and 3 million in teenagers. Of all sexually active high school students, 1 in 4 gets a sexually transmitted disease before graduating. With about 1/4 of American women becoming pregnant before the age of 19 and with teenage pregnancy occurring in every social group, all adolescents should receive sex education.

Sex education frequently persuades young people to delay starting sexual activity, use condoms, and have fewer sex partners. It works best in preventing pregnancy when it begins in elementary school before the strong feelings of biological urges and young romance make an adolescent unwilling to seriously consider advice about sex. Parents usually don't know when their children first have sex, and adolescents today face great peer pressures to have it, with a majority of high school students nationwide having already had sex. Of these sexually active students, 42% don't use condoms, and many use birth control inconsistently or improperly, with the youngest children having sex being the least likely to understand or practice safe sex. Half of all premarital pregnancies occur within the first 6 months of sexual activity. Many teenagers become sexually active before receiving any sex education in school. Of course, it is better to discuss sex with your child late than never, but before puberty is best.

If you are very uncomfortable talking about sex, practice using the words and talking about the issues beforehand using behavioral roleplays. Don't memorize a lecture; just become comfortable talking about the subject. You may even admit to your child that you grew up never talking about sex and you feel nervous or uncomfortable doing so. Your child will admire your honesty and courage. If you can't discuss these things openly, show your child parts of this discussion and give good books or pamphlets from the library, health clinics, or social service agencies such as Planned Parenthood. Or you might find a relative, friend, or preacher who will help inform your child.

Teach both boys and girls about menstruation, penile erections, and wet dreams before puberty, certainly before they occur. You should also talk about masturbation. Don't let your child feel guilty or worried about horrible consequences from this common, normal act. Describe the whole range of sexual activity, including embracing, kissing, caressing, cuddling, manual stimulation of the genitals, coitus, and oral sex. Don't use the word *foreplay,* which describes all other forms of sex as only a prelude to coitus. Stress that many people find affectionate activities more emotionally satisfying than coitus. Also reduce overemphasis on coitus by pointing out people may also reach orgasm by embracing each other and rubbing their bodies together, manual stimulation of the genitals, or oral sex.

Be sure to clear up the misconceptions adolescents often have about sex. Tell your child women can get pregnant from their first sexual experience, infrequent sex, sex during menstrual bleeding, or sex while standing up. Explain pregnancy may result from sex without orgasm in one or both partners, sex without insertion, sex if the male withdraws his penis before reaching orgasm, and manual play if any of the male's fluid reaches the vagina. Make it clear engaging in sex doesn't make you grown up or mature and doesn't necessarily make you happy. Point out a national survey of 16- and 17-year-olds with A or B averages found 70% have never had sex and that well over 1/3 of the 30% who have had sex wished they hadn't.

Discourage one-on-one dating before age 16 and early, frequent, steady dating. Explain that you learn more about people's character and you make better choices if you date around before settling down. Take a strong stand against girls dating much older boys and boys dating much younger girls— this often leads to more risky sexual behaviors. Instruct your children sex demands great responsibility because it stirs up deep feelings, because people are vulnerable when they become sexually involved, and because pregnancy and sexual diseases are possible. Stress that it is immature and immoral to feign affection, lie about your feelings in a relationship, or lie about your feelings or actions in other relationships. Teach the importance of having a good reputation in all areas of life, including sex.

Emphasize people must protect themselves from pregnancy and sexual diseases whenever they have sex. Instruct boys they have as much responsibility for avoiding pregnancy as girls do and as much responsibility after the fact. Teach your children about the kinds of birth control, their success rates, and their proper use. Make sure your children fully understand the responsibilities of parenthood and the consequences of unplanned pregnancies, including the poverty that often results. Chapter 19 details this information and describes helpful information for children about the foolish reasons sometimes influencing a teenager's decision to become pregnant. Discuss abortion with your children, too, including its legal, moral, and emotional aspects.

Adolescents should know how to recognize and prevent sexually transmitted diseases (STDs). Teenagers are now one of the at-risk groups for getting HIV, the virus leading to AIDS. They should know STDs often don't initially result in symptoms, yet are dangerous to leave untreated and can lead to sterility, cancer, or death. For example, HIV often shows no unusual symptoms for ten years before causing AIDS, human papillomavirus often shows no symptoms before causing cancer, and gonorrhea often shows no symptoms before causing sterility. Girls may not notice the early symptoms of syphilis, and these will go away before syphilis causes such problems as paralysis, insanity, and death later. Public health clinics can provide brochures on STDs. Emphasize it is immoral to have sex without warning your partner if you suspect or know you carry one of these infections.

Confusion between true love and the intense feelings associated with sex is one of the reasons for teenage pregnancies and for the very high divorce rate in teenage marriages. Teach your children good sex simply involves certain kinds of stimulation people can perform selfishly with no true love, but sex reaches its most ecstatic joyfulness and greatest fulfillment in a deeply loving and respectful relationship. Use chapter 2, Love, to describe the kinds of caring, closeness, tenderness, actions, trust, loyalty, and sharing predominating in deeply loving relationships. Point out a deeply loving relationship makes intimacy worthwhile and beautiful. Boys especially need this kind of emphasis because they often learn to view sex in selfish, pleasure-seeking ways. Help your child understand marriage has its ups and downs and it takes plenty of effort, communication, and compromise for love to endure.

Teach your children people can misuse sex in selfish ways. Many people pursue sex as a conquest, with little caring about the other person. People often falsely pretend they care and feel affection, sometimes for months and months, simply to have sexual intercourse, or they may pretend never to have felt this way before or never to have wanted someone so much before. Warn your children about the selfish ploy "If you really loved me, you would do it." Point out that many girls who have sex to keep a boyfriend end up losing him anyway and feeling extremely hurt and used. Warn girls of the selfish boy's pretense that he needs sex desperately because he is in physical pain without it.

Teach all children that loving sex is always a mutually desired expression of affection. Emphasize that the use of force or intimidation to get sex is not only vicious and immoral, but also criminal. Explain a desire for affection is not the same as a desire for sex, that people often want different degrees of sexual intimacy, and that misunderstandings can lead to unintentional date rape. Use the information in chapter 36 to describe what rape is, explain common misunderstandings between men and women, and teach your children how to avoid rape. For example, they should know how consensual sex can be rape, how verbally pressuring someone for sex can be rape, and that being drunk is no legal defense against accusation of rape, nor is consensual sex play before unwanted intercourse or a previous sexual relationship with the girl.

The most effective way to help your children avoid pressures to have sex is practicing saying no with behavioral roleplays. Make up situations where dates are pressuring them and ask them to respond. Create a variety of pressuring statements: about how all the cool people have sex, ridicule about being afraid or a baby, arguments you're uptight and sex will really relax you, promises to marry or to provide for the baby, complaints about needs, threats or hints about ending the relationship, etc. Make sure your children develop and practice many good responses about self-respect, unwanted pregnancy, sexual diseases, life goals, etc. Teach them to be assertive, to keep repeating no, to complain about the pressure, to describe how the pressure makes them feel about the relationship, and to refuse to discuss it further. Urge them to avoid becoming very sexually excited with a partner because it is so easy to fail to stop, even with every intention of stopping.

Discuss homosexuality with your children, too. Adolescents sometimes worry excessively about homosexuality despite having no homosexual desires, and may end up homosexual because of early homosexual experiences or misunderstandings about normal feelings and behaviors. Explain curiosity about sex organs is normal, but homosexuality means a preference for sexual partners of your own sex, not any other mannerisms or character traits. Because 9% of men and just over 4% of women have had homosexual sex at some time since puberty, often as teenagers, and most parents will never know about their teenager experimenting in this way until a strong homosexual identity develops, it is wise to help your children understand this situation. Tell your child many heterosexual people try homosexual acts and such experimentation doesn't necessarily lead to a homosexual lifestyle, but sex is very addictive and continuing such acts will lead to a homosexual lifestyle. Therefore, any person who doesn't want to be homosexual shouldn't experiment with these kinds of acts. Explain that because homosexual acts often have traumatic effects on self-esteem and heterosexuals often reject homosexuals, engaging in homosexual acts can make it much more difficult to develop heterosexual relationships. If you ever find out your child has experimented in this way, you can make whatever rules you feel are appropriate, but help your child avoid establishing a permanent self-label of homosexual by explaining some of these facts.

If you discover that your child has some pornography, you might simply ignore it. If it troubles you, you have every right, as a parent, to throw the pornography away and impose a punishment. If you do, however, try to discuss the issue in a calm and understanding way with your child. Simply explain your feelings about the influence of pornography, perhaps stating that true love is much more beautiful and satisfying than simple sexual gratification.

When discussing sex with your children, don't use scare tactics, yell, or try to force your attitudes onto them. This often makes them less willing to discuss sex honestly with you or to come to you with concerns or problems about sex. Instead, let your children express opinions, and gently try to help them grow in wisdom. Also, don't pry into the intimate details of your teenager's sex life. Teenagers need privacy in this area as much as other people do.

Teenagers

The teenage years are a period of transition in which children grow in independence, yearn for more freedom, experiment with different interests and goals in life, start to develop romantic relationships, and begin to assume more adult roles in life. Allow some of the freedoms your teenager desires, within normal limits for other children the same age. Teenagers need freedom to grow in independence and responsibility. Although it appears that less than 10% of families have serious problems with their teenagers, you can reduce the likelihood of problems by raising your children in the ways described previously. Developing a wide variety of interests and activities in your children helps a great deal. Showing your love, early training in virtues and problem-solving skills, setting a good example, and reducing the need for discipline in the ways described previously also help a great deal.

Of course, teenagers need firm, clear limits, parental vigilance, and firm consequences for problem behaviors. Get to know their friends, where teenagers are going, when they will come home, and what they do. You might allow a trustworthy teenager to come home alone from school and check on the teen every day with a phone call. If you work and your teenager has gotten in trouble, however, enroll your teen in some kind of after-school program. Teenagers face many problems and temptations and often want their parents' involvement and support, yet too many parents fail to maintain closeness during these critical years. Although 75% of the parents of 9-year-olds claim high or medium involvement, only 55% of parents of 14-year-olds do. Research shows parental involvement is the most important factor in preventing teenage drug use. Take the time and trouble to learn about pressures facing your child at school. Family activities or games can help improve communication in a subtle way. Teenagers also need your trust that improvement will come when problems occur.

The previous discussion about giving children the freedom to choose their own opinions, interests, likes and dislikes, friends, and goals is especially important for teenagers. Trying to regulate such aspects of teenagers' lives unnecessarily creates antagonism between parent and teenager and often makes the forbidden much more attractive. Although you may forbid outlandish clothing or hair styles, in general, don't force your opinions and personal tastes on them. If you take your teenager out, you have the right to require appropriate clothing, but the teen should also have the right not to go. Remember, each generation of the family is a product of their own times, and the teenage years are a time of experimentation and change. Don't judge your teenager when you differ in opinions or values—simply respect each other's opinions and leave it at that.

Never prohibit your teenager from having a particular friend. This often provokes a power struggle that strengthens the friendship and may force your child to start lying to you. If you don't trust one of your teenager's friends, you might allow meetings only under direct supervision, though unfair bias against any friends because of race, religion, social status, or stereotypes based on looks or clothing will make your teen lose respect for you. You can help teenagers make wise choices in friendships, however. Feel free to discuss your impressions of their friends, but make sure you do so calmly and rationally. Encourage teenagers to associate with several peer groups, not just one, thus reducing the chances of them becoming influenced by the wrong kind of friend. Encourage group interests and activities that may naturally lead to different peer groups. For example, lifting weights, taking karate, playing in the band, and joining a photography club may all lead to different circles of friends. This can also help if your child feels shunned by classmates. Another excellent social outlet for rejected teenagers is volunteer work. This develops responsibility, a sense of pride and importance, and provides a better perspective on how fortunate they are.

Encourage teenagers to date a variety of people before going steady with one person. This helps make them a better judge of character and human nature. People with plenty of dating experience choose better mates and are less likely to settle for an unfulfilling, explosive, or abusive relationship.

Make teenage curfews somewhat flexible. Although you may insist that your teenager arrive home by a certain time on school nights and by a later time on weekends, make allowances for special occasions. Teenagers also need some privacy. Although you should know their friends and whereabouts and you should maintain a rapport that encourages them to share their problems with you, don't interrogate them about their personal lives and feelings. Never read your teenager's mail or private journals without permission, unless you have good reason to suspect criminal activity or addiction.

The teenager's struggle for freedom and independence and the parent's need to control, protect, correct, or improve the teenager often pits them against each other in periods of conflict and strain. This is a normal part of the transition from childhood to adulthood, but teenagers need your steady, reliable love the most when they hate you the most, and despite explosive anger and strained relations during these years, most teenagers end up feeling very close to their parents in adulthood. One good way to reduce your anger is to think back on how you felt and acted during conflicts with your parents in your teenage years. Another helpful activity is for the parents and the teenager to make lists of all the things they like or appreciate about each other, including personal qualities, behaviors, skills, etc. Parents and teenagers can also reduce some of their bitterness and hostility by making a list of things they would like to apologize for.

Certain things are nearly indispensable to most teenagers, and parents can use these things as highly motivating rewards or penalties. These include spending money, a learner's permit for driving, the use of a car or motorcycle, and perhaps the right to buy a car or motorcycle or the right to participate in sports. Disrespectfulness might result in the loss of spending money. You might require that your teenager maintain good grades in school to earn the privilege of riding a motorcycle or using the family car, or you might pay a set amount for certain grade point averages or for each A or B. This last suggestion has worked effectively with juvenile delinquents in group homes using large rewards. Don't remove your child (especially a potential career athlete) from a sports team unless the problem is severe, such as a second episode of stealing. You can make your teenager earn these rewards with a number of behavioral changes by using a reward system. You might require the earning of spending money or use of a vehicle each week, but vehicle ownership and the learner's permit for driving make good long-term rewards.

Contracts and reward systems are very useful with teenagers. Use friendly, informal contracts exchanging improvements in your teenager's behavior for desired privileges or rewards whenever possible because written contracts and reward systems emphasize the parents' authority and more often lead to power struggles. If your behavior toward your teenager could improve, exchange your own improvement for that of your teenager's. Showing this fairness increases cooperation. One way to find useful terms for contracts and reward systems is for the teenager and the parents to make lists of what behaviors they would like changed. Teens may include on this list new privileges they would like. Giving them some input into the terms of the contract or reward system improves the terms and increases cooperation.

Discussing alcohol and drugs with your children during early grade school and frequently thereafter reduces the chances of teenage alcoholism or drug abuse. Parental disapproval is one of the most common reasons children give for not using drugs. One survey found for every type of drug and every age group, drug use was higher among students who reported little or no parental discussion. The more parents spoke with their children about the dangers of drugs, the less frequently the children used them. Parents tend to underestimate their children's drug exposure, a "not my child" syndrome. Surveys found 14% of the parents interviewed thought their teenagers could have experimented with marijuana, but 47% of the teenagers reported having tried it. One survey found 33% of parents thought their teenagers viewed marijuana as harmful, but only 18% of the teenagers felt that smoking marijuana was risky.

Ask your children what they have heard about alcohol or drugs from peers or older children. You may find that peer pressure toward using alcohol or drugs already exists. In 4th grade, 25% of students report pressure to try marijuana. Peer pressure is the most important reason for children trying drugs, and the median age for beginning the use of alcohol and drugs is 11. Surveys show 2/3 of 8th-grade students have tried alcohol and 1/4 say they are current drinkers. A national survey in 1997 found half of high school seniors and nearly 1/3 of 8th-grade students reported using illegal drugs.

Teach your children some very important facts from research. The younger a child begins the use of an addictive substance, the more likely is addiction, the quicker addiction generally develops, the more difficult it is to stop, the longer it generally continues, and the more likely the child is to advance to harder drugs. Experts also agree that addiction before adulthood is especially devastating because it interferes with the tasks of growing up. These tasks include developing a positive personality and lifestyle, learning to constructively deal with life's sorrows, developing satisfying social relations, achieving a good educational foundation, and learning to work toward long-term goals. Addicted adolescents show more behavior problems and more often fail to complete school than do other adolescents. Emphasize that for these reasons, children should wait until they become adults before using alcohol or any other addictive substances.

Teach your children how TV, movies, and music promote alcohol and drugs. Monitor the TV shows they watch and movies they go to. Teach them to ask who is going to a party and whether the parents will be home before accepting, so they won't face pressure to use illegal drugs. Use behavioral roleplays to prepare them to deal successfully with peer pressure. Act the part of the peer or older child urging alcohol or drug use. Coax your child by saying things like: "Oh come on, try it," "Just have a little bit," or "What's the matter, are you afraid?" Let your children think up lines to use to turn down alcohol or drugs. Practice the roleplays until they perfect lines they would feel comfortable using in real life. Point out many people will respect and admire a person who turns down such offers, and even the person pressuring the child will generally feel some admiration for this stance, although that person probably won't admit it.

Develop responsibility and keep teenagers busy with chores at home and extracurricular activities at school. Research shows experimenting with drugs is more likely when teenagers are unsupervised and have little to do. Forbid children's use of tobacco and alcohol because these drugs often lead to use of other drugs. One study found children who smoke tobacco are 11 times as likely to smoke marijuana as are other children. Another study found adolescents who drink alcohol are 10 times more likely to smoke marijuana and 11 times more likely to use cocaine than are other adolescents. As noted previously, parents should set a good example of abstinence or moderation with addictive substances. Don't teach your children to seek pleasure in heavy drug use by your occasional drinking of large amounts of alcohol, and don't teach them that drugs make acceptable crutches by chronically using coffee or tobacco.

Point out that besides the danger of addiction, alcohol and drugs can make you do dangerous things or things you regret later. Alcohol and drugs are common factors in date rape, unsafe sex, and promiscuity or acquiring a bad reputation sexually. Driving high can kill or maim you or someone else. Be sure you never drive drunk, and tell any adolescent who drives, goes on dates, or goes to parties where people drink alcohol to call you to avoid being a drunken driver or riding with one. Explain no matter what the hour of day or night, you will arrange transportation or taxi fare without complaint. Warn your children drinking and driving or driving high will result in the loss of car privileges until they are 18. You can explain they are too valuable to lose. Warn children near 18 the penalty for driving high is losing all rights to your car forever, so they must buy their own car.

Scare tactics with adolescents about the physical dangers of addictive substances and the possibility of going to jail don't work. When they hear about peers smoking marijuana at parties and still getting A's or successful athletes drinking, they question your knowledge. Nowadays teenagers often know much more about drugs than their parents do, although they often don't have a real grasp of the likelihood and seriousness of chemical dependency. Discuss drugs in realistic, factual ways, rather than with hysteria or uninformed stories about dangers of drugs that may close the door to further discussion. Use chapter 33 to educate yourself and your child about drug effects and signs of addiction. Chapter 33 also describes signs of drug use in children that parents should be alert for. If you want to learn more about drugs, community centers for drug abuse can provide additional information.

If you suspect or find out about alcohol or drug use, reassure your teenager you won't overreact and calmly ask for the truth. Remaining calm gives you the best chance of uncovering a problem and helping the teen with it. Try your best to show understanding, and find out how your teenager feels about it. Don't try to find out how much your child uses until after you show you will remain calm. This reduces the likelihood that your teen will feel the need to lie about it. Don't make or discuss any plans to deal with the problem until after you learn what your teenager uses, how often, how your teen feels, and what led to the behavior.

There is a world of difference between the occasional, moderate use of alcohol or drugs and addiction. Even so, moderate use easily escalates into addiction. You may need to talk to your community center for drug abuse to get a better idea of how serious the situation is. Parents can use many of the consequences discussed previously for alcohol or drug problems. You might refuse the use of the family car to an addicted teenager until you see one month of sobriety. One of the home kits available in drug stores for detecting drug abuse, such as Dr. Brown's, Parent's Alert, At Home, or First Check, helps in establishing more control. Think carefully before taking this step, especially if your teenager is not yet abusing drugs—it can worsen difficult parent-child relations. You will need extra vigilance, but sometimes helping your teen deal with contributing personal problems will solve the problem. Please refer to chapter 33 for a thorough description of how to deal with this serious problem.

Community-based approaches can also help. Many towns have drug-free dance clubs for teenagers that don't serve alcohol, where uniformed security guards enforce the rules. If your town does not, you might start a club like this. (This can be a moneymaking venture.) One high school sends home a family agreement at the beginning of each school year for parents and children to sign. In it, families agree to prohibit alcohol and drugs at teenage gatherings in their homes, the parents will provide adult supervision, and parents will welcome calls from other parents to verify these conditions when they plan a party. The school compiles a directory of those who sign and makes it available to all families, so parents can insist their children attend only parties at the listed homes. You might ask or petition your local high school to do this, too.

A parent with fears or concerns about how a particular situation will go with a teenager can prepare for it by rehearsing with behavioral roleplays. Using meditation or deep relaxation before the confrontation may help. Be sure to breathe deeply and to stretch or to relax muscle tension in your body just before and during the situation. If you really can't bring yourself to set firm consequences alone, get your spouse, a friend, or another parent to help you. The physical presence of the other person may be all you need to stand firm, or perhaps your friend can take over for you when you need it. The support groups Because I Love You or Toughlove International (see the end of chapter) can help a great deal.

When teenagers continue to do wrong despite the consequences their parents set and communication between them and their parents is poor, it is important the parents get help early, before the teen becomes deeply involved in drugs or crime. For example, get help early if communication is poor and your teenager gets suspended from school more than once, regularly stays out overnight without permission and gets into trouble, steals more than once, has more than one alcohol blackout, uses drugs chronically, or commits assault. You may need to read chapters 40 and 41 and get professional help for your child or your family. Of course, many teenagers with problems refuse to go to counseling. If this happens, hold a loving group confrontation in the ways described in chapter 12, Help from Other People, to persuade the teen to go. As discussed in chapter 12 too, the more concerned people who become involved in monitoring the teenager's progress, the better. If your child breaks any laws, you could bluff and threaten to report it to the police unless the teen goes to counseling. If this bluff doesn't work, don't undermine your credibility by repeating it.

If serious problems continue and your teenager refuses to go to counseling, consider getting police involved. This certainly gives you more power and control because the court can insist on such things as curfews, school attendance, or drug counseling and because the police can look for the teen at friends' homes, etc. Don't let embarrassment stop you from doing this—it can help get your teen back on the right track—but never do it in anger or without careful thought. Before doing it, talk to a local juvenile court police officer or social worker to find out what laws in your state apply to the problem, whether your child will spend time in a detention center, etc. Sometimes facing the consequences sooner rather than later for activities such as stealing, assault, or drug use prevents further problems, but many teenagers who go to detention centers come out with more criminal knowledge and more problems than before.

Carefully consider the possible consequences before deciding whether to turn your child in to the police. How might the teen and other friends and family members react? Your teenager may respect you for laying down the law, may hate you, may leave home, or may become even more troublesome. Friends and family members may support you or become angry with you. If abuse exists in the family or the family situation is completely unworkable, there is a chance the authorities will take your child away from you and put your child into state custody or a foster home. If you decide to turn your teenager in to the police, share your deep regret at needing to take this painful action and express the hope that facing the consequences sooner rather than later will avoid a life of crime or addiction.

If your teenager runs away from home, call police because they can search for the child or possibly identify a child who is hurt or in trouble in another state. If your teenager has been gone for long, realize that minors often find it difficult to get a job and many minors must resort to stealing or prostitution to make money. Both boys and girls can make quick money in these ways. Runaways resort to this kind of life much more often than their parents would like to believe. Prepare yourself to be loving, concerned, and understanding in case your child calls home. Express your love for your teen in words during the phone call. Emphasize your concerns about your child's comfort and safety. If you respond angrily to the phone call home, your teenager may hang up and never call again. Asking too many questions before your child is ready to share may also end the phone call. Two runaway hotlines (see the end of the chapter) can give you advice or help with negotiations between you and your runaway. These hotlines will also give teenagers information on finding legal help, temporary shelter, food, etc.

If your runaway teenager wants to come home, the National Runaway Switchboard (see the end of the chapter) can arrange for a free ride home from Greyhound Bus Lines, or you can buy your child a nonrefundable, nonexchangeable bus ticket home. When your teen gets home, try not to scold too much. Instead, show your great happiness about your child's return. You could arrange to first meet your teenager in the presence of a social worker, runaway counselor, police officer, or some family friend to help negotiate important issues. You could ask a court to order such things as curfew hours, school attendance, or alcohol or drug counseling, although the previous warnings about possible consequences apply here, too. Another possibility is to arrange for your teenager to stay temporarily with a friend or relative and to refuse permission to come home until the teen agrees to make certain changes, such as entering a drug treatment program, meeting reasonable curfew hours, etc.

Teenagers usually don't run away from home unless there is a long history of problems there. Things may go well for a time when a runaway first comes home, but eventually problems usually erupt. Admit serious problems exist and work on good communication and problem-solving skills and making contracts trading freedoms your teenager wants for improved behavior. When problems develop, you could temporarily send your child to live with a friend or relative until tensions calm down. If you can't make improvements on your own, read chapters 40 and 41 and get family counseling. In severe cases, the family may need to give up custody of an unmanageable teenager to the state or a foster family.

If your son or daughter is 18 years old or older, you have the right to throw the adult child out of the house for troublesome behavior of any kind. You could do this if an adult child uses drugs and won't work, for example. Also, you have no obligation to give money to a lazy or irresponsible adult child or one in legal trouble. For example, you might refuse to bail an adult child out of jail. These painful decisions can sometimes result in great improvement by forcing these people to face the consequences of their actions and become independent. If you do any of these things, make it clear you regret needing to do it, but you hope it pushes your child to improve.

Disabled Children

You can often make a great difference in your disabled child's level of functioning by spending extra time working with the child. Many people successfully improve or overcome various disabilities, sometimes even those judged hopeless by doctors, by sheer determination and persistent effort. People often live very productive, happy lives despite lifelong disabilities. My father is a good example. Despite lifelong deafness, he had a successful career as a research chemist, became a skilled glassblower, fixed all kinds of household appliances, took apart and rebuilt a car engine, and learned to do all his own plumbing, carpentry, and electrical wiring in the house. His many interests include astronomy, developing his own photography, growing a vegetable garden, and teaching sign language classes to hearing people. After he retired, he built one house and renovated another.

Work with professionals to find out as much as you can about your child's disability and what you can do to help. The slow progress of many disabled children, especially that of mentally disabled children, may frustrate you, but you can make great gains by working with your child persistently. Don't make the mistake of constantly catering to a disabled child and of not developing self-reliance. If you don't expect much from them and don't require improved behaviors from them, they won't live up to their potential. In fact, in the past, many normal children placed in institutions ended up functioning as mentally disabled because nobody helped them live up to their potential. These normal children may have first been institutionalized because their parents were too poor to raise them or because of family problems or physical disabilities such as deafness. Staff members in institutions often expected little of institutionalized children and rewarded quietness, compliance, and dependence to make taking care of many patients easier. These normal children lost many of the social and intellectual skills they had when they entered the institutions. The point is that all children, and especially disabled children, need training, encouragement, and high expectations placed on them if they are to improve themselves.

Whenever possible, break down new tasks into simpler parts and teach each step, one at a time. Use plenty of praise and encouragement each step of the way. At first you may need to praise disabled children for doing something vaguely like what you want them to learn. Later, expect more and more precision.   Help your child with schoolwork, but don't become frustrated and give the answer without helping your child understand. Mentally disabled children need more practice to memorize rote facts (such as addition or subtraction) than do other children. With mentally disabled children, work toward good language and social skills. You may need to start by teaching them to reduce odd mannerisms and facial expressions or how to walk normally. Teach self-care skills such as how to cook, wash dishes, scrub floors, do shopping, pick clothes that match, find their way around town, take buses, etc. Unfortunately, many parents of mentally disabled children simply give up and take care of their children all their lives. When the parents die, these adults still lack many self-care skills and often end up living in institutions.

Like all children, disabled children need loving attention, respectful treatment with good communication skills, firm and consistent discipline, and a variety of interests and activities. Developing skills in such things as cooking, photography, or a craft can greatly boost their self-esteem. Emphasize what disabled children can do, rather than what they can't do. Rejoice with them when they accomplish something, even if it would be routine to anyone else.

The books listed at the end of this chapter *Helping Your Exceptional Baby* and *Steps to Independence* are very helpful in training disabled babies and children.   Of course, the earlier section in this chapter on Making Learning Fun and Developing Skills is also very useful in working with these children.

Whose Problem Is It?

A parent's personal problems often interfere with the skills of raising children. Habits of yelling in anger teach children by example to argue and fight. Nagging, constantly scolding, regular use of negative labels or insults, and other poor communication skills frustrate children and develop poor self-image in them that contributes to problems. Inconsistent discipline and unenforced consequences teach children not to take you seriously. An angry parent who feels strongly that a child's behaviors must change, generally contributes to the child's problems without realizing it in some of the above ways. That parent's behaviors often must change in order for improvement to occur. A problem child often shoulders the full burden of blame despite the parents' very real contributions to the problem.

Depressed, anxious, or addicted parents often role model negative behaviors, giving up quickly, and low self-esteem. Studies have found depressed mothers to be less playful and responsive to their babies, to use less structure and discipline with their children, and to shout more and show more disapproval and anger to their children. Some parents cause problems by being too involved in their children's lives or trying to live through their children. These parents may push children to meet their own needs, put too much pressure on them to achieve, or meddle too much in older children's lives. They may overprotect children, depriving them of opportunities to develop their own independence, assertiveness, conflict resolution skills, and full social life.

Sometimes issues from a parent's own childhood interfere with the ability to raise children. Many parents repeat their parents' problem behaviors when they raise their own children. If issues from your past seem to interfere with your present happiness or parenting skills, please refer to chapter 38, Understanding Yourself, for help in exploring these issues and chapter 37 for help in resolving the painful past.

If you are the parent of a problem child, it is important to consider very carefully how your parenting skills could improve and what other personal problems you might need to work on. Are you emotionally needy? Do you have a satisfying life, with plenty of friends and a wide variety of interests and activities? Work on only one or two behavioral changes at once. Use the advice in chapters 11, 12, and 13 to increase your chances for successful change. You may want to use interpersonal roleplays to explore situations of family conflict.

Fortunately, little children can be remarkably resilient. When a parent improves, little children often improve, too. Older children may reject their parents' efforts to establish better rapport, however. These parents may need to wait for a long period of very slow improvement. Despite the fact most parents could improve their skills in raising children, parents do not have total responsibility for how their children turn out. Don't waste your time blaming yourself for your children's problems—they may go wrong without any parental neglect or mistreatment, perhaps by getting involved with the wrong crowd. If you use the advice in this chapter, however, you have the best chance of helping your child get back on the right track.

Recommended Additional Readings:

Your Baby & Child: From Birth to Age Five. 2nd ed. rev. ed. by Penelope Leach.
    NY: Alfred A. Knopf, 1989.

The Emotional Life of the Toddler. by Alicia F. Lieberman. New York: Free Press, 1993.

The Discipline Book: Everything You Need to Know to Have a Better-Behaved Child—From Birth to Age Ten. by William Sears and Martha Sears. Boston: Little, Brown, and Co., 1995.

Solve Your Child's Sleep Problems. by Richard Ferber. New York: Free Press, 1993.

ADD/ADHD Behavior-Change Resource Kit: Ready to Use Strategies & Activities for Helping Children with Attention Deficit Disorder. by Grad L. Flick. West Nyack, NY: Center for Applied Research in Education, 1998.

Attention Deficit Disorders: Assessment and Teaching. by Janet W. Lerner, Barbara Lowenthal, and Sue R. Lerner. Pacific Grove, CA: Brooks/Cole, 1995.

Steps to Independence: A Skills Training Guide for Parents & Teachers of Children with Special Needs. 2nd ed. by Bruce L. Baker, Alan J. Brightman, Jan B. Blancher, Louis J. Heifetz, Stephen P. Hinshaw, and Diane M. Murphy. Baltimore: Paul H. Brookes, 1989. contains excellent, practical advice for the parents of disabled children on training crawling, handling objects, dressing, self-care skills, home-care skills, and independent living skills, such as handling money and telling time.

Helping Your Exceptional Baby: A Practical and Honest Approach to Raising a Mentally Handicapped Child. by Cunningham, Cliff, and Patricia Sloper. New York:: Pantheon Books, 1980. has excellent, practical advice for helping babies meet developmental milestones by exercising them and teaching head control, sitting, visual development, grasping, reaching, rolling, manipulating objects, supporting weight on the elbows, crawling, pulling up, object permanence, and vocalization.

The Movie Mom's Guide to Family Movies. by Minow, Nell. New York: Avon, 1999. helps select fun movies and videos for family viewing by listing them according to the values they teach, such as honesty, courage, respect, tolerance, and problem solving. For information on new releases, check their web site at www.moviemom.com

The Date Rape Prevention Book: The Essential Guide for Girls and Women. by Lindquist, Scott. Naperville, IL: Sourcebooks, 2000. has details about warning signs, how to communicate and act defensively in threatening situations, and how to escape.

Support Groups, Hotlines, and Resources:

Kids Stuff catalog 877 363 0500 carries a folding wood potty chair with a removable tray helpful for toilet training children because you can easily keep them on it while entertaining them with books, toys, or snacks.

DRI Sleeper 800 795 7466 an electronic device that helps older children who wet their beds. It has two parts: a small pad with a sensor to detect wetness, which clips into a disposable diaper, and a small beeper unit that immediately sets off an loud alarm at the first sign of wetness. on-line: www.DRI-Sleeper.com

Recall List, CPSC, Washington DC 20207: address to write for the most important recalls of dangerous products or hazards, including infant car seats with defective handles, toys, old cribs that don't meet safety standards. on-line: www.cpsc.gov

Stuttering Foundation of America 800 992 9392 information, referrals. on-line: www.stutteringhelp.org

Screenit.com: gives detailed ratings of movies, with plot summaries, ratings of sex, violence, profanity, also tells you if scenes show disrespect, tense family situations, alcohol or drug use, weapons, smoking, etc. (Please note the similar web site listed above under the suggested reading Movie Mom's Guide.)

FreeNSafe: a free family friendly Internet service provider, so that you don't need computer filtering software. on-line: www.freensafe.com (America Online is a service provider that charges fees but offers parental controls as an option.)

Because I Love You 310 659 5289 or 818 882 4881, PO Box 473, Santa Monica, CA 90406 support groups for parents with children of all ages who have behavioral problems. on-line: www.becauseIloveyou.org

Kid Save 800 543 7283 information, referrals, shelters, counseling, sexual abuse, substance abuse, family counseling, residential care, foster care. on-line: www.kidspeace.org

National Mentoring Partnership 703 224 2200 resource for finding or becoming a mentor, also establishing mentoring programs. on-line: www.mentoring.org

Youth Crisis Hotline 800 448 4663 counseling and referrals for teens in crisis.

Teen Help Adolescent Resources 800 400 0900 refers struggling teens to long-term residential programs. on-line: www.schoolsforteens.com

Toughlove International 800 333 1069 support group for dealing with an out of control family member. on-line: www.toughlove.org

Girls and Boys Town National Hotline 800 448 3000 crisis hotline, information, referrals, for children and families. on-line: www.girlsandboystown.org

National Runaway Switchboard 800 621 4000 information, support, referrals, help negotiating, parent-child message center, give teenagers information on finding legal help, temporary shelter, food, runs a Home Free program with Greyhound Bus Lines that will give any runaway a free bus ride home.

Parents Without Partners 800 637 7974 information, newsletter, support groups. on-line: www.parentswithoutpartners.org

Family Pride Coalition 202 583 8029 for gay and lesbian parents, support, information, referrals, newsletter. on-line: www.familypride.org

23. Divorce

You can only change yourself, not others.

Learn from your mistakes.

Divorce has become very common in recent decades, with about 50% of new marriages in America failing. Reasons may include changes in attitudes so divorce does not carry the social stigma that it used to, the increased independence of women, the longer life span of Americans, and perhaps the increased emphasis on our rights to happiness and personal freedom. Black people in America have higher separation and divorce rates than white people.

In most of 186 sampled preindustrial societies, divorce is common. In Japan, Africa, and other parts of the world, divorce is a private institution. Most Japanese couples divorce by informing a registration office of their decision. European marriage once involved only a private contract between two families, but the Roman Catholic Church pushed countries to regulate marriage and outlaw divorce. The Eastern Catholic Church never forbade it. Chile forbids divorce, but Roman Catholic marriage annulments are very common there. In many Central American countries, such as El Salvador, Panama, and the Dominican Republic, the majority of couples never marry. Until very recently in the Arab world, the Koran made it very easy for husbands to divorce but nearly impossible for wives. For example, in Tunisia, men could divorce by simply saying "Talak" three times in front of witnesses, but women could only divorce if a judge ruled their husband refused to provide shelter or food or harmed the wife or children. Laws have changed there, but traditional practices often rule.

Until the 1800s, Western cultures traditionally gave custody to fathers because people considered children the father's property. With men working away from home in the Industrial Revolution, the notion young children needed their mothers' superior caregiving grew. In most of the 1900s, mothers got custody unless they were unfit or judged at fault in the divorce. Now sex roles have changed and custody depends on the child's future best interests, but most judges still seem to prefer maternal custody, with 86% of children living with their mothers after divorce. Divorce is most likely early in marriage, and women initiate between 2/3 and 3/4 of all divorces. The lowest divorce rate is in traditional homes with male breadwinners and full-time homemaker wives.

People considering divorce need to understand all marriages face serious disappointments, conflicts, and periods of unhappiness and marital dissatisfaction, but these marital problems contain hidden potential for constructive changes that can lead to a deeper, stronger marriage. Any couple can save their marriage if they put enough effort into making the necessary changes. Even when only one spouse actively works to improve the marriage, that spouse can make much progress. Anyone considering divorce should read chapter 21, Marriage, for a full discussion of these issues and how to improve a marriage.

Divorce is not an easy decision to make. There are many things to consider. Don't let your spouse fool you by proclaiming great love if you receive few loving actions of kindness, helpfulness, patience, compromise, unselfish problem solving, forgiveness, etc. Even abusive people may proclaim their love with great intensity and fervor. Use actions, not words or promises, to gauge your spouse's willingness to work to improve the problems in the marriage.

Consider whether you will really be happier without your spouse. Most divorced people report loneliness and you may never find another mate. Over one-third of mothers with custody never remarry. Depression is common, especially in mothers with custody of young children or three or more children. You may have to give up a comfortable home and sacrifice many other luxuries in life. Women's incomes fall after divorce despite child support, increased hours at work, and public assistance. Courts award child support to only 63% of mothers with custody, and of these, only half receive full or regular payments. Even if they receive full payments, most child support awards are not enough. With divorce reform laws, alimony, now called rehabilitative maintenance and seen as temporary money to help the woman become self-sufficient, is awarded in only a small percentage of cases and for only a short time. Of families headed by women, 40% live in poverty. Overall, divorce increases poverty levels in women and decreases poverty in men. You may have to go to work. Yet many studies suggest most divorcing people feel happier several years afterwards than they did during the marriage.

Consider your children's welfare, too. Psychologists agree that children are better off in a happy single-parent family than in a family headed by quarreling, unhappily married parents. Divorce may not improve the children's lives, however. A chaotic life after divorce, with unhappy parents who remain angry at one another and cannot cooperate, is likely to be worse for children than life with parents in a quietly unhappy marriage.

Although you may want to ask your friends for their opinions, other people cannot tell you whether to get a divorce. Every marriage is unique, and people considering divorce have their own unique priorities. Even psychologists avoid giving such advice, preferring instead to help their clients explore their feelings, sort out their priorities, and make their own decisions. Ben Franklin's procedure for simplifying difficult decisions, described in chapter 9, Problem Solving, can help. You can also explore your feelings about divorce by holding your own therapy session as described in chapter 9 or with the chapter 14 roleplay technique of dialoguing.

Before making your decision, you should talk to a lawyer who specializes in divorce. With enough information from you, these lawyers can often tell you what kind of settlement to expect. Be honest so the lawyer can give you a realistic appraisal of the situation. Violence, threats of violence, verbal abuse, bouts of screaming, bouts of heavy drinking or drug use, or other indications of emotional problems will hurt a parent's case for custody. A lack of time spent with or concern for the children will also reduce a parent's chances of gaining custody. In a court custody battle, either side to the dispute may bring in friends or neighbors as witnesses.

Women with children whose husbands have been the sole provider seldom receive more than 33 to 40% of the husband's income. States have set child support guidelines, based on percentages of the noncustodial parent's income or joint family income and designed as minimum awards, but courts often use them as maximum awards instead. In Illinois, for example, a noncustodial father of two children would typically pay 25% of his income in child support, with a few lucky women receiving an additional 10% in rehabilitative maintenance, limited to 6 years. Wives of the rich can generally expect a settlement that accommodates them in the lifestyle to which they have become accustomed. If you will have very little money after the divorce, ask your lawyer about what kinds of financial help from the government you might qualify for.

Divorce laws vary from state to state, and a divorce lawyer can tell you how the laws in your state will affect you. Every state now has some version of no-fault divorce laws, by which a couple can divorce without proving either party guilty of misbehavior. The state may grant the divorce when both spouses request it or when they have lived apart for a specific amount of time, generally 6 months or a year. In no-fault divorce, extramarital affairs are generally not a problem. Many states retain various fault grounds for divorce as an option. In this case, the first spouse to file for divorce brings charges against the other spouse, and the other spouse must defend against the charges. Ask your lawyer if an extramarital affair will affect the custody decision or if moving out of the home and leaving the children with the other spouse will affect the custody decision or award of the family home. If moving out could cause problems, suggest your lawyer draft a statement that moving will not prejudice your case. Your lawyer can help arrange temporary financial support and temporary custody until you complete the divorce. You may also need a restraining order to stop harassment from a spouse or prevent any sale of property before the divorce.

If you get a divorce, be sure to close any bank account or credit card that you both share. If you don't, you are liable for debts contracted by your previous spouse after you divorce. Although divorce lawyers normally split the debts of the marriage, the lenders are not party to your separation agreement. Never take a bank or credit card company's word over the phone that they have made a change, even if you no longer receive statements. Sometimes statements go to one party but both are still on the account. After calling, follow up with a dated letter and keep a copy of it as proof. Get a copy of your credit report after the divorce, which will show you which cards remain in your name. If you didn't do this right away and an unfair credit problem appears on your name, put a statement in all of your credit reports explaining what happened. The three major credit bureaus and their phone numbers are listed at the end of the chapter under hotlines.

Some couples manage to divorce in a respectful, cooperative way. Some even help each other begin dating again by going out to bars together as friends. A respectful, cooperative divorce is much less stressful and traumatic for both you and your children than a chaotic, angry divorce. With effort and determination, any couple can separate in a friendly way. Research suggests perhaps half of all couples end up with a good divorce, where the parents continue good relationships with the children and cooperate as families despite the changes. The best of these couples work together as close friends, whereas the others act as cooperative colleagues in the work of raising the children.

You will feel conflicting emotions of love, anger, pain, relief, joy, sadness, etc. Strive to recognize your emotions, share them with each other using good communication skills, and accept each other's feelings. Some couples can stay cordial throughout most of the divorce; others need time before they can establish this kind of working friendship. The person leaving should expect anger and give time and space for it. Money issues and new relationships tend to cause the most anger. Remember, anger and spitefulness will only increase stress and make the divorce a crisis for everyone. Vent your anger with friends and family members but not around your children. Use hand signals to stop any escalating argument in front of the children and wait for a calm or private time to continue discussing the issue. If you explode in anger or try to hurt or retaliate, apologize after you calm down.

Soften your own anger with objectivity by keeping in mind your own mistakes and contributions to the marriage breakdown. We often contribute to the collapse of a marriage not only by misdeeds, but also by lack of action: neglecting to take an interest in the other person, to nurture the warmth in the marriage, etc. Compile a list of things you did and things you neglected to do that may have contributed to the divorce, and read this list regularly to soften your anger. This learning experience can also help you succeed in future relationships.

Of course, many couples wage war with one another during the divorce and refuse to cooperate. Besides being stressful and traumatic, this can result in delays and increase the cost of a divorce from thousands of dollars to tens of thousands. Some people have lost businesses because of the financial drain of a bitter divorce. If the two of you cannot cooperate, be sure to consult lawyers, psychologists, social workers, clergy, or mediators who specialize in divorce. These professionals can help you reach a satisfactory settlement, including financial matters, custody issues, and visitation rights.

Experts in law and mental health agree that lawsuits and our country's adversarial legal system contribute to the anger, bitterness, and conflict of divorce. Because of this, mediation, using a neutral third party to help settle disputes, has become much more popular. Thousands of years ago, the Chinese used mediation for most disputes. Both African lineage spokesmen and rabbis in Jewish rabbinical courts act much like mediators. Mediation by professionals other than lawyers gives the spouses complete control of the decisions and the most control over the procedures used to reach them. This increases satisfaction in both parties, even the party who loses a dispute. If you use mediation to reach an agreement, both parties should hire a lawyer to review it—this protects you from dramatically unbalanced outcomes.

Some communities have conciliation courts or family counseling services associated with the court system that help in reaching a settlement without a court battle. Courts in 25 states require child custody disagreements to go through mediation. Mediation usually takes from one to three months, meeting one hour each week, depending on the number of issues and whether child custody is a problem. The American Arbitration Association, a nonprofit organization with offices in many cities, offers mediation services.

Avoid a court battle whenever possible because of the emotional trauma and additional expense. However, mediation may not work if one spouse lies, hides assets, refuses to keep an agreement, bullies or blackmails the other, is untrustworthy, or has ever been violent toward the other spouse. Women's rights advocates suggest that abused women skip mediation and go directly to court because battered women often feel too intimidated to assert themselves in meetings with the abusive man.

Divorce requires many adjustments in one's emotional, financial, social, and sexual life. You will probably experience such things as a profound sense of loss, depression, guilt, anger, fear, anxiety, regret, isolation, loneliness, feelings of failure, and perhaps a loss of self-esteem. It often takes one or two years to work through the emotional pain of the divorce completely and find much satisfaction in your new lifestyle. Continued hostility toward your previous spouse or dwelling on love fantasies or desires for reconciliation interferes with your adjustment. Keep busy and use the advice in chapter 4, Thinking, to avoid dwelling on such thoughts. The chapters on Depression (27), Anger (28), Interests and Activities (8), and Social Life (15) also help a great deal in adjusting. Remember, having a good network of friendships, ranging from casual to intimate, and having a wide variety of interests and activities help you cope better with life's misfortunes.

Divorce is a factor in 50 to 75% of child mental health referrals. There is great controversy over the effects of divorce on children's adjustment, with some researchers arguing for substantial long-lasting problems and other researchers arguing for relatively few psychological problems. Most of the research supporting substantial problems studied samples with psychiatric histories or identified problems. Many studies did not control for children's problems that long predate the divorce, caused by family conflict, nor for the academic and behavior problems associated with lower income levels. Children of high-conflict families show more problems than most children of divorce. A bad marriage is worse for children than a divorce, and good quality parenting can protect children's adjustment through several divorces and remarriages.

Emotional distress is certainly common in children after divorce, but psychological disturbance is not. Despite the practical and emotional struggles divorce presents, most children cope successfully with time and do well. The research consistently points to children's resilience. Yet children frequently express disappointment, longing, and resentment, even years later. Behavior problems such as disobedience and aggression are more consistently linked to divorce than are internal problems such as fears, depression, and low self-esteem. Toddlers may regress in toilet training, feeding, or dressing themselves, demand more time and attention, or become more upset about separation from the parent during daytime and bedtime routines, clinging and crying more. Toddlers and older preschool children may become more irritable, with more anger and temper tantrums, and may suck their thumbs more.

Studies suggest toddlers under age 3 tend to have less trouble than children from 4 to 6 years old. Of all the age groups, older preschool children are the most likely to think their behavior problems caused the divorce. One study noted that preschool children seemed more likely to develop worse problems when there was no explanation about the divorce given to them by the parents. Children between the ages of 5 and 9 may also show problems of anger, but intense sadness is more likely. Sometimes they show bodily problems such as stomach aches, headaches, nightmares, or bedwetting. Divorce may affect school performance in any child of school age, triggering trouble concentrating or lower grades. Children between 9 and 12 are more likely to throw tantrums or become moody, contrary, or rebellious. They may take their anger out on their peers or younger siblings. Boys express their anger strongly more than girls do.

Children in junior or senior high school may start lying, ignoring curfews, cutting school, abusing alcohol or drugs, or acting out with sexually irresponsible behavior, even many years after a divorce. Some adolescents do better in school, coping by concentrating on schoolwork and perhaps sports and hobbies. This is very healthy as long as the adolescent doesn't deny or chronically avoid feelings about the divorce. Many adolescents worry about having relationship problems or overreact to the inevitable conflicts. Rates of cohabitation without marriage, teenage parenting, and divorce are higher for children of divorce, suggesting problems with trust, intimacy, and commitment. Some fear abandonment and cling to troubled relationships.

There are many reasons why children show these problems. First, children naturally imitate their parents and divorcing parents often teach hostility and fighting by the poor example they set. Parental arguments upset the children and add a great deal of stress to their lives. Whether the parents are married and no matter what the custody arrangements, research consistently shows that conflict between parents strongly predicts children's adjustment. Divorcing families are often chaotic as household routines and roles break down. A parent's personal problems may cause both divorce and strains between parent and child. Divorcing parents often become more irritable, wrapped up in their own problems, and less sensitive in raising their children, often giving them less time and attention and disciplining less consistently. If a previously unemployed parent must now go to work, the children lose much parental time and attention and generally receive additional chores and responsibilities at home.   Although reasonable additional responsibilities can have a maturing influence, they do add stress. Moving can increase stress by disrupting many of the children's friendships and forcing them to make new neighborhood and school friends. In addition, a loss of family income may reduce material comforts and money for recreation and special treats. Finally, many of these problems may act to lower the children's self-esteem, which contributes to their problems.

Fortunately, the worst problems in children of divorced parents generally resolve by one year after the divorce. Children normally learn to cope satisfactorily by this time, unless the parents continue their hostilities toward one another or their other major problems. Parents can do many things to make the divorce easier on their children and to reduce the likelihood of children's problems. First, because the parents' emotional state is so important in the lives of children, all the coping strategies suggested earlier for divorcing couples are important. Try your best to remain civilized about the divorce. Use the advice in chapter 28 to help control your anger, and use good communication skills to express your anger in constructive ways, discussing topics that may provoke anger in private, not in the presence of the children.

Tell your children about the divorce shortly after you make the definite decision. This reduces stress by giving your children as much time as possible to prepare emotionally for the changes to come. Be sure to discuss it at least two weeks before a parent moves out, so the children have access to that parent for some time to process feelings. Both parents should tell the children together to reduce the temptation to blame the other spouse. If your spouse can't be with you for some reason, act as if the other parent is there, to avoid the name-calling and blame that will only hurt and confuse your children about the meaning of love. Choose a free block of time when the children are not sick, tired, or busy. Tell them you're sorry about the hurt and pain, but the decision is final. Explain what will happen and how the children's lives will change: where you plan to live, if an unemployed parent needs to find a job, if the children will get less spending money, if the children must help more with the household chores, etc.

Make sure to tell your children that although you're not in love anymore, you still care about each other and the family still needs each other. Remind them they can always call the other parent on the phone. Tell them you both still love the children, and emphasize you both will continue to love them after the divorce. Young children will need regular reassurance about your love. Toddlers will need repeated explanations and reassurances, sometimes daily. You can help toddlers, too, by using picture books, cut out pictures, photos, action figures, dolls, or collages to help them express feelings and visualize the new home arrangements and family structures. With action figures, you might use cereal boxes for houses.

Children often feel somehow at fault for the divorce, especially if the parents have argued about the children in the past. Make it very clear the separation is not their fault and that none of their actions caused the divorce. Emphasize that any fighting between the parents about the children was just one of many ways in which the parents didn't get along. Because young children are egocentric and especially likely to feel at fault, repeat these reassurances to young children several times during the divorce.

Use great care in describing the reasons for the divorce and in criticizing each other to the children. Children adjust to divorce better if they still respect and love both parents afterwards. Don't turn your children against the other parent, and don't try to convince the children the other parent was at fault. Instead, describe how differences between the two of you led to the divorce. If you argued regularly with your spouse, point this out and tell your children they will be better off in a peaceful, separated family. It will reassure them if you can honestly say that although you are not in love anymore, both parents still care about each other. If the children ask who is to blame, explain that both parents are responsible for the divorce. Try your best not to blame the other parent when talking to other people in the presence of your children. Regularly reading a list of the ways in which you contributed to the divorce (as described previously) can help you maintain the objectivity that you need to avoid damaging your children's respect and love for the other parent.

This does not mean you should never criticize the other parent or that you should sacrifice honesty to preserve your children's respect for the other parent. Don't lie about reasons for the divorce. Children can handle the clear, painful truth much better than deceit or ambiguity. It is especially important that you honestly discuss severe problems that the children have seen, such as addiction or physical abuse. Hiding painful truths may confuse a child or damage the child's trust in you. Explain reasons for the divorce in simple terms they can understand. In describing an extramarital affair, for example, you might simply say that you love and want to live with someone else rather than the other parent. You don't need to discuss personal matters the children know nothing about, however. For example, parents need not explain sexual problems in the marriage.

Children can learn from a realistic appraisal of the good and bad points of the other parent when you give the evaluation in a logical, calm way. Exercise caution so that you balance the need for honesty and for teaching your children with a tactfulness that strives to preserve your children's respect for the parent. Avoid hostile, excessive, or petty criticism and don't use negative labels such as bad, mean, or inconsiderate. Focus your criticism on specific, observable behaviors to avoid exaggeration or the excessive hostility often shown in vague complaints. Balance criticism of the other parent by admitting your own faults and mistakes. Children respect parents who can admit their own mistakes.

Helping your children cope with the divorce involves plenty of listening, answering questions, sharing feelings, and emotional support. Try to explore the feelings of each child and to share your own feelings without going to extremes and becoming overwhelmed by them. Sharing your feelings helps children accept and cope with theirs. Help your children to identify and accept feelings such as sadness, anger, and shame. Point out that their feelings will change and improve. Describe life as full of joys and sorrows, and emphasize the need for acceptance and for a focus on forgiveness and love. Explain things and answer questions until there are no questions left, again and again. Don't feel obligated to answer very personal questions, however. You can simply point out the personal nature of the question and say you would rather not discuss it.

Any of your children's peers whose families have been through divorce can help a great deal. Ask such a peer to help your children by listening and sharing experiences and advice. Simply knowing that others have gone through similar things can comfort children a great deal. If you find it difficult to discuss divorce with your children, use children's books or movies about divorce to open up honest communication. If you notice problems such as avoiding play with neighborhood children, you can use dolls, puppets, or action figures to set up a similar scene and ask how the doll feels. It may be easier for your child to discuss things indirectly by talking about play situations. Explore feelings, reasons for them, and alternative solutions. You can discuss things a little at a time, in many small conversations, to avoid getting overwhelmed. Tell your children that you can discuss it in bits, different times, whenever they want. If you can't discuss your divorce with your children in a calm manner, find a friend or relative who will explain things and help them express and accept their feelings.

Reduce the stress on your children during this time by keeping the changes in their lives to a minimum. If possible, arrange it so they can see their old friends, stay in the same school, visit relatives as usual, etc. Familiar places, schedules, and routines all help. If you must send your child to a new school, try to do it either at the beginning of the school year or after Christmas vacation. Preserve family rituals such as bedtime stories, and invent new ones, perhaps Saturday brunch at dad's. Help toddlers with visual aids like large calendars marked with mom days and dad days, or a red lunch box when mom will pick them up and blue when dad will. Calendars marking scheduled visits also help early elementary school children. Notify your child's teachers, guidance counselor at school, and anyone else who has regular contact with the child, so they can help.

Pay particular attention to your skills in raising children. A long-term study of divorced mothers found they make fewer demands for mature behaviors, are less affectionate with their children, and less consistent in disciplining them. Try not to let your personal problems make you more negative with your children. Notice and praise good behaviors frequently. Use good communication skills and the techniques in the section on Reducing the Need for Discipline in chapter 22, Raising Children. Because children of divorcing parents tend to feel less loved with the loss of a parent from the home, the chaos, and the realization that love may not endure, show more affection and spend extra time playing and talking with each child. Understand that your children may act out more, but don't let your personal problems interfere with consistency in enforcing discipline. Remember, inconsistent discipline causes behavior problems in both married and divorced families. Don't let your children manipulate you by saying things like how much better things are in the other parent's house. Unfortunately, many noncustodial parents are too lax in discipline and try to make up for limited contact with endless entertainment or gifts. Encourage your children to cope by helping them spend time with friends and relatives, renew old friendships, make new friends, and spend time on many interests and activities. Relatives can help you a great deal with child care and as an ally and consultant in discipline.

Custody decisions are very important matters with great impact on the children. If possible, make your custody agreement without a court battle, perhaps by using the services of the professionals mentioned previously. A court battle for custody is not only traumatic for the children, but also very expensive. A judge may order a custody investigation or hear testimony from people such as friends, neighbors, teachers, etc. A judge may also talk to your children (judges often do this privately) and ask them about family life and their custody preferences. Courts in some areas give great weight to a teenager's custody preferences. If you can't avoid a court battle for custody and if your children do give testimony, make it easier on them by telling them you will love them no matter what happens.

The parents themselves are the real experts in matters of custody. They know themselves and their own children far better than anyone else does. As long as parents cooperate, fix their minds on what is best for the children, and avoid letting anger or revenge enter the process of decision making, parents can make the best custody decisions. Children need love, training, discipline, and plenty of time and energy from parents. Which parent can best provide these things? Does one parent easily explode in anger when dealing with the children? Who is more sensitive to their feelings? Which children feel closer to one parent than the other? Which parent wants the responsibility of raising children? It is not wise to force a child on a parent who doesn't want the responsibility.

You should ask adolescents and children nearing puberty about their feelings on custody, and you can give their answers great weight in making your decision. You don't need to ask younger children. The question is a great responsibility and the burden can overwhelm a young child. A child who has strong feelings about custody will probably let you know. If you ask children for their feelings, make it clear the parents will make the decision. Young children are unable to consider all the factors involved and their feelings shift easily. In asking a child of any age about custody, phrase your question so you don't force your child to give an opinion or choose one parent over the other. For example, you might ask "Do you have any ideas or feelings about which parent you should live with?"

Joint physical custody, now available in all fifty states, keeps fathers more involved and benefits children when the parents' relationship is very cooperative. When conflicts continue, this arrangement is worse because children often get caught in the middle of hostilities, power struggles, and battles over rules in the two homes. In this case, sole custody with structured visitation seems better. Dual home arrangements work best when parents live very close to each other and share the same child care worker. If parents live in different neighborhoods, the children may have practical problems in seeing friends daily and coordinating clothes, schoolwork, and medicine. Younger children need security and stability and more often feel upset over moving back and forth between homes. Women leaving abusive men should avoid joint custody—it is unrealistic to expect cooperation from an abusive man, and coparenting will only increase opportunities for danger to her.

The best custody agreements are very detailed about everything. This cuts down on the need for communication between the parents and thereby reduces opportunities for conflicts. Try to quickly decide the plans for visits with the noncustodial parent, even if you must begin with a temporary plan. Children cope better when they know what to expect, even if there is a dramatic reduction in contact. Infants and toddlers don't really understand the ideas of future or next week, so more frequent, shorter visits work better for them. Don't forget you can revise custody arrangements as needed. Avoid problems by quickly establishing how communication between the parents will take place and clear methods for exchanging the children. Most angry couples do better if they exchange the children at daycare or school without seeing each other or by using another neutral place, with minimal contact between the ex-spouses. Use weekly phone calls or lunches at set times to discuss health issues, discipline, and schedules of events. Couples in conflict may need to avoid all other contact, except in emergencies.

If possible, arrange regular visits with the noncustodial parent. Children cope better when both parents continue to spend time with them after divorce. Weekends of one, two, or three overnights are common times for visiting, perhaps with a weekday visit for a few hours if there are weekends without visits. In joint custody, the schedule might reverse during summer vacations or the parents may have weekly or two-week rotations, exchanging on Sundays. Consider birthdays, school vacations, holidays, and traditional family events. If a holiday is more important to one parent than the other, you could make it a fixed holiday. You might divide the longer holidays or alternate the place for each holiday each year.

Attempting to buy your children's love by showering them with gifts or special activities spoils your children. Children need parents who enjoy sharing everyday life with them and who will train and discipline them. The best visiting arrangements include a little flexibility, so either the parents or children can change the plans when they want to schedule an extra visit or cancel one. Too much flexibility can be a problem, however. Many parents rely on scheduled visits to get chores done or to make their own plans. Try to follow your visiting schedule religiously. Let your children call the noncustodial parent (if it is a local call) and write letters whenever they please. It is also very nice if the noncustodial parent calls the children between visits.

Try to coordinate rules about homework time, bedtime, TV, and diet, including sweets, in the two houses. Consistency reduces discipline problems. Younger children need coordination the most. A toddler could have real trouble sleeping with a parent in one home but not the other, for example. Children can learn to live by different rules when parents can't agree, however. Conflicts and arguments between parents are much worse than somewhat different bedtimes or radically different diets in the two homes. You need to make decisions on choice of schools, religious training, and how to deal with the costs of medical and dental care, child care, school supplies, camps, summer trips, clothing, activities, and perhaps a computer or musical instruments. Some couples plan for their children's college expenses by opening an account and making contributions, agreeing to continue child support through the college years, or agreeing to make payments on it proportional to income when the time comes. You should require three months warning to allow for renegotiations if there is a move more than thirty miles by one parent. Annual reviews are helpful because circumstances change so much, with moves, new relationships, etc.

For the sake of the children, cooperate in a friendly manner whenever you pick up or drop off your children for visits. Let the other parent know as early as possible when you must change visiting plans. Make sure the children are ready for the other parent on time, pick up and return them on time, and call the other parent when you must be late. Young children feel especially hurt by lateness—after waiting all week, one or two hours may seem like an eternity to them. Don't argue in front of the children, in person or by phone. Remember that hostility between parents may be as bad for the mental health of the children whether the parents are unhappily married or bitterly divorced. Never ask your children to relay important messages about feelings or problems between you and the other parent. This unfair practice places your children in the middle of your conflicts. Discuss problems with the other parent, so you can present a united stance on discipline and other important decisions. Try to support each other's decisions because children tend to take advantage of disagreements between parents.

Children see their nonresidential parents infrequently on average, with various studies reporting between 21 and 52% of divorced fathers had no contact with their children at all in the past year. Too many also hurt their children by making occasional, but very unreliable, visits. Younger children often hope against hope for visits, only to repeatedly face disappointment, and adolescents often reject the irresponsible parent. Avoid continuous disappointment by not telling your child about visits until the parent actually arrives. Don't make up excuses; dishonesty damages your own relationship with the child. Instead, describe the truth in a calm, logical way to help your child see the situation realistically. You might say that although the other parent loves and cares about the child, that parent fails to visit reliably and the child will be much happier not knowing about or counting on the visits until they happen. When an uninvolved parent never visits, rarely visits, or rarely shows love, explain that the parent is unable or unwilling to act as a loving parent. Make it clear that the irresponsible parent is at fault, not the child. Help your child express and accept feelings about the situation.

Research highlights the importance of financial support by noncustodial parents in the adjustment of children. You can often adjust child support awards for inflation or update them when a parent's income increases. Child support depends on the parent's involvement, so avoid refusing visitation as a punishment when a parent falls behind in child support—this can lead to a vicious circle of refusing to pay in retaliation, refusing visitation, etc., sometimes leading to long-term alienation and noncooperation by the noncustodial parent.

If the court has ordered child support but a parent doesn't pay or constantly falls behind and the government workers take too long or can't find the person, you can contact a private child support agency (see under hotlines at the end of this chapter) for help. Interview a number of agencies before deciding which to use, and ask about their application fees, commissions, court costs, and legal fees. Don't pay a huge application fee— it should be $35 or so. Check the agency's reputation with your state attorney general's office.

Don't let your children become your only source of emotional support or make them feel responsible for taking care of your psychological well-being. These are unfair burdens to place on them. Your emotional needs should never take priority over their emotional needs. You may be in danger of this if you start encouraging your children to sleep with you or you treat a teenager as a peer and confidant or coparent. Instead, carefully shield your children from your worries about the future. Look for and lean on adult support, not your child's. Spend time with your friends, renew old friendships, and make new friends, so you don't become too needy of your children's attentions. The support group Parents Without Partners (see the end of this chapter) is a good resource for friendship, advice, and emotional support for single parents. Single parents often feel isolated from their married friends and from their single friends without children because these people don't fully understand the great burdens of raising children alone.

Today, nearly 90% of divorcing people get remarried or develop a new committed relationship within 3 years, and 1 in 3 Americans is part of a stepfamily.   When a parent remarries, the children must make many adjustments.   The new stepparent changes the living arrangements in the home and adds a new style of raising children to the family. The children lose time and attention from their biological parent to the new marital relationship. If the new stepparent brings children to the marriage, even more complications arise. The children lose time and attention from the biological parent to the new stepchildren. Life in the larger household becomes more complex and chaotic. An oldest child may now have older siblings, or a youngest child may have younger ones. The children may still feel loss and carry the burden of other issues related to the divorce. Love and loyalty to the noncustodial parent may interfere with a child's acceptance of the stepparent and stepchildren. It should come as no surprise that jealously and anger often occur. Your children may even reject the new stepparent in anger, perhaps saying something like, "I hate you! You're not my father!"

Problems with children contribute to a higher divorce rate early in remarriage, even when the spouses have good relations, but after the transitional period, the divorce rate goes down to normal. Help your children cope by talking about the coming changes once you decide to remarry. Emphasize every family member must help by showing extra kindness, helpfulness, and cooperation. Help them to understand the new stresses they face and to express and deal with their feelings. You might live with your new partner only on weekends at first, for a more gradual transition. Some cope by moving into a new home together, so nobody feels personal territory is being invaded and nobody has to give up a room.

At first let the natural parent take full responsibility for discipline. Of course, you can follow the lead of the natural parent in enforcing the boundaries of discipline when necessary, but the stepparent's first goal is to be friends with the stepchildren. Again, you can prevent many problems by frequently noticing and praising the children's good behaviors, giving loving attention to each child, encouraging plenty of interests and activities, and using good communication skills and consistent discipline. The techniques in the section on Reducing the Need for Discipline in chapter 22, Raising Children also help, as do using your sense of humor and doing fun things together. Spend time with the new family members in some of their favorite activities. Gradually, the stepparent can take a more authoritative role. It will take time for caring relationships and love to grow between the new family members.   Never force or pressure your children to express affection, but gently encourage affection to the stepparent and other new family members. Remember successful family integration may take years.

Courts generally don't consider your remarriage a sufficient excuse to reduce your child support payments, no matter what your new circumstances. When an ex-wife remarries, many men fear they are supporting the new family's purchases and become angry. You might calm him by discussing and planning exactly how to spend the money on the children. He may prefer to pay for specific bills, such as school, dentist, medical, music lessons, etc.

Recommended Additional Readings:

Divorce and New Beginnings: An Authoritative Guide to Recovery and Growth, Solo Parenting, and Stepfamilies. by Genevieve Clapp. NY: John Wiley & Sons, 1992.

The Good Divorce: Keeping Your Family Together When Your Marriage Comes Apart. by Constance Ahrons. New York: HarperCollins, 1994.

Families Apart: Ten Keys to Successful Co-parenting. by Melinda Blau. New York: G. P. Putnam's Sons, 1993.

Support Groups, Hotlines, and Resources:

Rainbows 800 266 3206 peer support groups for children or adults grieving divorce, death, or other painful family transitions. on-line: www.rainbows.org

Divorce Care 919 562 2112 church sponsored, nondenominationl support groups for separation or divorce. on-line: www.divorcecare.com

Parents Without Partners 800 637 7974 information, newsletter, support groups. on-line: www.parentswithoutpartners.org

Stepfamily Association of America 800 735 0329 information, support groups, free literature. on-line: www.saafamilies.org.

Child Support Services three national companies that can help find a parent who isn't paying court-ordered child support or help enforce payment if a parent constantly falls behind. Kids Limited 800 729 2445 on-line: www.collectchildsupport.com, SupportKids.com 800 723 5437 on-line: www.supportkids.com, Association for Children for Enforcement of Support 800 537 7072 on-line: www.childsupport-aces.org

To avoid credit problems, get a copy of your credit report after your divorce to make sure which credit cards remain in your name. If you didn't do this right away and an unfair credit problem appears on your name, put a statement in all of your credit reports explaining what happened. The three major credit bureaus: Equifax 800 685 1111, Trans Union 800 888 4213, Experian 888 397 3742.

24. Middle Age and Old Age

We are always the same age inside. (Gertrude Stein)

For 90%of people, middle age presents no unusual problems, no midlife crisis, but some people do experience dissatisfaction or unhappiness. The aging process, with its loss of strength, youthful looks, and sexual powers, may lead to unhappiness. Most people in middle age report very good or excellent relationships, but less time for friends than at any other time in their lives. In the *empty nest syndrome,* all the children grow up and move away, leaving the unemployed homemaker lonely and unhappy, with little to do. Some people reevaluate their lives and think about whether they really want to continue following the same path. Some consider a change in careers. People who married early may yearn for the freedom of the single life, and single people may yearn for the secure, deep love of marriage.

Personal problems that arise in middle age are no different from other personal problems, however. Use the appropriate parts of this book to cope. Ben Franklin's method of decision making, described in chapter 9, Problem Solving, can help in making great personal decisions. Some people simply need a deeper acceptance of their situation in life, perhaps by using more humor and positive thinking habits. Middle-aged and older folks should read the section on Sex in Old Age in chapter 18 for a description of the normal sexual changes associated with aging and what you can do about them.

In old age, satisfaction in marital life seems to increase, especially after children move away. Many old folks enjoy retirement, work and leisure activities, visiting children, and grandchildren, but certain problems may occur. Retirement can lead to boredom or depression and even marital tension if you don't fill your time with friends, interests and activities, volunteering, or part-time work. Seniors must confront bodily changes, sexual changes, and perhaps illnesses, too. Loneliness is common with the loss of husband or wife, friends, and relatives to death. Many old folks also face poverty. The loss of loved ones naturally results in grief, and any of the above stresses may lead to depression. The appropriate parts of this book can help. An acceptance of life's sorrows, a good sense of humor, positive thinking habits, and appreciation of simple things in life (nature, food, etc.) are all important assets in facing the problems of old age.

A great deal of research emphasizes the importance of exercise and good nutrition for health in old age. For example, a study of 17,000 college graduates from 1916 to 1950 showed that those engaging in energetic activities tended to live longer than inactive people. Certain cultures noted for longevity all farm mountainous terrain with no retirement age, so even the oldest people get plenty of exercise. One woman tea picker retired in her 130s and a 121-year-old man insisted that the people next door couldn't build their house without his help. Strength training can bring dramatic reversals in the loss of muscle, even among frail people in their 90s and those who have never exercised before, leading to improved balance, strength, mobility, and mental outlook. Even short-term exercise can build strength and mobility and help reduce injuries from falls in old age. (Experts estimate 30% of people over 64 years old have had falls and that half of those falls caused serious injury.) Seniors who want to begin exercising should first consult their doctors and read the section on Exercise in chapter 10, Stress.

The peoples in the long-lived cultures also consume a very healthy diet with many fewer calories, more vegetables and grains, and less meat and dairy products than the average American eats. A recent study of people over 100 years old in America reports that obesity is rare in this group. Unfortunately, older Americans are one of the groups at greatest risk for poor nutrition, which increases their chances of illness and slows recovery when they get sick. Doctors often overlook poor nutrition as a cause of anemia, weight loss, leg swelling, repeated infections, poor wound healing, pressure sores, and weakness. Depression, constipation, excessive use of alcohol, and certain prescription or over-the-counter drugs can lead to deficiencies by reducing appetite. Poor nutrition in old folks may come from financial problems, isolation, severe arthritis or other medical problems that limit food preparation or shopping, poorly fitting dentures, or other tooth or mouth problems. Doctors or dentists can often help. Look for government sources of economic assistance. Or you may need to find meal programs at group sites or provided at home through an agency.

Regular mental activity such as reading is important in old age. The regular use of memory and mental abilities helps maintain them. The phrase *use it or lose it* is as true of mental abilities as of muscle strength. People who believe in the myth that old age inevitably means mental and physical deterioration often allow their activities to dwindle in old age and then deteriorate in a self-fulfilling prophecy. Doctors believe that only 5 or 10% of people over 65 years old and about 20% of people over 80 have diseases causing senility. The more common loss of memory and mental abilities in old age comes from a simple lack of use. Throughout life, both mental and physical activity help protect against memory loss and Alzheimer's disease.

In chapter 1, Happiness, we noted a variety of studies suggest close relationships with other people help promote longevity. For example, a 13-year study of 2,761 people age 65 and older found the most socially active folks lived 2 and 1/2 years longer than the least socially active, despite no difference in health or physical activity levels. A study of younger men between 42 and 60 years old found increased rates of death in the men who were not active in clubs or volunteer organizations, felt dissatisfied with the quality of their relationships, gave or received little social support, or were single. Marriage and a fulfilling social life appear to protect against Alzheimer's and other dementias associated with old age. Feelings of being useful, needed, and loved may contribute to the longevity of the cultures noted above, with close-knit families respecting old folks for their wisdom.

These observations emphasize the importance of personal qualities and skills that improve social relationships, such as the ability to truly love, good communication and social skills, and productive interests and activities. These things become especially important when, in old age, you lose your closest friends and loved ones to death. Many seniors who have lost loved ones do volunteer work to keep busy, feel useful and needed, and satisfy social needs. Participate in a senior citizen's center that offers planned activities and perhaps group meals. Consider getting a pet. Studies suggest owning a pet may increase longevity. One study found people who survived heart attacks lived longer if they had pets at home. Some nursing homes allow birds and other pets in order to decrease boredom, helplessness, and loneliness and perhaps increase survival.

We all have an obligation to take care of our aging parents if they need our assistance. Parents spend 18 years or more working to provide food, a home, training, and discipline to their children. Even if you feel your parents did you wrong, forgive them and help them in their old age. Remember that your parents were a product of their own times, their parents, and the problems they experienced in their lives.

To maintain functioning, allow your parents to continue doing things for themselves and for you as much as possible. Old people deteriorate more when other people do everything for them. Contributing also helps make them feel useful, needed, and competent. Unfortunately, many old folks passively accept help they don't really want, and others may gratefully appreciate help they don't really need. Encourage seniors to make decisions, go places, help around the house, read, keep busy, and do things for themselves, even if they can't do certain things as well or quickly as they could in the past. Encourage them to remain as active as possible within the limits of their disabilities. Regular exercise can sometimes eliminate the need for a cane or walker for mobility.

Some relatives or friends take advantage of the isolation or physical deterioration of old folks and use intimidation to change wills or take money from them. Protect yourself by getting your checks sent directly to the bank, getting your routine bills paid automatically by the bank, keeping in touch with friends and relatives, and asking your bank about any questionable activities. Relatives should check on old folks who live far away. Always carefully check the references of anyone hired to take care of a senior citizen. Often a legal power of attorney robs the senior of assets, perhaps including his or her home. If you need someone to do business for you, make sure the power of attorney you choose is someone you trust. Consider limiting the control of your power of attorney, requiring annual accounting of income and expenses to your lawyer or financial planner. Explain the arrangement to the power of attorney, too, so the person knows somebody will be checking.

If your parents are growing old, be alert for signs of deterioration in physical or mental health. These include not eating regularly, significant weight loss, increasing falls or accidents, growing social isolation, unpaid bills, cigarette burns on furniture, burn marks on cooking pots, dressing inappropriately, acting suspicious, or difficulty finding words. Never assume that someone is senile without a doctor's evaluation, because some curable conditions may mimic senility: many physical problems, depression, poor eyesight, poor hearing, etc.

If problems develop, consider the parent's desires, needs, functioning, family finances, and the personal circumstances of each child in deciding how to take care of a parent. Parents may live in their own home, their children's homes, a nursing home, or a senior citizen's retirement community or apartment complex. Assisted living residences provide meals, housekeeping services, social activities, and some help with dressing and bathing, but not nursing home care. Continuing care retirement communities accept healthy people with a large entrance fee and offer independent living in a retirement community, with assisted living or nursing home care assured for life if and when they become needed.

Many communities have seniors' centers for recreation and socialization, exercise programs, meals delivered to the home, adult day care, and counseling. Home health services can provide visiting nurses, physical therapy, social workers, and perhaps help with household chores. Some communities offer chore services, transportation, or daily telephone calls that trigger police followup if the old person doesn't answer the phone. Because long-term caregiving is so stressful, use the available resources, get help, and be sure to take breaks from your responsibilities at least once a week.

Choose a nursing home carefully because many old folks die of neglect in nursing homes. In 1999, the government found more than 1/4 of all nursing homes had deficiencies that caused harm or risk of serious injury or death. A study of all deaths in California nursing homes from 1986 to 1993 showed more than 7% died because of preventable problems like untreated bedsores or infections or a lack of food or water. Many relatives never find out their loved ones died of preventable problems. When lawsuits occur, nursing homes generally settle quietly and pay only in return for silence. Federal regulations are weak, poorly enforced, and don't even specify how much staffing a nursing home needs. Instead of surprise inspections, many states inspect nursing homes only at precise yearly intervals during business hours, so the nursing homes have time to hide neglect and abuse.

In one recent year, state inspectors reported 5,458 nursing homes (1 in every 3) to federal officials, requesting these homes be barred from collecting money for new patients, but the U.S. only barred 156. Of 5,974 state requests to order special training for staff or fines for violations, the U.S. did so for only 331 homes. According to federal reports, each year, more than 1/4 of all nursing homes have health or safety violations that harm residents or place them at risk of death or serious injury.

Even beautiful, expensive nursing homes may have severe problems, with residents inactive and warehoused in their rooms. First, look at only Medicare and Medicaid approved facilities. Ask the nursing home to show you their recent inspection reports. If they can't or won't, it is a bad sign. Check the performance of nursing homes yourself using the National Citizens' Coalition for Nursing Home Reform or the federal Health Care Financing Administration web site (both are listed at the end of this chapter). In the reports, many violations will be minor, but pay particular attention to nursing problems. A lack of enough linens might just mean the industrial washer was broken for a few days, but serious problems include continued lack of proper staffing or an excessive rate of bedsores (decubiti).

Visit the nursing home unannounced. If they don't allow this, they may have something to hide. Talk to staff and residents and see if they both enjoy being there. Notice how the staff talks to patients. Understaffed homes may have slightly impatient or annoyed staff. Watch the time it takes staff to respond to the call lights residents use; more than five minutes is too long.

See if residents are clean and well-groomed. Discreetly try to notice oral hygiene. See if residents are walking the halls or common areas using canes, walkers, or wheelchairs. Poor nursing homes will have far less resident activity than good ones. Look for obstacles or puddles in halls that could cause falls in residents with poor vision. If medically possible, residents should at least be up in chairs for long periods each day; this is important for physical and emotional health.

Approved nursing homes must post their menus, but go to a meal and check if the meal served is what they claim. See if the staff helps feed those who can't feed themselves. They should serve the main meal at noon, with a lighter meal in the late afternoon or early evening, and they should provide juice and snacks in the afternoon and at bedtime. Most nursing homes occasionally smell of urine or feces, but there should be no persistent or stale odors. Strong disinfectant or deodorizer smells might mask problems. Many nursing home laundries close on weekends, so don't check for smells on Monday morning. Watch for residents in restraints, too; the more you see, the more leery you should be. After choosing a home, visit frequently. Residents with regular visitors tend to receive better care than those with few or rare visits.

A large majority of seniors spend their final days at great expense in nursing homes or hospitals in advanced stages of mental and physical deterioration. Because of aggressive treatment by doctors trained to preserve life no matter what the cost, many patients now experience needlessly prolonged pain or suffering before dying. One study found nearly 40% of critically ill patients who died in five major hospitals spent at least 10 days in an intensive care unit, kept alive by machines. According to a Gallup poll, 84% of Americans would refuse life-support systems if they had a terminal illness or injury with no hope of recovering, yet only 20% have a living will, which states what medical professionals should do in such circumstances. Discuss the option of a living will with your parents early, so they can have some choice in these important final matters before they become emotionally traumatic, last minute decisions.

If you don't want to be kept alive by artificial means and heroic measures, your local hospital or library can help you find information on writing a living will. Refusing artificial or extraordinary life-sustaining procedures is not enough. These vague terms are subject to interpretation and may allow many burdensome treatments. Be specific about procedures and terms such as cardiac resuscitation (compression or defibrillation), feeding tubes, respirators, impaired mobility, irreversible brain damage, or functional memory. What kinds of mobility or mental abilities? How do your wishes change in various circumstances? Be sure you require health care providers to give you excellent pain relief, despite your refusing other medical interventions. Update your living will every few years.

To get your wishes met, you need to do more than just make a living will. The study of critically ill patients in five major hospitals mentioned above also found doctors don't listen to what patients want. Only 49% of the critically ill patients who requested do-not-resuscitate orders actually got them, and 2/3 of doctors who received reports on patients' wishes about life-sustaining care didn't even look at the reports.

After making your living will, give a copy to each of your next of kin and loved ones. Ask these people to read it together if the time comes when they must make a decision for you about your medical care. Because none of us can predict every possible situation, give one person who knows your wishes durable power of attorney for health care that begins when you become incompetent. Find a doctor who agrees to honor your wishes and agrees to be your advocate, even if another doctor will treat you. Give a copy to your lawyer and local hospital. Your lawyer can advise you on state laws regarding living wills and on whom to notify and in what form.

Some people carry a card in their wallet indicating they have a living will and where to find it. Some ambulance companies have a living will form on which you can refuse various medical procedures. You might make sure that those involved in your care will not call an ambulance if you can't express your wishes in an emergency. Unless the ambulance personnel know your wishes, state laws often mandate that they administer life-saving measures. Another option is a MedicAlert bracelet or neck emblem indicating that you have a living will on file (see hotlines below). These devices give emergency personnel critical information regarding your life support wishes.

Some people band together to form caregiver networks in which friends take turns helping sick people with their daily needs. This is most common when a sick or dying person has no family left or when the family is uninvolved, but loving friends may establish such a group just to give family members regular breaks from the burden of ministering to the ill person. Begin by calling a meeting of all the friends who care enough to help, making a list of names and phone numbers, and scheduling whatever the person needs for the next month or two: meals, transportation to doctors and pharmacies, help with household chores, supervision of medicines, bathing, etc. You might coordinate the group's activities to supplement community services such as visiting nurses and meal services. At times, a caregiver network may eliminate the need for a nursing home.

Recommended Additional Readings:

Shaping Your Health Care Future with Health Care Advance Directives. a free publication from the American Association of Retired Persons and the American Bar Association on writing a living will. It helps you think through and write down your wishes. You can get it by writing to AARP Fulfillment (EE0940), 601 E St. NW, Washington, DC 20049.

Support Groups, Hotlines, and Resources:

National Council on Aging 800 424 9046 free information. on-line: www.ncoa.org

Federal Administration on Aging 800 677 1116 referrals to services for old folks, information on preventing abuse, age discrimination, employment, raising grandchildren, Alzheimer's, retirement, financial planning, housing options. on-line: www.aoa.dhhs.gov

Partnership for Caring 800 989 9455 counseling for dying people and their families, living wills, medical power of attorney.   on-line: www.partnershipforcaring.org

Care Guide 800 777 3319 information on caring for aging parents or elderly people, referrals for counseling or support groups. on-line: www.careguide.net

National Family Caregivers Association 800 896 3650 support, information, referrals, literature. on-line: www.nfcacares.org

Alzheimer's Disease and Related Disorders Association 800 272 3900 support group referrals. on-line: www.alz.org

federal government performance evaluations of nursing homes across the U.S., also how to choose a nursing home, alternative living arrangements. on-line: www.medicare.gov/Nursing/Overview.asp

National Citizens' Coalition for Nursing Home Reform 202 332 2275 gives the number for your state ombudsman's office so you can get recent state inspection reports on any nursing home, information on choosing a nursing home, nursing home abuse, long-term care insurance. on-line: www.nccnhr.org

American Association of Homes and Services for the Aging 202 783 2242 nonprofit agency giving information on choosing a nursing home, alternative living arrangements. on-line: www.aahsa.org/public/consumer.htm

American Health Care Association 202 842 4444 gives information on choosing a nursing home. on-line: www.ahca.org/info/informat.htm

MedicAlert 800 432 5378 bracelet or neck emblem indicating to emergency personnel that you have a living will on file regarding your life support wishes. on-line: www.medicalert.org

25. Death and Suicide

Death is but part of the circle of life,
teaching those almost caught in its reach
how beautiful and precious life is,
and teaching those who grieve
how much love they have inside.

Dying people need their friends more than ever. Try not to avoid a dying person because of your own discomfort with hospitals, illness, or sadness. When visiting a dying person, take the time to show you care. Never hurry. Don't worry about what to say—the important thing is simply that you care. Take a loving interest in how the person feels, but don't pry into feelings or problems. Tactfully allow either privacy or personal sharing. If the person feels like talking, listen carefully. Show understanding about any strong feelings expressed. Feel free to share your feelings or to let your feelings show. You may be able to cheer a dying person by sharing news about your own life or friends you have in common. Dying people often enjoy reminiscing about the past or experiences you shared together. Feel free to laugh—the person needs fun and humor. Don't let silence bother you; just spending time there shows you care.

Touch from close friends and relatives is often very comforting. You might hold the person's hand, stroke it, or stroke the person's hair. Use sensitivity and judgment, however, because not everyone feels comfortable with affectionate touching. Many dying people feel very weak or tired. If they fall asleep during your visit, you can show your love by staying nearby and waiting for the chance to visit during waking periods, or you may want to come back at another time. If you plan to come back later, ask when is the most convenient time for you to come. Because of the great stresses of facing illness and death, dying people may sometimes become overly emotional or inappropriately angry at caretakers or close friends and relatives. Try to understand such episodes and to emotionally support the person. If excessive anger becomes a regular problem, you should set limits on it. Firmly refuse to tolerate such behavior, while emphasizing your love and desire to help.

Some people band together to form caregivers networks, in which they take turns helping a dying loved one with daily needs or giving family members or primary caretakers needed breaks. Please refer to the end of the previous chapter for a description of this loving network and of how to begin one.

When someone dies, people often visit and give sympathy cards or gifts of food to help the family with the hectic week of the funeral. There are many other things you can do: offer child care services, help in arranging the funeral, drive them to grocery stores or doctor's appointments, or help with household chores such as vacuuming, yard work, washing the car, doing dishes or laundry, etc. You might offer lodging and transportation for relatives in town for the funeral or help with addressing and stamping thank-you notes. You might send a card or letter with pictures of memories of the deceased or listing things you offer to do to help.

People who have lost loved ones to death really need their friends more than ever for months and months, not just for a week or two. It can be very lonely for a grieving person when everyone else gets on with their lives. Continue helping and giving emotional support for months. The family members may greatly appreciate even an occasional letter, telephone call, or invitation. Often a grieving person will turn down invitations soon after a death but become much more receptive later.

Funeral costs are rising several times faster than the cost of living, with national chains often buying a funeral home, keeping the name and hiring the previous owner, but greatly increasing fees. Caskets are often marked up five times over cost, and homes often show only midrange to expensive ones, knowing most people will avoid the cheapest ones they see. Some sell expensive caskets that seal and protect the body from the elements, but these let anaerobic bacteria devour the body, producing gas that can burst the casket, sometimes spraying or leaking decomposed fluids out or even blowing the front off the crypt.

Don't let funeral directors take advantage of you in your grief. Take your time, leaving the body at the hospital or nursing home while you compare prices without giving much detail about your finances. Ask about hidden charges such as the use of common areas, restrooms, or parking lots. Save money with cremation or by ordering your casket yourself. A funeral home cannot refuse your casket or charge to handle it, nor require your presence for delivery. Holding visiting hours or a memorial service at your church or home without the body saves money, too. Any funeral director who claims state laws require something must show you the law to prove it. Cemeteries may sell a grave marker, then charge hundreds for placement and inspection. See the resources at the end of the chapter for saving money.

Don't prepay for your own funeral. Some funeral homes steal money or lose it in poor investments. Plans are often nonrefundable or nontransferable if you move or change your mind. Hidden fees may sharply raise costs when the time comes. Instead, you can use a certificate of deposit or life insurance policy to help your loved ones pay for your funeral or open a savings account with a family member with the right of survivorship so that your money is not taxed.

Because people now die in institutions such as hospitals much more often than they die at home, young children may not understand death very well. You may need to repeatedly explain that the deceased person will never come back. Speak in simple, realistic language, perhaps using the death of a pet or insect as an example. Young children may fear they were somehow responsible for the death or fear repeated loss or abandonment by other family members. Reassure them nothing they have done has contributed to the death, angry thoughts or wishes for harm could not have helped bring on the death, and the other family members still love them and will help and take care of them.

You can help a child understand that death is final by allowing the child to attend the funeral or view the body at the funeral home. Even adults often find this makes it easier to accept emotionally the reality of the loss. Allowing children as young as two or three years old to view the body does no harm, but never force children to go up to the casket or touch the body. Parents may decide whether their children should go to a funeral, taking into account how close the children were to the deceased and whether the children are mature enough to sit through the service. Or you may allow your children to decide about going. If your child is not familiar with funerals, be sure to describe what will happen and how people may express their emotions, before you invite or take your child.

Don't try to make children hide their sadness or grief. As we shall see in chapter 26, Grief, expressing emotions is an important part of healing. The end of that chapter gives more advice for helping children cope. On those rare occasions when a grieving child or adult loses control at a funeral and causes a disturbance, someone should take the upset person away to calm down.

Each year, almost 30,000 Americans take their own lives. Many experts believe this reported number may be half the true number of suicides. The most common methods of suicide are firearms, hanging, and drug overdose, with alcohol consumed along with medications in over 20% of attempts. Unfortunately, there is no reliable biological, chemical, or psychological test that can predict whether or not a person will commit suicide. Professionals do use a number of criteria to help guess at suicidal tendencies, however. The danger of suicide rises with increasing severity of problems and with more of the following criteria applying to a particular person, but the prediction of suicide potential is rather primitive, even for experts in the field.

Always take very seriously any talk or threats of suicide or talk that implies suicide, because most people who commit suicide do give warning beforehand. Take very seriously statements such as: "I'm so tired of living," "I'd be better off dead," or "I'm just a burden to my family." How often suicidal thoughts occur also helps indicate the risk. Frequent suicidal thoughts are much more serious than occasional, momentary thoughts about it. Developing a specific plan for suicide is much more dangerous than simply having vague ideas about wanting to commit suicide. The risk increases when a person chooses a particular method for committing suicide, and especially a particular time and place. Consider the lethality of the chosen method and the likelihood of rescue. Suicide plans involving guns, hanging, or jumping off tall buildings or cliffs are more dangerous than those involving cutting your wrists or taking aspirins or other pills. A plan to commit suicide alone in a motel room is much more dangerous than a plan to commit suicide at home, with your family likely to discover you in time. Another serious indication of risk is the making of a will or other unusual preparations for absence in a seriously depressed person.

A serious suicide attempt indicates especially high risk for the first few months after the previous attempt and high risk for several additional years. Studies suggest that approximately one-third of people who commit suicide have tried to do so before. Assess the lethality of the chosen method and the likelihood of rescue in the previous suicide attempt. A previous attempt of low risk doesn't raise the subsequent danger nearly as much as does a very lethal suicide attempt that didn't succeed. Consider the person's beliefs and intentions, too. Some people who desperately want to die choose methods with low risk because of ignorance, and other people who feel more ambivalent about dying choose a very fatal method because of ignorance. For example, a person may poorly estimate the lethality of the kind and amount of pills taken in a suicide attempt.

Some low-risk suicide attempts are cries for help in which people, on some level of their personality, want to call attention to personal problems to make other people understand the depth of their despair. Other people design low-risk suicides to manipulate loved ones such as parents or a boyfriend or girlfriend. For example, a suicide attempt in the presence of a spouse during a heated argument generally involves low risk, interpersonal motivations, and certain rescue. Even so, any previous history of attempted suicide indicates danger because even attempts using methods of low lethality may accidentally prove fatal.

Age, sex, and race also help in evaluating risk. White males account for 70% of all suicides in the United States. Suicide rates among blacks are roughly half that of whites, for both men and women. Hispanics kill themselves at a rate between those of whites and blacks. The overall rate in Native American Indians is even higher than that of whites, but there is great variation in rates among different tribes. Available information suggests that Chinese, Japanese, and Filipino male suicide rates are generally lower than those of American males, except in the oldest age groups. Males die by suicide 4 or 5 times as often as females do, but females make suicide attempts 2 or 3 times as often as males do. This is because women more often make low-risk attempts with better chances of rescue.

Overall, suicide becomes more likely with increasing age over 40, whereas younger people more often make low-risk suicide attempts. This trend holds true although suicide rates have decreased in older people and increased in younger people over the last 40 years. Overall, senior citizens commit suicide at two or three times the rate of adolescents, but in Hispanics and in Native Americans, the highest rates occur between the ages of 20 and 24. Since 1980, the rate in 10- to 14-year-old children has doubled overall and quadrupled among blacks, although the number of suicide attempts remained the same. Officials blame the increased availability of guns. (American children under 15 years old are 12 times more likely to die by gunfire than are children in 25 other industrialized countries.) More than 50% of those under 25 who kill themselves use guns.

Of course, depression plays an enormous role in suicide. The more depressed a person is, the greater the danger of suicide, especially if severe depression results in poor daily functioning and chronic fatigue. The danger increases when a depressed person withdraws from other people, perhaps spending very little time with friends, never sharing troubled feelings with others, or avoiding help. Another important clue is the person's social support system. The risk increases when a depressed person has few or no available close friends and decreases with a number of supportive, close relationships. Single, divorced, separated, or widowed people commit suicide more often than married people, especially married people with children. For example, separated and divorced women commit suicide almost 3 1/2 times as often as do married women.

Personal problems also help indicate risk. Great anger adds to the danger. People often intend the suicide to hurt or to punish other people in their lives, such as a spouse or parents. Angry suicidal people often enjoy the fantasy of upsetting others and making them feel sorry for past events by committing suicide. The danger also increases with great anxiety, severe insomnia, or drug or alcohol problems. Suicide is 30 times as common in alcoholics as it is in other people, and substance abuse plays a role in the majority of teenage suicides. A history of school, sexual, or social problems also adds to the risk. Terminally ill people are at especially high risk. Research suggests that suicide is 15 times as common in cancer patients as it is in the general population. Personal problems increase the danger the most when the person is impulsive, aggressive, unstable, confused, paranoid, or schizophrenic. The reaction to previous counseling for personal problems also provides a clue. Satisfaction with previous counseling is a good sign, but dissatisfaction indicates a higher risk.

Severely stressful life events, too, increase the chance of suicide. Many people react to the death of a loved one, becoming chronically ill or disabled, or a great loss of money or prestige with thoughts of suicide. Divorce, separation, the health problems of old age, or even the loss of a job may lead to suicidal thoughts. A history of suicide in the person's family increases risk, especially when suicide involves the parent of the same sex. Rates of suicide are higher in urban areas than in rural ones. Contrary to stereotypes, adolescents who commit suicide are more likely to be aggressive, acting out types than shy and introverted. Additional risk factors in young people include loss of a parent, family disruption, homosexuality, being a friend or family member of a suicide victim, media emphasis on suicide, and easy access to a gun.

What can you do if you notice depression, withdrawal from other people, or other unusual changes in a friend or loved one that suggest the potential for suicide? First, tell the troubled person you care, you notice some changes in behavior, and you would like to help. Remember, showing your concern and love may make the difference between life and death. If the person shares personal problems with you, use the helpful listening skills described in chapter 6, Communication Skills, and give emotional support, saying, "I'm here for you." Suggest this book or give it to the person as a resource for working on personal problems. If the conversation leads you to believe the person feels hopeless and you still suspect a potential for suicide, feel free to bring up the topic of suicide. Most people with suicidal thoughts feel relieved to share their feelings with a trusted and concerned friend or relative. If the person shares thoughts of suicide, express your sorrow things are so bad the person wants to die.

Encourage anyone who thinks about, threatens, or attempts suicide to get professional help. A professional will evaluate the need for emergency hospitalization to prevent suicide. The decision about hospitalization will depend on the person's functioning, the available social supports, and the risk factors described previously. If necessary, a doctor or psychiatrist can use legal procedures to hospitalize a dangerously suicidal person against that person's will. The doctor may also decide the person needs medicine to help with depression, anxiety, anger, or mood swings. Sometimes you can avoid expensive emergency hospitalization despite great danger by arranging for friends and relatives to take turns staying with the suicidal person 24 hours a day until the suicidal crisis ends and long-term counseling has begun. Never use a family member alone to carry out a suicide watch—most family members cannot maintain perspective. An important precaution is to remove any methods of self-injury, such as guns, sleeping pills, rope, or other poisons, from the person's environment.

Try to make a contract with the person about staying alive. Begin by expressing your love and perhaps by saying how important the person is to you. Then point out most suicide attempts are not fatal and that many people who leap from buildings or shoot themselves in the head end up living with severe disabilities such as brain damage, loss of vision or hearing, legs or arms that don't function, etc. Even overdosing with pills can severely damage the liver and cause a slow, agonizing death. Next, ask the person to agree never to commit suicide and also to talk to you first about suicidal feelings before making any suicide attempt. Try to get agreement to both of these things. If the person refuses, try to get an agreement not to attempt suicide for as long as possible: two months, two weeks, etc. Later, but before the period ends, try to renew the agreement and extend the time.

This contract should also include other important points. Ask the person to get enough food and sleep, and remove anything useful in attempting suicide (even if a 24-hour watch is unnecessary). Make a list of people and phone numbers to contact if thoughts of suicide grow strong, and make a list of activities to keep busy and avoid brooding over problems. It can help to write down the contract, including how long it lasts, and have the suicidal person and any favored chosen friends or family members sign it.

Find out why the person feels suicidal and try to help the person work on personal problems. Encourage anyone who is lonely or isolated to get out more, join various groups, and perhaps move in with friends or relatives. People who are unhappy at work, unemployed, or who often change jobs may benefit from occupational training and placement.   If the person goes to counseling, you can simply take an interest in the developments and give your emotional support.   Be careful not to nag about working on personal problems.   This may interfere with the person's progress by provoking resentment and rebellion. Please refer to chapter 12 for a discussion of how to help someone work on personal problems in a tactful, sensitive way. Suicidal people will need plenty of encouragement and help to counter their own negativity, develop interests and activities, etc. At times you may need to give them commands, but use plenty of praise and good communication skills and make sure they want and appreciate your help. Occasionally ask the person if you push too hard or if they feel nagged.

When a child or adolescent attempts or commits suicide, the principal of the school should call all teachers and staff for a mandatory meeting before school the next morning to share information about what happened, explaining faculty and staff should answer student questions but not initiate a discussion of suicide. Excuse upset students from class to spend time with the school counselor or other crisis team members. Refer any questions from worried parents or news media to one designated person for accurate information and the school's response.

Support Groups and Hotlines:

Partnership for Caring 800 989 9455 counseling for dying people and their families, living wills, medical power of attorney. on-line: www.partnershipforcaring.org

Funeral Consumers Alliance 800 765 0107 nonprofit organization that offers lists of reputable, low-cost funeral homes. on-line: www.funerals.org

Make A Wish Foundation 800 722 9474 grants wishes to children with serious illnesses. on-line: www.wish.org

Sunshine Foundation 800 767 1976 grants wishes to chronically ill and terminally ill children ages 3 to 21. on-line: www.sunshinefoundation.org

To save money by buying a new casket directly, call Direct Casket on the East Coast at 800 732 2753 and on the West Coast at 800 772 2753 on-line: www.directcasket.com. To buy a used casket, call Consumer Casket USA at 800 611 8778. Both businesses ship within 24 hours.

Resources:

Please refer to the end of the previous chapter, Aging, for resources on living wills and caregivers, and please refer to the end of the next chapter for resources on grief or loss.

26. Grief, Trauma, and Crises

*We are healed of a suffering only by
experiencing it to the full. (Marcel Proust)*

The tree of wisdom is watered by tears. (Swiss proverb)

Trials give you strength, sorrows give understanding and wisdom.

Some animals clearly show the emotion of grief. Two rhesus monkeys carried their dead babies until the babies became skeletons with skin. After its mother died, one baby chimpanzee avoided others, stopped eating, spent hours hunched over, rocked back and forth, and died of starvation. Gorillas, baboons, elephants, and dogs, too, sometimes show grief or a need to deny death. After her mate of 34 years died, one elephant in a zoo in France rejected food for over 4 weeks and died. One Tokyo University professor's dog would accompany him to a railroad station on his way to work, then wait for him all day until he came home. After just over one year of this routine, the professor died and the family moved to a distant part of Tokyo. The dog found its way back to the railroad station and continued to make this daily journey for ten years until its death. The Japanese erected a statue of the loyal dog in the railroad station and issued a postal stamp in its honor.

The death of a loved one is one of life's greatest sorrows. People of various cultures react to this loss in very different ways. In parts of the world, people often amputated a thumb or finger joint in grief. In some African cultures, women often try to throw themselves on their husband's graves. In other cultures, people show only subdued reactions. Ute American Indians believed the best way for relatives to honor the dead was to immediately forget them. The Buddhist Thai-Lao villagers of northeast Thailand subdue all emotions to free themselves from attachment to desire and the material world. In their culture, observable grief after loss of a family member rarely lasts for more than one week, even when the death comes suddenly and unexpectedly.

Grief is our natural response to a major loss or affliction, such as the death or severe injury of a loved one, end of a love relationship, becoming disabled in an accident, or onset of severe physical or mental problems. The more severe losses or afflictions are just as traumatic as crises like rape, kidnapping, mugging, violent victimization, wartime combat, and natural disasters.   A *trauma* is an event that is shocking, terrifying, and overwhelming, resulting in feelings of intense fear, helplessness, and powerlessness. We discuss grief and trauma together in this chapter because many of our reactions to both are very similar, they take around the same amount of time to recover, and they share coping methods, such as the importance of expressing feelings during the first few months.

In our culture, crisis reactions and grief after the loss of a loved one such as a parent, child, or spouse normally last between approximately six months to one or two years, although the worst of the symptoms diminish or end by about two to four months. Most people become relatively free of symptoms by approximately one year afterward. Full recovery, however, doesn't completely end all the sadness. People often feel sadness and pain whenever reflecting upon the crisis or loss for the rest of their lives.

A number of things may affect the intensity of grief, responses to trauma, and the time needed to recover. People with many close friends or with some very close relationships left after the loss or crisis generally recover more easily than do people with few social supports. People generally find it much more difficult to accept sudden crises or deaths with little or no warning than deaths after prolonged illnesses. Perhaps this is because death after illness often brings relief from pain and suffering to the deceased and gives the other people plenty of time to prepare emotionally for the coming loss. Murders and suicides are more difficult to accept and resolve than are other deaths. When you feel responsible for the crisis or death in some way, you tend to have a more difficult time coping. Responses to trauma and grief are more troublesome, too, during times of great stress or after other recent major crises. Grief also becomes more complicated when the previous relationship with the deceased person had been tumultuous, with mixed feelings and with good and bad times. Finally, when one has been overly dependent on the deceased person, with few outside relationships and interests and activities, resolving the loss becomes more difficult.

Crisis reactions or grief can result in a variety of symptoms, some of which may frighten people or make them fear or wonder if they are going insane. The first reaction is often a short period of shock, especially if the crisis or death was sudden and unexpected. During this period, the person may feel confused, find it hard to believe what happened, deny that it occurred, or temporarily feel nothing or little emotion. The controlled response of feeling little emotion and telling it in a matter-of-fact way may happen for weeks, but before long, the person faces reality and feels the full force of the crisis or loss. Depression may become a regular problem, or sadness and sorrow may overwhelm the person.   Crying may occur occasionally or frequently.   Some people prefer to deal with the intense emotional pain, at first, by withdrawing from all but their closest friends and relatives.

Thoughts about the event or dead person may preoccupy your mind. In grief, you will probably think about the person, experiences you shared, or events leading up to the death. Many people try to avoid these thoughts but feel unable to stop.   Some people become afraid that this extreme preoccupation for day after day or week after week is unhealthy.   Some people respond to grief by either avoiding or saving and treasuring reminders of the deceased. Extreme examples of the latter are people who keep the dead person's room exactly as it was during their lifetime.

After childhood physical or sexual abuse, a rape, violent attack, or wartime combat, intensely arousing memories may trouble you greatly. Driving by the place where it happened, being in a similar place, or seeing or smelling anything similar may bring back intense feelings. The worst of the troublesome memories are *flashbacks*, sudden illusions in which you relive the traumatic episode emotionally, cognitively, and through your senses, usually in response to a trigger or cue associated with the trauma. After you repress a trauma, flashbacks begin as perceptual fragments such as images or sensations you weave into a coherent story over time. A national study of memory loss and delayed recall noted over half the memories started coming back because of seeing something in the media related to the issue of the trauma. Other triggers for memories included similar events, conversations, dreams or nightmares, or violence. For example, a phrase, gesture, or cologne used by your abuser or weather like that of wartime experience may trigger flashbacks. In a study of sexually abused people, one-third reported that a consensual sexual relationship triggered the return of memories. Sometimes the death of the abuser or a changed relationship with that person triggers the memory of sexual abuse.

Burying emotions by ignoring them every time they arise is a common method of coping with grief or crises. We often prefer to ignore and avoid painful emotions. This can work. Research suggests some people benefit from denying, repressing, and avoiding unpleasant emotions and memories. Traumatized people may minimize what happened or its seriousness, dissociate, deny, numb themselves emotionally, forget, or rewrite their personal history. If these coping techniques repress the memories, you have no conscious memory of them. There is great controversy over how much this actually happens, however. Research on the frequency of memory loss for trauma followed by delayed recall has found a range from zero to 2/3 of those experiencing traumas. A study with a national sample of men and women found 20% had temporary complete amnesia for trauma and that another 20% had temporarily forgotten important details of the trauma. The traumas that disrupt memory tend to start in early childhood and repeat (such as child sexual abuse), to include penetration or violence, and to affect children or adolescents rather than adults. Even so, psychologists agree most people who were sexually abused as children remember all or part of what happened to them.

Grief or trauma may also lead to depression, perhaps including apathy or fatigue. In grief, loneliness in living without the deceased is common. The death of a loved one may bring some feelings of relief, especially if taking care of the person was your burden or if the deceased had been suffering for a long time or suffered a painful death. Anger is also common. People often experience anger at what fate has brought, at people who contributed to the crisis, from irrational feelings of abandonment through death, or at the deceased person for contributing to the death by neglect—the overuse of alcohol, refusing medical attention, etc. You may feel guilty about having anger toward the deceased. Many people feel guilty over not having thought to do something that may have prevented the crisis or death. In grief, we often feel guilty over not having been kind enough before the death, especially in cases of suicide. When one person survives an accident, military combat, or some other cause of death and the other person doesn't, the survivor often feels guilty for surviving while the other person died.

There are many other possible symptoms after crisis or the death of a loved one: anxiety, nervousness, oversensitivity to noise, restlessness, irritability, mood swings, insomnia, nightmares, dreams about the deceased, a lack of appetite, shortness of breath, tightness or tension in the body, an upset stomach, or headaches. You may increase your use of tobacco, alcohol, tranquilizers, or other drugs. Some people develop the feeling life doesn't seem quite real anymore. Many grieving people experience hallucinations in which they see or hear the deceased person or delusions in which they simply sense the presence of the dead person. Although some people fear these things indicate insanity, most people experience them as comforting. In fact, these hallucinations and delusions are common, especially among long-married widows and widowers. Several researchers report approximately half of all the widowed people studied reported such experiences. One study noted these hallucinations or delusions were more likely in people who had lost their spouses after age forty. Many American Indians consider it normal to hear voices of dead relatives.

Psychologists diagnose posttraumatic stress disorder when a trauma results in certain symptoms lasting over one month and causing significant distress or impairment. The diagnosis requires repeated reexperiencing of the trauma, perhaps in intensely arousing memories, troublesome dreams, flashbacks, or actions or play related to the trauma. Other requirements involve avoidance and numbing responses, such as avoiding thoughts or triggers for memories, numbed feelings, or loss of pleasure in life or closeness to others. Finally, there must be two or more of the following: sleep difficulties, irritability or outbursts of anger, difficulty concentrating, hypervigilance, or exaggerated startle response. Symptoms of great stress often begin immediately after the trauma, but there can be a delay of months or years. Complete recovery occurs within three months in about half of cases. Various studies indicate between 3 and 66% of at-risk people, such as combat veterans, prostitutes, child sexual abuse victims with penetration, or victims of crime and between 1 and 14% of the population have experienced this disorder. Antidepressants can help with the anxiety, depression, insomnia, nightmares, and flashbacks associated with the disorder.

It should come as no surprise we become so preoccupied with thoughts about a crisis or deceased loved one and we can experience so many emotional and physical symptoms, because these things profoundly affect our lives, altering many of our familiar behaviors and circumstances. Crises are great stresses and often make us feel powerless and vulnerable. Natural disasters may force us to start all over gathering material goods. A rape or crime victim can find trusting others very difficult. The loss of a loved one truly means that a part of our life is gone, eliminating many opportunities for closeness, sharing, and emotional support, and perhaps changing family relationships. Along with family changes, come changes in familiar roles and self-image. The death of a loved one may end your marriage, your parenthood, or mean that you no longer have a parent to rely on. The death may also affect your finances and force you to work for the first time, move to a less expensive neighborhood, or pay your own way through college.

Sad feelings and repetitive thoughts are part of a healing process, which ultimately leads to recovery. Psychologists believe crisis reactions and grief help us to heal and integrate a major loss into our lives. It may be detrimental to your functioning if you don't allow and express the sadness and pain or don't completely work through or finish the feelings. Doing these things is called grief work. When people avoid or bury their feelings, they may develop prolonged depression, drug or alcohol problems, delayed grief reactions, exaggerated grief reactions later to a minor or less important loss, or anniversary grief reactions involving grief or depression at the same time of year in following years. Some societies provoke grief work by traditionally hiring people after a death to wail, cry, groan, and moan the name of the deceased person until the family members cry.

Share your sorrows with close friends and family members. Talk about the crisis or death, your feelings, your relationship with the deceased, and fond memories of the past until you have nothing left to say. Do this repeatedly whenever you feel the urge, not forcing yourself to act cheerful. Don't be afraid to cry. Allow yourself to cry until you can't cry anymore. It is an excellent way to release and finish emotional pain. The crying may come and go. Ask or allow a loved one to hold you in your grief or pain— this is a wonderful way to experience emotional support and may give you strength. Be proud of your grief, not ashamed. Your painful grief is a part of the love you feel for the deceased person. If you didn't love so deeply, you wouldn't grieve so deeply. Accept your grief and realize you are not alone, that everyone has great joys and great sorrows in life.

Take good care of yourself while you grieve or after a crisis. Eat well, get plenty of sleep, avoid the abuse of addictive substances, spend time relaxing, and get some exercise, perhaps by going for walks. Please refer to chapter 10, Stress, for more suggestions on coping during this difficult time. If possible, resume your normal routine fairly soon. This will reduce time for drowning in negative emotions and thoughts. After a crisis such as a rape, it will help you feel in control of your life again. Don't make major decisions or great changes in your lifestyle (such as selling your house or moving to a distant city) immediately afterwards because you might regret overreacting later.

Some people channel their grief or pain into writing, an excellent way to express and work through your feelings, whether you write immediately after the crisis or death or long afterward. You might write about how it affects your feelings and view of the world (days seem so empty and long, meals seem dull, etc.). If you think you may be stifling anger or guilt, write about and exaggerate the emotion to express and finish it. Many of your feelings may result in very touching poetry.

In grief, writing about your past life with the deceased also helps. Make a list of touching personal moments, other good experiences you shared, and the person's qualities. Spend hours or days thinking over the past and adding new memories as they come back to you, describing some of your fondest memories in detail. Keep this list as a memoir of the deceased person. You might also make another list of unpleasant memories, disappointments, times when you felt angry or upset with the deceased, and the person's negative traits. You may not want to keep this list for very long, but it helps in understanding your relationship more realistically and in finishing the past more completely. The negative list is especially helpful if your relationship had been tumultuous, with mixed feelings and plenty of good and bad times.

You can speed your recovery in a number of ways. Following the previous advice for fully experiencing and expressing feelings will help, and religion helps many people. If your sadness interferes with your daily life 4 months after the crisis or death, make an effort to quit brooding and start life anew. You probably don't have enough interests and activities or a full enough social life to get your mind off the crisis or loss. Work on these problem areas using chapters 8 and 15. As noted previously, changing your behavior is often the fastest way to change your feelings. Begin acting the way you want to feel. Pretend you have completely recovered. Act cheerful and do fun things to contact the fun-loving, happy part of your personality, which your pain or grief masks. Go to a party or nightclub and dance, for example. Think about getting a pet. One study reported that widows who recently lost a husband coped better if they had a pet beforehand.

If you can't overcome excessive pain or grief 4 months after the crisis or loss, please refer to chapter 27 for help. It describes the importance of negative thinking in depression and discusses how to motivate yourself to develop interests and activities. Replace the negative thoughts that prolong your pain or grief with more positive thoughts every day as described in chapter 4. Helpful alternatives might include thanks for your blessings, thanks that the person's suffering ended, and statements like: "I can't change the past. What can I do to improve my life now and have more fun?" and "She's gone forever and it's time to start living life fully again." Counter thoughts of regret over the past ("If only ....," etc.) with more helpful alternatives. For example, after a suicide, you might regularly read statements like: "There was no way I could have known," "I was concerned. I just didn't know how to get through to her," and "It's not my fault. I did what I could. He wouldn't get help." If excessive pain or grief persists despite your working on all of these areas, read chapter 37, Getting over the Past, for more helpful activities. You could also join one of the self-help groups for grieving people.

When a close friend or loved one grieves or experiences a crisis, make yourself available to do plenty of listening. Understand and allow talking repeatedly about the event, feelings, and the past. Allow privacy, however, if the person wants it. Ask before intruding to visit and don't push for talking and the sharing of feelings. Show your love by helping with daily tasks (as detailed in chapter 25, Death) and perhaps by hugging or holding the person. Continue listening, giving emotional support, and helping for at least the first few months. Reassure these people that the symptoms of grief or crisis reactions previously described are normal, and encourage crying as a healthy release. Realize that upset feelings and stressful changes may lead the person to sometimes become irritable or inappropriately angry at you.

The symptoms of grief or crisis reactions in children are very similar to those in adults (shock, denial, preoccupation with it, sadness, anger, headaches, stomachaches, etc.). Don't push them to stifle their feelings; allow them to express their grief or pain. Let them cry, share their feelings, share their memories, etc. Reassure young children that you love them and will help and take care of them. Share your own feelings with your children and help them label and accept their feelings, striving for an honest discussion without going to extremes and drowning in misery. Emphasize an acceptance of the joys and sufferings in life. Spend extra time talking to and playing with children after the crisis or death to counter the stress or loss in their lives. Encourage plenty of interests and activities, both new and old, spending more time with friends and relatives, and developing new friends. These things will help the children cope and recover from the pain or grief.

If your child develops any problems and avoids talking about it, you might open communication by setting up a similar situation in play with dolls, puppets, or action figures. Ask how the doll feels, then explore reasons for the feelings and alternative solutions. Young children may not understand death, fear they were somehow responsible for the death, or fear repeated loss or abandonment by other family members. Help young children to understand death in the ways described in chapter 25.

Recommended Additional Readings:

How to Survive the Loss of a Love. by Melba Colgrove, Harold H. Bloomfield, and Peter McWilliams. Los Angeles: Prelude Press, 1991. for the end of a relationship, whether by breaking up, divorce, separation, or death.

Beyond Grief: A Guide for Recovering from the Death of a Loved One. by Carole Staudacher. Oakland, CA: New Harbinger Publications, 1987. for loss of a spouse, parent, child, helping children with grief, accidental death, suicide, and murder.

Support Groups, Hotlines, and Resources:

Compassionate Friends 630 990 0010 support groups for parents and siblings grieving the death of a child. on-line: www.compassionatefriends.org

Rainbows 800 266 3206 peer support groups for children or adults grieving death, divorce, or other painful family transitions. on-line: www.rainbows.org

AARP's Grief and Loss Division 202 434 2260 referrals to support groups for old folks grieving loss, service of the American Association of Retired Persons. on-line: www.aarp.org/griefandloss

Parents of Murdered Children 888 818 7662 also for the violent death of someone close to you, support group referrals, help in keeping the murderer behind bars— blocking parole, second opinions on unsolved cases, complicated cases, and cases labeled suicide when the family doesn't believe it.

National Victim Center 800 394 2255 information and referrals, support groups, on-line: www.ncvc.org

National Mental Health Association 800 969 6642 referrals for treatment, brochures on grief, posttraumatic stress disorder, and other topics. on-line: www.nmha.org

If your trauma was rape or abuse, please refer to the resources at the end of chapter 36. Grieving or traumatized people can also use the resources at the end of chapter 5, Emotions.

316 Psychology Made Easy

27. Depression

Remember sadness is always temporary. This, too, shall pass.

Can't, If, When, and But never did anything.

Trials give you strength, sorrows give understanding and wisdom.

Depression involves sadness, pessimism, a preoccupation with personal problems, and perhaps feeling sorry for one's self, anguish, crying, and hopelessness. Depressed people often lose interest in many activities and social contacts because of loss of pleasure in and enthusiasm for their usual activities. They may become apathetic or socially withdrawn. Low energy, chronic tiredness, excessive sleeping, and insomnia are common. Other possible symptoms include poor appetite, heavy eating, weight loss or gain, feelings of inadequacy or worthlessness, anxiety, regrets, decreased productivity, poor concentration, or recurrent thoughts of death or suicide. Four out of five cases of severe depression clear up without treatment within six to nine months, but half of the people with severe depression experience it again later.

Depression is twice as common in women as men. Approximately one of five adult women has experienced severe depression; about one of ten adult men has. Although the reasons for this are not clear, differences between the sexes in genes, hormones, social status, and learned social roles may play a role. Some of the many physical diseases causing depression are more common in women than in men. Premenstrual mood fluctuations and *postpartum depression,* depression after childbirth, may involve hormonal tendencies toward depression in women. The social status of women seems important because women are more subject to physical and sexual abuse than men, because homemakers raising children often experience poverty after divorce due to a lack of job skills, and because women generally hold jobs that pay less than men's jobs. Learned social roles may make women more open to expressing emotions and admitting depression. A passive role in women may lead to depression through a failure to resolve life stresses, or a role of emotional dependence may lead to depression after the woman tolerates abuse. Men may be more likely than women to use alcohol and drugs or violence as outlets for depression; men are twice as likely as women to be alcoholics.

Severe depression occurs about twice as often in the families of depressives as it does in the general population. Studies of identical twins, fraternal twins, and adopted children show some inherited genetic factors influence depression, but also the family of upbringing, environment, and life stresses play important roles. For example, when one identical twin has severe depression, the other twin shares this problem in half the cases.

Some severely depressed people need medicines to control their depression, but most people can conquer depression by following the suggestions in this chapter. Even those people on prescribed medicines for depression will benefit from the suggestions in this book. If you feel severely depressed, most psychiatrists will use trial and error to find a drug that will help you. But certain blood and urine tests can detect biological depression, pinpoint which drugs are most likely to be effective, and reduce the risk of depression recurring by determining when the biological imbalance ends. For the fastest, most effective treatment of severe depression, find a psychiatrist who will use the *dexamethasone suppression test (DST),* the *thyrotropin-releasing hormone (TRH) stimulation test,* and the *MHPG urine test.* In both the DST and TRH stimulation test, the psychiatrist administers a hormone and monitors your body's response with blood tests. Using these tests finds imbalances and predicts the effectiveness of antidepressants. The MHPG urine test helps in choosing among antidepressants. The *tricyclic dose-prediction test,* involving a test dose of antidepressant and a blood test 24 hours later, predicts therapeutic dose, minimizing dose changes and side effects. When psychiatrists prescribe an antidepressant, they should order one or more blood tests to make sure your blood level of the drug is in the effective therapeutic range.

The chronic use of alcohol or other drugs often leads to mood swings, personal problems, and depression. One study of severely depressed opiate addicts found that 95% of them became depressed only after the use of opiates. Moderate use of amphetamines or cocaine may result in depression. Using alcohol or other drugs to improve your mood is especially risky because addictive substances often intensify pre-existing mood or personality problems. Even prescribed medications (many tranquilizers or sleeping pills, many high blood pressure medicines, hormones such as oral contraceptives, some anti-inflammatory or anti-infection drugs, some ulcer medicines, etc.) may lead to severe depression. Conquering drug dependence or changing your prescribed medications may eliminate depression.

A personal loss often triggers depression: death of a loved one, becoming disabled in an accident, divorce, separation, end of a love relationship, physical or mental problems from old age, loss of a home or job, or a great loss of prestige or money. The more traumatic of these may result in grief or crisis reactions with shock, anger, preoccupation with the loss, etc. If you have experienced a traumatic loss, please refer to the previous chapter for a description of the time it takes to recover, the possible symptoms, the importance of allowing and expressing feelings in the first few months, and helpful suggestions for coping.

Many stressful events or major changes may also help bring on depression. People often become depressed about marital, romantic, or family problems. Research suggests marital problems often precede depression. For example, one study found an unhappy marriage increased the risk of clinical depression 25 times over untroubled marriages. Another study found marital problems in newlyweds married for 6 months predicted symptoms of depression at 18 months. Going away to college or moving far away from family and friends after getting married may lead to depression. Depression may arise from a loss of self-esteem due to experimentation with such things as promiscuity, homosexuality, or crime. No matter how much you wanted to have a child, the resulting loss of freedom may cause depression. When children grow up and leave home, you may become depressed. Retirement can lead to depression because of loss of work activities to fill the day and loss of friendships with coworkers.

Depression may occur without any loss or great stress to trigger it, however. Personal problems often lead to depression. Many depressed people lack the well-rounded interests and activities so important to happiness, social life, and mental health. Chapter 8 details the importance of interests and activities and points out a narrow range of interests and activities tends to become boring at times and does little to combat depression. Simply developing more interests and activities may conquer depression.

Many depressed people lack the close relationships with others so important in happiness and mental health. Perhaps your marriage lacks a confiding relationship of sharing feelings and receiving acceptance, understanding, and emotional support. Good social skills and a good network of friendships ranging from casual to intimate ones help prevent depression and speed recovery. Depressed people often have problems interfering with their social lives. Research shows they are more likely than other people to interact with spouses and children in ways characterized by hostility and anger. Poor social skills may include negative communication habits, problems in meeting people, making friends, maintaining friendships, flirting, or dating. Problems in assertiveness or in controlling anger may also alienate other people and contribute to negative feelings about themselves. Some depressed people long for friendship and love but alienate other people with negativity or with clinging neediness because of lack of enough socializing or interests and activities. Many depressed people make the mistake of hunting for romance to satisfy their unhappiness, poor self-esteem, or other problems. (The section on dating in chapter 15, Social Life, describes why this approach often fails.)

Negative thinking habits play a very important role in depression. Research shows depressed people are more negative about their experiences, themselves, their futures, and their world than people who don't feel depressed. Depressed people tend to minimize their accomplishments, talents, and qualities. They tend to see themselves as inferior and incompetent, despite being comparable to other people in qualities and skills. Their thinking habits focus on or exaggerate problems and faults and minimize or fail to see the good things in their lives. They tend to recall negative things more often than positive things, and they tend to minimize, overlook, or forget feelings of pleasure in their lives. They may feel preoccupied with loss or personal problems, perhaps wallowing in thoughts about self-pity, inability to cope, or escaping their problems. Depressed people are pessimistic and tend to attribute their successes to other people or outside circumstances but to blame themselves when they fail. Their pessimism makes their efforts seem futile, so they give up easily and bring on failure in self-fulfilling prophecies. Their pessimistic thinking also leads them to reject many enjoyable activities.

Many psychologists believe depression involves anger turned toward the self. Certainly depressed people have many complaints and negative feelings about things and about themselves. Buried anger often seems related to depression. Unassertive people who often bury feelings of anger and suffer mistreatment in silence can easily become depressed. One research study on facial expressions also supports the notion depression involves anger. In this study, researchers asked people to try to create in their minds the thoughts and feelings of a typical day in their lives and used electrodes to measure resulting changes in facial muscles. People without psychiatric problems showed facial muscle patterns similar to the happiness profile of muscle patterns when they thought of their typical day, but the depressed patients in the study showed facial muscle patterns resembling a mixture of sadness and anger profiles.

Many psychologists believe depression involves a learned helplessness in which people lose motivation and deteriorate in mood because of thinking there is no hope for things to get better. Certain animal experiments provide evidence for this theory and help us understand the phenomenon. When researchers placed dogs in cages and shocked them occasionally, the dogs soon learned that nothing they could do would prevent the shocks. They gave up trying to escape and became submissive to their fates. When the researchers changed the experiment and tried to teach the same dogs to cross to the other side of the cage to avoid further shocks, the dogs wouldn't respond. Even when the researchers left the door open and dragged the dogs out, the dogs didn't learn to avoid the shocks on their own until the researchers dragged them out repeatedly. Researchers have performed similar learned helplessness experiments with cats, fish, birds, rodents, primates, and humans, with similar results. For example, newborn rats can swim for up to sixty hours before drowning. Yet when researchers trained newborn rats in learned helplessness by repeatedly holding them until they quit squirming and gave up trying to escape, and then put these newborn rats into water, many of them never tried to swim and all of them drowned within half an hour.

Depressed people, like the animals in these experiments, lack motivation because of feeling helpless about improving their fates. They pessimistically expect dissatisfaction and failure. Feeling unable to change the unhappy fate they expect, depressed people often avoid trying new activities, passively resign themselves to problem situations, and fail because of giving up easily. Sometimes their lack of motivation involves not knowing what to do to improve things or fear of making the needed changes.

Unfortunately, it seems the problems of depressed people can sometimes worsen in a cycle of deterioration. Because of their negativity, depressed people often passively allow personal problems to accumulate, their range of interests and activities to narrow, and their social lives to diminish. These changes reduce satisfactions and pleasures in their lives and tend to deepen the depression. In this way, many psychologists believe depression can lead to a cycle of further problems, less pleasure and satisfaction in life, worse depression, even more problems, etc.

How can you overcome depression? You must work on your personal problems, making sure you avoid becoming overwhelmed. Work on only one or two simple things at a time, breaking large or complex problems into goals you can easily accomplish and using the other advice in chapter 11, Easy Changes, to help ensure success. Use rewards, friends, family, and support groups as in chapters 12 and 13, too. You will find good support groups listed at the end of this chapter. Reexamine your expectations or priorities in life and, if necessary, adjust them to suit reality better. Depressed people often think they can't be happy without certain things, such as a lover, a particular lover, material possessions, a much higher income, etc. You can eliminate such problems by changing your negative thinking and learning to accept the situation. Certain situations or troublesome people simply won't change. When you can do something about a problem, however, you should. For example, you may need to leave an alcoholic spouse or to go to school to prepare for a better job.

Take a long, hard, honest look at yourself for personal problems, paying particular attention to repeating problems in your life. Do you abuse alcohol or other drugs? Do you need more interests and activities to avoid boredom and keep your mind off negative thoughts? Do you feel lonely? Do you alienate other people with any of the communication problems listed in chapter 6? Depressed people who avoid confrontations and bury their anger at mistreatment from others should work on assertiveness. If you let frustrations mount and sometimes explode in anger, work on expressing your anger in constructive ways using good communication skills. If painful issues from the past still trouble you, use chapter 37 to work on resolving the feelings of the past, perhaps including buried anger. Certain people in your life may contribute to your depression by things they do. Are certain people inconsiderate, unkind, overly critical, or overly hostile toward you? You may need to become more assertive with these people, to reduce your contact with them, or even to eliminate them from your life.

Many depressed people tend to give up and blame their problems on fate, bad luck, other people, circumstances, or themselves. Don't give up and allow your problems to continue. Instead, take responsibility for them and work on them using this book. What negative or stressful situations exist in your life? What can you do about them? Instead of burying anger over problems, learn to solve problems. Brainstorm solutions and ask other people for ideas. Some depressed people reject all the possible solutions, finding reasons to eliminate each one as unacceptable, unpalatable, or unworkable. Don't let your negative thought habits interfere with problem solving. Keep an open mind to all possible solutions.

If you don't know why you feel depressed, look for clues by comparing and contrasting your life now with a happier time in your life. The best way to understand your depression is to study it carefully as in chapter 9, Problem Solving. Use the scale of zero to 100 to rate your depression many times throughout the day, and observe and record all the thoughts, circumstances, and events associated with it. Ideally, you should make your observations and rate your depression hourly. If you think over your day and rate your depression at the end of it, you will tend to rate your moods more negatively because of your negative thought habits. Even if you feel you know your stresses and problems, you can learn from studying your depression in these ways. By frequently rating depression, people generally discover their moods are not always low. Depressed people usually feel better when they keep busy (at work, cooking, visiting, etc.) and worse when idle (weekends, evenings, etc.).

As noted previously, the fastest way to change an emotion is often simply to act the way you want to feel. Act happy, smile regularly, act friendly toward other people, and participate in plenty of interests and activities, including fun things such as dancing. Don't wait to be in the mood to do these things—you may never feel like it. Depressed people who keep practicing these behaviors find themselves feeling more cheerful. With practice, these behaviors gradually become more comfortable and natural. Other people generally respond in positive ways to these changes, so you receive more pleasure and satisfaction in your life from them. Work on improving nonverbal behaviors that convey depression. Don't use a slow, quiet, bored, monotonous tone of voice. Show some pitch variation and enthusiasm in it. Use erect posture rather than drooping posture with downcast head and eyes. Use good rates of eye contact (chapter 7, Nonverbal Communication) with other people and don't frown.

People need a healthy balance between pleasure and work. A few depressed and overwhelmed people need to quit pushing themselves so hard, relax more, and eliminate some work activities, but most depressed people need more interests and activities. Idle time often leads to negative thinking and depression. Please refer to chapter 8 for a full discussion of the importance of interests and activities. Choose more of them from the list in chapter 8, including those you once enjoyed and could resume, and ask yourself which ones you might do if you didn't feel depressed. As you develop interests, share them with other people.

Aaron T. Beck, the psychologist who pioneered in working with negative thought habits of depressed people, recommends depressed people schedule plenty of activities on a weekly chart. Make a chart every week of your planned activities for next week. Put every waking hour of each day on the left side of your chart, the days of the week across the top, and fill in the chart with work and leisure activities. If your depression only troubles you during certain times, however, you may need to fill only those times with activities. Use your old charts to help plan next week. Schedule more of the activities you found the most satisfying during previous weeks.

Many doctors and psychologists recommend regular exercise for depression and note it improves the mood. Exercise invigorates you, giving you more energy. Deep relaxation also helps combat depression and especially helps anxious depressed people. Relaxation helps people find peace within themselves. Please refer to chapter 10, Stress, for a complete description of these issues, advice on exercising safely, advice that helps maintain interest in exercise, and a discussion of the kinds of meditation and other relaxation techniques.

If you find it difficult to motivate yourself to develop more interests and activities, stop prejudging and avoiding activities because you believe you wouldn't enjoy them or wouldn't be good at them. If you force yourself to start, you will often find that you do get some pleasure from and gain some skill in the activity after all. Depressed people tend to overlook and discount feelings of pleasure and accomplishment. Learn to recognize these feelings. Stop several times a day to jot down the little things you have done or enjoyed (made a nice breakfast, arrived at work on time and did a good job, read a news magazine, called a friend, etc.), even if the feelings of accomplishment or pleasure were minimal. Develop these slight feelings and take pride in your activities. It is especially important to look for and emphasize such feelings when you try a new interest or activity. Repeat those that give you slight feelings of accomplishment or pleasure. You can develop them into very rewarding activities.

Motivate yourself with rewards for engaging in new activities and getting things done. You might decide you must buy your groceries and finish all your laundry before you take a nap. If you smoke cigarettes, you might avoid smoking until you try a new activity from the list in chapter 8 or accomplish something. Ask friends and family members to help motivate you in the ways described in chapter 12. Chapter 11, Easy Changes, describes useful techniques for motivating yourself.

Work on replacing negative thoughts with positive thought alternatives every day as described in chapter 4. That chapter includes many examples of negative thoughts in depression. Humor helps a great deal in facing life's problems without drowning in negativity. If you find it difficult to motivate yourself, work on changing the thoughts that block your improvement. You probably have negative thoughts about lacking energy, not being in the mood, hating exercise, etc. Replace these with more helpful thoughts such as: "I'll feel more like it once I start," or "Let's just give it a try." When you try a new interest or activity and dislike it, replace your negative thoughts with an emphasis on slight feelings of pleasure and accomplishment and with reminders that you can learn to enjoy it.

If you tend to blame circumstances or other people for your depression, combat these thoughts of helplessness by reading or by repeating, "I made myself depressed over that. I didn't have to respond that way." Use assertiveness skills, good problem-solving skills, or more positive thinking the next time a similar situation arises. If you often assume other people think badly of you, read or repeat "I can't read other people's minds." To combat negative thoughts and feelings about yourself, follow the suggestions for low self-esteem in chapter 31.

Certain kinds of written records help combat depression. Compile a journal or list of joyous experiences you remember. Describe your most special moments, including beautiful nature scenes, especially close moments with loved ones, fun times, a series of events that you particularly enjoyed, or spiritual experiences. Make another list of your positive attributes. Include your talents, qualities, virtues, accomplishments, etc. (Anyone who wants to help a depressed person can make such a list and give it to the person.) Make a list of blessings you can be thankful for, too. Compile a collection of inspiring thoughts, quotes, poems, prayers, or affirmations. *Affirmations* are inspiring statements you write and then repeat throughout the day for self-improvement or emotional well-being. For example: "I will strive to be an example of peace and love for my fellow human beings," or "Let calmness and serenity fill my heart." Keep adding new items to these journals or lists as you think of them, rereading them regularly to help keep your mind focused on good, rather than negative, things.

When you complain, cry, talk of sad feelings, or discuss problems, your friends and loved ones probably respond with sympathy and tender loving care. Unfortunately, these loving responses reward and help maintain the depressive behaviors. Some friends or family even take over chores for a depressed person who stays in bed or asks for help. Again, this rewards the passive or dependent behavior. Perhaps you reward yourself when you drown in negative thoughts or self-pity. Many depressed people eat, spend money excessively, abuse addictive substances, or have sex without love to feel better. Eliminate these and any other subtle rewards for depressive behavior.

Stop seeking consolation with complaints, sighs, sad looks, and crying. Work to make your social interactions more positive by showing warmth toward other people, taking an interest in them, developing and sharing interests and activities, etc. Ask your friends and loved ones to ignore your depressed behaviors and to cut telephone calls and visits short when you dwell on complaints or drown in self-pity, spending more time with you and showing more warmth and interest when you act in more normal ways. Asking them to do this is very important because close friends and loved ones generally take appropriate behaviors for granted and try to cheer you up with extra warmth and attention when you feel depressed. Tell them to avoid taking pity on you and feeling guilty for not catering to your depression, and ask them not to take over chores and duties you can do for yourself.

Marital relationships are often particularly important in depression. An appreciative, complimentary, supportive marital relationship can protect you from depression or relapse despite challenging life stresses, and as noted previously, marital problems often lead to depression. Work on increasing the positive behaviors described in chapter 21, Marriage. Develop a confiding relationship of sharing feelings, not just facts, and receiving acceptance, understanding, and emotional support from each other. Ask your spouse to compliment you more and to say many of the things normally taken for granted, to show appreciation for the routine things you do every day.

Conquering your depression may take months or years, depending on its severity, how long you have had negative thinking habits, your personal problems, and how much effort you put into making the necessary changes. Don't overwhelm yourself; work on making just one or two simple changes at a time. By following the advice in this book, you learn skills that can help prevent depression in the future.

Recommended Additional Readings:

The Good News about Depression: Cures and Treatments in the New Age of Psychiatry. Rev. ed. by Mark S. Gold and Lois B. Morris. New York: Bantam Books, 1995.

The Feeling Good Handbook. by David D. Burns. NY: Penguin Books, 1989. for feelings, thinking habits, communication skills, anxiety, fear, and phobia.

Feeling Good: The New Mood Therapy. by David D. Burns. NY: Avon Books, 1980. for feelings, thinking habits, anger, guilt, depression, and love addiction.

Getting Your Life Back: The Complete Guide to Recovery from Depression. by Jesse H. Wright and Monica Ramirez Basco. NY: Free Press, 2001. self-help handbook for depression, helps assess severity of depression, information on cognitive, behavioral, biological, social, and spiritual aspects of depression.

How to Survive the Loss of a Love. by Melba Colgrove, Harold H. Bloomfield, and Peter McWilliams. Los Angeles: Prelude Press, 1991. for the end of a relationship, whether by breaking up, divorce, separation, or death.

Support Groups, Hotlines, and Resources:

National Depressive and Manic Depressive Association 800 826 3632 information, referrals to support groups, newsletter. on-line: www.ndmda.org

National Institute of Mental Health Information Line 800 647 2642 information, free literature on depression, including in old folks, women, students, and in the workplace. on-line: www.nimh.nih.gov/publicat/depressionmenu.cfm

Emotions Anonymous 651 647 9712 support groups for any personal problem, pen pals. on-line: www.emotionsanonymous.org

Recovery Inc. 312 337 5661 support groups for any personal problem, on-line: www. recovery-inc.com

Those who are upset over the end of a love relationship can attend Divorce Care 919 562 2112 church sponsored, nondenominationl support groups, on-line: www.divorcecare.com

National Mental Health Association 800 969 6642 referrals for treatment, brochures on depression, grief, and other mental health topics. on-line: www.nmha.org

Co-Dependents Anonymous 602 277 7991 support groups for love or sex addictions or dealing with a loved one's problems. on-line: www.codependents.org

Overcomers Outreach 800 310 3001 Christ-centered support groups for any personal problem. on-line: www.overcomersoutreach.org

28. Anger

Anger dies quickly with a good man.
(English proverb)

Kill your anger while it is small.
(Slovakian proverb)

Anyone can improve a bad temper by working at it and refusing to give up. Anger occurs in response to frustrations or provocation from other people in conflicts. Conflicts occur because people have different views, needs, desires, and lifestyles. The target of anger is usually a person rather than an inanimate object or an institution. More often than not, the target person is either a loved one or someone you know well and like. Close contact with friends and loved ones brings more opportunities for conflict, makes it more likely that the emotional burden of conflicts will accumulate, and gives us more reason to want to change their behavior.

Use your anger constructively to motivate yourself to solve problems. Used in this way, anger can increase understanding, harmony, and closeness in a relationship. Never feel shame or guilt over simply having anger. Shame and guilt are reasonable when you express your anger in explosive outbursts, threats, insults, other communication problems, acts of revenge, grudges, etc. Use shame or guilt over such acts to motivate yourself to improve your behavior.

Although angry outbursts may sometimes succeed in getting what you want, regular outbursts of anger carry a high price in interpersonal relationships, destroying much of the closeness and trust and interfering with open, honest communication. Anger may mount in those who yield to your angry outbursts, as you neglect their needs and desires. Problems in the relationship often remain unresolved and become chronic. Many people who deal with regular angry outbursts from a loved one feel very justified in lying or deception by omission. Thus, the quality of the relationship suffers. We also degrade ourselves when we inflame our anger. Both self-esteem and respect from other people suffer when we fail to control our anger.

Besides causing a great deal of stress in our lives, anger is a common part of a wide range of adult and childhood psychiatric disorders and it may have health consequences. High degrees of anger and hostility are often associated with interpersonal problems, lack of social support, low self-esteem, and poor coping skills. Children with excessive anger are at higher risk for limited social skills, peer rejection, academic problems, and later truancy, drug abuse, teen pregnancy, school dropout, theft, serious violence, crime, becoming a physically or sexually abusive parent, and mental problems. Studies suggest highly hostile people tend to engage in excessive eating, smoking, drinking, and substance abuse, all of which can lead to various health problems. A variety of studies suggest hostile attitudes and frequent anger increase one's risk for high blood pressure, atherosclerosis, strokes, and heart disease. One study finds people who are highly prone to anger are nearly three times more likely to have a heart attack, even after researchers take into account other major risk factors.

The first step in improving a bad temper is to admit you have the problem, but you may not like to admit, even to yourself, a problem with anger, ignoring it until it becomes painfully obvious in a bout of explosive anger that disrupts your interpersonal relationships. You also may find it difficult to apologize for angry episodes. Use the advice in chapter 11, Easy Changes, to fight denial, stay aware of the problem, and keep working on it. Learning to apologize for yelling or angry outburst also helps in facing the fact you lost control.

Common folklore has long held that you can release anger and thereby reduce your anger toward someone by attacking inanimate objects (hitting punching bags, pounding pillows, etc.). Research, however, shows this is a false and dangerous notion. Never hit or break things to vent your anger; this only keeps you angry. Many people also recommend writing very heated, angry letters to release anger and then tearing these letters up and throwing them away, symbolically ending the anger, but our study of the importance of thinking in our emotions indicates these letters unnecessarily prolong our anger.

Becoming comfortable with expressing your feelings is an important step in learning to use your anger constructively. People who explode in anger range from chronically violent people with little impulse control to very unassertive people who only rarely explode, but all of these people bury their anger in many situations. By failing to assert yourself about minor irritations, you allow your frustrations to mount until you explode in anger. Anger often covers up feelings of hurt, insecurity, inadequacy, or fear, so learn to recognize all your feelings and express your anger appropriately when other people frustrate you. Practice expressing your feelings at least twice a day with "I feel ..." statements using the list of emotions in chapter 5. If you are unassertive, please refer to chapter 16 for useful advice.

Learn to recognize your anger early, so you can do something about it quickly, before it escalates and gets out of control. Use the techniques in this chapter when you first recognize your anger, not after it escalates. Unassertive people who chronically bury their anger may need much practice to learn to recognize it. It is especially important that people who have ever been violent learn to recognize their anger early. These people should study themselves and learn their earliest bodily indications of anger, so they can learn to control their anger in time to prevent violence.

Mounting anger often causes your speech to become louder, faster, more tense, or more demanding. You might stand up, pace, use exaggerated gestures, pound your fist, move too close, or stamp your feet. Your eyes may flash, narrow, stare, or glare. A very common clue is tension in the body. You may use stiff posture, clench or grind your teeth, clench your hands, or bite your fingernails or lips. You may notice tense muscles or a tight feeling in your face, mouth, neck, arms, legs, or stomach. A frown may accompany tension in the face or mouth. Faster heartbeats and faster breathing are common. Other possible clues to underlying anger include: depression, withdrawal, becoming quiet, tears in the eyes, headache, poor concentration, dizziness, a pounding heart, extra energy and overstimulation, or churning in the stomach. Anger can even cause backache, anxiety, trembling, nausea, cold hands, chilliness, feeling flushed or warm, sweating, weakness, difficulty eating or sleeping, or eating or sleeping more than usual. Your breathing may become faster and lighter or deeper and slower. You may even gasp for air or experience a choking sensation. (Many of these symptoms relate to the bodily arousal of adrenaline.) When angry, many people become sarcastic, act viciously, fail to follow through on commitments, or blame other people. Instead of recognizing their anger, unassertive people may respond to frustrations with one of the above reactions, by laughing or using humor, or by being extra nice and trying to please.

Once you recognize your anger, make a polite request. If a polite request works, you don't even need to express your anger. If it doesn't work, use good communication skills to direct your anger into pressing for negotiation and problem solving. The anger will pass if you accept it and express it respectfully. Angry people tend to show many of the communication problems listed in chapter 6 (yelling, blaming the other person, bringing up old resentments, avoiding issues, insulting, etc.). Use chapters 6 and 9 to work on your communication and problem-solving skills. When you complain, make sure you focus on specific behaviors (actions, words, tone of voice, and facial expression), rather than on vague complaints, blaming, or attacking the other person's character. Use good listening skills to understand and clarify the other person's point of view.

Anyone who has occasional arguments with another person will benefit from establishing regular complaint and problem-solving sessions. Husbands and wives, in particular, often find them useful. One problem-solving session per week is often enough, but some people need them more often and others less often. Select a time when neither person feels tired and you have plenty of time to problem solve without distractions. Both people must accept criticism and try to learn from it. Use the advice in chapter 9 about problem-solving sessions. Write down any agreement you make in order to avoid arguments about the terms of the agreement later. If you fail to find solutions to several problems, you can often make contracts swapping one concession for another (I will do ..., if you do ...).

Discuss your problem-solving skills after each session. Were we logical and calm? Did we listen well? Did we define problems and solutions in specific terms about behaviors? Did we exhaust each topic or find a solution before moving to another? Which communication problems in chapter 6 were we guilty of? Were we both willing to compromise? Did we brainstorm and evaluate a number of possible solutions? What should we do differently next time? Use these questions to learn from your mistakes.

There is an excellent, simple way to calm down a heated discussion or argument, so both parties listen carefully and problem solving can occur. It is also the best way for people who often argue to hold a problem-solving session. Use this technique whenever anger rises in either party (voice becoming louder, etc.). Take turns listening quietly while the other person explains feelings and viewpoints about the problem issue right down to the last detail. During the other person's turn to speak, the listener may speak only to ask questions that help clarify the speaker's perspective.

There are two more excellent, simple strategies for controlling anger. Anytime you can't maintain a calm, respectful tone of voice and carefully listen to the other person, you should use them. First, take a few deep breaths, relax the tension in your body, and count slowly until you calm down, whether this takes 5 seconds, 10 seconds, 25, or more. Imagine your parents and grandparents, a preacher, a respected and well-loved teacher or boss, your counselor, or several policemen are watching how you respond. If you can't use a calm tone of voice to respond tactfully and respectfully, start counting again and pretend the authority figures are watching.

If this doesn't help, leave the situation and do something else until you calm down (time out). If your anger is intense or explosive, don't bother with counting—leave immediately. People with a history of violence should leave the home and should use this technique several times a week for practice, even if they feel only mildly irritated and don't really need to leave. Avoid angry thinking during your time out by getting things done or doing what you enjoy. Work on a hobby, read a good book, work on projects around the house, etc. Practicing meditation or deep relaxation (chapter 10, Stress) is an excellent way to calm yourself. Physical activities, such as going for a walk, jogging, exercising, or bicycling, help by releasing tension. Don't punish a loved one by leaving for more than an hour or two, however. Don't use alcohol or other drugs. Be very careful to avoid driving a car dangerously in anger. If you return and can't use a calm tone of voice to respond tactfully and respectfully, leave again and do something else. As you gradually improve in dealing with your anger, you should be able to reduce the time you need away from the situation to calm down.

Be sure to avoid angry thinking when you count or leave to calm down. Most angry people tend to repeatedly think about the upsetting episode and to blame other people or circumstances for their anger, but nobody can make you angry except you yourself. If you tend to blame other people or circumstances for your anger, read or repeat every day, "Nobody *makes* me angry. I make myself angry over certain situations and only I can change this." Learn to counteract angry thoughts with humor and with more helpful thought alternatives every day in the ways described in chapter 4. Some possible alternatives include: "Stay calm. Getting upset will only interfere with solving this problem," "Don't take it personally. People say things they don't really mean when they are upset," "I'm getting upset, so it's time to get away for a while," and "I want to get along with people better, so I'm going to learn to be patient and keep my voice calm when I'm upset." More examples of positive thought alternatives for anger appear in chapter 4.

Negative thought habits contribute to problems with anger in other ways, too. Many people never put much energy into working on their bad tempers because they think they can't control their anger, and many people avoid responsibility for their violence or angry behavior by blaming it on alcohol or other drugs. Other people believe they sometimes must defend their reputation by fighting, and some men feel a need to prove they are tough by acting callously and explosively. All of these sadly mistaken beliefs maintain problems with anger and wreak havoc in people's lives. Counter such destructive thoughts with more sensible, helpful alternatives in the ways described in chapter 4. Some examples include: "I can change my bad temper if I keep working on it and never give up," "Drinking alcohol is no excuse. I was really vicious last night," "People respect a man for walking away from a fight," and "Being tough is one thing, but I need to learn to be gentle with my wife."

When you can't change or avoid a troublesome person or situation, you must learn to accept it. Vent frustrations by sharing your feelings with trusted friends who can give you emotional support. Use humor to release tension and increase acceptance. Don't dwell on angry thoughts; they only waste your time and keep you upset. To get your mind off the problem, spend time with friends or pursue interests and activities. In these ways, you can be happy despite a major problem in your life.

When someone is angry at you, make a special effort to remain calm. Take a few deep breaths, relax bodily tension, speak slowly, and keep your voice soft. Staying calm encourages the other person to calm down and helps prevent escalation of the conflict. Say "I'm sorry you're upset." Don't act impatient, treat these people as stupid or immature, nor make a fool of them in front of other people. If the angry person yells at you or speaks loudly, point out what needs to happen in a positive, rather than negative, way. For example, don't say "Stop yelling!" Say something like, "Let's sit down and talk this over calmly." Reassure angry people that you can both work together to find a solution when they calm down. If you have overcome worse problems in the past, say so. Don't attempt problem solving until you feel sure the other person is completely calm. When you do discuss things, watch for vocal and bodily clues of anger. If anger is rising in either party, insist on a break from the negotiations, so both parties can think things over and relax.

Occasionally allow angry people to save face with excuses. Use the good listening and communication skills to clarify feelings and issues and show understanding. Make sure you work on only one problem at a time. Start with the simplest issues first in order to have some success in negotiating. Point out the need for both people to compromise to find a good solution. To reduce hostilities, agree with them when you can, try to find something good about them to praise, and try to find positive feelings about them you can express. Backing down on one of your minor points can help, but doing so regularly without concessions from the other person shows unassertiveness and allows the person to take advantage of you.

If you have occasional arguments with a spouse, parent, child, or close friend, try stopping to feel the love underneath your anger. Think about the good times you have shared, things the person has done for you in the past, and any qualities you appreciate.   Perhaps taking the person's hand or hugging the person will help you contact the love underneath.

Anytime you feel angry, the following questions can help you analyze the situation and get a better perspective on it. You can read and think about these questions or you can write your answers to them. Writing helps you organize your ambivalent feelings and think carefully and rationally about the questions. Aggressive people can particularly benefit from using this list because they tend to pay little attention to social cues and to make decisions quickly, while wrongly perceiving hostile intent in other people.

Questions for Analyzing Angry Situations and Getting a Better Perspective on Them

Why am I angry?

What else contributed to this state of mind?

What other feelings do I have? Am I feeling rejected? Hurt? Shocked?
   Threatened? Am I afraid of change or of losing something? Am I feeling
   vulnerable? Bewildered? Guilty? Insulted? Harassed? Manipulated? (Use the
   list of emotions in chapter 5.)

What were my expectations in this situation?

Did I check to see if my impressions are correct? What is the proof? How else
   could I interpret this? And how else?

Am I overreacting or blowing things out of proportion?

Who am I angry at?

Am I venting my anger at someone other than the source of my frustration?

Am I overlooking the good aspects of my relationship with this person?

Is the event really less important than I first thought?

Am I blaming someone for the anger I responded with?

Did the person intentionally hurt me?

Could a difference in lifestyles, values, opinions, or upbringing play a part in this
   conflict?

How do the other people involved in this situation probably feel? In what other
   ways could they possibly feel?

Am I being selfish and forgetting the needs and desires of other people?

How can I best bring about the changes I need? Do I need to learn to accept a
   situation that won't change?

What would I say to a friend in this situation if I were trying to help?

What would a counselor, teacher, or minister trying to help say?

Carefully study the situations in which you become angry using the advice in chapter 9, Problem Solving (this is especially important for people with a history of violence). You may find some simple triggers for your anger (clothes left on the floor, a blaring television, etc.) that you can eliminate with a little extra effort or help. Your detailed record and frequency counts provide a basis for rewarding yourself for improvement. Ask your friends and family members to help you work on your bad temper in the ways described in chapter 12. Chapter 11, Easy Changes, discusses how to keep motivated, how you should best deal with failure (episodes of explosive anger), and the importance of regularly monitoring your continued progress after you feel you have conquered your problem with anger.

You can also use behavioral roleplays to rehearse constructive responses to situations that typically anger you. Be sure to do this if you have a bad temper or if you have ever been violent in anger. For example, a man who wants to eliminate drunken brawls should roleplay with a friend ways to reject a challenge to fight. If you find it difficult to express your feelings about common irritations, practice doing so with behavioral roleplays. The interpersonal roleplay can deepen understanding of past angry episodes in a fun way that relieves tension while it helps each person see things from the other's perspective.

Both people and animals tend to become angry, fight, or attack others more readily when they are in pain or feel frustrated. This suggests that all personal problems probably aggravate a bad temper. It is wise, then, for anyone with a bad temper to look for and work on improving all personal problems. Don't overwhelm yourself, however. Work on making only one or two small changes at a time. It may also help to practice meditation or deep relaxation every day. Such daily practice can increase feelings of peace and reduce the stress in your life that aggravates your problem with anger.

For further reading on the problem of violence in America, its history, the reasons for it, its effects, the characteristics of violent people, and treatment, please refer to chapters 36, Abuse, and 42, Preventing Violence and Crime. Anyone who has been violent or dealt with violence from a loved one should certainly read chapter 36 for helpful advice.

Recommended Additional Readings:

Anger Kills: Seventeen Strategies for Controlling the Hostility That Can Harm Your Health. by Redford Williams and Virginia Williams. NY: HarperCollins, 1993.

Couple Skills: Making Your Relationship Work. by Matthew McKay, Patrick
   Fanning, and Kim Paleg. Oakland, CA: New Harbinger Publications, 1994.
   marital communication skills, finding and fighting automatic thoughts about your
   mate, coping with anger, separating your partner from your childhood parent
   issues.

Feeling Good: The New Mood Therapy. by David D. Burns. NY: Avon Books,
   1980. for feelings, thinking habits, anger, guilt, depression, and love addiction.

Support Groups and Hotlines:

Emotions Anonymous 651 647 9712 support groups for any personal problem, pen
   pals. on-line: www.emotionsanonymous.org

Recovery Inc. 312 337 5661 support groups for any personal problem, on-line:
   www.recovery-inc.com

Overcomers Outreach 800 310 3001 Christ-centered support groups for any
   personal problem. on-line: www.overcomersoutreach.org

Co-Dependents Anonymous 602 277 7991 support groups for love or sex addictions
   or dealing with a loved one's problems. on-line: www.codependents.org

29. Anxiety, Worry, Fear, and Phobia

Don't worry over little things, and remember,
when you look at the big picture, everything is really little.

In silence is peace and joy.
Once you find it, use it as an anchor in the rough seas of life.

Anxiety is common and normal in unfamiliar situations such as moving to a new area, change in lifestyle, becoming lost, a large party with few familiar people, etc. Interpersonal conflict often leads to anxiety. Many people become anxious when they receive criticism or hostility from others or must refuse or complain. We tend to become anxious on very important occasions, such as weddings or decisive business meetings, and when other people evaluate our performance in interviews, tests, public speeches or performances, etc. Many people react with anxiety when rejection is a possibility, such as in flirting, dating, or attempts at making a friend. Common fears include the dark, snakes, spiders, rats, dogs, bees, wasps, blood, injury, pain, death, and heights. Normal fears do not interfere with a person's adjustment and functioning and may help us avoid danger. Fears are particularly common in childhood, and social anxieties are common in adolescence.

Some people experience excessive worrying, chronic or severe anxiety, panic attacks, or phobias. Worriers make themselves anxious with habits of negative thinking. *Generalized anxiety* is chronic and has no particular focus. *Panic attacks* are sudden, severe attacks of anxiety, fear, or terror, with cardiovascular and other physiological symptoms, often compounded by thoughts of losing control, going crazy, or dying. Originally thought to be rare, community studies show 5 to 9% of the population has experienced panic attacks. This common problem can cause difficulties in social, family, and occupational functioning as severe as those caused by clinical depression. Patients with panic disorder frequently have clinical depression and show a high rate of alcohol or drug abuse.

A *phobia* is excessive or irrational fear of an object, activity, or situation that either causes much distress or interferes with the person's functioning. The most common phobias involve dogs, snakes, mice, spiders, other insects, heights, and closed spaces. Social phobias involve the excessive fear and avoidance of certain situations in which other people may evaluate you, such as eating in public, using a public lavatory, or speaking in public. Twice as many women as men have phobias and panic disorder, and most problems with phobia and panic develop during the person's adolescence, twenties, or thirties.

Agoraphobia is a fear of panic symptoms that leads to avoiding many situations in which escape or getting help is difficult or embarrassing. Agoraphobic people may avoid being alone outside the home, standing in lines, or being in crowds, elevators, bridges, tunnels, automobiles, or public transportation. They may avoid most outside activities and insist that family members go with them when they do go out. In severe cases, they cannot leave the home without a companion. Psychologists now see agoraphobia as a complication of panic attacks, in which the social and occupational disabilities come from living in dread of future panic attacks.

Anxiety, panic, or phobia may result in trembling, restlessness, twitches, bodily tension, an inability to relax, sweating, high heart rate, pounding of the heart, or skipped heartbeats. It can cause choking sensations or tightness in the throat, shortness of breath, high breathing rate, chest pains or pressure, muscle pains, upset stomach, nausea, diarrhea, constipation, or appetite disturbances. Other possibilities include numbness, tingling or prickly sensations in the hands or feet, cold or clammy hands, hot or cold flashes, flushing or pallor, light-headedness, dizziness, poor concentration, loss of balance, weakness, fatigue, or insomnia. Feelings may include sudden fears for no reason, feelings of unreality, dread of anxiety attacks, feeling on edge, irritability, panic, or terror. Thoughts may include fears of going insane, dying during an attack, or losing control.

Anxiety, fear, and phobia may develop in various ways. Some anxieties and fears may be ancestral to humans, remnants of instincts about danger to primitive human beings. Examples include fears of the dark, snakes, spiders, rats, dogs, heights, closed spaces (where you can't escape), and open spaces (where you can't hide). Anxieties about interpersonal relationships may have helped us nurture strong ties to the protective family group. We may learn other fears by their association with pain, danger, or stressful experiences. Examples include fears of doctors, dentists, bees and wasps, blood, and funerals. A traumatic experience, such as a kick from a horse or falling off a bridge, may lead to an extreme fear. Panic attacks often begin after major stresses or negative life events or just before, in anticipation of such events. Sometimes a phobia comes from a previous trauma you have forgotten or repressed.

Children often learn specific fears (spiders, snakes, etc.) from their parents. Family members of people with phobias or panic attacks are more likely than unrelated people to have them. This may indicate the learning of such feelings and behaviors, shared stresses, or genetic predisposition. Many cardiovascular, endocrine, neurological, and respiratory problems and medicine side effects may also cause anxiety or panic attacks. The medical diagnoses most commonly related to panic are endocrine problems such as thyroid disorders or hypoglycemia, adrenal gland tumors, mitral valve prolapse, and temporal lobe epilepsy. Any person with chronic or strong anxiety or with panic attacks should consult a doctor to check for medical causes.

The use of caffeine (coffee, soft drinks), amphetamines (diet pills), cocaine, or marijuana can lead to anxiety problems or panic attacks. Caffeine intoxication, chronic use, or caffeine withdrawal can cause panic attacks or chronic anxiety with no particular focus. Many panic patients notice that caffeine triggers or intensifies panic and cut back on coffee consumption. Excessive coffee intake has, at times, caused psychiatric hospitalization. Simply eliminating the drug use may solve the problem. Abruptly stopping alcohol, barbiturate, tranquilizer, sedative-hypnotic, or opiate abuse, too, may cause severe anxiety.

Anxiety often comes from personal problems or from inner conflicts and may relate to depression, marital or relationship problems, poor social skills, unassertiveness, low self-esteem, etc. When you relieve stress by resolving personal problems, even seemingly unrelated anxieties may improve or disappear. For example, a phobia may disappear when marital problems improve. Obviously, anxiety is closely linked to stress. In fact, the body's adrenaline and other hormonal responses to stress can cause all the physical symptoms of anxiety or panic noted above. Working on personal problems often helps resolve anxiety.

Abnormal breathing patterns are commonly associated with anxiety, especially with panic attacks. Hyperventilation can cause most of the physical symptoms of anxiety or panic. *Hyperventilation* is excessive breathing that disturbs the proper levels of many components of the blood. Some people hyperventilate only occasionally and others do so chronically. You may hyperventilate by breathing too fast with short, shallow breaths, breathing too deeply in a normal speed, or both. Hyperventilation often involves breathing from the chest instead of from the abdomen, frequent sighing, frequent yawning, frequent sniffing, or frequent clearing of the throat. Chronic hyperventilation may make you more vulnerable to intense symptoms, but it can be very difficult to identify, and most panic patients are not chronic hyperventilators. Acute hyperventilation is frequently present during panic attacks, but it generally follows, rather than precedes, the onset of panic. It usually plays a role when people suddenly feel unable to breathe. Breathing from the chest taxes the muscles and can result in chest pain and sensations of breathlessness. The simple fact that you can't hold your breath very long should reassure these people that, despite their immediate sensations, their bodies won't allow them to go without the oxygen they need.

No matter what leads to the first episodes of anxiety, psychologists believe panic attacks or phobias may develop in a vicious cycle of deterioration. Perhaps the first episodes of anxiety relate to major stresses, personal problems, learned fears, a disturbing episode of hyperventilation, or a startling awareness of a medical abnormality, such as a palpitation of the heart. Your anxiety may result in the release of adrenaline and other hormones or in hyperventilation and may cause symptoms that frighten you even more. The more frightened you become, the more bodily symptoms may arise. This can become a vicious cycle and lead to panic and terror. In attacks of anxiety or panic, physical escape from the feared object or situation seems to be your only alternative. After one or more attacks, people usually carefully try to avoid the fear. Because escape or avoidance brings immediate and temporary relief, people often develop a phobic lifestyle based on avoidance and escape. Regularly using avoidance and escape reinforces your belief you cannot cope with anxiety or panic. Sometimes the phobic avoidance becomes increasingly widespread and debilitating as more situations become associated with the anxiety attacks by coincidence.

Severely anxious people and some phobic people need prescribed medicines to control their anxiety or panic attacks, even when there is no disease causing the anxiety. High potency benzodiazepines (Valium, Librium, etc.) reduce panic attacks but cause drug dependence, withdrawal, and rebound panic. Newer medicines like fluoxetine (Prosac) or buspirone (Buspar) are better, working well without causing dependence or rebound panic or anxiety. After prolonged, continued success, learn to decrease your use of medicines. Many researchers believe anti-anxiety medicines may interfere with the full experience and acceptance of bodily symptoms needed to succeed in the long run. Most people can conquer their anxieties and fears without prescribed medicines by following the advice in this chapter. Even people who need prescribed medicines will benefit from these suggestions. It is best to work on problems of anxiety, panic, or fear early, before they become chronic and before you develop a lifestyle of phobic avoidance.

Begin by studying the situations in which you feel anxious as described in chapter 9, Problem Solving. Be sure to rate and take notes on panic attacks immediately afterwards. People who report at the end of the day or week claim much worse and more frequent attacks because of negative thought habits. Studying the anxious situations may indicate the importance of personal problems such as unassertiveness or poor flirting and dating skills. If so, work on the problems using the appropriate chapters in this book. Whenever possible, prepare in advance for situations that often provoke anxiety by using behavioral roleplays.

Many anxious or fearful people lack enough interests and activities. Please refer to chapter 8 for a full discussion of the importance of interests and activities in mental health. Cultivate them to prevent worries or anxious or fearful thoughts. Interests, activities, and work tasks make good substitutes whenever these negative thoughts arise, too. The best replacement activities are enjoyable but require some concentration or involve other people. If it is inconvenient or impossible to do most things, distract yourself from anxious or fearful thoughts with simple activities such as talking with someone about pleasant topics, whistling, or mentally going through one of your favorite songs or prayers. Another possibility is making a constant mental commentary or description of the colors and details of people and things you see in your environment, such as architecture, nature, clothing, etc. Or you could read a book or solve crossword puzzles that you keep with you for such occasions.

Use deep muscle relaxation (chapter 10, Stress) for at least twenty minutes, twice each day, to combat the body's hormonal responses to stress found in anxiety and fear. Relaxing deeply can increase your daily level of calmness. After you develop some skills in relaxation, you will find them very useful when you worry, feel anxious or fearful, and before situations that you know will provoke anxiety. Even without regular practice, paying particular attention to relaxing your body by breathing deeply, stretching, or allowing your muscles to fall with gravity can help during episodes of anxiety or fear.

A careful study (chapter 9) of your anxiety will also determine your most common negative thinking habits. These play an important role in causing problems with anxiety, worry, fear, and phobia. Depending on the individual and the specific problems, many of the categories of negative thinking listed in chapter 4 may relate to the anxiety. Work on replacing your worries or anxious or fearful thoughts with more helpful thought alternatives every day as described in chapter 4.

Some people don't worry much at all, but chronic worriers, probably about 15% of the general population, often worry throughout much of a typical day. Most people fall between these extremes, worrying occasionally during the day, and some people find a moderate amount of worrying to be comforting or useful. If you want to worry less, a number of approaches can help. We have already mentioned three strategies: keeping busy with interests and activities to help prevent worrying and as a substitute when worries arise, practicing relaxation to reduce your general level of stress and each time you worry, and substituting positive thought alternatives each time you worry.

A thirty-minute session of intensive worrying every day can also help. Hold the worry session at the same time and place every day, so you can train yourself to worry only in this situation. Every time a worry arises, tell yourself you will worry about it later during the worry session and then substitute another activity. Spend the thirty minutes each day worrying about everything you can possibly think of to worry about. In several research studies, people who followed this procedure for one month reduced worry time an average of 35%. Bombarding yourself with all your worries at once may emphasize how silly the worries really are.

Combat your worries and anxieties by making a complete list of them. Then go through your list and cross out all the items that are unrealistic, unlikely, or past events. Next, problem solve and brainstorm solutions on each item left whenever possible. What can you do about each? What can you do to prepare for forthcoming items? Use realistic thoughts to combat unrealistic or unlikely worries or anxieties. Learn to accept the past and things you can't change, using positive thinking and humor. Sometimes it helps to take a long-range perspective. Ask yourself if things you can't change will really matter to you in future years.

The best way to conquer a fear or phobia is to face the fear in real life. The fastest way is to put yourself in the most fearful situation you can tolerate, stay there for two to four hours until your anxiety reduces quite a bit, and repeat this procedure often, preferably several times a week. For example, you can conquer a phobia of snakes the most quickly by regularly going to a zoo, walking up as close to a gigantic snake as you can tolerate, and staying there until your anxiety reduces quite a bit (at least two hours). Eventually, you could even ask the caretaker at the zoo to allow you to touch the snake. Research shows exposing yourself to the feared object or situation for only half an hour or an hour each time may make you worse. In short exposures like this, your anxiety may remain high the whole time. Ten exposures of two to four hours each normally conquer a phobia.

You can also do this procedure by putting yourself in the feared situation more gradually. This involves more exposure sessions, but people with strong, overwhelming phobias often need this more comfortable approach. The difference is you only go close enough to the feared object to feel moderately or mildly fearful. These procedures work for phobias of bridges, elevators, dogs, snakes, mice, spiders, other insects, heights, etc. Adapt the procedure to your problem. If you fear eating in public, start with a candy bar or soft drink. If you fear being in crowds, start with places and times that are less busy.

Most phobic people begin their exposure sessions accompanied by a therapist, friend, or family member for emotional support. This is a helpful technique for facing any fear. As you improve, the other person can accompany you less closely, so you face the situation alone, yet you can still quickly get your friend's help if you need it. Eliminate the companion soon, so you learn to function alone. Support groups in which people help each other overcome anxiety attacks, fears, and phobias are a great help, but those for personal problems in general can also help (see list at the end of the chapter).

One reason support groups help so much is the influence of other members who are good role models. Role models can also help children with fears. Showing a child who fears large dogs the actions of another child who overcomes a fear of large dogs, often helps the first child to overcome the fear. If you use this technique, ask the role model to express the initial fear vividly, to say it turned out to be easier than feared, and to help encourage your child. Then encourage your child to imitate the behaviors of the role model. This strategy works the best when the role model is similar to your child in age, sex, and initial level of fear.

Success in overcoming anxiety attacks, panic attacks, fears, and phobias comes from learning to experience and accept the symptoms fully. Don't wage an internal battle to fight your feelings of anxiety or fear—this only increases your bodily arousal and symptoms. Never run away from the situation; this can also make the problem worse. Instead, you must abandon yourself to the feelings, experiencing and accepting them fully, in order for them to decrease. Be sure to stay in the situation for at least two hours. Panic attacks and phobic fears strike with severe intensity but don't stay at this level for long. You will find that the intensity of such feelings rises and falls as your thoughts change and that a significant decrease in fear generally occurs in the second hour.

People who fear internal sensations can deliberately expose themselves to such sensations by holding their breath, breathing through a straw, overbreathing, spinning (perhaps in a chair), or shaking their heads from side to side. To create heart, breath, chest symptoms, tingling sensations, numbness, dizziness, or shakiness, you can use exercises like walking, running in place, repeatedly going up and down a flight of stairs, or tensing the whole body for a minute or longer. To cause chest symptoms, exhale completely, wrap your arms in a tight squeeze around your chest, and then pull in air. Psychologists call this technique *internal exposure*. The purpose is to learn some triggers for panic attacks that seem to arise suddenly for no reason and to learn that you can deliberately produce some of your feared sensations, thus you can modify or control them by other behaviors discussed in this chapter. You might breathe rapidly and shallowly (25 to 30 breaths per minute) through your mouth for 3 minutes and see if you begin to feel any mild versions of symptoms you associate with anxiety. Look for shortness of breath, difficulty breathing, rapid heartbeat, pain or tightness in the chest, tingling sensations, numbness, dizziness, etc. When you try each of the above activities, try to identify as many internal physical cues, behaviors, or thoughts associated with panic as you can.

During anxiety attacks, panic attacks, or phobic fears, first remind yourself the symptoms you feel relate to anxious or fearful thoughts, to bodily tension and arousal from the release of adrenaline and other hormones, and to hyperventilation. Just understanding the cause and realizing the symptoms are not dangerous can help calm you, especially if your fears include feelings that you are unable to breathe, having a heart attack, or going crazy.

When you panic or feel very anxious or afraid, you are probably thinking about the most horrible things that could possibly happen, despite the fact these things are very unlikely. Your thoughts may focus on such things as falling from a tall building, insects or mice crawling all over your body or face, being stuck in an elevator forever, being unable to breathe, dying, being paralyzed in fear, going insane, or losing control and screaming frantically in public. Poor thinking habits such as these help build an overwhelming state of distress. As noted previously, you must study your anxious or fearful thoughts and practice positive alternatives every day in the ways described in chapter 4. For example, "I want to learn to accept my feelings and symptoms. They will pass and with more practice, it will become easier." Chapter 4 includes more examples of positive thought alternatives.

We have already noted the importance of interests and activities and of relaxation in combating anxiety, panic, or fear. Use them as described previously. You should also learn good breathing techniques to help avoid hyperventilation. Practice breathing about once every five to eight seconds, breathing from the abdomen instead of the chest, and perhaps holding your breath briefly between each inhalation and exhalation. To learn breathing from the abdomen, place your hands on both your chest and stomach, with the little finger of the hand on the stomach just above the navel. Then breathe so your chest stays still and your stomach does all the moving. Passively breathe through your nose and work toward a breathing cycle of eight seconds, inhaling four or five seconds and exhaling for three or four seconds. It may help to visualize pouring thick oil from one barrel to another. If you want, you can breathe in for three or four seconds, breathe out for two or three seconds, and hold your breath in between cycles for one to three seconds. Do whatever you find most comfortable, without breathing too deeply. Eliminate habits of regularly sighing, yawning, sniffing, or clearing your throat. It is especially important to practice relaxation and these breathing techniques for controlling hyperventilation during panic attacks and phobic episodes.

Use the above coping tactics as soon as your anxiety or fear begins to arise. Don't wait for a full-blown panic attack or phobic fear to overwhelm you. Keep a list of the above suggestions and a list of your helpful thought alternatives in your pocket or purse, and look at these lists as soon as you notice your anxiety or fear beginning. Rate your level of anxiety or fear at different times on a scale from 0 to 100 as described in chapter 9, Problem Solving. By occasionally rating these feelings, you can see for yourself that you can control your level of anxiety or fear with your own thoughts and actions.

You cannot expect to eliminate panic attacks or phobic fears quickly and completely. Instead, you can gradually learn to function, to carry on despite the anxiety or fear you feel. This is the first step in eventually conquering your panic attacks or phobic fears. Your progress won't always be smooth, however. Panic attacks will return unexpectedly, and phobic fears of things you thought you had conquered will recur. These setbacks simply mean you need to keep practicing your coping strategies. Never give up because of the unexpected recurrence of the problem. Think of these setbacks as opportunities to study the problem situation and practice your coping skills. Research shows those who continue to practice and use their new skills generally continue to improve. As time goes on, you will overcome your anxiety or fear with increasing ease.

A strong phobia may make it impossible to take direct action. You may become paralyzed with fear and feel unable to work on the problem, even from a distance. If you cannot work on it, even with medicine, you must first use a less effective technique, *systematic desensitization*, to desensitize yourself to the fearful situation. This technique also helps when you can't arrange direct exposure (for example, sexual anxiety in a single person). When the anxiety relates to a lack of skills, however, it is better to work directly on the appropriate skills than to use systematic desensitization. For example, if you feel very anxious about socializing, dating relationships, rejection, or assertiveness, you should work on the appropriate skills rather than use systematic desensitization. Use behavioral roleplays, positive thought alternatives for negative thinking, relaxation, and plenty of practice to develop the skills you need.

Systematic desensitization involves learning to relax deeply while imagining the situation that provokes anxiety or fear. Prepare to use systematic desensitization by spending several weeks learning deep muscle relaxation as described in chapter 10, Stress. Deep muscle relaxation physically combats the body's hormonal responses in anxiety and fear. After you learn to relax your body thoroughly, imagine a series of increasingly anxious or fearful situations while practicing relaxation. Begin by relaxing while imagining an easy item that produces only a little anxiety or fear. Move on to the next, more threatening item only after you can imagine the first item while staying relaxed and without feeling any anxiety or fear. This procedure continues over a number of sessions until you can imagine the most threatening item while relaxing and with no anxiety or fear. Then you are ready to confront the anxiety or fear in real life, beginning with the least threatening situations. You may need 10 to 100 sessions of systematic desensitization before you are ready to confront the anxiety or fear in real life.

Create your list of items for systematic desensitization during the weeks in which you practice deep muscle relaxation. Add new items as you think of them, until you have eight to twenty items, arranging them from least to most threatening. Two sample lists follow.

Fear of Heights

1. A child climbs a tree while you watch.
2. A cat climbs to the first large branch of a tree and can't get down. You must get a ladder and rescue it.
3. You stand on the tenth floor of a building and look out a large picture window.

4. You stand on the thirtieth floor of a building and look out a large picture window.

5. You climb up high in a big, old, sturdy oak tree.

6. You stand at a scenic overlook and your friend urges you to come closer to the railing.

7. You have climbed as far as possible in an old oak tree, and the branches that support you sway with the wind.

8. You sit in an airplane and look down at a break in the clouds and the land far below.

9. You stand at the edge of the railing at the Grand Canyon.

10. You stand at the top of the Empire State Building, overlooking New York City.

Fear of Funerals and Death

1. You read in the newspaper that a distant relative you hardly know has died.

2. While walking by a cemetery, you think of all the dead bodies there.

3. While waiting at a red light, you become startled by a funeral procession crossing the intersection in front of you.

4. You visit the grave of a dearly loved friend in a cemetery.

5. You think to yourself that your parents will die someday.

6. You must visit a friend who is terribly sick in the hospital.

7. You drive slowly in a funeral procession for a family friend toward the cemetery.

8. Your brother has died and his wife cries at the funeral.

9. You receive a phone call from your mother saying your father has died.

10. Your father has died and you view his body in the casket.

Just because you have a fear of heights doesn't mean the above list would suit you. Some people with a fear of heights don't fear riding in an airplane at all. Create your list to suit you. A person with a fear of doctors and dentists might start a list with items about calling for an appointment, move on to items about routine health matters, then end the list with embarrassing examinations or surgery. A person with severe anxiety about sexual intimacy would begin with items about expressing affection while fully clothed and work up to items including nakedness and sex acts. For extreme marital jealousy, you might create a list by starting with your spouse talking to and laughing with a friend on the telephone and then moving on to progressively more threatening situations. Distance often helps in creating items of greater and lesser fearfulness for phobias.

Begin each session of systematic desensitization with about five minutes of deep muscle relaxation, preferably while lying down. Then imagine yourself in the situation described by your first item, the least threatening item, for about thirty seconds or until you begin to feel anxious or afraid, whichever comes first.   Anytime you feel anxious or afraid, stop imagining the scene and practice deep relaxation until you feel very comfortable again.   Then go back to the imagined scene as often as necessary to imagine it without becoming anxious or fearful.   Spend about thirty seconds relaxing between imagined scenes.   Never go on to the next item in your list until you have successfully imagined the previous item for at least thirty seconds, three times in a row, without becoming the least bit anxious or afraid.   This may happen after imagining the scene only three or four times, or you may need to imagine one scene thirty or more times before successfully imagining it three times in a row, so you can move on to the next item.   Each session should last thirty minutes to one hour, and each session should begin with the easiest item and progress to more difficult ones.

If you find that one item is much more difficult than the previous one, try to find others that fall midway between these two in the amount of anxiety or fear they provoke.   You can make the procedure easier by tape recording each item, with a pause between each.   Then just play your tape and pause it to spend as long as you need on each item.   If you can't imagine the items clearly enough to bring on your anxiety or fear, obtain photographs of the feared object or situation to look at during the procedure.   If you use photographs, sit in a comfortable chair with the pictures on a table in front of you.   Turn the photographs over one by one when you need them, and shut your eyes for the relaxation parts of the procedure.   With continued practice of systematic desensitization, you will eventually be able to begin practicing real life exposure to your least threatening situations.

Enlist your family and friends to help you conquer your anxiety or fear in the ways described in chapter 12.   In systematic desensitization, helpers can read the items for you or turn on and off the tape recorder, so you can relax more completely.   Look for ways in which other people may contribute to your problem with anxiety, fear, or phobia.   Do you stay at home or avoid your problems in other ways because of the help of friends and family members, such as in shopping and errands?   Do you get extra attention and pity for your problems?   This acts as a reward for your phobic behavior.   Ask people to stop contributing to your problem in these ways and to become involved in more helpful ways.   Ask them to ignore you when you complain about your symptoms, and ask them to accompany you on errands, instead of doing the errands for you.

Self-imposed rewards and penalties help a great deal in working on problems of anxiety, worry, fear, and phobia. Use the advice in chapter 11, Easy Changes, to keep motivated in working on your anxieties and fears, too. After you succeed in overcoming your problem, check on your own continued progress regularly and renew your efforts at self-improvement whenever necessary, as described in the last paragraph in chapter 11 to ensure long-term success.

Recommended Additional Readings:

Master Your Panic and Take Back Your Life: Twelve Treatment Sessions to Overcome High Anxiety. by Denise F. Beckfield. San Luis Obispo, CA: Impact Publishers, 1994.

Beyond Shyness: How to Conquer Social Anxieties. by Jonathan Berent and Any Lemley. NY: Simon & Schuster, 1993. for shyness, social anxiety, social phobia.

The Anxiety & Phobia Workbook. 2nd ed. by Edmund J. Bourne. Oakland, CA: New Harbinger Publications, 1995.

Worry: Controlling It and Using It Wisely. by Edward M. Hallowell. NY: Pantheon Books, 1997.

The Feeling Good Handbook. by David D. Burns. NY: Penguin Books, 1989. for feelings, thinking habits, communication skills, anxiety, fear, and phobia.

Support Groups, Hotlines, and Resources:

National Institute of Mental Health Information Line 800 647 2642 information, free literature on panic, posttraumatic stress disorder, generalized anxiety disorder, phobias, obsessive compulsive disorder. on-line: www.nimh.nih.gov/anxiety/anxiety/

Anxiety Disorders Association of America 301 231 9350 information, support group referrals. on-line: adaa.org

A.I.M. 248 547 0400 for anxiety disorders, literature, referrals to support groups, newsletter, pen pals. on-line: anny@Ameritech.net

Phobics Anonymous 760 322 2673 support groups.

National Mental Health Association 800 969 6642 referrals for treatment, brochures on anxiety disorders, phobias, and other topics. on-line: www.nmha.org

Emotions Anonymous 651 647 9712 support groups for any personal problem, pen pals. on-line: www.emotionsanonymous.org

Recovery Inc. 312 337 5661 support groups for any personal problem, on-line: www.recovery-inc.com

Overcomers Outreach 800 310 3001 Christ-centered support groups for any personal problem. on-line: www.overcomersoutreach.org

30. Guilt

Guilt is the doorway to self-improvement and forgiving yourself.

People with no sense of guilt are monsters, sociopaths.

Guilt is a feeling of responsibility or painful regret for real or imagined offenses. Guilt over wrongdoing is a noble, helpful emotion. Use your guilt over real offenses to motivate yourself to make reparation, learn from the mistakes, and change your behavior. Ideally, you should apologize and make up for the offense by paying for physical damages, by performing extra acts of kindness for hurt feelings, etc. If it is impossible to make up directly for what you did, perform completely unrelated good deeds or acts of service to other people. Analyze the best responses to the problem and resolve to do better in similar situations in the future. After you do these things, forgive yourself. Burdening yourself with the past is a waste of time and emotional energy.

Guilt often comes from the value systems we learned in our family, culture, or religion. Just understanding that your guilt arises from value systems learned early in life can help you overcome it. If your guilt arises from such training, decide for yourself whether you agree with these standards. If so, work on improving your behavior. If you decide your previous values are not realistic for you at this point in your life, feel free to behave according to your true beliefs. Because of the difficulty of rejecting a lifetime of training and beliefs, however, guilt may continue to plague you over behaviors you enjoy and believe to be morally right. This is normal but guilt from the new behaviors will diminish as you continue the behaviors and become accustomed to your new lifestyle.

Sometimes other people induce guilt in you by pressuring you to satisfy them or live up to their standards. These people may control you by complaining, acting the martyr to get pity and help, scolding you, telling you what you should do, pressuring you to achieve, or silently judging you while conveying their feelings with facial expressions. In such cases, you must decide whether you really want to meet their expectations. You may decide you have certain duties toward them but that in other areas, you must live for yourself. Remember that you can't please everyone. Learn to stand up for your own rights and to say no comfortably when you really want to (chapter 16, Assertiveness). Perhaps you need to spend less time with a person who induces guilt in you. If so, you might develop new interests and activities or make new friends who better understand your needs.

Guilt may be simply unrealistic. People sometimes assume they caused a problem when, in fact, they did not. When you feel at fault, ask yourself if someone or something else may have caused the problem. Perhaps you mistakenly thought you hurt someone's feelings. Feedback can clear up matters such as these. Ask for feedback from other people in the situation.

Guilt may come from being overly strict with yourself. Are you demanding too much? You can't be perfect. Everyone makes mistakes. It is normal to become angry occasionally at people you love. Did you deliberately act in an immoral, unfair, or hurtful way? Sometimes we take one mistake or wrongful act far too seriously. Would you be so hard on someone else who had acted in this way? Will this one act really matter to anyone a year from now? Are you overlooking the balance of good in the affected relationship that far outweighs the evil in this one act? Will this act permanently damage your relationship with the person? Telling trusted friends about the act and receiving understanding and forgiveness often helps relieve the burden of guilt. Ask your friends if they have ever made a similar mistake. People often feel horribly alone in their guilt, although the truth is thousands of other people have done the same thing.

If you have followed the relevant advice above and guilt still plagues you, work with your guilty thoughts as negative thinking in the ways described in chapter 4. Quit making yourself feel guilty with guilty thoughts and write more positive thought alternatives to read several times each day and each time the guilty thoughts arise. Some possibilities include: "Other people may feel differently, but I feel this behavior is right for me," "It's only human to make mistakes," "I made a mistake and acted improperly, but that doesn't make me a bad person," "I've made up for what I've done and learned from my mistake. Now it's time to forgive myself and forget about it," and "It's over now. I can't change it. Why waste time and energy worrying about it?"

Recommended Additional Readings and Support Groups:

Please refer to the end of chapter 5, Emotions, for helpful readings and support groups for negative thought habits.

31. Self-Esteem

Each time you do your best, you grow,
and as you grow, your best will be more each time.

Self-esteem comes from honesty,
hard work, kindness, and generosity.

Low self-esteem may develop in a variety of ways. You can learn low self-esteem early in life from parents who have low self-esteem and other problems. It may develop after a series of failures in school due to a disadvantaged home environment or parents who don't stress the importance of school and homework. Low self-esteem may come from early experiences with vicious childhood teasing or overly critical parents. It may also come from personal problems or relate to lack of certain skills or behaviors.

Look for personal problems by honestly and carefully evaluating each area of life described in this book. Studying the times when you feel the most troubled by low self-esteem in the ways described in chapter 9, Problem Solving, can help define the most relevant issues in your problem. Chapter 38, Understanding Yourself, can also help you explore personal problems and conflicts. Working on and improving personal problems does much to alleviate low self-esteem. Accomplishing your goals in life also improves self-esteem a great deal. Make sure your goals are realistic and attainable and plan how to reach them. Discipline yourself to avoid giving up until you reach your goals.

Certain parts of this book are particularly important to self-esteem. Of course, happiness is closely linked to self-esteem. It is especially important to perform good acts, develop qualities in yourself, strive for ideals, and develop well-rounded interests and activities. Please refer to chapter 1 for a full discussion of the reasons why these things are important. Work on your favorite interests and activities until you build some expertise you can take pride in. A satisfying social life with several very close friends and a number of other friends also contributes a great deal to self-esteem. For this reason, controlling your anger and developing good communication skills are important.

Healthy self-acceptance is an integral part of self-esteem. There will always be other people who are more beautiful, handsome, successful, intelligent, athletic, and popular than you. And there will always be other people who are less fortunate than you in these respects. Develop an acceptance of your physical body and your limitations. Strive for improvement but don't demand perfection of yourself. Realize we all make mistakes and resolve to learn from yours. Use your sense of humor about faults, frustrations, losses, and other problems to promote self-acceptance.

Low self-esteem always involves negative thinking habits about the self. Remember that negative thoughts can lead to overly pessimistic perceptions, to giving up too easily, and to failure in a self-fulfilling prophecy. This occurs in social life, academic work, working toward goals, etc. Work on replacing negative thoughts about the self with more helpful thought alternatives every day as described in chapter 4. Many of the categories of negative thinking and positive alternatives given as examples in chapter 4 are important in problems of low self-esteem.

Practice saying only positive things about yourself. People with low self-esteem often say negative things about themselves, using statements like those in the examples of negative thoughts in chapter 4. Combat this tendency to insult yourself by practicing speaking about yourself in positive ways for 10 or 15 minutes at a time. You can practice doing this alone, with a trusted friend, or into a tape recorder. Continue practicing until you can talk easily and naturally to strangers about yourself in positive ways.

Make a list of your qualities, virtues, accomplishments, and talents. Add to this list whenever you think of additional items. Ask a good friend to make such a list about you or to add to your list. Then read this list every day and whenever you feel negative about yourself, to combat your low self-esteem. You can also make a list of your good deeds or kind acts and things you did well. Include even minor things, such as cleaning the house or acting kindly despite being provoked by someone. Add to this list every few days. Regularly reading these lists combats the tendency to think only negative things about yourself.

Does anybody contribute to your problem of low self-esteem, perhaps by insulting you with negative labels or by criticizing you unfairly? Confront the person with your feelings and ask for a change in behavior. Learn from criticism about your behaviors, but refuse to accept overgeneralizations or negative labels. If an overly critical person in your life won't change, you may need to spend less time with that person or even to eliminate the person from your life.

Because of inadequacy and a need for love and acceptance from others, it is easy for people with low self-esteem to allow others to use them.

Carefully avoid pleasing other people at the expense of your own needs and desires. Work on assertiveness in saying no when you really want to and in making requests and demands of other people. Never tolerate unsatisfying friendships or romantic relationships. If you need to evaluate the quality of a relationship, please refer to the section on Is This Relationship Good for Me? in chapter 15. Another mistake often made by people with problems in self-esteem is looking for a romance to satisfy their unhappiness. As detailed in the section on dating in chapter 15, this is an unwise, poor approach to dating. Finally, if upsetting past events (such as teasing by other people or overly critical parents) contribute to your problem, work with the past in the ways described in chapter 37 to understand, accept, and finish these issues.

Recommended Additional Readings and Support Groups:

Please refer to the end of chapter 5, Emotions, for helpful readings and support
groups for negative thought habits.

32. Insomnia

Learn to enjoy resting and sleep will come naturally.

In a government study, people allowed to sleep as long as they wanted averaged 8 1/2 hours and felt more energetic and happier than when they slept their habitual amount, a little over 7 hours. Journals before electric lighting indicate people averaged 10 hours sleep each night, yet a Gallup poll found only 28% of American adults sleeps 8 hours a night. Another study found 31% of us sleep less than 7 hours a night. Needs between 5 and 10 hours a night are common, and some people function well with only 3 or 4 hours of sleep a night. As we age, sleep gradually becomes lighter and we wake more easily and more often. Many people notice this by age 65. Frequent and prolonged wakening is common in the elderly, although many of them make up for this with daytime naps. Over age 65, a higher percentage of people need only 3 to 6 hours of sleep a night.

Nearly everyone experiences insomnia at times because of noise, overcrowding, weather extremes, schedule changes, pain, or stresses like the loss of a loved one, work pressures, marriage, or divorce. The average adult falls asleep in 20 minutes, but over 1/4 of us have trouble falling asleep. Those with insomnia may need an hour or more and often have trouble staying asleep. If you need more sleep, you may doze off during the day or notice a loss of energy and initiative, fatigue, lapses in attention, distractibility, or increased irritability. Missing 2 hours of needed sleep each day for 5 days decreases motor coordination. Because the need for sleep varies so much, psychologists don't consider insomnia a problem unless it results in daytime fatigue or the other symptoms noted here.

Insomnia has many causes. Anxiety, depression, stress, drug and alcohol dependency, certain medicines, and chronic pain are some of the most common. The overuse of beverages that contain alcohol or caffeine (coffee, tea, or soft drinks) or drinking them during evening hours can cause insomnia or disturbed sleep, even in people who believe otherwise. Avoid caffeine for six hours before going to bed, and avoid alcohol for a few hours before going to bed. Many over-the-counter medicines contain caffeine and often cause insomnia in older folks. Tobacco also has stimulant effects, so sleep may improve after you quit smoking. Work on problems of anxiety, depression, or stress using the appropriate chapters of this book. If you have chronic pain, take over-the-counter or prescription painkillers before going to bed.

Check with a doctor to find out if medicine or a physical problem, such as a hormonal imbalance, causes your insomnia. Many antidepressants and high blood pressure medicines can do this. Restless legs syndrome causes insomnia by forcing sufferers to constantly move their legs to get relief. An iron deficiency, antidepressant drugs, alcohol, renal failure, or diabetes can contribute to this syndrome. A bed partner might notice the symptoms of sleep apnea, which causes loud snoring, periodic snorts and gasps, and periods of stopped breathing. Sleep apnea is the most common sleep disorder, found most often in middle age, overweight men. Sleep apnea can eventually cause hypertension, heart disease, stroke, or disordered thinking. Over 95% of cases can be cured with a soft mask and machine that provides continuous airway pressure.

About 10% of sworn insomniacs sleep soundly when they come to a sleep clinic but think they've been awake all night. We often sleep without even realizing it. When researchers measure brain waves and wake people during stages of sleep other than the short dreaming stage, many people don't even realize they have ever been asleep. This is because most stages of sleep don't contain long dreams but contain less visual, less story like, less bizarre dream fragments, many of which are memories of recent events or thoughts about daily concerns and difficult to distinguish from waking thoughts.

Psychologists do not recommend sleeping pills for insomnia. Because of physical tolerance, all sleep medications become ineffective by about two or three weeks of daily use. This tempts you to increase the dosage, a dangerous practice whether you use prescription or over-the-counter sleep medications. Prescription sleep medications are addictive and interfere with the most important parts of sleep. Eliminating them may cause increased insomnia and unpleasant withdrawal symptoms, even after cautious, restrained use. After having used only one sleeping pill each night, some people experience mild withdrawal symptoms of insomnia, irritability, anxiety, weakness, or nightmares. The use of alcohol to get to sleep can also cause all the above problems. The Journal of the American Medical Association reports chronic use of the hormone melatonin as a sleep aid may aggravate depression, cause eye (retinal) damage, reduce fertility, or lower male sex drive. Most brands of melatonin are manufactured without rigorous quality control, so the dosage may vary and other unwanted ingredients may be present.

Get plenty of exercise during the day, so you will feel tired at night. Many insomniacs report low levels of physical activity, and regular exercise helps combat insomnia. However, vigorous exercise less than six hours before bedtime or moderate exercise less than four hours before bedtime can cause insomnia. Use quiet, relaxing activities before bedtime, such as a warm bath or light reading. When you go to bed, make sure you feel as comfortable as possible. If your feet feel cold, wear socks to keep them warm. Occasional loud noises can disturb sleep even if you don't wake up. If a noisy household or neighborhood interferes with your sleep, earplugs or white noise will help. White noise is even, low-level background noise, such as a fan turned on or the radio set in between radio stations, that helps mask other bothersome noises. Ocean sounds help, but don't use radio stations or the TV—they have louder peaks that will interfere with sleep. A new alternative is a white noise machine.

The most effective way to fight insomnia is as follows. Stay out of bed if you aren't tired or sleepy and don't feel like resting. Don't eat, read, or watch TV in bed. If you go to bed and don't fall asleep in ten or twenty minutes, get up and do some quiet activity until you feel sleepy again. Many people enjoy reading during this time. Daytime naps, sleeping late in the morning to make up for a restless night, and irregular sleep habits contribute to insomnia. No matter how tired you feel, don't do these things. Get up at the same time every morning. In over half of the insomniacs studied, this routine helps.

Deep relaxation skills (chapter 10, Stress) can also help. People who practice deep muscle relaxation often become surprised when they note the amount of muscle tension held in their faces and bodies when they rest in bed and try to go to sleep. Learn to notice and eliminate bodily tension as described in the section on Relaxation Skills in chapter 10, and use these skills in bed to get to sleep. After having used deep muscle relaxation throughout all of your body parts several times to rid your body of excess tension, use breathing meditation until you fall asleep. Meditating on relaxed, rhythmical breathing helps because it is repetitive and monotonous.

Habits of negative thinking play an important role in insomnia. Worrying about not being able to fall asleep keeps you anxious and awake. Please refer to the list of thoughts related to insomnia in chapter 4 for examples of troublesome and helpful thoughts. Replace worries about getting to sleep with more helpful thoughts about enjoying resting until you do fall asleep. Learn to be tolerant of occasional sleeplessness. If you tend to look at the clock and worry about not getting to sleep, turn the clock backwards or put it somewhere else, so you can't see it from your bed. You can get up after ten or twenty minutes by guessing. Don't obsess about the exact number of minutes. If worries keep you awake at bedtime, chapter 29 can help you control them. If you continue to have problems despite all this advice, ask your doctor to refer you to a sleep clinic for evaluation.

Because sleepwalking, sleeptalking, and night terrors occur mostly in childhood, please refer to the bedtime section in chapter 22, Raising Children, for a discussion of these topics. In adults, episodes of sleepwalking are often related to fatigue, stress, sleep deprivation, drug use, or psychiatric disorders. Most people have experienced at least one episode of talking in their sleep, and most of these episodes are brief and don't involve negative emotions. Talking to the person can prolong the episode, and some even laugh, sing, or cry. Because talking in your sleep causes no problems, psychologists don't treat it. You will find the topic of nightmares discussed in the bedtime section in chapter 22, Raising Children, in chapter 39, Dreams, and in the second book below.

Recommended Additional Readings:

No More Sleepless Nights. rev. ed. by Peter Hauri and Shirley Linde. NY: John Wiley & Sons, 1996. comprehensive book on insomnia, medical causes, sleep apnea, narcolepsy, restless legs syndrome, many other sleep related problems, jet lag, night work, shift work, how to quit a habit of using sleeping pills, list of sleep disorder clinics, when to go to a sleep disorder clinic.

The Sleep Rx: 75 Proven Ways to Get a Good Night's Sleep. by Norman Ford. Englewood Cliffs, NJ: Prentice-Hall, 1994. good discussion of insomnia, medical causes, snoring, sleep apnea, narcolepsy, restless legs syndrome, jet lag, reprogramming nightmares, etc.

33. Substance Addictions and Gambling

*Beat addiction by keeping busy, making friends who
don't use, avoiding temptation, and finding
better ways to relax, have fun, and deal with emotions.*

Russians drink three times the hard liquor per person as people here or in China, which helps cause their declining life expectancy, now 58 years for Russian men. We discuss gambling in this chapter along with drug addictions because most of the strategies for overcoming drug addictions are also useful for gambling. Alcohol and tobacco are, by far, our worst drug problems. Approximately 2/3 of the adults in the U.S. regularly or occasionally drink alcohol. About one out of six drinkers is an alcoholic with personal, family, work, or social problems due to alcohol. About 1/4 of adults here smoke cigarettes and 43% of our high school students use tobacco. Marijuana is the next most common drug problem, making up about 80% of the nation's illegal drug use.

The Institute of Medicine estimates that 2/3 of addicted people are men and that 1/3 have more than one addiction. Addicted people are notorious for denying their problems, even to themselves. Alcoholics, gamblers, and other addicts often prefer to believe that because they hold jobs and carry on social lives, they can handle their vices. They may believe they are not addicted because they only indulge after work or during weekends, because they don't use hard liquor, or because they have never experienced withdrawal symptoms. But the vast majority of addicts are not bums. They hold jobs, carry on social lives, and often support families. Less than 5% of alcoholics fit the stereotype of the hopeless drunk. The truth is you may be addicted despite indulging only occasionally, never using hard liquor, and never having experienced withdrawal symptoms.

Although many Americans enjoy bingo, a lottery, horse racing, or slot machines, an estimated 2% are problem gamblers who suffer because they cannot control it. Some lose their savings and homes, neglect their children, or resort to stealing or attempt suicide because of gambling. Some children die when their gambling parents or caretakers leave them in a hot vehicle for hours. Some people have passed out because they were so obsessed with gambling, they didn't eat or drink anything for 48 hours. Some casinos have had to replace fabric slot-machine stools with vinyl covered ones because of problem gamblers who won't stop to go to the restroom.

The following list describes characteristics of addicted people. Certain items apply only to alcoholics or gamblers, but most items apply to any person with a drug addiction. Many of the items about drinking also apply to chronic gamblers. To use this list for other drug addictions or for gambling, simply replace *alcohol, drinking,* and *drunk* with *drug, drug use, drug intoxication,* or *gambling.* If more than a very few of the early items apply to a person, that person either has an addiction or is close to becoming addicted. Later items indicate severe addiction.

Characteristics of Addicted People

often thinking about and looking forward to occasions for use

increasing physical tolerance, it now takes a greater amount to produce the same degree of intoxication (Gamblers may increase tolerance for higher and higher bets)

drinking because of depression, anxiety, nerves, anger, insomnia, disappointments, arguments, or problems at home, at work, or in school (Such incidents often lead to addiction. Repeatedly drinking in response to these problems is characteristic of addiction.)

drinking to feel more competent at work, build up self-confidence, feel more witty and charming, flirt, have fun at a party, complete chores more enjoyably, etc. (Such incidents often lead to addiction. Repeatedly drinking for such purposes is a characteristic of addiction.)

intending to have one or two drinks and getting drunk instead (gambling more than planned)

getting drunk without having planned to drink

drinking before going out to get in the right mood for the bar, party, etc.

drinking alone

drinking in the morning

a friend or loved one feeling embarrassed by your use

a friend or loved one complaining about your use

unusual behavior for you while drunk

disappointing someone else by failing to meet the person as scheduled due to the use of alcohol

failing to live up to a responsibility or promise due to the use of alcohol

occasionally getting too drunk and regretting it

other people thinking you drink too much

having excuses for your drinking or reasons why you drink as much as you do

minimizing how much you drink or how often you drink

lying about your drinking

hiding alcohol on your person for use where it is not served

hiding alcohol

drinking more than most of your friends

gambling again after losing to "get even"

borrowing money or doing without other things to buy alcohol

drinking extra without other people knowing it

gulping your drinks (or using drugs quickly)

having ever missed school or work because of alcohol

regretting things that you said or did while drunk

injuries (cuts, bruises, etc.) due to the use of alcohol

having ever had a blackout, a temporary loss of consciousness or a loss of memory for events due to the use of alcohol or other drugs, or any of the more serious physical problems (see the following nine pages) due to use of a drug

dreaming about alcohol

drinking replacing your interest in various activities

growing apart from nondrinking friends and spending more of your time with drinking friends

drinking for hours each day or whenever you have free time

deciding never to get so drunk again and then repeating the problem

repeated episodes of behavior while drunk that you later regret

drinking affecting your work on the job or at school (occasional absenteeism, reduced performance, etc.)

difficulty stopping after one or two

inability to turn it down or never turning it down when it is available

continuing to drink despite social problems, psychological problems such as anxiety or depression, physical problems, or work problems from it

repeatedly trying to quit or cut down on your drinking

failing to cut down on your drinking

drinking when you know you really shouldn't (before driving, at work, before a job interview, etc.)

a traffic violation due to alcohol

loss of friends due to alcohol

needing to drink at certain times; discomfort, irritability, or distress without it

unable to stop using for two months

choosing a work schedule or job to accommodate your drinking

changing values due to alcohol

choosing friends or lovers on the basis of access to alcohol

having blackouts or any of the more serious physical problems (see the following nine pages) due to use of a drug

fights, arguments, or getting into trouble due to alcohol

an arrest related to alcohol use

financial problems due to alcohol

traffic accident due to alcohol

loss of a job due to alcohol

severe family problems (unruly children, threat of divorce or separation, etc.) due to alcohol

loss of your spouse due to alcohol

neglecting good nutrition

medical problems due to alcohol

suicidal feelings when drinking

withdrawal symptoms when you stop using alcohol

Now let's consider some basic information on commonly abused drugs. The following list presents possible physical effects of each drug, ranging from initial effects to the extreme effects associated with high doses. Individuals vary in their physical reactions to drugs, however, and physical tolerance may reduce certain effects. *Physical tolerance* is the phenomenon in which regular use of a drug causes reduced physical effects from the same doses used previously. Physical tolerance occurs in all the drugs of abuse. Because a more detailed discussion of alcohol, nicotine, and marijuana follows, this list doesn't include the long-term physical effects of these drugs.

Drug Effects

Central Nervous System Depressants (alcohol, barbiturates, tranquilizers, sedative-hypnotics, and opiates): relaxation, euphoria, lowered inhibitions, relief of anxiety, slowed reaction time, impaired motor coordination, drunken behavior, drowsiness, relief of physical pain, nausea, vomiting, coma, failure to breathe, and death. The opiates (opium, morphine, heroin, etc.) also cause narrowed pupils. Combining any of the central nervous system depressants (for example, drinking alcohol and taking barbiturates) is very dangerous because it multiplies the effects of each, rather than simply adding the effects of each drug used. This leads to many accidental overdoses on these substances. A dangerously uneven physical tolerance develops to the effects of alcohol, barbiturates, tranquilizers, and sedative-hypnotics. With these drugs, tolerance develops for the anxiety relief, euphoria, relaxation, and sleep-inducing effects but not for the physical mechanisms that cause coma and failure to breathe. Thus, you can build up a tolerance to the effects of these drugs that you desire and you can die without even attaining these effects. This doesn't happen with the opiates. The opiates produce tolerance to the physical mechanisms that cause coma and failure to breathe, along with the tolerance for the anxiety relief, euphoria, relaxation, and sleep-inducing effects.

Caffeine (coffee, tea, nonprescription pills for staying awake, many soft drinks, chocolate): alertness (counteracts drowsiness), enhanced energy, increased heart rate, heart palpitations, decreased appetite, restlessness, insomnia, anxiety, irritability, stomach complaints, nausea, diarrhea, and muscle tremors (the shakes). Although just seven to ten cups of coffee each day may cause the above problems, people generally use small doses of caffeine and avoid major problems. Heavy use of caffeine increases the risk of heart disease, however, and an overdose of caffeine can cause delirium, convulsions, failure to breathe, and death.

Nicotine (tobacco): relaxation, increased heart rate and blood pressure, restlessness, anxiety, stomach complaints, and nausea. The first episodes of tobacco use may result in anxiety, stomach complaints, or nausea, but regular use produces mostly stimulant effects (increased heart rate and blood pressure) and mild feelings of pleasure or relaxation. Despite feelings of relaxation, the stimulant effects seem to cause chronically increased anxiety (making you feel you need another cigarette) and can cause insomnia.

Marijuana: euphoria, reddened eyes, subjectively intensified sense perception, time distortion, increased heart rate, heart palpitations, increased blood pressure, dry mouth, slowed reaction time, and impaired vision, motor coordination, concentration, and short-term memory. Chronic, heavy use decreases pleasure from use, but physical tolerance is not great. Many users have experienced short-lived episodes of anxiety, paranoia, or panic from the use of marijuana, but in rare cases strong anxiety and paranoia may last a few days.

Cocaine, Amphetamines (prescription diet pills, "speed"): alertness (counteracts drowsiness), euphoria, enhanced energy, increased activity, increased heart rate and blood pressure, heart palpitations, increased breathing rate, talkativeness, decreased appetite, widened (dilated) pupils, restlessness, insomnia, anxiety, impaired concentration, irritability, suspiciousness, repetitious behavior such as nervous habits or overcleaning, aggressiveness, nausea, vomiting, muscle tremors (the shakes), sweating, chills, paranoia, confusion, panic, an itchy feeling as if bugs are crawling under your skin, hallucinations, paranoid schizophrenia, convulsions, failure to breath, heart failure, and stroke. After the use of even moderate amounts of cocaine or amphetamines, many people experience a period of fatigue, depression, nervousness, or irritability, called the "crash." Cocaine and amphetamines are particularly dangerous for people with heart conditions, epilepsy, and high blood pressure. Chronic sniffing of these substances can destroy nasal tissues and cause holes in the nasal cartilage.

Inhalants (glues, spray paints, gasoline, cleaning fluids, solvents, correction fluid, nail polish and remover, nitrous oxide, amyl or butyl nitrate): euphoria, slurred speech, impaired motor coordination, restlessness, coughing, sores in or near the nose or mouth, decreased or increased heart rate and blood pressure, heart palpitations, fatigue, anemia, weak muscles, headache, dizziness, impaired memory, irritability, double vision, nausea, fainting, vomiting, lead poisoning, hallucinations, muscle spasms, brain damage, kidney damage, liver damage, lung damage, coma, suffocation, heart failure. Children or adolescents who don't understand the dangers most commonly use inhalants. The high is generally short-lived, but effects and dosages are unpredictable. Even first time use may result in death through suffocation or heart failure (especially if followed by exercise).

Abruptly stopping the chronic use of a drug may lead to withdrawal symptoms. Withdrawal symptoms greatly depend on the amount of drug that the person chronically used and the physiology of the individual. Moderate use may produce no withdrawal symptoms, but chronic use of very large amounts of certain drugs invariably leads to the severe symptoms described below. Because of physiological and psychological differences, two people using the same amount of a drug may experience very different withdrawal symptoms. Psychological factors such as one's expectations and attitudes toward withdrawal symptoms affect negative emotions experienced during withdrawal and may affect the intensity of the milder physical withdrawal symptoms.

Withdrawal Symptoms

Central Nervous System Depressants (alcohol, barbiturates, tranquilizers, sedative-hypnotics, and opiates): irritability, anxiety, depression, weakness, restlessness, insomnia, increased nightmares, aches and pains, sweating, dizziness, stomach cramps, nausea, vomiting, hyperactivity, muscle tremors (the shakes), muscle spasms, confusion, disorientation, hallucinations, convulsions, and death from heart attack. Withdrawal from opiates may also include watery eyes, running nose, diarrhea, and hot and cold spells. A mild case of withdrawal from opiates may appear to be a bout of flu. Withdrawal from alcohol typically begins within 4 to 12 hours of stopping or reducing use, peaks during the second day of abstinence, and generally ends in 4 or 5 days. Withdrawal symptoms from central nervous system depressants may last from 3 days to 2 weeks, and convulsions and death may occur as long as 2 weeks after the person stops using these drugs. Withdrawal from large amounts of alcohol, barbiturates, tranquilizers, or sedative-hypnotics is much more likely to lead to convulsions and death than is withdrawal from large amounts of opiates. Withdrawal from large amounts of minor tranquilizers such as diazepam (Valium) can easily mislead people because no withdrawal symptoms may occur for as long as 5 to 10 days after stopping the drug, yet the withdrawal may still include convulsions and death.

Caffeine (coffee, tea, nonprescription pills for staying awake, many soft drinks, chocolate): headache, anxiety, irritability, restlessness, poor concentration, increased hunger, and fatigue. Many people experience no withdrawal symptoms from heavy daily use, but other people report some mild withdrawal symptoms, sometimes from ending habits of as little as 5 to 10 cups of coffee each day. Few people, if any, have trouble switching from coffee to decaffeinated coffee, however.

Nicotine (tobacco): anxiety, irritability, increased coughing, a slight sore throat, increased eating (as a replacement nervous habit), headaches, light-headedness, insomnia, fatigue, drowsiness, constipation, and diarrhea. Many people experience no withdrawal symptoms from heavy daily use, but other people report some mild withdrawal symptoms.

Marijuana: anxiety, irritability, insomnia, tremors, and chills, lasting a few days. Many people experience no withdrawal symptoms from heavy daily use, but other people report some mild withdrawal symptoms, which do not generally cause marijuana use throughout the day for avoidance.

Cocaine, Amphetamines (prescription diet pills, "speed"): increased appetite, depression, irritability, anxiety, insomnia or prolonged sleep, fatigue, and slowed movements. Many people experience no withdrawal symptoms from heavy daily use, but other people report some symptoms beginning hours or days after stopping and lasting up to several weeks.

Inhalants (glues, spray paints, gasoline, cleaning fluids, solvents, correction fluid, nail polish and remover, nitrous oxide, amyl or butyl nitrate): Withdrawal from the chronic use of certain inhalants may result in headache, chills, abdominal pain, muscular cramps, muscle tremors (the shakes), and hallucinations.

A closer look at the three most common drugs of abuse, alcohol, tobacco, and marijuana, helps illustrate the serious dangers of drug abuse. Although illegal drugs greatly increase crime rates, lower employee productivity, lower student achievement, and increase family problems, alcohol is a worse drug problem than any of the illegal drugs, with an overwhelming impact on society. Alcohol results in more deaths than all other illegal drugs together. Alcohol plays a role in between 41 and 55% of traffic fatalities, an even higher percentage of single-car fatalities, and 50% of fire and drowning deaths, fatal falls, and fatal boating accidents. It contributes to 54 to 65% of murders and attempted murders, 75% of marital violence, 66% of violence toward current or former romantic partners, about 48% of robberies, about 35% of suicides, and 37% of violent crimes. Many heavy users of alcohol (40%) report their use has resulted in fights. Alcohol plays a role in over 50% of rapes and in 35 to 60% of cases of child abuse, including sex crimes against children. It contributes to 25% of admissions to psychiatric hospitals. Alcoholic parents produce approximately 35% of the delinquent children in the United States.

Alcoholism and medical problems related to alcohol result in 30% of hospitalizations. Alcohol reduces the ability of the immune system to fight diseases. It causes liver problems including fibrous tissue, internal bleeding, decreased enzyme function, hepatitis, and cirrhosis. Alcoholic cirrhosis alone causes 29,000 deaths per year. Alcohol increases the risk of cancer of the mouth, anemia, and gastric ulcers. It causes miscarriages, stillbirths, birth deformities, and mental retardation in babies born to a drinking mother. It increases the risk and severity of heart disease, pneumonia, and tuberculosis. Studies suggest between 1/3 and 1/2 of chronic male alcoholics have low sexual desire and that between 1/10 and 1/2 experience impotence. Chronic alcoholism reduces male fertility, and in rare cases severe alcoholism causes a male's testes to shrink and breasts to grow. Alcoholism lasting ten years can cause permanent impotence in males and is the most common reason for impotence after previous sexual functioning in men between 40 and 60. Alcohol can inhibit ovulation in females. Alcohol can damage nerves in the arms, legs, hands, and feet and cause permanently slower reaction times. It can also cause diseases of the brain with memory loss for events that have just occurred.

Alcohol causes medical problems through its direct effects on many physiological processes in the body, but it also contributes to medical problems by providing calories without nutritional value and by reducing the absorption of the vitamins and minerals folic acid, niacin, B-1, B-6, B-12, zinc, and magnesium. If you drink alcoholic beverages regularly, make sure you get a nutritionally well balanced diet. Take vitamin and mineral supplements whenever you drink alcohol and don't eat right.

The legal drug tobacco also causes a variety of medical problems, including diseases that eventually kill about 1/3 of all smokers. Starting smoking as a teenager is especially dangerous, causing permanent genetic lung damage that forever increases the risk of lung cancer, even if the person quits and never smoked heavily. And the younger you begin smoking, the more of this damage is done. Tobacco smoke contains about 4,000 chemical compounds, including 200 known poisons. Carbon monoxide, nicotine, and tar do the most damage to the health of cigarette smokers. Other dangerous chemicals in tobacco include ammonia, acetone and benzene (two powerful solvents), formaldehyde (a component of embalming fluid), carboxylic acids, hydrogen cyanide (the poison used in gas chambers), ketones, nitrosamines, sulfur compounds, alkanes, alkenes, arsenic (used in rat poison), and various insecticide residues. The average smoker inhales twice the legal industrial limit for carbon monoxide. The tar in cigarettes contains 30 chemicals known to cause cancer. Unfortunately, a person who smokes a pack of cigarettes each day inhales one cup of tar each year.

Smoking tobacco is the most common cause of cancer and emphysema, causing 85% of all cases of both. Smoking multiplies your risk of lung cancer up to 25 times and multiplies your risk of emphysema 11 times. Emphysema is a horrible disease in which people cough deeply and fight to breathe because of extra lung fluids. Because cigar and pipe smokers consume less tobacco than cigarette smokers, cigar smokers increase their risk of lung cancer 9 times and pipe smokers, 8 times. Smokers are also more likely to get cancer in the throat, mouth, esophagus, larynx, pancreas, urinary bladder, kidney, cervix, and uterus. Smoking keeps the lungs constantly irritated and inflamed, but smokers notice nothing, except perhaps shortness of breath when exercising or a smoker's cough. The inflamed lungs make colds, flu, bronchitis, and other infections of the lungs more likely in smokers than nonsmokers.

Smoking tobacco increases blood pressure and heart rate and increases the risk of strokes and heart attacks. Cigarettes cause 80% of cardiovascular deaths in people under 50 years old. Smokers are 5 times as likely to suffer heart attacks in their 30s and 40s as nonsmokers. Female smokers who also use oral contraceptives have 10 times the risk of heart attack and 20 times the risk of stroke as nonsmokers. Smoking can also impair circulation in the hands and feet, sometimes becoming severe enough to result in gangrene. In men, circulation problems can weaken penile erections. Smoking during pregnancy increases your risk of miscarriage, stillbirth, premature birth, cleft palate and lip birth deformities, and low birth weight babies (which makes vision, hearing, and speech problems, learning disabilities, Attention Deficit Disorder, mental retardation, and cerebral palsy more likely). Smoking also triples the risk of mothers losing a baby to crib death.

Tobacco reduces the ability of the immune system to fight disease, so chronic smokers are hospitalized more often for many medical problems. Smoking increases the risk of gastric ulcers, osteoporosis, gum disease, and cataracts. It doubles the risk of age-related macular degeneration, an eye disease that is the leading cause of blindness in people over 65 years old. It doubles the risk of Alzheimer's disease and other dementia. It also aggravates allergies, interferes with the metabolism of vitamins B-12 and C, and reduces taste bud sensitivity. It increases the likelihood of premature facial wrinkles more than 3 times, more than 12 times if you also get plenty of exposure to the sun. Up to age 65, twice as many smokers die as nonsmokers in the same age groups. People who smoke two packs of cigarettes per day die, on the average, eight years earlier than do nonsmokers.

Tobacco companies pretend lower tar and nicotine cigarettes are safer than other cigarettes and cite studies with smoking machines, but heavy smokers don't behave like smoking machines. Without noticing it, heavy smokers who switch to low tar and nicotine cigarettes tend to use larger and more frequent puffs, inhale more deeply, and hold the smoke in their lungs longer to receive the same amount of nicotine, which brings even more smoke into their lungs than before. New evidence links low tar cigarettes with a different type of lung cancer that reaches deeper into the lungs. Tobacco companies also mislead people by naming their cigarettes as light or mild, whether or not the cigarettes actually contain low levels of tar and nicotine.

Even nonsmokers receive dangerous exposure from the tobacco smoke of other people. About 2/3 of the smoke from cigarettes and a higher percentage of the smoke from cigars and pipes escape into the environment. Because of a difference in electrical charge, human bodies attract smoke. Secondhand smoke, the smoke that escapes, contains two times as much tar and nicotine, three times as much carbon monoxide and ammonia, and even higher concentrations of many cancer-causing substances as does the inhaled smoke. Researchers estimate secondhand smoke causes 3,000 deaths from lung cancer and 30,000 to 50,000 deaths in nonsmokers in the United States each year. Close contact with a smoker for even one hour each week thickens arteries about 40% as much as smoking does, which is like being a light smoker.

Because children weigh less and breathe faster than adults, they receive more pollutants from environmental tobacco smoke in ratio to adults. Babies and children of smoking parents develop chest colds, ear infections, tonsillitis, bronchitis, and pneumonia more often than do those of nonsmoking parents. The EPA blames secondhand smoke for causing an extra 150,000 to 300,000 respiratory infections a year in children under 18 months old in the United States. The EPA also concluded that secondhand smoke causes as many as 26,000 new cases of asthma in children each year and aggravates asthma in at least 200,000 children each year in the United States.

There has been a great deal of research on marijuana in recent decades and although marijuana is dangerous, it has shattered one myth. There is no evidence that marijuana causes an amotivational syndrome (a loss of ambition or motivation). Research studies in Jamaica, Costa Rica, and Greece comparing long-term heavy users to nonusers found no evidence of intellectual or neurological damage, no changes in personality, and no loss of the will to work or participate in society. Other studies of long-term users in the United States, India, and the Caribbean show no evidence of mental or physical deterioration. However, smoking marijuana increases a middle-age person's risk of heart attack nearly five times in the first hour after smoking, because of the increased heart rate and blood pressure it causes. Laboratory studies of marijuana have shown temporary damage to cells of the immune system, but researchers have not found any increased danger of infectious disease or cancer because of these changes. Although marijuana affects sex hormones and lowers sperm counts, there is no evidence that these changes affect male sexual performance or fertility. Researchers know of no case of death from marijuana overdose. Animal studies suggest the toxic dose is perhaps thousands of times higher than the amount needed to get high.

Marijuana smoke contains over 400 different chemical compounds, including the same cancer-causing chemicals as tobacco, usually in somewhat higher concentrations. Regularly smoking marijuana irritates and inflames the lungs and narrows its air passages, increasing the likelihood of bronchitis, emphysema, and lung cancer. Of course, emphysema and cancer develop slowly and smokers will probably notice nothing until it is too late. Marijuana also impairs attention and motor coordination and slows reaction time, so it is dangerous to drive or operate any dangerous machinery while intoxicated. Marijuana certainly contributes to fatalities on our highways.

Marijuana is also dangerous during pregnancy. Preliminary evidence suggests the heavy use of marijuana may increase your risk of low birth weight babies, premature babies, miscarriage, stillbirth, and birth defects. Even if marijuana only caused low birth weight babies, this would increase your baby's risk of vision, hearing, and speech problems, learning disabilities, Attention Deficit Disorder, mental retardation, and cerebral palsy. Pregnant women should avoid marijuana.

The toll on people's lives from drug abuse goes far beyond physical problems, however. The previous list of characteristics of addicted people contains many items reflecting the damage that drugs can do to people's personal and social lives. If you want to learn more about drugs, go to your local public library or any drug treatment center for more detailed information.

As detailed previously in the section on Teenagers in chapter 22, research shows children are much more susceptible to addiction than adults, and childhood or adolescent addiction often has devastating effects. The younger a child begins using an addictive substance, the quicker and more likely is prolonged addiction. Please refer to the section on Teenagers for advice on preventing and dealing with childhood alcohol or drug problems. Help and encourage any addicted child or adolescent to use the techniques in this chapter, too.

Parents should learn to recognize the signs of drug use in children. Slurred speech, drunken behavior, or excessive drowsiness indicates the use of central nervous system depressants. If you notice any of these things, look for the smell of alcohol, the chemical smell of inhalants, or the narrowed pupils of opiate use. With barbiturates, tranquilizers, or sedative-hypnotics, none of these extra clues will exist. Other signs of inhalant use include empty spray cans, empty tubes of glue, or rags, plastic bags, paper bags, or soda cans with chemical smell or paint on them. You can recognize marijuana use by its distinctive odor on the breath, reddened or bloodshot eyes, increased coughing due to smoking, impaired concentration, or impaired short-term memory (forgetting the topic of conversation, where they just placed something, etc.). People often cover the smell of marijuana with breath mints or mouthwashes and hide the reddened eyes with eye drops, however. Discovering your child owns eye drops for redness suggests the use of marijuana.

Cocaine and the amphetamines cause widened (dilated) pupils and may cause increased energy and activity, talkativeness, restlessness, repetitious behavior such as nervous habits or overcleaning, insomnia, decreased appetite, or weight loss. Anxiety, paranoia, or hallucinations may indicate the use of cocaine, amphetamines, or hallucinogens, although inhalants may also cause hallucinations. A runny nose without allergies, a cold, flu, or sinusitis may indicate the inhalation of cocaine or amphetamines. The most serious sign of drug use is needle marks from injecting drugs. People usually inject drugs into the prominent veins in the arm, until these veins become too weak and they resort to the leg. Many intravenous drug users cover the needle marks by wearing long sleeves.

Other changes in behavior may suggest but do not prove drug use. Signs of possible drug use include mood swings, irritability, personal problems, deterioration in school performance, loss of interest in previous interests and activities, or loss of ambition. Drug use may also cause secretiveness, withdrawing to their room more often, increased rebelliousness, refusal to talk about where they go or what they do, or decreased communication and closeness with family members. Great changes in your child's social life, such as becoming a loner or dropping old friends for a new circle of friends, may occur. Such behaviors may simply come from the many changes that teenagers go through in establishing independence and developing their own personalities, but these behaviors do warrant parental concern and extra vigilance. A child's finances also provide a helpful clue to drug use. Does your child seem to go through money quickly and always to need money? Can your child account for all the money spent?

Children of alcoholics are three times as likely as other children to enter inpatient substance abuse programs, but children with no alcohol or drug problems of their own may suffer serious psychological consequences from their parents' addictions. We have already noted the increased rates of marital assault, child abuse, and delinquent children in families headed by alcoholic parents. Children of alcoholics are more likely than other children to repeat grades in school, be truant, drop out of school, or be referred to school counselors. Both alcoholics and their children may have personal problems such as depression, poor control of anger, low self-esteem, etc. Young children, often the object of the alcoholic parent's anger, may feel responsible for their parent's problems. Older children often feel ashamed of their alcoholic parent and may deny problems or avoid discussing it with other people. Some older children of alcoholics take on adult roles early in life, such as giving parents emotional support, helping raise younger children, and perfectionism. Some of these people, as adults, feel as if they have never had a childhood.

Many children of alcoholics learn to deal with their parent's mood swings by burying their own needs and emotions to avoid problems. Therefore, they find it difficult to let other people know what they need and to identify their own feelings and express them. Children who have often felt disappointed and hurt may develop severe problems with trusting other people that interfere with adult love relationships. Having learned early in life not to expect much from loved ones, they often feel uncertain and fearful in intimate relationships. They may have great conflicts about feelings of dependency, may fear losing control of their own feelings and behaviors, or may easily feel controlled by others. If you have an addicted parent, please refer to the advice at the end of this chapter on how to best deal with addicts. Depending on the circumstances, you may need to use many other chapters in this book. If you have difficulties with identifying or expressing your emotions, chapters 5, Emotions, and 6, Communication Skills, can help you. You may need to work on assertiveness, depression, getting over the past, controlling your anger, improving your self-esteem, etc.

In most cases the best way, by far, to overcome any addiction is to stop the behavior immediately and maintain complete abstinence. The only exception to this rule is the chronic use of high doses of one of the central nervous system depressants (alcohol, barbiturates, tranquilizers, sedative-hypnotics, or opiates). Because these drugs may result in dangerous withdrawal symptoms, you should consult a doctor or a drug treatment facility for advice on whether you must withdraw from use gradually and for the medical attention that you may need to safely go through this period.

Many addicted people hope to achieve moderation and refuse to completely abstain from their addictions. Unfortunately, even the most happy, stable people often spend years trying to control their addictions because of refusing to abstain completely. Attempts to behave moderately or to gradually reduce use often fail because each occasion of use or of gambling is an opportunity to go to extremes. Of course, even a mild state of intoxication lowers the inhibitions and interferes with good judgment, making a setback more likely. Although addicted people often succeed in behaving moderately for months at a time, they also tend to become overconfident, less strict with themselves, and to eventually overdo it. Refusing to abstain completely makes it extremely difficult to succeed in overcoming an addiction. Research shows the vast majority of alcoholics who try to drink moderately end up simply going in cycles of improvement and deterioration. Experts believe less than 10%, and perhaps as little as 1%, of people who abuse alcohol can succeed in moderation for the rest of their lives. Addiction most often takes a chronic course with periods of improvement, perhaps including abstinence, and periods of deterioration.

Although complete abstinence is by far the best strategy, this chapter includes helpful information on how to control use for people who foolishly insist on trying to overcome their addictions without complete abstinence. Attempting moderation is especially foolish for people who don't feel completely happy, don't have completely satisfying and very harmonious social and family relations, or don't have a good, stable work record. If more than a very few of the early items in the list of characteristics of addicted people in the beginning of this chapter apply to you, you would be very foolish to attempt moderation. Another important criterion is the ability to easily abstain from your addiction for two consecutive months. Test yourself. If you can't easily do this, you would be extremely foolish to attempt moderation.

Of course, the first few weeks of abstinence are the most difficult and abstinence becomes easier as time goes on. Physical withdrawal symptoms only last a few weeks, at the most. One year followup research on alcohol, tobacco, and heroin addicts after treatment programs shows most failures in abstinence occur during the first three months after the end of the treatment program. After two or three months, people become more accustomed to abstinence and maintaining it becomes much easier. Keeping this in mind can keep you motivated during the difficult first week or first month.

Keep busy with tasks and interests and activities to prevent many of the addictive desires that arise when you feel bored. Keeping busy also helps a great deal in coping with urges and cravings when they do arise. The exhilaration of heavy exercise and the excitement of participating in a sport make good substitutes for the euphoria of addiction. The best replacement activities are enjoyable but require some concentration or involve other people. If it is inconvenient or impossible to do most things, you can often talk with someone, whistle, or mentally go through one of your favorite songs or prayers. Another possibility is making a constant mental commentary or description of the colors and details of people and things you see in your environment, such as architecture, nature, clothing, etc. Or you could read a book or solve crossword puzzles you keep with you for such occasions.

Please refer to chapter 8 for a full discussion of the importance of interests and activities. Boredom is common in addicts. Many have forgotten the things they used to enjoy doing before they became addicted. Use the information in chapter 8 to develop a wide range of interests and activities and to plan what you will do to keep busy. To avoid problems, make a chart every week of your planned activities for next week. Put every waking hour of each day on the left side of your chart and put the days of the week across the top. Fill in the chart with drug-free work and leisure activities, making sure you have at least half an hour each day of relaxing or fun activities you really enjoy.

Many people habitually indulge in their addictions to unwind at the end of the day. Find more constructive ways of relaxing. Good alternatives include a hot soak in the bathtub, paying for a massage, trading massages with someone, sunbathing, pleasurable interests and activities, meditation, or relaxation. Very busy people may need to make time for relaxing or fun activities, at least half an hour each day. Daily meditation or practice of any of the relaxation skills in chapter 10, Stress, can increase inner peace and help overcome addiction. With continued practice of meditation or relaxation, many people begin to experience peak moments of joy and serenity. Practicing relaxation also makes a good substitute for addictive behaviors whenever desires or cravings occur.

Simple temptation often leads to a setback or failure. The common mistake of keeping such things as alcohol, cigarettes, ashtrays, drugs, or drug paraphernalia in the house often leads to problems. Other sources of temptation include certain people and places such as parties, bars, gambling places, trips out of town where friends or family members won't know what you do, homes of friends who use the drug, or a person who deals drugs. Avoid temptations if possible. If passing by a particular place tempts you, choose a path that avoids it. Never tempt yourself just to test your control over the addiction.

If you must place yourself in a tempting situation, plan strategies for success. If going out of town on business tempts you greatly, you might call your spouse early and late each evening to make yourself act responsibly. If you must pass a place of temptation on your way home from work, read a list of your reasons for abstaining every day before passing the place. Even when you feel extremely confident about withstanding a particular temptation, plan ways to increase your chances for success. Before going to a bar, you might inform family members and ask them to check on you after you arrive home, to make you feel more accountable for your actions. Upon arriving at the home of friends who use drugs, announce your decision to abstain and ask that they not tempt you with any offers.

All addicted people should use behavioral roleplays to practice saying no to temptations from friends. Practice both simple offers and situations in which other people repeatedly urge you to drink, use, or gamble. Practice dealing with repeated requests that come with flattery, insistence, begging, or taunts such as, "Oh, come on! Are you too good for us now?" Find and perfect a number of good responses you feel comfortable using when other people pressure you. Use good eye contact and a clear, firm, unhesitating voice. Change the subject or turn away from the person to show you don't want to discuss it anymore.

Study your problem as described in chapter 9 to understand your high-risk situations for failures in abstinence. You must learn to change your routine habits of addictive behavior. Many people indulge in their addictions at parties, picnics and cookouts, beaches or nature parks, fishing or boating, card games, playing billiards, watching television or sporting events, vacations, traveling, etc. Many people indulge to celebrate when happy, joyous, or excited, and some people are at high risk any time they possess much money. Plan to use strategies from this chapter that will help you in these situations. For example, if having money is a problem for you, let your spouse or parents take control of your paycheck for several months until you are in better control. Read your list of reasons for abstinence just before attending any celebration, party, family outing, trip, or sporting event, and ask all of your friends and family members to remind you and urge abstinence whenever temptations arise.

It is especially dangerous to use an addiction to cope. Pay particular attention to any high-risk situation in which addiction seems to help you cope. If you don't have much fun at a party without alcohol or marijuana, you need to learn to have fun at parties without becoming intoxicated. If you can't flirt comfortably in bars or at parties without alcohol, you need to learn to flirt without drinking. Whenever you can't do something nearly as well, nearly as comfortably, or nearly as enjoyably without your addictive crutch as you can with it, you need to practice that skill until you can do it as well without the addictive behavior.

Negative emotions are very common high-risk situations. Unpleasant emotions, interpersonal conflicts, and temptations from friends account for 3/4 of the failures in abstinence reported by alcoholics, cigarette smokers, and heroin addicts. Stresses such as a baby, unruly children, job pressures and deadlines, or financial problems may lead to trouble. Don't use addictive behaviors to cope with frustration, disappointment, irritation, anger, boredom, restlessness, anxiety, worry, sadness, depression, grief, or loneliness. If any of these sometimes lead you to drink, use, or gamble, please refer to the appropriate chapters in this book (problem solving, raising children, assertiveness, etc.) to learn how to deal with the negative emotion or problem situation in more constructive ways. Learn to voice frustrations and problem solve before tensions mount and explosive anger leads to drinking.

Thoughts play a very important role in maintaining the confidence, hope, and determination needed to conquer any addiction.   Addiction treatment programs sometimes claim exaggerated success rates because psychologists realize that the client who has confidence in the program gains the advantages of the placebo effect and the self-fulfilling prophecy. Please refer to the list of negative thoughts and helpful thought alternatives associated with addiction in chapter 4, and consider the impact of such thoughts on a person's confidence, hope, and determination. Some people never even attempt abstinence because of negative thoughts about their ability to succeed! Study your own negative thoughts about addiction and replace them with positive thought alternatives every day as described in chapter 4.

Don't dwell on your thoughts of desire and build urges up into intense cravings. Urges and cravings will arise, peak, lessen, and go away over time, usually within 15 minutes. Study the problem situation and learn to avoid the people, places, thoughts, and feelings that trigger urges and cravings. Cope by distracting yourself with activities, talking it out with a supportive friend, or using helpful thought alternatives like, "If I just wait, this urge will go away," or "Don't give up now. Remember how hard it was on the first day?" Strengthen your determination with thoughts such as, "I'm going to make it. It'll take time and plenty of work but I'm not giving up!"

Positive thinking can even help you deal with withdrawal symptoms. The results of an experiment with alcoholics emphasize the importance of thinking in withdrawal symptoms. Withdrawal symptoms such as muscle tremors (the shakes) and cravings for alcohol often improved when researchers misled alcoholics into believing they had consumed some alcohol. Cultivate the attitude that you won't experience withdrawal symptoms and that you can ignore or tolerate any withdrawal symptoms you do experience. For example, "A little headache and irritability won't stop me! The important thing is it'll be over soon and I'll be through with this addiction at last!" (As noted previously, the dangerous withdrawal symptoms from ending the chronic use of high doses of alcohol, barbiturates, tranquilizers, sedative-hypnotics, or opiates require a doctor's supervision.)

Your thoughts about failures in abstinence are especially important. Never lose hope and give up because of a setback, even for just a few days; this is the most dangerous time. Addicted people often let one mistake lead to a spree of drinking, using, or gambling. Instead, renew your commitment and ask for help. Learn from the mistake. Identify seemingly irrelevant small decisions as early as possible in the chain of events that led to the problem. Plan and practice better responses to similar future situations as described in chapter 11, Easy Changes. Even if you have often failed, there is always hope. Many people succeed in conquering an addiction only after having tried and failed many times. Inconsistent progress is normal.

Be sure to use the techniques for fighting denial and keeping motivated described in chapter 11. Use the previous information on characteristics of addicted people and on the negative effects of addictive substances to list negative things about your addiction. Be graphic about the worst possible outcomes, including items such as *losing my spouse and home because of my addiction, endlessly coughing and fighting to breathe in the hospital with emphysema because of cigarettes, raising a mentally retarded and deformed child because of alcohol,* and *becoming impotent because of alcohol.* Ask your friends and relatives to think of times when they felt embarrassed, disappointed, worried, angry, hurt, or upset by your problem behavior.

Perhaps you failed to do something as scheduled or promised because of your addiction. Add these episodes to your list of negative items. A list of the benefits of abstinence could include *increased respect from other people* and *saving the money I used to waste and buying a car.*

Use the information in this chapter about common patterns to make your list of high-risk situations. Your list of coping techniques should include behaviors suggested in this chapter and helpful thought alternatives such as: "I always fool myself by thinking that just one drink won't hurt, then I get loosened up and keep on drinking. I've got to beat this pattern. Don't even have one drink," "Celebrations are my weak spot. I'll spend my time with the nondrinking people in the group," and "I'm doing great so far with 12 days of abstinence. Let's not mess up now!" Read all these lists every day. Keep the list of negative things about your addiction and the list of coping techniques with you, so you can read them whenever desires or cravings arise or you face a temptation or a high-risk situation.

Involve as many of your friends and family members as possible in helping you change, using the advice in chapter 12. Ask all your friends and loved ones not to offer you the opportunity to drink, use, or gamble. You may also need to ask these people to abstain in your presence. Try to find a friend or loved one who will quit an addiction along with you, even if you have different addictions. You can help and encourage each other as described in chapter 12, especially during times of great temptation. Spending more time with people who abstain is one of the most important things you can do. Bring an abstinent friend with you to parties and tempting places. Make new friends who abstain. The more your social life revolves around people who abstain, the more likely you will succeed. Go places and do things where alcohol is not available.

Support groups in which people help each other overcome addictions (see the end of this chapter) are also excellent resources. A new eight-year study by the federal government found Alcoholics Anonymous was just as successful in reducing drinking sharply as two types of psychotherapy. Internal surveys of Alcoholics Anonymous members suggest that new members who remain for at least three months have more than a 50% chance of abstaining for the following year and that if abstinence lasts one year, members have an 86% chance of remaining abstinent a second year.

Increase your chances of success by rewarding yourself when you accomplish specific goals. You might want to celebrate each of your first four weeks of abstinence and then every month of abstinence thereafter, or you could set aside money that you normally would have spent on your addiction for special rewards for yourself.

Personal problems cause stress that can help maintain an addiction or cause a failure in abstinence. Improving personal problems such as marital troubles, problems with children, job dissatisfaction, loneliness, or bad temper may help you permanently conquer your addiction. Carefully consider each of the problem areas of this book to find and work on your personal problems. Don't overwhelm yourself, however. Work on only one or two simple problem areas at a time (chapter 11, Easy Changes).

Because moderation in addiction is such a dangerous, difficult thing to attempt, people who foolishly refuse abstinence should make and faithfully follow very strict rules about how and when they will indulge. Make rules in terms of specific situations and amounts, and make them strict enough to greatly reduce the danger of an uncontrolled episode. A married alcoholic might use the following rule: he may drink alcohol only when he and his wife go out and have only one beer or wine every hour and a half. Another alcoholic attempting moderation might limit herself to two cups of wine during any evening, once a week. Someone addicted to marijuana might indulge in three inhalations from a pipe, one evening a week. Limit both the amount of time and the money available for the addiction, bringing only enough money for the drinks you plan.

People who refuse abstinence should also pay close attention to their feelings and reasons for drinking, using, or gambling each time they do so. Take a time out of twenty minutes anytime you want to indulge, and pinpoint your feelings and think about why you want to indulge. This helps avoid impulsiveness and helps in understanding the patterns associated with your problem. If the urge relates to stresses, negative emotions, or interpersonal conflicts, find more appropriate ways of dealing with the problem.

Alcoholics should switch from straight hard liquor to beer, wine, or mixed drinks with only one ounce of hard liquor and should use nonalcoholic drinks between alcoholic ones. Avoid your favorite drinks and sweet drinks, which mask the taste of liquor and go down quickly. Spend more time on both alcoholic and nonalcoholic drinks by slowly sipping very small amounts and by setting your drink down and waiting at least one minute before taking another sip. In bars, you can add ice or additional mixer or refill your cup with water and sip it slowly as if it was hard liquor. Never drive a motor vehicle while intoxicated. Take a taxi, sleep overnight with your friends, ask a friend to drive you home, or take turns with a friend, date, or spouse remaining abstinent to drive.

Alcohol and drug treatment programs are an excellent resource. You can receive weekly addiction counseling sessions or you can live in a residential treatment facility while you learn to adjust to abstinence. The American Psychiatric Association (APA) guidelines now recommend that addicts whose lives focus on substance abuse, who lack social and vocational skills, and who live in drug-infested surroundings with few drug-free friends to help them should enter residential treatment programs for at least three months. If you have a severe addiction and you don't know whether you need a residential program, read chapter 41 before getting a professional opinion because many privately owned addiction treatment hospitals tend to recommend hospitalization rather easily to make money. If you do need a residential program, perhaps your friends and family members can provide 24-hour supervision as a cheap alternative as described later in this chapter. The APA guidelines indicate most cocaine addicts need intensive outpatient treatment, meaning counseling sessions more than two times a week.

Some medicines can help. Bupropion (Zyban or Wellbutrin) doubles the success rate in quitting smoking cigarettes. Doctors can prescribe naltrexone (Previs) to block the high of heroin or other opiates or reduce the craving for alcohol. Disulfiram (Antabuse) helps reliable, motivated alcoholics by making them violently ill if they ingest alcohol, but it can be dangerous if you don't follow your doctor's instructions carefully or if you have certain other physical conditions. Acamprosate is another new medicine for alcoholism. Some heroin or opiate addicts can quit, but many will need long-term maintenance on methadone or on LAAM. There are also medicines for certain withdrawal symptoms. These drugs can help a great deal but alone they are not enough. You should also get counseling, go to support group meetings, and work on the things in this chapter with all your friends helping.

Even if you succeed in remaining abstinent or moderate in your addiction for months, you may resume your addiction months or years later. As noted previously, addiction usually takes a chronic course with addicts going in cycles between improvement and deterioration. Research suggests sobriety requires three to five years to become stable. Therefore, check on your own continued progress regularly and renew your efforts at self-improvement whenever necessary as described in the last paragraph in chapter 11, Easy Changes, to ensure long-term success.

Alcoholics should learn to use a variety of nonalcoholic drinks to satisfy their thirst and serve to company. Some possibilities include fruit juices, carbonated beverages, hot or iced tea mixes, and bouillon. Try blending two or more juices or blending juices with carbonated drinks. Hot juices taste good served with spices such as cinnamon. You can mix yogurt, crushed frozen banana pieces, or crushed ice with fruits and juices in blenders for tasty drinks, and you can crush ice in blenders for slushes flavored with fruit juices or with carbonated beverages. Some people enjoy drinking tonic water or soda water instead of alcohol.

The addiction to tobacco includes a nervous habit: the hand and mouth movements of smoking. The prescription Nicotrol Inhaler meets these needs while providing nicotine to reduce withdrawal symptoms. Many other hand or mouth movements help, too. Try puffing on plastic straws cut in half to mimic cigarettes or nibbling or sucking on toothpicks, perhaps the flavored variety. You may prefer to slowly sip a glass of cold water, chew sugarless gum, suck on a clove, or nibble on carrot or celery sticks whenever you feel the urge to smoke. You can also use foods such as fruits, vegetable slices, crackers, nuts, or cheese, but nibble on mostly low calorie foods. If you begin to gain weight, switch to straws, toothpicks, cold water, sugarless gum, cloves, or lower calorie foods. It also helps to keep your hands busy by doodling, playing with a pen or pencil, knitting, gardening, etc.

Fortunately, people generally find the urge to smoke tobacco passes in a few minutes if they don't dwell on it, especially if they keep busy. Spending time in libraries, museums, movies, and other places with rules against smoking can help during the difficult first weeks of abstinence. If you miss the stimulant action of nicotine, which wakes you or perks you up, substitute naturally stimulating activities. These include a cool shower, drinking ice water or cold juice, eating a frozen juice bar, melting ice cubes in your mouth, stretching, jogging in place for a minute, a brisk walk, or exercise.

Tobacco smokers often smoke after meals or when drinking coffee or alcohol. Plan strategies to help you overcome these habits. Possibilities include brushing your teeth and then washing the dishes or going for a walk immediately after meals, switching from coffee to tea or hot spiced juices, and reading your list of reasons for quitting tobacco before drinking alcohol.

Nicotine patches, available without a prescription in over-the-counter sales, reduce tobacco withdrawal symptoms by providing a steady, precise dose of nicotine directly to the bloodstream through skin absorption. Nicotine gum, a less convenient alternative also available over the counter, can cause upset the stomach if you don't follow the directions carefully and can stick to dental work such as false teeth or caps and cause damage. It also requires avoiding all foods and especially acidic drinks like soda pop, coffee, fruit juices, and beer for 15 minutes before using the gum because they interfere with absorption of the nicotine. Like smoking, doctors recommend pregnant women and nursing mothers avoid nicotine patches and gum.

One study suggests that the best way to quit smoking may be to use the clock to gradually increase the time interval between cigarettes before quitting. In the study, smokers cut back by 1/3 the number of daily cigarettes each week until they reached 2 to 4 cigarettes a day, then the next week, they quit smoking completely. However, they could only smoke at the scheduled time. For example, if the day's limit was 16 cigarettes, they could have one at each hour while they were awake. If they didn't smoke by five minutes past the hour, they had to skip the cigarette and wait for the next hour. When compared to those who quit cold turkey or those who cut down gradually without scheduling by the clock, people who reduced by the clock had fewer withdrawal symptoms, less tension during the quit week, and more success in abstinence at followup one month, six months, and one year later. Timing cigarettes by the clock probably helps break the habits associated with smoking, and it also gives you practice in quitting for longer and longer periods of time.

Don't carry cigarettes with you when you want to abstain, on errands, for example. Smoke less of each cigarette and make sure you don't increase the number of cigarettes you smoke. Finally, if you can't quit smoking tobacco on your own, many hospitals and local chapters of the American Lung Association, American Cancer Society, and American Heart Association (see under hotlines at the end of this chapter) all offer free or low-cost treatment programs.

We shall conclude this chapter with information and advice for the close friends and family members of addicts. Unfortunately, people often unknowingly contribute to the addictions of their loved ones in subtle ways, sometimes by denying problems long after evidence for the addiction exists. For example, "He's a heavy drinker, but he's no alcoholic!" You may deny the problem because of shame, because of your inability to face the truth, or to protect your loved one. Denial by friends and loved ones helps addicts deny their problems and avoid improvement. Don't be afraid to face or admit the truth! If you sometimes wonder whether a loved one has an addiction, use the list of characteristics of addicted people near the beginning of this chapter to better understand the situation.

A fruitless battle of wills over the addiction can easily contribute to the problem, too. Close friends and family members may plead, beg, criticize, nag, argue, scold, yell in anger, hide or discard the alcohol or drug, or make telephone calls or physical searches for the person to interfere with the drinking, use, or gambling. Addicts usually resent attempts to control their behavior and often respond with further addictive behavior to assert their independence ("Nobody is going to tell me what to do!"). They may also resort to further episodes to relieve negative feelings such as anger, guilt, or depression that come from the criticism or anger of loved ones. We shall soon describe some useful ways to confront and coerce an addict, but a prolonged battle of wills does more to promote addiction than to end it.

Loving acts of loyalty, help, and protection can make it easier for the person to continue the addiction. This pattern begins innocently enough when loved ones help smooth over the rare problems caused by early episodes of the addiction. As addicts become less reliable, their loved ones often find themselves comforting the person (during hangovers, after gambling losses, etc.), hiding problems, making excuses (to friends, school authorities, employers, etc.), taking over chores, or making family decisions or paying overdue debts for the person. As the addiction progresses, loved ones may cover bad checks, find the addict a new job, fix a wrecked automobile, or bail them out of jail. These acts of loyalty shield addicts from the full consequences of their actions, teach them they won't have to take care of problems they create, and make it easier for them to deny their problems and continue their irresponsible ways.

The closest loved ones try their best to cope and sometimes go to great lengths to help. They may, at times, worry so much they can't get to sleep. They may feel they had no choice but to take over responsibilities for the person. The wife of an alcoholic, for example, may exhaust herself because she feels she must run the family alone, try to keep her husband out of trouble, and minister to his shifting moods. All too often, the family becomes socially isolated. Friends may drift away as the addiction and family problems intensify. Family themselves may turn down invitations and eliminate many social activities because of shame or fear of embarrassing episodes. Family members often become less close with their friends, too, because they feel reluctant to share their problems and emotional pain. Sometimes spouses and parents sacrifice their own interests and activities to keep an eye on the addict.

If you contribute to an addiction in any of the above ways or if an addicted person's behavior interferes with your happiness, use the following advice to help promote the addict's recovery and to become as happy as you can despite the problems. First, make sure you have a full and satisfying life of your own. Besides helping you cope, this will make you best able to help the addict.   As detailed previously in chapter 8, you need well-rounded interests and activities. Keep busy so you won't dwell on the other person's problems and become upset. If you feel lonely or have become isolated because of the other person's addiction, develop new friends as described in chapter 15. Reestablish ties with old friends and relatives. You should have several very close friends and a number of other friends, some closer than others, but all free of addiction.   If you have children, help them do these things, too.

Work on any problems you have using the appropriate chapters of this book. You may need to work on your marriage, on getting over the past, or on problem emotions such as anger, worry, depression, or low self-esteem. Don't scold, nag, lecture, preach, blame, act like a martyr, yell, threaten, punish, or retaliate. Instead, notice and praise good behaviors and use the good problem-solving skills of chapter 9 and communication skills of chapter 6. Make sure when you complain, you focus on specific behaviors (actions, words, tone of voice, or facial expressions), rather than on vague complaints, blaming, or attacking the person's character. Use good listening skills to understand and clarify the other person's point of view. Use chapter 28 to help prevent and minimize anger in your relationship with the addict. Never try to confront, argue with, or reason with an intoxicated person. Do these things only when the person is sober. Refuse to blame yourself for the addict's problems, even if you are the parent. They are not your fault.

Use the group confrontation technique described in chapter 12, Help from Other People, to persuade the addict to go to counseling or make drastic steps toward improvement.   Each participant should prepare for the confrontation by using the list of characteristics of addicted people near the beginning of this chapter to help remember episodes from the past. Parents can send their children for alcohol or drug evaluation or treatment, including sending addicted children into alcohol or drug treatment facilities for detoxification, against the minor's will. Any parent considering a residential alcohol or drug treatment center for their child should read chapter 41 for important advice before getting a professional opinion.

If addicts agree to work on the addiction but refuse to get professional help, you can still help them in many ways. First, help them use all the advice in this chapter. The more friends giving emotional support and monitoring their progress, the better. Encourage them to join Alcoholics Anonymous, Narcotics Anonymous, or Gamblers Anonymous. Parents can use one of the home kits available in drug stores for detecting drug abuse, such as Dr. Brown's, Parent's Alert, At Home, or First Check, to confront a child with the truth or to enforce consequences. However, be careful, especially if your teenager is not yet abusing drugs—it can worsen difficult parent-child relations. These tests are especially useful for the relatives and loved ones of people recently released from drug abuse rehabilitation centers. Although people can beat these tests unless you use them daily, they do help fight denial and increase responsibility.

If necessary, friends or family members can provide 24-hour supervision and take control of the addict's finances and automobile. This can often work as a cheap alternative to hospitalization when there is no threat of dangerous withdrawal from chronic, heavy use of alcohol, barbiturates, tranquilizers, sedative-hypnotics, or opiates. You can deprive addicts of the opportunity to indulge if you always stay with them except for work and school, keep their car keys, and drive them to and from school or work. Pick up their paychecks with them, and give them only the money they absolutely need, with strict accounting of where all the money goes. With cooperation from the addict, this procedure is only necessary during the first month or two of abstinence until the addict develops enough self-control to stay abstinent.

Adapt this procedure to the circumstances. The addicted person may need to move back home to the family, or family and friends may take turns staying with the addict. You may also need to seize credit cards and bank checkbooks, prepare bag lunches so the addict can't hoard lunch money, and ask concerned coworkers to verify the amount spent on lunch. If necessary, ask friends to drive the addict to and from work or school, or ask concerned friends or neighbors to report the time the addict arrived home from work or school on the bus. In some cases, you may even need to keep the car keys on your person at night or to lock up money, credit cards, and bank books at home, in a bank safety deposit box, or at a trusted friend or relative's home.

Parents of an addicted teenager can enforce such a regimen without the permission of the teenager, but obviously, providing constant supervision and taking control of an adult's finances and automobile requires some sort of submission, no matter how reluctant or complaining. This procedure has the greatest chance of success when the addict agrees to the need for such drastic measures, although even reluctant submission indicates at least part of the person agrees to the need.

You might push for change by temporarily breaking off your friendship or romance, leaving the person and living somewhere else, or throwing the person out of your house until long-term abstinence occurs. A parent can't throw a minor out, however, without providing another place to stay such as a relative's home, a tent in the backyard, or the home of a willing friend. You can give notice that you plan to do one of these things if the addict doesn't begin treatment or doesn't show great improvement within a specified time. Don't angrily threaten the person. Express your love, say you cannot tolerate the addiction any longer, share your regret at needing to take this action, and express the hope that this consequence pushes the person to improve. Make sure the person feels your love and understands you want to help. You may find it very difficult to follow through on this, but these drastic measures may provide the addict with the motivation to change. If change or improvement doesn't occur, at least you will be better off in the long run without the addict.

Some friends and family members resort to calling the police on addicted people who use drugs or who drive while intoxicated. You can warn addicts that you plan to call the police if serious problems continue and they refuse to go to counseling. Before calling the police, however, carefully consider all the possible consequences. Never do this impulsively or in anger. First, find out what laws in your state apply to the situation, so you know the likelihood of a jail sentence or probation. Realize, too, many people acquire criminal knowledge in jail, jail may add to a person's personal problems, and prison records may interfere with finding jobs and career advancement. Will time in jail result in job loss and hardship on the family? How may the addict and other friends and family react? The addict may respect your decision and improve, hate you for it, leave you, or become even more troublesome. Friends and family may support you or become angry with you. If you do decide to call the police, share your regret the action is necessary and express the hope that facing the consequences sooner rather than later will help prevent a life of addiction.

You can bluff about breaking off a friendship or romance, changing living arrangements, or calling the police, but you lose credibility if the other person doesn't cooperate and you fail to follow through. If you can make a second bluff sound more serious than the first, it may work, but don't bluff repeatedly without any resulting improvement; this only teaches the addict not to take you seriously.

If a planned confrontation worries you, practice it in behavioral roleplays until you feel comfortable dealing with all the possibilities that might occur. Using meditation or deep relaxation before the encounter may help reduce anxiety. Breathe deeply and stretch or relax muscle tension in your body just before and during the confrontation. If you can't bring yourself to set firm consequences alone, get someone to help you. You may need only the physical presence of a friend or family member in order to stand firm, or the other person can take over for you when you need it.

Instead of carrying on a prolonged battle of wills, accept the fact the addiction is ultimately the responsibility of the addict. Concentrate on developing a satisfying life for yourself despite the addict's problems. Don't compromise yourself. Refuse to ride with an intoxicated person who insists on driving. If the addict regularly puts you in this position, carry a set of car keys, leave early so you can drive yourself home, and arrange for someone else to take the intoxicated person home. If a teenager smokes marijuana at home with friends when you leave the house, take away the teenager's keys, so the teen can't misuse your house in this way. Don't compromise yourself by joining in an addiction, either. Never drink more alcohol to keep up with an alcoholic and never try drugs to prove yourself understanding or to deepen rapport with an addict.

Always act sensibly about addictive substances. If you have a party, encourage snacks and activities more than alcohol. Toward the end of the party, put the alcohol away and serve snacks or some of the drink alternatives previously mentioned. Because of the dangers of secondhand smoke, insist that people go outside to smoke cigarettes or set aside one room for smoking and open a window there enough to ventilate the room. Remember that blowing the smoke away from adults or children is not enough.

Let addicted people suffer the natural consequences of their behaviors. Don't tend to needs or solve problems resulting from an addiction. Refuse to make excuses for the addict to friends, school authorities, or employers. You don't need to offer information that will cause problems; just let the addict deal with it. You should, however, talk in a calm and honest way to children in the family about the problem to help relieve their fears and worries. Don't comfort a gambler after a big loss, help an alcoholic to bed, comfort or clean up after a vomiting alcoholic, nor comfort an alcoholic with a hangover. Call emergency help, however, if a helpless drunk vomits and might drown in it or if a very confused or incoherent drunk progresses to seeming asleep but doesn't respond to shouting or pinching (coma) or stops breathing. Don't do laundry for or clean up after an addicted teenager who doesn't help around the house. Don't pay overdue debts, cover bad checks, nor fix a wrecked automobile for an addict. If an addict loses a job, gets thrown out of school, or lands in jail, let that person deal with the problem without your help. Even parents and spouses have no obligation to bail an addict out of jail or pay for addiction counseling or treatment. The sooner addicted people must deal with and pay for the problems they create, the better.

Letting addicts take responsibility for their own problems helps them and generally makes your life easier, too. Don't give up if the addict becomes angry at you or if other people criticize you for this approach. Simply explain psychologists recommend this approach as a way of forcing addicted people to take responsibility for their own actions. If refusing to bail the addict out of jail will probably cause the loss of a job, however, carefully consider the needs of the whole family. If the family really needs the money and a comparable job will be difficult to find, you probably won't want to risk paying such a high price to teach the addict one lesson.

It is only natural that your relationship with the addicted person will improve if abstinence or great improvement occurs. Be sure to show you feel closer to the person during these times and to express more joy in the relationship. These natural consequences help. Regularly notice and praise any nice, helpful, or caring behaviors you see. Refuse to go to movies and other events when the person has been drinking. If the drinking improves emotional communication or facilitates sex, work on improving these things without it.

If the addict tries to improve, help in any way you can. Encourage interests and activities as substitutes for addictive behaviors, give rides to support group meetings, monitor progress, praise improvements, ask the person to call you when cravings occur, etc. Use the information in chapter 12 to help without interfering. Show patience, too; addicts often have setbacks. If a setback occurs, get a renewed commitment and encourage learning from the mistake in the ways described previously. Do this quickly—don't wait for things to get bad. Finally, support groups for people with addicted loved ones are excellent resources (see below).

Recommended Additional Readings:

The Recovery Book. Al J. Mooney, Arlene Eisenberg, and Howard Eisenberg. NY: Workman Publishing, 1992. excellent, comprehensive book dealing with all phases of recovery including deciding to quit, inpatient treatment, rules for detoxification, medical aspects, recognizing addiction in a child, etc.

Support Groups and Hotlines:

National Drug and Alcohol Hotline 800 662 4357 (Spanish 800 662 9832 9am to 3am EST) referrals to local treatment and counseling centers, information on drug and alcohol issues.

National Clearinghouse for Alcohol and Drug Information 800 729 6686 information and referrals. on-line: www.health.org

Alcohol and Drug Hotline 800 821 4357 referrals to support groups and treatment centers.

National Council on Alcoholism and Drug Dependence 800 622 2255 or 800 475 4673 information, literature, referrals to treatment. on-line: www.ncadd.org

Alcoholics Anonymous 212 870 3400 information and referrals to support groups. on-line: www.alcoholics-anonymous.org

Cocaine Anonymous 800 347 8998 or 310 559 5833 information and referrals to support groups. on-line: www.ca.org

Narcotics Anonymous 818 773 9999 information in several languages and referrals to support groups. on-line: www.wsoinc.com

Gamblers Anonymous 213 386 8789 information and referrals to support groups. on-line: www.gamblersanonymous.org

Families Anonymous 800 736 9805 information and referrals to support groups for family members and friends concerned about a loved one's drug or alcohol abuse. on-line: www.familiesanonymous.org

Al-Anon/Alateen 888 425 2666 or 800 356 9996 for support groups for those dealing with alcoholic loved ones. on-line: www.al-anon.org

Adult Children of Alcoholics 310 534 1815 information, support groups for those who suffered from their parents' alcoholism. on-line: www.adultchildren.org

Secular Organizations for Sobriety 310 821 8430 support groups without an emphasis on spirituality or religion. on-line: www.secularsobriety.org

Women for Sobriety 215 536 8026 on-line: www.womenforsobriety.org

American Lung Association 212 315 8700 information, referrals to support groups for quitting smoking tobacco. on-line: www.lungusa.org

American Cancer Society 800 227 2345 information, referrals to support groups for quitting smoking tobacco. on-line: www.cancer.org

American Heart Association 800 242 8721 information, referrals to support groups for quitting smoking tobacco. on-line: www.americanheart.org

34. Nervous Habits

Substitute either healthy or hidden, tiny actions for bad habits.

Nervous habits include such things as biting or picking fingernails, pulling or twirling hair, tapping fingers, and folding lips. Begin working on a nervous habit by studying the kinds of situations in which it usually occurs. Because of embarrassment, many people do it mostly in private or only around family members.   Nervous habits often occur when you watch television, study, or read. If problem emotions such as boredom or anxiety trigger it, work on them using the appropriate chapters in this book. Make a list of the situations in which you usually do your nervous behavior, and read it daily as a reminder of the high-risk situations that need special attention.

Urges to engage in a nervous habit normally last only a few seconds or minutes, and you can easily replace them with other things. Substitute any of the relaxation techniques in chapter 10, Stress, both when urges arise and when you notice yourself absent-mindedly engaging in the habit. Even very simple relaxation skills such as improving your posture, stretching, and releasing bodily tension help as substitutes, and you can also substitute tasks, interests, or activities for urges. When it is inconvenient or impossible to do most things, substitute simple activities such as chatting with someone, whistling, or mentally going through one of your favorite songs. Activities that keep your hands busy, such as doodling, playing with a pen, doing crossword puzzles, knitting, and gardening, make especially useful substitutes.

In any situation, you can replace nervous habits with finger pressing. Lightly press a thumb and finger together or press a finger on the arm of your seat, on a book while you read it, or on the steering wheel of an automobile. Do this finger pressing so lightly that nobody would notice it. Avoid the prolonged use of substitute activities like doodling, playing with a pen or pencil, and finger pressing, however, because this may build a new nervous habit.

Conquering a nervous habit will get easier as time goes on, but many people resume such habits automatically after a short period of determined effort. Therefore, check on your own continued progress regularly and renew your efforts at self-improvement whenever necessary, in the ways described in the last paragraph in chapter 11, Easy Changes.

35. Obesity and Eating Disorders

Lose weight by keeping busy, finding better ways
to deal with emotions, eating better, and exercising.

Standards of beauty change over time and differ between cultures. Although modern Western culture is obsessed with excessive thinness, most other cultures prefer fleshy, plump women. Primitive and farming cultures more often prize heavy women than thin women, perhaps because they view heavy women as strong, healthy workers and perhaps because the threat of famine makes obesity a sign of success and prestige. Certain societies viewed massively obese women in the king's harem as the ultimate female sex partners. Some cultures preferring fat women even send young women away from home for fattening up before marriage for up to two years. Paintings show people of Western cultures, too, preferred fleshy women in the past.

Unfortunately, prejudice and discrimination against fat people is now widespread. People often view fat people as unattractive, lazy, lacking in self-discipline, emotionally troubled, or plagued with physical problems. Prejudice against fat people results in harassment in school, rejection in dating and romance, diminished closeness in relationships, and marital and romantic abandonment. Obese women are far less likely to marry than other women and when they do, they are far more likely to fall in social class. Discrimination against fat people exists even in college admissions and employment, especially against fat women. One study found obese women stood only one-third the chance of acceptance in college of thinner women, despite the same levels of intelligence and achievement. There is evidence for discrimination against fat people in hiring, job placement, promotion, discipline at work, and wages. Other studies suggest almost half of employers prefer not to hire obese women and that weight loss often results in increased employment or better pay.

Many women struggle all their lives not to become too fat because our society views physical attractiveness as more important for women than for men. A recent study of 800 adult women of all ages found nearly half felt dissatisfied with their bodies overall. Other studies suggest many people of both sexes perceive their bodies to be larger than they really are, with women exaggerating size more than men. Our cultural obsession with thinness also affects children. Research on children in middle school suggests about half of young adolescent girls want to lose weight because they feel they look fat.

Because of ingrained prejudice and discrimination, many obese people suffer from low self-esteem, depression, loneliness, etc. Eating in response to negative feelings can lead to a vicious cycle in which gaining additional weight causes more personal problems, you feel bad and eat more, you gain more weight, etc. Unfortunately, many people become truly obese after and partly because other people have labeled them fat and ridiculed or rejected them. Resorting to food for comfort and resigning themselves to the social role of obesity, the negative label can become a self-fulfilling prophecy. Don't eat in response to frustrations. Instead, use the appropriate chapters in this book to deal with negative emotions constructively.

Sometimes obesity is a safe refuge that helps avoid dealing with sexual relationships. Because obesity provides a convenient excuse for rejection, overweight people who feel inadequate sometimes find it easier to become obese than to compete in dating popularity. Overweight people who have experienced rejection in romance may find it easier to become obese and avoid sexual relationships than face the possibility of repeated painful loss, or a spouse may become obese, in part, as a way of avoiding unsatisfying marital sex. If you think you might use obesity in this way, work on more constructive ways of dealing with problems in self-esteem, socializing, dating, or sex using the appropriate chapters in this book.

Obesity can also become, in part, a weapon for revenge, to punish other people. Wives may punish their husbands with obesity, and children, their parents. If you think you might use obesity in this way, work on expressing your anger in more constructive ways or on getting over the past. Spouses using obesity for revenge need to work on improving their marriages.

Researchers link obesity with an increased risk of many physical problems: heart disease, high blood pressure, strokes, arthritis, gallstones, diabetes, gout, respiratory disorders, kidney disease, cataracts, foot problems, asthma, sleep and breathing problems, and cancers of the uterus, cervix, breasts, ovaries, gall bladder, prostate, and colon. Obesity slows wound healing and increases the risk of infection after surgery. Obese pregnant women have higher rates of babies with neural tube defects such as spinal bifida. Weight loss reduces the symptoms of arthritis, gout, and diabetes and reduces the chance of heart disease, stroke, and kidney disease. Losing just five pounds greatly lowers the risk of high blood pressure, reduces aches and pains, and makes everyday activities easier. The National Institutes of Health says that weighing even just 20% more than your ideal weight is an established health hazard. Over 60% of all Americans weigh too much for their own good and 26% are obese (grossly overweight).

Experts believe hereditary diseases, hormone problems, and brain damage cause only 5% of obesity, yet studies of twins and adopted children indicate genetic factors play an important role. Studies of adopted children, however, show family food and exercise habits also play an important role. Family food and exercise habits often make married couples similar in obesity and often make family members in a household increase and decrease in level of obesity together. The best way to maintain weight loss in any obese person with obese family members is to teach the whole family better eating and exercise habits. Genetic factors and family habits add up so that having one obese parent gives you a 40% chance of obesity in adulthood and having two obese parents gives a 70% chance.

Metabolism is all the physical and chemical processes that occur in a life form to use food and produce energy. The larger the body, the higher the metabolism. Because of individual differences in metabolism, some people put on weight rather easily and other people eat plenty of food but cannot gain weight. Two people of the same age and height who get the same amount of exercise and eat the same number of calories each day may differ in changes in weight. Metabolism also varies in the same person over time. For example, becoming overweight causes hormonal changes that make the body more efficient at making and storing fat, and these changes diminish when an overweight person loses weight. During a diet, the rate at which the body burns calories decreases as much as 15 to 25%. This helps the body conserve energy during times of famine, but makes it more difficult for people to lose weight.

Exercise should play an important role in any weight loss program. It burns more calories than does quiet activity. Exercise increases the rate at which the body burns calories for a time afterward. It may minimize the decline in metabolic rate that usually accompanies weight loss. Hunger reduces after strenuous exercise. Exercise causes the body to switch to burning more fat for fuel, probably even after exercising. If you exercise enough to build up extra muscle, you will constantly burn more calories, even while sleeping, because muscle burns more calories than fat does. Many studies show that when obese people begin exercising, their appetites do not increase. Studies show the one strongest factor in maintaining weight loss is exercise, with 95% of the people who lose weight and keep it off for 5 years having some kind of regular exercise program. Exercising regularly helps in losing weight, and quitting increases your chances of gaining weight again.

Moderately obese people succeed in losing weight more often than do extremely obese people, probably because of long-term behavior habits.

Obesity dating back to childhood tends to be more severe and less likely to change than obesity beginning in adulthood, especially in women. About 30% of obese women lose weight, but about 70% of obese men do. The earlier in life you treat obesity, the more likely you will succeed. Parents should teach their children to control their weight before severe obesity develops. Don't worry about fat babies—many of them grow into children of normal weight. If obesity increases during the years of school attendance, however, help your child eat a more healthy diet and increase physical activity. Don't use a low calorie diet on your child. Experts point out doing so may interfere with a child's growth.

Numerous frauds prey on the American public to make money because no United States law requires anyone making claims about diet advice to have any medical, nutritional, or scientific expertise. Many advertisements make false claims about spot reducing, the reduction of fat from one part of your body in particular. The truth is no equipment, exercise, or treatment can take fat off mostly one part of your body. Men tend to accumulate fat mostly on the abdomen and women on the buttocks, thighs, hips, and breasts. Diet and exercise can remove fat from the whole body, not from one part in particular, and exercise always makes muscles longer and wider. Exercise may firm an area of the body, but it will not trim that area unless you lose enough weight to overcome any increase in muscle size.

Waist belts and body wraps or suits for losing weight are also frauds. Some of these simply cover the body and others use heat or air inflation. Some retailers sell creams or pills for use with them. Retailers often claim using them will break down fat, but any weight loss really comes from sweating and lasts only until you become thirsty and drink water. The same thing happens in a sauna. In fact, excessive and rapid water loss can be dangerous. The risk of heat exhaustion or heat stroke is much greater while wearing a rubber or plastic suit. Avoid treatments for cellulite, supposedly a special kind of hard-to-remove fat. With age or excessive weight, skin loses elasticity and may show a dimpled appearance, but researchers agree there is no such thing as cellulite. Pills, lotions, special clothing, and other treatments for cellulite are frauds. Other common frauds involve electrical stimulation as an easy method of exercising or ridiculous claims about new medical discoveries for eating as much as normal and losing weight anyway.

Many unscientific theories about metabolism and weight control, often proposed by doctors, are also frauds. The idea that certain foods or food combinations somehow help in burning off calories faster has no medical basis whatsoever. One popular version is the grapefruit diet, often called the

Mayo Clinic diet, although the famous Mayo Clinic denies any association with the fraud. Grapefruit pills for dieting are a similar fraud found in many health and nutrition stores. Theories, diets, and products involving enzyme breakdown, enzymes working for you, or the reduced absorption of foods are just frauds. Unfortunately, many popular diet books that have become best sellers actually recommend unbalanced diets that can lead to nutritional deficiencies and health problems. Liquid protein diets have caused 59 deaths. High protein diets, low carbohydrate diets, low protein diets, fructose diets, fruit diets, and protein formula diets can result in such things as dehydration, dangerous breakdown of tissues in bodily organs, dizziness, weakness, nausea, heart problems, ketosis, gout, kidney stones, gastric ulcers, and even death.

Diet pills for curbing the appetite are unwise because of side effects, psychological addiction, and their ultimate ineffectiveness. Even over-the-counter diet pills can have dangerous side effects, particularly in combination with coffee, cold pills, or some medicines. All diet pills help for only several weeks, until your body builds up a physical tolerance and you need higher doses for the same effects. This tempts people to increase the dosage, a dangerous act with any diet pill. Also, diet pills substitute a temporary chemical reduction of hunger for the changes in habits you really need to maintain weight loss. Most people who use diet pills later regain all the weight they have lost. If you insist on using diet pills despite these problems, alternate one month of using them with one month dieting without them to reduce your physical tolerance every other month and practice good eating habits without the pills.

Elimination of excess water causes the impressive speed of weight loss often noted in the first week or two of any diet. After this, the rate of weight loss slows. In fact, you shouldn't lose more than two pounds per week. Hunger sensations diminish after the first week or two of a diet, not because the stomach shrinks, but because we become accustomed to eating less and perhaps because of hormonal changes in the body. Stomachs do stretch with food and this may help us feel full, but we don't feel the full effect of a meal until 10 or 15 minutes after we finish it. This explains the common experience of feeling fine immediately after a holiday meal but becoming uncomfortable later and deciding you have eaten too much.

Consult a doctor before beginning any diet or reasonably vigorous exercise program, especially if you have health problems. Sometimes a doctor will find a physical reason for the obesity. People with diabetes, bone or joint problems, stomach or intestinal problems, heart disease, kidney disease, liver problems, chest pain, or dizzy spells should definitely see a doctor before beginning any diet or exercise program. You should also see a doctor first if you have irregular heartbeats, more than 80 heartbeats per minute while resting, or a family history of high blood pressure or heart disease. The same is true if you weigh 15 pounds more than you should or use any addictive substance (tobacco, alcohol, etc.) in a fairly heavy way.

A realistic diet improves your chances of success. Don't push yourself too hard in your diet; this often leads to eating binges. Eat between 1000 and 1300 calories every day. Very thin women use the least energy but they still use up 1250 to 1350 calories each day. If you eat less than 1200 calories a day, take a multivitamin and mineral pill each day because it is almost impossible to meet these needs from food sources alone. Whenever you eat less than 1000 calories per day, your body begins to break down vital organ tissues to help meet energy needs—don't do this without a doctor's supervision. By eating between 1000 and 1300 calories each day, the average person can lose one or two pounds each week (after the first week or two of quick water weight loss). Measure your progress by weighing yourself at approximately the same time of day once a week, because weight fluctuations after meals can mislead you. Women often gain a few pounds before menstruation because of water retention.

Make sure you eat a well-balanced variety of foods from all the major food groups. Barring allergies, everyone should eat fruits, vegetables, grains, dairy products, and foods with plenty of protein, such as meat, fish, eggs, beans, peanut butter, and other nuts. Fiber-rich vegetables, fruits, and whole grains help satisfy hunger with fewer calories and less fat. With equal calories, carbohydrates satisfy hunger better than fat does. A strict diet that forbids all fattening foods will probably lead to eating sprees. Instead, create a realistic, flexible diet emphasizing nutritious foods and occasionally including small amounts of fattening foods. In this way, you learn the good eating habits you need to maintain your ideal weight after the diet.

Drink several glasses of water or juice to eliminate sensations of hunger. Drinking three glasses of water before meals reduces the amount of food you must eat to feel full. Keeping busy with tasks, interests, and activities helps prevent many of the thoughts about and desires for food that arise in boredom. When people distract themselves from hunger with activities, they often find they don't feel hungry after all. Another useful trick is to spend more time in places where you can't eat, such as libraries, museums, or walking in the woods with a canteen of water. This will eliminate many thoughts of food. Students can do their homework at the library every day instead of at home. Drink from a water fountain whenever you feel hungry in public places.

If you don't start a program of vigorous exercise, at least increase your level of daily activity. One popular form of exercise is walking fast, probably because it is cheap, easy, and very safe. Go for walks in shopping malls, parks, and the countryside. Substitute walking for short trips in which you normally use the car, perhaps to a nearby store or a friend's home. Carry your grocery bags to the car instead of taking the shopping cart. Do household chores such as yard work and washing floors more often to burn more calories and make your home more presentable. You can also get more exercise by doing household chores without modern conveniences, perhaps washing the dishes without the dishwasher, washing laundry in the bathtub, etc.

Participate in group or shared activities such as dancing, walking or bicycling with a friend, family outings, volleyball games, gym classes, health spas, etc. Exercise companions and group activities can provide extra pleasure and keep you motivated. Many new interests and activities, such as gardening or camping, add plenty of exercise. Even less strenuous activities, such as volunteer work and crafts, can add to the amount of exercise you get. Of course, calisthenics and vigorous sports such as jump rope, basketball, or tennis help a great deal.

Build up your level of activity or exercise gradually in short time periods, so you don't become tired of your regime and quit. Work on increasing walking or other exercises until you reach at least 10 minutes, 4 times daily. One study found instructions to increase exercise gradually to 10 minutes, 4 times a day, resulted in more exercise and weight loss than instructions to increase exercise gradually to one 40-minute period each day. Please refer to the section on Exercise in chapter 10, Stress, for a more detailed discussion of exercise and related health issues.

Find a diet program that plans nutritious, well-balanced meals for each day of the week. In one study, people who followed such a plan lost 50% more weight than those who attended similar meetings without detailed meal plans. Following a good plan reduces snacking by providing breakfast and lunch regularly, dictates that you buy enough fruits and vegetables, and teaches more regular and healthy eating habits.

Learn about the number of calories in various foods and put this information to use in your diet. For example, mayonnaise, butter, margarine, and vegetable oil have over twice the calories per teaspoon of sugar, brown sugar, and maple syrup. This makes fried foods, sauces, and salad dressings more fattening than equal amounts of many sweets. Meat skins, fish skins, and meat drippings used in gravies are almost entirely fat. Always remove skins from meat and fish before cooking them and either quit making gravies or make them an occasional treat. Bake, stew, or broil your meats and fish. Stores sell small books that list foods and the numbers of calories found in servings of particular sizes, and some of them include listings for many commercial brands of foods. Buy one and study it or use the government recommended web site listed at the end of this chapter. You might count all the calories you eat, perhaps using a small kitchen scale to weigh everything.

Pay attention to the labels on food products. Many of them list calories per serving and size of serving. Unfortunately, most commercially prepared foods contain unnecessarily high amounts of calories. Most cereal brands, canned soups, and frozen precooked meals include so much sugar or fat that they are very fattening. The sugar content in many sweetened cereals is higher by weight than the sugar content in cake. One cup of yogurt with fruit contains enough added sugar to total 250 calories, equivalent to a piece of cheesecake, one of the most fattening cakes. One can of creamed soup has 250 calories, too. Fruit juices and fruit drinks often contain sugar or corn syrup. Avoid fruit drinks and choose only the fruit juices that don't include sugar or corn syrup. Make your own lemonade and limeade without sugar or with much less sugar than commercial brands. Pay careful attention to the calories you consume in alcoholic beverages, too. Alcohol has no nutritional value but has many more calories than an equal amount of sugar.

Replace sweet snacks and desserts with naturally sweet fruits and juices and with artificially sweetened products. You can also replace sweets with something sour, such as a slice of lemon or lime or some cucumber with vinegar. This satisfies you by stimulating your taste buds. Use low calorie foods such as fruits, cherry tomatoes, and vegetable sticks for snacks. Freeze juices or diet drinks in small cups or ice trays for snacks. Good alternatives for salad dressings include tomato juice, lemon or lime juice, vinegar, soy sauce, salsa, and various combinations of these things, perhaps with herbs or spices. A little bit of plain yogurt makes a nutritious salad dressing, but one cup of plain yogurt has 160 calories.

Plan your grocery list and go shopping on a full stomach. This helps avoid impulsive grocery shopping. Emphasize a well-balanced variety of low calorie foods on your list and then buy only those. Dieting becomes much easier if you make fattening foods unavailable in your home. Make and pack low calorie meals for work. Don't skip any meals because this can lead to eating binges. Drink plenty of water and eat low calorie snacks. Eating smaller amounts of food more often during the day, rather than the same amount of food in one or two big meals, combats the hormonal changes that make obese bodies better at making and storing fat. When you cook a large amount of food, put the extra food away before you eat. Leaving extra food out while you eat only tempts you to eat second helpings. When you cook leftovers or just one meal, cook only the amount of food you need, not enough for second helpings. Smaller plates or bowls can also help you eat smaller amounts.

Eat slowly while paying attention to each bite. Studies show obese people chew less often per bite than other people and often finish their food so fast that they get second and third helpings while other people are still eating their first helpings. Counter habits of eating quickly by chewing your food thoroughly, putting down your fork or spoon between bites of food until you have carefully chewed and swallowed, and stopping to talk more often during meals with other people. Eating with smaller utensils such as a tiny cocktail fork or teaspoon can help. You can eat less and still enjoy your food more if you eat like a gourmet, paying careful attention to each taste and savoring each bite before you swallow it.

Don't eat to finish your plate, eat the last of the food to avoid waste, nor eat to become full. When you feel just satisfied or no longer hungry but not full, throw away the rest of the food on your plate. Put away any family leftovers, no matter how small. When other people eat dessert, either limit yourself to just one or two bites or eat a low calorie alternative such as fruit. Remember that you will feel more full 10 or 15 minutes after a meal than you do the moment you finish eating. Use this fact to help you eat less. Stop before you feel completely satisfied and wait to feel the full impact of your meal. If you finish your allotted portions and you still feel hungry, drink water, skim milk, juice, or a diet beverage to fill up.

Study your eating patterns as described in chapter 9, Problem Solving, to find eating habits contributing to your weight problem. Many people snack while watching television, reading, studying, or attending movies or sporting events. While absorbed in such activities, you tend to eat in an automatic way without thinking about it. Avoid this problem by strictly limiting the times and places in which you eat, perhaps by eating only at the kitchen table with a plate. You may want to chew sugarless gum or drink diet beverages as a substitute for food in these situations. Another common pattern is eating in response to personal problems, interpersonal conflicts, or negative emotions. Do you eat when you feel frustrated, angry, lonely, depressed, anxious, bored, or restless? If so, plan better coping strategies with the appropriate chapters in this book.

Despite the tempting food at social occasions, plan strategies for success. Don't go on an empty stomach; base your meals that day on what you think you will eat. Drink plenty of water there to fill up. For extra motivation, you might announce you won't eat any snacks or desserts. Plan in advance what you will eat at the party, restaurant, or holiday meal and follow your plan strictly. In restaurants, you can ask for broiled or baked fish without a rich sauce, vegetables, and a baked potato with lemon juice, soy sauce, salsa, mozzarella cheese, or tomato sauce as a topping. Salad makes an excellent choice for supper or a snack if you either skip the salad dressing or request a low calorie salad dressing, such as a little lime juice and soy sauce or tomato juice with a little vinegar or lemon juice. When snacking in a restaurant with friends who order desserts, choose fruit or a diet drink. In all but the most formal situations, you can bring your own low calorie food to eat, perhaps explaining why in advance. You can even bring low calorie foods to a restaurant when you go with friends who buy meals or snacks.

Another good strategy is to eat less during the week before a special occasion, saving up calories so you can splurge on the day of the festivities. Never splurge at a social occasion and promise yourself you will make up for it later, however. Few dieters live up to such promises. Use behavioral roleplays to practice responses to repeated offers of snacks or desserts, until you find and perfect several responses you feel very comfortable using. For example: "No thanks, I'm eliminating all snacking between meals," and "I really don't want any. Please don't ask me again." Tightly fitting clothes can help you monitor your eating at restaurants, during the holidays, and other social occasions. Tight clothes help you notice becoming full more quickly than you might otherwise.

Your thoughts can help you succeed or demoralize you and drive you to failure. Don't dwell on the discomforts of dieting: "I wish it was time for supper right now," "I'm starving!" or "Everyone else gets to eat whatever they want, but I have to go hungry all the time!" Instead, drink water when you feel at all hungry and replace thoughts about hunger with more helpful thought alternatives such as: "Keeping busy will help keep my mind off food. I guess I'll read this magazine," and "I'm not really all that hungry. I can wait." Remember how psychological hunger can be.

Other negative thoughts that shatter confidence, hope, and determination and lead to failure include: "I just can't stop eating sweets. It's too hard," "I'll never lose all of this weight," "I've always been fat and I always will be," and "I've gone on a million diets, but I've always regained all the weight." Some people never attempt to lose weight because of negative thoughts like these. Replace the thoughts with more positive alternatives. Examples include: "It will get easier as I get used to dieting," "I'll lose all this weight if I keep trying and never give up," and "I'm learning to eat properly with a flexible diet, not dieting and going back to my old fattening eating patterns." Study your own negative thought habits about obesity and use the advice in chapter 4 to write positive thought alternatives and practice them every day.

Never give up because of eating too much or splurging on a fattening food. Dieters often give up and overeat for days or even quit their diets altogether because of one mistake. The sooner you go back to work on your diet, the better. Instead of dwelling on negative thoughts about having failed, learn from your mistake and plan and practice better responses to similar situations for the future in the ways detailed in chapter 11, Easy Changes. If you never allow yourself to taste some of your favorite foods, change your diet regimen to make it more satisfying and realistic. Make up for splurging on fattening foods by eating less until you have saved the same number of calories you ate while splurging.

Make and use the lists for keeping motivated described in chapter 11. Your list of reasons for losing weight might include such items as fewer dates, less chance of getting married, feeling unattractive, times when people made fun of you for your size, increased risk of illnesses, and job discrimination. Read this list whenever you feel like splurging. Putting a picture or a drawing of such animals as a pig, elephant, or whale on your refrigerator as a reminder can help. Imagine yourself in a bathing suit every time you feel like splurging. Looking at yourself nude in the mirror every day adds extra motivation, too. Use the information on common patterns in this chapter to make your list of high-risk situations. Your list of coping techniques should include both behaviors suggested in this chapter and helpful thought alternatives such as, "I'm doing great so far. Let's not mess up now!" Keep your lists in the strategic places described in chapter 11 and read them every day and whenever you feel the urge to splurge.

Increase your chances of success, too, by rewarding yourself when you accomplish specific goals such as weeks or months in which you lost weight, the loss of five pounds, or ten days under your calorie limits. Your rewards might include favorite foods, a movie, special trips or purchases, visits to the beauty salon, etc. Penalties may involve extra exercise, giving money away, etc. Use the advice in chapter 12 to involve your friends and family. Ask them to encourage you to be more active with interests and activities, to participate in activities with you, and to remind you of your diet whenever temptations arise at parties, restaurants, family gatherings, etc. Ask all your friends and loved ones not to offer you fattening foods. If you feel it necessary, ask them not to eat fattening foods in your presence. Try to find someone who will go on a diet with you. You can help and encourage each other as described in chapter 12, especially during times of temptation. Bring a friend with you to social occasions such as parties who will remind you to eat sensibly when temptations arise. Weight loss support groups (see the end of this chapter) are also excellent resources.

Finally, when you reach your ideal weight, you can eat more food, but continue to eat sensibly and moderately, so you won't regain the pounds you have lost. Check your weight every week or two, and renew your diet whenever you reach five or ten pounds over your desired weight.

Anorexia, Bulimia, and Binge Eating Disorder

Many experts believe the rates of anorexia and bulimia are rising because of our unhealthy obsession with excessive thinness. Both disorders appear mostly in Caucasians in industrialized countries with the modern, Western prejudice against obesity, especially for women. But African Americans and other ethnic groups are increasingly developing these problems. Cross-cultural studies suggest those at risk in Third World societies come from the higher socioeconomic classes with Western cultural values. Before television came to Fiji in 1995, large size was considered beautiful but within 38 months, the number of high school girls who vomited for weight control increased 5 times.

Although men can develop anorexia or bulimia, over 90% of cases involve women. Perhaps the most famous case is Diana, the English Princess of Wales who struggled with bulimia. The risk is higher than average for models, dancers, gymnasts, long-distance runners, figure skaters, actors, wrestlers, jockeys, other people in professions or activities that require or emphasize thinness, and perhaps also for homosexual men.

The disorders usually begin in adolescence or early adult life, with 1 in 150 young women in America developing anorexia and another 1 in 50 developing bulimia. About 3/4 of those with bulimia and 1/3 of those with anorexia eventually recover, and most eventually show some improvement. The consequences can be severe, with 1 in 10 cases leading to death from starvation, cardiac arrest, or suicide. Those who use drugs to vomit, laxatives to move the bowels, or diuretics to urinate are in the most danger, as these things increase the risk of heart failure.

People with anorexia or bulimia have low self-esteem and a real fear of and preoccupation with becoming fat. They are intensely afraid of gaining weight and very dissatisfied with their weight, thinking they are overweight or too fat in certain body parts. Their self-esteem is highly dependent on their body shape and weight. Many of them, but not all, live in families with a great deal of conflict or came from such families. They often report feeling criticized, devalued, and powerless or helpless. Despite stereotypes, most studies suggest they are no more likely than other people to have been sexually abused. Their low self-esteem makes them overly sensitive to other people. In trying to please others, they often bury their anger. Many of them are perfectionists who pressure themselves to live up to high expectations. They seem to handle conflicts, stress, anxiety, and self-esteem concerns by using eating behaviors to control their bodies and gain approval from others. Girls with eating disorders often have brothers or fathers who are overly critical of their weight or mothers who are overly concerned about their weight or attractiveness.

In anorexia, people intentionally starve themselves and fail to maintain a minimally normal body weight, yet are convinced they are overweight. The diagnosis requires the person to be at least 15% below normal weight, but children and adolescents may simply fail to make expected weight gains while growing in height. Because of hormonal problems from starvation, women with anorexia lose their regular menstrual periods and men with anorexia often become impotent. Losing weight doesn't calm anorectic bodily concerns; these people often become more concerned about gaining weight even while they lose it. Although some may admit they are thin, most feel they are too fat, even when they become bone thin. Those who admit they are thin generally deny the serious medical consequences of the problem.

Anorexia often begins after a stressful life event, such as leaving home for college. In anorexia, self-esteem depends on losing weight, and gaining weight is an unacceptable failure. These people may lose weight by dieting, fasting, excessive exercise, diet pills, self-induced vomiting, laxatives, diuretics, or enemas. Some exercise rigorously many hours every day. Most obsess over thoughts of food but restrict themselves to a narrow range of foods. Many develop compulsive behaviors of collecting recipes or hoarding, concealing, crumbling, or throwing away food. When they become seriously underweight, the starvation may cause tiredness, depression, social withdrawal, irritability, excess energy, poor concentration, insomnia, cold intolerance, ritualized eating behaviors, constipation, abdominal pain, and less interest in sex. Starvation and the abuse of laxatives, diuretics, and enemas can cause many physical problems, including infertility, increased susceptibility to infections, and blood, liver, kidney, heart, hormone, digestion, muscle, dental, skin, hair, bone, and brain problems. Even those who look well, claim to feel fine, and have normal electrocardiograms may have heart problems and die suddenly.

In bulimia, people go on uncontrolled eating binges from a few times a week to several times a day. Some bulimic people eat as much as ten times what the average person eats. The food varies but typically involves sweets or junk foods. The binge often continues rapidly until the person is uncomfortably or painfully full. Negative emotions, interpersonal conflicts, intense hunger from dieting, or feelings about body weight or shape and food trigger the binges. The binge may improve their mood briefly but guilt, depression, self-criticism, or disgust at themselves often follows. They may panic at the thought of gaining weight. Afterward, they try to make up for it in some way. Approximately 85% of them vomit after binges. Most become very good at vomiting and can eventually vomit· at will. Some binge primarily to vomit and some vomit even after small meals. About one-third of all bulimic people abuse laxatives to reduce the absorption of calories. Dieting rigorously between binges is common. Many make up for binges by fasting, exercising excessively, or using diet pills, and a few abuse diuretics or enemas. The hunger from excessive dieting after binges leads to further binges and a cycle of binges and purges.

Regular vomiting can burn and inflame the esophagus and dissolve and decay tooth enamel. Those who use their hand to stimulate vomiting may show calluses or scars on the knuckles or top of the hand from repeated trauma from the teeth. Those who abuse laxatives may become dependent on them to stimulate bowel movement; some end up with a nonresponsive large colon requiring surgical removal. Vomiting and laxative use may lead to bleeding and anemia or even esophageal or bowel perforation and death. Some people of normal weight with bulimia develop the metabolic and hormonal adaptations of starvation from their chronic dieting or purging. Some develop fatigue, less interest in sex, irregular menstrual periods, puffy face from swollen salivary glands, stomach bloating, ruptured stomach, nerve damage, muscle damage, kidney problems, swelling, or heart failure.

Bulimia is uncommon but possible among moderately obese or very obese people. Most bulimic people are of average weight, with some being slightly underweight or slightly overweight. Research suggests many of them were overweight before the bulimia developed, however. Bulimic people often hide the disorder for years, bingeing and purging in secret. They are ashamed of their behavior, but they believe it controls their weight. They may develop unusual interest in food or strange eating rituals. Many have symptoms of depression or anxiety and about one-third abuse drugs, usually alcohol or stimulants. Their impulsiveness may also result in shopping sprees, shoplifting, promiscuity, or self-mutilation.

Binge eating disorder resembles bulimia in the uncontrolled eating binges and associated feelings, but the person does not regularly try to make up for binges with rigorous dieting, fasting, excessive exercise, vomiting, enemas, or using laxatives or diuretics. Although some people with this disorder have never been overweight, most are obese with a history of weight fluctuations and many diets. Between 20 and 30% of people in weight control clinics seem to have this disorder. Among the general population, estimates range from 5 to 8%. The pattern often begins in late adolescence or early adulthood after significant weight loss from dieting. Compared to other people of the same weight, these people generally feel more depression, anxiety, and self-loathing and report more interpersonal and work problems from their eating or weight.

It is best to treat eating disorders early, before they become chronic, long-term habits. It may be extremely difficult to detect these disorders or to get the person to go to or stay in treatment, however. Denial, lying, and poor cooperation are common. Watch for unusual patterns. Signs of trouble include a teenager eating 1,000 calories a day or less or anyone regularly disappearing to the bathroom for periods after meals. Anorectic people may bundle up in plenty of clothes to stay warm and hide how thin they are. Consider an eating disorder if anyone begins avoiding meals with the family or if large amounts of food (cakes, ice cream, etc.) disappear regularly. Many people with eating disorders hide food, try to inconspicuously throw food away during meals, or spend time cutting up food and rearranging it to make it look as if they have eaten. Excessive exercise is another clue, especially if it interferes with the person's social, academic, or work life.

The first step in treatment of anorexia or bulimia is a complete physical examination by a doctor. Although professionals can treat most bulimic people and some anorexic people as outpatients, medical danger may require hospitalization. If the person needs it but refuses, the doctor can obtain a court order for hospitalization. Conditions warranting hospitalization include excessive and rapid weight loss, serious metabolic disturbances, dehydration, fainting or dizziness, persistent muscle cramps, vomiting of blood, chest pain, suicidal risk, severe binge eating and purging, or psychosis. Ideally, the treatment team will include a doctor, nutritionist, and psychiatrist or psychologist, all experienced in treating eating disorders. Team treatment is now standard because these patients are often difficult to work with.

Medications can help control medical complications, depression, anxiety, and compulsive thoughts and behaviors. Bulimic people often benefit from antidepressants, even if they don't feel depressed. Professionals must slowly refeed starving people because this may cause heart failure and many other unpleasant symptoms. Eating a normal amount for a few weeks increases the metabolism from starvation mode but may frighten patients because of initially fast weight gain, which is mostly water weight. In some cases, forced tube feedings are necessary.

Treatment also teaches about the medical realities and consequences of eating disorders. For example, using laxatives is a very ineffective way to limit calorie absorption because laxatives act in the large colon rather than the small intestine. Laxatives, like diuretics, only give the illusion of weight loss because of dehydration, and the weight comes back in the next day or two as you absorb fluids again. Using ipecac to vomit can damage the gastrointestinal system, nerves to the muscles, and heart. Constipation from laxative withdrawal requires a high-fiber diet, adequate fluid intake, stool softeners, and education about the frequency of normal bowel movements.

Nutritionists help in correcting mistaken ideas about nutrition and teaching good eating habits. People with eating disorders often have distorted ideas about what foods are fattening or healthy, energy intake needs, and ideal body weight. They must learn that eating regular meals is essential in gaining control over binge eating and in normalizing metabolism. Some of them may also need dental work.

Counseling is intensive, once or twice a week, and helps people with eating disorders learn to deal with underlying emotional issues. They learn how our culture's unhealthy obsession with excessive thinness drives many people to abuse their bodies. Binges are repeatedly described as the result of excessive dieting and hunger. They learn to monitor eating patterns with a detailed food diary that includes not only amounts of foods at meals, snacks, and binges, but also events, thoughts, and emotions triggering eating behavior. Work on rigid negative thinking habits involves writing and repeatedly reading more positive thought alternatives as described in chapter 4.

Gradually, using rewards for improvements, the person learns to eat avoided foods and control eating behaviors. You may need to eat meals mechanically at first, no matter how you feel. Recovery normally includes relapses; don't get discouraged and give up. You may need work on social skills, assertiveness, anxieties or fears, and deep relaxation skills. Anxieties about eating with other people or in public situations may require much work. Group therapy can help a great deal.

The family members also need therapy to understand the eating disorder and learn how to best support the needed changes. Trying to control the person's problem behaviors will fail. Never try to force eating. Don't tell the person when to stop eating and don't ask what the person ate or will eat. Avoid stressful topics and fighting at mealtime. Don't follow the person to the bathroom after meals to prevent vomiting or laxative use. If you can't follow these rules, eat separately until you can.

If you have a friend or family member with an eating disorder, let the person know you care. Help by listening and giving moral support. Use the advice in chapter 12, Help from Other People, to encourage change without doing any nagging. Encourage going to treatment, using the information in this section to explain the danger to the person. Be persistent. You might use the loving group confrontation technique described in chapter 12. Once these people are in treatment, they will need plenty of understanding and encouragement to stay in it.

Recommended Additional Readings:

Tipping the Scales of Justice: Fighting Weight-Based Discrimination. by Sondra Solovay. Amherst, NY: Prometheus Books, 2000.

Prevention's Your Perfect Weight: The Diet-Free Weight-Loss Method Developed by the World's Leading Health Magazine. by Mary Bricklin and Linda Konner. Emmaus, PA: Rodale Press, 1995.

Make the Connection: Ten Steps to a Better Body—And A Better Life. by Bob Greene and Oprah Winfrey. NY: Hyperion, 1996.

Jenny Craig's What Have You Got to Lose? A Personalized Weight Management Program. by Jenny Craig and Brenda L. Wolfe. Rocklin, CA: Prima Publishing, 1997.

The New Living Heart Diet. by Michael E. DeBakey, Antonio M. Gotto Jr., Lynne W. Scott, John Foreyt, Mary McCann, Suzanne Simpson, and Diane Branch. NY: Simon & Schuster, 1996.

Controlling Eating Disorders with Facts, Advice, and Resources. by Raymond Lemberg, ed. Phoenix, AZ: Oryx Press, 1992.

Support Groups, Hotlines, and Resources:

government recommended web site listing foods and their composition, including calories: www.cyberdiet.com/ni/htdocs/index.html

Overeaters Anonymous 505 891 2664 information, referrals for support groups. on-line: www.overeatersanonymous.org

Take Off Pounds Sensibly 800 932 8677 information, referrals for support groups. on-line: www.tops.org

National Association of Anorexia Nervosa and Associated Disorders 847 831 3438 information, referrals, support groups. on-line: www.anad.org

National Association to Advance Fat Acceptance 800 442 1214 information, support groups, activism, pen pals. on-line: www.naafa.org

36. Abuse and Rape

A wise person avoids close relationships with those with bad tempers.

Nobody can continue to abuse you without your permission.

Definitions

Abuse is treating another person in a harmful, injurious, or offensive way. It is not normal moodiness or anger in a relationship. Abuse often refers to violence or cruel acts of intimidation and control, such as temper tantrums, threats, throwing objects, destroying personal property, hurting pets, public humiliation, isolation, child corruption (crime, drugs), sexual exploitation, or rape. Abusive behavior interferes with the emotional or physical welfare of the other person. Therefore, frequent criticism and regular insults may qualify as verbal abuse. Any slap, hit, or other act of violence or discipline that results in a mark or bruise lasting more than one hour or results in an injury requiring medical treatment is an act of abuse. Abuse includes pushing, punching, beating, kicking, biting, tearing out hair, inflicting burns, or attacks using weapons, scissors, plates, chairs, etc. Some abusers attempt to drown, smother, strangle, or blind their victims. Abusive acts can, but often don't, result in cuts, bruises, broken bones, burns, internal injuries, broken teeth, miscarriage, or disfigurement. After their abusive acts abusive people often do apologize and act in extremely loving, kind, and attentive ways.

Rape is vaginal, oral, or anal sexual contact committed without the other person's lawful consent. The victim may physically resist but be overcome by force, or the rapist may prevent resistance with threats of bodily harm, perhaps with the use of a weapon. Date rape often involves alcohol or drug use and generally involves verbal pressure or physical strength to force sex, rather than weapons or threats of violence. Sex with someone who has drunk too much and passed out or who is out of control is rape. Legally, sex with consent from an underage person or a person with some abnormal mental condition is also rape.

Most physical child abuse deaths come from angry, stressed father figures who blow up in rage over an infant's crying, feeding problems, or failed toilet training. Head trauma is the leading cause of child abuse deaths. The *Shaken Baby Syndrome* is so deadly that up to 25% of its victims die and most survivors suffer brain damage. *Neglect*, the most common form of child abuse, occurs when a parent or caretaker fails to provide adequate food, clothing, housing, supervision, or emotional warmth for a child. Examples include bathtub drowning, starvation, abandonment, allowing sexual abuse, isolation, or chronic ignoring or rejection. Many physically neglectful parents live chaotic lives, and many emotionally neglectful parents are depressed and unresponsive to their children or interact mechanically, with little joy. Mothers cause most deaths from neglect, but neglect may occur because of poverty or ignorance. For example, one baby almost died of starvation because the mother believed it was full when it spit up food. The vast majority of abused and neglected children are under four years old. There is no disease, natural disaster, or trauma that kills more children under four than abuse and neglect.

Child sexual abuse is a sexual act between a child and either an adult or an older child. It includes fondling, touching sexual organs, sex play, oral sex, vaginal intercourse, or anal sex. The abuser may force the child into the sexual act, perhaps violently, or simply lead the child into it. Child sexual abuse may occur without any physical contact. For example, indecent exposure, telling your child to take off her clothes, or the photography of nude children qualify as acts of child sexual abuse when the purpose is sexual gratification, or a father might get a child to masturbate while he watches.

Sexual harassment is a form of verbal, emotional, or physical abuse with unwelcome sexual attention or the creation of a sexual environment that causes discomfort. It may involve threatening to make a personal relationship or verbal or physical sexual acts a part of a job, condition for employment, or part of job evaluation, promotion, or pay increase. The harassment may come from a person of your own sex. A pattern of hiring or promoting sex partners over more qualified people is sexual harassment. Even nonsexual harassment may qualify if it occurs because of the person's gender, such as when men haze women in traditionally male jobs. Unwanted sexual attention may be requests or advances, invitations, personal letters or phone calls, pressure for dates, comments, jokes, gestures, teasing, brushing the body, or touching. Some clear examples of sexual harassment are looking over a person's body, leering, staring, making insulting or obscene comments or gestures, sexual threats, spreading sexual rumors, or throwing things to hit private parts. Others include pinching or poking, kissing, an uninvited hug that is too tight or lasts too long, cornering a person, fondling or grabbing private parts, or sexual activity through force, threat, restraint, or domination. Displaying sexually suggestive objects, photographs, cartoons, magazines, books, or graffiti may be harassment, especially in work or school settings. Other situations, such as pats, squeezes, dirty jokes, flirting, suggestive comments, remarks about a person's attractiveness, whistling, or sexist statements, may or may not constitute harassment, depending on the situation and how the other person feels. In general, behavior becomes sexual harassment when it crosses the line from friendly to hostile or when it continues or repeats despite the other person's displeasure, discomfort, complaint, or refusal to return the affection. The most commonly reported types are verbal comments about a woman's body, jokes about sex, sexual innuendoes, and sexual invitations that persist despite the woman's response.

Stalking involves repeated pursuing and following with no legitimate purpose, harassment, or unwanted communications, surveillance or lying in wait, trespassing, refusing to leave when warned, or intimidation, if the behaviors would cause a reasonable person fear or emotional distress. Many victims live in fear and change their lives significantly to find safety and freedom from harassment. Experts understand any stalking suggests danger of injury or death, even when the stalker makes no threats.

Statistics

Because so many cases of abuse never get reported, it is impossible to determine the precise numbers that occur. Experts believe that, excluding sexual harassment, over 3 million children in the United States suffer abuse each year, with at least 2,000 children dying from it each year. Only 25 to 50% of the deaths from child abuse are cases known to child abuse agencies before the deaths occurred. A 1996 study by the U.S. government reported estimates of 1.22 million abused children, 1.96 million neglected children, and 565,000 seriously injured children in 1993. Children of single parents had an 80% greater risk of serious injury or harm from abuse or neglect than children living with both parents. The stresses of poverty are closely linked to abuse. Children from families earning less than $15,000 a year were 22 times more likely to suffer maltreatment, 22 times more likely to receive serious injury, and 18 times more likely to become sexually abused than children from families with incomes above $30,000.

Approximately 1,400 women and 500 men in the U.S. are killed by their intimate partners each year. In 50% or perhaps 60% of all families with battered women, children also suffer physical abuse. Intimate partners rape approximately 1.5 million women and 800,000 men each year. Nearly 25% of women and about 7% of men have been raped or assaulted by a current or former partner. Research suggests mentally disabled people are at least four times more likely than other people to be targets of both sexual assault and other violence. The Justice Department found 2/3 of all sex offenders in state prisons attacked children. Children make easier targets for sexual abuse— they are easier to intimidate into silence and they may not understand anything is wrong until much later.

Many studies indicate around 50% of women have experienced physical violence from a husband or boyfriend. Around 900,000 women and 160,000 men are attacked by intimate partners each year and report it to the police. About 20% of all marriages include repeated physical violence, such as thrown objects, hitting, forceful pushes, etc. Experts believe 5 to 7% of all women experience severe battering from their mates and that husbands or boyfriends beat from 2 to 4 million women each year. Abuse at home is the most common cause of women's injuries, occurring more often than automobile accidents, rapes, and muggings combined. Current or former boyfriends or husbands attack, rape, and kill women more often than do any other kind of person. Most murders, assaults, and rapes of women occur behind closed doors in private, whereas men become victims in more public settings. Between 22 and 35% of emergency room visits by women come from domestic abuse. In various studies, between 34 and 75% of physically abused women also report sexual attacks, with forced anal sex being one of the most common types. Abuse by a husband or lover kills around 50% of all adult female murder victims.

Almost 5% of women say a partner has stalked them. Men stalk women in about 75 to 80% of cases. Most are young or middle-aged. Most stalkers had a previous personal or romantic relationship with the victim before the stalking began, but about 20 or 25% are obsessed with a complete stranger or a casual acquaintance. These stalkers generally have mental disorders and fantasies or delusions of a personal relationship with the victim.

Research indicates approximately 1 out of 4 or 5 girls is sexually abused before the age of 18 and approximately 1 out of 7 girls and 1 out of 15 boys has a sexual experience with an adult before puberty. Most incidents of child sexual abuse do not involve penetration or violence, which results in the most trauma, especially with multiple episodes. Experts believe about 1/4 of child sexual abuse occurs to children under 7 years old, and children between the ages of 8 and 12 are at the highest risk. Although women do sometimes sexually abuse children, a Justice Department study of imprisoned sex offenders found 97% of child molesters were male. A third of these molesters had attacked their own child or stepchild, and another half of them had attacked other relatives, friends, or acquaintances. Family members, relatives, neighbors, or trusted friends most often sexually abuse children, although unrelated people, strangers, and acquaintances sexually abuse boys much more often than girls. Child molesters exist in cities, suburbs, and rural areas and may be highly respected members of the community.

History

Abuse is nothing new, of course. In early Roman law, fathers had the right to sell, abandon, offer in sacrifice, devour, or kill their children. In Rome, people often raised abandoned children as slaves, prostitutes, or beggars, and people often deliberately mutilated children by gouging their eyes out or breaking up or amputating their arms, legs, or feet to make better beggars of them. In the 1500s, Germans buried children alive under the doorsteps of public buildings, continuing an ancient, widespread custom meant to insure the durability of important structures.

During the early days of the Industrial Revolution in the late 1700s, factories used pauper children with no parents as workers in the mills 16 hours a day. The management often starved and beat these children, sometimes riveting irons around their ankles to keep them from running away. Children working day and night as chimney sweeps in narrow flues during the late 1700s usually had masters burning straw under them to hurry them up. These children often suffered mental and physical deterioration, serious accidents, cancer of the scrotum, and tuberculosis.

Early in the 1800s, both English and American courts held husbands had the right to beat their wives. In London of the 1800s, nurses often collected their fees and then killed illegitimate babies people put out to nurse. In the 1870s, church workers in New York couldn't persuade legal authorities to remove a regularly beaten and seriously malnourished child from her home until a court finally labeled the battered girl an animal, so laws enacted to prevent cruelty to animals could protect her. Even as recently as about 30 years ago in both Texas and Italy, a husband who caught his wife in extramarital sex could legally murder both the wife and lover.

Reasons for Violence

Abuse continues in our civilized world for many reasons. First, our society accepts violence in many circumstances. Courts sentence criminals to death, most people accept war as a necessary evil, soldiers often get medals and special privileges for killing the enemy, and parents discipline children with spanking. The widespread acceptance of physical punishment in disciplining children links love and violence during the formative years of the personality and means that parents set an example of using violence to deal with frustration and stress in the family. It also makes it more difficult for parents and other concerned people to recognize the difference between ordinary discipline and abuse. As noted previously, five European countries—Denmark, Austria, Finland, Sweden, and Norway—have outlawed physical punishment of children, including spanking.

Doctors now consider violence a public health epidemic in the United States. Only in some developing countries is there a higher incidence of violence than in the U.S. Our gun laws contribute to this problem. In a survey of 102 countries, nearly all foreign countries have a comprehensive national system of gun control. History, traditions, and culture also contribute to these differences, however. Murder rates without guns are also much higher in the U.S., and certain social groups, such as gangs, see prestige and honor in violent acts. Violence also continues because people gain rewards through it. Nations use war to gain in resources and territories, criminals to attain sex, material goods, or power in organized crime, husbands to force compliance from their wives, children to acquire the use of toys, to stop insults and teasing, etc.

Unfortunately, violence is also very exciting. Today, violent sports replace the Roman passion for feeding Christians to lions. Crowds love to see fiery crashes in automobile races and boxers beating each other until one of them falls unconscious. Some careers in violent sports (automobile racing, boxing, football, etc.) result in death or permanent disability. Certainly violence in art speaks to us of the human condition—think of Greek drama. But movies and television have become increasingly violent since they began. Comedy often portrays insults, threats, and violence between marital partners, family members, or friends as trivial, humorous events rather than as serious ones. Toy stores offer many violent toys (handguns, rifles, bazookas, fighter planes, etc.), so children can happily and realistically pretend to murder and destroy things.

Experts on abuse believe our acceptance of violence in entertainment also helps breed rape, child abuse, and wife beating. In the section about television in chapter 22, Raising Children, we detailed research that shows violent acts portrayed in the media do cause violence in both children and adults. Many countries refuse to allow as much violent TV programming as Americans accept. Sweden has banned all toy weapons and war toys to eliminate the training in violence these toys provide.

Sex role expectations and stereotypes contribute to date rape. Too many people still believe that men are aggressors in sex and women are sexually passive and ambivalent, often saying no but meaning yes. Men who date rape generally hold these views and very often don't see themselves as rapists—they feel some aggression is normal in sexual and romantic relationships. In *Sex in America* (Michael et al., 1994), the comprehensive, scientific survey of sexual behaviors, 22% of women said a person had forced them to do sexual things they didn't want to, usually someone they loved, but only 3% of men admitted forcing themselves on women. Apparently, men and women misunderstand each other's signals about sexual desires and have very different ideas about what constitutes forced sex. One study found 75% of women who reported rape by an acquaintance didn't identify the episode as rape. These women believe in the sexual stereotypes and therefore don't realize how respectful, mutual, and loving sex should be.

Many abusive men and abused women hold traditionally stereotyped family and sex roles. They often believe men should rule the household and women should take care of the children and domestic chores. These traditional views of male authority may eliminate the negotiation and compromise that satisfying relationships require for good problem solving. Traditional sex roles concerning emotions and chores hold that men should be unemotional and provide the income for the family, and women should be gentle, loving housewives. These traditional roles provide little opportunity for abusive men to develop their gentler sides and for abused women to develop assertiveness and financial independence. Even when an abused woman wants to disagree, refuse, go out, get a job, or go to school, the abusive man often uses traditional views of male authority to control the woman and keep her dependent upon him.

Cross-cultural research links violence toward women and sexual inequality. Out of 90 societies studied, family violence was rare or nonexistent in 16 of them. All 16 had a strong emphasis on peaceful solutions to conflicts, stable marriages, sexual equality in decision-making in finances and the household, and no double standards in premarital sex and other freedoms.

The traditional attitude about men having absolute rule over their households also helps spousal rape and abuse continue. Men who batter their wives often feel they have the right to discipline them. Unfortunately, many people act as if they agree with this. One research study compared the reactions of strangers to the same level of verbal and physical abuse in three different kinds of situations: between two men, between a man and a woman, and between two women. Strangers intervened much more often in fights between two members of the same sex than in fights between a man and a woman. Interviews showed the strangers often assumed the man and woman were married and felt they had no right to become involved in a marital quarrel.

Another problem is many people believe family violence is less serious than violence between strangers ("It's just a family quarrel!"). Certainly awareness of domestic violence has grown, but many people fail to understand how common domestic violence is and how dangerous the violence often is. Unfortunately, as detailed in chapter 42, Preventing Violence and Crime, laws classify most domestic assaults as misdemeanors, even though the same act by others would often be felonies of rape or aggravated assault, and domestic violence misdemeanors cause more injuries than do felony rapes, aggravated assaults, and robberies. In the vast majority of cases, family violence does not result in prosecution and when conviction occurs, sentencing is generally quite lenient with few offenders spending time in jail. Many women fail to show up for court because of intimidation, retaliation, or fear of losing family income, alimony, or child support if the person goes to jail. Prosecutors could subpoena the victim or use victim advocate testimony or videotapes of initial victim interviews, however. Overall, the legal system seems sexist, devaluing women.

The dominance of males in the police force, criminal justice system, medical system, mental health services, and religious organizations adds another problem. Men in these positions of responsibility often identify with the man and fail to intervene in cases of wife beating. Research documents a tendency for male authority figures to believe the man's version of the events and reject the abused woman's version. Policemen often think abused women are overreacting and becoming hysterical. Male doctors may tell the abused women to behave. Male psychologists often believe abused women somehow enjoy or want the abuse, and often label these women masochistic. Experts agree, however, that women do not normally fabricate or exaggerate abuse, abused women are not masochistic, and abusive men usually deny their violence and act calm and friendly when faced with people intervening.

The mistaken notion that abusers must be abnormal or obviously different from regular, nice people also helps rape and abuse continue. People find it difficult to believe that normal people could rape or act abusively, but abusive men and abusive parents can be very charming and often appear perfectly normal. In fact, verbal abuse is quite common, with one nationally representative survey finding that parents verbally abuse 2/3 of U.S. children, averaging 12.6 times a year. This generally causes no lasting harm because of the low frequency, intensity, and duration of the abuse. People who act more abusively have severe problems in controlling their anger, so they take their frustrations out on their families.

The vast majority of mentally ill people are not violent; people with no mental illness commit the vast majority of violence. People with less serious forms of mental illness but who engage in substance abuse have the highest risk of violence. Schizophrenics are less likely to be violent than people with other mental illnesses. Psychopaths, charming, self-centered people who lack remorse and can't control antisocial impulses, may be most likely to be violent. Although many abusers feel like losers, some are successful, widely respected people with excellent social skills. Although many abusive men have criminal or prison records, most abusive men do not. Rape and severe abuse occur in cities, suburbs, rural areas, and all races, ethnic groups, income groups, levels of education, occupations, and religious groups. Younger women and women living in poverty are at higher risk than other women for both marital and nonmarital violence. Women living in poverty are at especially high risk for severe and life-threatening assaults.

Many people experience abuse in their childhood families and repeat the pattern as adults, creating a cycle of abuse. Most studies of the childhood experiences of men who abuse women, abused women, child abusers, and the mothers of child abuse victims find much higher than average rates of wife or child abuse in their families of origin. Most adults in jail for child sexual abuse were themselves child victims of sexual abuse. But most abused children don't repeat the pattern as adults. Research suggests perhaps 30% of abused children go on to become abusive parents. Many abusers, abused women, and mothers of victims didn't experience abuse or witness marital violence as children. Research suggests experiencing violence in childhood leads to different behaviors in men and women: men tend to become abusers, whereas women tend to become victims.

The abuse of alcohol or other drugs, especially cocaine or crack, methamphetamines, and heroin, often plays an important role in rape and family violence. Many studies find high rates of alcohol abuse in child abusers, including child sexual abuse, and in men who abuse women. Alcohol plays a role in most rapes. Chapter 33, Substance Abuse, gives estimates of violence linked to alcohol. Many abusers drink alcohol moderately and don't use drugs, however. Although many abusers and victims believe alcohol always causes the violence, careful thought usually reveals that the violence also occurs without alcohol. The alcohol or drug use lowers impulse control, provides a convenient excuse for the abuser, and provides a comforting explanation for the victim, but research indicates alcohol or drug use tends to result in more dangerous assaults and more severe injuries, including murder.   Men's shaky employment status and alcohol abuse are important factors in domestic violence, but ethnicity plays almost no role.

Sexual Harassment

If you experience sexual harassment, assert yourself. In a clear, strong voice, say you don't like what the other person has said or done and it makes you very uncomfortable. If other people are around, say this loudly enough so that others will hear it. Demand an end to the behavior. If possible, get away from the person. If it happened at work, tell the person's boss. If it happened at school, tell a trusted teacher, school counselor, or the principal of the school. Children should tell their parents, other relatives, or the group activity leader.   The most effective response is immediate, strong confrontation and reporting to authorities. The longer you delay, the less credible your complaint.

Many victims feel uncomfortable or fear retaliation and prefer privacy, but it is usually a serious mistake to do nothing. At the very least, confront the person verbally or with a written note and keep a record of the confrontation. A written note keeps the matter private, yet creates a clear record of your complaint. If the person argues the appropriateness of the behavior, argues your authority to complain, denies the episode, or asks what you are talking about, carefully describe the offensive behavior and offer to take the issue to a higher authority. Make it clear you will report further problems. Even if your complaint seems to end the problem, make a record of what happened, its date and time, what you did about it, and the response you got. You never know when the problem might resurface with you or other people or when retaliation might occur. Document every episode, get your notes on serious problems notarized, and give a copy to a trusted friend. Thorough, detailed records help enormously in convincing others if you find you must go to authorities later.

If you can't or don't wish to confront the person yourself, or you don't feel safe around the offender, ask a friend to do it or get a third party to do it. Even if you are not ready to file a complaint, a supervisor or harassment officer can support you, advise you on how to speak to the offender, or speak to the offender for you.

Always report serious offenses. Large companies often have human resources personnel or sexual harassment professionals on site or by contract who can help. Ideally, both male and female harassment officers are available for those who are uncomfortable speaking to the opposite sex about it. Small companies may just contract with lawyers when necessary. Your union can also provide support and information about what you can do, perhaps including legal help.

Both males and females can also report sexual harassment to the police or file a lawsuit against the offender. This is a good idea if you do not feel satisfied with your company's response or if the person is the only boss in a small company and the harassment continues despite your complaints. Continued sexual harassment can make your job unbearable, interfere with thinking and productivity at work, and lead to shame, low self-esteem, or any of the symptoms of trauma noted in chapter 26. Courts may hold companies financially liable for an employee's behavior, even if unaware of it and even if the company has a policy against sexual harassment. A company may severely punish or fire an employee found guilty of harassment. Very few cases get filed as lawsuits; most get resolved through organizational procedures. Most cases that are filed get settled before they reach trial.

If you file a lawsuit, find a lawyer with experience in sexual harassment. The lawyer will help you decide whether to file against the organization, the offender, or both and whether to file under state laws or the federal Equal Employment Opportunity Commission (EEOC). Timing is very important, as laws often require filing within 180 or 300 days from the date of the alleged harassment. Sometimes the nearest EEOC or state agency can recommend a lawyer or, in certain circumstances, provide some funding toward hiring one or take the case on themselves. Legal clinics associated with women's organizations or law schools may offer reasonably priced services, but most sexual harassment lawyers take cases on for a part of the settlement, usually 33 to 40%. Settlements may involve awards for personal injury and compensation for lost wages and legal fees. State and federal sexual harassment lawsuits have strict award limits, but juries in personal injury lawsuits can award large punitive damages. You may be able to file a lawsuit combining both federal violations and personal injuries. Few cases go to trial, however. Most are settled, withdrawn, or dismissed by a judge.

If someone accuses you of sexual harassment, don't try to deal directly with the person. This can lead to suspicions that you are trying to silence, intimidate, or retaliate against the person. Instead, deal respectfully through a mediator, apologize, and show a desire to learn why others see your behavior as a problem.   Find a mediator with expertise in this area and experience in pursuing opportunities for resolution.   The right lawyer or a human resources staff member can often help prevent escalation of the conflict.

Rape

Rape is a major crisis that can cause physical pain and emotional, social, and sexual problems.   Most rapists are men under 35 years old. Although most victims are single women between the ages of 12 and 24, victims range from 6 months old to the oldest of the elderly.   Rape incidence is highest for girls between 16 and 19 years old.   Most date rape victims are between 15 and 24 years old.   Despite stereotypes, the following facts are true.   Men do rape men, and women sometimes rape men.   Rapists are more likely to use force or threats than weapons such as guns or knives.   Most rapists attack women of the same race and socioeconomic class as themselves.   Most victims, both male and female, are raped by acquaintances: a peer, coworker, authority figure, date, or lover.   In the comprehensive, scientific sex survey *Sex in America* (Michael et al., 1994), nearly half the women who had experienced forced sex reported they were in love with the men who forced them and strangers raped only 4%. A variety of studies show the impact is just as devastating whether a stranger or a date rapes you.   Most rapes occur in either the victim's or the rapist's home.   The next most common location is a car.   Rapes by acquaintances are more likely to occur indoors than are rapes by strangers.   Preliminary studies suggest more than half of male victims of rape by men are heterosexual and that perhaps half the men who rape other men are heterosexuals who have sexual relations with consenting females.   One study suggests male victims are perhaps more likely to be gang raped or brutalized than female victims.   Although only 20% of female victims report their rapes, males are less likely to talk about or to report rapes.   Sadly, knowing your rapist makes it less likely you will reveal the rape to anyone, seek help, or report it to authorities.

Everyone should understand using verbal pressure alone to have sex is rape if the woman feels intimidated, and you can prosecute the man in court for it.   Many victims report that the fear they felt based on the man's size and physical presence was the reason they did not fight back or struggle.   Men need to recognize that no means no and if they don't accept a woman's no, they risk raping her while thinking she meant yes.   Men need to understand that desire for affection is not the same as desire for sex.   Men also need to know being drunk is not a legal defense for rape, nor is the woman dressing or acting provocatively or beginning sexual activity and then changing her mind. Everyone needs to understand having had a relationship for a long time or living together without being married is not a legal defense for rape. Nearly every state allows the prosecution of marital rape.

Unfortunately, people often accept rape and sexual violence. A study of 1,700 middle school children found 65% of the boys and 57% of the girls believed it is acceptable for a man to force a woman to have sex if they have been dating for 6 months. Around 25% of the boys said it was acceptable for a man to force sex on a woman if he had spent money on her. Other studies of high school and college students report similar findings. Even in states where marital rape is illegal, going to court or jail for it is almost unknown. In South Carolina in 1992, a court acquitted a man of marital rape despite his videotaping rape after tying up his wife and putting duct tape on her eyes and mouth. He commented "How can you rape your own wife?" Such attitudes are common in the U.S., so that in about 30 states, prosecutors can treat marital rape less seriously than rape by a stranger. For example, a prosecutor may charge a felony for stranger rape and a misdemeanor for marital rape.

Reduce your risk of rape by avoiding rides with strangers, using routes with good lighting whenever possible, having a companion at late hours and in rough neighborhoods, and avoiding going home with strangers. Trust your intuition whenever you feel uneasy about a stranger or date. Realize charm, offering help, and persistence are tools of the sociopath, with help accepted making you thankful and less likely to resist further requests or intrusions. Avoid strangers who offer help and ignore your "No thank you," or offer unrequested promises ("I'll just carry it in and go, I promise.") to convince you of their good intentions. A virtuous person and those who can truly love, honor the word no. A firm, confident, stronger no often sends a sociopath looking for a more hesitant, fearful, or yielding victim.

Promiscuity gives more opportunities for rape. The scientific survey *Sex in America* found women who reported forced sex were more likely to have had ten or more sex partners in their lives, anal sex, and group sex. Over half of all rapes involve alcohol. Avoid drinking too much or using drugs on a date, especially early in a relationship. These things lower inhibitions and may lead your date not to respect your feelings or lead you to do something you regret. To avoid "date rape" drugs, watch the bartender make your drink, never let anyone you don't know well bring you a drink, and never leave your drink unattended. If you don't know your date well, don't spend time in his home. Instead, double date or go to a crowded place like a mall, movie, or restaurant. Always carry a telephone calling card or cellular phone and enough money to get home. To avoid date rape, avoid giving mixed signals by playing hard to get, trust your feelings about pressure for unwanted sex, and act on these feelings early by getting angry and setting strong, firm limits.

Talk honestly about your feelings and views on sex. Look for dates whose views closely match yours. If you can't agree on what is right, find someone else whose beliefs are closer to your own. Be very clear about your firm limits in sex, and don't let pressure or a passionate moment change them. Remember that someone who really loves you will respect your feelings and limits. If you get a double message, stop and ask what your partner really wants. Some men report feeling forced or pushed into sex, so women need to understand men don't always feel interested in or ready for sex.

A loud and forceful "No!" or "Stop it!" may end a date rape attempt. If it doesn't end the pressure, get away fast. If others are nearby, yelling "Fire!" attracts attention better than yelling "Help!" Always take emergency money with you on dates, in case you need to call for help. Realize dressing provocatively may attract harassment or rape. Be suspicious of people who stare at you too much or talk or act like they know you more intimately than they do. Get away fast if someone sits or stands too close and seems to enjoy your discomfort or if someone grabs or pushes you to get their way. If anyone tries to block your way, run to escape, screaming if necessary.

Please refer to chapter 26, Grief, Trauma, and Crises, for a description of the common symptoms after rape, the time it takes to recover, the importance of allowing and expressing feelings during the first few months, and helpful suggestions for coping. At first it may be very difficult to be around any man. Even a reassuring touch or someone trying to sympathetically hold your hand or move close to you may feel like a personal violation. Distress levels seem to peak at around three weeks after the rape, with depression and great anger and perhaps irritability, difficulty concentrating, apathy, uncontrollable crying, or suicidal thoughts.

If the rapist is a friend, acquaintance, date, or lover, you are likely to experience severe trust issues and fear of people you know, and you will probably doubt your ability to evaluate friendships and relationships. If the rapist is a stranger, fear of strangers predominates, especially in unfamiliar situations, and may limit your social interactions or willingness to go out alone. Nightmares, waking up in a panic, or fears of crowds, of being alone, or certain places trouble many victims for a long time after rape. One half of all rape victims feel a temporary aversion to sexual contact. Even sex with someone you love may cause great anxiety or physical difficulties. Males may develop difficulties with erection or ejaculation. These problems can become long lasting.

Deep shame, humiliation, embarrassment, and feeling dirtied are nearly universal. Guilt or anger is also very common. Victims wonder what they did to bring it on, regret where they were or what they wore, wonder if they should have fought or fought harder, etc. Rape is an act of power and violence that can happen to anyone, and you only submitted to survive, or perhaps you felt paralyzed with fear. Males are more likely than females to respond to rape or child sexual abuse in a very controlled manner, hiding their feelings and perhaps never talking to anyone about it. This is probably due to sex role training for boys to be tough and unemotional. Some victims manage to forget the whole incident or to pretend to adjust fine, but may need help later when anger, depression, fear, or other symptoms come back. Many feel better and have fewer symptoms if they get away for a while, perhaps staying with friends or relatives. Some move to a new neighborhood or town; many get an unlisted phone number. If the victim presses charges, the process means telling the story to lawyers and in court if the rapist pleads not guilty, and perhaps demeaning accusations by the defending attorney.

Men often respond to male rape with a masculinity and self-esteem crisis and with confusion about their sexual orientation, feeling the attack took away their masculinity or perhaps that they were not man enough or strong enough to stop the attack. Strength and sexuality are important parts of men's self-image, and it is humiliating to get beaten but much worse to be used sexually. Many people mistakenly believe male victims of rape by males must be effeminate, weak, and homosexual or else they would have fought off the attack. If the rapist stimulated them and they had an erection or ejaculation, they are particularly likely to feel abnormal, self-blame, and confused about their sexuality. (Women can also respond to rape with sexual arousal and end up feeling confused and angry at themselves.) Sexually inexperienced men who are raped by men may conclude from the attack that they are homosexual and develop a homosexual lifestyle. Many men raped by other men think the rapist must be homosexual and develop a great fear of or hatred toward homosexuals. Even men raped by women may develop problems in self-esteem, feeling inadequate because of the extreme reversal in sex roles or feeling abnormal for responding with an erection or orgasm.

Work performance after rape may suffer for 8 months or more. Anxiety, fear, problems in self-esteem, and sexual problems may last for up to 18 months. Studies suggest perhaps 25% of women report continuing negative effects several years after rape. One study found even after 4 to 6 years, 30% of raped women still reported negative effects on their sex lives, including lack of desire, fear of sex, and problems with arousal. Some women respond by becoming unattractive to avoid sex. Long-term medical complications include gagging, gastrointestinal complaints, menstrual or premenstrual problems, and chronic pain disorders in the head, jaw, face, back, or pelvis.

After a rape, before cleaning, changing any clothes, or washing your body in any way, you should immediately go to a doctor's office or hospital for an examination, even if you don't feel physical pain. Bring a change of clothes because unwashed clothes may contain blood, hair, or DNA evidence of the rapist. Make sure the doctor who sees you knows how to treat rape victims and collect evidence. Unfortunately, rape victims often don't receive the care that emergency room protocols require. Ask if they have a rape kit, the examination tool that collects evidence in the way courts need. Your local rape crisis center or police station can give you the names of some doctors with experience in this area. Medical evidence can often prove forcible as opposed to consensual sex, even in women who have been sexually active for a long time. In consensual sex, the woman tilts the pelvis to accommodate the penis. In rape, she is trying not to accommodate the man and reddening or bruises may result. If it is just reddening, it fades fast and you need to identify it quickly. Evidence of semen can last for 48 hours if not washed away. Even combing pubic hair or material from under the fingernails may provide evidence. You may need a followup appointment to check for venereal diseases or pregnancy. A 1991 study estimated 30% of rape victims acquire sexually transmitted diseases and 5% become pregnant. Yet a recent national study found 39% of rape victims who received medical attention did not get any information or testing for venereal diseases. Many states now pay for health examinations for rape victims through victim's assistance programs. Ask your local rape crisis center or district attorney's office about these programs.

Get a medical exam and report the rape to the police immediately, even if you think you don't want to press charges. Many people change their minds later when they don't feel so overwhelmed. If you decide to press charges, the evidence will help a great deal. The sooner you report to the police, the more likely the police will find and arrest the rapist. Reporting immediately helps in remembering details that may make a difference in catching the criminal. In many states, reporting the rape to the police will qualify you for money for medical, abortion, and mental health counseling expenses from the federal Victim of Crimes Act of 1984, whereas reporting it to a hospital emergency room or providing a statement from a victim service agency will not. Ask your local district attorney about these funds. In many states, delaying the police report beyond a certain time limit will disqualify you from money for abortion if you should become pregnant from the rape. The sooner you report, the stronger the criminal case will be, as a delay makes the victim less believable. For example, in one case of gang rape by seven men, a rapist was able to plea bargain down to a misdemeanor because the victim waited a month before reporting the rape.

Remember, if you are not comfortable explaining what happened to a policeman, you can request a female police officer. You can also have a friend with you or ask a trained advocate from the rape crisis center to go with you. Be very careful to admit the whole truth. Don't try to improve your story because of embarrassment. This may make you less believable. For example, one woman said she kissed the rapist but it wasn't sexual. A jury will see right through that, knowing kissing someone you just met is a sexual act. Another woman felt too embarrassed to admit she accepted a ride from a stranger. Because she corrected her story before the trial, the defending attorney argued that if she lied about that, she may have lied about the whole thing, and the jurors found the man not guilty. Reporting is a good idea even if you are late, you have no evidence, or you don't want to prosecute and go to court—your information may help the police put together another case.

Don't worry about feeling overwhelmed and unable to tell your story in court. The trial won't happen right away. You will have plenty of time to cope with the attack and get ready for court. If you don't report immediately, write down as much as you can remember about what happened, including where you were, what the rapist did and said, his physical characteristics, how you responded, etc. A detail that seems unimportant now may be important information later. Sometimes just writing everything down helps in facing what happened and makes the rape less overwhelming.

Prosecuting a rape is a good idea. A prosecuting attorney will present your case free of charge. (In many states, men prosecuting rape by other men will use the charge sodomy rather than rape.) Even if you can't prove the case and put the rapist in jail, thereby making the community safer, at least the rapist faces the law and this may help prevent other rapes. Many victims feel a sense of personal power from prosecuting that helps a great deal in healing, especially if the rapist goes to jail. Deciding to prosecute is a very personal decision, however. If acquittal is likely, the woman may prefer not to face the additional trauma of testifying. Unfortunately, rapes by strangers are much easier to prosecute than are rapes by dates, friends, neighbors, or acquaintances. Date rape is especially difficult to prove. In a study of 800 rape cases, a victim's "questionable" character was the best predictor of an acquittal. Things like whether the victim had been drinking, frequents bars, has had multiple sex partners, has birth control pills, has had an abortion, or has had sex outside of marriage tend to sway juries the most. Nearly all the states have laws making details of the victim's sexual history inadmissible in rape trials. Even so, defending attorneys often bring these issues up anyway, which prompts an objection by the prosecutor that the judge sustains, but the jury has already heard the damaging information. This emphasizes the importance of an immediate medical evaluation to get physical evidence and an immediate report to the police.

Many people need counseling after a rape to deal with emotions and relationship issues that arise. Rape crisis centers (look under hotlines at the end of this chapter) often provide counseling free. Attending programs in self-defense or street fighting can help in regaining a sense of power over your life. If your friend or loved one is raped, reassure her that it was not her fault, even if she didn't fight back. Never accuse or judge her. Don't ask blaming questions like, "Why did you talk to him?" or "Why didn't you scream?" Remember that victims often submit to survive or they may feel paralyzed by fear. Don't gossip about the rape. Allow your friend to decide who knows about it. Read chapter 26, Grief, Trauma, and Crises, to understand what she is going through and how you can help tactfully. Gently encourage her to do the kinds of things described there and in the section in chapter 10 on Coping with Stress.

Close friends and family members may feel shock, great anger, shame, confusion, helplessness, and other feelings. Recognize and accept your own feelings and help her to recognize and accept hers and those of other important people in her life. Reassure her she has your unconditional love, you will work through this crisis together, she is just as virtuous as she was before the rape, and you respect her as much as before. If you are her lover, reassure her she is just as faithful and desirable as before. You may need to work through feelings of rage and a desire for revenge, but don't contact the rapist or threaten to take revenge. The victim doesn't need to worry about further legal problems or your safety. If you can't be fairly calm and rational about your anger, the victim may avoid confiding in you and lose your loving support because she doesn't want to upset you. Be patient and don't become angry because she needs you so much. Remember that some people take longer than others to recover. A rape survivor support group can help a great deal. Check with your local crisis center to find a group for members of your own sex. Small towns probably won't have a group for men, however.

If the victim is your sexual partner, realize the rape will probably affect your sex life temporarily. The victim may need abstinence for a time or she may experience reduced sexual responsiveness. Many rape victims have flashbacks during sexual relations. Victims of extremely violent rapes or victims of multiple rapists often have an especially difficult time. Show your affection and love in other ways now. Encourage the victim to talk about how she feels about affectionate behaviors and sex. Let her decide how or when to resume sexual relations. If you push her to have sex, it may remind her of the rape. Get counseling if problems persist for too long.

Child Sexual Abuse

Father figures abusing daughters account for most cases of incest, but other relatives can be sexual abusers, including mothers. The abusers, whether family members, friends, or strangers, often tempt the child to participate with bribes or special kindness and attention. The abuser insists the child keeps the sex a secret and often uses threats to help ensure keeping of the secret. A sexually abusive parent may reassure the child sex is a normal way to show love for the parent. Parents can develop sexual relationships with their children by turning normal affectionate caresses more sexual or by using orders and threats of punishment. For all of these reasons, the child often does little to resist sexual activities. The child may find pleasure in them, may enjoy them mostly for special attention, or may find them terrifying and unwanted, painful, or even physically damaging. The victim may *dissociate* to cope, creating emotional distance by reducing awareness, emotions, memory, or perception of the environment. This may involve becoming emotionally or physically numb, imagining it is happening to someone else, trying to think of other things until it is over, pretending to be someone else or elsewhere, observing it from a distance as an out-of-the-body experience, or retreating into a trance or fantasy life.

Some sexually abused children carry a huge burden of guilt and shame for participating in the sex and some feel incredibly low and dirty. Contrary to clinical impressions, however, most do not blame themselves for what happened. Sexually abused children are more likely than other children to be depressed or suicidal, to have low self-esteem or substance abuse problems, or to show posttraumatic symptoms like fear, anxiety, and concentration problems. Substance abuse helps numb negative feelings. Victims of parental incest, being trapped in their own homes with no safe place to go, often feel especially devastated. Often the incest is a continuing horror they feel hopeless about changing. They may remain silent because of shame, because they fear beatings for telling the truth, they think other people won't believe them, or they fear the problems that can result from disclosure, such as foster placement or the family provider going to jail. If they do tell, they may feel guilt and a burden of responsibility for the resulting problems.

Sexual abuse results in a profound feeling of betrayal that can make it difficult to trust others. It causes great anger and may result in unstable relationships and shifting moods. Many victims hunger for closeness and love but feel confusion and mixed emotions and may test or sabotage relationships because closeness and trust were so dangerous for them. They may avoid trusting others, manipulate other people, act out angrily, cut or burn themselves, or become involved in further damaging, exploitative relationships. Profound feelings of powerlessness often contribute to the angry acting out, and the child may respond by exploiting other people. On the other hand, the vulnerability and powerlessness of being a victim may result in dissociation, forgetting, denying, emotional numbing, rewriting personal history, minimizing what happened or its seriousness, running away, anxiety, flashbacks, phobias, or sleep, elimination, or eating problems. Some victims suffer severe effects, though others seem to have no symptoms. Children report no distress more often than do adolescents, but this may be an inability to express themselves, or perhaps adolescents show delayed responses after growing to understand the situation better.

Victims of parental incest experience confusing mixtures of great love and great hate for the abusing parent. They may crave love from the abuser while hating the person for using and betraying them. Incest victims battle with intense emotions when they testify against their own parents in court, where the possible consequences are so severe. Some of these victims feel so much love for their parental sex partners that they refuse to testify against them. Some victims feel angry at the other parent who failed to recognize the signs of abuse or failed to put a stop to it. Sometimes the other parent truly has no idea of what is going on. Sometimes physical abuse, neglect, or spousal abuse play a role, and sometimes the other parent denies signs of abuse because of the pain of facing it and the risk of family disruption, jail, loss of income, and scandal. Spouses with unresolved experiences of sexual abuse from their own childhood may have a particularly difficult time in facing the sexual abuse of their children.

Child Abuse

If you have reason to believe that any kind of child abuse has occurred, *immediately* report your suspicions to child abuse authorities at the local branch of your state health department. Don't wait for repeated episodes of abuse and don't wait until you feel sure the abuse is going on. A child's emotional welfare, health, or life may be at stake. Report your suspicions quickly because a successful investigation depends on the documentation of evidence such as injuries. You may report it anonymously, and laws protect people reporting suspected abuse from any possible legal damage suits, even when authorities find no evidence of abuse. Laws require all doctors, nurses, medical examiners, dentists, teachers, social workers, mental health professionals, daycare workers, and law enforcement personnel to report evidence of child abuse. About twenty states require reporting by anyone who suspects child abuse.

We noted previously the high risk of child abuse for children of abused women and parents who themselves experienced abuse as children. Research also indicates unwanted children, children in temporary foster care, stepchildren, disabled children, physically limited or deformed children, and perhaps hyperactive children are all at higher risk of child abuse than are other children. Girls living with no mothers or invalid or chronically ill mothers are at higher risk of sexual abuse from their fathers than girls with healthy mothers, especially if the father is a loner with no close friends. Girls who live with stepfathers or their mothers' live-in boyfriend are also at higher risk. One study found this risk was five times higher than when girls live with biological fathers.

These generalizations about the risk of child abuse say nothing about individual cases because most of the children in these categories don't become abused. What other signs provide clues that should help raise suspicions? Certainly we should take very seriously and investigate any child's report of injuries from parents, physical or sexual abuse, or neglect. A child's fear of a parent or fear of going home also indicates abuse. Some abused children come early or stay late at school to avoid their troubled home life. Parents may dress their children in inappropriate clothing to hide bruises. Physically abused children may show little response to pain and may not cry when they get hurt. Some physically abused children become apprehensive when other children cry. Abused children may not trust other people easily, fear adults in general, or feel wary of adult touch.

Physical signs, of course, provide the most direct evidence. As noted previously, any act of violence or discipline that results in a mark or a bruise on a child lasting more than one hour is an act of child abuse. Parents may accidentally inflict one bruise during physical punishment in an isolated incident, but more than one such bruise indicates child abuse. On a child less than one year old, even one bruise or mark lasting more than one hour from parental discipline indicates child abuse. Any bruise or lasting mark on the child's face or genitals inflicted by a parent indicates child abuse.

Other signs include unexplained bruises, welts, cuts, abrasions, burns, fractures, limping, or painful movements. Contradictory explanations for such injuries also signal child abuse. Injuries that regularly appear after absences from school, weekends, or school vacations indicate child abuse. Although freak accidents do happen, improbable explanations for injuries may suggest child abuse, especially when the parent or child gives the explanation nervously. Delays or reluctance in seeking medical treatment may suggest abuse, as may constantly changing doctors for treatment. Long periods during which you never see a child outside the home and the child never attends school may suggest abuse. The parent may have locked the child up or be waiting for injuries to heal. Bruises, welts, abrasions, or burns from child abuse may take the form of objects used to inflict the injuries, such as belt buckles, electrical cords, rope, hot electric stove heating elements, burning cigarette or cigar tips, or hot clothes irons. Immersion burns may cover hands or feet up to the height of the immersion or may appear in a doughnut shape on the buttocks or genitals.

Physical signs of neglect include abandonment, chronic health problems, chronic hunger, or malnutrition. Malnutrition may result in an underweight child, perhaps sickly, weak, or lacking in endurance. A hungry, neglected child may beg, steal, or hoard food or rummage in garbage cans for food. Unattended physical problems or unmet medical needs also signal neglect. The child may desperately need eyeglasses or dental work, be chronically dirty and unkempt, or untreated cuts may regularly become infected. The child may often wear inappropriate clothing for the weather, or all the child's clothing may be ragged, very worn, or outgrown. A chronic lack of supervision, especially in dangerous activities or for long periods of time, indicates neglect. Emotionally neglected infants (rarely held or played with) become unresponsive to people and disinterested in the environment, perhaps eating weakly, regurgitating often, and becoming malnourished or even dying. Emotionally neglected toddlers lack curiosity, may not go to their parents for comfort or help, or may seldom laugh, smile, or play.

Neglected children are more likely than other children to show withdrawal and developmental and intellectual delays.

Signs of child sexual abuse include pain or itching in the genital or anal areas, difficulty in walking or sitting, or torn, stained, or bloody underclothing. Child sexual abuse may cause bruises, sores, swelling, or bleeding in the genital or anal areas. Vaginal infection, discharge, or venereal disease indicates sexual abuse, especially when found in children under the age of puberty. Child sexual abuse may also result in pregnancy. Sexually abused children may become upset when bathed or when the abusive adult touches them. A child's fear or intense dislike of being left somewhere or with someone may also signal sexual abuse. Some sexually abused children respond to physical contact with people of a particular sex with anxiety or a startle response. Sometimes inappropriate sexual talk or behavior or sophisticated sexual knowledge suggests sexual abuse. Sometimes a child refuses to change or participate in gym class to hide injuries from abuse or stained underwear.

Many other problems in children may suggest abuse but can also come from other family or personal problems without abuse. These problems may include bedwetting, thumb sucking, stuttering, excessive crying, biting, rocking, great fears of the dark or at bedtime, nightmares, insomnia, or mood swings. Others are hyperactivity, anxiety, oversensitivity, nervousness, fears, worries, low self-esteem, depression, hopelessness, temper tantrums, excessive hostility, cruelty, fighting, or aggressiveness. The child may show habitual lying, destructiveness, excessive compliance, poor appetite, headaches, stomachaches, asthma, ulcer, social withdrawal, few or no friends (isolation), poor peer relationships, or bizarre social behavior. Some have fantasies of a different home life, often arrive late for school, truancy, poor academic performance, or chronic fatigue in school. Others have alcohol or drug abuse, steal, delinquency, run away from home, or show self-injury, suicidal behavior, psychosis, or perhaps multiple personality. All these problems are general signs in children of a stressful life.

These general signs may occur in any child for a short time and may relate to problems other than abuse, such as divorce. Therefore, these general signs never prove the existence of abuse. Problems such as these should at least serve to raise the question of abuse, however, especially when the problems become chronic, when one child exhibits many of the above problems, when the problems appear suddenly, or when behaviors or functioning deteriorates. For example, if your child suddenly withdraws from close friendships, suddenly develops a number of problem behaviors, or grades suddenly drop, you should carefully consider the possibility of abuse, watch for negative feelings about or unusual relationships with certain people, and encourage your child to share personal problems with you.

Certain family characteristics that tend to go with child abuse may help raise suspicions, especially in combination with other signs. Families in poverty or with many personal problems (divorce, marital problems, unemployment, drug or alcohol abuse, etc.) may resort to child abuse as an outlet for personal frustrations. Abusive families are sometimes isolated, with few or no close friends or less frequent contact with extended family and friends. Consider child abuse, too, when parents criticize their children excessively, discipline their children harshly, or hold unrealistic expectations for child behavior. Abusive parents often fail to follow through on requests from school authorities or fail to keep appointments people make with them concerning their children. Of course, these characteristics may simply reflect poor skills in raising children and not child abuse.

Unfortunately, child abuse often escapes detection and causes many problems. No effect of abuse is universal in children. Psychological abuse, present in probably 90% of cases of physical abuse, is strongly correlated with low self-esteem, depression, and self-blame for negative events later in life. Physically abused children are consistently rated as more aggressive, with more problems with peer relationships and more antisocial behavior than nonabused children. Neglected children, too, often act angry and rebellious, but they can also be withdrawn, dependent, or inattentive. Severely abused children, especially neglected ones, often fall behind their peers in language development, learning, reading, and muscle coordination skills. Abused girls appear more likely to withdraw, feel depressed or anxious, hurt themselves, and develop physical problems related to stress, and abused boys appear more likely to feel angry, take risks, and show aggressive behavior.

Research shows childhood abuse increases the chance of learning and reading problems, repeating grades, and becoming juvenile delinquents, runaways, addicts, teenage mothers, unemployed adults, criminals, or psychiatric patients later in life, although most abused children do not become involved in crime, nor mentally ill. Approximately 50% of families reported for abuse later had a child taken to court as delinquent or ungovernable. Experts estimate 20% of physically abused children become delinquent. A parent has physically or sexually abused perhaps 2/3 of the estimated 1 million runaway children. Two large studies suggest around 60% of teenage mothers suffered sexual abuse as children. Both men and women in prison report rates of childhood abuse twice as high as those for men and women overall. The physical and sexual abuse rate is high in convicted rapists, child molesters, murderers, and serial killers. Many studies establish the link between abuse and psychological problems or mental illness, and symptoms tend to be worse with more than one kind of abuse. Estimates of childhood physical abuse in psychiatric inpatients range from 18 to 50%.

Studies suggest perhaps 70% of teenage drug addicts and prostitutes suffered sexual abuse, but the majority of sexually abused children do not become prostitutes, drug addicts, rapists, or child molesters. Around 20% of adults sexually abused as children have serious mental disorders, with major depression, anxiety disorders like phobias or panic, and posttraumatic stress disorder most common. Many report problems with anger and some report negative responses to touch, headaches, gastrointestinal problems, or back or pelvic pain. Some cater to other people's needs at the expense of their own to get love. Childhood sexual abuse may also result in excessive seductiveness, promiscuity, sexual excitement responses to abuse and dominance, power and control issues in sexual relationships, repeated sexual victimization, sexual addiction with guilt and shame, prostitution, sexual problems, or sexual identity problems. A variety of studies suggest childhood sexual abuse doubles the likelihood of revictimization by rape in adulthood. This may come from patterns of sexualized play, learning to gain attention, affection, and privileges through sex, and not recognizing danger cues. Feelings of powerlessness, helplessness, hopelessness, and depression may lead to poor limit setting and toleration of further abuse, feeling bad and dirty and deserving of abuse, or expecting disappointment and abuse. Learned responses to trauma of denial, numbing, and dissociation may play a role.

What can you do about child abuse? Parents should protect their children from sexual abuse early in life, preferably before school attendance, by discussing the possibility in simple language and your child's best responses. Do this as described in the section on Discussing Sex with Your Children in chapter 22. This discussion is not sexually explicit and becomes just one normal part of training your child about safety rules. You should also make sure your child's daycare center and any other activity freely accepts parent volunteers. A daycare or scout group that doesn't welcome parental participation may have something to hide. And make sure your daycare center or activity leader knows who will pick up your child on any given day.

Child molesters often join church, school, or sports activities to get closer to children. Pay attention to any adult who develops a relationship with your child beyond the group activities, perhaps by buying gifts. Ask your child questions after visits with someone like this, finding out if your child had fun, who was there, what they did, etc. Don't allow overnight visits, especially if the person lives alone, unless you know the person very well. Child molesters often have a history of joining various children's group activities, never staying too long. Some move on before they get caught, and others relocate and start over after legal problems from molesting.

If a child reports abuse to you, believe the child. Children rarely lie about abuse. Try your best not to become upset, horrified, or overly alarmed about it. Your reaction is critical to the child's view of the situation. Research indicates the reactions of the adults children tell and from whom they seek help and understanding strongly influence a child's recovery from abuse. Meet the child at eye level. Let the child speak without you verbally suggesting abuse or specific actions. Praise the child's bravery in telling you about it. Never blame the child for sexual abuse. Children tend to feel very guilty and responsible for what happened anyway and don't need this extra burden. Instead, say you care, reassure and support them, explain both they and your relationship with them are still just as good as before, and emphasize what happened is not their fault. Say you will do everything you can to make sure the child is safe. As soon as possible, write down the actual words the child used in first disclosing the abuse—the exact words can be important.

Next, contact your local branch of the state health department and report the abuse to the professionals. Do not contact the suspected abuser or a daycare or program where you believe the abuse occurred. Make sure a doctor with the appropriate experience and training in detecting physical or sexual abuse does a medical examination. Health department child abuse workers, children's hospitals, or medical societies can recommend a doctor with expertise. In cases of sexual abuse, you should talk to other parents whose children may be at risk, so they can look for unusual behaviors, talk to their children, or look for physical symptoms in their children.

Then find an agency or individual with expertise in evaluating and counseling physical or sexual abuse victims (the National Child Abuse Hotline at the end of this chapter gives referrals in your area). In cases of incest, the whole family must receive psychological treatment to help resolve intense feelings such as anger, betrayal, fear, shock, confusion, and guilt and to help establish more healthy family relationships. The abuser must take responsibility for what has happened. The victim must deal with intensely conflicting emotions and damaged self-esteem and must learn assertiveness skills to prevent any future sexual abuse. The family must learn to get over the past and learn effective communication skills that will thwart any future sexual abuse.

Child sexual abuse, like other kinds of child abuse, may or may not result in legal action. Prosecution for child abuse depends on the severity of the abuse, local laws and procedures, whether the abuser is a relative of the victim, and the wishes of the family. Official abuse reports indicate about 40% of sexually abusive families and about 20% of physically abusive or neglectful families go to court. When legal action against a parent occurs, jail, loss of family income, and/or foster or state placement for the child may result. However, only about 20 to 25% of reports of sexual abuse and somewhat less than 20% of reports of physical abuse result in foster care. Instead, when the family wants to stay together, professionals generally try to work with them to improve family life and eliminate the danger. In areas with inadequate social services, however, the only way to protect the child may be to jail the abuser or put the child in foster care.

One real advantage of going to court when social services for abuse exist in the community is the threat of jail enforces the sentence of psychological treatment for abuse and addictions. This is important because many abusers who voluntarily agree to treatment quit therapy before completing it and many repeat the crime. Preliminary studies suggest between 40 and 75% of child sexual abusers repeat the crime. A real problem with pressing charges is the child victim may have to detail the abuse for police and court interrogations in front of strangers. Some victims find this even more traumatic than the sexual abuse.

Many communities are improving the court procedures to reduce trauma to sexual abuse victims. When social service and legal agencies coordinate to investigate together with joint interviews, more accurate and complete information results, with less stress on the child. Ideally, one person will question the child and other personnel watch behind a one-way mirror or see the videotape. Such methods may avoid a child's testimony at grand jury and preliminary hearings. Special sexual abuse prosecution units can use the same prosecutor for all stages of the case. Children may receive an advocate in court who might brief them on what will happen, introduce them to the judge, and allow them to visit the courtroom beforehand, perhaps even sitting in the witness chair and speaking into the microphone. Alternatives to testifying in open court include testifying in private with the judge, using one-way mirrors, screens to hide the defendant, closed-circuit TV, videotaped testimony, or closing the courtroom to spectators.

Although children appear more relaxed, confident, fluent, and consistent testifying by closed-circuit TV, studies suggest jurors are more likely mistrust children and the testimony has less impact when delivered in this way.   One study found children cry less when the judge closes the courtroom to spectators and that allowing parents or loved ones to stay in the courtroom during a child's testimony results in the child's improved ability to answer questions and less fear.

Whether or not legal action occurs, abusive parents need professional help to reduce the danger to their children.   Many communities offer programs that teach parenting skills and techniques for controlling anger to physically abusive parents (see under support groups and hotlines at the end of this chapter).   Some programs also provide trained aides to help in the home.   Professionals such as child abuse workers, social workers, and psychologists help abusive parents and their children work on controlling anger, communication, parenting, interests and activities, marital problems, problem solving, relaxation, social life, depression, self-esteem, addiction, etc.

Be sure to choose a counseling program specifically for abusive parents or to read chapter 41 and choose a counselor who sees the behavioral skills of controlling anger as the first priority for physically abusive parents. Traditional psychological counseling more often fails to stop the violence. Learn to recognize your own anger early using the bodily clues discussed in chapter 28, so you can do something about it before it escalates and gets out of control.   Any time you can't maintain a fairly calm, well-controlled, respectful approach to discipline, count or remove yourself from the situation as detailed in chapter 28 until you calm down.   Always work to recognize your anger early and use these techniques frequently, even for minor irritations when you don't really need to count or leave to calm down. Frequent practice of these responses will help you change your habits of explosive anger.   Use plenty of behavioral roleplays to practice appropriate responses to situations that typically anger you, too.   This can help a great deal.

Learn to be firm with your child without raising your voice very often. You will get more cooperation from your children if you learn to treat them more respectfully.   Study and use the advice in chapter 22, Raising Children, especially the sections on Helpful Ways of Showing Your Love, Setting a Good Example, Reducing the Need for Discipline, and Discipline.

Physically abusive parents should also arrange for friends or relatives to help them in the following ways.   Ask them for permission to phone them when you feel too angry to deal with your child appropriately, explaining that you want emotional support and help in calming down until you can treat your child more respectfully. Find some people who are willing to provide emergency babysitting services when you feel so angry that physical abuse becomes a possibility. A daycare center can help during business hours, but you will also need friends, neighbors, or relatives who are available at other times.

As noted in chapter 22, all parents need at least a few hours away from their children every week, both individually and together as a couple. Abusive parents are often in dire need of such free time. Take turns relieving each other of parenting duties, take turns supervising group play with friends who have children, and use babysitters occasionally, so you can get this important time for yourself and your marriage.

Woman Abuse

Excluding murder and rape, women may assault husbands and boyfriends as often as men assault wives and girlfriends, but men assault women more severely. Men are more likely to perform multiple aggressive acts in a single incident, men are much more likely to injure women in attacks than vice versa, and men normally inflict more serious injuries during assaults than do women. Women are about 8 1/2 times as likely as men to receive treatment in hospital emergency rooms for abuse from a spouse or intimate dating partner, and men kill about 9 of every 10 murder victims, whether male or female. Violence by either husband or wife is strongly associated with later violence by the other spouse, and men are much less likely to repeat their violence when their women abstain from violence.

Besides the kinds of abuse described in the first paragraph of this chapter and stalking, woman abuse may also include behaviors designed to upset the woman. Examples include not showing up as scheduled for activities or dates, embarrassing or offensive behavior while intoxicated, or excessive flirting with other people in the presence of the woman. Sexual exploitation may involve unwanted sex, rape, coerced or forced oral or anal sex, orgies, forced sex with other men for voyeurism or money, penetration with objects, bondage, or sadistic acts such as choking or head-banging during sex. Battered women who are sexually assaulted by their partners tend to experience more severe physical assaults than other abused women.

Experts note certain common characteristics in abusive relationships. Low self-esteem is very common in both partners. Abusive men feel ashamed of their own violence and many feel like losers or underachievers in life, although these men typically deny and bury these feelings while maintaining a front of tough manhood. Whether or not the woman had problems in self-esteem before the abuse, acts of abuse and humiliation wear down her self-esteem. Many women continue to tolerate abuse because of low self-esteem.

We have already noted the traditionally stereotyped family and sex roles that reduce compromise and negotiation, men's kinder and gentler sides, and women's assertiveness and independence. Another common characteristic in abusive men and especially in abused women is social isolation. Many abusive men have no truly close friends and make it very difficult for abused women to maintain friendships, deliberately alienating her friends, throwing jealous tantrums, or beating her for socializing. Eliminating outside friendships helps abusive men keep the woman dependent on them. Abused women may also lose intimacy in their friendships as shame causes them to hide the abuse from friends and relatives, or they may lose friends as their situation grows worse and unpleasant scenes alienate others.

Abusive men usually find it very difficult to admit they have been violent toward women, probably because of taboos against violence toward women, which relate closely to social codes of manhood. They may deny their own violence, minimize the extent of it, or attempt to shift the blame for their violence onto the woman for not behaving properly. For example, some men hold excessively high expectations in housework or in the control of children and then abuse the woman for not living up to their requirements. Other abusive men are overly jealous and suspicious of the woman and attempt to blame their own anger and violence on imaginary social slights or sexual affairs. Such a man may constantly interrogate the woman about her every activity, throw tantrums or beat her for socializing, lock her in the house, or force confessions of nonexistent sexual affairs.

Of course, there is never any acceptable excuse or reason for abusive behavior, not even drunkenness. Although arguments over such things as finances, housework, jealousy, sexual relations, children, or addictions may lead to violence or abusive behavior, many assaults occur without any prior domestic conflict. Some women report beatings that began during their sleep. The real cause of abusive behavior is the abuser's severe problem with controlling anger.

Experts agree the violence in abusive relationships tends to increase in both its frequency and severity as time goes on. Studies of both dating and marriage find violence generally begins after the partner has made a major commitment. Between 73 and 85% of abused wives report the violence began after the marriage. Most abused women experience recurring violence and some experience daily violence. Although many women attempt to fight back during beatings, most women who do so find retaliation either is futile or results in beatings of increased severity. Experts also note abuse may begin with the woman's first pregnancy and that pregnancy tends to increase violence in abusive relationships. Of course, pregnancy signals the end of the honeymoon and the coming burden of parenthood. Violence toward pregnant women may even be attempts at inducing abortion or miscarriage, as the man often directs blows and kicks at the abdomen. Violence toward pregnant women may result in hemorrhage, fetal fractures, rupture of the uterus, liver, or spleen, premature labor, miscarriages, stillborn babies, birth defects, or the baby's mental retardation.

Abused women are normal people. Contrary to prevalent stereotypes, they are not masochists. The myth that abused women are masochists seems to explain why they would stay in abusive relationships, but women often leave their abusers. For example, the rate of abuse is much higher among separating or divorcing couples than among other married couples. Many obstacles to leaving exist, however. First, after a few violent episodes, many women still hope for improvement and trust the abuser's promises to reform. The fact that abusive men often apologize and act in extremely loving, kind, and attentive ways for a time after violent episodes encourages women to trust them. Many women think if they change their own behavior to please the man more, the abuse will stop.

Women also stay in abusive relationships because of sex roles. Women grow up practicing nurturing roles, looking forward to love relationships, and viewing love and marriage as central to their future identities. They often love the man despite the abuse, and they often feel they should do everything they can to make their marriages work. Thus, a woman may stay with an abusive man because she feels he needs her, or she may return to him because she feels sorry for him when he talks of unbearable loneliness and of how much he loves and misses her. Women may also stay because they think children need two parents in the home. Psychologists agree, however, children are better off with one nonviolent parent than with two parents in an abusive relationship.

Even when a man repeatedly beats a woman and the woman has given up hope for improving the relationship, there are many obstacles to leaving. Finances are often a great obstacle. Women with few job skills who have devoted their lives to keeping house and raising children often face a life of poverty if they leave. Understandably, many feel reluctant to deprive themselves and their children of material pleasures by leaving. Some women stay while they prepare themselves for leaving, by going to school or acquiring job skills. Women with prosperous husbands may choose to endure the beatings rather than to give up social status and an affluent lifestyle. One study emphasizes the importance of finances in women's responses to abuse; most of the women whose earnings primarily supported the family immediately ended the relationship with the abusive man, and women immediately ended their relationships with unemployed abusive men more often than with abusive men who held jobs.

Of course, leaving involves much more than money. People often fear change and prefer to accommodate themselves to an unpleasant situation rather than make drastic changes in their lives that may have uncertain consequences. Some women fear loneliness and others fear the great responsibilities of raising children alone. Some women wait until the children start school or grow old enough to help around the house, so their lives as single parents will be easier. Socially isolated women may stay with abusive men because they think they have nowhere else to go. Some women stay because they feel ashamed to seek help and they prefer to keep up the image that everything is all right.

Depression, diminished self-esteem, or negative thinking may make the practical problems involved in leaving seem overwhelming and insurmountable. Negative thoughts may include such things as: "I could never earn a living and take care of the children all by myself," "I would hate living all by myself," or "I'm too old to find another man." In addition, psychologists believe an abuser's unpredictable mental and physical abuse despite the woman's constant efforts to soothe and change him may result in a state of learned helplessness in which the woman passively resigns herself to the abuse. Please refer to chapter 27, Depression, for a full discussion of learned helplessness.

Many women also stay because of the reasonable fear that the abuser will harm them if they try to leave. Abusive men often become the angriest when their women attempt or threaten to leave them. Many of the most severe beatings, including murders and use of weapons, occur when women attempt to end abusive relationships. Approximately 25% of reported cases of violence against wives and 40 to 50% of all marital murders occur after the couple no longer lives together.

Finally, some women stay in abusive relationships because they experienced abuse as children and are therefore accustomed to the feelings and behaviors in them. These women grew up accustomed to mixtures of love and emotional or physical brutality that make them fairly comfortable with chaos and danger, not trusting their loved ones, not having their needs met, and a kind of unsatisfying love that includes much hate, anger, and pain. These women can tolerate great amounts of emotional ambivalence, and they don't expect much from other people. They are accustomed to stifling their anger, yielding during conflicts, silencing themselves, smoothing things over, apologizing despite being wronged, and unfair blame. They may also be accustomed to feeling pity for, covering up for, and helping their loved ones take care of problems they bring on themselves. These women may not understand how profoundly gentle and kind marital love can and should be.

Experts agree abused women are not masochists. These women simply don't know what signs to look for to avoid men with violent potential and how to protect themselves once they become deeply involved with violent men. Most abused women go through a slow process of trying to salvage the abusive relationship and gradually giving up hope for improvement. Many show great courage, resourcefulness, and perseverance in dealing with the abuse and finding ways to leave. They must carefully pacify the abuser and protect the children, while functioning as a parent and wife under constant mental and physical abuse. Many develop a plan of action for leaving and slowly gather up the money and resources over long periods to be able to leave. Because of the many obstacles to leaving, it should come as no surprise that women often leave their abusers three, four, or five times before permanently leaving.

Understandably, the unpredictable, traumatic experiences of abuse often result in emotional problems or stress-related medical complaints in victims. Anger, fear, anxiety, shame, and depression are common. Rage is often buried and unrecognized. She may fear for herself, her children, and perhaps her family of origin. Terror may immobilize her during abusive episodes. Anxiety may result in restlessness, insomnia, nightmares, or hypervigilance. With damaged self-esteem from a process similar to brainwashing, she may come to blame herself, feel guilty for not pleasing her man, or feel deserving of abuse. Depression may include fatigue, loss of appetite, or suicide attempts. Psychosomatic symptoms may include headaches, backaches, gastrointestinal problems, asthma, etc. Anxiety, depression, a fear of intimacy, paranoia, and disturbing memories may last long after the woman ends the abusive relationship, and paranoia may cause inability to trust others and difficulties with reality.

No person should tolerate abuse. Experts encourage all women to leave abusive men because abusive men often increase the frequency and severity of their violence as time goes on. Even without physical violence or sexual abuse, you should not tolerate verbal or emotional abuse that undermines your confidence, self-esteem, or self-respect. If you end the relationship, be especially careful. The two most dangerous times are when the abused woman attempts or threatens to end the relationship and when she starts a new relationship with another man. Some women choose to leave without warning to avoid trouble. If you plan to leave when the man is not at home, be sure to have either the police escort you (preferably) or several friends with you in case he shows up while you are moving. Prepare for leaving by placing everything you will need in easily accessible locations, without doing so in obvious ways.

Take your children with you. If you leave in an emergency without your children and then decide to end your relationship with the man, go back with a police officer and get your children as soon as possible. Some abusers claim abandonment by the mother and get temporary custody of the children. Judges often fail to consider the difficulties in such emergencies and view mothers who leave the children behind with the husband as neglectful. You may want to pick up your children at school, but never go back to your home for children or personal belongings unless you have the police escort you (preferably) or several friends with you.

Friends, relatives, or shelters for abused women (see hotlines at the end of this chapter for referrals) can give you a place to stay and help you arrange a new life for yourself. Call the National Domestic Violence Hotline at the end of this chapter to find local resources. You can also get help from crisis centers, psychologists, social workers, police, courts, doctors, and clergy. Don't stay with any single man who is not a relative—this suggests adultery and may result in loss of alimony or child custody. If you evict the abuser from a shared residence or if he may have extra keys to your home, change the locks on the doors and make sure the windows fasten tightly. If he will know where you live, consider the safety precautions of living with a friend, roommate, or guard dog. Working women should car pool, get rides to and from work, or ask coworkers to watch for their safety in the parking lot before and after work.

Abused women should request court orders for protection (called restraining orders or injunctions in some areas), based on previous threats, intimidation, violence, or misdemeanor arrests. You will not have to prove criminal conduct beyond a reasonable doubt. In most areas, these court orders can order the man out of a shared residence (even if it is in his name) or to avoid all contact with you (including telephoning and writing). They can order him to participate in counseling or to pay for your new shelter, moving expenses, medical treatment, counseling, attorney's fees, property damage, or time lost from work. Court orders for protection can also limit visitation rights to children (perhaps allowing visits only in the presence of a third party), require exchange of children in a safe setting such as school, require child support, or give you exclusive use of his car.

Call your local court and find out what court orders for protection apply to your case and whether you need a lawyer to get them. If you do need a lawyer and you can't afford one, check with the county Bar Association, city or county court prosecutor's office, social service agencies, or women's organizations to find out what is available. Try to find a lawyer with experience in woman abuse.

Ask the police, prosecutor, or a lawyer about the stalking laws in your state. Crossing state lines or to stalk, harass, or injure someone or violate a protective order is now a federal crime, as is doing these things on federal property or other places within federal jurisdiction, whether or not the victim is or was a spouse or intimate partner. More battered women are filing civil personal injury lawsuits against their abusers, especially when the divorce settlement is unjust. These lawsuits can provide money for emotional distress and all the expenses mentioned above. Sometimes the judge will set aside a prenuptial or divorce agreement that you signed under pressure or distress.

Arresting your abuser may or may not help, and the research on counseling for batterers gives little basis for hope. These are two more reasons why experts insist abused women should leave their men. Research suggests arrest reduces rates of further violence in employed or married offenders, but it may increase violence after a reduction in the first 6 months or year in "bad risk" offenders. These offenders are unemployed men, unmarried men, men who never finished high school, and those with previous arrests or a criminal history. Most episodes of violence against women in which someone calls the police do not result in an arrest or even a report. The police often don't arrest the man unless the violence results in severe injury, he uses a weapon, or he assaults the woman when the police are there. When arrest occurs, prosecution generally doesn't, and when conviction occurs, sentencing is generally quite lenient with few offenders spending time in jail. Because of this, many batterers see arrest as "no big deal."

Couple's therapy without a clear focus on violence is dangerous for abusive women. In counseling, the couple examine and discuss many of their most difficult and emotional issues, which can easily lead to violence. The batterer going to abuse counseling very often persuades women in shelters to return to the man, but experts now question if this is wise—batterers' counseling programs may actually increase the woman's risk by leading to a false sense of security. The vast majority of abusive men in counseling go reluctantly, only because a court forces them or the abused woman has left and refused to return until they go.

The research suggests counseling for abusive behavior often fails, even when men complete the program, but most men quit counseling shortly after the woman returns, including those sentenced by the court to counseling. Thus, the outlook for changing an abusive man is poor. Please refer to chapter 42, Preventing Violence and Crime, for a full discussion of arrest policies and their effects, the unhelpful attitudes of many prosecutors and judges, the ineffectiveness of counseling, and new legal responses to domestic violence.

With some assertiveness, you can use the legal system effectively, however. First, when calling the police in an emergency, don't mention that the attacker is your husband, ex-husband, boyfriend, or ex-boyfriend. When the police arrive, describe what happened in detail, show the police any injuries or damaged property, and tell them about previous episodes of violence. Even if you don't want the police to arrest the abuser, ask them to file a report about the incident and to give you the case number of the report, so you will have some evidence in case further assaults occur. Ask the police for their badge numbers, too, writing down the case number of the report and the badge numbers.

If you want the man arrested and the police won't arrest him, you can force the police to do so by telling them you want to make a citizen's arrest and you want their help in taking the abuser to the police station and filling out the arrest forms. If the police refuse to do this, report them to their commanding officer or, better yet, to the Civilian Complaint Review Board for failing to perform their duties. You can also go to the police station, immediately or the next morning, and sign a warrant for the abuser's arrest. You can do this without a lawyer. Explain where he works and encourage the police to arrest him at work, where he will feel social consequences for his violence. In most cases, the police will release the man shortly after his arrest.

You will need a lawyer (preferably one experienced in woman abuse) if you are ending a marriage or separating from the father of your child. Ask your local police department or court if your community has any victim compensation programs. Shelters for abused women may provide you with victim advocates who will help you deal with the legal system. If your community has no victim advocates, bring a friend with you for moral support whenever you deal with the legal system. Prepare to stand firm in case the prosecutor tries to talk you out of filing criminal charges. If the prosecutor refuses to prosecute your case or seems unresponsive to your needs, ask for a different prosecutor or insist on talking to the prosecutor's supervisor. You may want to ask for help in dealing with your prosecutor from the victim's assistance program in the criminal court building, from a legal aid lawyer, a shelter for abused women, or a local chapter of the National Organization for Women (NOW).

If the abuser threatens to hurt you if you don't drop the charges, insist the violence is a criminal offense, that only the prosecutor or judge can drop the charges, and you can do nothing except tell the truth in court. This stance may persuade him to plead guilty in court. Insist that the police arrest the abuser if he assaults you again. By standing firm, you stand the best chance of changing his violent ways. If possible, bring photographic evidence and medical records of injuries, police report numbers, police badge numbers, torn or bloody clothing, and any witnesses with you when you go to any hearing or trial, including a hearing for a court order for protection. Signed statements may provide evidence when a witness cannot appear in court, and even your children may act as witnesses in court when no other witnesses exist. Dress well and conservatively every time you go to court, and never show any anger toward the judge or toward your abuser in court. The judge's opinion of your character may influence the decision in the case.

A jail sentence is unlikely for first offenders unless the abuse resulted in severe injuries or the man is already on probation or parole. If you don't want him to go to jail, tell the prosecutor you prefer that the court order probation and mandatory counseling, checking with you for three years of followup, with further violence or intimidation being a violation of parole. Call the police and let your prosecutor know every time the abuser violates court orders for protection or probation requirements, even if the only violation has been verbal harassment, threats, or quitting counseling. If you show the police the court order and tell them what happened, the police should arrest him. Normally, the police will release him soon after the arrest and tell him when to appear in court. You must attend this court hearing and present any evidence (witnesses, photographs, signed statements, etc.) to convince the judge the violation occurred. If the court finds the abuser guilty, the judge may impose a severe penalty, perhaps ordering him out of the house or putting him in jail.

Abusive men often use custody, money, or sentimental possessions as weapons after the woman leaves. Find out from a lawyer in your state what a court might award you and what you can legally take with you. Unless a lawyer says you can't, take half the money in any checking and savings accounts before the abuser has a chance to take your name off the accounts. Realize he may take your name off joint credit cards or change the locks on all the doors to your home. Take any family photographs or heirlooms and items of sentimental value with you, so he can't destroy them. Ask a lawyer about child custody issues, too. If an abuser with child visitation rights still gives you trouble, exchange children by picking them up or dropping them off at school or ask friends or relatives to deliver them and pick them up.

If your abuser is your boyfriend, former lover, or divorced husband, you can charge him with a crime if he enters your house without permission, forces you to have sex with him, assaults, or threatens you. Many abusers continue harassment despite the woman moving out or court orders for no contact. This is stalking and suggests danger. Report any harassment or threats to the police. You will be safer if you install adequate outdoor lighting around your home and solid core doors with dead bolts and peepholes. Trim back bushes and vegetation in your yard that provide places to hide. Tell trusted neighbors and coworkers about the problem and give them a photo of him and any vehicles he may drive.

Vary the routes you use when you go places regularly, such as stores or restaurants. Anytime you go out of the home or workplace, try to find a companion and to stay in public areas. If you jog or go for walks, be sure to do these things. If you ever need help, yell "FIRE!" People respond to this word more than any other. Generally it is best never to meet the abuser except in a public place with plenty of people around and only when absolutely necessary.

If he calls you on the phone, feel free to hang up. Ask coworkers to screen all phone calls and visitors. Screen calls at home with Caller ID devices or an answering machine to avoid his calls. If you can afford it, use an answering machine on a published phone number and use a private unlisted phone line for close friends and family, so he won't realize you have another line. Label and date answering machine messages, make a list of Caller ID dates and times, and save written letters as proof of continued harassment.

Severe beatings often cause abused women to give up hope in the relationship and leave permanently. All too often, the emergency forces them out of the house unprepared to leave permanently. Whether or not you currently plan to leave the abusive man, you should prepare for this possibility in advance. Make sure you know the financial assets of the marriage. If you don't know them, hunt for papers concerning properties, car registrations, bank accounts, stocks, loans, insurance, etc. Make copies and make extra car and house keys and a list of telephone numbers you might need (including those of creditors), keeping them at a safe place, perhaps the home of a trusted friend or relative. Think about where you might want to live and find out about housing in your price range, either by checking ads or investigating public housing or welfare. Find out what papers you will need to show to qualify, then gather them and make copies. Make new friends. Get job skills through on-the-job training, classes, or volunteer work. You might join a support group.

Whether or not you plan on filing criminal charges or leaving the abuser, you should gather evidence for the abuse. You will need this evidence if the beatings become worse and you decide to press criminal charges, if either of you sues for divorce, or if child custody ever becomes an issue. Take color pictures of any bruises or injuries shortly after the beating. Get a medical or dental examination for further proof, telling the doctor or dentist what really happened. This establishes the date beyond any doubt and helps in detailing minor or internal injuries that may not show in photographs. Save any torn or bloody clothes for evidence. Take pictures of any damaged or vandalized property. Keep all of this evidence where the abuser will never find it, perhaps with a trusted friend, and ask witnesses to remember the violence in case you ever need the evidence.

Protect yourself in other ways, too. First, remove any guns from the house. If that is impossible, install trigger locks, unload the guns, and keep the ammunition in a separate place or get rid of it. Teach children in the house who are old enough to use the telephone how to call for help whenever they see or hear violence in the home. Ideally, you should teach them to call the police or the emergency number 911 and to give your address. Less effective alternatives include instructing them to call a friend, relative, or neighbor. Teach them to run to a neighbor's home and ask the neighbor to make the emergency call whenever violence occurs and they can't reach the telephone unnoticed or without risking danger. Explain the situation to your closest neighbors and ask them to call the police if they hear any suspicious noises. You can also establish a code word so family, friends, or coworkers know when to call the police, and a visible signal for neighbors to call, such as whenever a particular shade in your house is down.

A woman who refuses to call the police and stays in the house when a man becomes violent not only risks danger, but also shows the man she will tolerate more violence. Leaving, even temporarily, asserts your rights and gives you leverage to insist on improvements. You should leave and go to a safe place whenever violence occurs, even if it is only pushing you around or breaking things. Don't waste your time trying to reason with a violent man; just gather the children if you can and go to the home of a friend or relative, a member of the clergy, a shelter for abused women, or a police station. Stay away at least until you feel quite sure the man is calm. You should probably stay away overnight, and you may need to stay away for several days or more.

Plan for these emergencies in advance. Set aside money for going or staying elsewhere when necessary. Keep enough money on your person to pay for a taxi to a safe place. Make habits of keeping your car full of gas and backing your car into the driveway, for leaving quickly in emergencies. During arguments, avoid rooms with no exits, such as the bathroom, or rooms with weapons, such as the kitchen. Find trusted friends or relatives who will help you in an emergency. Give them extra copies of your house and car keys, the extra cash, a list of telephone numbers you might need, and a change of clothes for you and your children. Keep medicines, birth certificates, social security information, passports, and other necessities easily available. If you have no close friends or relatives in town, memorize the phone number of the nearest shelter for abused women or police station and learn how to get there from your house. You may need money for one or more nights in a motel. Women being stalked (even if the stalking is only harassment so far) can keep a packed suitcase in the trunk of their car. Working women may decide to keep extra keys, clothes, and papers at work.

If you can predict the man's rages, leave before he explodes in anger. If you can't predict the rages, pay close attention to events leading up to violence. Perhaps complaining about petty things, cursing, and yelling at the children often build up to a violent rage, or perhaps a quiet, sullen mood and heavy drinking often lead up to violence. Perhaps his eyes make him seem emotionally unreachable or his speech gets faster. An inability to listen to you is common when anger builds. Any time you suspect the likelihood of violence, leave the house before problems arise. You might slip out of the house unnoticed, perhaps by saying you hear the baby crying and going out a back door or window. You might pretend you need something from the store in order to bake or that you had promised the children they could go visiting. Develop excuses to go outdoors that won't make him suspicious. Make a habit of walking the dog twice a day and of taking the garbage out late at night. Develop a signaling system to alert your older children to call the police, either at home or by sneaking out to go to a neighbor's house. Get out and stay at a safe place until you feel sure his mood has greatly improved.

Unfortunately, most abused women struggle with the question of whether to leave, and many feel tempted to go back when the man says he misses them terribly, begs them to return, and promises to improve. If you wish you had the courage or opportunity to leave or you feel tempted to return but dread doing so, your reasons for staying or returning probably include practical problems you blow out of proportion with negative thinking. Some examples appeared earlier in our discussion of the obstacles to leaving.

Replace your negative thoughts about practical problems with positive thought alternatives every day as described in chapter 4. Positive alternatives include: "I can make it on my own. The women's shelter will provide counseling and help me get started," "I can make friends at church, look up old friends, and join clubs so I won't feel too lonely," "Plenty of women raise children alone. It will certainly be better than putting up with violence." Reading statements like these every day will help give you courage to leave or stay away from the abuser. Make a list of reasons for leaving, including that abuse tends to get worse over time, that counseling usually fails to help, and all the episodes of abuse you remember experiencing. To strengthen your determination, read this list every day and spend time remembering and imagining some of the worst experiences on it.

If you go back (a foolish decision), at least use your leverage in the relationship at this point to insist on some changes before you return. Insist that he go to counseling. Tell him if he quits counseling or doesn't improve his anger, you will leave him again.

Be sure to choose a counseling program specifically for abuse or to read chapter 41 and choose a counselor who sees the behavioral skills of controlling anger as the first priority for abusive men. Traditional psychological counseling more often fails to stop the violence. Abusive men must learn to recognize their anger early using the bodily cues discussed in chapter 28, so they can do something about their anger before it escalates and gets out of control. Every time you can't maintain a calm, respectful tone of voice or can't quietly listen to the other person's point of view, count and imagine the presence of an authority figure or remove yourself from the situation as described in chapter 28 until you calm down. Always work to recognize your anger early and to use these techniques frequently, even for minor irritations when you don't really need to count or leave to calm down.

Frequently practicing these responses will help you change your habits of explosive anger. Use plenty of behavioral roleplays to practice appropriate responses to situations that typically anger you, too; this can help a great deal. If possible, join a support group (see end of this chapter).

Eliminate excuses for the violence such as: "It was the alcohol," "If she didn't do ..., I wouldn't have gotten angry," and "I couldn't control myself!" Practice taking responsibility for your violence by writing and daily reading sentences like: "I have a severe problem with anger," "No provocation, no matter how severe, can cause my violence. It is my fault," and "I have beaten the woman I love." Because abusive men so often return to their violent ways, they and their partners should regularly review their lives for his continued progress in the ways and time intervals described in the last paragraph of chapter 11, Easy Changes. If you find any instances of explosive anger or violence, renew your efforts at self-improvement.

Abused women who stay with their men need counseling, too. Observations of marital interactions have found violent couples lacking in communication skills and engaging in fewer positive and more negative behaviors than other couples. Both partners must work on their marital problems and on replacing negative communication habits with good communication and problem-solving skills. If you can't discuss certain topics without someone getting upset, discuss these issues in counseling that focuses on the violence. Both partners often need work and improvement in relaxation and stress reduction, interests and activities, loneliness or social isolation, self-esteem, appropriate assertiveness, getting over the past, depression, raising children, and addiction. Use the appropriate chapters of this book to work on these problems one simple step at a time (chapter 11), so you don't overwhelm yourself trying to work on too many things at once.

Even when abusive men refuse to work on their problems, women who make the dangerous choice of staying in the relationship can work alone to improve things. Use this book to work on the marital problems, your own communication and problem-solving skills, and any other needed areas. If you tend to feel guilty for not behaving perfectly and take the blame for the abuse you receive, counter such feelings with more realistic thoughts such as: "It's not my fault he's angry. He's throwing a temper tantrum!" and "He's in the wrong, not me!" If you have become emotionally numb because of the abuse, get in touch with your feelings using the advice in chapter 5, Emotions. Recognizing your feelings helps you to accept and overcome them and provides the basis for assertive communications and problem solving.

The best time for a woman to demand changes in an abusive relationship is when the woman leaves and the man wants her back. The next best time to demand changes is after the man beats her, when he feels very sorry and acts very kind. If neither of these things happens, choose a time when you are getting along better than usual. If you have been afraid to make new friends, go to school, or get a job because of his reactions, start doing these things during one of these safer times, even if you still have a black eye. If you wait until the bruises fade, he won't be so sorry and you might get beaten again for trying. Demand that he work on his anger using the following rule. Every time he can't maintain a calm, respectful tone of voice and quietly listen to your point of view during a conflict, you will point out this problem and he must use one of the two techniques for controlling anger detailed in chapter 28. He must count and imagine the presence of an authority figure or he must leave the situation. Explain that any time he refuses to use these techniques, you will leave the house and stay with friends or relatives until his mood improves a great deal. Copy this rule down on piece of paper, including the complete description of these two techniques from chapter 28, and make him sign it.

Explain that you plan to work on improving your negative communication habits, too. If you yell in arguments, follow the same rule about counting or leaving the situation until you calm down. If you don't yell in arguments, choose your most common communication problem from the list in chapter 6 and work on it. If possible, get the abusive man to read the chapters on anger, problem solving, communication skills, and marital problems. Don't try to make too many changes at once, however. Each of you should work on only one or two things at a time until you succeed at making these changes for a period.

Chapter 28, Anger, contains the most important advice for abusive men. Help him work on recognizing his anger early, expressing his feelings several times each day, defining problems in very specific, observable actions, and avoiding angry thinking that prolongs his upset feelings. Hold regular problem-solving sessions at least once or twice a week, taking turns listening quietly as described in chapter 28. Use the helpful list of questions for analyzing anger. Copy it and keep it where you can both refer to it whenever you feel angry. Lavish praise on the abusive man whenever he counts or leaves a conflict to calm down, negotiates or compromises, and reads any of the chapters in this book. He needs to know you feel proud of his efforts. Consistently praising him for good behavior actually helps him change.

Never let him shift the blame for an angry outburst onto you for not acting properly. Every time he tries to do this, tell him, "Nobody *makes* anyone else angry. We are all free to respond to upsetting situations in many different ways. You make yourself angry over certain situations and only you can change it." If he blames alcohol for his angry outbursts, tell him alcohol is no excuse. If he blames a loss of control, tell him "You must take responsibility for your own bad habit of exploding in anger. With effort, you can change this problem." Make a copy of the relevant sentences and refer to them when necessary. If possible, get him to read them every day.

Abusive men have long-term habits of poorly controlled anger. You will need to repeatedly assert yourself for months to change him. Use the techniques in chapter 16, Assertiveness, to practice making your needs and desires known, saying no, putting forth your opinion, complaining about treatment you don't like, refusing sex when you so desire, etc. Keep insisting on your rights and the changes you need until he takes you seriously. The following list contains examples of statements you can use.

Assertive Statements for Abuse

Your voice is getting loud. I'm not going to discuss it until after you go and do something else to calm down.

I want to solve this problem with you, but first you must calm down. Why don't you go visit ... for a while?

You're upset. Your voice is very loud. If you don't go and do something else until you calm down, I'll have to leave and take the kids to visit ...

I have the right to say no.

I won't tolerate this kind of treatment.

I have a right to bring up problems affecting me. And I demand that you help me find a solution.

You have no right to insult me like that. If you don't stop right now, I'm going to visit ...

I am your wife (girlfriend) and I deserve some kindness and cooperation.

Petty criticisms like that are unfair. I've worked all day taking care of the children and fixing supper.

Conflicts require negotiation and compromise on both sides.

I have the right to change my mind.

You can't control me with intimidation anymore.

I'm going to visit ... until you are in a better mood.

If you find it difficult to assert yourself in confrontations, practice using behavioral roleplays. Ask a friend to portray the abuser, and practice asserting yourself in explosive situations until you become very comfortable doing it. Use previous episodes you remember and new episodes you make up.

Like grief over the loss of a loved one, the emotional pain of abuse will diminish with time but may always remain with you to some degree. If you have experienced abuse in the past, either as a child or in an adult love relationship, be very cautious in choosing love relationships. Realize a stable and kind relationship may seem dull in comparison to a chaotic abusive relationship with its roller coaster fights and reconciliations. Realize trusting someone before the person earns your trust is dangerous. Go slowly in dating and romance. Date a variety of people and don't slip quickly into sex and the dependency of strong emotional involvement. Date any new romantic prospect for months and months before becoming deeply involved, so you can begin to evaluate his selfishness, control of anger when upset, and kindness when disappointed. Use the section on Is This Relationship Good for Me? in chapter 15, Social Life, to help make good decisions in romance. It includes some important clues to danger in a relationship that might eventually become violent.

In addition, be wary of very jealous men who think you will become unfaithful just because you talk to another man, dance with an old friend, etc. Be wary of men who don't seem to like your having too many friends, who feel hatred or disgust for women from previous romances or for women in their family, or who abuse alcohol or drugs, have spent time in jail, or experienced abuse as children. Previously abused women often fall in love with troubled men and hope to change them for the better. For your own happiness and safety, don't make this mistake!

Instead, learn to quickly end new relationships that trample on the borders of respect. Assert yourself with good communication skills anytime you feel the least bit uncomfortable about how boyfriends or other people treat you. Practice making your needs and desires known, saying no, and complaining about treatment you don't like. Most abused women are unassertive and overly compliant, but many also tend to be overly suspicious. Learn to recognize when slights and disappointments are not deliberate attempts to hurt you. Don't worry about losing your boyfriend by practicing assertiveness. Losing a selfish boyfriend is much better than risking the nightmare of abuse later! Never submit to pressure that seems the least bit unfriendly. End the relationship if you regularly find yourself stifling anger, smoothing things over, catering to the other person to avoid trouble, apologizing despite mistreatment, or receiving unfair blame or criticism. If you don't do these things, you make it easy for other people to use or abuse you.

Recommended Additional Readings:

You Can Be Free: An Easy-to-Read Handbook for Abused Women. by Ginny NiCarthy and Sue Davidson. Seattle, WA: Seal Press, 1989.

Violent No More: Helping Men End Domestic Abuse. by Michael Paymar. Alameda, CA: Hunter House, 1993.

The Date Rape Prevention Book: The Essential Guide for Girls and Women. by Lindquist, Scott. Naperville, IL: Sourcebooks, 2000. has details about warning signs, how to communicate and act defensively in threatening situations, and how to escape.

Recovery from Rape. 2nd ed. by Linda E. Ledray. NY: Henry Holt and Co., 1994.

If You Are Raped. 2nd ed. by Kathryn M. Johnson. Holmes Beach, FL: Learning Publications, 1998.

If She Is Raped. 2nd ed. by Alan W. McEvoy and Jeff B. Brookings. Holmes Beach, FL: Learning Publications, 1991.

Victims No Longer: Men Recovering from Incest and Other Sexual Child Abuse. by Mike Lew. New York: HarperCollins, 1990.

Sex, Power, and Boundaries: Understanding and Preventing Sexual Harassment. by Peter Rutter. New York: Bantam Books, 1996.

Sexual Harassment on the Job. by William Petrocelli and Barbara Kate Repa. Berkeley: Nolo Press, 1992.

Obsessive Love. by Susan Forward and Craig Buck. NY: Bantam Books, 1991. good for those who want to leave an abusive relationship but feel addicted to the love or sex.

How to Survive the Loss of a Love. by Melba Colgrove, Harold H. Bloomfield, and Peter McWilliams. Los Angeles: Prelude Press, 1991. for the end of a relationship, whether by breaking up, divorce, separation, or death.

Please refer to the suggested resources at the end of chapter 28, Anger.

Support Groups, Hotlines, and Resources:

Rape, Abuse, and Incest National Network, RAINN 800 656 4673 information, support, referrals, gives rape crisis centers in your area. on-line: www.rainn.org

National Child Abuse Hotline 800 422 4453 information, support, crisis counseling, referrals for reporting, evaluations, or counseling. on-line: childhelpusa.org

National Domestic Violence Hotline 800 799 7233 (deaf people call 800 787 3224 with TDDs) information, support, referrals for shelters for abused women and counseling. on-line: www.ndvh.org

Batterers Anonymous 909 355 1100 (leave message) support group referrals. on-line: www.genesisnetwork.net/users/goffman/ba210.htm

Parents Anonymous 909 621 6184 referrals to professionally led support group treatments for abusive parents, many have groups for their children, too. on-line: www.parentsanonymous.org

Molesters Anonymous 909 355 1100 (leave message) support group referrals. on-line: www.genesisnetwork.net/users/goffman/ba210.htm

Survivors of Incest Anonymous 410 893 3322 information, referrals, support groups, literature, newsletter, pen pals. on-line: www.siawso.org

Voices in Action 800 786 4238 information, referrals to treatment, newsletter, support groups for victims of child sexual abuse.

Victims of Child Abuse Laws 800 745 8778 referrals to psychologists and lawyers for wrong accusations of child abuse, newsletter. on-line: www.nasvo.org

False Memory Syndrome Foundation 215 940 1040 for people falsely accused of child sexual abuse based on recovered memories and for those questioning their memories.

Equal Employment Opportunity Commission (EEOC) 800 669 4000 a federal agency that investigates cases of sexual harassment. on-line: www.eeoc.gov

If you want to leave an abusive relationship but feel addicted to the person, please refer to the support groups for sexual or love addictions at the end of chapter 18, Sex.

37. Getting over the Past

Visit the past but don't live there.

Certain upsetting life experiences interfere with happiness for a long time. Physical or sexual abuse, rape, wartime combat, disaster, or the sudden and unexpected death of a loved one are the most traumatic of these, but a wide variety of stresses may result in long-lasting emotional pain. Some of the most common include parental or peer problems from childhood, divorce, bad experiences in romance, and the death of a parent or a loved one. If you can't resolve painful feelings about the past, you may remain unforgiving and alienated from a loved one, your feelings about the past may interfere with new relationships, or you may repeat patterns of behavior you experienced as a child, such as abuse, victimization, or addiction. Although the suggestions in this chapter can help a great deal in getting over the past, the emotional pain may always remain with you to some degree. Getting over the past always involves a healthy acceptance of the painful event and of the emotional pain you feel. Please refer to chapter 1, Happiness, for a discussion of the importance of fully accepting life's joys and sorrows.

Negative thinking often interferes with acceptance. You may dwell on the past, wallow in self-pity over past events, or blame the past for your failures in life today, instead of working to conquer your problems. Study the negative thoughts keeping you focused on emotional pain over the past and replace these thoughts with positive thinking alternatives every day (see chapter 4). For example, a person who still feels upset over excessive criticism in childhood from a parent might write "I am a good, talented person and I'm finished with all that criticism now and forever." The sections Rejection in Romance, Chained to the Past, Depression, and Excessive Grief in chapter 4 include more examples of negative thoughts about the past and positive alternatives.

Sometimes we remain preoccupied with our painful past relationships or experiences because we lack enough pleasures, interests, activities, friends, or time spent socializing. Carefully consider this possibility. Do you have a well-rounded variety of interests and activities you enjoy? Do you have a network of friends, including several very close friends and a number of other friends, with whom you share different interests, activities, and parts of your personality? Do you spend enough time with your friends every week to truly enjoy your social life? Are you often lonely or bored? Are you afraid of becoming deeply involved in a new relationship because of past experiences? Improving problems in these areas may be the most effective way of getting over your painful past. Please refer to chapters 8 and 15 for a full description of the importance of interests, activities, and social life and for a description of how to best make improvements in these areas.

Sometimes we remain preoccupied with painful feelings from the past because other problems, perhaps problems caused by the painful past, interfere with our present personal growth. Look through the table of contents in this book and consider whether other problems (such as depression, low self-esteem, or lack of assertiveness) may interfere with your progress in getting over the past. If so, work on these problems using the appropriate chapters. Many people fall into a victim role, feeling hurt repeatedly, perhaps by jumping into relationships too quickly or perhaps by allowing their depression, negative thinking, poor assertiveness skills, or poor control of anger to sabotage relationships.

Sometimes the past still plagues us because we avoid our painful emotions. We noted burying emotions and memories by ignoring them every time they arise is a common method of coping with grief and trauma. We may also stifle our emotions to hide personal problems, because of feeling emotions are a sign of weakness, to hide emotions that seem illogical, selfish, or childish, or because we feel boys or adults shouldn't cry or emotions are feminine. After divorce or rejection in love, we may hide emotions to avoid giving other people the satisfaction of knowing how much they have hurt us.

Unfortunately, avoiding our emotions sometimes backfires and the problem emotion keeps returning. In such cases, keeping very busy with interests, activities, and socializing may be running away from the problem rather than solving it. If an upsetting past relationship, loss, or experience still plagues you, you may need to spend more time understanding and deeply experiencing the past to finish it more completely. Chapter 5, Emotions, details the rationale for getting over the past by thoroughly understanding, deeply experiencing, and working through the troubling emotions. Psychologists often refer to unresolved issues such as anger, hatred, frustration, pain, guilt, love, and appreciation as *unfinished business*. Properly resolving or finishing these issues helps in forgiving other people and in bringing a new happiness and vitality to your present life.

The most thorough way to resolve unfinished business is to use as many of the following exercises as apply to your situation, feeling free to use only as many of the exercises as you need to contact, express, and resolve your feelings about the past. Two kinds of roleplay, interpersonal roleplay and dialoguing, help a great deal in resolving unfinished business. Please refer to chapter 14 for a full discussion of these two kinds of roleplay, so you will understand the discussion that follows. And please consider the warning in chapter 14 about the danger to certain people of using these techniques. You may need the help of a psychologist to explore and resolve the past.

Interpersonal roleplay can be particularly powerful (and dangerous) when the participants are the same people whom your painful past event actually involved. These people may not be sensitive enough to help you deal with intense emotions as they arise. Usually, however, others portray the people from your past in the roleplay and you must instruct the participants on how to feel and act, describing the personalities from your past. You can use reversed roles and asides to help illuminate the perspectives in the situation. Always use the first person singular and the present tense (I feel, I wish, etc.) in your interpersonal roleplays or dialogues, so you can better contact your feelings. If you work with a childhood episode, don't use large, difficult words. If you dialogue with a person from your past, a picture of the person (preferably) or an empty chair can help by symbolizing the person's presence.

Before starting any roleplay or dialogue on painful experiences, spend time remembering as much detail as possible about the events. Where were you? What did the place look like? Who was there? How old were you? What kind of mood were you in before the episode took place? Exactly what happened? What did you see and hear? What feelings did you experience? What were you thinking? What did you do? How did other people react? What happened next? Spend at least twenty or thirty minutes trying to remember, picture, and hear the situation clearly in your mind.

Begin your work by simply trying to reexperience the upsetting situation in an interpersonal roleplay (preferably) or dialogue. In an interpersonal roleplay, you can coach the other participants to make the dramatization more effective. You may need to repeat part or all the roleplay or dialogue a number of times to contact or fully express the painful emotions from the past. If you never expressed your emotions in the original past episode, the next step is to create a new version of the incident in which you do express your thoughts and feelings. Express your grief, outrage, and other feelings emphatically. Say the things you wish you could have said. Ask the things you didn't dare to ask. Feel free to accuse, rant and rave, scream, stomp on the floor, cry, etc. Ask the other people in the roleplay to react as you suspect the people in your past would have reacted.

If you can't contact your long-buried feelings in these roleplays, spend plenty of time experimenting with possible feelings. Keep repeating sentences that express emotions you suspect you have, such as: "I feel sad," "I am so angry," "I resent ...," or "I hate you!" Act the feeling using the sentences until a real feeling breaks through. Pretending to cry may help, and repeating angry sentences louder and louder can bring out buried anger. Exaggerate or magnify any tiny flickers of emotion you experience. You may need to repeat important or upsetting parts of the roleplay until your feelings break through. Try starting sentences with: "I wish ...," "I wish you had ...," "If only ...," "Why did you do ... to me?" or "How dare you ...!" Try out emotions you don't even think you have but could occur in the situation, such as anger in grief. If you experiment with an emotion and it feels false, reject that approach.

If you contact and express buried emotions about a past event that still truly affects you, you should feel a sense of relief at releasing the buried emotions. Reexperiencing the painful past can be very difficult and may even leave you trembling, but venting intense, long-buried emotions is also a great relief and helps you get over the past. The next roleplay exercises go beyond the repetition of the past to explore various aspects of the painful past. Our goals are to experience fully and understand the event in all of its complexity and to express fully other feelings that relate to the situation.

Now create a version in which you explain how the past has affected you over the years and affected other problems in your life. Freely express your present thoughts and feelings about the past. In this version, create responses from the people in your past from their own perspectives. Prepare for this by considering the effects of the past on you, how the other people must have felt at the time, and why they acted the way they did. What stresses or problems were they dealing with? What in their past or childhood helped make them the way they are? What had they grown up believing? Don't be afraid to let the other people in your roleplay react with brutal honesty.

Next, explore what you wish had happened or how things should have been. Create a happy fantasy in which the people in your past act wisely and either avoid the problem or help you deal with it. Spend time picturing and enjoying this improved version of the past. If someone truly did wrong to you in the painful past event, create another roleplay in which you act assertively and prevent the problem from happening. Then create another roleplay in which the painful event occurs, you confront the other person, and the response is wise or occurs in the way you wish the person could have responded. These techniques help you explore the ideal responses to the situation and avoid repeating the patterns of the painful past.

If the painful event occurred long ago, create a dialogue between you as you were then and you as you are now. In this dialogue, allow your present self to use the extra experience in life you have gained over time and increased emotional distance you now have from the painful past to comfort your past self that still feels freshly upset over the incident. This puts your own wisdom to work for emotional healing.

If you need to resolve feelings about a person in your life, you should also spend time paying attention to the person's qualities and to the good aspects of your relationship. This helps in reaching a more balanced understanding of the past and resolving it more thoroughly. Create a dialogue in which you show your appreciation and love, thanking the person for all the good times, all the love the person showed, things the person did for you, etc. Name a variety of specific events and actions you found especially helpful, joyous, and good. Make a written list of the person's qualities, of good times, kind acts, and other things you appreciated. Add new items to this list whenever you think of them. Occasionally rereading this list is especially helpful.

All the above techniques help in dealing with prolonged emotional pain over the death of a loved one. In dialogues with the deceased, speak to either a picture of the deceased or the gravesite (preferably), or perhaps to an empty chair. Close your eyes if this helps you pretend you are speaking to the deceased person. Roleplay the death trauma as it actually happened and create a new version of the death in which you totally and freely express your shock and grief. You may need to keep repeating emotional sentences and to act emotions until the buried ones break through. Experiment with anger in your roleplays, too. People often feel anger is inappropriate and bury it after the loss of a loved one, but we may feel angry at what fate has brought us, the deceased person's self-neglect that helped bring on the death, or because of feelings of abandonment by the deceased.

Create another dialogue in which you tell the deceased how the death affected you and describe the importance of your relationship to the person. For example: "I still miss you so very much," and "You were my most loyal friend and you really understood me." To bring out things you regret, experiment with sentences beginning with: "I wish ...," "I wish you had ...," "I wish I had ...," and "If only ..." People often feel guilty, especially after suicide, about not having been kinder or not having thought to do something that may have prevented the death. Some people may want to start a sentence with, "I felt very little at the time of your death, but ..."

Next, use interpersonal roleplays or dialogues to re-create major conflicts or arguments that occurred between you and the deceased. Create new versions in which both of you explain your own feelings, views, and reasons for acting the ways you did. Imagine how it would have been if the two of you had acted wisely, and then create a version of the death in which you both express love, reminisce over good times, resolve personal conflicts, and forgive each other. Forgiveness by the deceased in a roleplay may seem silly but is really a way of forgiving yourself.

Make sure you spend time remembering all the good things about your relationship. Make a list of these as described above for a permanent record. If the death occurred when you were a child, create a dialogue in which you as an adult comfort the child that experienced the loss. The last step in resolving your feelings about the death is to say good-bye forever to the loved one. The best place to do this is at the gravesite. Spend time picturing the burial or cremation in your mind, and then use your own words to admit you will never see the person again and to lay down this emotional burden forever, so you can get on with your life. This may be very difficult.

Writing also helps a great deal in getting over the past. Interpersonal roleplay and dialogue, with their action and speech, tend to be better than writing at bringing out buried emotions, but careful written work often results in a more thorough understanding of the past and other people's perspectives in the past. Writing leaves a permanent record that you can occasionally review. All the above techniques for remembering, working with, understanding, and finishing the painful past may take the form of written letters to and from yourself rather than roleplays. Roleplays followed by written work is the most thorough approach, of course. Sharing these personal letters to yourself with a trusted friend can be a healing experience. Also, as detailed previously in chapter 5, channeling your painful emotions into creative mediums such as art, poetry, short stories, music, or interpretive dance can help a great deal.

Sometimes communication and feedback with the people involved in painful past episodes can be healing. If you do discuss painful events with people who were there, do so in a careful, gentle way. Don't alienate them by scolding or belittling them. Instead, explain what you felt and how the episode affected you, and ask these people what it was like for them. Gentle, constructive feedback may help the other person avoid repeating the problem with someone else.   Outcomes including apologies, forgiveness, and expressions of love are very healing, but prepare yourself to face negative outcomes such as shallow excuses, denials, or a refusal to discuss the situation, especially if the other person was clearly at fault. Even people not directly at fault may be unable to face the truth, unwilling to talk about it, or angry at you for bringing it up.

Forgiveness is an important part of healing. Forgiving the past and showing love to the other person helps you finish your own resentment and emotional pain. Angry thoughts or a preoccupation with the painful past wastes energy and depresses you. By forgiving, you rise above the past, increase your self-esteem, and find more peace in the present. If you want to forgive but don't feel it in your heart, read your list of good times and things you appreciated about the other person every day until you can. Forgiveness does not mean forgetting or pretending it never happened. It may be wise not to trust the person or to maintain only a superficial relationship in which you avoid sharing deep feelings and being vulnerable. Certain acts, especially repeated acts of abuse, may be nearly impossible to forgive. If you can't forgive or don't want to forgive the person, you may find more peace by eliminating the person from your life, home, or circle of friends.

Rituals can also help in getting over the past, so people all over the world use rituals for dealing with death, such as wearing black for a time and various funeral rituals. After working to finish the past in the above ways, make a list of the painful events, tear it into very tiny pieces, and throw them all into a waste basket while saying, "With this action, I hereby lay to rest all these problems forever."

If emotions from the past continue to trouble you greatly despite your use of the above exercises, consider whether other past events may play an important role in your troubling emotions.   If so, explore your past relationships and buried emotions as described in chapter 38, Understanding Yourself. If you discover more painful past events or emotions, work with them as described here. If this doesn't help and emotions from the past still trouble you greatly, work on the areas described first in this chapter: acceptance, negative thinking that keeps you focused on the past, interests, activities, socializing, and other personal problems that interfere with your having a full and satisfying life now.

Working with the painful past as suggested in this chapter should help reduce the frequency of intensely arousing memories and flashbacks. Keeping busy can help, too. When these things occur, however, you can do several things. Orient yourself to reality by focusing on things around you, asking other people to talk to you, or becoming involved in some activity to take your mind off the past. The best refocusing activities are enjoyable but require some concentration or involve other people. Even if it is inconvenient or impossible to do most things, you can talk with someone, whistle, or mentally go through one of your favorite songs or prayers. Another possibility is making a constant mental commentary or description of the colors and details of people and things you see in your environment, such as architecture, nature, clothing, etc. You could read a book or solve crossword puzzles you keep with you for such occasions. During severe flashbacks, friends or loved ones may need to sharply remind you of the time, place, who they are, and what is going on around you.

Understanding that the troublesome memories are often unpredictable but can be harnessed for healing will help. After studying your own patterns in the ways described in chapter 9, Problem Solving, you can often avoid situations that trigger memories. When you feel ready to do so and in convenient circumstances, you may occasionally choose to spend time with painful memories or flashbacks to learn more about the painful past, accept it more fully, and thereby weaken its hold on you. You can also choose to change the memory to make it less threatening. When it begins, you might shrink the size of the abuser, imagine yourself getting revenge, or imagine the abuser facing embarrassing situations or consequences. Examples of embarrassment include the person's pants falling down in a crowd, false teeth falling out in a business meeting, or all your friends and neighbors scolding the person.

If lovemaking triggers flashbacks of sexual abuse, opening your eyes or turning on a light often helps. Tell your partner about the problem and explain how to help you when this happens. You may want your lover to hold you and talk, or you may want no touching but to talk. Use whatever works best for you. Finally, certain medicines can help in reducing the frequency and severity of flashbacks. If the flashbacks interfere with your life in significant ways, a psychiatrist can prescribe one of these medicines for you.

Recommended Additional Readings and Support Groups:

Please refer to the end of chapter 5, Emotions, for helpful readings and support
  groups for negative thought habits.

Part 3: Conclusion

May you always learn and grow, and
may your life be full of hope, peace, joy, and love.

Understanding yourself is true peace, and
knowing your weaknesses helps make you strong.

Part 3 contains two chapters that help in understanding yourself better and working with your feelings and conflicts. The first, Understanding Yourself, includes information on ways people often misperceive their own personal problems and misperceive other people. The chapter on Dreams describes techniques for working with dreams for personal growth.

The next two chapters, Warnings about Psychology and Important Advice about Counseling, describe things you should understand about the profession of psychology. These include how to avoid incompetent psychologists, how to best choose and work with a psychotherapist, where to go for an unbiased opinion about whether you need a residential treatment program, and how to leave a mental hospital early, before your doctor releases you.

The last chapter in the book, Preventing Violence and Crime, has some advice for individuals, but mostly describes research suggesting ways we might reduce these two important social problems.

38. Understanding Yourself

Don't be afraid to see yourself through someone else's eyes.

*Everything that irritates us about others can lead us
to an understanding of ourselves. (Carl Jung)*

You can learn about yourself by asking your friends or relatives for feedback about your personal characteristics, virtues, and faults. Don't settle for short, superficial responses.   Explain you want to learn more about yourself and keep asking for more responses.   Whenever you don't understand or don't agree with an answer you get, ask for specific examples of observable behaviors. Find out exactly what you did on various occasions that made the person give you this feedback. You can also take turns with a willing friend pointing out characteristics, virtues, and faults in each other.

Take very seriously any criticism you receive, whether or not you requested the feedback. Always evaluate criticism with an open mind because we often fail to recognize our own faults, even when other people repeatedly point out the same faults. People often fail to recognize their own problems because of either rationalization or projection. *Rationalization*, first described as an important psychological concept by Sigmund Freud, involves believing your motives or explanations for your behaviors are more noble or healthy than is actually the case. For example, we can sometimes detail plenty of plausible reasons or excuses for behaving in a manner other people recognize as essentially selfish. We may fail to recognize personal motives such as anger, cruelty, revenge, greed, lust, etc., or we may realize these selfish motives play a role but fail to recognize their true importance.

Projection, also discovered by Freud, is believing your own thoughts, feelings, or conflicts occur in other people and not in you. We project them from ourselves onto other people.   Everyone sometimes interprets other people and events in biased ways because of projection, but projection occurs more often in people with personal problems. Examining the extreme case of paranoia helps in understanding projection. A paranoid woman may believe everyone hates her and that everyone plots against her, but the truth is she projects her own upset feelings and hatred onto other people. A paranoid man may believe everyone thinks, says, or insinuates bad things about him and that everyone makes fun of him, but the truth is he projects his own negative thoughts and feelings about himself onto other people. Or a paranoid man may believe everyone considers him a homosexual, but the truth is he projects his own fears of being a homosexual onto other people.

Similarly, a man who feels upset over "constant" disgusting sexual approaches by homosexuals actually has a problem with his own sexual feelings and may even think a sexual gesture occurs every time another man licks his lips. A woman who feels upset over the sexual immorality of acquaintances or strangers actually has a problem with her own feelings about sex, and a man who feels upset that evil overruns the world actually has a problem with his own feelings about good and evil. If you think most strangers or dates are untrustworthy, you project your own personal problems with trust onto other people. If you often feel upset with authority figures, you have a personal problem with issues of power and submission. When you feel upset about competition from other people, you often fail to recognize your own strong needs to compete and often think you face extremely competitive people.

In interpersonal conflicts, we often fail to recognize our own feelings and project feelings such as anger and hatred onto others. People often loudly insist that they don't feel angry, while thinking the other person in the conflict feels very angry. Projection may result in statements like, "She hates me! I know she does!" Even people who admit they feel angry, often project some of their own anger onto the other person in the conflict and misinterpret the other person's feelings. Another very common example of projection involves feelings of inadequacy. People with low self-esteem often believe other people look down upon them.

Consider the possibility of projection whenever you react to someone else with strong negative feelings, overreact to something, or imagine how other people feel or think about you. Projection is particularly likely when the same problems occur repeatedly in our lives with different people or situations or when we blame other people for our own problems and behaviors. Whenever you do any of these things, carefully consider the possibility that the feelings, issues, or problems you see in other people might be your own. Are you being realistic in this situation? Could your feelings bias your perceptions of other people? What did you do that may have helped cause this problem? What could you do to help prevent problems like this in similar situations? Fight projection by writing sentences clearly identifying the emotions, thoughts, and issues as your own. Start these sentences with the word "I." For example: "I feel ...," "I have a problem with ...," or "I'm the one who thinks ..." List any behaviors contributing to your problem and list any better alternatives that can help avoid similar problems in the future. Read these things every day as a reminder to improve.

You can also make lists for self-exploration and finding areas in which you need improvement. Try making lists under the following headings on separate pieces of paper: My Values and Goals; My Talents and Skills; My Interests and Activities; How I Have Dealt with Family, Emotional, Physical, Social, or Financial Crises in My Life; Things I Dislike; and My Mistakes, Faults, Problems, and Weaknesses. Use the table of contents in this book and the list of communication problems in chapter 6 to help you think of items for these lists.

Explore your past and present relationships with other people by labeling one or more pages with the name of each parent, each sibling, any other important family relationships, and each important friend and romantic relationship in your life. Then list good and bad experiences that stand out in your mind, good and bad characteristics of these people, feelings you experienced, and behaviors you chose in responding to them. Use the list of emotions in chapter 5 to search for good and bad feelings you associate with certain people. Much of our personality comes from important early relationships. Looking at old photographs, perhaps in an album of pictures from your childhood, can trigger forgotten memories. If you have forgotten details of early traumas in your life, try gathering information from siblings or other family members. How are you similar to the important people in your early life? Do you see characteristics or patterns of behaviors in yourself that developed early as responses to other people?

Spend plenty of time compiling these lists and add items over a period of several days or weeks as you think of them. The lists about relationships and about crises can help you notice negative patterns you repeat in your life. After all of this personal exploration, think about what you should change in your life. Do you have a well-rounded variety of interests and activities? What behaviors should you eliminate? What behaviors should you practice or learn? Work on resolving problem emotions or behaviors using the appropriate chapters of this book.

Awareness of both your pleasant and unpleasant emotions is an important part of understanding yourself. Please refer to chapter 5 for a discussion of the importance of being in touch with your emotions and for advice on how to recognize and express your emotions. Chapter 5 also details how sinking deeply into a problem emotion can help you understand its sources and help you resolve it. Spend at least one hour with the problem emotion to allow images, thoughts, ideas, urges, expectations, ambivalent feelings, and fantasies that relate to it to arise.   Remember what was happening, how you felt, and what you wanted and thought during previous episodes. Thinking about your first experience of it and strongest experience of it may be particularly helpful. Even if you learn nothing from spending time with the problem emotion, your willingness to face and accept it may help finish or resolve it. As detailed in chapter 5, expressing your negative emotions in creative mediums such as art, poetry, short stories, music, or interpretive dance can also help. Chapter 37, Getting over the Past, describes many other ways of contacting, expressing, and finishing painful emotions.

Unfortunately, with the passing of time, we often forget many of our most touching, beautiful, or joyous experiences.   An excellent way to remember such peak experiences is to keep a journal or list of them. Describe beautiful nature scenes, special close moments with loved ones, fun times, a series of events you particularly enjoyed, and spiritual experiences. Include enough descriptive details to help you remember it many years later. Compile a collection of inspiring thoughts, quotes, poems, or prayers. Refer to these things occasionally, especially if you feel sad, want to reminisce, or want some inspiration.

Dialoguing (chapter 14) can help you explore your feelings and conflicts and understand yourself better. Because of the danger to certain people of dialoguing (see chapter 14), you may need the help of a psychologist to explore your emotions and conflicts in this way. If you have expressed a negative emotion in a creative medium, you may want to dialogue with your creative work to explore your emotions.   Start by telling the creative work how you feel about it, what it reminds you of, and asking what it means or how it relates to your life and problems. You might ask why it has a particular ingredient such as a color, feeling, image, texture, or event or why it has so much of a particular ingredient.

Dialoguing will be a trite exercise with meaningless results unless you dialogue about important issues, conflicts, feelings, or situations in your life. How can you find clues to parts of yourself that are in conflict? One good source is your conscience. Think carefully about times in the past when your conscience bothered you. Think about things you should do and things you think you should feel. Write as many "I should ..." statements as you can. Criticize yourself, too. These activities indicate ambivalent feelings between two parts of yourself.   In all these activities—thinking about when your conscience bothered you, writing "I should" statements, or criticizing yourself—one part of yourself moralizes and another resists the conscience and makes excuses. Describe these two sides of the conflict to name the parts of the self.

Simply describing yourself can also define inner conflicts. Make a list of your personal characteristics (not physical ones), feelings, and values. Now consider the opposite of each item on the list. This is the side of yourself that you suppress or de-emphasize or you never developed. Whenever the opposite side of a characteristic seems to tell you nothing, try making the characteristic extreme before thinking of its opposite. For example, a man might consider himself aggressive with women, but the opposite, passive with women, seems undesirable and sheds no light on his personal work. When he takes it to the extreme, however, aggressive with women becomes pushy and selfish with women, and its opposite, he decides, is gentle and considerate with women. Now he realizes some women may perceive him as pushy and selfish, and he may need to develop the more gentle and considerate parts of his personality.

In chapter 14, we noted dialogues for personal exploration may begin with physical symptoms that seem to be outlets for buried emotions. In addition, sometimes even characteristic gestures such as scratching your chin or pushing the hair off your face, characteristic postures such as rigidness or slumping in a chair, or characteristic speech patterns such as "er," "uhm," and "you know" may indicate unrecognized parts of yourself. Try exaggerating the action and giving it a label such as lazy, nervous, etc.

Some people have a strong inner voice they can use to find conflicts. The great psychologist Carl Jung pointed out some people have a well-developed inner life with a voice for their conscience, an inner critic that comments on many of their actions. The comments, conflicts, issues, and themes from this inner voice make very useful data for understanding the self.

Many of the conflicting parts of yourself you find in the above ways won't reflect important conflicts. Use your own experience and feelings to decide which are important and which are not. If you discover feelings or problems needing work, perhaps an appropriate part of this book can help. After dialoguing with the more interesting or important conflicts, consider possible solutions and use what you have learned about yourself to make changes in your life as described in the discussion of dialoguing in chapter 14. If a dialogue seems important but doesn't lead to any answers or decisions, think about what a very wise person would decide to do.

39. Dreams

Listen to your inner voice. You know what is right and true.

The interpretation of dreams was important for healing and problem solving in primitive and ancient cultures all over the world (Aztec, Babylonian, Egyptian, Greek, Roman, Hindu, Chinese, etc.). Some of the earliest books, on cuneiform clay tablets in Assyria, were guides to dream interpretation. It played an important role in Christianity until Thomas Aquinas emphasized reason in the 1200s. One tribe of native Australians deserted their homeland because of a dream of an owl that elders interpreted as a warning from a spirit that other tribes were planning to attack them. When the Chinese Emperor Wu Ting (1324-1266 B.C.) lost his aged and most trusted advisor to death, he offered ritual sacrifice to the ruler of the gods and asked who should replace the advisor. Wu Ting dreamt the face of the new advisor but didn't find the man until he sent a portrait of his vision throughout the empire. Because of the dream, Wu Ting gave the post of Prime Minister to a common workman from a distant province.

Even today, many people in India, Greece, Lebanon, and some North African countries perform rituals requesting dreams for advice or healing and pay for dream interpretations or advice on healing rituals suggested by dreams. Until the 1700s, people often believed that demons caused nightmares. The word *nightmare* comes from this belief. In Old English, mare was the spirit or demon who inhabited the soul during sleep.

Dreams sometimes lead to scientific discoveries or masterpieces of creativity. Elias Howe had been trying unsuccessfully to design a sewing machine until he had a nightmare. When he woke up, he realized the spears used against him by hostile tribesmen in the dream, like the design of the needles needed by the sewing machine, had holes near their points. The chemist Friedrich August von Kekule struggled for years with the structure of aromatic carbon compounds until he dreamt of atoms whirling in a circle and discovered their molecular ring structure, revolutionizing organic chemistry. Dreams helped Nobel Prize winners Niels Bohr to realize electrons in an atom must follow specific, fixed paths and Otto Loewi to discover the nervous system uses chemicals to transmit information to and from the brain. Albert Einstein considered his whole career and his theory of relativity to relate to a strikingly beautiful dream during adolescence about sledding faster and faster until the stars distorted into a dazzling array of patterns and colors. People reported Benjamin Franklin found answers to difficult problems in his dreams.

Samuel Taylor Coleridge wrote his masterpiece poem "Kubla Khan" by describing a sequence of magnificent visions in a dream, and dreams inspired John Milton's *Paradise Lost*. The Italian composer Giuseppe Tartini wrote "The Devil's Trill" after hearing it in a dream in which he sold his soul to the devil in return for the violin composition. Robert Louis Stevenson often based his adventure stories on dreams, sometimes even dreaming successive installments night after night. His most famous story based on a dream was *The Strange Case of Dr. Jekyll and Mr. Hyde*. The painter Francisco Goya had many nightmares and sometimes based his paintings on them.

Scientific research has increased our knowledge about dreams, yet important questions remain unsolved. Most dreams and all the longer dreams occur during REM sleep, a sleep characterized by rapid eye movement, unpredictable changes in heart rate and breathing, very little body movement, and usually physical sexual arousal. People woken up during REM sleep report dreams 80 to 90% of the time. Babies dream in the womb and newborn babies dream as soon as they fall asleep. At first babies spend nearly 50% of their sleep time in REM sleep, but by 6 months, it is 30%. By adolescence, it reaches the adult level of dreaming 20 to 25% of the time you sleep. Children's dreams have less complex plots, imagery, and organization compared to those of adolescents and adults. People deprived of sleep or just REM sleep for too long (72 to 250 hours) will develop memory, concentration, and irritability problems and may begin to hallucinate. After going without enough REM sleep for too long, your body will make it up by dreaming almost constantly when you sleep. This often happens during alcohol detoxification, for example.

The great majority of dreams include at least one other person besides the dreamer. Exotic or bizarre dream settings are unusual. Routine chores and manual labor are not very common in dreams, either. Dreams involving misfortune, aggression, and other bad experiences are more common than dreams involving success, friendly acts, or other pleasant experiences. Approximately 2/3 of dreams are emotionally negative and typically become more unpleasant as the dream goes on. Fear and anxiety dominate about 1/3 of our dreams, and anger dominates another 15%, but violence and other dream events that should cause great emotion, often don't.

Nightmares are quite common in preschoolers, common in grade school children, and not unusual in teenagers and young adults, with college students reporting an average of one nightmare every month or two. The frequency of nightmares seems to decrease in adulthood and to stabilize at around age 40, with the average adult reporting several nightmares each year. Probably around 30% of grade school children, 15% of high school and college students, and 5 to 8% of adults have regular nightmares. About 10% of adolescents and college students have at least one nightmare each week, but only 1% of healthy elderly persons report that many. Regular nightmares may relate to trauma, mental illness, certain medicines and drugs, depression, anxiety, or stress, but many sensitive people such as artists, musicians, teachers, and therapists report regular nightmares. Carefully studying your dreams, of course, will uncover more nightmares.

You can reduce the frequency of a recurring nightmare or eliminate it in the following way. First create a new dream based on it, changing the action before it gets bad. If a large dog growls and runs toward you in the dark, make the street suddenly brighten with plenty of lights and the owner call the dog and befriend you, so you end up petting and playing with the dog. Each night in bed, practice deep relaxation techniques and then visualize the new dream. With enough practice, the nightmare will probably end the new way and bother you less often or stop bothering you.

The meaning of dreams is very controversial. Sigmund Freud argued that dreams were a "royal road to the unconscious." Carl Jung believed dreams balance our rational thinking lives by expressing our deeper, buried feelings. Researchers are accumulating evidence that both early, slow wave sleep and the dreams of REM sleep help the brain to make new connections and consolidate learning and memory storage. Other research suggests dreams may involve random electrical discharges or may clear overloaded circuits and help us to forget.

Many psychologists believe dreams carry important symbolic messages about conflicts from our inner selves that can help us solve our personal problems. New positron emission tomography (PET) scans provide support for this notion, suggesting dreams during REM sleep may activate our emotional memory bank without allowing much logical processing by the frontal lobes of our brains. The PET studies showed increased blood flow in inner brain structures involved with memory, emotion, and orchestrating visual scenes, but decreased blood flow in frontal areas. Changes in blood flow reflect changes in neural activity. No matter how the physiology of the brain creates dreams, any sincere, honest work with your own conflicts can be productive simply because this work involves your own ideas and feelings, and dreams provide fascinating material for personal work.

There have been many systems of dream interpretation in psychology and throughout history, but most psychologists today prefer a flexible approach that allows people to find their own meanings in their dreams. This flexible approach to dreams combines the insights of Sigmund Freud, Carl Jung, and Frederick (Fritz) Perls.

Collect your dreams as soon as you wake. If you don't, you will quickly forget most of the details. Even talking to someone for just one minute will interfere with your ability to remember details, unless you describe the dream to the other person. Keep a tape recorder or a notebook with a pen or pencil right next to your bed and immediately record any dreams every time you wake up. To avoid disturbing other people at night, you may want to write your dream on paper in the dark and copy it in better form later. Write your dream in the present tense to keep it fresh and powerful. For example, use *I ran ...*, not *I was running ...*

Many psychologists believe repetitive dreams may be repeated messages from the inner self about a personal problem that persists, either because you don't recognize it or because you refuse to change. And many psychologists believe strikingly beautiful or very emotional dreams (happy, upsetting, etc.) may hold important messages for you. Even if dreams don't carry important symbolic messages about conflicts, these kinds of dreams are ideal for personal exploration because they are interesting.

Begin your work on any dream by looking for similarities between the events, feelings, people, or behaviors in the dream and those in your real life. Consider each of these areas one at a time. What conflicts occur in the dream? Do they remind you of any in your past or present life? For example, a violent attack on you in a dream might symbolize the vicious lie someone recently told about you. Do any of the events or feelings in the dream remind you of other situations in your past or present life? Dreams of threatening forces chasing you, perhaps accompanied by paralysis or an inability to run away, may relate to unresolved fears.

Dreams about people you know may tell you about that person or your relationship. For example, dreaming a friend tells a lie or a loved one hurts you may help you realize the person is untrustworthy. Perhaps dreams informing you of such things result from clues in your life you had not particularly noticed. People in your dreams can also symbolize other people in your life or even parts of yourself, however. Do any of the people in the dream remind you of other people in your life? Do any of the people in the dream remind you of parts of your own personality? Do any of the behaviors in the dream remind you of things you or other people in your life have done? In the following dream, one person obviously symbolizes another. While out of town on a long business trip, a man learned that a close friend back home had suddenly died. Soon he had a dream in which his best friend in adolescence had died and in which he was crying and sympathizing with the upset family of the deceased. Although the friend who suddenly died had no family left, this dream accurately portrayed the sharing of feelings among friends he felt he had missed by being out of town during the funeral.

Dreams often relate to recent events. Watching a horror movie may cause a nightmare, or a dream may relate to the day's events. Emotions in a dream may parallel emotions in your recent life. Keep striking events from your day in mind when analyzing your dreams. Think about recent arguments, troubling experiences, problems with authority figures, etc.

Most dreams don't relate so clearly to people in your life, recent events, or personal conflicts, however. You will often have to decipher the meaning of the dream images as if they were a lost language. Dreams often have several levels of meaning. One symbol, element, or part of a dream may represent two different ideas or two people in two completely different meanings. Consider the previous dream about the death of a man's best friend in adolescence. If this man also felt the closeness in the dream was greater than any closeness or sharing in his life today, he might decide the dream also serves as a graphic reminder that he shouldn't wait for a calamity to express love and share feelings with his loved ones. In this case, the close sharing with the family of the deceased in the dream has two separate meanings for him.

Explore your dreams with *free association*, too. In this technique, you picture a dream element and let your thoughts and feelings wander freely onto other ideas or feelings that you associate with the dream element. Free association to dream elements often tells you the subject matter of the dream. For example, a woman had a dream about a series of problems in trying to find a mansion she had seen. Her free association to the mansion in her dream resulted in the following series of ideas: a fine home filled with art treasures, a home for my soul filled with beauty and love, Michael. This free association quickly showed the mansion symbolized her deceased husband. She decides, then, the dream symbolizes the troubles she has experienced in trying to find a new husband.

You can also find the meaning of dream elements by making a list of their characteristics and seeing what this list reminds you of. For example, a man dreamt about eating a peach with a kitten's face on the skin of the peach. The kitten smiled and felt happy about his eating it. Here is his list of characteristics for a kitten: independent, soft, warm, playful, and intelligent. Here is his list of characteristics for a peach: wet, juicy, tangy, soft, round, and delicious. These two lists together reminded him of his girlfriend and told him the kitten and peach symbolized his girlfriend.

Once you find what you feel is the subject of a dream using similarities between the dream and your real life, free association, or lists of characteristics, study the rest of the dream with these techniques for further understanding. Other episodes in the dream or other dreams may add further dimensions to the basic feelings, ideas, or conflicts you are exploring. For example, the woman's dream about a series of problems finding a mansion included various episodes that she could explore with free association. One seemingly unimportant dream segment involved her landlord painting one of her chairs white to brighten her apartment. She stopped him and wiped the wet paint off the chair because she preferred the natural wood. Remembering that an old friend gave her the chair, she concluded the chair symbolized Ron, a regular date who reminded her of the old friend in certain ways. The landlord's attempt to brighten her apartment reminded her Ron truly did brighten her life, but the unacceptable white paint emphasized her feelings Ron's lifestyle didn't fit her own. Thinking over these feelings, she decided she should clearly define her relationship with Ron as just a friendship and not a romance. Removing the white paint in the dream symbolized removing the romance from the relationship.

Dialoguing (chapter 14) also helps in exploring dreams. You might ask a dream element who or what it symbolizes, why it occurs or acts the way it does, or what it means. You might ask the whole dream what it means, says, or wants you to change or do. You can ask questions of feelings from dreams, allow dream elements or parts to speak to you, allow two dream elements or parts to argue with one another, two people in the dream to discuss issues with one another, or body parts or body tension in the dream to talk. Use "I" and the present tense to identify with the dream part that speaks. Imagine how the dream elements might feel or think, and create an argument between them. Be silly and experiment! Exaggerate and magnify views or emotions you find in each part of the dialogue. Do these parts remind you of parts of yourself? If so, dialogue with the parts of yourself to explore the conflict. Experiment with the opposite side of each view or emotion. Is this a neglected or buried part of yourself? Whenever a dialogue reminds you of any other feeling, issue, situation, or person in your past or present life, you can switch to a new dialogue based on that, dialoguing for hours on one dream.

Ideally, you should use all the above techniques and work with many of your dreams. Feel free to switch around among the various techniques. Be sure to switch to another technique when your work seems fruitless. Working with a variety of dreams opens many more possibilities for personal exploration than does working with one or a few dreams. Even when working on only one problem issue in your life, various dreams help you see more facets of the issue, so working with a whole series of dreams helps you see the situation more completely. Feel free to occasionally spend days working on one particularly interesting dream with a variety of techniques. Dreams can hold many levels of meanings and you can study one dream to explore many different personal issues, one at a time.

You are the final judge of whether any dream interpretation is correct or helpful. Correct dream interpretations promote growth and feel relevant to your life, meaningful, helpful, and alive. Incorrect dream interpretations feel boring, doubtful, meaningless, pointless, and dead. If your dream work feels difficult or frustrating, you may be struggling with the burden of an incorrect dream interpretation or you may be tackling important personal issues you need to face. If you then interpret the dream correctly, however, the dream work will feel relevant, important, striking, or alive.

Dreams may directly reflect your personality and issues in your life. Teenagers may dream about dating problems, college students who work very hard for good grades may dream about problems in preparing for class tests, and sexually promiscuous people may dream about flirting and sex. Dreams can also compensate for things that are missing or buried in your personality. For example, people with few sexual feelings in real life may dream about sex, or unassertive people who try too hard to always show kindness may dream about mean acts or acts of aggression. We can easily see when dreams directly reflect our own personalities, but most people find it difficult to recognize and admit when dreams vent buried impulses. Consider both possibilities. Ask yourself if you might neglect or bury emotions or behaviors that come out in you or others in your dreams. If so, you may need to incorporate the neglected or buried parts of yourself in socially acceptable ways in your waking life.

Dreams about people we don't know or don't know well or people from the past we don't keep in touch with any more, usually symbolize parts of ourselves, other people in our lives, strangers, authority figures, lifestyles, or principles. Dreams about people we were very close to a long time ago often symbolize parts of ourselves that are like that person. Dreams about anonymous children may symbolize playful or growing parts of ourselves or parts that need development or remain stuck with childhood conflicts. Dreams about dead people or people from the past sometimes identify unfinished feelings or issues concerning those people that need further work, perhaps with the techniques for Getting over the Past in chapter 37.

Most animals in dreams are symbolic, except for dreams about animals that play an important role in your present life. The wilderness may represent your instincts or natural, animal self. Houses and rooms in dreams often symbolize your inner mental world, personality, marriage, or interpersonal relationships. The front yard may be your public self and the back yard may be the deeper, hidden parts of you. Vehicles (cars, trucks, trains, etc.) often symbolize the direction and energy in your life, or perhaps the direction in which a relationship is going. For example, problems in dreams such as a truck going out of control or a car or train accident may indicate problems in your goals, behaviors, feelings, or relationships.

You may want to create paintings or drawings based on dreams or to finish a dream by making up the rest of it and work with this product just as you would with any other dream. Review all your dreams occasionally, looking for subjects, feelings, or conflicts that occur repeatedly, for patterns, and for change and development. Compiling lists of symbolic meanings from dreams can help you keep track of your own personal dream symbols and how they evolve. Devote one page to each important symbol or action in your dreams. Every time the symbol or action appears in your dreams, add another note to the page listing the date and describing the meaning of the symbol in that dream.

Start or join a group devoted to dream work. Experts lead some dream work groups, but other groups are leaderless. Local libraries or universities may have information on established dream work groups. You can start your own group with friends or post notices in churches, schools, libraries, etc. Limit the number of people to five or ten and choose a place and time to meet regularly. During each meeting, participants take turns describing and analyzing their own dreams. After each presentation, the group may give feedback and offer suggestions.

40. Warnings about Psychology

Trust your own feelings. There are many false prophets.

The profession of psychology has greatly expanded in recent decades. In 1959, there were 2,500 members of the American Psychological Association who counseled clients in professional practice. By 1989, there were 40,000 of them, 16 times as many. We also have psychiatric social workers, psychiatric nurses, and paraprofessional counselors in mental health clinics and hospitals, drug and alcohol programs, child abuse programs, crisis centers, adoption agencies, and weight loss programs. The ideas of psychotherapy for every age group, for couples, and for families and of psychological consultation for businesses, schools, courts, athletic teams, the military, and even animals no longer seem strange.

Nicholas Cummings, a past President of the American Psychological Association, said in his presidential address, "It may be that the mental health movement has promised the American people a freedom from anxiety that is neither possible nor realistic." Some critics argue the profession of psychology creates, in part, the illnesses it treats, by encouraging us to see life's normal difficulties as problems that need treatment. Dr. Joyce Brothers claimed 75% of all marriages fall short of their potential because of "sheer, spirit-crushing boredom." Whole books detail the midlife crisis but most people don't experience one. The great sex therapists Masters and Johnson claimed "at least half of all marriages have major degrees of sexual dysfunction or disorder," but is there really anything wrong with two people who love each other deciding they are not interested in sex anymore?

Psychologists tend to focus on conflicts, frustrations, and negative emotions and may see problems where none exist. A famous study is a classic example of this. In the early 1970s, David Rosenthal of Stanford University and seven other normal people made appointments at psychiatric hospitals and complained in their interviews of hearing voices saying the words "empty," "hollow," or "thud." Except for falsifying their names and addresses, all of them told the truth about their lives. After the hospital admitted them, all of them stopped complaining of psychological symptoms and acted normally, but all of them received diagnoses of schizophrenia. In another study, therapists and therapy students listened to what was supposedly a first therapy session. Actually, an actor played a relaxed, confident, productive man who said he was curious about therapy. When the therapists and students rated his mental health, 43% said he was psychotic or neurotic, 19% said he had adjustment problems, and only 38% said he was healthy.

Many people in therapy for one problem find they and their therapists disagree on when to end therapy. When they feel ready to stop, the therapist argues other issues need work. Many feel insecure about leaving against the expert's advice, especially if the therapist says it is unwise and hints at dire consequences, but psychologists in private practice need clients to make a living, and everyone has negative emotions and personal issues that could use work.

Psychology is an infant science. There are many theories of psychology, each with its own experts, ideas of relevant phenomena, rules of evidence, methods of psychotherapy, books, journals, and jargon. There is no agreement on fundamental issues. Unfortunately, what little we know about the science of psychology is not very encouraging about the profession of psychology. First, diagnoses have become increasingly important mainly because the government and private insurance companies require diagnoses before they will pay for hospitalization or therapy. Unfortunately, the reliability and validity of psychiatric diagnoses are unimpressive. The poor reliability means when different psychiatrists or psychologists evaluate a client, they often end up with different diagnoses. There is a great deal of overlap between the symptoms of various diagnoses. The poor validity means the diagnoses have little meaning—they don't predict a person's future functioning nor how the person will respond to treatment. As noted in the Introduction, many famous, very productive people have diagnosable disorders.

Growing numbers of researchers and psychologists debate the value of using strict sets of symptoms to distinguish mental illness from mental health. Researchers now argue that many people meet the psychiatric definition of a mental disorder but may neither experience severe impairments in their daily lives nor need mental health treatment, with many of them probably only having temporary setbacks due to stressful events in their lives. In a survey of how psychiatrists use the *Diagnostic and Statistical Manual of Mental Disorders* (American Psychiatric Association, 1994), nearly half of the 557 responding psychiatrists expressed doubt about the validity of diagnostic criteria, and 35% wouldn't use the manual if they didn't have to. Studies of serial killers suggest, by the criteria of the diagnostic manual, many qualify as utterly normal. This highlights the absurdity of psychiatric diagnoses.

Definitions of mental disorders change over time, and recent revisions of the diagnostic manual have expanded the criteria for some disorders, increasing the numbers of people labeled mentally ill. Conduct disorder, added as a diagnosis for children in 1980, lumps all children misbehaving in certain ways together, whether in response to a bad environment (such as sexual abuse or dangerous neighborhoods) or not. Nearly 1/2 of all adults have had a diagnosable mental disorder at some time, and almost 1/3 have had one in the previous year. The most common is major depression; it appears in 17% of the population, with 10% reporting it in the previous year. Next comes alcohol dependence, with a lifetime rate of 14% and 7% in the previous year. Then come social and simple phobias, strong fears of things like speaking in public, bridges, heights, or flying. Phobias appear in 13% of all adults, with 11% in the past year. About 1/6 of the population suffer from three or more mental disorders over the course of their lives.

Some psychiatrists and psychologists argue diagnoses are insulting and oppressive nonsense. Some apologize for the diagnostic labels, explaining they must label to get paid and asking the client please not to pay too much attention to the label. They hope to avoid making clients feel unable to change because of an unreliable, invalid diagnosis. Of course, the diagnoses do represent ongoing work in understanding emotional patterns and such things as prevalence, family rates, course, and associated features.

Traditional psychological assessment is very unscientific. The most commonly used test, the Minnesota Multiphasic Personality Inventory (MMPI), was poorly constructed, using very small samples and a very bad control group: friends and family members visiting hospitalized patients. The MMPI will often find mental illness where there is none. Researchers have long known that the famous Rorschach inkblot test and sentence completion tests are completely invalid. Critic Robyn Dawes warned against using any psychologist who evaluates you by asking you to draw anything or respond to inkblots or incomplete sentences. His warning came in the 1994 book *House of Cards: Psychology and Psychotherapy Built on Myth*, a scientific critique of psychology. *Contemporary Psychology*, the most important review journal in the field, described this book as "extremely important," as "well documented," and as must reading for all clinical psychologists. His book summarizes the meaning of a great deal of research and forms the basis of points in the next three paragraphs.

The science of psychology tells us that psychologists and psychiatrists are no better than intelligent, minimally trained people at diagnosing mental problems or at predicting what people will do. In some studies, psychologists do worse than people with no training at all. Well-made tests based on obvious variables that correlate with group outcomes predict much better than do expensive, experienced psychiatrists or psychologists. For example, past violence best predicts the likelihood of future violence, and the number of past convictions best predicts success on parole. Although the courts often ask psychiatrists to predict a person's dangerousness, experts agree there is no way to do this beyond what any judge knows. Despite the training, expertise, and wisdom many psychiatrists and psychologists pride themselves on, impressions from interviews or decisions based on clinical experience never helps and often makes prediction worse.

Furthermore, over 500 scientific studies show psychotherapists' credentials and experience are not related to patient improvement from counseling. Psychologists and psychiatrists with 30 or 40 years of experience are no better at helping people than are intelligent, minimally trained lay people. Even self-help groups often do as well as professional psychologists, and many members of the clergy do good counseling with little or no training. A December 1996 8-year study by the federal government called Project MATCH found Alcoholics Anonymous was just as successful in sharply reducing drinking as two types of psychotherapy administered by trained psychotherapists, including cognitive-behavioral.

Research suggests the helpful aspects of psychotherapy are simply the client receiving attention, acceptance, warmth, respect, empathy, understanding, encouragement, reassurance, and emotional support. But professional psychology organizations have spent a great deal of money lobbying the government to establish psychologists as well-paid experts and to stop other people from providing counseling services much more cheaply. Despite the scientific evidence, taxpayers and insurance companies foolishly continue to fund overly expensive counseling and lucrative, but invalid, psychological testing making paternalistic, limiting judgments about people in both clinical and legal settings. And despite the evidence, judges and juries continue listen to very expensive so-called expert consultants on both sides who often disagree and offer confusing, subjective, jargon-ridden testimony.

Research shows psychotherapy need not be long-term, as brief therapy is just as effective. Research also shows most psychotherapy clients do not perform basic procedures such as deep relaxation techniques daily as instructed, even if they are suffering from problems such as anxiety or headaches. The people who benefit the most from counseling are those who practice the new behaviors constantly and never give up until they succeed.

Unfortunately, many psychologists and psychiatrists don't keep up with the field. Once you get your license in psychology, you can ignore the science of psychology and do foolish things. A number of licensed psychologists specialize in helping people whom extraterrestrial aliens have abducted and hypnotized to forget it. Others use hypnosis or guided imagery techniques to explore people's past lives. Psychologists all over the country charge plenty of money for biofeedback, despite research showing biofeedback is no better than simple deep muscle relaxation techniques you can do at home with no equipment. Subliminal audiotapes sold to do such things as speed weight loss, improve memory or self-esteem, or bring peace of mind are another scam. These tapes don't work as advertised and many of them don't even contain subliminal messages.

Diagnoses and treatments in psychology are often fads and some of them are dangerous. In the 1940s and 1950s, psychiatrists were performing lobotomies, drilling holes in the skull and destroying parts of the brain with tools like ice picks, often without seeing what they were cutting. Dr. Moniz, the inventor of this procedure, won the Nobel Prize in medicine, and highly respected psychiatrists and neurosurgeons everywhere recommended it despite its dangers and side effects. Many of the victims were mental patients in state hospitals, long abandoned by their families.

There is great controversy among former patients and mental health professionals over electroshock therapy (ECT) for depression and manic-depressive illness. Patients normally receive it only after multiple failures with medicines, when health reasons prevent the use of medicines, or to combat strong suicidal feelings. The evidence for short-term improvement is strong, but the problems frequently come right back. The major side effects are confusion and memory loss, which are usually short term but sometimes long lasting. Approximately 100,000 people each year receive ECT, with people over 61 years old being the largest age group receiving it. ECT has caused many deaths, but most occurred before recent developments in anesthetic technique.

Historically, as Dr. Peter Breggin details in his book *Toxic Psychiatry*, people have used ECT in horrible ways to eliminate memories and even identities, usually those of women. (Dr. Breggin led the fight against lobotomy and the courts held that Breggin, not the American Psychiatric Association, summarized the psychosurgery data accurately.) H. C. Tien published a detailed account in 1972 of using ECT to change an abused woman who wanted to leave her spouse into a new, more passive wife with little memory of the marital abuse. In the late 50s and early 60s, the CIA paid

D. Ewen Cameron in Canada to learn how to brainwash people and wipe out their memories with ECT. This led to a lawsuit with many of Cameron's victims dividing a settlement in 1988. One of Dr. Cameron's patients was unable to state her name, the year, or her location during her hospitalization and became incontinent of urine and feces. She continues to have no memory of her life before her treatment at age 26. In Ossining, New York's Stony Lodge hospital, patients received shock until they became unable to talk, incontinent of both bowel and bladder, and in need of spoon-feeding. Some doctors and psychiatrists have quit jobs and risked their careers by speaking out against ECT.

New studies of modern ECT show brain abnormalities do not usually result and most cognitive symptoms are short-lived. A review in the July 1994 *American Journal of Psychiatry* concludes ECT interferes with memory formation for a few weeks, so people rapidly forget newly learned material and lose events during and surrounding the time of ECT. Within weeks, however, the ability to learn new information returns to normal. This review also notes some patients will lose memory for events before the time of the ECT and that this memory loss can be long lasting. But damage to the brain may result, especially for patients who undergo numerous courses of treatment, and the use of general anesthesia carries its own risks.

In *Toxic Psychiatry*, Dr. Breggin argues modern ECT is perhaps more dangerous because the anesthesia and sedatives used to prevent broken bones mean they must use higher doses of electricity to cause convulsions. He notes a large percentage of ECT patients report serious memory blanks and difficulties for years after treatment, and the elderly are more likely to have severe reactions, including confusion, falls, and cardiorespiratory problems. He believes the American Psychiatric Association (APA) claims the effectiveness and safety of ECT to prevent lawsuits on this very profitable business. He points out the APA successfully lobbied the Food and Drug Administration to reverse its 1979 decision to classify ECT as having an unreasonable injury risk. One-third of the cities in the United States have laws against the use of ECT. Now the powerless elderly receive more ECT treatments than any other age group.

One of the newer fads in psychology is recovered memory therapy. Because of the enormous publicity given to sexual and physical abuse, recovered memory therapists all over the country prey on their suggestible clients and seem to uncover sexual abuse, ritual satanic abuse, and perhaps multiple personality, with faulty, leading techniques. The first cases of satanic abuse came out in 1983, a time when rumors and media reports about teenage Satanism and satanic lyrics in heavy metal music were common. Cases usually began when one child made a comment that upset adults. Flimsy allegations gathered momentum as suggestible children made more and more accusations under repeated questioning. Children as young as three accused their parents, grandparents, teachers, and neighbors of animal mutilations, murders, sexual abuse, and baby sacrifices in ceremonies, with their stories growing from believable to absurd.

This kind of hysteria is nothing new. Stories of Satanists devouring babies go back to early Christian times. In the 1500s and 1600s, authorities in Europe put to death half a million people because of these beliefs. In the 1980s, diagnosing and treating the victims became a big business. Lecturers with few credentials taught police, therapists, and social workers in seminars on satanic cults. Special hospital wards gathered insurance money to treat the victims. After the FBI spent 8 years studying claims of satanic abuse, a 1992 report stated that although many people certainly experienced sexual and physical abuse, there was little or no evidence for the kinds of inflated claims being made. In a typical example, one woman claimed a cult bred her to have babies for ritual sacrifice and her parents forced her to have a Cesarean section, but the investigation showed she had no Cesarean scars. The consistent lack of evidence when law enforcement agencies investigate such claims shows the vast majority are fantasies. There are child sex rings and there have been bizarre religious cults practicing sexual abuse, but most allegations of ritual satanic abuse are false.

The emphasis on recovering lost memories has continued, however, breaking up thousands of families and leading to hundreds of lawsuits. Over half the states have passed new laws allowing lawsuits based on recovered memories. The demand for sexual abuse therapy has skyrocketed and both psychotherapists and residential treatment centers gather insurance and government money for recovered memory therapy. While most psychologists have never seen a patient who reported ritual abuse memories, a few report large numbers of cases. Recovered memory therapists often mistakenly believe most clients are victims of sexual or ritual abuse or that common symptoms such as depression, anxiety, eating disorders, or fears of fires, knives, blood, dying, animals being hurt, coffins, cemeteries, snakes, or spiders are evidence of sexual or ritual abuse. A client not remembering abuse does not convince some therapists; they see this as evidence of repression, the burying of memories until there is no conscious awareness of them. These therapists view doubts about what they say as denial and evidence of repression, so they go on to use a variety of faulty techniques to probe for memories.

Recovered memory therapists don't understand how memory works and may use hypnosis, truth serum, barbiturates, support groups, free association, guided visualizations, age regression, trance writing, body manipulation and massage, dream work, imagery exercises based on dreams, and artwork to uncover lost memories. All of these techniques can lead to false memories, especially with unhappy, suggestible clients who may be prone to fantasy. (This is a form of *self-fulfilling prophecy*—when people's actions and expectations lead to the predicted result.) The therapist's suggestions, phrasing of questions, tone of voice, comments, emotions, arguments, and leading techniques cause the client to imagine scenes, then details, then elaborate stories. Clients who need to feel special may unwittingly respond to therapists' interest and fascination by creating more details and confusing fantasy and reality in the trance-like states produced by many of the above techniques. Support groups run by recovered memory therapists encourage troubled people to participate by sharing memories and reward them with attention, companionship, warmth, and a sense of belonging. Many people go to a group without clear memories and then get them during the meetings. Of course, books, articles, media publicity, and movies on the occult, physical and sexual abuse, incest, and satanic themes create fears and expectations, make the imagination run wild in susceptible people, and encourage bizarre ideas and stories. Some hospitals punish denial with the loss of privileges and require clients to produce memories before the hospital will discharge them.

Clients have recently begun suing their therapists for leading them to make false accusations against their parents and disown their families. Four cases have ended in settlements of between $1 million and $2.67 million. One of these cases involved a woman who came to believe horrible things through counseling. She thought that her clergyman father regularly raped her between the ages of 7 and 14, her mother sometimes helped by holding her down, and her father twice impregnated her and forced her to abort the fetuses herself with a coat hanger. Doctors found she was in fact a virgin who had never been pregnant. Most clients who uncover ritual satanic abuse in therapy had no memory of it before therapy.

Researchers know memories are easy to manipulate. The National Institute of Justice reported on 28 prisoners set free from jail after DNA tests proved their innocence. Court records showed eyewitnesses had testified against 24 of them. Sadly, if a detective leads a witness on, the witness often becomes highly confident even when wrong. In a famous case of poor psychological techniques leading to false memories, a man may or may not have been guilty of sexually abusing his two daughters. After 5 months of interrogation and suggestions from a psychologist to visualize scenes, he confessed to an ever-expanding list of rapes, assaults, and child sexual abuse and to participating in a satanic cult that murdered 25 babies. A prosecution psychologist decided to test his credibility by presenting a false rape situation and asking him to visualize and pray on it. Several hours later, the man developed detailed memories and wrote a confession.

The science of psychology doesn't really know what causes multiple personality, now called Dissociative Identity Disorder. Before the book *Sybil* in 1973, there were only about 75 cases of this disorder in recorded history, mostly between 1876 and 1920, with only 8 reported between 1960 and 1970. One expert now estimates 40,000 diagnosed cases. Some believe multiple personality is finally receiving the attention it deserves. Other experts see it as a fad diagnosis popular in the recovered memory movement. After the famous cases of Eve and Sybil received publicity, some patients went from therapist to therapist until they found one who believed them. Again, the vast majority of psychologists and psychiatrists have never seen a single case, while a very small minority of clinicians report the great majority of cases. And again, special hospital units collect huge amounts of insurance money to treat the disorder. It is not unusual for the treatment of one multiple personality patient to cost $1 million. One case cost $2.75 million. When one woman reached her $1 million insurance limit, the hospital dumped her into a state facility, which then determined she had no significant mental illness and discharged her.

Some experts argue psychotherapy causes multiple personality through comments, leading questions, suggestions, encouragement, excessive probing, argument, and hypnosis. They point out the average time in therapy before the diagnosis of multiple personality is six or seven years. Supporters of the diagnosis give several explanations for this delay. First, patients are ashamed of their symptoms and afraid to trust authority figures because of their childhood abuse. Also, most therapists have little training in diagnosing this problem and the bureaucracy of psychology is very slow to change. Finally, the supporters say society cannot deal with sadistic incestuous abuse and its implications for the family and for power and sexual relations.

Critics of the diagnosis also make the following points, however. The great majority of patients are white people with good finances or health insurance allowing access to prolonged work with therapists in private practice. No case descriptions seem to be of lower class, poor, or homeless patients. If trauma caused multiple personality, one would expect many more cases involving black people because available statistics suggest blacks are more likely to suffer traumas than whites. In addition, multiple personality is a North American epidemic, with only occasional cases reported elsewhere by therapists with American training or similar viewpoints. In England, Europe, and other parts of the world, the diagnosis is rare.

Many patients say they couldn't believe the diagnosis of multiple personality but they finally learned to accept it. Of course, those who refuse to go along would simply leave the therapist. Most patients show no symptoms of multiplicity before treatment and don't know they have the disorder until the therapist helps uncover it. The most troubling symptoms—switching between adult and child personalities, howling like an animal, speaking as the devil, slashing their wrists, inflicting burns on themselves, or voicing desires to kill the main personality—don't normally appear until after a great deal of therapy.

Recovered memory therapists may see evidence for multiple personality in many common things like headaches, depression, poor concentration, mood swings, ambivalent feelings, forgetfulness, or daydreaming. They see evidence for it in talking aloud to yourself, missing part of what someone is saying, hostile fantasies, or bad habits you can't control. They even see it in being called a liar, meeting people who insist they have met you before, having no memories for periods of your life history, drug abuse, sexual feelings or behaviors causing guilt, or uncharacteristic actions. They believe cure comes only from uncovering all the personalities, the histories of each, and the trauma that led to the formation of each, so the person can finish the feelings and integrate the alternate personalities. These therapists probe endlessly, encouraging you to label different feelings and conflicts or parts of yourself (sadness, parts that enjoy playing with children, etc.) as separate personalities. If you complain, they may accuse you of being in denial or threaten that healing is impossible without letting all the personalities out. The most common way to uncover evidence of multiplicity is hypnosis, with leading suggestions and requests for the alternate personalities to come forth, but searching for alter egos in therapy or through hypnosis or barbiturates may become a self-fulfilling prophecy.

Even the character of multiple personality seems to have changed following the recent lore of the diagnosis. People didn't consider childhood abuse the cause until after the book *Sybil* in 1973 and subsequent movie. Cases before 1920 were only occasionally associated with child abuse. Now most patients report histories of childhood sexual abuse and many tell increasingly bizarre tales of satanic ritual abuse. In some treatment centers, 80% of multiple personality patients recover memories of ritual satanic abuse. Before the 1940s, most cases reported had only two or three personalities. Many early cases showed transitional periods of sleep, and often convulsions, between alternate personalities. In recent decades, the average number of alters is 15 or more, with no sleep or convulsions between them. Now many therapists report clients with over 200 personalities, including some that are animals, inanimate objects, or demons. One expert claims a case with more than 4,500 alters, an improbable number that seems difficult to measure. In the first cases, therapists rarely reported the existence of a self-destructive alter personality that tries to cut, burn, or mutilate the person or commit suicide. In the last decade, however, the rate of destructive alters in multiple personality cases seems to have grown from perhaps around 20% to nearly 50%.

Many experts argue these changes come from the preconceived notions of recovered memory therapists, people who promote the diagnosis, and their organizations. Many multiple personality patients and therapists participate regularly in workshops and conferences on the topic, in self-help and therapy groups focused on it, and have access to national newsletters on it. The idea of therapists causing multiple personality disorder is not far-fetched when you consider how many alien encounters and past life regressions clients uncover using faulty techniques.

Many psychologists note speaking to alters or showing much interest in them rewards them and makes psychotherapy less effective in treating symptoms such as depression or alcoholism, but that directing the client's attention away from the alter personalities leads to their decline. One former multiple personality client asked her therapist, "Don't you think it is odd that no one is getting better and that everyone wants to go out and kill themselves after they get into therapy with you?" Even experts who support the diagnosis of multiple personality agree excessive preoccupation with exploring alternate personalities, therapist fascination, the overuse of journaling, or pressure to uncover traumas prematurely are serious clinical problems that can worsen the disorder.

Some clients, including Sybil, have admitted playing the role of multiple personality to please the therapist and feel relieved when a new therapist doesn't want to emphasize these patterns. When Sybil and her psychiatrist Dr. Cornelia Wilbur were unable to make progress in therapy, Dr. Wilbur referred her to Dr. Herbert Spiegel for diagnosis and additional therapy. He also worked with Sybil later when Dr. Wilbur went on summer break. At first he didn't understand when Sybil would say, "Do I have to become Helen or can we just discuss this?" She explained, "When I'm with Dr. Wilbur, she wants me to be that person." Dr. Spiegel left it up to her and found that Sybil didn't. Dr. Spiegel feels these personalities were "created by the therapist."

Dr. Spiegel reports no mention of the diagnosis of multiple personality until after Sybil quit therapy with him and the author of *Sybil,* Flora Schreiber, and Dr. Wilbur began collaborating on the book. When Schreiber asked for Dr. Spiegel's files and cooperation and mentioned the diagnosis of multiple personality, Dr. Spiegel objected to the diagnosis. Schreiber argued the book would never sell without the diagnosis, Spiegel refused to cooperate, Schreiber became very angry and left, and both Schreiber and Dr. Wilbur wouldn't talk to Spiegel after that. Dr. Spiegel says Sybil's mother was definitely schizophrenic, but the sexual abuse had never been corroborated. Sybil made some profoundly unlikely claims, including detailed incidents from the ages of six weeks and six months, times when ordinary brain development would not maintain such complex memories.

Eve admitted she was "having fun being a multiple." After uniting into one personality, she wrote "the magic had gone out of my life." Eve changed her story of originating trauma several times, as can be seen by reading her books, but her doctors could not find any trauma terrible enough to cause the disorder. She had seen two dead bodies in her early years, and relatives asked her to touch her dead grandmother at age five, a custom believed to help in ending grief. Her parents, by all accounts, were extraordinarily supportive and loving.

One psychiatrist used hypnosis and other suggestive techniques to convince a woman of many horrible things. She thought she had childhood physical and sexual abuse, was in a satanic cult, ate babies, was raped, had sex with animals, was forced to watch a young friend's murder, and had 120 personalities, including angels and a duck. The psychiatrist also performed exorcisms on her, one lasting 5 hours. When she realized the memories were false, she sued and settled out of court for $2.4 million.

If the foolish techniques of recovered memory therapists actually cause multiple personality disorder, psychologists cause these patients to deteriorate, which in some cases even leads to suicide. Why would anyone want to make up stories of ritual satanic abuse or multiple personalities? First, these troubled, unhappy people may want the special concern, attention, and emotional support that come with the diagnosis, both in therapy and elsewhere. (Many multiple personality patients also claim experiences of ESP, clairvoyance, reincarnation, astral travel, poltergeists, and similar phenomenon.) These insecure people may also need the sense of belonging they find in the workshops and support groups. These claims also give a framework to explain the anger or rage, pain, and emotional abandonment these patients may feel. It is easier to tell dramatic stories of abuse than it is to talk about your real problems, honestly study yourself, and take responsibility for and work on your personal problems. Finally, the techniques psychologists use may simply confuse them into thinking their stories are true.

Many experts see recovered memory therapy as a horrible mistake causing enormous harm. The American Medical Association (AMA) in June 1994 warned of the danger of creating false memories with the techniques used by recovered memory therapists, but the use of memory-distorting techniques continues. An informal survey of therapists around the country found misconceptions about memory and hypnosis abound. Many think memory records things like a videotape; researchers rejected this notion over twenty years ago. Many believe people can remember things from their first year of life. There is no scientific evidence you can remember anything from before the age of two or three. Many therapists thought you couldn't lie under hypnosis or that reporting a trauma under hypnosis proved it was true.

Memory is a process that alters, reworks, interprets, and reconstructs bits of information. Our moods and beliefs influence what we recall, and we build memories by filling gaps with probable scenarios, general knowledge, and the way we see things now. Mood distorts memories: we often call up memories fitting our present mood and interpret memories or fill in gaps with our present mood. How you feel about a person affects what you remember about the person's past actions and how you interpret them. Emotions like guilt, rage, or competitiveness can also distort memories. Memories we first claim unsurely very often become stronger as time goes on, so we later have no doubt about them. Memories are greatly influenced by the kinds of questions asked and the status of the person asking. Hundreds of studies show you can easily introduce falsehoods into memories by suggestion. Telling someone there was blood, broken glass, a tape recorder, or even a barn in a scene with no buildings at all often results in agreement and further details. With repetition, it is easy to convince 20 or 25% of people they had a severe ear infection, got lost in a shopping mall as a child, or knocked over the punch bowl at a family wedding, spilling the punch on the bride's parents.

During hypnosis, studies show asking a question will interject the idea as a reality. The great psychologist Sigmund Freud stopped hypnotizing patients when he realized hypnosis mixes fantasies, desires, and fears with real details. The American Medical Association has taken a stand against using hypnosis to refresh memory, arguing that this increases gullibility, responsiveness to suggestion, and false memories. Their report noted hypnotized people who recalled disturbing things sometimes remained disturbed. Hypnosis increases confidence in memories, whether or not they are true. Because of this, memories brought out in hypnosis are no longer admissible in court.

Experts believe approximately one out of four therapists has faulty beliefs and practices, such as believing certain presentations are associated with abuse, or the use of one or more suggestive techniques to explore abuse. Abuse therapists often encourage blaming, hatred, and false reports against relatives, while doing nothing to solve current or past problems. Therapists who don't keep up with the science of psychology are incompetent and may harm their clients. As we shall see in the next chapter, many psychologists and psychiatrists receive their training in and continue to use unscientific types of psychotherapy. Traditions in the bureaucracy of psychology change very slowly. Despite decades of scientific research proving the uselessness of traditional psychological testing, universities still teach the same tests and clinicians everywhere still use them. Psychiatrists still use ECT and claim improvements, while former patients complain and states and cities outlaw it.

The Freudian viewpoint has led to an extreme emphasis among many psychologists and psychiatrists on seeking to contact early trauma, recall it in depth, and reexperience it emotionally in order to finish it. Too many therapists believe we can't heal ourselves without doing this, but we still have no scientific proof that, as Freud theorized, doing so leads to increased happiness and productivity. Some people recover memories of alien abductions or past-life regressions and feel much better afterwards. The truly sad thing is people who enter therapy may drown and deteriorate in endless discussions of the horrible past, whether true or imagined.

Many psychologists exaggerate the importance of childhood experiences and blame people's parents for their problems. Both the Freudian viewpoint and the more recent family systems viewpoint in psychology have contributed to this problem, most obvious now in the phrase "dysfunctional family." This vague, overused term blames parents for our own unhappiness without specifying any clear behaviors at fault and implies the damage from our childhood is irreversible. No family can act in perfectly healthy ways all the time. We often see one unhappy person labeling the whole family as very dysfunctional, while other family members feel it is healthy but the one person has problems.

Long-term studies show that although abused and neglected children show higher rates of emotional problems, delinquency, arrests, and psychiatric hospitalizations, most abused and neglected children don't show these problems. Children are remarkably resilient and many triumph over a disadvantaged and deprived childhood and even abuse. A classic study of 400 famous and highly achieving people found 1/4 had physical handicaps and 3/4 grew up in poverty or came from broken homes or abusive families. Overcoming disadvantages can provide the motivation for great achievements. Because of our tendency to retrieve memories fitting our present mood, it is easy to think of childhood problems and blame our parents for all our problems, but our childhood history does not doom us forever.

Good therapy does not allow us to wallow in misery over the past, nor to blame all our problems on it, even if it was abusive. Understanding how the past affected us can be important, of course. Most psychologists believe contacting and expressing avoided or repressed emotions is important and helpful, but very often we feel preoccupied with our painful past because of negative thinking, lacking enough pleasures, interests, activities, friends, or time spent socializing, or other problems interfering with our present personal growth. Good therapy will look at our lives today to see what we can do in these areas and will explore what we do now that keeps us feeling hurt and injured in the familiar role of victim.

41. Important Advice about Counseling

Don't be afraid or too proud to ask for help;
asking for help when you need it shows strength and wisdom.

If you experience any of the following symptoms, you definitely need psychotherapy and you may need medicines: suicidal thoughts, prolonged severe depression with apathy, social withdrawal, or growing inability to cope at work, in your social life, with personal problems, or with emotions. The same is true if you experience extreme highs and lows in emotions, extreme anxieties or fears, many unexplained physical problems, severe flashbacks, difficulties in concentrating, confusion, or irrational or bizarre thoughts. *Delusions* are false ideas that resist change by reason, such as strong concerns that other people read your mind or paranoid beliefs that other people persecute you and try to hurt you in various ways. *Hallucinations* are experiences of seeing or hearing things that don't exist. If you have either delusions or hallucinations, you definitely need psychotherapy and you are likely to need medicines. The one exception is the common experience of seeing, hearing, or feeling the presence of a deceased loved one during grief. These hallucinations or delusions do not require psychotherapy or medicines. If you abuse other people or violate codes of sexual decency, you also definitely need psychotherapy. People with anorexia or bulimia need to work with a doctor and a psychologist or psychiatrist who both have experience in working with eating disorders.

Anyone who feels overwhelmed by personal problems or feels unable to conquer a personal problem without help should go to counseling. Counselors can provide direction and emotional support and can help you avoid denial, sort priorities, work on problems, and stay focused on working to change. Even if you feel you function fairly well and that you can conquer your personal problems by yourself, counseling may help because people often remain remarkably blind to their own personal problems. Counselors provide objectivity in identifying personal problems and their effects.

When beginning counseling, most people feel overwhelmed and somewhat helpless about their personal problems and expect the counselor to guide them along the path to improved emotional well-being. Unfortunately, some counselors have little training and experience in psychotherapy, and some have personal problems that interfere with their counseling skills. Also, many counselors use theories and techniques that often fail to solve personal problems, and some counselors act in unprofessional or unethical ways.

In choosing a counselor, first consider the person's qualifications. If your symptoms include severe anxiety or depression or confusion that interferes with your daily functioning, severe flashbacks, irrational or bizarre thinking, delusions, or hallucinations, you should look for a psychiatrist. Only a psychiatrist has the medical knowledge and license to prescribe the medicines you may need. If you don't have any of these severe problems, you can go to a psychologist for psychotherapy or to a social worker, nurse, or member of the clergy who provides counseling. Realize, however, other counselors don't have the extensive training and expertise in counseling that psychiatrists and psychologists must have. Nevertheless, many social workers, nurses, and members of the clergy have good counseling skills. Don't be fooled by the terms psychotherapist or counselor. You must have a license to call yourself a psychologist or psychiatrist, but in some states there are no rules about calling yourself a psychotherapist or a counselor.

There are various types of psychotherapy, but one type is much better than all the others. A great deal of research on rates of improvement suggests the effectiveness of only cognitive-behavioral psychotherapy. In studies of the effectiveness of therapy, researchers seldom even try to beat placebo effects with any other type. Psychiatrists and psychologists who keep up with the field, no matter what their training or theory of psychology, are now incorporating cognitive-behavioral techniques into their work. Cognitive-behavioral psychotherapy works toward eliminating problem thoughts and behaviors and learning more helpful thoughts and behaviors such as those described in this book. This type of psychotherapy saves you plenty of time and money by focusing on the specific changes and goals you need rather than focusing on endlessly exploring feelings and past events.

Unfortunately, many psychologists and psychiatrists receive their training in less effective forms of psychotherapy. For example, Freudian psychoanalysis usually involves years of expensive therapy endlessly analyzing childhood experiences, dreams, and wandering thought processes called free associations. Freudian theory holds that childhood sexuality during the preschool years greatly affects adult mental health, that all little boys desire their mothers sexually and fear the revenge of castration from their fathers, and that all little girls experience penis envy for the "more desirable" male organ. A special program about the legacy of Sigmund Freud on educational television (PBS) admitted Freudian theory is now discredited. He discovered the unconscious mind, the importance of childhood experiences on adult emotional life, the effects of repressed traumas, the importance of reexperiencing and working through buried feelings, the importance of interests and activities, rationalization, and projection. Freud also revived interest in dream interpretation and opened the field of sexuality, but Freudian beliefs about unconscious childhood sexual wishes have prevented many therapists from seeing incest, even when evidence for it exists. Freudian psychoanalysis and its descendants (Jungian analysis and other psychodynamic therapies) rely on unscientific, vague theories and provide types of psychotherapy that are more suitable as long-term hobbies for the rich than to solving personal problems quickly.

Family psychotherapy can refer to any type of psychotherapy with families. When a behavioral or cognitive-behavioral psychotherapist provides family therapy, you receive effective family psychotherapy. Unfortunately, however, most family therapists receive their training in the family systems theory of psychology. Family systems theory is as vague, unscientific, and unproven as is Freudian theory. It has actually accused parents and especially mothers of causing all the following problems in their children: schizophrenia, drug addiction, juvenile delinquency, manic-depressive illness, anorexia, homosexuality, epilepsy, rheumatoid arthritis, colitis, ulcers, and asthma. According to this theory, the parents cause these problems through certain styles or patterns of communication, through certain family alliances, through overly low or overly high tolerance for individualism in the family, and through other vague faulty family relationships.

Family systems psychotherapy is very bad at treating abuse. It tends to hold both husband and wife responsible for patterns, even when the man abuses the woman. Many of these therapists think the violence will stop if the woman changes her behaviors. Family systems theory has contributed an important emphasis in psychology on involving family members in working on your personal problems to increase the chances of success. It has also contributed insights in the areas of possible family dynamics and troublesome communication styles, but family systems psychotherapy lacks a scientifically proven approach to solving personal problems.

Cognitive psychotherapies such as rational emotive therapy focus mostly on negative thinking habits and neglect a more practical focus on ways of changing problem behaviors. Rogerian or client-centered psychotherapists use the helpful listening skills discussed in chapter 6, Communication Skills, to bring out the views and feelings of the client. In this way, Rogerian psychotherapists help their clients explore their priorities and decide what they want to do about their personal problems. Carl Rogers, the great psychologist who founded Rogerian psychotherapy, has contributed an important emphasis on these strategies for staying focused during counseling on the client's needs and values, but this kind of psychotherapy also neglects a more practical focus on ways of changing problem behaviors. Gestalt psychotherapists use mostly the dialoguing techniques described in chapter 14. Fritz Perls, the founder of gestalt psychotherapy, contributed some very useful approaches for exploring conflicts and for contacting, reexperiencing, and working through feelings from the past, but gestalt psychotherapy also neglects a more practical focus on ways of changing problem behaviors.

Perhaps it seems strange that so many types of psychotherapy could flourish and gain acceptance when most of them are not proven effective. Many personal problems improve over time, however, with or without psychological treatment. For example, people don't usually feel extremely depressed, so if you feel that way, it is likely to change. And any kind of psychotherapy contains placebo effects that help worried or desperate people feel better. The client receives attention, acceptance, warmth, respect, empathy, understanding, encouragement, reassurance, and emotional support, all of which help increase self-esteem. Taking action against your problem by going to a knowledgeable expert you trust and by following the expert's advice creates the expectation of a forthcoming cure, reduces fear, inspires hope, and gives you a sense of direction and of mastery. The expert also gives you an explanation for the problem that helps in making sense of confusing feelings and helps you see the past and present in less threatening ways. Other helpful placebo effects include the release of emotions, the confession of past mistakes or wrongdoing, and the sharing of dark secrets and fears.

In fact, shamans (the medicine men of primitive cultures who act as religious leaders, doctors, and psychologists) use all of these helpful elements in their work. The work of the shaman is not nearly as bizarre as it appears. Long, exhausting ceremonies help emotional release. States of trance allow people to express plenty of emotions and buried parts of themselves. (People often express personalities markedly different from their own during the trance state.) Like psychologists, shamans sometimes rely on relaxation, hypnosis, exploring the past, reenactment of the past, long-term therapy relationships, the participation and emotional support of friends and family members, or the removal of the client from stress. In both psychology and the work of shamanism, too, the treatment benefits from the whole weight of the culture's coherent systems of beliefs about illness and healing.

These facts help explain why many people seem to gain emotional benefits from various kinds of psychotherapy and from religious healing techniques, such as those found in voodoo. Thus, some psychiatrists in

Brazil, Mexico, Bali, Africa, and Asia coordinate treatments with traditional healers and refer patients to them. Personal testimonials about cures from therapy prove about as much as do testimonials about the effectiveness of products on television. Scientific proof of effectiveness in psychotherapy, however, must go beyond normal improvements over time and the effectiveness of the placebo effect.

In choosing a counselor, you have the right to shop around and ask questions. People with problems often feel small compared to the psychiatrists, psychologists, and counselors who specialize in personal problems, but you shouldn't feel intimidated by these professionals. Remember that some are better than others and some are incompetent. Avoid any counselor who seems overly nervous or has obvious signs of personal or emotional problems. Be sure to ask about the therapist's training, experience, credentials, and type of psychotherapy, and avoid any counselor who specializes in abuse unless you already remember abuse. As detailed in the previous chapter, recovered memory therapists may do more harm than good.

It is not uncommon to go to therapy for treatment shortly after the onset of upsetting imagery and symptoms. If you have some memories of childhood abuse, the therapist should not argue for or against the memories but should maintain a respectful, neutral stance and help you examine both sides of the issue using your conflicts and experiences. If you express uncertainty about a memory and your therapist says you are in denial, you should find another therapist. A good therapist's first concern and overall emphasis will be on healing—establishing emotional safety, stability, and improving functioning. Responding to, interpreting, or uncovering the past should only come slowly, in a controlled way, when you do not feel emotionally overwhelmed. At this time, you may learn to predict and regulate the troublesome memories, so you can most effectively deal with and understand them.

Because counseling involves a detailed and sometimes difficult discussion of very personal matters, it is essential you feel comfortable sharing your deepest thoughts and feelings with the counselor and you feel a good rapport. Avoid any counselor whose personality or beliefs interfere with your ability to share your deepest thoughts and feelings. Choose an understanding counselor who can accept you as you are. Reject any counselor who seems unable to understand you, seems unable to relate to your lifestyle or values, seems judgmental of you, or seems to looks down upon you as inferior. You should like and respect the counselor and feel they like and respect you. A good counselor is warm, supportive, caring, and sensitive to your feelings and needs. Avoid those who seem distant, cold, or aloof or whose friendliness or concern seems forced or fake. Also, reject any counselor who seems uninterested in or insensitive to your feelings or problems. Trust your own impressions in making these judgments. Your feelings will help you find the right counselor for you.

Pay attention to how productive your time in counseling has been. Good counselors will help you recognize your personal issues and problems, choose your priorities among them, and take concrete steps toward overcoming them. They will help you define problems and goals in ways that make sense to you and meet your needs. Unfortunately, many counselors waste time letting you ramble on about your thoughts and feelings without an effective focus on defining and solving problems. Other counselors are too passive and do very little except to encourage you to talk ("Tell me more," "How do you feel about that," etc.) or to occasionally signal that they are listening (nodding, "hmm," "mm-huh," etc.). Some of them waste your therapy time talking about themselves, bragging, or trying to impress you. A good counselor won't talk as much as you do.

If your counselor makes any of the following serious mistakes, you should definitely stop going to that person and find another counselor. Quit any counselor who becomes angry and treats you with disrespect, humiliates you or insults you with negative labels, or yells at you, unless the counselor is matching your intensity because you are already yelling. If a counselor tries to seduce you, immediately stop going to that counselor and report the incident to the state licensing bureau. Any large library can help you find the appropriate address or phone number for such complaints. Never tolerate sexual advances by a counselor; they are highly unethical. If the therapist is a member of the professional organization, you can also report psychologists to the American Psychological Association and psychiatrists to the American Psychiatric Association. These organizations can scold, impose penalties, require supervision, or kick the person out of the organization.

Studies suggest perhaps as many as 5% of male psychiatrists have become sexually involved with a client. The leading cause of lawsuits against psychologists is therapist-patient sex, and an increasing number of states consider this a felony. In some areas, victim programs give money for therapy to deal with the aftermath of this problem. Even if you don't file criminal charges, you can file a malpractice suit, which may result in some monetary award. These lawsuits have time limits, but judges may extend them due to your inability to act because of your psychological response to trauma. Many lawyers will take these cases with no money up front, for a part of the settlement. Realize, however, that the defense may try to portray you as promiscuous or ask questions of your sexual history.

Women seeking help for abuse should watch out for signs the counselor is overly sympathetic to abusive men or holds outdated beliefs about women abuse. Reject any counselor who labels you as overly demanding, masochistic, overreacting, or hysterical or who suggests you enjoy the abuse, you behave and stop upsetting the man, you try to become more pleasing to the man, or that the outbursts of anger are not really that serious. Codependency groups are not particularly helpful for abused women because they tend to blame the victim as an enabler rather than to place full responsibility for the violence on the abuser. For the reasons noted previously, avoid any therapist whose training was in family systems psychotherapy.

Almost any kind of couples or family therapy can be dangerous if you live with an abusive man—the man may threaten you before sessions or beat you for bringing up problems in sessions. Couples or family therapy seems to trigger some murders. For couples or families with problems of violence, experts recommend only behavioral therapy specifically focused on the violence. Group therapy can help a great deal, but abused women and abusive men should be in different groups, and the focus of the abusers' group should be on behavioral therapy for the violence. Abused women find being in groups with their men intimidating.

Never waste your time and money with any counselor who fails to meet these requirements. Never feel pressured into scheduling another appointment. You have the right to reject another appointment or to tell the counselor you haven't decided yet and will let the person know later whether you want to return. You can also go to other counselors before deciding whether to continue with any particular counselor.

People who can't afford to pay for counseling can go to many counseling services sponsored by the government. Check with your local crisis center or social service agencies for details. Even when you receive free counseling services or those that charge according to your income, you have the right to choose a competent counselor you feel comfortable with. Feel free to request another counselor if you don't feel satisfied with the one assigned to you.

If you have severe problems and you don't know whether you need a residential treatment program, as opposed to weekly counseling sessions and perhaps medicines, get a professional opinion from someone with expertise in your type of problem. Don't go to a private hospital for help in making this decision. Many of the privately owned psychiatric hospitals or residential treatment centers tend to recommend hospitalization rather easily to make money. Counselors in private practice are not the best choice either because they have an economic interest in finding clients. Instead, go to a public counseling or treatment facility funded by the government or affiliated with a public hospital or university.

If you voluntarily sign to enter a psychiatric hospital or residential facility (as opposed to being ordered to enter by a court), remember you can leave against medical advice by giving notice of your decision. The hospital must discharge you within 72 hours in most states and within 48 hours in a few states. If you have insurance and do this, your insurance will still pay, although some facilities will claim otherwise.

Recommended Additional Readings:

The Rights of Mental Patients: The Revised Edition of the Basic ACLU Guide to a Mental Patient's Rights. by Bruce J. Ennis and Richard D. Emery. New York: Avon Books, 1978. an excellent book by the American Civil Liberties Union discussing the legal rights of mental patients in both voluntary and involuntary hospitalization, criminal proceedings, institutions, and the community.

The Rights of Patients: The Basic ACLU Guide to Patient Rights. 2nd ed. rev. ed. by George J. Annas. Totowa, NJ: Humana Press, 1992. an excellent book by the American Civil Liberties Union discussing patient rights advocates, the right to see medical records, the meaning of competence, how to use law and medical libraries, and many other issues common to all patients.

42. Preventing Violence and Crime

Don't be afraid to become involved.

An ounce of prevention is worth a pound of cure.

We have already discussed some things that can prevent violence. Chapter 36, Abuse and Rape, presented statistics on violence and explained helpful attitudes and strategies for preventing and stopping various kinds of violence, including suggestions for rape that can help avoid other violence. Alcohol and drug treatment programs can help because of the link between abuse, crime, and these substances. The section in chapter 22 on Discussing Sex with Children gives advice that can prevent child sexual abuse. School programs offering this kind of information greatly increase children's telling authorities about ongoing or isolated incidents of sexual abuse. Much of the chapters on Raising Children and Marriage helps reduce crime because juvenile delinquency tends to occur in families with parents in conflict, parents using discipline inconsistently, those who supervise their children loosely, and those who reject or act coldly toward their children.

Gun Control

Guns kill around 31,000 people and seriously injure another 65,000 people each year in the United States. More teenagers die by guns than by all natural causes combined. In America, children under 15 are almost 12 times more likely to die by gunfire than the children in 25 other industrialized countries combined. Between 1990 and 1995, no children died from guns in Hong Kong, the Netherlands, Singapore, Japan, and Kuwait. The U.S. is the most heavily armed nation, with guns in 40% of our households. In a survey of 102 countries, nearly all foreign countries have a comprehensive national system of gun control. The widespread availability and social acceptance of guns here make violence in America particularly deadly.

Gun control laws reduce murders and suicides. Nations with strong gun control laws have much lower death rates and the weaker the laws, the higher the death rates. In the U.S., local laws restricting guns quickly and sharply reduce murders and suicides, even when nearby areas have no restrictions on gun ownership. Tightening our rules on licensed gun dealers reduced the number of dealers over 65% between 1993 and 1996, and this lowered pistol production almost 60%, with even greater decreases in the making of cheaper pistols, the junk guns (or Saturday night specials) preferred by young killers. Gun control is probably part of the reason for our nation's falling rates of gun violence.

Only one of four adults in America owns a gun, and a large majority of these people foolishly believe having a gun makes your home a safer place. Gun companies, dime-store novels, and movies of the Old West have created this shoot-up-the-bad-guys myth, but until the 1850s, fewer than 10% of Americans owned guns, half of those guns were not working, and towns like Dodge City and Tombstone had strict gun control laws.   Dodge City confiscated all guns at the city limits. Gun ownership does not protect men, women, or children—it makes your home much more dangerous. About half of our gun owners always keep their guns loaded, leading to many fatal accidents among children. Guns kept in the home for self-protection are 22 times more likely to kill someone you know than to kill in self-defense. Guns in the home make murder 3 times more likely and increase the risk of suicide 5 times. Using a gun in self-defense during a violent crime increases your risk of being attacked by a gun 7 times.

Special interest groups lobby extensively and dominate the gun control debate here, focusing our attention on stranger crime rather than on the way guns are more often used—between family members and acquaintances. The National Rifle Association (NRA) spends $1.5 million a year lobbying to defeat every gun law proposed.   They have lobbied shamelessly against banning machine guns, plastic pistols, and police-killing bullets designed to pierce bulletproof vests. Although all Supreme Court decisions agree the Second Amendment of the Constitution does not protect any right to own guns, the NRA has convinced most Americans that it does.

Recent polls have found up to 80% of Americans, including most gun owners, favor stricter gun laws. Strict gun control would reduce the cost of health insurance and taxes, because gun injuries cost over $23 billion annually in direct and indirect costs. Many people wrongly believe gun laws are doomed to fail because guns are everywhere and often stolen. The truth is gun ownership is steadily decreasing, crime guns are usually new guns, 75% of robbers nationwide don't use a gun, and a large majority of youths involved in crimes, including gang members, don't own guns.

Many laws can help without putting major restrictions on gun owners. The overwhelming majority of Americans support limiting gun sales to those thought to be irresponsible or potentially dangerous, such as people with criminal histories or under 21 years old. Federal law already outlaws the purchase or possession of firearms by convicted felons, people found legally mentally defective, and those with dishonorable discharges from the U.S. military.   It also prohibits those with misdemeanor domestic violence convictions from owning handguns.   Whenever a complaint of domestic violence includes the report of a gun in the home, even if it is not involved in the incident, we should check to see if the owner has legal possession of it.

Arrests for violence rise sharply for boys through the teenage years. A government study found 18- to 20-year olds, just 4% of the population, commit 24% of all gun killings and lead all other age groups in rapes, assaults, and robberies using guns.   Yet in 27 states, juveniles may own shotguns and rifles.   Handguns are especially dangerous because they are easily hidden.   Federal law prohibits people under 18 years old from possessing them, but 27 states have no restrictions or background check requirements for 18 to 21 year olds buying handguns.   We should at least outlaw teenagers buying military assault weapons.

No federal law stops people convicted of violent misdemeanors other than domestic violence, such as assault, from purchasing handguns, although some states do.   Research shows people convicted of any misdemeanor are 6 times more likely to be charged with a new violent offense after buying a handgun than are those with no prior criminal history.   Handgun buyers who had more than one prior misdemeanor conviction were more than 10 times as likely to be charged with another crime and 15 times as likely to be charged with murder, rape, robbery, or aggravated assault.   We should deny firearms to any adult convicted of a violent crime, even as a juvenile.

A national law banned semiautomatic assault weapons (popular with drug dealers and violent criminals) except for use in war, but two loopholes keeps these dangerous guns on the market.   Any of these guns that were legally manufactured and sold before the ban can still be sold or transferred. One company, S.W. Daniel, sells assault weapons through the mail by selling the frame and an easily assembled kit separately.   We should eliminate these loopholes and outlaw high capacity ammunition clips.

Most youths and criminals buy guns in off-the-record transactions from acquaintances, family members, gun shows, flea markets, pawn shops, illegal gun dealers, or the Internet.   Criminals do this to avoid detection, and traces of guns used in crimes often can't go any farther than the first sale.   An average of 340,000 guns are stolen in our country each year.   Many private gun sales, including many at gun shows, involve stolen guns or gun parts. Driving a car requires a license, yet owning a gun doesn't.   A few states now wisely require gun manufacturers to provide police with spent shell casings carrying the ballistic fingerprint of every new handgun sold.

Ideally, we should require licenses for owning a gun and background checks for all gun transfers. Law enforcement officials should have complete and accessible records of criminal records, military discharges, and legally adjudicated mental health records because laws alone do not stop all illegal transactions. The FBI's background checks lack important information like domestic abuse misdemeanors, court restraining orders, and mental health records. States don't have the money to pursue most felony arrest warrants or pay extradition if a suspect is found, so probably an average of less than 20% of these warrants get sent to the FBI. A 5-day waiting period would provide more time for reviewing records. Requiring records of all gun transactions and computerizing gun sale records from out-of-business gun dealers would help us trace crime guns and find illegal gun dealers. Often, police must now go and retrieve files manually from warehouses. The vast majority of Americans favor requiring licenses for owning a gun, gun registration, and background checks for gun purchases.

Varying laws make the same guns more expensive in certain cities and states than in others. Gun traffickers make huge profits by buying many guns in areas with weak laws and selling them where the illegal market price is much higher, sometimes selling from car trunks in high-crime neighborhoods. Gun manufacturers sell too many guns right outside the city limits of towns with strict gun laws and sell dozens of weapons to a single buyer who resells them to criminals. Manufacturers oversupply southern states with weak gun laws, knowing the guns end up used by criminals up north. Some companies design and advertise guns for criminals, like the weapons and bullets designed to pierce bulletproof vests and the TEC-DC9 assault weapon that offers "excellent resistance to fingerprints." We should outlaw gun ads or at least those suggesting guns increase personal or family safety.

State laws restricting handgun purchases to one per person per month are very effective in disrupting and shifting the illegal movement of guns across state lines. When Virginia adopted this law, the likelihood that a gun used in a crime in the Northeast would be traced to Virginia instead of other Southeast states with weak laws dropped by 66%. Making this a national law would make a huge difference and most Americans, both gun owners and nonowners, support this restriction.

To reduce the transfer to guns to criminals, we could outlaw owning or selling to any one person more than a few guns. Because many people go out of town to buy guns when they can't get them locally or to avoid local gun registration laws, we could outlaw selling guns without following the gun laws of the buyer's hometown. We should increase penalties for illegal gun sales. You can get more jail time for selling crack on the street than for putting thousands of guns in the hands of criminals.

Gun violence is concentrated in areas of poverty in inner cities, often using illegally obtained handguns. Half of all homicides occur in our 63 largest cities, which have only 16% of the population. In Kansas City, paying police overtime to patrol one high-crime area and seize guns carried illegally by motorists reduced crimes involving guns by 43%. Indianapolis copied these tactics and found similar results. Aggressive programs for getting guns off the streets in New York and Boston helped reduce murder rates in those cities. Research shows gun buyback programs don't work, however.

Toy guns must meet consumer product safety regulations but despite 31,000 deaths a year, real guns are exempt! In 1999, major car makers put latches inside the trunks of new cars because 11 children died the year before by suffocating inside locked car trunks. Opening a bottle of children's vitamins is more difficult than shooting most handguns, and electric drills use safer triggers than revolvers do. We should require child safety devices that meet minimum government safety standards on all handguns. Some safety locks are made of such flimsy plastic you can easily crush them. A poll found 86% of all Americans favor laws requiring childproofing of new handguns. We should require safety features such as combination or key locks, devices with a color coded display or a pop-up pin to show when a seemingly empty clip has a bullet in the firing chamber. Another possibility is rings or bracelets with encoded chips so only the owner (or owners) can fire the gun. Many cars now unlock with the owner's remote control. Colt already has a Smart Gun for police that uses radio signals so only authorized people can shoot it, and Colt has applied for a patent on a civilian version.

Although violent crime has declined in the last seven years, states with strict laws on carrying concealed weapons (CCW) and the seven states that prohibit them have seen the greatest drops in violent crime. Unfortunately, most states allow people with criminal convictions for violent or drug-related misdemeanors to get CCW licenses. Weakening CCW laws increases gun-related murders. In the first six months of 1997, concealed handgun license holders in Texas had twice as many gun crimes as that of the general population of Texas. A survey shows 2/3 of all Americans and more than 3/4 of those living in urban areas don't support carrying concealed weapon laws.

A 1993 survey found 59% of school children in 6th to 12th grade said they could get a handgun if they wanted one, and a third of them said they could get one within the hour. We could pass a national child access prevention gun law. In 15 states, such laws penalize adults with jail time or large fines if they don't use a trigger lock or safe, locked storage when children may be around and an injury results from a child using the gun. Florida's law required gun dealers to warn customers of the penalties, and sales of safety devices rose dramatically. One study found these state laws reduced children's accidental firearms deaths by 23%. We should require a 72-hour holding period for children who bring guns to school.

We could limit the total number of guns manufactured or ban low quality, easily concealable "junk guns," which are dangerous, unreliable, inaccurate at a distance, and not useful for sport. Experts agree the ideal approach would be outlawing all handguns and assault rifles. England has one of the toughest gun laws in the world, but they do allow pistols of antique or historical interest, starting pistols, and shot pistols with very small caliber charges that people use against rats, mice, and other pests. All but the last of these laws would preserve people's hunting rights. Any of them would save tax dollars for police protection and medical expenses for violence, injuries, disability, and deaths. Think of how many accidental deaths, murders, rapes, and other crimes we could prevent. Don't we deserve a safer society?

Sex Education, Birth Control, and Adoption

Most Americans want sex education in the schools and favor allowing women the right to choose for themselves birth control options, but few Americans realize how important these things are. Pregnancies that were unintended at the time of conception, either mistimed or unwanted, are linked to later child abuse, children's psychiatric problems, juvenile delinquency, and crime. Several comprehensive government studies conclude that preventing child abuse should begin with pregnancy planning and affordable birth control services. This makes sex education, birth control, adoption, and abortion very important ways to prevent violence and crime.

Most pregnancies (57%) in the United States are unintended, either mistimed or unwanted. Rates of unintended pregnancy are higher for teenagers, women living in poverty, and never-married women, and probably especially high for homeless women, teenage school dropouts, and women heavily abusing alcohol and illegal drugs. We could avoid many problems if Medicaid covered surgical abortion, abortion pills, and morning-after pills.

The World Health Organization of the United Nations says sex education frequently persuades young people to delay starting sexual activity, use condoms, and have fewer sex partners. Sex education works best in preventing pregnancy when it begins in elementary school before puberty, biological urges, and sex and before the strong feelings of young romance that can make an adolescent unwilling to seriously consider advice about sex. Parents usually don't know when their children first have sex, and adolescents today face great peer pressures to have it. Recent surveys by the Centers for Disease Control and Prevention (CDC) have found 50% of high school students in the U.S. have had sex, and 16% of students have had sex with four or more partners. A nationwide survey found about 17% of 7th- and 8th-grade students have had sex. Unfortunately, many teenagers become sexually active before receiving any sex education.

Even with recent decreases, teen pregnancy rates in the U.S. are much higher than in England or Canada, 8 times as high as in the Netherlands, and 10 times as high as in Japan. Studies document widespread misconceptions about sex in American teenagers and major gaps in adults' and parents' knowledge about basic sexual information, probably because many children here learn about sex only from their peers. In contrast, children in England, many other European countries, and Japan learn about sex very early in school and learn about the various contraceptives before puberty.

The CDC survey shows 42% of sexually active students in high school don't use condoms, but many more don't use contraceptives consistently or don't understand the proper ways to use them, with the youngest children having sex being the least likely to understand or practice safe sex. Half of all premarital pregnancies occur within the first 6 months of sexual activity.

When given the choice of excusing their children from sex education classes, less than 5% of parents do. Although most states require or recommend sex education in the schools, many states have rules limiting its effectiveness, such as greatly limiting or refusing discussion of contraception or introducing these topics too late. Conservative lawmakers recently required schools to preach only abstinence in order to receive any of $250 million for sex education. If a school uses the word condom, it doesn't get a cent. Research shows this is foolish—detailed knowledge of contraception is much more important than knowledge of reproduction in reducing teenage unprotected sex.

Lawmakers who bow to conservative fears and limit sex education and family planning services actually contribute to higher rates of venereal disease, AIDS, teen pregnancy, child abuse, juvenile delinquency, and crime. Conservatives need to understand that the best sex education is very concerned with values and good decisions. It teaches about the consequences of unintended pregnancies and early parenthood, including the poverty that often results. It teaches abstinence, teaches against risky behaviors, and it uses roleplay to train effective ways of saying no, avoiding sex and unprotected sex, and dealing with pressure. The best programs teach the advantages and disadvantages of each form of birth control and detail the complex skills of how to use each effectively. The Quaker religion has taken the stand that it is immoral to withhold information about safer sexual behavior because of the health implications.

The programs most effective in reducing pregnancy rates provide information on where and how to get birth control, adoption, and abortion, how much it costs, and where to find subsidized care if finances are a problem. Research indicates these services do not increase teenage sexual activity, nor do free condom programs in high schools. More comprehensive school-based programs combine good sex education with career training and employment, perhaps with tutoring. Many studies suggest special school programs for teen mothers offering medical services, parenting classes, and counseling help reduce subsequent additional children. Of course, adding infant and toddler child care to these programs helps increase participation.

Providing easy access to birth control near schools but not on school grounds reduces problems with confidentiality. Fear of discovery is a major reason for unprotected sex in teenagers. Community-based centers can serve students, school dropouts, and suspended or expelled students and are open weekends, after school, and during vacations, unlike school-based programs.

All around the world, even in the United States, inadequate access to birth control causes high rates of unplanned pregnancy and abortion. More than 1/5 of all pregnancies end in abortion, with similar rates in both rich and poor nations, despite abortion being illegal, expensive, and unsafe in many poor nations. Laws don't stop abortions—they just put women in the hands of butchers and make it much more dangerous. In poor countries that outlaw abortion or where legal abortion is widely unavailable, women die from abortion complications between 275 and 1,650 times as often as they do in developed nations. Before abortion became legal in the U.S. in 1973, it is estimated that women obtained 1 million illegal abortions each year, with about 100,000 of those requiring hospitalization for dangerous complications. Before 1973, illegal abortions were the major cause of maternal death in the United States.

Because of a vocal, militant minority of abortion foes, women now have a much more difficult time getting a surgical abortion than at any other time since the 1970s. Anti-abortionists have committed 8 murders, 11 attempted murders, and over 2,000 documented acts of violence. In January 1996, a sold-out banquet of more than 100 anti-abortion extremists honored those people known to have killed abortion providers. In February 1999, a jury found abortion foes guilty of illegal threats for creating a web site listing abortion doctors, their photos, home addresses, daily schedules, license plate numbers, and the names and ages of their children. When three doctors were killed, their names on the list were crossed out like items on a grocery list.

Understandably, many doctors won't provide surgical abortions anymore. Now 84% of U.S. counties and nearly 1/3 of all metropolitan areas have no providers and in many rural areas, women must travel hundreds of miles to get this kind of abortion. Improving access to abortion helps prevent child abuse, children's psychiatric problems, juvenile delinquency, and crime. Unfortunately, abortion clinics are an easy target for violence, with each clinic facing an average of 100 violent acts per year. Requiring all large medical (not psychiatric) hospitals with no conflicting religious affiliation to provide surgical abortions would eliminate the need for abortion clinics and would avoid the travel and lodging expenses for many women.

Many women don't realize birth control is safer than childbearing and that oral contraceptives have health benefits including protection against benign breast disease, ovarian and endometrial cancer, and pelvic inflammatory disease. Morning-after pills (high dose oral contraceptives) reduce the chance of pregnancy by 75% but can cause nausea and vomiting. There are two kinds on the market, Preven and Plan B. The name morning-after pills makes most people think anything after the next morning is too late, when in fact, they work up to 72 hours after sex. You can get a kit for them from a doctor at the last minute, if necessary, or just to keep at home in case you need it. The American Medical Association has recommended the government make morning-after pills available over the counter. An older alternative, emergency birth control by IUD insertion after sex, is nearly 100% effective.

Only 1/3 of all large group insurance policies cover oral contraceptives and only half pay for any contraceptives at all. A few states have passed legislation requiring any insurance company that pays for prescription drugs to pay for contraceptives. Making this a national law would save a great deal of money in the costs of births, abortions, and later child abuse, children's psychiatric services, juvenile delinquency, crime, and violence.

The abortion pill mifepristone (Mifeprex, previously called RU-486) is highly effective (92-95%) and safe for chemically aborting pregnancy at home without the need for surgery. Women must take it within three weeks after missing their menstrual period. It takes several days and some miscarriage-like cramping and bleeding before it is complete, however, and failures require surgical abortion.

We need to reduce bureaucratic delays to help those who want to adopt children. The U.S. has 500,000 children in foster care, but only 46,000 of them were adopted in 1999. This system of legal foster care and adoptions through public agencies makes up only about 30% of all adoptions. Meanwhile, about 45,000 adoptions go through private agencies or lawyers, at a cost of $10,000 to $30,000 per child, and Americans adopt over 13,000 children from overseas at great cost.

Several obstacles unnecessarily keep children in foster care. One survey suggests 40% of families who want to adopt would accept children of other races, and most overseas adoptions involve Latin, Asian, or black children, but many white families find it nearly impossible to adopt transracially. Despite a 1996 law banning racial discrimination in foster and adoptive placement and despite research showing good adjustment in the children of transracial adoption, many social workers hold outdated attitudes, acting like these children belong to their races in a property-like way.

For over 30 years, public agencies have focused on preserving the rights of the biological family, even when the parents have severely abused the children. In some cases, parents found guilty of murder or of causing their own children's deaths by abuse have been given custody again. Don't abused children have any rights? We certainly have many people willing to adopt them.

A 1997 law requires agencies to terminate birth families' rights and begin adoption for any child who has been in foster care for 15 out of the last 22 months, but this is not enough. The median number of years spent by children in foster care is 3 years. Research shows this is a disaster. Adults who grow up in temporary homes have many problems. Between 15 and 56% never finish high school or earn a GED. Many become pregnant when they are released from foster care at age 18. Up to 50% spend time on welfare. Most hold low paying jobs, and drug use is common. Nearly 1/3 of the males commit crimes as adults. A government study of homeless people found 27% reported a childhood history of foster care or institutional placement.

We spend $3.5 billion a year for foster care, with half of that going to administrative costs, including social worker salaries. In some states, the annual turnover of social workers is 70%. Some states have a patchwork of fragmented policies because each county has control over foster care. Speeding up adoption would save huge amounts of money.

Texas has made some important improvements. Texas doesn't require family preservation efforts for families with records of severe mistreatment of children. Texas requires ten weeks of parent training for all foster and adoptive parents, and social workers who discriminate racially can be fired.

Home Visits to Parents

Intensive family preservation services provide social support, education on parenting, marital, and social skills, counseling, and referrals to community services such as welfare, employment services, housing, food banks, financial, legal, and medical aid, and child care to very troubled families to try to prevent state custody or foster placement. These programs generally provide the services on a short-term, crisis basis, with workers on call 24 hours for emergencies. The better programs offer intensive, long-term services and followup, recruit the help of extended family, friends, and neighbors, and refer to community agencies and resources for further help. Unfortunately, research shows even model programs often fail to change these very troubled families.

Experts now understand that offering services to abusive families after the fact is too little, too late. Child Protective Services spend a great deal of time and resources investigating reports of abuse, but nobody reports most abused children to them, and many of the cases they determine unproven involve families and children in serious need of services. Many of the proven cases were reported previously but found unproven, thus missing an opportunity for earlier intervention. A nationwide survey found more than 1/3 of confirmed cases of abuse received no services. Understaffed programs often have poor training and high turnover. In New York in 1991, for example, 77% of child abuse investigators transferred to other agencies, resigned, or were laid off. Child Protective Services today has become mainly an investigative agency rather than a service provider, and the main intervention has become foster care, although the agency uses it in only a small portion of abuse cases.

All the leading national organizations concerned with child welfare now agree that it doesn't make sense to wait until abuse happens before we respond or help parents. We must emphasize prevention services. Many studies show weekly home visits for new parents, whether by nurses, social workers, preschool teachers, psychologists, or trained paraprofessionals, prevents child abuse and the associated increased rates of juvenile delinquency and crime. In high-risk families, studies have found 75% less juvenile delinquency when the infants reach the teenage years. In several European countries, all families with new babies must accept in-home visits by trained nurses. Research shows teaching just parenting skills to the parents of emotionally disturbed toddlers with severe behavior problems results in normal school and work outcomes when the children grow up.

Ideally, home visit programs should provide infant health care information, household hygiene, social support, education on parenting, marital, and social skills, counseling, and referrals to community services such as welfare, employment services, housing, food banks, financial, legal, and medical aid, and child care. They should teach developmentally realistic expectations and warm child rearing and discipline styles, with the parents roleplaying the desired interactions.

Home visits for new parents are an excellent way to avoid problems and save huge amounts of money for police, courts, and jail. Many studies suggest a good, warm parent-child relationship can prevent children's future problems despite multiple stresses such as poverty, family conflict, and neighborhoods full of drugs or crime. By intervening early in life with comprehensive services, we may be able to prevent delinquency even when one parent is alcoholic, a drug abuser, or emotionally disturbed.

We should repeatedly offer services to all new parents and other referrals because many people would avoid a program for abusive parents. Offering services to new parents at hospitals works best because most new parents have many questions. Other possibilities include using the Women, Infants, and Children program (WIC) to reach high-risk families or accepting referrals from health and child welfare agencies, but this risks stigma that makes many people refuse to participate. The most effective programs use early and long-term contact with high-risk families (at least one year, preferably two).

Daycare

We need high-quality daycare for children, even during evening or night hours when many parents work. In most other industrialized countries, the government heavily subsidizes child care and it is cheap for parents. The average American family spends about $4,600 each year for the care of one child, with the working poor often paying 25% of their income for daycare. Affordable child care can remove children in high-risk families from stresses that can lead to child abuse. High-quality daycare can provide emotional support, social skills, and the foundations of academic skills to children, reducing school failure and the delinquency, violence, and crime linked to it. High quality daycare can increase cooperation and reduce temper tantrums, hitting, and whining, compared to child care alone or with one or two other children. In low-quality daycare, children learn more slowly, show less consideration for others, and aren't prepared to learn in kindergarten.

Unfortunately, most child care workers earn salaries near the poverty line, and the average zoo keeper earns more than the average child care worker. Poor pay results in a high average turnover of 36% of the staff each year, which is not good for children's emotional well-being. Children in centers with higher staff turnover have less developed language and social skills.   Well-educated teachers and low child/staff ratios contribute to children's intellectual and social growth.

Long-term benefits of early educational programs for disadvantaged children such as Head Start often include reducing rates of school absences, repeating grades, and assignment to remedial or special education classes. Academic performance often improves for two or three years. The best child care programs can double rates of completing high school, going to college, and employment at age 19 and cut in half rates of juvenile crime and teenage pregnancy. The most effective programs actively involve parent and have low child to adult ratios (averaging 5 to 1). Georgia now offers free preschool to all 4-year-old children. Both New York and California have plans to develop similar programs, with California planning to include 3-year-olds.

The quality of care is poor in most daycares. Head Start programs and those based in public schools tend to be much better than those run by for-profit chains. The for-profit chains hire fewer teachers per child, fewer teachers with college degrees, pay their teachers less, and have much higher turnover in staff than do independent for-profit centers. The quality of child care in family daycare homes is usually better in regulated homes than in unregulated homes.   Referral agencies do little to gather or provide information on the quality of local daycares, although inspection results and consumer complaints are in the public record.

We need to increase standards for daycares and streamline the procedures for regulation, eliminating unnecessary burdens. Most states have low standards, and although inspectors can revoke a daycare's license, this burdensome process (often requiring lawyers, extensive documentation, and frequent site visits) rarely happens. Many states need to establish a range of penalties that can help force improvement without closing centers down, from monetary fines to probation, perhaps rewarding high-quality centers with less frequent or shorter inspections. We should revise the rules for government funding to make poor-quality centers ineligible, adding financial incentive for improvements. States should be able to post notices at the daycare itself for at least one month about the quality or problems found. States should ensure that local libraries have information on inspections and complaints, so parents can judge the quality of local daycares.

Because many family daycare providers avoid regulation or go out of business when regulation begins, we should increase government funding along with regulation. Perhaps we should offer services to regulated providers such as a van service for field trips, a toy lending library, or a list of substitute providers in case of illness or for vacations. The federal government should encourage states and businesses to invest in child care by matching them dollar for dollar and should encourage businesses to provide part-time work, flexible work schedules, job sharing, and work-at-home options by computer for parents. Neighborhoods and towns should eliminate rules or zoning requirements prohibiting daycare centers or making it difficult for family daycares to operate.

The Justice Department recommends employers use the FBI's fingerprint records to screen for criminal history all caregivers hired to work with children, the elderly, and the disabled. Congress should pass federal legislation eliminating state barriers to doing this. Churches and schools can donate space for child care if they don't want to run a daycare. Using elementary schools greatly reduces parents' transportation problems and reduces costs by using playground, cafeteria, library, and gym facilities. Hiring a district-wide director, separate from the school administration, avoids giving principals extra work.

School, Youth, and Gang Programs

Contrary to stereotypes, isolated and rejected children are normally no more aggressive than their peers, aggressive children are often very popular with both peers and teachers, and aggressive children (like violent criminals, spouse abusers, rapists, and gang members) often have unrealistically high self-esteem. Aggressive children often see themselves as less aggressive, more popular, smarter, more friendly, and more socially competent than other people rate them. Boys bully by taunting, threatening, and using physical violence, but girls more often spread rumors or use social rejection.

The best time to get help for angry children or bullies is as early as possible. Early elementary school children are much more workable than late elementary school children, and adolescents in trouble are notoriously difficult to change. Many children from problem families may be difficult to change by third grade, which highlights the importance of home visit programs for parents, high-quality child care, and early childhood educational programs for disadvantaged children.

Schools should offer preventive mental health services instead of using counselors to treat children with serious problems after the fact. Early childhood patterns of impulsiveness, annoying social behaviors such as interrupting conversations, negative and defiant behavior, and aggressiveness such as poking, pushing, or bullying are high-risk behaviors that can reliably predict later aggression and anti-social behavior. As noted previously, children with excessive anger are at higher risk for limited social skills, peer rejection, academic problems, and later truancy, drug abuse, teen pregnancy, school dropout, theft, serious violence, crime, becoming a physically or sexually abusive parent, and mental problems. Hostile behaviors in school predict these serious problems better than do race or social class. Victims of bullying often become adults with depression and low self-esteem.

Four states (NY, CA, WA, and CT) have taken the lead in preventive mental health services. A mental health professional or school counselor selects, trains, and supervises nonprofessional child associates, who establish a warm, trusting relationship with the child and use play to gently explore feelings and teach improved behaviors. This cheap, effective program reduces problem behaviors in school and increases social, emotional, and academic competence, which can prevent many severe problems later. It has even helped many children improve in Harlem, despite its very high rates of poverty, unemployment, health problems, infant mortality, teenage pregnancy, and drug use. Most of the cost of the program is simply paying the nonprofessional child associate. In 1995, the estimated average cost of seeing a child through the school year was less than $500, but the program saves huge amounts of money by avoiding special education placements and long-term residential placements. For a description of these programs and how to start them in your school, please refer to the book *School-Based Prevention for Children at Risk* (Cowen et al., 1996).

Research shows an early lack of certain skills leads to later violence. These important skills are empathy (recognizing other people's feelings, taking their perspective, and expressing concern), impulse control, problem solving, and anger management. Early intervention with comprehensive long-term programs training social skills prevents delinquency, crime, and substance abuse. Learning empathy is particularly important for impulsive children in preventing aggressive behavior and learning problem solving. Teachers should use roleplays and literature for children, model skills by thinking out loud, and provide prompts, cues, suggestions, feedback, and praise. Encourage children to stop, look, listen, think, notice cues, make suggestions, take time brainstorming and evaluating alternatives before choosing a solution, give feedback, and praise each other. If you don't use the skills in real life as everyday problems arise in the classroom, you lose most of the benefits of the program. High-risk children can receive extra training in pull-out groups. The best programs teach concepts over multiple years, repeating previously learned skills and expanding on them with more depth and complexity as the children mature

Drug Abuse Resistance Education (D.A.R.E.) is the most frequently used substance abuse prevention curriculum in the U.S., used by over 70% of school districts, but studies show it doesn't work. Similar drug prevention programs that emphasize teaching about drugs and their effects, emphasize the risks of drugs (to instill fear), emphasize moral approaches, or focus on building self-esteem or responsible decision-making all don't work. What does work is focusing on teaching students how to resist peer and social pressures to abuse substances, especially when this is part of a comprehensive social skills training program. Again, the most effective programs use role modeling and frequent roleplays to give children plenty of practice with the skills, not a lecture and discussion format.

Group counseling is popular in many prevention programs for youths at risk or in trouble, but studies show it is ineffective and can cause more delinquency and crime, especially in teenagers. Putting troubled youths together often encourages negative behaviors, and frequent talk in these groups about problems with parents may weaken respect for parents and family closeness. Peer mediation programs teaching troubled youth to intervene with anger management and conflict resolution skills can lead to increased violence. Individual counseling doesn't improve delinquency, but behavioral family counseling can. Arresting juveniles for minor offenses increases future delinquency, compared to simply police giving warnings.

A large study shows one in three students between 6th and 10th grades are either bullies or victimized by bullies. Another study found by high school, 25% of students fear victimization by their peers. Several states now require schools to have policies against bullying. One of the best programs for reducing delinquency is Olweus' program for bullying (Olweus, 1993). It reduced bullying by 50% or more, improved order, discipline, and student satisfaction, and reduced other antisocial behaviors such as vandalism, fighting, theft, drunkenness, and truancy in 42 schools. It uses readings and roleplays to focus on violence and the related problem of social rejection by peers. All the teachers outlaw bullying, discuss episodes so problem children can get special attention, and intervene quickly and consistently whenever they suspect bullying. Teachers reject assurances, even from the victim, the whole thing was just for fun, and follow this with careful attention to the children involved. Children learn that failing to intervene or report bullying is being an accomplice by passive participation.   Teachers encourage friendliness and including isolated children and ask popular students to disapprove of bullying, help victims, and help include everyone.

This program consistently punishes bullying by taking away privileges, making the student stay close to the teacher, sit outside the principal's office during breaks, or go to a class of younger students (to emphasize their immature actions) to work for a while.   Coordinating privileges and punishments at home based on bullying at school helps, too, but don't use corporal punishment. Sometimes after consulting with parents, the school splits up a gang or group of aggressive children into different classes or schools. The possibility of moving an aggressive child can pressure a child to improve. The program also gives special attention to supervision on the playground, at lunch, and in restrooms, noting that the greater the number of teachers supervising, the less bullying occurs.   If possible, the school eliminates secluded areas on the playground. Because older children often bully younger ones, arranging separate lunch and break times and physical locations or areas helps.

School failure is a very important risk factor for alcohol and drug abuse, teen pregnancy, delinquency, violence, and crime. Each year in the United States, 1 million or 25% of children enrolled in grade school or high school drop out, with males dropping out more than females. In many inner city schools, over half the students drop out. About 75% of all dropouts are white and 62% live in the suburbs.

Because success in school often prevents problems in at-risk youth, all schools should use early intervention with plenty of tutoring by volunteer or paid tutors, with summer school programs when necessary. Even relatively small doses of tutoring have led to academic improvements. Some studies show aggressive approaches to truancy, whether by police working with social service agencies or by outreach workers tracking truants and offering services to their families, helps reduce crime.

Smaller class sizes help reduce discipline problems and give teachers more time for each student. A government study showed reducing class sizes to less than 20 students improves student behavior and increases the average student's academic performance from the 50th percentile to above the 60th percentile. Most good private schools have 15 to 18 students per class. Smaller schools help, too. Smaller schools allow students and teachers to know each other better, give more children opportunities to express themselves in sports, band, student council, and other extracurricular activities, and are associated with better grades, better attendance, lower dropout rates, and less fights and gangs. Chicago, New York, and Los Angeles have recently opened high schools with 500 or less students, sometimes splitting one large school into several schools within a school. A recent study of 33 middle schools nationwide where students keep the same teachers for two or three years found not only that this arrangement reduces discipline problems and fosters better learning, but that most students and teachers preferred their longer-lasting bonds.

Studies show when high-risk children from problem families become very productive adults, strong, warm, trusting connections with one or more responsible adult role models, often teachers or coaches, play an important part. This adult encourages them and constantly challenges them to set goals. The message is "Don't mess up your life. I believe in you." Many schools set up mentoring programs matching at-risk youth with school or community adults who play this role. Mentors should meet with a child once a week or more, for at least several hours each time. One study of 959 high-risk youngsters in Big Brothers/ Big Sisters of America's excellent program found youth with volunteer mentors were 45% less likely to start using drugs, 27% less likely to start using alcohol, 32% less likely to commit assault, and skipped 52% fewer days of school. This program recruits and carefully screens, trains, and matches mentors and youth and costs only $1,000 per match. Unfortunately, Big Brothers/ Big Sisters desperately needs more volunteers. Federal support of this program would probably be very cost-effective in preventing problems.

About 5 million children in our country go home unsupervised after school, making the hours between 2pm and 8pm the time when 50% of all juvenile crime occurs. Community recreational programs in high-risk neighborhoods provide adult supervision, social skills, and educational activities, along with fun activities like sports, music, and hobbies. Children often relate to the adults supervising after-school activities more than they do teachers and guidance counselors because of the fun activities, so these adults make potent role models. This doesn't have to cost much money—all you need is volunteers and a place such as a church, playground, park, social service center, or a YMCA.

But these programs can backfire and increase crime by grouping high-risk youth together. Some studies find higher rates of delinquency in youth from recreational programs, and one Philadelphia nightclub shooting came after a fight that began on a recreational center basketball court. Also, the youth most at risk are the least likely to become involved in these programs. School-based leisure-time enrichment programs, including supervised homework and self-esteem exercises, fail to reduce delinquency risk factors or drug abuse. We need more research on how to run these programs effectively.

Summer job, subsidized work programs, and short-term non-residential job training programs for at-risk youth have no effect on earnings or crime rates. Job Corps is expensive but promising in helping at-risk youth. The residential requirement disrupts social contacts with bad influences and removes youth from opportunities for illegal earnings. Job Corps lasts long enough to raise poor reading skills, and the vocational focus and close connection to the job market give academic training in a supportive environment. Teenagers under 17 aren't very worried about work, and there is growing evidence that early work makes children too independent, leading to earlier sexual activity and increased rates of dropping out of school and substance abuse. This emphasizes the importance of helping children succeed in school so they can find better jobs.

Poverty, child abuse, and school failure are important risk factors for gang membership. In 1995, 28% of students between ages 12 and 19 reported spotting gangs in school, including 40% of those in central cities, 26% of those in suburbs, and 20% in rural areas. Some symptoms of gang involvement include not going home for several nights, substance abuse, quick changes in behavior, unexplained money or possessions, requests for money, and special clothing, hairstyles, or symbols. Communities with gang problems need schools with no bullying policies and social skills and anger management training, tutoring, mentoring, early grade school programs that emphasize dreams and goals and teach the consequences of drugs and gang life, interesting curriculum, drug dog locker searches, gang tattoo removal, and volunteer service activities. Offering special activities like camp experiences or horseback riding to those who promise never to become involved with gangs may also help.

Photos or videos of deadly drug-related violence may help educate about the consequences of gang activity. But "Scared Straight" programs that bring minor juvenile offenders to maximum security prisons so the inmates can tell them horror stories about prison life fail to reduce crime rates and sometimes increase crime, perhaps by giving troubled youth tough, hard role models. Both juvenile and adult correctional boot camps using traditional military basic training fail to reduce crime. And juvenile residential programs in rural settings using wilderness, challenge, or counseling programs fail to reduce delinquency.

Whether gangs exist or not, school systems can make problem schools safer by using hand-held metal detectors, giving staff members self-defense training, giving students ID cards, and giving teachers pepper spray, telephones, panic buttons, or two-way radios, and photo ID badges. Of course, all schools should have zero-tolerance policies for violence. Schools should get help immediately from police if gang violence occurs in school, train staff and security personnel in recognizing gangs, control visitors and school access points, maximize the visibility of security personnel with strategic locations, confiscate all weapons, and remove graffiti as quickly as possible. Instead of allowing students to spend time with gangs by getting themselves suspended, whenever the student is not dangerous, in-school suspensions and community service make better alternatives.

Many communities have tried using street workers to guide gang members to more appropriate activities and resolve conflicts, but no studies prove effectiveness in reducing crime, and some have found increased crime. It seems helping gang members get along better may make them better at working together in crime. Police efforts using federal funds to suppress gangs and jail members may increase violence by providing glory to the sad lives of the members. Mediating between rival gangs sometimes helps, and street workers who emphasize encouraging individuals to leave gangs sometimes helps. Boston has reduced juvenile violence with close cooperation among schools, police, and social services, close surveillance and gun checks of known gang members, probation officers riding with police to enforce curfews and other terms of parole, and massive police response to shootings, getting anyone even indirectly involved in trouble. This last approach may give gang members a convenient excuse to avoid planned conflicts.

Policies for Abuse

The laws for mandatory reporting of child abuse are overly strict in some states, requiring personal contact with the abused child's behavior. In these states, you cannot get any visit to investigate because of complaints you hear unless you can persuade a source with direct contact to tell. Many people who complain to their friends about abuse are unwilling to inform authorities because they are victims themselves who feel overwhelmed and fear retaliation or because they use drugs and fear any investigators.

Domestic violence is widespread and highly underreported. Most family violence against women reported to the police does not result in arrest or even a police report, even when evidence of physical violence exists. The police often don't arrest the man unless the violence results in severe injury, he uses a weapon, or he assaults the woman when the police are there. In 40% of the cases when police have sufficient evidence to arrest, the man is gone from the scene and few courts or police agencies bother to issue arrest warrants unless the victim requests one by making a burdensome trip to the court. The chance of conviction for an arrest for misdemeanor domestic assault is as low as 1%, and sentencing is usually lenient, with the chance of going to jail as low as zero per 400 cases.

Laws classify most domestic assaults as misdemeanors, even though the same act by others would be a felony. For example, more than 1/3 of misdemeanor domestic violence cases would, if done by others, be called rape, robbery, or aggravated assault. In 42% of the remaining misdemeanor cases, an injury occurred, which means more people became hurt in these less severe domestic cases than in the felony rapes, robberies, and aggravated assaults. Violating a court order for protection, too, is a misdemeanor in most states and merely a cause for civil contempt in many states.

Police and prosecutors often feel cases of domestic violence are less serious than cases of violence against strangers ("just family quarrels") and that they are a waste of time because so many women drop the charges. Most women deny their initial complaints or fail to show up for court because of intimidation or retaliation or fear of losing family income, alimony, or child support if the person goes to jail. Many prosecutors discourage abused women from filing criminal charges for their families' sake, and most prosecutors freely allow abused women to drop charges. It is not surprising then, that newspapers continue to report domestic murders following numerous police reports of assaults that accomplished nothing.

Every state now has a "probable cause" provision allowing police to arrest batterers even if the victim refuses to press charges, and most big city police agencies have pro-arrest or mandatory arrest policies for family violence, but the acceptance and honoring of these policies varies greatly. Rates of arrests for domestic abuse 911 calls in different cities vary from under 10% to 39%. Because of differing attitudes, prosecutors and judges in the same area often vary in how many abuse cases and restraining order violations get dismissed. Prosecutors often informally drop most cases because they have no extra staffing for them. Some judges rarely dismiss cases and others may dismiss up to 75% of them in certain circumstances.

Arrest reduces rates of further violence in employed or married offenders and those living in areas where most families have an employed adult, but arrest increases violence in "bad risk" offenders: unemployed or unmarried men, those who never finished high school, and those with previous arrests or a criminal history. Perhaps it is foolish to expect arrest or court orders for protection to help when prosecution is uncommon and conviction often results in lenience. The abuser may view the results as "no big deal."

Court-ordered counseling is common as a condition for plea-bargaining or for dropping charges before trial or as a part of sentencing after conviction. Often the court suspends the sentence if the batterer goes to counseling. Many programs only require six months to one year of counseling, supervision is often poor, and most men don't complete even these programs.

Unfortunately, the research on counseling for batterers gives little basis for hope. Couple's therapy without a clear focus on violence is dangerous for abused women, because discussing your most difficult and emotional issues can easily lead to violence. Most abusive men refuse counseling. The vast majority of the ones in counseling go reluctantly, only because a court forces them or the abused woman has left and refused to return until they go. Men who go because the woman has left them, often quit counseling shortly after she returns.

Going to counseling often fails to end the violence. Researchers don't yet know if completing counseling for physical abuse reduces rates of further violence. The batterer going to counseling very often persuades women in shelters to return to the man, but experts now question if this is wise— batterers' counseling programs may actually increase the woman's risk by leading to a false sense of security.

Battered women's shelters provide a safe place during the high-risk time immediately after assaults, but we don't have enough of them. In New York in March 1995, shelters turned away an estimated 300 women and children because of lack of space. Research suggests going in a shelter is not enough—one study found increased rates of violence after shelter stays unless the woman took additional steps to change her life and found that additional steps only lowered rates of violence for six weeks.

Many researchers suggest arrest without comprehensive followup is not enough. Perhaps the ideal legal response would be arrest, prosecution, conviction, and mandatory court-ordered counseling (for both abuse and substance addiction when needed), with close monitoring by prosecutors or probation officers, long-term followup, and jail time for quitting counseling, quitting followup, or any further violence. We could verify batterers' maintained improvement by private contacts with the victim for three years followup after counseling and provide additional counseling for further problems. Research suggests a major lifestyle change requires three to five years to become stable.

We should train police to arrest, not counsel, in domestic disputes, even when the victim refuses to press charges. Police officers should separate the couple before taking their statements and should always take photographs of injured victims for evidence. Ideally, we should videotape initial victim interviews for evidence in strong cases and use victim advocate testimony in court. Police should give written information to victims on the procedures and available resources to prevent further harassment and violence. If the abuser leaves the scene before police arrive, police should mail arrest warrants to the suspect. This reduced further violence in a study in Omaha. Police should never base arrest decisions on the consent or request of the victim and shouldn't consider the relationship of the parties in deciding appropriate response. We should require police to write incident report forms with the allegations, their response, and reasons for their actions.

Prosecutors should make sure there is time before a trial to talk to victims and collect evidence. Prosecutors should pursue strong cases even without victim cooperation, using the police as complainant so the case doesn't depend on the frightened victim's testimony. They should refuse to allow domestic assault cases to plea-bargain down to disorderly conduct, and they should never replace prosecution with counseling unless there is no previous conviction involving violence and no previous diversion to counseling for an offense. Judges should never ask victims for suggestions on sentencing while the attacker is present in court—this puts victims at risk.

Judges should not allow the financial status of the victim or the relationship status of the couple to influence decisions.

Victim advocates may contact abused women as soon as possible after the assault and explain court procedures and help with paper work such as court orders for protection. Some programs provide monetary compensation to victims. Allowing victims to file criminal charges in another county than that in which the abuse occurred helps eliminate transportation problems for women who move away to avoid problems with the abuser. Some areas require the police to act on victims' requests to evict an abuser or require the police to arrest abusers at work in order to bring social consequences.

Some states make violation of court orders for protection a felony. All states should make violating any protection order a criminal offense, with arrest and jail time for violations. Police should aggressively enforce these orders. Because most officers confronting abusers have no idea if a court order for protection exists, all police departments should have a computer database of such orders along with arrest warrants. Court clerks should notify police departments when the orders expire. States or jurisdictions that require lawyers or filing fees for orders of protection or criminal charges should make sure no abused person need fear the costs of filing.

Personal radio alarms worn as necklaces for emergencies can signal police to come. Liverpool, England rotates their use among women involved in the most recent and serious cases, because research shows the first day and month after an assault is the most dangerous time. Electronic monitoring devices attach to the abuser's ankle and signal an alarm in a monitoring control center when the man nears the woman that notifies police to respond and provides proof of violation of court orders for protection.

Hawaii, Los Angeles, Chicago, and other large cities use family courts for divorce and domestic abuse cases, or perhaps courts specializing in abuse. The personnel are better trained and more sympathetic to the victims and handle requests and enforcement of protective orders faster and more effectively. In Philadelphia, one courtroom remained open evenings and nights for emergency restraining orders, reducing the time spent getting one from three hours to thirty minutes. Another way to do this is to authorize court clerks working nights to issue protective orders without requiring a judge's signature.

If a court finds the man guilty, the judge may order him out of a shared residence (even if it is in his name), to avoid all contact with you (including telephoning and writing), or to participate in counseling. The court may order him to pay for your new shelter, moving expenses, medical treatment, counseling, attorney's fees, property damage, or time lost from work. The court can also limit visitation rights to children (perhaps allowing visits only with a third party present), require exchange of children at daycare or school (without parental contact) or in another safe setting, require child support, or give you exclusive use of his car.

In fact, court orders for protection (called restraining orders or injunctions in some areas) can do all these things based on threats, intimidation, or previous misdemeanors and do not require proof of criminal conduct beyond a reasonable doubt. The few courts that don't allow all these things should do so. More battered women are filing civil personal injury lawsuits against their abusers, especially when the divorce settlement is unjust. These lawsuits can provide money for emotional distress and all the expenses mentioned above. Sometimes the judge will set aside a prenuptial or divorce agreement that you signed under pressure or distress.

Crossing state lines to stalk, harass, or injure someone or violate a protective order is now a federal crime, as is doing these things on federal property or other places within federal jurisdiction, whether or not the victim is or was a spouse or intimate partner. Every state now has some form of law against stalking, but most define stalking as "the willful, malicious and repeated following or harassing of another person." Some states require both a verbal or written threat of violence and the appearance that the person intends to and can carry out the threat. States that require a credible threat of violence may use laws against harassment for other stalking offenses, but these laws usually carry only misdemeanor penalties. Most states consider first stalking offenses as misdemeanors and second offenses or later violations of protective orders a felony.

The National Institute of Justice urges all states to make stalking a felony. Experts understand any stalking suggests danger of injury or death, even when the stalker makes no threats. Thus, the states requiring threats in their definition of stalking should eliminate this requirement. The word *malicious* in the definition is also problematic. States should not require evil intent or the intent to cause fear because many stalkers have delusions and believe their target wants to reunite with them. Perhaps a better definition of stalking is the one given in the first section in chapter 36, Abuse.

Because 20 to 25% of stalkers have no previous personal relationship with their victim, the states allowing orders of protection only to former spouses or intimates should eliminate this requirement. Some helpful state stalking laws allow police to arrest without a warrant if probable cause exists or do not allow bail for stalking in certain circumstances (such as immediate danger to the alleged victim or a third offense). Other helpful state laws provide automatic court orders for protection, require psychological treatment for stalkers, consider previous convictions for stalking in other states, consider previous offenses against different victims, or define stalking to include threats made to or toward the victim's family.

Drug Policy

Our drug laws give us one of the highest crime rates in the world. We spend nearly $40 billion a year building prisons and holding inmates, with $24 billion of that used to jail 1.2 million nonviolent, mostly drug-related offenders. Our country builds a new prison every week, and states now spend more money on prisons than on higher education. There are 100,000 more people in prison in America for drug offenses than all the prisoners in the European Union (EU), even though the EU has 100 million more citizens than the US. Retired drug czar and General Barry McCaffery, previous Director of the Office of National Drug Control Policy, compared our policies to those of Russia by calling our prison system an "American gulag."

Between 1980 and 1997, the number of people put in jail for drug offenses has increased by 1040%. In 1997, 4 out of 5 drug arrests were for possession, with 44% of those for marijuana. More people are doing life for marijuana possession in California than they are for murder, rape and robbery combined. We foolishly waste our anti-drug budget spending about 66% of it on policing and prosecuting drug offenders and less than 15% on treatment. Over 80 years of prohibition have failed, making illegal drugs one of the largest industries in the world, creating criminal empires, corrupting governments, and costing the lives of police officers.

Because of mandatory minimum sentences, prisons must release career criminals early (many serve only 20% of their time) to make room for first-time drug offenders, and nonviolent drug offenders crowd prisons. Each one costs $25,900 per year. Many judges, law enforcement officials, and crime experts, including most federal judges, agree mandatory minimums are foolish and often unjust. Congress has found that mandatory minimum sentences are discriminatory and are decimating the black community. Yet 36 states have mandatory minimums laws for drug offenses.

Mandatory minimums, particularly for crack cocaine, have resulted in sentences that are often longer than for rape and murder. These laws have put a mother of two children in jail for life for $40 worth of cocaine and a father of nine children in jail 10 years for growing marijuana. In places like New York, there are more black and Hispanic children in jail than in college. Many women helping boyfriends with drug sales receive longer sentences than their boyfriends because they lack the insider information to plea bargain or they refuse to inform on their boyfriends. Before mandatory minimums, judges could consider all the circumstances of a case in sentencing. Some states have weakened these laws. Georgia eliminated mandatory life sentences for second drug offenses after statistics showed 4/5 of those serving life had sold less than $50 worth of narcotics.

Experts agree drug treatment, not jail, is the best response, yet there is a severe shortage of treatment programs. Government studies show treatment is successful for 50 to 70% of those completing a program, but most addicts drop out and do not succeed on their first attempt. Every dollar spent on alcohol and drug abuse treatment saves $7 in health care costs, increased productivity, and reduced accidents. Treatment is cheaper and many times more effective than law enforcement in reducing substance abuse and related violence and crime. A California study found treatment reduced to 1/3 addicts' drug sales, drug-related prostitution, and theft. Unfortunately, less than 11% of our prisoners have access to treatment. One study found treating all addicts in the U.S. would cost $21 billion but would save more than $150 billion over the next 15 years. Arizona, New York, and California now emphasize treatment instead of jail for nonviolent drug offenses.

Unnecessarily putting people in jail ruins lives, removes parents from their children, puts more families on the welfare rolls, eliminates taxpayers from the working world, and causes violence by exposing these addicts to dehumanizing prison violence and rapes and to more experienced criminals who teach them how to commit crimes. Our overreaction to the drug crisis has taken away the basic right to freedom. We are destroying inner cities, people of color, and the future of many of our children.

We need to invest in treatment, not waste our money on punishment. We should accept that addiction is a chronic condition and use long-term followup, with easy access to treatment whenever slips occur, long before people lose their jobs and families or resort to crime. We should force insurance companies to cover addiction treatment without spending caps, deductibles, or high copayments.

Drug courts combine supervision with GED education, community service, job skills training, drug treatment, weekly testing for drug use (or more), and penalties to make nonviolent criminals quit using drugs. Drug court treatment of one addict costs about $1,250 a year, compared to about $11,000 a year to imprison that addict for a year. In some cities, rates of repeat offenses among drug court participants are as low as 4%. Ideally, drug courts should use intensive education and enforce at least three years of treatment and followup, sentencing all users, including those who sell drugs mostly to support their habits, to jail only if they refuse or repeatedly fail court-supervised treatment.

Of our 2 million prisoners in jail, over 80% were either high on drugs or alcohol when arrested, stole to buy drugs, or have a history of drug or alcohol abuse. Maryland tests all the state's parolees and people on probation for drugs twice a week. Staying clean can shorten probation and each failed test has escalating penalties, climaxing in a return to jail. In three months, the percentage testing positive went from 40% to less than 8%. This is a good way to find and help people in trouble.

Because alcohol results in more deaths than all other illegal drugs together and alcohol causes more crimes of violence, including murder, rape, assault, and child and spouse abuse, than any other drug, we should regulate it more strictly. Research shows the more police focus on drunk driving, the more they can reduce deaths. Improving bar practices with codes of practice, legal liability of bartenders, and training for alcohol servers, bouncers, and police may reduce assaults, drunk driving, and traffic accidents. Government studies show rates of sexually transmitted diseases in youth drop when states increase taxes on beer or raising the legal drinking age.

We need to eliminate all advertising for alcohol and tobacco. Many European countries ban tobacco advertising, and the World Health Organization is working on a global treaty that will urge all nations to ban tobacco advertising and sponsorship of major cultural or sports events. Tobacco and alcohol companies here would probably fight restrictions on advertising as a free speech issue, but the Supreme Court would be wise to allow this exception to the First Amendment. Lowering the legal drunk driving limit to 0.08% blood-alcohol concentration will save 500 lives a year. Canada, Japan, Australia, and most of Europe have legal limits of 0.08 or lower. We should stop selling alcohol at gas stations, to discourage drinking and driving. We need harsh penalties for people and businesses that provide alcohol to underage drinkers. Because 43% of college students and 80% of fraternity and sorority members binge on alcohol, more colleges should offer substance-free dorm rooms and nonalcoholic parties, concerts, and dances, and more fraternity and sorority chapter houses should ban alcohol.

The experience of European countries shows legalizing marijuana increases use, but decriminalization of marijuana does not lead to increased use of hard drugs. A government study here found less than 1% of marijuana users become regular users of cocaine or heroin. European countries have found government-supplied drugs to registered addicts greatly reduce crime on the streets. Many studies show methadone helps heroin addicts lead productive lives and stay out of trouble, yet it is available only in special clinics and five states outlaw its use. Our nation's drug policy chief recommended allowing doctors to dispense it in their offices. A three-year study of Switzerland's policy of heroin and methadone distribution by doctors to addicts found a big drop in crime among addicts. The study noted a huge improvement in the health of addicts, an increase in the number of those with steady housing and jobs, and promising signs that some would try to kick the habit. The Dutch parliament also distributes heroin to addicts.

Registering addicts with the government providing drugs to them cheaper than street prices would greatly reduce both crime and prison costs, eliminate most high-volume pushers, and collect money toward intensive drug education and counseling. We could then divert many addicts to new treatments, such as buprenorphine, which stops cravings for heroin without causing addiction. Researchers are working on a drug that will do the same for cocaine and on drugs that can immediately eliminate PCP and cocaine from the brain, thereby calming addicts who have overdosed on these drugs.

Many government studies agree programs exchanging addicts' dirty needles for clean needles work in greatly reducing AIDS and in giving drug counselors helpful, trusting contact with addicts that lead some addicts into treatment, without any increase in drug abuse. According to studies by the Centers for Disease Control and Prevention (CDC), 33 people a day or 12,000 people a year get AIDS from dirty needles, and this causes 90% of new AIDS cases in women and 93% of new cases in children. Unfortunately, the U.S. has banned federal government funding of clean needle programs since 1988, although 15 states and about 100 communities in the U.S. authorize these programs.

Other Legal and Police Improvements

The insanity defense, which is being used more often in recent years, excuses violent behavior and allows dangerous people to roam the streets long before felons with matching crimes get out of prison. A study in Michigan found 1/3 of people acquitted because of insanity get discharged from the hospital immediately and another half get discharged within 100 days of commitment. This often results in lawsuits charging hospitals or their staff with negligent discharge.

Some states allow the release of people found not guilty of dangerous acts because of insanity only by court approval or a release panel. However, judges concerned about reelection may ignore such people and thereby overcrowd psychiatric hospitals. Ideally, a panel like Oregon's Psychiatric Security Review Board, which has a psychiatrist, a psychologist, a parole official, a lawyer, and a private citizen, would set terms of conditional release, enforce recommended mental health treatment, and reconfine the offender when necessary, with immunity to lawsuits for its decisions.

When psychiatric treatment has reached maximum possible benefit but the board feels the need for further confinement, authorities should transfer the offender to the most appropriate jail. Some argue that in the majority of states, which do not allow confinement because of dangerousness alone, this last possibility is unconstitutional because the court found the offender not guilty by reason of insanity. Therefore, it would be best if we changed the term *not guilty by reason of insanity* to *guilty but mentally ill.*

In chapter 40, Warnings about Psychology, we noted psychologists cannot predict dangerousness any better than judges using the history of the defendant and that psychiatric diagnosis and assessment are not reliable nor valid. We also learned that intelligent, minimally trained paraprofessionals using good techniques from behavioral manuals often do counseling as well as psychologists with thirty or forty years of experience. Even so, we need the judgment of psychologists and psychiatrists in court to help explain the patterns associated with various categories of behavior that affect decisions about mental state, mental illness, ability to resist impulses, dangerousness, competence, and criminal responsibility. Without expert opinion, we would have to rely on mostly the defendant's biased friends and relatives.

When experts testify, they often must do so by using interviews with the defendant long after the criminal act and perhaps after the person receives treatment and legal advice. This makes the professional judgment even less valid than usual. Judges and juries must make decisions based on technical information and theories they don't understand, often handicapped by contradicting expert opinions given by the professionals hired by the two sides, plaintiffs and defendants. Lawyers hiring psychiatrists have led to such absurdities as the "Twinkie defense" in a murder case in San Francisco, in which psychiatrists testified (without offering any evidence) the killer had become deranged by eating too much junk food.

We need a new system, using a large pool of eminent scholars whose research uniquely qualifies them to give expert testimony. These experts should prepare the legal briefs for individual cases, called amicus briefs, not for either side—just one for the court. Peer review of the brief by the whole pool of experts would help ensure impartiality. The American Association for the Advancement of Science and the American Bar Association have both proposed this arrangement.

Racial and economic injustice contributes to anger and violence, so we should work to eliminate it. We need to correct the massive racial disparities in police work and the justice system. We should outlaw racial profiling, fire police caught using it, and allow lawsuits for it. Black youth are more likely to be locked up than white peers, even when charged with a similar crime and when both have no prior record. Nearly twice as many black people go to jail for drug offenses, although there are 5 times more white drug users than black ones. In 15 states, black men are admitted to state prison for drug charges at a rate that is 20 to 57 times the white male rate. Mandatory minimums for crack cocaine are 100 times as heavy as those for powdered cocaine (more often used by white people). Most crack users are white people, but police target inner city black neighborhoods and jail black users at a far higher rate.

Race and social class often determine who will live and who will die. Between 1977 and 1998, 81% of the 500 prisoners executed had killed a white person, even though about half of all murder victims are black. A black person killing a white person is 22 times more likely to face the death penalty than is a black person who killed another black person.

Experts agree only poor people face the death penalty, because rich defendants can hire good lawyers. Court-appointed lawyers are poorly paid and are often the most inexperienced or the worst lawyers. The National Law Journal found lawyers for death row inmates in six Southern states had been disciplined, suspended, or disbarred up to 46 times as often as other lawyers in those states. In states with little money for court-appointed lawyers, courts often try cases with no experts for the defense and no investigators. Some court-appointed attorneys fall asleep during trial or come into court drunk. The Texas appeals court has upheld three death sentences in which defense lawyers slept through parts of the trials. In Louisiana, about a dozen death row inmates have no lawyer at all. Studies show over 2/3 of the 4,578 death sentences given between 1973 and 1998 were later overturned, most often because of incompetent defense lawyers or police or prosecutors suppressing important evidence. We should follow California's example and pay court-appointed lawyers well and pay for investigations. Doing the trial right the first time would save money by giving far fewer grounds for appeals.

Eyewitness testimony is very unreliable, like memory (see chapter 40, Warnings about Psychology). One study of 205 mistaken felony convictions found 52% due to eyewitness identification. In a government study of 28 prisoners freed after DNA tests proved false convictions, eyewitnesses had testified against 24 of them. People are often highly confident about identification even when wrong, and confidence has no correlation with accuracy. In one study, 172 college students watched a murder on videotape from a convenience store, and researchers asked them to identify the killer by looking at photos, like most police investigations. Although the real killer was not in the photos, every student chose one of them as the killer in the video. Reasons for mistakes include time between the crime and identification, the effects of stress on perception, racial factors, the rate of forgetting, and the tendency to believe you saw a person in one time and place when you really saw the person elsewhere. Another reason is the tendency of witnesses who have talked to reinforce each other's identifications.

We should never use the death penalty in cases relying on witness testimony and circumstantial evidence. We should use it only with compelling physical and other corroborating evidence. All states should keep DNA data banks for all convicted felons, with nationwide computer links between them, and we should keep DNA evidence at least as long as the defendant remains in jail, in case we need to use it after conviction. Wrongful convictions also come from false testimony from jailhouse snitches claiming to have heard a defendant's confession. Another problem is false confessions, which occur much more often than police recognize. Children and those with mild mental retardation often try to hide their lack of understanding by trying to guess the "right" answers to police questions.

The average prisoner in maximum-security facilities costs $75,000 per year. Most states have a death penalty, but most don't have enough government lawyers, so appeals prolong cases for many years. Most inmates sentenced to death wait ten years before execution, and the most frequent cause of death on death row is natural causes. Most Americans support the death penalty, but the current situation is unfair, expensive, wasteful, and ineffective. Like a parent who threatens a punishment and fails to follow through, a rarely enforced death penalty cannot act as a deterrent to crime. The safest countries in the world with the least crime are those that use fast, severe punishment for crimes, including the death penalty.

If we make executions much more fair, we should be able to streamline the constitutionally mandated appeals. Fairness would involve paying court-appointed defense lawyers and investigators well, establishing certification for both death penalty lawyers and forensic experts, limits on the use of jailhouse snitches, recording all police interrogations, the DNA collection procedures suggested above, and using the death penalty only in cases with physical evidence. By eliminating most of the nonviolent drug population in prison and with greater use of a more fair death penalty, we could have much more money to work with the remaining, less violent prison population and perhaps to spend more on the kinds of prevention programs discussed earlier.

Our courts use fines, but often jail poor people who can't pay them. This injustice may add to anger and our crime rate, too. In Western Europe, fines are the most common sentence for crimes and they are set according to both severity of the offense and the person's income. Copying this system would save prison costs, make our system much more fair, and increase respect for the law.

Funding for additional police and police overtime is normally based on population, but studies suggest it would be much more effective if concentrated in high crime areas. Each additional police officer assigned to a big city prevents six times as much serious crime each year as an officer assigned nationally by population. Programs targeting guns and alcohol, in particular, can help control crime hot spots. Ideally, Congress should revise police funding to fit the need on the city, neighborhood, and block level.

Yet flooding high crime areas with extra police has led to race riots in the past. Research consistently suggests rude or hostile police can provoke anger, reduce respect for the law, and increase the risk of future crime, especially in juveniles, while polite police work, using good manners, greater respect to offenders, and simply listening to the offender's side of the story, may reduce future crimes. For example, men arrested for domestic violence are much less likely to be arrested again for this when they feel police had treated them respectfully and listened to their side of the story.

Our country clearly has a problem with unfair police treatment of minorities, with harassment and violence against them commonplace in some urban areas. Police beatings repeatedly outrage the country. Blacks file much higher rates of complaints of police misconduct than whites, police shoot at, injure, or kill blacks in disproportionate numbers, and many black people win significant monetary awards from the police in civil damage suits. Too many officers feel it is a war on the streets.

People are more comfortable voicing complaints against police when civilians perform intake in an office located away from the police building. These complaints should then go to police internal investigations department, which has the expertise to judge them. Ideally, a member of the civilian review board, independent of the police (not a former law enforcement official or prosecutor), with expertise in conducting investigations, should work with the police, acting as an outside monitor for poor administration or wrong attitudes. This civilian monitor should have the power to subpoena witnesses and access to police disciplinary records. After the investigation, the civilian board should receive the records and recommend actions.

The federal government should require this police investigation and civilian board oversight process. It is much cheaper than paying the lawsuits when police are out of control. (Studies show completely separate civilian review board investigations duplicate efforts and tend to be conservative, rubber stamping police department decisions. Nowhere do citizen review boards find more officers guilty of malpractice.) All police departments should use publicity to invite complaints.

We can greatly reduce both justified and unjustified police shootings through strict guidelines on police use of force, enforced with reviews of all these situations and extra training or punishment when necessary. Requiring a detailed national system for reporting all use-of-force incidents would improve both police training and tracking of unjustifiable homicides and civil rights violations. Although the 1994 Crime Control Act requires the Attorney General to collect such data, there are no uniform definitions of force, no laws to force local police to report such data, and many do not. A national reporting system would help us find injuries to victims, repeated complaints against certain officers, and complaints with no criminal charges or only the charge resisting arrest (often used after injury to hide police misconduct).

We should analyze critical incidents, actions that led to complaints, officers' use of force, actions that led to officer injury, and actions showing officer restraint and defusing of street situations, to identify every decision made and better alternatives. Officers normally learn of violent situations from a distance and can often structure their response to minimize problems. In Los Angeles, experts used a database of 8,000 use-of-force incidents to develop improved training in arrest techniques, with refresher courses every 18 months. The research showed most problems end up with officers and suspects wrestling on the ground, so training now emphasizes ground fighting, joint locks, and dodging punches and kicks. When first grabbing a suspect's arm, the use of a loose "C grip" reduces angry responses.

Ideally, every police department would have weekly leaderless discussions of the above kinds of incidents to learn better ways to prevent violence. Run by rank and file officers, they help each other avoid problems and perhaps save their careers in this buddy system. This is a good place to voice and learn from complaints between police officers. Police need a nonverbal signal to remind colleagues to calm down when on the verge of losing control. Once we set up a reporting system, we should monitor arrest reports and give officers feedback to make sure they file reports as required.

Initial police training should include roleplays in realistic conditions, both indoors and outdoors, where other police play citizens and troublemakers. This is much more effective than videotaped simulations. Training should teach police not to take personally any insults and attacks and to choose words carefully when arresting someone to help talk the person into jail. Cross-cultural training should teach the norms of local minorities and their ways of dealing with authority figures. Unfortunately, in some areas, untrained police officers (especially part-time officers, reserve officers, and those from small towns) carry guns and make arrests.

Final Suggestions

In general, poverty and social injustice leads to anger and violence. There is something terribly wrong in a world where the three richest men (Bill Gates, Warren Buffet, and Paul Allen) have $20 billion more in assets than the total gross national product of the 43 poorest countries, with a population of 600 million people. The fact that drug companies refused to bend patent rules to help Africa with AIDS for so long, while doctors overprescribed antibiotics to millions of paying customers who can't benefit from them, causing new, dangerous antibiotic resistant germs, shows our priorities are appalling.

Violence is more common when people have little hope for the future, yet our nation does less for our own citizens than any other democracy on earth—less health care, child care, housing, and support to families. These basic needs are critical to long-term family functioning. In the U.S., about 1 out of 5 children now lives in poverty, more than at any time in the last 30 years, with more than 1 million children homeless. There are 43 million Americans below Medicare age with no health insurance and this problem is growing, with the rate accelerating. Many welfare-to-work people are losing Medicaid but getting jobs with no health coverage. It is getting harder for the uninsured to get health care. We need a comprehensive system of health care and improved services and living conditions for the poor.

Government policies have helped create our problems. Community characteristics correlated with violence, such as residential instability and high rates of poor, single mother households, seem to come directly from our concentrating low-income public housing units together in areas with few job prospects. Another very likely cause was urban renewal in the 1970s, which demolished 20% of all black homes in urban areas, breaking the protective bonds of dense friendship networks. Banks and insurance companies have emphasized more lucrative areas and compounded the problems. Inner city segregation has increased over the last three decades, so now we have more extreme race and class segregation than at any other time in the history of our country. This has led to hopelessness in dangerous inner cities with few services or opportunities, a proliferation of bars and guns in poor areas, high rates of alcohol and drug abuse, the growth of gangs, and changes in values that increasingly oppose authority and favor gaining respect through violence.

A study of working poor (with incomes no more than twice the poverty level) found they are more willing to work long hours and to sleep less to get ahead than other people. A government study of homeless people found 44% had worked at least part time in the previous month and 42% said they needed a job more than anything else. We need more child care, job training, and access to transportation to help these people succeed. We need the economic revitalization of urban areas, perhaps through Enterprise Zones. In Florida's Miami-Dade county, a tax of 1% on food and beverage sales only in restaurants with annual revenues of $400,000 or more gives $6 million a year to the state for emergency shelter, transitional housing, job training, and drug treatment. Needy people often don't find jobs or receive social services because they lack an address or phone number where others can reach them. Seattle assigns voice mailboxes to unemployed and homeless people who can't afford phones, so they can use pay phones to keep in touch.

We need more low-income housing spread out in suburban and affluent areas. Chicago moved over 6,000 poor families, mostly single mothers, to suburban areas and found these women were more likely to have jobs 5.5 years after moving and their children were less likely to drop out of school, much more likely to go to college, and less likely to be unemployed. Programs finding inner city people jobs in the suburbs and providing transportation may help, but leave children in the same bad environments.

Neighborhood Watch and other community mobilization programs don't work, with high crime areas being the least likely to organize. Structural changes, such as reducing pedestrian flow in large apartment complexes and closing off streets to make more dead ends, may reduce crime by blocking or hindering escape. Closing streets may also help reduce cruising for prostitution and drive-by shootings, by making circular driving patterns more difficult.

Mothers raising children with little or no help from their ex-husbands are a primary cause of poverty today. About 60% of mothers don't receive the court-ordered amount of child support they are due. Of families headed by women, 40% live in poverty. We should identifying fathers more often and enforce and update child support. Periodic updates of child support help because most fathers have little income when the child is born, but many earn much more in the following years. The government should be able to suspend driver's licenses, hunting licenses, and professional work licenses and even boot cars for falling behind on child support payments. The state of Virginia booted cars successfully in a pilot program. Establishing a national registry of parents who owe child support would improve collections through wage withholding.

Men are most likely to be involved with their children immediately after birth. We should tell them establishing paternity gives them rights in adoption, visitation, and custody. We should require all women having babies in hospitals to identify their children's fathers. Legal paternity allows children access to medical records and Social Security or military benefits. Because perhaps 5% of all marital children are not the biological children of the husband, we should limit men's right to challenge paternity to two years after the birth of the child.

We should coordinate better between computer systems within and between states to track all arrest warrants. This would cut down on the estimated 80% of felony arrest warrants that don't show up in gun background checks, help us enforce all the laws, including child support, and reduce the threat to public safety from criminals going years on the streets without paying for their first crimes. It would also help us stop felons, fugitives, and probation and parole violators from receiving tens of millions of dollars each year in illegal SSI, Medicaid, Medicare, and welfare benefits.

Mandatory minimum laws cause real injustices in other areas besides drug offenses. A man in Los Angeles got 25 years to life for stealing pizza. In Iowa, a man got 10 years for stealing $30 worth of steaks from a store and struggling with a store clerk who tackled him. Although mandatory minimums are politically popular, many experts agree they are very costly and aren't working. Even many hard line conservatives who had previously supported these laws have changed their minds.

We should require life skills programs in both elementary and high school, including the topic of sexual abuse, beginning in kindergarten, because children are terribly vulnerable. By high school, these classes should cover marriage, relationship, and parenting skills. This may help reduce the high costs of welfare for divorced mothers, mental health and special education services for the children of abusive or addicted parents, or the associated crime rates in these children. Florida requires a marriage class for high school graduation and several other states are considering doing this.

Because at-risk families have many needs and because pooling resources saves money and increases effectiveness, model programs now integrate various social services in a centralized administrative structure. In high-risk areas, we can improve rates of participation by providing transportation or offering services in housing recreational areas. Ideally, you should maintain long-term contact with a small number of helpers because building a good relationship with the client improves program effectiveness. Long-term followup helps because people often return to habitual patterns.

Rewards and penalties help increase the likelihood of change. In Rohnert Park, CA, a police program for school truancy combined with the possibility of delaying a teenager's driver's license for repeated truancy reduced daytime burglary by 86%. Whether you are working with new parents, at-risk families, abusing families, children, teenage parents, prisoners, or any other population, you can use desired services such as programs for weight reduction or quitting smoking to reward participation in other programs, such as child management or household hygiene.

The most effective way to reduce adult prisoners' crimes after release is education, job preparation, and job training. Age generally reduces rebellion and risk-taking and increases the desire for stability. Teaching prisoners to read can reduce the rate of getting arrested again after release by 40%. Nationally, about 60% of released convicts get arrested again and about 40% go back to jail. When inmates receive education, however, recidivism drops to 15.5%, with inmates having at least two years of college education only getting arrested again at 10%. Rehabilitation is most effective when it combines education and job training with skills training roleplays on the prisoner's specific behavioral problems: anger, drug use, or antisocial attitudes. Counseling focused on support, insight, or self-esteem does not help.

Unfortunately, we continue to fund ineffective programs and many proven programs have never served most of the eligible needy people. We spend most of our meager funds for school-based crime prevention on D.A.R.E. for substance abuse and on group and individual counseling, when both are proven ineffective and research shows other programs are much more effective. In recent years, lawmakers have made the situation worse by reducing funds. For example, in 1990, there were 350 programs for prisoner education; by 1997, only 8. Because of cutbacks in insurance coverage, half the nation's addiction treatment programs closed in five years in this decade, with 60% of adolescent addiction treatment centers closing in seven years.

The emphasis now seems to be on lawmakers looking tough on crime by funding more prisons, rather than using our resources wisely and funding programs that we know fight violence and crime. Without reliable, long-term funding, programs become much less effective because the program directors must focus on fund-raising. We need to remember "An ounce of prevention is worth a pound of cure!"

Recommended Additional Readings:

Much of this chapter is based on the National Institute of Justice's excellent review of the scientific literature on preventing crime. on-line: www.preventingcrime.org

The Gift of Fear: Survival Signals That Protect Us from Violence. by Gavin de Becker. Boston: Little, Brown, and Co., 1977. teaches how to recognize signals of possible danger from others, including characteristics of employees that signal possible violence, hiring practices that can help avoid violent employees, and ways to safely fire a troublesome employee.

Support Groups and Hotlines:

National Victim Center 800 394 2255 information and referrals, support groups. on-line: www.nvc.org

National Literacy Hotline 800 228 8813 information and referrals for both volunteers and those needing literacy services. on-line: www.ed.gov/

National Mentoring Partnership 703 224 2200 resource for finding or becoming a mentor, also establishing mentoring programs. on-line: www.mentoring.org

Planned Parenthood 800 829 7732 information, support, referrals for contraception (even emergency), abortion, adoption. on-line: www.plannedparenthood.org

Internet site for emergency contraception information: www.not-2-late.com or http://ec.princeton.edu

Internet sites for adoption information, including avoiding fraud: www.adoption.com, www.adoptioncenter.com

Select Bibliography

Ahrons, Constance. *The Good Divorce: Keeping Your Family Together When Your Marriage Comes Apart.* New York: HarperCollins, 1994.

Al-lssa, Ihsan, ed. *Handbook of Culture and Mental Illness: An International Perspective.* Madison, CT: International Universities Press, 1995.

American Psychological Association. *Working Group on Investigation of Memories of Childhood Abuse Final Report.* Washington D.C.: American Psychological Association, 1996.

American Psychiatric Association. *Diagnostic and Statistical Manual of Mental Disorders.* 4th ed. Washington D.C.: American Psychiatric Association, 1994.

Asnis, Gregory M. and Herman M. van Praag. *Panic Disorder: Clinical , Biological, and Treatment Aspects.* New York: John Wiley & Sons, 1995.

Baker, Bruce L., Alan J. Brightman, Jan B. Blancher, Louis J. Heifetz, Stephen P. Hinshaw, and Diane M. Murphy. *Steps to Independence: A Skills Training Guide for Parents & Teachers of Children with Special Needs.* 2nd ed. Baltimore: Paul H. Brookes, 1989.

Barkley, Russell A. *Attention Deficit Hyperactivity Disorder: A Handbook for Diagnosis and Treatment.* New York: Guilford Press, 1990.

Beck, Aaron T., Fred D. Wright, Cory F Newman, and Bruce S. Liese. *Cognitive Therapy of Substance Abuse.* New York: Guilford Press, 1993.

Bellack, Alan S. and Michel Hersen, eds. *Handbook of Comparative Treatments for Adult Disorders.* New York: John Wiley & Sons, 1990.

Bergin, Allen E. and Sol L. Garfield, eds. *Handbook of Psychotherapy and Behavior Change.* 4th ed. New York: Wiley, 1994.

Blau, Melinda. *Families Apart: Ten Keys to Successful Co-parenting.* New York: G. P. Putnam's Sons, 1993.

Bornstein, Marc H. *Handbook of Parenting.* Mahwah, NJ: Lawrence Erlbaum Associates, 1995.

Brasswell, Lauren and Michael L. Bloomquist. *Cognitive-Behavioral Therapy with Attention Deficit Hyperactivity Disorder Children: Child, Family, and School Interventions.* New York: Guilford Press, 1991.

Breggin, Peter R. *Toxic Psychiatry.* New York: St. Martin's Press, 1991.

Briere, John, Lucy Berliner, Josephine A. Bulkley, Carole Jenny, and Theresa Reid, eds. *The APSAC Handbook on Child Maltreatment.* Thousand Oaks, CA: Sage Publications (in cooperation with the American Professional Society on the Abuse of Children), 1996.

Brown, Sarah S., and Leon Eisenberg, eds. *The Best Intentions: Unintended Pregnancy and the Well-Being of Children and Families.* Washington D.C.: National Academy Press, 1995.

Brownell, Kelly D., and Christopher G. Fairburn, eds. *Eating Disorders and Obesity: A Comprehensive Handbook.* New York: Guilford Press, 1995.

Buzawa, Eve S., and Carl G. Buzawa. *Domestic Violence: The Criminal Justice Response.* 2nd ed. Thousand Oaks, CA: Sage Publications, 1996.

Cairns, Robert B., and Beverley D. Cairns. *Lifelines and Risks: Pathways of Youth in Our Time.* Cambridge, Great Britain: Cambridge University Press, 1994.

Capuzzi, David, and Douglas R. Gross, eds. *Youth at Risk: A Prevention Resource for Counselors, Teachers, and Parents.* Alexandria, VA: American Counseling Association, 1996.

Cohen, Lewis M., Joan N. Berzoff, and Mark R. Elin, eds. *Dissociative Identity Disorder: Theoretical and Treatment Controversies.* Northvale, NJ: Jason Aronson, 1995.

Cowen, Emory L., A. Dirk Hightower, JoAnne L. Pedro-Carroll, William C. Work, Peter A. Wyman, and William G. Haffey. *School-Based Prevention for Children at Risk: The Primary Mental Health Project.* Washington D.C.: American Psychological Association, 1996.

Cunningham, Cliff, and Patricia Sloper. *Helping Your Exceptional Baby: A Practical and Honest Approach to Raising a Mentally Handicapped Child.* New York: Pantheon Books, 1980.

Dawes, Robyn M. *House of Cards: Psychology and Psychotherapy Built on Myth.* New York: Free Press, 1994.

Emery, Robert E. *Renegotiating Family Relationships: Divorce, Child Custody, and Mediation.* New York: Guilford Press, 1994.

Faller, Kathleen Coulborn. *Child Sexual Abuse: Intervention and Treatment Issues.* The User Manual Series. National Center on Child Abuse and Neglect, Department of Health and Human Services, 1993.

Freeman, Arthur, and Mark A. Reinecke. *Cognitive Therapy of Suicidal Behavior: A Manual for Treatment.* The Springer Series on Death and Suicide. New York: Springer, 1993.

Furlong, Michael, and Douglas Smith, eds. *Anger, Hostility, and Aggression: Assessment, Prevention, and Intervention Strategies for Youth.* Brandon, VT: Clinical Psychology Publishing Co., 1994.

Geller, William A., and Hans Toch, eds. *Police Violence: Understanding and Controlling Police Abuse of Force.* New Haven, CT: Yale University Press, 1996.

Glaser, Ronald, and Janice K. Kiecolt-Glaser. *Handbook of Human Stress and Immunity.* San Diego: Academic Press, 1994.

Gold, Mark S., and Lois B. Morris. *The Good News about Depression: Cures and Treatments in the New Age of Psychiatry.* rev. ed. New York: Bantam Books, 1995.

Goleman, Daniel. *Emotional Intelligence.* New York: Bantam Books, 1995.

Gorman, Jack M., and Robert M Kertzner, eds. *Psychoimmunity Update.* No. 35 of *Progress in Psychiatry.* Washington D.C.: American Psychiatric Press, 1991.

Gormley, William T., Jr. *Everybody's Children: Child Care as a Public Problem.* Washington D.C.: Brookings Institution, 1995.

Hampton, Robert L., Pamela Jenkins, and Thomas P. Gullotta. *Preventing Violence in America.* Vol. 4 of *Issues in Children's and Families' Lives.* London: Sage Publications, 1996.

Hester, Reid K., and William R. Miller, eds. *Handbook of Alcoholism Treatment Approaches: Effective Alternatives.* 2nd ed. Boston: Allyn and Bacon, 1995.

Jacobson, Neil S., and Alan S. Gurman, eds. *Clinical Handbook of Couple Therapy.* New York: Guilford Press, 1995.

Kernodle, William D. *Panic Disorder: What You Don't Know May Be Dangerous to Your Health.* 2d ed. Richmond, VA: William Byrd Press, 1993.

Kohn, Alfie. *Punished by Rewards: The Trouble with Gold Stars, Incentive Plans, A's, Praise, and Other Bribes.* Boston: Houghton Mifflin Co., 1993.

Koss, Mary P., Lisa A. Goodman, Angela Browne, Louise F. Fitzgerald, Gwendolyn Puryear Keita, and Nancy Felipe Russo. *No Safe Haven: Male Violence at Home, at Work, and in the Community.* Washington D.C.: American Psychological Association, 1994.

Laumann, Edward, Robert Michael, Stuart Michaels, and John Gagnon. *The Social Organization of Sexuality: Sexual Practices in the United States.* Chicago: University of Chicago Press, 1994.

Leathers, Dale G. *Successful Nonverbal Communication: Principles and Applications.* 2d ed. New York: MacMillan, 1992.

Lemberg, Raymond, ed. *Controlling Eating Disorders with Facts, Advice, and Resources.* Phoenix, AZ: Oryx Press, 1992.

Lerner, Janet W., Barbara Lowenthal, and Sue R. Lerner. *Attention Deficit Disorders: Assessment and Teaching.* Pacific Grove, CA: Brooks/Cole, 1995.

Lew, Mike. *Victims No Longer: Men Recovering from Incest and Other Sexual Child Abuse.* New York: HarperCollins, 1990.

Lewis, Michael, and Jeannette M. Haviland, eds. *Handbook of Emotions.* New York: Guilford Press, 1993.

Lieberman, Alicia F. *The Emotional Life of the Toddler.* New York: Free Press, 1993.

Loftus, Elizabeth, and Katherine Ketcham. *The Myth of Repressed Memory.* New York: St. Martin's Press, 1994.

Lorion, Raymond P., Ira Iscoe, Patrick H. DeLeon, and Gary R. VandenBos. *Psychology and Public Policy: Balancing Public Service and Professional Need.* Washington D.C.: American Psychological Association, 1996.

Lynn, Steven Jay, and Judith W. Rhue, eds. *Dissociation: Clinical and Theoretical Perspectives.* New York: Guilford Press, 1994.

McNally, Richard J. *Panic Disorder: A Critical Analysis.* New York: Guilford Press, 1994.

Michael, Robert T., John H. Gagnon, Edward O. Laumann, and Gina Kolata. *Sex in America: A Definitive Survey.* New York: Little, Brown, & Co., 1994.

Minow, Nell. *The Movie Mom's Guide to Family Movies.* New York: Avon, 1999.

Monahan, John, and Henry J. Steadman, eds. *Violence and Mental Disorder: Developments in Risk Assessment.* Chicago: University of Chicago Press, 1994.

Ofshe, Richard, and Ethan Watters. *Making Monsters: False Memories, Psychotherapy, and Sexual Hysteria.* New York: Charles Scribner's Sons, 1994.

Olweus, Dan. *Bullying at School: What We Know and What We Can Do.* Oxford, United Kingdom: Blackwell, 1993.

Petrocelli, William, and Barbara Kate Repa. *Sexual Harassment on the Job.* Berkeley: Nolo Press, 1992.

Prager, Karen J. *The Psychology of Intimacy.* New York: Guilford Press, 1995.

Rutter, Peter. *Sex, Power, and Boundaries: Understanding and Preventing Sexual Harassment.* New York: Bantam Books, 1996.

Slovenko, Ralph. *Psychiatry and Criminal Culpability.* New York: John Wiley & Sons, 1995.

Sobell, Mark B., and Linda C. Sobell. *Problem Drinkers: Guided Self-Change Treatment.* Treatment Manuals for Practitioners. New York: Guilford Press, 1993.

Solovay, Sondra. *Tipping the Scales of Justice: Fighting Weight-Based Discrimination.* Amherst, NY: Prometheus Books, 2000.

Sutker, Patricia B., and Henry E. Adams, eds. *Comprehensive Handbook of Psychopathology.* 2nd ed. New York: Plenum Press, 1993.

Thompson, Ross A. *Preventing Child Maltreatment Through Social Support: A Critical Analysis.* Thousand Oaks, CA: Sage Publications, 1995.

Walker, Lenore E. A. *Abused Women and Survivor Therapy: A Practical Guide for the Psychotherapist.* Washington D.C.: American Psychological Association, 1994.

Wassil-Grimm, Claudette. *Diagnosis for Disaster: The Devastating Truth About False Memory Syndrome and Its Impact on Accusers and Families.* Woodstock, NY: Overlook Press, 1995.

Williams, J. Mark. *The Psychological Treatment of Depression: A Guide to the Theory and Practice of Cognitive Behaviour Therapy.* 2nd ed. New York: Routledge, 1995.

Wright, H. Jesse, and Monica Ramirez Basco. *Getting Your Life Back: The Complete Guide to Recovery from Depression.* NY: Free Press, 2001.

Index*

*Bold page numbers refer to the most important or complete discussion of the topic.